BILLY RILEY

The Man, the legacy

Dr. Stephen Greenfield MBBCh MRCGP
Mark De Courcy

Billy Riley The Man, the legacy
Copyright © 2014 by DG Library

All rights reserved. No part of this book may be reproduced or transmitted in any form or by any means without written permission from the author.

ISBN (978-1503252189)

Dedication

This book is dedicated to our coach Roy Wood. Without his help in introducing us to the families of the wrestlers, and his patience in recounting the many stories that fill these pages, this book would not exist.

Table of Contents

FOREWORD 7
PREFACE 8
INTRODUCTION 9
THE MAN AND HIS FAMILY 10
WRESTLING – THE EARLY YEARS 18
TOURS ABROAD 25
THE 'ALL IN' ERA 44
RILEY'S COACHES 61
BILLY RILEY – THE COACH 73
BILLY – THE PROMOTER 87
TO IRELAND, IN STYLE 93
BUILDING A LEGEND 100
A CHANGE OF FOCUS 103
THE JAPANESE AND WIGAN 107
REBIRTH OF THE SNAKEPIT 116
THE WRESTLERS 120
ERNIE RILEY 122
BILLY JOYCE 128
JOE ROBINSON 138
JACK DEMPSEY 140
GEORGE GREGORY 148
CHARLIE CARROLL 150
KARL GOTCH 152
BILLY ROBINSON 164
BILLY HOWES 187

JIMMY HART	**190**
MELVYN RISS	**191**
FRANCIS SULLIVAN	**194**
JIMMY NIBLETT	**200**
JOHN FOLEY	**202**
SEAMUS DUNLEAVY	**208**
TONY ZALE	**212**
JOE CRITCHLEY	**214**
BRIAN BURKE	**217**
HARRY LITHERLAND	**221**
LEN WEATHERBY	**222**
ALAN WOOD	**224**
JACK FALLON	**228**
JACK CHEERS	**231**
PAUL DUVAL	**234**
JOHN NAYLOR	**236**
TOMMY HEYES	**238**
ROY WOOD	**241**
RESULTS	**247**
Billy Riley	*248*
Jack Atherton	*251*
Ernie Riley	*254*
Billy Joyce (Bob Robinson)	*261*
Joe Robinson	*288*
Jack Dempsey (Tommy Moore)	*289*
George Gregory	*327*
Karl Gotch	*338*
Billy Robinson	*350*
Billy Howes	*391*
Jimmy Hart	*426*
Melvyn Riss	*428*
Francis Sullivan (Alan Latham)	*443*

Bob Sherry (Jimmy Nibblett)	464
John Foley	467
Seamus Dunleavy	471
Tony Zale	472
Joe Critchley	473
Brian Burke	475
Harry Litherland	482
Alan Wood	483
Jack Fallon	496
Paul Duval	498
John Naylor	499
Gene Riscoe (Tommy Heyes)	502
Roy Wood	503

Foreword

It is a great honour for me to write the foreword for this book. Both Steve and Mark have dedicated endless hours and commitment to help preserve the history of Catch wrestling and ensure that our truly great sport and the great people involved can be recognized and remembered,
I feel this it is so important that facta are documented to allow people with a sincere interest in Catch to have a factual source to refer to.
It is a privilege to call them my friends and I cannot thank them enough for all they have done and continue to do.
Roy Wood
October 2014.

Preface

This book would not have been possible without the help of many people and we would like to thank the following for their help in the research and writing of this work

    Roy Wood – Our coach
    Jayne Byrne – Billy Riley's daughter
    Karen Lynch – Alan Latham's daughter
    Joan Burke – Brian Burke's wife
    Pauline Cheers – Jack Cheers daughter
    Jacqueline Wood and Andrew Wood – Alan Wood's family
    Seamus Dunleavy
    Tommy Heyes
    Raymond Plunkett – Wrestling historian for his tireless work with the results section
    Jackie McCann – who helped introduce me to a number of people who have helped with the book
    Eddie Rose – for kindly allowing me to print some of his stories

All photogrpahs in the book are taken from the Snakepit archive (collected by Roy Wood over a period of nearly 50 years), Jayne Byrne, Karen Lynch, Joan Burke, Andrew Wood or from our private collection.

Introduction

When we began training in Lancashire Catch as Catch Can wrestling under Roy Wood, we knew little of the rich history behind the art and the gym at which we trained. After each training session with Roy Wood we would meet in the Gerard Arms pub and he would tell us stories of his training under Billy Riley, and of the other wrestlers that trained in the gym. Some were funny, some sad, some inspiring, and some were downright unprintable. But the more we heard the more we became intrigued and wanted to find out more about the great men that had preceded us. Although some of the wrestlers such as Billy Robinson were well known in the professional wrestling and Catch as Catch Can communities we felt it important to try and ensure that the history of the great man himself Billy Riley and the gym its wrestlers wasn't lost. And so we set off on a two year long journey that consisted of many hours in the Wigan library as well as getting to meet the families of the great men that had emerged from the gym.

No work can record every fact, and for some of the wrestlers it was difficult to gain any information on them, however we have presented all that we found out. In the case of interviews we have left them in their original colloquial language. We hope that it will serve as a record for the great men and their achievements and stimulate further study.

Chapter 1

The man and his family

Born in Leigh, Lancashire in 1896[1] Billy was one of five boys. His father James Patrick Riley, a master plasterer from county Cavan Ireland was born in 1859, his family had moved to Wigan when he was a small boy. James Riley met and married Jayne Boylan. Jayne was born in 1863. Her father John Boylan was born in Ireland later living in Wigan and his wife Rosannah Boylan was born in Wigan. James and Jayne had six sons John Edward Riley (1890-1971), who went on to marry Ellen McGeever, Joseph E Riley (1892-1924), James Riley (1893-1966) who married Ellen Bibby, William H Riley (1896-1977) and Thomas E Riley (1899- 1919).

Billy's eldest brother John later went on to be a mayor of Wigan and was given freedom of the borough. His brother Jim was a professional boxer, but also knew the wrestling business and would later coach in the gym if Billy was away[2]. According to Jayne Byrne, Billy Riley's daughter, her uncle Jimmy was a very good boxer but unlike his brother Billy didn't have the same training ethos, as he "couldn't be bothered". He once had a match beating a boxer who had beat the champion Max Baer[3]. In 1899, when Billy was just 2 years old his father travelled to America leaving Billy's mother with 5 sons, the eldest being 11 years and the youngest 6 months. He sailed from Liverpool on the SS Campania on the 14th of January landing in New York on the 21st. The immigration documents stated he was a plasterer, aged 42, from Leigh and was single, it is possible he was travelling with a female as they are grouped together on the document, her surname was Byrne and she was aged 40. He arrived in New York and possibly travelled to Pennsylvania. His father sent money home for the first year but then Billy's mother stopped receiving any contact from him, there was some notice that his sister in America had died after about 10 months of him being there. However despite not hearing from him, Billy's mother never had him declared dead and therefore

SS.Campania

was unable to receive the widow's pension. Jayne Byrne, his daughter says that this lack of a fathers love affected the not only the way he was with he was with his own children and grandchildren but also the way he was with the boys in the gym later in life, where he became more of a father figure to them not just a coach [4].

Jayne Riley or Granny Riley as Billy's daughter Jayne called her always wished for a daughter but only had 5 living sons. She took in a niece Agnes after she had visited the girl's family and noticed Agnes had a mark on her face. On questioning, the child, she was told it was the stepmother that had done it and so she took her home Agnes was 12 and she stayed until she married a gentleman named Jimmy Lowe[5]

One of the youngest in the family, Granny Riley's mother had given birth to her whilst in her 40s. With little entertainment, she used to tell her granddaughter Jayne she remembered people visiting the house, and telling ghost stories and fairy tales for entertainment as well as sharing local news and gossip. She remembered being sat in her nightie near the fire and her mother telling her "C'mon Jayne you've got to get up to bed now, it's time for bed". And she'd say, "Oh, do you think I could have a crust of bread because I wanted to listen to the ghost story". Although she didn't have a formal education she had to fend for herself and her 5 children. She was strict, keeping them on the straight and narrow. Jayne said she was ahead of her time and very

work easier for the housewife. Later when she had some money she would lend money to local people, as she knew what it was like money being short.

Billy Riley's mother

Although she didn't have a formal education she used to say "I can count money" and she rented a little shop. Following this she took up the position of the landlady of the White Bear public house. This was a decision she questioned however as recalled by Billy's daughter "She said the night she took the White Bear she was walking around one of the corridors and she said she was howling 'what have I done all my sons will turn out to be drunkards' " however two of her sons turned out to be teetotal (Billy and Jimmy).[6]

Billys mother outside the White Bear pub

modern in her thought, she used to say "I was born a century too early", believing in any devices that made

Like many of the local lads, Billy only had a basic education. In an interview in 1939 Billy remembered that his teachers and sport masters tried hard to make him change his affection for wrestling to cricket and soccer, sports that the school excelled in. However it was his mother who encouraged him in his early days, and it was at the age of 15 whilst working in a molders shop that he made his first appearance and started his professional wrestling career[7]. In fact in an interview in 1939 he commented to the reporter "Don't forget to tell Ringsider readers that it was my mother who helped me from the beginning…she was a wonderful lady"[8].

On the 9th February 1924 Billy's older brother Ernie (Joseph) died aged 32.

Billy as an apprentice molder

John Riley

Billy Riley got married in 1925 [9] (1926[10]) to Sarah Birks. Sarah Birks, born 1902, was the daughter of George Henry Birks and Ellen Holland. She was one of 9 children (Anne, Mary Agnes, Samuel, Charles, James, Elizabeth, George and Ellen) George and Ellen were both from Wigan.

Sarah had attended St.Patricks schools the same as Billy, however she attended some five years after her future husband had left to start his wrestling career[11]

Although professional wrestling was providing an income, as he would advise his students to in future years, he also learned a trade to fall back on. He was a molder in Walker brothers engineering works [12]. It was a dirty, physically demanding job in a very hot environment. Later one of his students, Roy Wood would go on to become a molder too.

Both his children Jayne and Ernie were born in the White Bear pub. The pub was located in Wellington Street Scholles. There was a room in the back of the pub that was used to train and Ernie Riley recalls wrestlers always coming back and fore[13] later Billy took on the Crispin arms and moved there when Jayne was about 18 months old with Billy's mother going with them[14]. In the Crispin arms there was a clubroom upstairs and here the wrestling practice was held. Ernie remembers American wrestlers Such as Benny Sherman coming to the pub. "There was this

Billy and his wife Sarah

American man, tanned wearing a light tailored suit walking into a pub full of men in flat caps, some of them recognizing him form the film newsreels, he stayed there a few days, also Jack McGrath the wrestler and promoter came there arriving outside the pub in a car like an American gangster"[15]. When Billy travelled to South Africa his wife ran the pub. On returning home from his visit to South Africa they gave up the pub, taking up residence for 6 months in Beech hill[16] and ran an off license. It was at this time he acquired land to build a house. The house in Beech hill was a stopgap until the new house was finished[17]. He had a house built in Great Acre by Tom Winners, who later went on to sell him the land the gym was to be built on [18]. Although known for being a tiger in the ring he was a gentleman and family man out of it. Always being able to come down to the level of a child he took great pleasure of telling his grandchildren stories sometimes to the chagrin of his own children. His daughter Jayne recalls "He'd talk about all daft stories to the children and they'd say well granddad said, and I'd be 'don't be taking him in at all.' Rubbish he'd talk about and see Luke there, I remember my daughter, she's married and lives in Madrid. She said, she was only about 13 'You know granddad, he didn't know there was a Father Christmas until he was 14.' Don't be listening to your granddad, he honestly thought there was a Father Christmas until he was 14 mum. They're sat like listening to him, y'know. 'Well, don't take any notice of him''. One of Jayne's children Michael remembers being told by Billy that he was in short trousers until the age of 18. It was not only his own children that he used to extend his time and care to "He used to take them all to the swimming baths. He used to have a row of them and then the neighbor of my mother said 'Would he take my two grandchildren?' He used to go to the swimming baths and he would have one of the lifeguards teaching them cause they knew my father nana when we get in if they had sweets because she'll give me a good hiding he used to say', 'oh, she's there now,'.'He bought us sweets nana' and he'd say 'oh don't hit me, don't hit me.' But you know like he'd come down to their level, but he was good fun wasn't he. He could take a joke and he could give a joke too. But wonderful, a good sense of humor, but oh, very cool, calm and collected, very calm and collected. He enjoyed every minute of his grandchildren and when we lived in Ireland he used to come for about nine weeks at a time and stay with us you know, he loved it."[19]

Although he was a landlord and owned an off license Billy was teetotal, on the rare occasions he did take a drink it had a big effect, his daughter Jayne recalled "He was sat down with the light on and he was saying to my mother 'God, you know I'm getting cramp,' now my dad was 79 at this stage, 'I'm getting cramp,' so Matt said look have a drop of whiskey, he said, 'I've never had a drop of whiskey in my life!' and he said well I'm telling you have a drop of whiskey it'll do you good for your circulation you know. Oh he said 'Aye,' so Matt got it and it was a, one of those very small sherry glasses so he said now get that and I'm going straight to bed and he said one time he was at my uncle John's, my uncle Johns had built Stanley Arms and then uncle John was like you see. He'd take them early in the morning and then they'd call for buns, so they could have rolls and soup when they got back home. He was warned by my mother not to buy them any sweets when they were coming home. He'd be saying 'don't tell your a councilor then some guy had come in and, my dad called to see him, uncle John said 'oh, come in Willy,' well they always used to call my dad Willy, the brothers. 'Come in Willy, there's such a body, you'll like to meet some,' oh it's very nice to meet you. And he said will you have a sherry and my dad had never had a sherry in his life, he'd never had a taste of beer in his life, He said, I must have been about 10 or something, my dad said, well, I've just had a sip of Sherry so me dad said, he, I don't know if he'd been up the waterside at that point, at the Douglas going where the gym used to be but you had to come that way along the river and he said I can remember coming off the path, and he said it's a narrow path, and I was thinking I hope nobody, this is in the afternoon, I hope nobody sees me he said because I felt as if I was walking up and I was lifting my legs up and when he came he said, I thought as soon as I get in the house I'll have to off to bed and he said when he got in he said 'I think I'll go lie down.' She said that's funny. So he went up to bed when he came in. so he's said 'I felt terrible, never in my life,' he must have only had that much because he wouldn't drink it. He said ' I don't know how they drink that stuff.' He never knew the taste of beer"[20]

Despite his many achievements he always remained humble, his grandson Patrick remembers being out and about with his grandfather in Wigan and him being stopped on the street "I always remember walking through Wigan with him. He'd be walking and then people would stop and talk to him, I'd have no idea who they were but he'd just stop me and he'd be talking to them. But he always had time to talk to anybody; it was always the grandkids that were dragging him away. He'd stop and talk to anybody. A mild, good-natured man. He was never like, 'I've been a world champion' this or that, he was never about that no matter who you are no matter what sport you were in there's always someone that will come along that is better than you. "[21].

On his 65th birthday a surprise party was held at

Celebration of Billy Riley's 65th Birthday

Wigans Golden Clog club. Billy Riley and his wife had attended believing they were having a simple night out instead they found themselves at the head of a table at a surprise dinner arranged in their honor. Over 70 wrestlers attended, well known throughout Europe as well as friend and partner Jack Atherton. On display were the belts of Billy Joyce, Jack Dempsey and Melvyn Riss. He was presented with an Italian silver coffee wagon and silver tea service. Bob Robinson (Billy Joyce) made a short speech " Just a small mark of appreciation on attaining the age of 65 from all the professional and amateur wrestlers who owe so much to your guidance'[22]. Bob Robinson commented, "his coaching has helped us all to earn a lot of money and we thought this was the least we could do in appreciation. Wrestlers have come from all over the world to be trained by Mr. Riley". There are some notable absences from the photopgraph, Billy Robinson, who was on a wrestling tour in Spain and Roy Wood wasn't old enough at the time to attend!.

Billy's friend and soul mate was Joe Robinson, brother of Bob Robinson. Both Billy and Joe used to go to Ernie's house for a sauna and he would take then a cup of tea, Joe would sit there with his glasses on and they would spend the afternoon reminiscing [23]. Although there was a great respect for one another there was also a rivalry as recounted in Billy Robinsons book Physical Chess.

Billy Riley fell ill in the September of 1977. Jayne his daughter remembered one of the wrestlers coming to see her father "On the Friday, he'd been in the gym and he'd just went to bed as he wasn't feeling so well. I remember there was one lad that came up to the bedroom and he was one of the hard lads going to the gym and me father was just propped up in his bed. I took him up to see my father and he stood at the foot of the bed and he went out of the bedroom and he was heartbroken crying and he was the same at the gym, he was one of the tough lads he'd seen my father and he couldn't believe it, that he was going to die. There were lots; the rugby players and everything were at his funeral. The funny thing is his great friend Jimmy Sullivan died the same day and the rugby players from Wigan rugby were at my dads and then they were going down Jim Sullivan's then, it was funny that. They died within hours of each other"[24]. Roy recalls returning home after a class in the gym and receiving a call from Ernie saying if he wanted to come and see his father one last time, now was the time to do it which Roy did. The next day Billy died.

When Billy died it affected Joe Robinson terribly, Jayne recalls "I remember Joe Robinson the day of the funeral the house was that full at my mother's house that in the hallway we had a row of seats on the back wall and Joe Robinson was sat in one, this is Bob's brother and he said 'Well, my soul mate's gone now and I'll be the next one after him,' and they buried him in November. I think he let his heart down. He loved my father like a brother."[25]. Ernie remembers Joe saying that Billy was "'the greatest fella who ever lived'"[26].

His obituary in the paper read *Riley died at his home in green acre Whelley aged 81. Service at St*

RUGBY LEAGUE - JAMES SULLIVAN

Mary's RC church Standish gate at 10 am with internment at Gidlow cemetery." Later a reception was held at nearby Haigh Hall.

---

[1] Ringsider January 25th 1939
[2] Ernie Riley interview A.Coleman
[3] Jayne Byrne interview November 2013 Greenfield
[4] Jayne Byrne interview November 2013 Greenfield
[5] Jayne Byrne interview November 2013 Greenfield
[6] Jayne Byrne interview November 2013 Greenfield
[7] Ringsider January 25th 1939
[8] Ringsider January 25th 1939
[9] Jayne Byrne interview November 2013 Greenfield
[10] Unknown newspaper article
[11] Unknown newspaper article
[12] Alan Latham interview, Wigan observer 22/5/51 'king of the wigan wrestlers'

[13] Ernie Riley interview A.Coleman
[14] Jayne Byrne interview November 2013 Greenfield
[15] Ernie Riley interview A.Coleman
[16] Jayne Byrne interview November 2013 Greenfield
[17] Jayne Byrne interview November 2013 Greenfield
[18] Ernie Riley interview A.Coleman
[19] Jayne Byrne interview November 2013 Greenfield
[20] Jayne Byrne interview November 2013 Greenfield
[21] Jayne Byrne interview November 2013 Greenfield
[22] The Wrestler October 1961 page 1 and 13
[23] Jayne Byrne interview November 2013 Greenfield
[24] Jayne Byrne interview November 2013 Greenfield
[25] Jayne Byrne interview November 2013 Greenfield
[26] Jayne Byrne interview November 2013 Greenfield

Chapter 2

Wrestling – the early years

Billy Riley began his professional wrestling career aged 14. In Billy's own words "I was a well built 14 year old, and had just landed a job as an apprentice molder at four shillings a week. In those days matches were made on Saturday night and we wrestled in the fields on Sunday afternoon for a couple of quid. Most of my opponents were young miners. At that time there were thousand pit shafts in Wigan. There isn't one colliery working today. Anyway.wrestling was the top sport then, bigger than Rugby league. I once wrestled before10,000 people at Springfield Park. I soon quit my apprenticeship and turned professional wrestler. As part of my training, I used to wrestle in the cellar under my mothers shop. She made bets on all my fights. As much as £500 a time when I was a champion. She wasn't daft. I never lost a bout where a side stake was involved"[1]. Encouraged by his mother he began wrestling in matches for side bets. One of his first reported matches was with Tom Bowling of Wigan. The match took place in May 1913 and took place at the West Wood grounds one Saturday. It was said a good crowd was in attendance for the match, which was worth £15. Betting was in favor of Riley at 2 to 1 on. The referee for the match was R Hamilton also of Wigan. Riley got the first fall by double elbows after 50 minutes. The second fall occurred just 12 minutes later by elbow and leg[2].

Billy aged 17

It was Ernie Riley, Billy's older brother that initially looked after Billy and chose and negotiated the terms of his matches[3].

At the age of 18 he had a match with the then Bantamweight champion of England, Jackie Burns.

The match ended in a draw, but proved Riley was a force to be dealt with and a promising career lay ahead [4].

In 1914, whilst a catch weight Billy had a match against fellow catch weight Peter Burns. The match took place at the Westwood grounds in Wigan on a Saturday afternoon in September. The match was for a sum of £30. Burns, who weighed less than Billy was a favorite at 6 to 4 on. The match started with Riley on the offense with Burns acting defensively for around 20 minutes. However Burns quickly seized Billy in a leg and arm and gained the first fall. Riley returned in fine form putting Burns though a grueling time, Billy wrestling for all he was worth with Burns responding with a "perfect exhibition of defensive work". After a further 80 minutes the men retired and the referee a Mr. G Simmons announced the match a draw [5].

In 1919 Billy Riley was to have a shot for the British Middleweight title against Billy Moores of Bolton. Although the match lasted the full 90 so a rematch was decided on. Due to much wrangling this wasn't to take place until 1922 when articles were agreed and signed for a return match. The agreed terms were to wrestle best two out of three falls, Lancashire style with 90-minute time limit. Riley's weight was not to exceed 7 SC and 8lbs (148lbs) and Moores 7Sc and 12 lbs. (152lbs). The purse was for £100 a side. In the event of no falls being won a decision was to be given on points.

Both men underwent training and preparation for the title match. Moores trained in Blackpool under the famous Lancashire wrestler Tommy Rode. Billy trained from home under Bill Duggan. The match was refereed by Jack Smith of Greenheys. At weigh in both men met their allotted weight targets.

On Saturday in October 2500 people met at Central Park football grounds, paying admission to witness the match.

The following is the account from the match from the newspaper at the time

"On getting together they worked mainly at the

Billy Riley's middleweight medal 1923

Opposite side (Billy Riley inscribed in centre)

minutes the referee was unable to decide on a victor and so the match was declared a draw. This was a situation and result unacceptable to either party and

neck. Moores making the work "plucking" at the head. At his second effort he brought Riley to his knees and practically finished at the back when Riley

19

by an effort cleared himself by a strong "walk out". Another pluck by Moores saw Riley win the trick and get at the back and continuing the rally he had Moores bridging to save himself. There was some exciting work as Moores tied to get on his feet to a breakaway and three times he was dropped heavily to the ground. Riley only failing by a fraction later to get Moores arm up his back in another fierce rally Riley reversed positions and attacked strongly. After failing at three lifts he climbed on top and then applied the scissors and the match hung in the balance, but Riley handled the situation well by clearing himself and finishing behind his man. Again he only just failed to get Moores arm up his back, but soon timing his attack he turned Moores by a far arm and looked like finishing his man with a half nelson. Moores however just cleared but Riley followed with a powerful three quarter hold and Moores was thrown in thirteen minutes.

After the interval Riley was not too disposed to take risks on the strength of his one fall advantage which in the absence of any further falls being registered would give him the match and most of the work done by Moores who had 77 minutes to equalize in and come into picture. Moores attacked strongly at the top holds and a deal of strength was used on both sides but Riley was quite equal to all the occasions they came along.

Moores was very lacking in variety with the result that it became more a trial of strength than all round wrestling. There were a few exciting passages but Moores was never able to make much headway and the 77 minutes for the second fall were gone through without a throw and Riley was declared the winner. The stakes were paid over immediately after the match."[6]

In July 1922 Riley met Walter Mooney captain of the Leigh Rugby football team. The match was to take place at Leigh athletic grounds. Mooney was catch weight whilst Riley was at 150lbs. The stakes were £100. Two thousand people paid to see the match making a gate receipt of £120. The match started 45 minutes late. After 90 minutes no fall came and the match was declared a draw by the referee[7].

However it is interesting to hear Billy's side of this match as recalled in an interview given by Alan Latham and Ernie Riley: -

Alan: I remember him telling us that he wrestled a fella from Leigh called Walter Mooney, who was a bit of a freak as far as build was concerned he was more like an ape because his hand used to come well down...

Roy Wood: He was a rugby league international

Alan: He was a rugby league international, and he wrestled him on was it Leigh football ground?

Ernie Riley: Yeah I think it was.

Alan: He started off in front of the stand and he kept backing away, backing away and backing away It's very hard to beat a fellow at wrestling if he keeps backing away, it's a lot easier if you can get 'em to attack ye because then you beat them on the counters. He backed away and backed away and they started off in front of the stand and they backed all round

Leigh rugby ground all round perimeter and finished up back in front of the stand

In 1931 a widely reported match was between Billy and Karl Reginsky a Greco-Roman wrestler who was on tour in the UK doing the music hall circuit. The match even made the papers in Australia. The match was refereed by the great George Relyskow, a former Olympic Champion.

Reginsky, who was German middle weight champion was on tour of England, had challenged Riley, and this was covered in the Wigan Observer

"Billy Riley the well known Wigan wrester and undefeated middle weight champion of the world has received a challenge from Karl Reginsky a young German wrestler who at present is touring great Britain with a troupe of international wrestlers, amongst whom he is the star turn. Riley has intimated his willingness to meet him in a deciding bout."

Wiganer born of Irish parents Billy Riley is a brother of councilor John Riley a Labour member of the Wigan town council he is 34 years of age and 11 years older than his German challenger but he is quite unperturbed as to the outcome of the meeting and is confident of retaining his world title for some considerable time to come. In addition to home experience he toured America a few years ago when he defeated all the leading champions out there. He is anxious for his meeting with Reginsky to take place in Wigan where the event is causing considerable interest amongst the wrestling fraternity as well as amongst wrestlers in Lancashire generally

Like Riley, Reginsky is an athlete of fine physique and at 23 years of age he is popular in national sporting club circles and his supporters particularly the German sportsmen have high hopes to take the championship from Riley since the German is appearing in many towns in this country during he tour whilst it would be a much coveted honor for Germany and would bracket with the heavyweight boxing championships present held by his country man Max Schelling. Amongst his successes Reginsky defeated Douglas Clarkes pupil Brookes in 2 min 11 sec. the match with be for either £50 or £100."[8]

In the same edition of the paper a letter from

Billy Riley (left) in his youth

Billy Riley was published

"To the editor of the Wigan observer

Sir – I am prepared to meet Karl Reginsky at any time of place suitable to him for £100 a side catch as catch can or Lancashire style. I hope he will meet me in either of these as I am the undefeated worlds champion and am prepared to uphold the honor and traditions of British wrestlers

Seeing that Lancashire is the hot bed of wrestling and most of the Worlds champions have hailed from that county I feel that Lancashire should have the preference of this match. It would also be convenient to many of the old time wrestlers to witness and would be an inspiration to the younger men.

Of course this might not appeal to Reginsky whose object is the championship honor. At the same time it would be well to have an audience who understand the different points of the game. In conclusion I am ready for Karl Reginsky and am confident of retaining the championship. Thanking you for the interest taken and the publicity given to wrestling

I remain your obedient servant Billy Riley

Crispin arms Birkett Bank Wigan"

On the 29th of January the articles of agreement were signed at the Wigan examiner "William Riley and Karl Reginsky would wrestle for the middleweight championship of the world in Lancashire style. The best of three pin falls in one hour to decide the winner. Contest and weigh in to take place at the empress hall Wigan 20-8-31"[9]

An account of the match is below

"Riley Retains world wrestling title

Great struggle with sporting German challenger
Billy Riley of Wigan retained his title of middleweight wrestling champion of the world when at empress hall Wigan on Thursday night he defeated Karl Reginsky the middleweight champion of Germany after an hours wrestling in the catch as catch can (Lancashire) style. The match was deiced on the best of three pin falls and as Riley secured the first two falls he took the match

Riley was the more experienced man as far as catch as catch can wrestling was concerned and he was the aggressor through out but the German fought magnificently and forty seven minutes elapsed before Riley obtained the first throw with a scissors and half Nelson hold. The second fall came quickly after the first Riley putting his man on his back with a hammerlock and a half-halch hold. Riley's victory was immensely popular with the crowd, which incidentally packed the empress hall to capacity, but the spectators also appreciated the great display and superb sportsmanship of Reginsky and he was given a great ovation. The fighters embraced each other after the match while the crowd went frantic with joy

The above description of the match conveys no idea of the thrills with which it abounded. Both men were magnificently fit and Riley was two pounds the heavier man (11st 4lbs) whilst his knowledge of Lancashire wrestling was also immensely superior to that of his opponents. On the other hand Reginsky who is only 23 years of age was eleven years younger than Riley who turned 34 last June while he was also very strong and agile. All things considered the stage was set for a great match. Regisnky pressed at the start but Riley wonderfully cool and composed quickly to the exchanges in hand and made all the running. Many time he nearly pinned his opponent down and once a fall appeared so certain that someone in the ringside seats ejaculate "he's down!" but Reginsky squirmed out of his opponents grip and grinned down boyishly at the pressmen. The match also was not without its comic side. In fighting the wrestlers were frequently off the mat to the ropes and almost out of the ring all together. There upon the referee tapped each man on the shoulder and these muscular he-men obediently scrambled back into the centre of the ring on their hands and knees like children in the nursery. The fight went on the mean heaving and sweating and Riley wonderfully calm. Once when he had his man pinned on his face Riley coolly relaxed whilst he rubbed away the sweat which was trickling down his nose. After 34 minutes by mutual consent the men declared a truce and rested. Then came the first fall followed by the second.

In Reginsky's favor it must be stated that he was not wrestling in his usual style. He is at present touring the music halls with a troupe of wrestlers and his manager Mr. King told an Observer representative at the ringside that as a rule wrestlers in the Greco Roman style which forbids holds below the waist. He has only been wrestling catch as catch can for six months. He was defeated but certainly not disgraced and he certainly appears to have a great future in the game as he possess great physical gifts and any amount of grit and fighting spirit In Riley he simply met a past master at the wrestling game.

Riley won the title in 1923 in New York when he beat Pinkie Gardner. He was trained by an ex champion Billy Charnock of Newtown and he has been wrestling since he was 15 years of age. Incidentally Reginsky had with him in his corner Joe Carol of Wigan an old wrestler and former middleweight champion of the world. The referee Mr. George Relyskow of Oldham was also a former champion wrestler he was an Olympic games champion in 1908 and has many honors to his credit.

The match on Thursday was for £50 a side[10]."

An Australian newspaper carried details of the match also

"WRESTLING MAD
Lancashire Move

Wigan; that hotbed of Lancashire sport, has been caught up in, a whirlwind of enthusiasm for wrestling, which bids fair to outrival the great wrestling fever of -the years shortly before, the war (says the 'Daily Mail' in- a recent issue). Recently, when the famous local exponent of the art, 'Billy' Riley, successfully defended his title of middleweight catch-as-catch-can champion of the world against the' young German, Karl Reginsky, packed crowds of women as well as men shouted themselves hoarse. There were amazing scenes in the Empress Hall, where the bout, which proved to be one of the greatest tests of endurance Lancashire has ever seen, was fought. Women stood on chairs by their menfolk, and at one period of the battle, when Riley appeared to be losing ground, I saw a smartly dressed girl, about 22 years of .age, with tears running down her cheeks.'MARVELLOUS, BILLY!'

That was when Reginsky had- for tire only time a winning hold on Riley, and the girl cried, 'Oh, stick it, Billy 'Don't let the- lad beat you.' -When, with a gigantic effort, Riley threw his opponent off his back, she shouted, 'Oh, marvelous, Billy!' 'The fight was-an epic. Riley, although 34, eleven years elder than the German, was from the start much the superior of his challenger in craft and guile. But the German was the stronger, and for a long time he tried- to wear out the older man. For 45 minutes the two were locked in a desperate embrace on the floor of the ring before Riley was able to pin down Reginsky's shoulders to the matting. The men perspired so much that neither could get a hold, and the referee had to order them to stop while their seconds gave them a rub down. At the end of the first stage Reginsky was obviously tired, and it took Riley only seven minutes to gain a second fall and the bout. Reginsky's trainer, Joe Carroll, who was champion of the world for 11years, said to me afterwards; 'Wrestling is coming back. Wigan, as it always has done, will lead the way. Lancashire will follow, and then the whole country will go wrestling mad again. Such was the enthusiasm in Crewe, where Reginsky had trained, that a special train was run to Wigan for the bout.[11]

Billy continued to have catch as catch can matches even during the 'All in' era of wrestling, one of the last of these that I could find an account for was in July 1932. He took part in a match in Poolstock Wigan. He fought Jack Owen who was part of the Leigh Wrestling club. The match was for £50 a side. Conditions were that Riley had to throw Owen three times within one and a half hours whilst Owen only had to throw Riley once. Shortly after beginning the match Riley secured a forearm and elbow hold to Owens chin and throat. Owen signaled he had enough. However Owen though that would only count for one fall whereas the referee understood this to mean he forfeited the whole match [12]

[1] Town that put wrestling on the map - Graeme Kent 1965
[2] Wigan Observer 13/5/13 – Wrestling match at west wood
[3] Tommy Heyes interview 9/7/14
[4] Unknown Newspaper article
[5] Wrestling Wigan Examiner sept 15th 1914, page 3
[6] "Wrestling - £200 match at Wigan" Wigan examiner October 17th 1922
[7] Pictoril history of leigh harriers A.C. page 135 Sutton and Taylor
[8] Wigan observer 18/7/31 page 119
[9] Tommy Heyes article – Wigans undefeated champion of the world – Past Times
[10] Wigan Observer 22/8/31
[11] Daily news Perth Saturday 10th October 1931
[12] Pictorial history of leigh harriers A.C. page 134 Sutton and Taylor

Chapter 3

Tours abroad

In October 1922, shortly after his match with Billy Moores, Billy Riley and his friend Jimmy Cox, who was a boxer under the name of Seaman Jimmy Cox set sail for America. They left Liverpool on the 24th October on the Steamer SS.Pittsburgh and landed in Boston November 2nd. The shipping records show the following: -

381607 – Cox, James, 28 Church street Wigan Boxer 24

381607 – Riley William, 29 Wellington street Wigan Wrestler 26

The SS.Pittsburgh maiden voyage was in 1922. Its route was Liverpool to New York and was part of the White Star line. Jimmy Cox's arrival was reported in an American newspaper stating that he was seeking the best men in the state to Box, it said at 127 lbs. he had claimed over 50 victories and 25 of those by knockout[1].

They settled for a time in Worcester MA which is where Jack McGrath who was to become a friend of Riley lived, as did Waino Ketonen who had helped train him years prior. It would seem that Jimmy Cox had relatives in the area[2]. On a subsequent American tour Jimmy Cox stayed at the Vernon Hotel and it's a possibility it was their base for the 1922/23 tour[3]. In a letter to the Wigan observer dated 13th March 1923 Jimmy cox reported that Billy Riley had a job at the Worcester academy college teaching the student wrestling team. It also reported that he had a big match coming on the 2nd of March and then planned to go onto Chicago for 2 matches[4]. The Worcester academy was founded in 1834 with the aim of it being " a school for the education of youth in languages, arts and sciences, for promoting habits of industry and economy, and for inculcating the principles of piety and virtue". Its motto is "Achieve the honorable". It relocated from downtown to the

Union Hill campus in 1846. It consisted of a number of buildings[5]. The campus was large and Billy would have worked out of the large Daniels Gymnasium, built in 1915 which now comprises of 2 basketball courts, a wrestling room, a weight room a four lane swimming pool. The running track is above the original basketball court.

Tommy Heyes recalls Billy Riley telling him about going to Chicago "Billy told us that he had been to Chicago stating that he arrived late in the day and about the same time the city was hit by a horrendous blizzard which continued through the night"[6]

Cox was also taking on matches, in the Modesto evening news it reported that Jimmy cox had won on a ten round decision over George Kidd Lee[7], and he fought and beat Frankie Quill Broxton, welterweight on the 19th March[8]

An article from a local reporter was printed in the Wigan Observer

"Willie Riley the English wrestler is making great hit with his daily workouts at the K of C gym the Englishman with his country man Jimmy Cox the boxer is a most conscientious trainer says an American paper. "Every morning they are up bright and early out on the road building up their leg muscles and breathing apparatus. Both of them are firm believers in the fruits of roadwork. They train a little earlier than most of fighters although Cox waits around in the gym until the local boys begin to arrive in order to swap punches with them. Riley takes anyone on who will stop on to the mat with him. He knows every trick in the game. It is easy to understand how he won both the welterweight and middleweight championship of Great Britain after watching him go through one of his workouts there are no false moves. Everything he does has a definite purpose. Competent critics who have watched him are of the opinion that he might beat Waino Ketonen in a match to the finish."[9]

The tour was to last approximately 6 months and Billy wrestled a number of matches including bouts in Boston, Chicago, Dakota and Wilmington Dellawhere. Whilst in America he met Jack

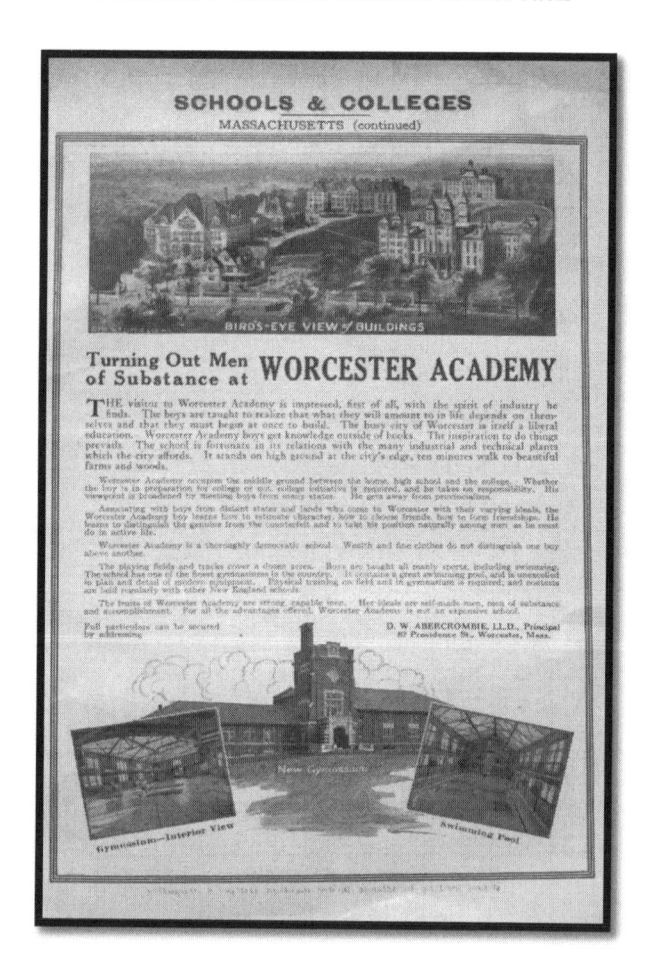

McGrath

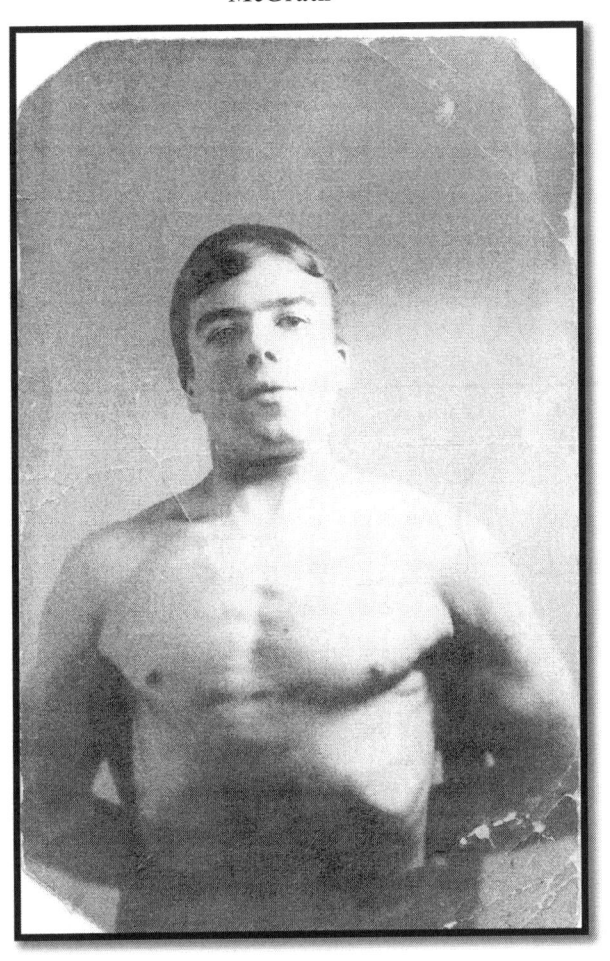

Seaman Cox

who was to become a lifelong friend[10]. He fought Pinkie Gardner In New York in 1923 to obtain the World Middleweight title[11]. The match took place in Albany New York. The match started at 11 o'clock lasted a grueling 2hrs and 5 minutes with Riley being declared champion at 1.05 am.

Carroll A Gardner was born in Poughkeepsie in 1894[12]. He moved with his family to Schenectady in 1900. His father Charles N. Gardner ran a monument's business 'Charles N. Gardner and Sons Monument Corporation'. Carroll began working in his father's company in 1917, in the State Street premises in Schenectady. Charles N. Gardner sadly passed away in 1926, at which point Carroll A. Gardner took the helm of the company along with his mother, brother Peter Gardner, and his sisters, Mrs. J. Harold Wittner, wife of the director of athletics at Union College, and Miss Mary Gardner. Carroll Gardner suffered loss in 1928 with the death of his brother Peter and his mother the following year in 1929[13].

Carroll Gardner began wrestling in 1911 as a hobby, and within a short space of time[14] entered the professional wrestling circuit. Carroll Gardner was a product of a Y.M.C.A school for wrestling; he was always interested in athletics and tumbling[15]. Carroll Gardner won the middleweight championship of the world by defeating Waino Ketonen. Carroll Gardner had won the middleweight championship in 1921 and 1922.

Pinky, as his friends and fans alike knew him, made a number of successful tours of Australia and in 1928, he came in as a runner up for the light heavyweight championship of Australia, unfortunately only being defeated by Ted Thye, the Champion. When asked how Carroll came by the moniker "Pinky" he replied that as a child '*he had cold in one of his eyes, and it took on a pinkish cast. One of his companions to get his "goat" called him Pink Eye, which afterward became "Pinky," and the name stuck ever since.*'[16]

Time and again when reporters wrote about 'Pinky' Gardner they referred to his physique and scientific knowledge of wrestling. '*I thought him the most perfect specimen of physical man outside of Eugene Sandow I had ever seen... He is like chain lightning.... He has a quick thinking mind, a clear eye and a forceful determination.*'[17] In a report of his match against Joe Turner at the New Nixon theatre attention is paid to Carroll's strength and flexibility when '*in bridging Turner grasped him about the neck and by jumping on him attempted to crush him to the mat. Instead of which Gardner slowly and surely lifted the prostrate body of the aggressor, and both men came up to a standing position.*'[18]

In a match against Waino Ketonen the bout was described as follows '*Ketonen won the first fall in 38 minutes using an arm and leg lock to gain the decision. In the second session Pink caught the champion in a head scissors and chancery and flattened his shoulders in four minutes. Waino didn't realize the round was over, so sudden was his opponent's victory and it was necessary for the referee, John Heracle to drag the gladiators apart. Ketonen retained his right to the belt in the third fall, when after running Pink a poor second for 11 minutes he caught the Charlotte lad's toe in a deadly hold that threatened to put him out of commission. For 65 seconds Pink endured the pain, then his face contorted with agony, he threw up the sponge. The official time was 12 minutes and 5 seconds. From a spectacular standpoint the match last night has seldom been equaled in Wilmington and never surpassed. It was the flashy, tricky general against the herculean and methodical plodder and the plodder won. Both men repeatedly pulled individual plays of brilliance that brought the spectators to their*

Gardner's Measurements

Height	5', 8½"
Neck	16"
Shoulders	21"
Chest—	
Normal	41"
Contracted	37"
Expanded	44½"
8th Rib Expansion	3"
Biceps	14½"
Forearm	13"
Wrist	7½"
Waist—	
Normal	30½"
Contracted	28½"
Expanded	32"
Hips	37"
Thigh	22½"
Knee	16"
8" Above Knee	18½"
Calf	14½"
Ankle	9½"

Pinkie's measurements in 1922

feet, and each saw to it that there was never a moment's rest for the other.'[19] Pinky Gardner was referred to as the '*Champion middleweight wrestler of the world,*'[20] in light of his defeat of Waino Ketonen in 1921. He was matched to face the Swede Hanson in May of 1921, whereby he was described in the light of his win over Ketonen as '*Gardner, clean cut, handsome and more than able…..Gardner is a gentleman as well as a wrestler and to know him is to like him.*'[21]

In various accounts of Gardner's matches he is described as an able wrestler with many technical holds attributed to him. '*Ranking as one of the best men the game affords…..Few men are cleverer than Pinky Gardner… Gardner is a leg wrestler in that he uses his legs as proficiently as do most men their arms and hands.*'[22]

Pinky Gardner made repeated tours of Australia with the usual cohort of wrestlers, the names of Mike Yokel, Waino Ketonen, Sam Clapham, Ted Thye, Clarence Ecklund, Jack Winrow, Ad Santel, John Kilonis, Billy Meeske regularly mentioned in connection with contesting for the World title and the wrestling season in Australia.23,24 In early 1929, Pinky Gardner travelled with Peter Limutkin from Melbourne, whilst going to holiday in Tasmania prior to leaving for England and America. They had given an exhibition together, which resulted in Gardner receiving an injured left shoulder, Limutkin weighed in at 15 st 4lbs.25

Pinky Gardner became the wrestling instructor at Union College, Schenectady in 1922.[26] Carroll was attributed as a Director of Athletics at a Northern College[27].

In 1929, Pinky broke his leg through an accident on a slippery sidewalk, which temporarily put paid to his wrestling activities. However, in 1930 he came back strong being a runner up for the National light heavyweight championship tournament run by the National Boxing Association losing to Joe Banaski in the final. Although he continued to defeat the cream of the wrestling crop in 1930, the double-edged nature of the continuing success in his monuments business limited Carroll's ability to devote to wrestling.

Carroll A. Gardner ran to be county sheriff for Schenectady as the Democratic nomination, eventually running 11 times. Carroll was affiliated with a number of fraternities in the area such as New Hope Lodge, F and A.M St. George's Commandery, Cyprus Temple, Champion Lodge, I.O.O.O.F. to name a few. Pinky Gardner was considered a '*keen patron*' of the stage.[28] Pinky Gardner acted as a guest speaker for a number of fraternities offering his insight and guidance on a range of topics. On one such occasion *'Speaking on the topic " Combative Defense." Mr. Gardner spoke of "rough and tumbling" fighting as taught to the agents of the Federal bureau of Investigation and to the Rangers of the united Stats Army. The talk was illustrated by Mr. Gardner, who demonstrated several tactics used by members of the armed forces in protecting themselves from the enemy in personal combat, including methods of disarming an enemy. Mr. Gardner, who resides in Schenectady, is now county clerk of Schenectady County, and is well known in sporting circles*[29.] Pinky had been a keen speaker to the youth of the America and had supposedly addressed 'Thousands of youths' on such things as the value of physical fitness.[30]

Pinky Gardner passed away unexpectedly at his summer home in Newfane Vt. whilst entertaining the annual outing of the Schenectady Oldtime Football Players Inc. at the age of 75 in 1969. Having worked in the family monument business most of his life, Pinky unveiled what was to be his own grave monument in 1951. The monument included two benches and a reproduction of the 300 B.C statue of 'The Wrestlers.'[31]

Matches

27th March 1916 Gardner defeats Con Albright; $200 and gate receipts; Charlotte, N.C Gardner wins the first fall in 32minutes with leg scissors and toe hold, second fall in ten minutes with overhead chancery and double leg lock, whilst Albright applied a leg scissors throughout the technique.[32]

24th Jan 1917 Gardner defeats Charlie Kaiser; first fall in 23 min Arm scissors and half-nelson, 2nd fall in 18 min double arm lock and leg scissors.[33]

In 1917, Pinky Gardner faced against Jack Ozar, Jack won after 59 minutes with a cross and half-nelson hold.

18th March 1918 Gardner fought Mike Yokel at the New Nixon Theater, Pittsburg after being thrown over the ropes sustained a concussion of the brain; Yokel and the referee George Fisher were taken into custody post match.[34]

In 1919, Gardner faced against Jack Ozar in Atlantic City and defeated Ozar with a combination toe hold and cross over leg-hold after 68 minutes.

15th May 1919 Gardner lost to Jack Ozar in Harrisburg; after 59 minutes secured an arm scissors and crotch hold on Gardner, 2nd fall in six minutes bout had degenerated into a general smash.[35]

18th July 1919, Gardner defeated Sam Cramer Of New York; Cramer broke his leg whilst wrestling.[36]

27th February 1920, Jack Ozar was scheduled to fight Carroll Gardner as a finish bout catch-as-catch-can, originally billed as the first instance of the two wrestlers meeting. This was organised under the Armory Athletic Association who also intended to schedule matches with Jack Winrow, Mike Yokel, Waino Ketonen recognised middle-weight champion and John Kilonis.[37] Jack Ozar won with the first fall in 52 seconds with a flying mare; the second fall was a hip lock after one hour and 35 min.

1920-1921 Wrestling season Australia; Promoter Ira W. Cates arranged for Waino Ketonen, Mike Yokel, Young Monday, Matty Matsuda, Pinky Gardner, Victor Seaholm, Cyclone Ress, Miaki Oishi, John Kilonis, Jean Westegard, Peter Dallas, Chris Jordan, Jack Ross, Bob Diary and Ole Peterson to wrestle middleweight. Pinky Gardner was a favorite amongst the Australian spectators *'No season could possibly be complete unless the fans had watched the Chesterfieldian Gardner in action. Pinky is probably more popular than any man who ever came here.*'[38]

10th November 1920, Pinky Gardner lost to Waino Ketonen, middleweight title holder. Ketonen defeated Gardner in the third fall with a toe hold '*he caught the Charlotte lad's toe in a deadly hold that threatened to put him out of commission. For 65 seconds Pink endured the pain, then his face contorted with agony, he threw up the sponge.*'[39]

In early 1921, Pinky Gardner defeated Waino Ketonen in Boston for the Middleweight Championship title of the world.[40]

5th May 1921, Pinky Gardner faced against the Swede Hanson at the Academy Mat in Wilmington, North Carolina.[41]

2nd September 1921, Pinky Gardner faced against Captain Walter Evans at the Elks Theater, Port Arthur, Texas. In the same article reference is made to Pinky Gardner winning a match against Mike Yokel due to aggressiveness and cleverness after wrestling for 2 hours and 57 minutes and no fall awarded.[42]

In 1922, Pinky Gardner recently defeated the likes of Pete Brown of Texas, Irslinger of Atlantic city, and thrown Yokel four times.

13th February 1922, Pinky Gardner lost two falls in a match against Bonnie Rueben of Chicago, in Wichita, Washington.

16th April 1923, Pinky Gardner faced against Jack Ozar for the fifth time. Pinky Gardner won two straight falls.[43]

In March 1924, Pinky Gardner was due to face Zeke Smith of Richmond, Virginia.

16th April 1926, the Swiss wrestler Martin Lodecke defeated Pinky Gardner[44]

3rd August 1928, Pinky Gardner defeated Clete Kauffman in two straight falls[45] Gardner had Kauffman in the Boston crab causing a submission fall, followed by a pinfall.[46] Mr. Alf Bridges (the referee) described Pinky Gardner as '*the most brilliantly scientific wrestler he had ever seen.*'

11th August 1928, Pinky Gardner was drawn to wrestle Jack Winrow in Melbourne[47]

10th August 1928, Pinky Gardner defeated George Zarinoff two falls to one in Melbourne[48]

2nd September 1928, Pinky Gardner defeated Mike Yokel. Gardner obtained the first fall with a body press on Yokel, but Yokel forced Gardner to submit by the Boston Crab in the seventh round. Gardner was awarded the match on points due to demonstrating versatility, and a variety of counter holds.[49]

On the 12th September, Pinky Gardner faced Professor Higami, '*champion Jiu-jitsu wrestler of the world*' at the Adelaide City Baths[9]. The Japanese wrestler was knocked out whilst escaping from a threatened halch from Gardner as his head struck the mat violently[50].

24th September 1928, Pinky Gardner defeated Bob Bullet Myers; they had each secured a fall although Gardner was awarded the match on points.[51]

20th October 1928, Clarence Ecklund successfully defended the world's light heavyweight championship against Pinky Gardner at the Melbourne Stadium. Gardner secured the first fall with a double wrist lock and leg hold. Ecklund gained a fall via leg scissors on both of Gardner's arms with a leg hold. Ecklund then pinned Gardner to win two falls to one.[52]

4th November 1928, Ted Thye defeated Pinky Gardner at the Melbourne Stadium, two falls to one.[53] Ted Thye was considered a master of wristlocks and true to his title secured a fall on Gardner via wristlock to force Pinky's shoulders to the mat. Gardner then secured a fall via submission from a leg and toe hold. Ted Thye secured a second fall by wristlock and body press.[54]

10th November 1928, Lost to Count Zarynoff.[55]

26th April 1932, Pinky Gardner threw John Kilonis at Cleveland, Ohio[56]

2nd May 1932, Caroll "Pinky" Gardner, Schenectady County's wrestling sheriff, today retained the world's light heavyweight wrestling championship. '*He threw Jack Kilonis of Manchester, N.H, former title holder, in a rough bout lasting 35 minutes here last night.*'[57]

Billy Riley would, according to an article from the Ringsider magazine, lose his title he had won from Gardner to Waino Ketonen. In the article it says, " I have always looked upon this fight as the greatest contest of my career. I enjoyed every minute of it. It was a ding dong battle from the sound of the bell and I realized that I had lost my title I got consolation in the fact that I had passed it on to one well worthy of it" [58].

In an interesting article in the courier, a journalist made comment on the effect of the travels to the US on Seaman Cox "Seaman Cox of Wigan used to be quite a good fellow and was always kept busy up and down the country. He too went in search of the irresistible dollar. I hope he brought some back with him but all I could discern when he met a Belgian Gaeerterts at the ring on Saturday last was a pronounced thick left ear and a very broad nose. He was not guilty of either when he left these shores. His performance amazed me. In a free and easy manner he stands with his right arm hanging by his side and his left wresting on his leg just above the knee. Luckily for him it needed very little defense to stop the Belgian from scoring but had the visitor been a little more experienced Cox would have paid dearly for his open stance"[59]

As an interesting aside in an interview given to Jake Shannon , Karl Gotch a one time student of Billy Riley seemed to have suggested that Billy had travelled to America and been soundly beaten and come straight back. This does not seem to be supported by the shipping records, newspaper reports or in fact by the family of Billy Riley.

Tommy Moore, who wrestled under the name Jack Dempsey, passed on another possible reason for the American tour to his son Michael. He told him that Billy had gone out to look for his father as well as to wrestle, and apparently it was with the help of a policeman who wrestled in New York that he found his fathers grave, and also found out that he had died of influenza.

They departed New York on the SS Adriatic in May 1923 arriving in Liverpool on the 20th May.

It was not only America that Billy would tour. It was his match with Reginsky that led the spokesperson for the Johannesburg sporting club to cable Riley approximately 6 weeks following the match. They offered him a lucrative sum and paid

SS Arundel Caste - the ship Billy travelled to South Africa on

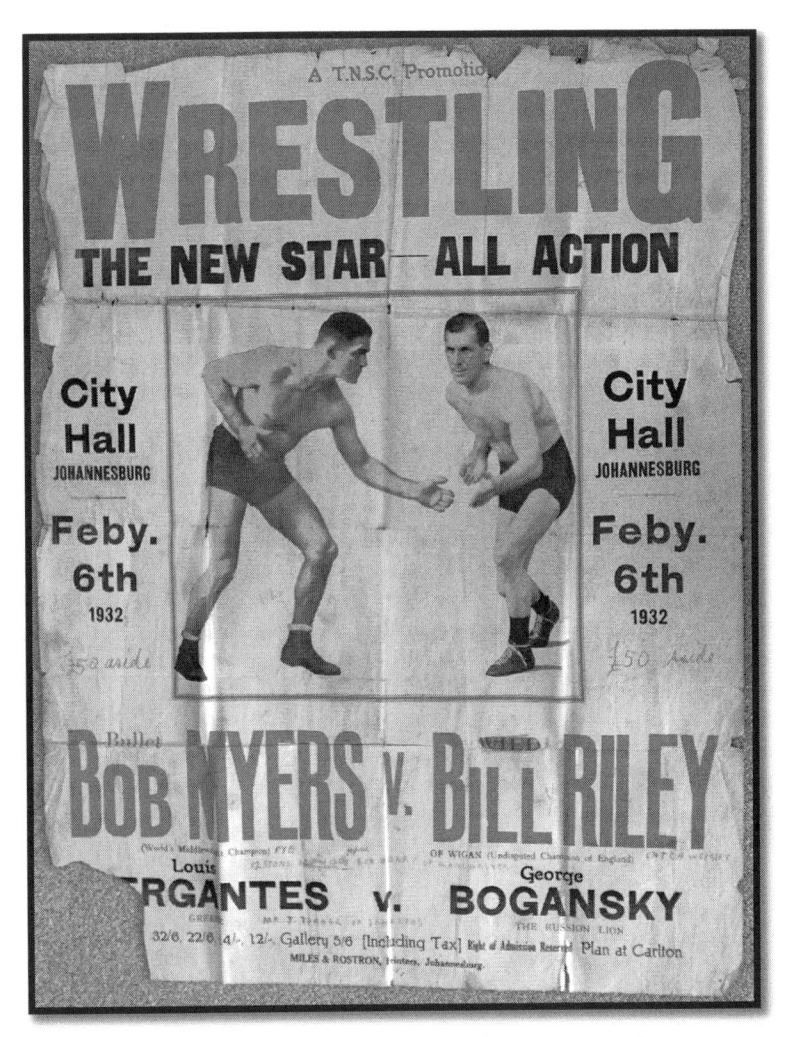

passage to go to South Africa[60]. The first tour was to take place in late 1931 and early 1932.

A wrestling correspondent wrote " *there was nothing in the quiet spoken almost insignificant man who arrived at the Park station one December morning to suggest that he was English all in middleweight wrestling champion. Indeed he had the reputation of being the roughest grappler in England. There was less still to suggest the ruthless punisher of the mat ring when he was first seen stripped for he had none of the statuesque muscle of his American predecessors who all looked the part*"[61]

City hall Johanesburg

His first match was with Ben Sherman, who was to become a long time friend of Billy Riley. Sherman, a Canadian, was firm favorite for the match. Sherman was a product of the Multumah Athletic club in Portland Oregon. He travelled to Europe in the 1930s and wrestled Bert Assirati. He would later come out of retirement in the 1950s to accept a challenge match. He spent a time in Honolulu under the moniker of the masked 'Scarlet Pimpernel'[62] It would be this match that would earn Billy the title of "Wild Bill" that would follow him through accounts of his tour. The match was described by a South African Wrestling champion D.MacDonalds and was printed in the Wigan observer.

"*Wrestling was beginning to go a bit flat here when Riley met the clever Canadian champion Ben Sherman the latter being hot favorite.*

This quiet unassuming little Englishman sits in his corner with a faint smile the gong sounds Riley is out of his corner like a flash down

Transvaal national sporting club committe

goes the Canadian with a crash Riley of top Sherman is on the defense fighting for his life as he gets to his feet but Riley is on him like a tiger and down again he crawls to the ropes. By this time the crowd is roaring and cheering everyman on his feet. Sherman is picked up and dashed down thrown over the ropes at the press table at last the round is over. The applause is deafening. The second round commences Riley is all over his man and in two minutes it is all over Sherman is battered to a standstill and finally thrown over the ropes he retires. Riley's is the winner. What wonderful applause he gets for the next few weeks one heard nothing but 'Riley'"[63]

Billy Riley had the following to say in a newspaper article about his encounter with Sherman "Referring to his opening fight against Sherman the young Canadian, as the result of which the Wiganer was given the title "Wild Bill Riley" he said the seconds were to blame for the wild scenes described in the report of the fight which was published in the "Examiner" "They climbed into the ring and began an altercation; the crowd got excited and about twenty of us finished up in the ring fighting" said Riley "It was a lively do"[64]

His next match was to be one with Bullet Bob

Bob Bootle and Billy Riley with the British Empire belt

Myers, holder of the middleweight championship of the world. Myers had beaten Walter Miller for the world welterweight in 1927[65].Some sources site that there were three matches between the two wrestlers[66] whilst others two[67]. Myers had defended his title against Jack Robinson in the October of 1931 winning by two falls to one[68]. Bob Myers, nicknamed Bullet, studied at the Multnomah athletic club in Portland Oregon alongside Benny Sherman[69].

The first meeting was recounted in the Wigan Examiner :-

"'Wild' Bill Riley of Wigan was converted from the maniacal uncontrollable rough man of the ring seen against Sherman into a more orthodox grappler at the City hall when his tactics against "Bullet" Bob Myers the worlds middle weight title holder whom he beat on points almost merited the changing of his name to that of 'Wild' Bill Riley.

The Wigans mans work was scarcely notable for delicate artistry but he certainly showed that he had a fairly extensive repertoire of holds confounding the critics who said that his actual knowledge of wrestling was nil and compared with his rough exhibition in the city hall his methods were almost anaemic. The flaming Riley who introduced himself to the rand some weeks ago with the swaggering bravado of a two gunned tobacco chewing "bad man" of a wild west film was this time only a smoldering fellow who had control of himself and except for occasional flashes of temper when he gave a glimpse of the snarling Riley of before, he did his rough tricks with a cool deliberation and with a definite object.

THE EXTRA ROPE

One thing that handicapped him in his exploitation of the spectacular was the new ring with an entire rope a foot about the highest of the old ring, this together with the fact there was an extra platform of three feet outside the ropes on to which the wrestlers occasionally fell were the special recommendation of the deputy commissioner of the Witwatersrand Police, Colonel Heatley Jones who expressed his appreciation of the arrangement to the promoters.

It is doubtful however if those who like to see a real Roman holiday in return for their admittance money appreciated the extra strand, which robbed the crowd of many a thrill. Similarly Riley, who boasts throwing out of the ring as one of his most effective forms of aggression must have viewed the new ring with disfavour as he frequently picked Myers up bodily and made a line for the ropes only to hear the derisive laughter of the crowd as Myers coolly held on to the extra strand and let the Wigan man exert his strength in vain. The new ring however certainly helped to give to hostilities of the evening more claim to the dignity of being called wrestling

Billy Riley vs Jack Robinson

thought there were occasional elements of a street brawl during the evening.

Fluctuating fortunes

The bout itself was a spectacular affair of fluctuating fortunes, which gripped the spectator throughout and sent a capacity house away well satisfied. There was little to choose between the men in eight grueling round of punishing work. But Riley perhaps just deserved the points decision given to him by reason of his greater aggression ad his solid work in the opening rounds. Myers rallied in theatrical style in the last two rounds, and having experienced a grueling time. The spectacle of Myers bleeding from a cut under the eye and generally bedraggled and battle worn making a heroic effort to recover his reserves and save himself from defeat in the closing minutes of the match appealed to the spectators sense of the dramatic. Every move of the champions was applauded and he received a warm ovation at the close. The very fact that the decision was in Riley's favour received a good reception seemed to indicate that he must have won more clearly than many good judges imagined.

Perhaps the two deciding factors of the match were Riley's physical strength and more especially the fact that Myers did not seem to have his usual speed. When the pair stood up to be introduced Myers seemed twice as broad in the shoulders and his classic figure made the Wigan man look almost puny by comparison. But handsome is as handsome does and Riley proved that it is not always the statuesque possessor of beauty that has the strength, by maintaining the aggressive in the first three rounds with sheer physical effort. With beady black eyes following the retreating Myers with the intensity of those of a snake Riley followed Myers relentlessly in the opening rounds. Myers unlike Sherman showed how level headedness could deal with his opponents aided by the top strand of rope which was at the right height for him to grasp it he backed with impunity to the ropes when Riley was obviously anxious to live up to public expectations by throwing him into the crowd. Faced by a calmer wrestler than Sherman and a tactician to boot Riley showed that his wrestling knowledge is not confined to mere roughness by producing a number of holds

Whether he would have been successful had Myers been as fast as usual was open to question. But the champion through a picture of fitness was sluggish and when he did apply good holds often had them broken by Riley's sheer force

Myers was in a bad way when he was pinned 2 min 3 sec after the fourth round had started. In the third round Riley had brutally gouged his antagonists eyes in a headlock and with blood coming from a nasty cut under the eye and half blinding him Myers looked to be waging a losing battle. He fought courageously against the inevitable, but a fall against the weakening Myers was merely a question of time in the fourth round and Riley seemed a certain winner after obtaining it. Myers however mad a great rally and seemed to gather both strength and spirit until in the sixth rough in contrast to his usual even-tempered methods he was stirred to kick his opponent after some unnecessary roughness but the Englishman.

When Myers actually obtained an equalizing fall in the seventh round the enthusiasm of the crown bordered on a frenzy.

With a fall back both grapplers wrestled themselves to a standstill in a last round in which each in turn seemed likely to pin the other in a style typical of the fluctuating tour of the match. It was a grueling match in which both men fully earned the good praise they received[70]

Next a follow up match was had with Sherman, but again Riley won, this time on points.[71]

His next match was with Jack Robinson holder of the British Empire belt. . This would not be their first match , a previous encounter had seen the match end with Robinson with a broken arm. The match was sponsored by the Johannesburg star newspaper. The proceeds were to be for charity and would go to the Seaside fund. Official receipts showed it to be the largest show they had ever had and took place at the city hall.

The following article regarding the background to the match was reprinted in the Wigan Examiner:

F.W.R writing in the "Johannesburg Starr "regarding Billy Riley of Wigan, the champion wrestlers says "It is said that distance tends

Jack Robinson

enchantment to the view This is often true of idols when too close scrutiny reveals them to have feet of clay. But there are times when it is not. Would you prefer to know Wild Will Riley for instance as the vicious specialist tin the most merciless phases of the "all in" wrestling game or a kindly family man outside the ring. The bowing hundreds who acclaim or hoot the methods of this stoic of the mat whose features are equally immobile whether he is torturing his opponent with some fiendish grip of himself being rucked with an equally painful hold, know him only as one of the hardest of the hard faced men of a hard game where mercy and the finer sentiments are unknown.

They would smile perhaps if you were to draw a picture of the same "Wild Will" as a family man dangling a toddler upon his knee with a beatific smile or the lined intense face known to the City Hall wrestling habitués .Yet this is true. Vicious Bill Riley who has playful thrown twelve stone opponents over the ropes is the mildest and least ostentatious looking individual outside of the ring. Quiet spoken, essentially reserved, obliging courteous and generous is this docile fellow whose enemies try to label him as one of the arch villains of the mat game.

This is the kind of man Riley is , in vivid contrast to some notoriously avaricious boxers we have had. During the week he was approached by "The Star" to appear in the big professional tournament to be staged at the city Hall on March 19 in aid of the seaside fund. It was explained he would only receive a small fee for meeting a most formidable opponent. Immediately he grasped this, the proceeds were to go to giving poor children a holiday by the seaside and so take them for a spell out of drabness to a comparative paradise of bathing, and sunshine he accepted eagerly."AI'll wrestle anyone you say anywhere and ah don't want nowt for it neither so long as it's for kiddies" he said in his best and slowest broad "Lancasheer"

So the picture of Riley who is gentle with the children with the same arms that have learnt to apply Killer headlocks is not merely a bit of 'sob stuff blurb" that might have come from Hollywood. Riley these days is a prosperous publican in Wigan, but he has seen harder days and struggles in childhood and has attuned his ear to ready responses to charity calls. His father disappeared when he was a toddling member of a family of six children for whom Mrs.Riley had to battle until her young brood grew up and made a way in the world for themselves until one of them became a Councillor in Wigan and another puny youngster grew up to overcome his disadvantages sufficiently to start in a public house out of his wrestling earnings and to reach the pinnacle of a match for the worlds title."Ah could a done with summit like a "Star" seaside trip myself when I was a nipper. It's a gradely idea" As Riley's was of disclaiming the credit of his offer to wrestle *for nothing. This is a Riley Mr Man in the Street does not know.*[72]

MacDonald's reported the match as follows

"Jack Robinson another English wrestler who is also here next claimed a match with Riley. The contest was for the British Empire middle weight championship and a valuable belt presented by Mr. H Carter chairman of the Transvaal national sporting club Johannesburg. The contest took place in the City Hall as did all the others before a crowded house. Robinson proved no match for Riley. Robinson hugged the mat crawled to the ropes in fact held on to anything and everything and retired after the second round completely exhausted."[73]

Riley himself gave the following account in an interview with the Wigan Examiner:

One of Riley's biggest nights was when he wrestled for the British Empire Title. The programme was organised by "The Johannesburg Star" and the proceeds were in aid of the Star Seaside Fund "It was a wonderful night" Riley told our reporter "and as a result, the fund was augmented to the extent of £1,000. I soon disposed of Robinson who retired in the third round and the crowd was disappointed that the fight had turned out to be such a fiasco. I wanted to give them value for money, so I stayed in the ring and wrestled three rounds with Bullet Myers. The crowd was delighted. The promoters wrote me a wonderful letter and told me that the proceeds would mean that three hundred poor children would get a fortnight's holiday at the seaside. Many of them would otherwise never see the sea"[74]

It would seem to be this match that Riley won "decisively on points" and was described as an exciting match, however this was not a championship match[75].

Next came the final match with Myers. The match again recounted by McDonalds was as follows:-

Riley next met Bob Myers on 9th April for the worlds middle weight title and after five rounds of exceedingly fierce and fast wrestling in which Riley was more than holding his own Myers secured a punishing Japanese arm lock the referee appealed to Riley to give in or his arm would break but Riley replied with a determined "no". With than something snapped the towel was thrown in and Riley's arm hung limp. A doctor who was called in forbade Riley to continue but in spite of this Riley insisted that he should wrestle on and advanced towards his opponent with one arm helpless at his side until the referee actually barred the way and declared Myers the winner on leaving the ring Riley received a greater applause than did Myers. Riley will always be welcomed back to Johannesburg in all his matches here he was giving away from 6 to 8lbs in weight even against Myers.

Riley is a fine example of a real clever and scientific Lancashire wrestler. I thought I knew all there is to know about catch as catch can until I met Bill Riley but he has shown me a few moves previously unknown to me although I have held both the middleweight and light heavy weight amateur championship of South Africa for 20 years, I also have taken part in the Antwerp in 1920 without being thrown and recently won the heavyweight amateur championships of South Africa although only 11 ½ stone and 49 years of age I have refereed all the top line contests here during the past three years and seamen Ike Walter miller ex worlds champion Henry Irslinger ex worlds champion Ben Sherman Fred Maracci, L Pergantes, JJ Van Benarurg G Bogansky and a host of others.

Riley is certainly the cleverer of the lot what a pity he was not 6lbs or 7lbs heavier after his first match he was looked upon and talked as a dangerous wild man and earned the name of wild Will Riley. the press was up in arms the dangerous man must be checked. New measures had to be drafted, an extra rope had to be put around the ring to prevent him throwing out his opponent the outer edge of the platform had to be padded but the critics were astounded when this wonderful little wrestler threw opponents half a stone heavier than himself over the additional rope which was particularly as high as himself. We are all sorry he has had to return but we trust he will return next season and bring Mrs. Riley with him. In the meantime we wish him every success.[76]

Riley himself had the following to say about his encounters with Myers:

"My stiffest fights were against Bob Myers, The Texan, and he's a good un" admitted Riley "I beat him and the he beat me when I wrestled him for the world title. For the fight there was a £2,000 gate and people were clamouring to get in; the City Hall was crammed to its fullest capacity. During the fight I had a bone in my arm broken, and could not go on. Myers was the only man to beat me during the tour. He is a full fledged middle weight, and can wrestle as well with his legs as with his arms".

According to the Johannesburg Press, Riley was a great drawing card in the City, for the excitable crowds want to see action all the time. "I gave them plenty" he remarked "In all my fights there was no time for stalling it was ding-dong all the time and a great feature of the wrestling was the fairness of the referees. One of the best was Duncan MacDonald"

A talkie film was taken of the title fight and Riley hopes to secure it so that it can be screened in Wigan[77]

According to the Ringsider magazine "They still talk of the contest that was staged at the city hall in Johannesburg, Billy was forced to retire after 58 minutes with a broken arm bone"[78]

Another account from the Wigan Examiner was as follows:

Billy Riley the Wigan wrestler who is on a tour of South Africa, was defeated in a thrilling contest with Bob Myers and the following account of the match is taken from the "Johannesburg Star".

"In a fiercely contested championship battle which contained many thrills Bob ("Bullet") Myers managed to retain his middleweight belt at the city Hall on Saturday night, but only after losing a sensational fall in the first round and taking a severe gruelling for another three and a half rounds from Bill Riley, did he manage to turn the table on his opponent.

"Riley lived up to his pseudonym of "Wild Bill"" with a vengeance. One of the mildest mannered men outside the ring, the scent of combat apparently convers him to an implacable opponent.

"The difference in the man can be sensed immediately he takes to the ring. His features assume a grave mask out of which his eyes gleam fiercely, and, while waiting for hostilities to commence his pent up energy found expression in beating a nervous tattoo with his fingers on the ropes. When he discarded his dressing gown in readiness for the fray, his tough, lean figure gave but a faint idea of his strength and endurance and compared ill with the Adonis like body of the champion.

Irresistible action

"But once the bell sounded Riley seemed to be galvanised with irresistible action. He darted on the

Canadian and crashed through an attempt to hand him off, seized a headlock and hurled him on his back with a good old fashioned cross buttock, Here he held Myers in a fierce headlock for one minute before the champion broke free with sheer strength. No sooner was Myers free on his feet than Riley was on him like a tiger breaking his strength through his resistance and crashing him to the mat in a headlock. Four times in quick succession he repeated his vicious headlock and cross buttocked bewildering the champion with his dynamic strength. But the fourth time he hipped his opponent with the cunning of the veteran he changed his tactics and instead maintaining the headlock he whipped round lie a cat on his feet and seizing him by the legs swung him round and in a second had secured the deadly Boston crab. There was no escape for the champion .It was a case of submitting a fall or sustaining a back injury and as Riley holding his man so that he could not move an inch, exerted pressure Myers could only yield a fall. He tapped the mat and Riley after holding on a little while to give the champion something to go on with reluctantly relaxing his hold. Thus, in 1 min 30 sec of thrilling action, Riley had secured the first fall.

Myers Shaken

The champion obviously surprised and badly shaken came out for the second round bent on standing for a rest, but Riley was there to prove the Lancashire men have nothing to learn about the catch as catch can style and that they can adapt themselves to the all in methods. He pounded on Myers like a cat on a canary and swung him round over the ropes with a body hold. Fortunately for Myers, particularly as the contest proceeded, an extra line of rope had been fixed round the ring and he was able to hook his arm around the top strand to break his fall. No sooner was he back than Riley seized him in a headlock and hipped him to the mat, where he converted to a reverse body hold into an arm hold and head scissors.

"Up to this stage it was all Riley, but Myers was gradually finding himself. When Myers finally got on top he proceeded to shake him and hammer him into the mat and then worry his man with an arm bar.

Riley took his medicine and returned the compliment when he knuckled Myers face when he was in a headlock , the bell going to the champion's relief.

Riley the master

"Riley was clearly the master to this stage and he proceeded to emphasise his mastery in the third round, when his all in tactics rattled Myers out of his wonted placidity, There was a little fray off the mat at the start of the round which had to be stopped by the referee. Then Riley threatened to obtain a second fall with a body scissors and arm bar, which gave Myers a bad time, the Lancashire crack varied his tactics of frequently throwing Myers out of the ring together with some magnificent ground wrestling, while Myers retaliated with what must have been very nearly a stranglehold on a couple of occasions. With tempers becoming ruffled, Myers landed a solid body punch to which Riley replied and it seemed for a moment a bout of fisticuffs was indicated.. When the bell rang Riley had Myers in a punishing hold which he was reluctant to release

"Myers trussed up the Lancastrian with a combination hold in the fourth round which must have tested all his fortitude but there was never that expression in his immobile countenance. Each turn secured punishing holds but Riley was providing most of the fireworks and every few minutes threw the champion over the ropes by way of variation to ground work.

The decisive fall

The decisive moment of the match came in the fifth round when Riley again twisted Myers over the ropes and fell on top of him. On this occasion it was the biter that was bit as when they came back through the ropes Riley was apparently dazed and Myers seized him in a crotch hold and threw him over the ropes. Failing to break his fall by grasping one of the strands of the ring as Myers had invariably done Riley fell on his head on the outer platform with a force that stunned him and from there he rolled on to the floor. The referee Mr Macdonald counted thirty the period permitted a contestant to return to the ring but Riley was clean "out" and his second realising the position threw in his towel. This would have better signalled the end of the contest as Riley was carried to his corner and despite the frenzied attentions of his second had only half revived when the bell sounded for the next round. Mr MacDonald might well have stopped the bout but he checked a couple of attempts of Myers to "shin" his man and the champion was content to put him down and pin him with a body press to win the contest by two falls to one. "While Riley sagged in his corner the triumphant Myers stood in the ring receiving the applause of the crowd while Mr Harry Carter the chairman of the Transvaal National sporting Club buckled the middle-weight belt around his waist"[79]

Myers would later try his luck at gold prospecting. He travelled to a rich reef near Rwanda in Southern Rhodesia.[80]. He lost his life in a mining accident[81].

The end of his tour was recounted in the Wigan Examiner:

"I never really felt at my best out there" he went on "but I was given a wonderful time and I know I should receive a warm welcome if ever I go back. Everybody I came across did all they could for me. I was never short of sparring partners and the people, particularly the members of the Transvaal Sporting Club, laid themselves out to show me round and give me a good time, I went round gold mines and I have brought back some fine souveniers back with me as well as trophies"

Just prior to his departure for home the secretary of the Transvaal Sporting Club wrote to Riley expressing the club's appreciation of his services he had rendered "You have always been keen and ready to assist at each and every tournament: stats the letter "by giving out your best and not only my club appreciates your efforts, but also the thousands of Rand supporters who have witnessed your performances. Your sterling work in the ring and your sportsmanlike demeanour , both inside the ring and outside has made you many friends throughout the Union of South Africa and we hope you will return to the country at no late date, and once again come under the arc lights of the Johannesburg City Hall. You have won a British Empire Middle Weight Wrestling Championship Belt under the auspices of my club and when you return we hope to stage you again in a title bout"

About two hundred friends gave Riley a rousing send off when he embarked on the "Warwick Castle" [82]

On arriving home a civic welcome was given by the Mayor (Councillor W.A.Hipwood) who was accompanied by the Mayoress (Mrs Hipwood) and members of the Corporation.

For the second tour we know he sailed on the SS.Arundel Castle in third class on the 11th of august 1933. The ship was of the Union castle line. The shipping records show him to be living in 47 Burkett Lane at the time and noted him to be a wrestler and 38 years old.[83] He returned home in the Janurary of 1934 and he arrived at the port of Southampton on the 5th February 1934, again on the SS Arundel Castle, he was passenger 125 , an interesting note is that the family had obviously moved in the meantime as it noted his address as Beach Hill, Wigan Lancs.[84]

The following is an account of his second tour in the Wigan Examiner:

Wrestlers return form South Africa
Billy Riley the Wigan wrestler who is the British Empire middleweight champions and belt holder has returned home from his second universally successful South African tour. As on his previous tour two years ago Riley was the guest of the Transvaal National Sporting Club and during his six months at the Cape he has had ten fights, winning five drawing one and losing four. To every opponent the Wiganer had to concede weight; there was a dearth of middleweights worthy of Riley's mettle and he met some of the best heavyweights in the country for the edification of the sporting crowds. Riley by his skill and pluck established himself firmly in the affections of the Rand crowds on his first tour and this time he was given a wonderful reception at every place he visited. "Wild Bill" Riley as he has become familiarly known was a general favourite. Leaving England on August 11th he landed at Cape town on August 28th and was met by Mr Harry Carther (chairman) Mr St John Dean (Secretary) and the following members of the

committee of the Transvaal National Sporting Club: Mr Bassett Davies, Mr Pat McCarthy, Mr Corner and Mr Gwillam. The last named gentleman by the way is a Wiganer hailing from the Marsh Green District.

Riley had been in training on the boat and two days after his arrival his first appearance at the city Hall, Johannesburg when he met Jumping Joe Ketos, the Australian heavy-weight and won by two falls to nil before an audience of between two to three thousand people.

His second fight against Louis Pergantes was one of the most terrific battles of his career. Pegantus who is a Greek is one of the cleverest heavy weights in the world. Riley was conceding over two stones in weight but was a match for the Greek in cleverness. It was unfortunate for Riley that in the fifth round Pegantes threw Riley to the mat with such force that the Wiganer was stunned and the towel had to be thrown in. In the return match with Pegantus at Bulaiwayo the men wrestled to a draw over six ten minute rounds.

Riley's next opponent was Dr Martin Murkes who also had a weight advantage of two stones over Riley. The fight took place at the Wanderine Sports Ground, Johannesburg in the open air. Rile secured the first fall but was eventually beaten by the odd fall in three.

Riley's defeats at the hands of much heavier men did not detract one jot from his popularity and there was once more a huge crown when he stepped into the ring to oppose Butch Prag. Riley won by the only fall of the match and in his next fight at Bloenfontein he defeated the hefty Van der Meyer a strong and difficult man to pin by two falls to nil. At Port Elizabeth he beat George …… another heavyweight on points but at the seaside town of East London Riley had to retire in his bout Ventor owing to a bad cut on his forehead, which had to be stitched.

For his ninth fight the Wiganer met Pat Henry the Capetown middleweight and pinned him twice in four rounds.

Riley's last bout before returning home was with his old opponent Ben Sherman who is now in the light heavyweight class. Neither man secured a fall, but when in the second round Riley was knocked unconscious by a bad fall when he was hurled to the mat on his head the fight was awarded to Sherman. The Wiganer was unconscious for nearly an hour.[85]

Jayne Riley's had the following to say about her

A momento made for Billy from gold containing rock from the mines he visited

father's travels to South Africa "he enjoyed South Africa, he didn't like the Apartheid thing though. No, he didn't like that, I can always remember when he was in the hotel there, he only started smoking when he went to South Africa. He never smoked, and wait a minute, he said, this day, they had a man look after them in the hotel and he said, he came in and he said, whatever his names was, 'listen, would you like some cigarettes?' he said, 'yes, I would' so me' dad he said 'here take some,' and he came like that to my dad, [hands shaped like a beggars bowl] and me dad said 'don't you ever do that to me again, you're my equal, you take them off me like I would take them off you, but don't ever do that to me again,' he didn't like that at all. Then he went down to, while he was there, there was some number that used to be at the school, I remember my brother was, and she'd gone out to say thank ye, looking after this little black children and he went to visit them and they donated his proceeds and it was to send them on holiday, somewhere in South Africa and he was very touched by that I think it was Sister Mary Peter's that used to be at St. Patrick's in Wigan. He went to visit her, so he enjoyed that y'know. I think he liked South Africa, he didn't like being away from home. He was a very home bird, he used to say 'well I like Wigan. They all come back to Wigan.' He said"[86]

Whilst in South Africa Billy met many ex-Wiganer's who were living in South Africa. He recounted his experiences in the Wigan Examiner *"Many Wiganer's domiciled in South Africa flocked to Riley's fights. "I met George Howarth, a Wiganer whose father was at one time in business in Mesnes-street and Tommy Tyrer, an engineer from Mesrs. Walker Bros. who is working out there, came to all my fights" said Riley. "David Booyson, the former Wigan Rugby Player, is doing fine back in his own country and I spent a few days at his home. He wishes to be remembered to all his Wigan friends. I also met Van Der Spay another ex-Wigan player and Bob Lester, a man from Newtown. They all wanted to know something about the old town"*[87]

Later Ernie Riley whilst staying in the Transvaal, 40 miles north of Pretoria was staying at the farm of a friend by the name of Andre Petiga, who was a Pentecostal minister but had also played rugby league for the Transvaal. Whilst on a grocery shop he travelled to a village 4 miles form the house to a local off license. A gentleman in his 80s who looked to be in great physical condition was in the off license. Ernie commented on his good shape and he said "I used to be a wrestler". Ernie laughed telling him that he was a wrestler too. He then said to the man " My father was out in South Africa in the 1930's" , the man replied" Who was your father" , when Ernie replied the man exclaimed "I knew him!". He was the brother in law of Bullet Bob Myers, who had married his sister. The gentleman's name was Bill Van der Velde [88].

Billy Riley told Michael Moore that whilst in South Africa he fell asleep in the sun getting badly burned. This was one week before one of his major matches, he felt very ill and despite being treated with ice baths the wrestling must have been extremely painful[89]

Although according to the Wigan Examiner Billy was offered favorable terms to return to America for another tour, however, the second tour in South Africa was to be his last. He was now keen on concentrating on his career at home and to answer the many challenges coming his way. As he told the Wigan Examiner "Let them come and put the money down"" he says "and let's have less challenging"

---

[1] Cincinatti enquirer eition page 3-11-22
[2] WIgan examiner June 21 1924
[3] Wigan Examiner 17th November 1923
[4] Wigan Observer 13th March 1923
[5] www.worcesteracadaemy.org/history - July 2014
[6] Letter from Tommy Heyes
[7] Modesto evening news 3rd March 1923
[8] Lynn Telegram news – 13/3/23
[9] Wigan Obsercer – 17th March 1923 Two wign boys in america
[10] Ernie Riley interview A.Coleman
[11] Wigan Observer 22-8-31
[12] Schenectady NY Gazette, 29th October 1931 p.8
[13] Schenectady NY Gazette, 29th October 1931 p.8
[14] Wilmington morning Star 28th March 1916
[15] Harrisburg Telegraph 10th May 1919
[16] Harrisburg Telegraph 10th May 1919
[17] Harrisburg Telegraph 10th May 1919
[18] Harrisburg Telegraph 10th May 1919
[19] Wilmington Morning Star 11th November 1920
[20] Wilmington Morning Star 1st May 1921
[21] Wilmington Morning Star 1st May 1921
[22] Wilmington Morning Star 2nd May 1921
[23] Referee (Sydney), Wednesday, 16th February 1927
[24] The Argus (Melbourne) Monday 23rd April 1928
[25] The Mercury (Hobart, Tasmania) Tuesday 8th January 1929
[26] News (Adelaide) Tuesday 11th September 1928
[27] The Bee, 15th March 1924
[28] Sunday Times (Sydney) 28th October 1928
[29] Troy Record, 29th March 1945
[30] Troy Record, 5th May 1950
[31] Times Record, 4th October 1969
[32] Wilmington morning Star 28th March 1916
[33] Charlotte News 24th Jan 1917
[34] Harrisburg Telegraph 20th March 1918
[35] Harrisburg Telegraph 16th May 1919
[36] Lebanon Daily News, 19th July 1919

[37] Schenectady Gazette, Thursday, February 19th 1920
[38] Wilmington Morning Star 14th Sept 1920
[39] Wilmington Morning Star 11th November 1920
[40] Wilmington Morning Star 1st May 1921
[41] Wilmington Morning Star 1st May 1921
[42] Port Arthur News, 2nd September 1921
[43] Daily Lebanon News 17th April 1923
[44] The Register (Adelaide) Friday, 28th May 1926
[45] Mirror (Perth) Saturday, 4th August 1928
[46] The Register (Adelaide) Monday 6th August 1928
[47] Referee (Sydney) Wednesday 27th June 1928
[48] Mirror (Perth) Saturday, 11th August 1928
[49] Recorder (Port Pirie) Monday 3rd September 1928
[50] The Register (Adelaide) Thursday 13th September 1928
[51] Barrier Miner, Tuesday 25th September 1928
[52] The Maitland Daily Mercury, 22nd October 1928
[53] The Maitland Daily Mercury, 22nd October 1928
[54] Recorder (Port Pirie) Monday, 5th November 1928
[55] The Daily News (Perth) Monday, 12th November 1928
[56] Charlestown Daily Mail, 27th April 1932
[57] Indiana Gazette, 3rd May 1932
[58] Ringsider magazine
[59] The courier 21/3/25
[60] Interview Tommy Heyes 9/7/14
[61] Unknown newspaper article 1971
[62] The Wrestler Magazine September 1962 – Page 19
[63] Billy Rileys South African Success – Wigan observer – 4/6/32
[64] Wigan Examiner June 11 1932
[65] Tommy Heyes interview 9/7/14
[66] Mascall?
[67] Billy Rileys South African Success – Wigan observer - 4/6/32
[68] Nottingham evening post 26/10/31
[69] The Wretsler magazine – October 1962 – page 23
[70] WIgan examiner 3rd March 1932
[71] Billy Rileys South African Success – Wigan observer - 4/6/32
[72] Wigan Examiner April 2nd 1932
[73] Billy Rileys South African Success – Wigan observer - 4/6/32
[74] Wigan Examiner April2nd 1932
[75] Billy Rileys South African Success – Wigan observer – 4/6/32
[76] Billy Rileys South African Success – Wigan observer - 4/6/32
[77] Wigan Examiner April 2nd 1932
[78] Ringsider magazine.
[79] Wigan Examiner April 9th 1932
[80] Aberdeen press and journal 21/1/36
[81] The wrestler– October 1962 page 23
[82] Wigan Examiner June 11th 1932
[83] Shipping Record ancestry.co.uk
[84] Shipping Recordwww.ancestry.co.uk
[85] Wigan Examiner February 1934
[86] Jayhe Byrne interview November 2013
[87] Wigan Examiner June 11th 1932
[88] Ernie Riley interview A Coleman
[89] Michael Moore interview 10/7/14

Chapter 4

The 'All in' era

In the mid 1920's wrestling's popularity had waned both in America and in Britain. In his book 'Blue blood on the mat' Sir Athol Oakley stated that it was Farmer Burns, famous catch as catch can wrestler and trainer of Frank Gotch, who came to the belief in 1925 that the only way in which wrestling could become popluarised again was to revise the rules of catch as catch can. The reasoning behind this was that men such as Padoubney Zybyszko due to his build and statue were almost impossible to pin under the Lancashire rules. He decided to add in the submission locks that were strictly forbidden in the old catch as catch can and Greco wrestling but utilised by the Japanese, as this was the only way to win against the 'unpinnable pachyderm' as he had christened Zybyzko[1]. However, it is difficult to say that all submissions were added by the Japanese there are accounts of matches prior to this point being decided on a submission and accounts of the use of the double wrist lock for example as present from 1910 onwards in the match accounts in the United States as well as holds such as the toe hold and body scissors for the purpose of getting a submission by means of the pain produced by the hold, so it is probably an over simplification on the part of Oakley, it must also be remembered his initial background was that of amateur wresting where such holds were prohibited. Lancashire wrestling's rules had changed between the early 19th and early 20th centuries. The means by which a win was decided changed also, certain holds were prohibited as a general rule such as that of the strangle hold, however sometimes individual matches would prohibit a certain hold such as the toe hold as a means of 'evening the odds', indeed in certain circumstances prohibited holds such as the strangle would be allowed to favour an individual, however these were generally rare and more to do with promoter wrangling than general recognized rule sets. There are even rare accounts of jackets being part of matches billed as catch as catch can in America, but it is likely this was down to misinterpretation of the rules and confusion with the Cornish style.

Oakley and Henry Irslinger were to introduce the new 'All in style' as it had been christened. A match was to be held at the Royal Albert hall. Bill Garnon, Oakley and Bert Assirati were taught the new all in style by Ben Sherman. The bill was to consist of Irlinger vs. Bill Modrich, Ben Sherman vs. Oakley and Billy Riley vs. Bill Garnon [2]. However there were issues with the work permits being issued[3]. So an alternate plan was formed. Two stadiums were to be used, namely the Olympia in London and the Bellevue in Manchester, both to open simultaneously on the 15th of December 1930. Irslinger vs. Modrich at the Olympia and Assirati vs. Oakley at the Belle Vue[4]. Also on the bill at the Belle Vue was Billy Riley who was to wrestle Bill Garnon. Newspaper articles of the event report Garnon and Riley wrestling under the new all in rules[5]. More than 6000 people turned out to see this first exhibition of all in at the Belle Vue. A newspaper report is included of the event below

Wrestlers fall from the ring

wrestler and then the other took turns at leg twisting and arm-twisting hair pulling and nose flattening.

While the contestants took their struggle so seriously that they toppled through the ropes out of the ring the crowd were so amused that they ignored any finer points which may have been displayed in the rough and tumble in the padded ring.

Hair pulling and nose flattening

More than 6000 people stayed after the boxing at Belle Vue Manchester last night to see the first exhibition in the city of "all in" wrestling.

Before the two contests the MC announced that under the new rules "holding with the hands gouging or kicking were barred"

Then Billy Riley of Wigan the champion of England and Bulldog Billy Garnon of Fishguard champion of Wales stepping into the ring

Within five minute the amazed crowd had seen some of the most extraordinary tactics. First one

Head Banged

Bulldog Garnon took great joy in banging the head of his prostate opponent on the floor about a dozen times while the man from Wigan exhibited his strength by twisting the Welshman round and round by the ankle and wrist and then hurling him half way across the ring until he sprawled, spread eagled and half stunned.

Fifteen minutes of this was endured before the Wigan man stood on the others head and was declared the winner[6].

Wrestling bouts

New style in Manchester

A new type of wrestling was introduced to Manchester last night. As seen at Belle Vue it was short of the butting bouncing hurling from the ring and gouging that are allowed in America but head locks the use of elbows and legs were permitted and Billy Riley of Wigan appeared to thrive on having his head bumped on the carpeted floor by Bill Garnon of Fishguard as he promptly tumbled Garnon out of the ring. Then he held him spread eagled fashion and tried to make him giddy by swinging him round in a circle before throwing him contemptuously from him. Garnon did not mind but after 23 minutes of very strenuous endeavor his shoulders touched the carpet for the necessary three seconds and Riley was declared the winner.[7]

However it seems a period of experimentation with the rules continued for a short time after. In the March of 1931 the Manchester guardian reported:

A programme comprised of what was described as all in wrestling was staged at Belle Vue Manchester last night, there were however, certain limitation compared with the conditions permitted in other countries and among them was the debarring of a competitor from throwing his opponent out of the ring which is a feat which has been seen in the Kings hall ring. Three of the principals engaged have been in Manchester within the last few weeks but the fourth George Bobanski billed, as the 'Russian lion' was a new comer. He met George Modrich of Serbia who was recently defeated by Henry Irslinger of America, who has now matched against Athol Oakley of England. The new American ruling of one fall deciding the match was introduced in the principal bout between Oakley and Irslinger. Irslinger gained the fall in the fourth round. Bobanski beat Modrich by one fall in

---

ALL-IN WRESTLING!!

THRILLS WITHOUT FRILLS

Stadium, Midland Street, Barnsley

FRIDAY, SEPTEMBER 27th, 1935

Doors open 6-30.   Commence 7-30.

Promoter - Mr. TOM COLEMAN.   Referee - Mr. TOM NOBLE, Manchester

Great Middleweight Contest—10 5-minute rounds

BILLY RILEY

WIGAN. Middle-weight Champion of the World and Belt holder. The only British Wrestler who has won a Gold Belt and Championship on Foreign soil. Winner of over 600 contests   VERSUS

BULL COLLINS

KANSAS. AMERICA. First appearance in this country. Accepted as the greatest Middleweight Wrestler that ever left the American shores. Defeated Spider Brooks in his last contest.

Don't fail to see the World's Best

8 5-min. Rounds Light-weight Contest

MAD O'MALLEY v. MAT O'NEIL

LIVERPOOL. The lad who holds up his name. Fears nothing   DENTON. Defeated Monte Casto, drew with Jack Tani, etc.

TWO SLOGGERS.

8 5-min. Rounds Contest (Challenge Match)

Miles KILVERT v. Johnny SUMMERS

SCOTLAND. Who claims to be the Fly-weight Champion of Scotland. Cunning, Clever and Fast.   SALFORD. Who will meet any lad in the World at his weight for sidestake. SENSATION. Match can be made at ringside.

Supporting Bout of the Evening. Welter Contest, 10 5-min. Rounds

BATTLING BILLY MILLS

DONCASTER. Winner of over 100 contests. Defeated Con Weston in his last bout at Holborn Stadium, London, Sept. 7th.   Versus

ISSY CAROL

HINDLEY. Met and defeated most of the leading Welter-weights in England. A real rough customer. An all-in demon. Look out for something you have not seen.

Popular Prices:

2/6 (Ringside Plush Tip-up Chairs); 1/3 Seating and Galleries (1000); Terrace 6d. (700) No 4d.

(all including Tax).

Seats can be Booked at any time of the day at the Stadium Office, Barnsley without extra charge.

The Management reserve the right to refuse admission. Bus stops at the door.

PLEASE NOTE.—Seats can be Booked by ringing Mr. A. Cheetham, Phone Royston 47.

Clayton & Utley, Printers, Dodworth Road, Barnsley. Phone 610.

the fifth round and Sam Walsh of Wigan beat Billy Blake of Newcastle by winning two falls out of three [8].

Even though rules were in place, as one article describing a match between Henry Irslinger and Athol Oakley would report facial punches were not stopped by the ref Stanislaus Zybezko, they were 'elastic'. However Irslingers tactics met with such disapproval by the crowd the referee left the ring[9].

Later that year the British wrestling board of control was formed "to observe that wrestling matches under the American rules are carried out in accordance with the regulations prevalent in other countries". The board was meant to be separate from the promoters and promoting body, and their main role was to punish or suspend any wrestlers for any breach of the rules, it was also meant to stop English wrestlers assuming foreign names to which they were not entitled. Licensing was introduced and no wrestler was allowed to wrestle without one[10].

An interesting citing of the rules occurred when the ban on wresting at the Hull Baths was lifted. It was said that the Baths superintendent had correspondence with the international wrestling syndicate and "all in" wrestling would mean "the amalgamation of the leading styles of wrestling in vogue namely judo (jujutsu) catch as catch can and Greco roman" to these would be added all moves and blows allowed in boxing with the exception of a direct punch to the face and with the addition of jujutsu rabbit and chop punches nerve knuckling on the body and face only ad the use of the forearm and the flat of the hand to the face. – a penalty of suspension added of 30-100 days for breaking rules."[11]

All in wrestling however was not to be met with universal approval and in fact some predicted its demise in a relatively short period. In the Manchester guardian in March 1932 all in wrestling was reported as a "queer music hall sport – a blood less orgy" and "it needs no sense of prophesy to predict for all in wrestling in its bloodless exaggeration what the critics call a short run"[12]. However it was the death of a wrestler, by the name of George Johnson, a 27 year old from Chesterfield that was to raise the profile of the new version of the ancient sport.

An opinion was expressed by a Sheffield jury today that all in wrestling is not a clean sport and ought to be prohibited.

George Johnson (27) of Brampton Chesterfield known as Strangler Johnson died following an all in bout at Attercliffe on March 3 – died of syncope from over strain. After being defeated by Carl Romsky Johnson collapsed in his dressing room. He died in a taxi on his way to lms railway statin.

Fouls 'gouging biting scratching nose ear or mouth twisting, offensive kicking knee grinding and hitting in the face with closed fists'

Police constable Ernest Clarke who was on duty described all in wrestling as 'savage and brutal' – DI Manifold declared it a particularly degrading method of entertainment

Coroner said that bills advertising the contests appeared to pander to the baser side of human nature and to attract the people to come and see something which was rather cruel[13].

Later the reporting's of the case were as follows

Sheffield jury opinion given that all in wrestling not a clean sport. And ought to be prohibited following the death of George Johnsons 'Strangler Johnson' died following all in match at Attercliffe 3/3/33- syncope from overstrain. Defeated by Carl Romsky , collapsed in his dressing room and died in a taxi on the way to lhm railway station. His brother saw the bout and thought it a fair one. Coroner Mr. J Kenyon parker asked questions re the rules and read a list of fouls including biting gouging scratching nose ear or mouth twisting offensive kicking knee grinding and hitting in the face with closed fists. Police constable Ernest Clarke who was on duty at the hall described it as 'savage and brutal' and declared it a particularly degrading method of entertainment. Addressing the jury the coroner said that bills advertising the contests appeared to pander o the baser side of human nature.[14]

Billy Riley The Man, the legacy

that he was making enquires into the death. The verdict had been death by heart failure. He commented "all in wrestling is not an English sport and out to be prohibited"[15].

The war meant that wrestling bouts were reduced but even then it still courted controversy leading to a ban in London in 1944. The Manchester guardian reported "London county council yesterday decided to prohibit all in wrestling in premises licensed by them. The public control committee in recommending the prohibition stated 'in our view all in wrestling cannot be regarded as wrestling in any sense. We do not consider that it contains any element of sport and we regard it as a degrading and unhealthy form of entertainment' – only four premises in London are licensed for public wrestling"[16].

In 1947 Admiral Lord Mountevans became president of the new British wrestling board of control. The aim was to regularize the sport and eliminate some of the more undesirable practices. Vice president was Commander A B Campbell and Mr. Maurice Webb MP. Mountevans was to provide championship belts as trophies which would become

The death was raised in the House of Commons. Sir John Gilmour the home secretary told the house

Billy Joyce's Lord Mountevans belt

48

known as the Mountevans belts in the following weights:-

Fly weight – 8st 12lb
Bantam 9st 0lbs
Feather 9st 11lbs
Light 10st 3 lb.
Welter 11st 5lbs
Middle 12st 2 lb.
Light heavy 12 st. 13lb
Heavy any weight.

Plans were made for a standard form of contract for use by promoters when engaging wrestlers.[17]

Billy Riley enjoyed a busy career in the "All in" era wrestling all over the country the following are extracts from match accounts of the period.

1931
February

The presence on the programme of a wrestling bout of the all in style between Billy Riley(Wigan) champion of England and Bulldog Bill Garnon Fishguard champion of wales was interesting in view of the recent contest in London which resulted in one of the men sustaining a broken rib. The match of the three ten minute rounds was put on immediately before the big fight. It certainly provided plenty of amusement and the spectacle of the contestants being pushed back through the ropes by anxious faced ringside seat holders in evening dress was unforgettable. Riley was awarded the verdict after the bout had gone the full course [18].

1932
Octoner

Jack Pye retires in grueling bout with Riley

In an all in wrestling match at Wigan last night Billy Riley of Wigan defeated Jack Pye of Doncaster. The Doncaster man retired on the advice of a doctor after taking the first fall when two minutes 25 seconds of the fifth round had gone. Pye had the better of matters at the start and seemed likely to force a fall in the first round, but the Wigan man wriggled clear and threw his opponent over the ropes and out of the ring. The Doncaster man climbed back and returned the compliment. A few minutes later after some desperate work Riley once more went over the ropes. The Wigan man was again almost down in the second round but once more wriggled clear. In the third round Riley attacked ferociously. Streaming with blood from a cut in the temple he got scissors hold on Pye but the Doncaster man showed great fortitude and strength throwing his opponent off. The fourth round was full of excitement and both men went over the ropes in turn. In the fifth round Riley managed to get two arm locks on Pye and with the second of these forced a fall. Pye went to his corner in great pain and it was stated that he had severely strained his arm.[19]

December

There was a wild scene at Olympia hall, Bradford,..... ...a six 10 minute round contest between Ben Sherman (America) and Mitchell Gill (Bradford) ended in a draw.

In a thrilling bout between Billy Riley (Wigan), the middleweight champion of the world and Leo Lightbody (Huddersfield) Riley who had been receiving punishment applied the reverse cart wheel grip in the last round and Lightbody had to give in.[20]

1933
January

Wigan man wins at Leeds

The keenly awaited return all in wrestling match between Harry Brook, the young Huddersfield pupil of Douglas Clark and Billy Riley (Wigan) the middleweight champion of the British empire at the Leeds Brunswick stadium last night ended in disappointing fashion brook being disqualified in the third round for butting. The match had gone on very even lines up to the beginning of the third round neither man having gained a fall. Brook was thrown clear over the ropes in the second round but though he was dazed he clambered back into the ring before the full count and lasted out the round.

He had fully recovered by the beginning of the third round and he quickly weakened Riley with some fierce blows to the body. Riley was thrown and seemed certain to concede a fall but brook allowed his enthusiasm to get the better of his discretion and he butted the other in what the referee adjudged was a low position and was disqualified. A return contest for £50 a side has been agreed to by both parties. Brook who was the heavier last night agreed to wrestle at 12st 4lb[21]

February

Three wrestlers had to receive medical attention as the result of injuries sustained at the all in tournament at the Leeds Brunswick stadium.

The principal contest was between Harry Brook (Huddersfield) and Billy Riley (Wigan), the middleweight champion of the British empire, each man threw the other out of the ring on several occasions and on one occasion the referee Mr. W Goosey who had climbed outside the ropes to the edge of the ring to gain a better view of the wrestlers was kicked from the ring by Riley. He fell and hurt his arm and it was massaged while the men in the ring fought on. Then when he attempted to climb back into the ring the referee was accidentally kicked again on the head by Riley.

There were no falls in the first two rounds but in the first half minute of the third stage Riley seized brooks arm and flung him over his shoulder brook fell heavily on the point of his left shoulder and lay still. The contest was stopped immediately in Riley's favour and book was taken to Leeds public dispensary. It was stated that Brook's collar bone was dislocated. the injury will prevent him wrestling for two to three weeks[22]

Wigan man wins at Leeds

The keenly awaited return all-in wrestling match between Harry Brook, the young Huddersfield pupil of Douglas Clark, and Billy Riley (Wigan), the middle-weight champion of the British Empire, at the Leeds Brunswick Stadium last night, ended in disappointing fashion, Brook being disqualified in the third round for butting.

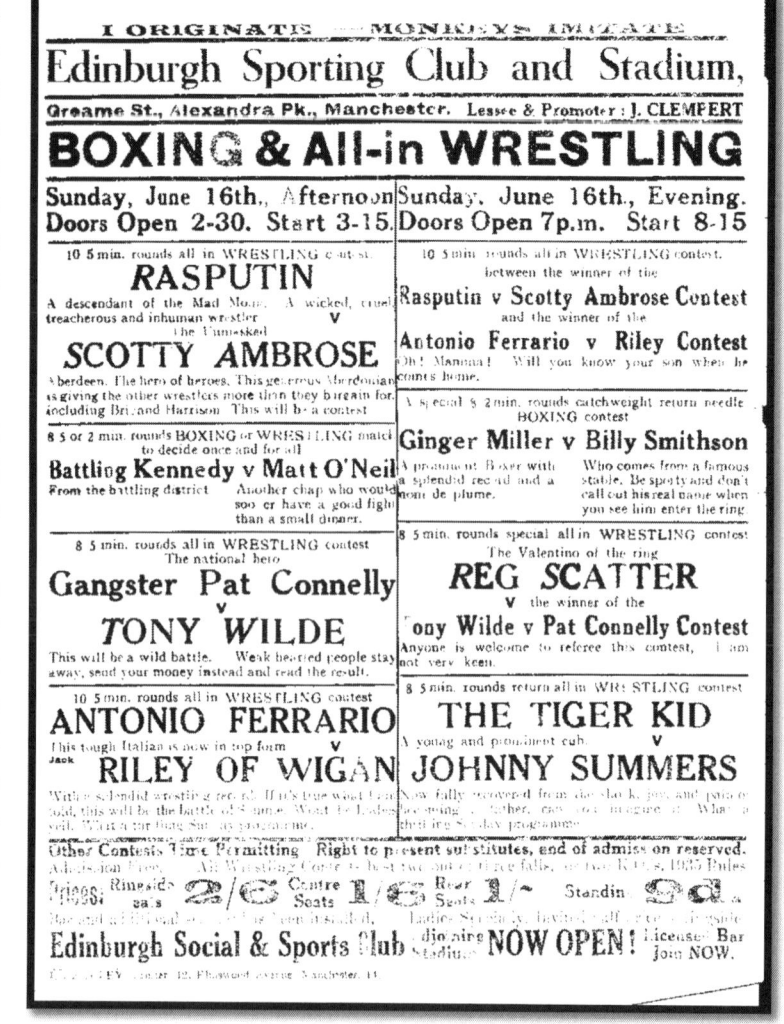

The match had gone on very even lines up to the beginning of the third round, neither man having gained a fall. Brook was thrown clean over the ropes in the second round but though he was dazed, he clambered back into the ring before the full count and lasted out the round.

He had fully recovered by the beginning of the third round and he quickly weakened Riley with some fierce blows to the body. Riley was thrown and seemed certain to concede a fall; but Brook allowed his enthusiasm to get the better of his discretion and

disqualified in the third round for butting. Brook was thrown over the roped in the second round but though ….he clambered back into the ring before the full count and lasted out the round. Brook had fully recovered by the beginning of the third round and he

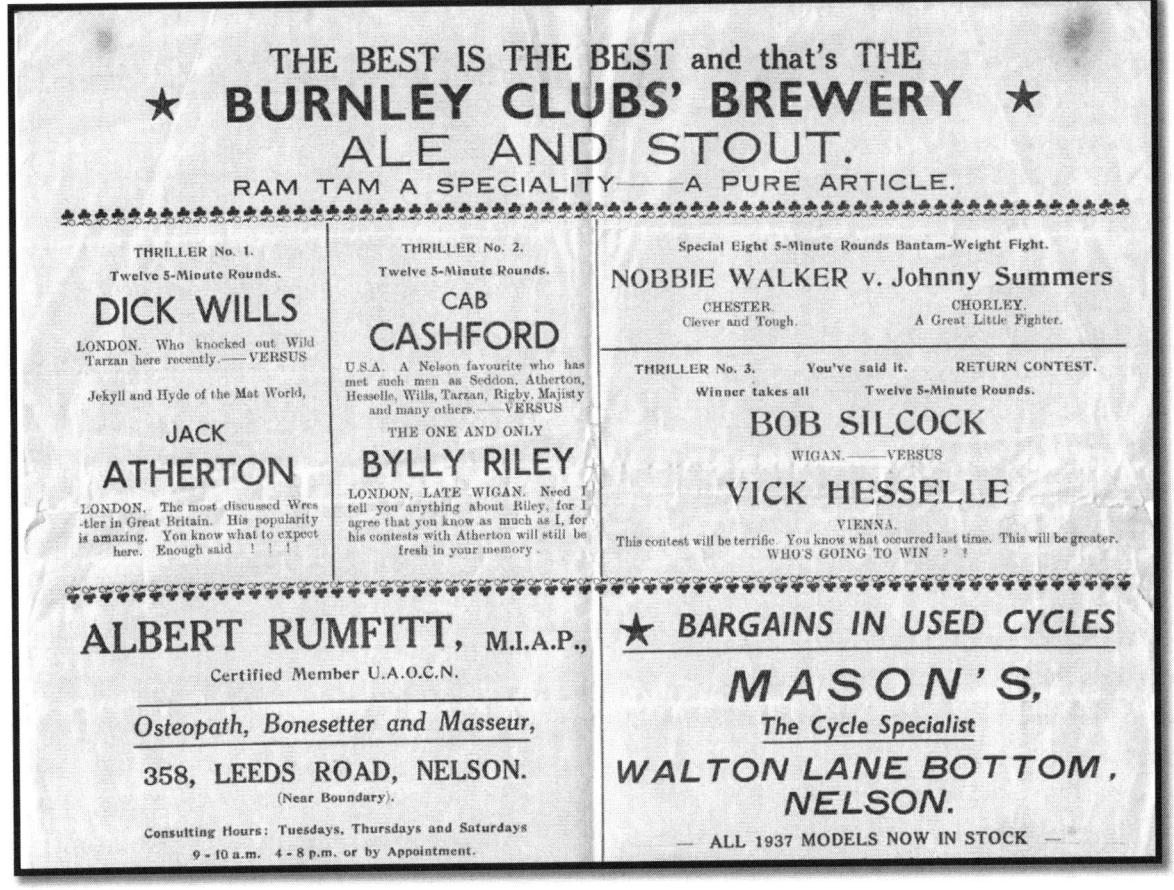

THE BEST IS THE BEST and that's THE
★ BURNLEY CLUBS' BREWERY ★
ALE AND STOUT.
RAM TAM A SPECIALITY——A PURE ARTICLE.

THRILLER No. 1.
Twelve 5-Minute Rounds.
DICK WILLS
LONDON. Who knocked out Wild Tarzan here recently.——VERSUS
Jekyll and Hyde of the Mat World,
JACK ATHERTON
LONDON. The most discussed Wrestler in Great Britain. His popularity is amazing. You know what to expect here. Enough said ! ! !

THRILLER No. 2.
Twelve 5-Minute Rounds.
CAB CASHFORD
U.S.A. A Nelson favourite who has met such men as Seddon, Atherton, Hesselle, Wills, Tarzan, Rigby, Majisty and many others.——VERSUS
THE ONE AND ONLY
BYLLY RILEY
LONDON, LATE WIGAN. Need I tell you anything about Riley, for I agree that you know as much as I, for his contests with Atherton will still be fresh in your memory.

Special Eight 5-Minute Rounds Bantam-Weight Fight.
NOBBIE WALKER v. Johnny Summers
CHESTER. CHORLEY.
Clever and Tough. A Great Little Fighter.

THRILLER No. 3. You've said it. RETURN CONTEST.
Winner takes all Twelve 5-Minute Rounds.
BOB SILCOCK
WIGAN.——VERSUS
VICK HESSELLE
VIENNA.
This contest will be terrific. You know what occurred last time. This will be greater.
WHO'S GOING TO WIN ? ?

ALBERT RUMFITT, M.I.A.P.,
Certified Member U.A.O.C.N.
Osteopath, Bonesetter and Masseur,
358, LEEDS ROAD, NELSON.
(Near Boundary).
Consulting Hours: Tuesdays, Thursdays and Saturdays
9 - 10 a.m. 4 - 8 p.m. or by Appointment.

★ **BARGAINS IN USED CYCLES**
MASON'S,
The Cycle Specialist
WALTON LANE BOTTOM, NELSON.
— ALL 1937 MODELS NOW IN STOCK —

---

he butted the other in what the referee adjudged was a low position, and was disqualified. A return contest for £50 a side has been agreed to by both parties, Brook who was the heavier last night agreed to wrestle at 12st 4lb.[23]

Contests at Leigh

At the wrestling tournament at Leigh last night, Fighting Ferguson (Leeds) was defeated by Billy Riley (Wigan) the champion middleweight wrestler of the world by two falls to none.[24]

The return all in wrestling match between Harry Brook the young Huddersfield pupil of Douglas Clark and Billy Riley the middleweight champion of the British empire at the Leeds Brunswick stadium ended in disappointing fashion brook being

quickly weakened Riley with some fierce blows to the body Riley was thrown and seemed certain to concede a fall but Brook allowed his enthusiasm to g the better his discretion and he butted the other in what the referee adjudged was a low position and was disqualified. A return contest for £80 a side has been agreed to Brook to wrestle at 12st 4lb[25]

June

Nelson – Billy Riley beat Fred Pierone (USA) by two submission falls

Wilf Charnock (Newtown) beat Paul Stirrup, Joe Robinson (Huddersfield) beat Paddy Kelly mayo

July

Lowerhouse sports ground

At the top of the bill is Billy Riley the British Empire champion who has held the title since 1912 against challengers all over the world, and W Strathcona the South African middleweight champion. They will meet in a contest, which is of six 10 min rounds.[26]

Referee mixed up in All-in Wrestling Match

There was a remarkable scene at an all-in wrestling match at Springfield Park, Wigan last night. The referee was thrown out of the ring.

The contest was between Billy Riley of Wigan, middle-weight champion of the British Empire and holder of the British Empire belt, and Jack Pye of Doncaster, light-heavyweight champion of England.

Towards the end of the contest Riley was entangled in the ropes while hanging out of the ring. Pye continued to fight, and when the referee Mr. Job Shambley tried to separate them he became mixed up in the contest and was eventually thrown out of the ring on to the Press table.

Earlier in the evening a large portion of the crowd standing in one of the enclosures about 50 yards from the ring broke through smashing a section of the railings and a number of chairs.

Seven thousand spectators watched the contest, which was a return match. Riley who weighed in at 11st. 4lb. won the previous match. Pye weighed 12 st.. 12lb. and was eight years younger than his opponent.

Riley scored the winning fall one minute 57 seconds after the start of the fourth round, after one of the most terrific fight that has been seen in the district for many years.[27]

Those who failed to see Billy Riley the British empire champion wrestling at old Burnley "a" team ground at Lowerhouse last Tuesday night should not miss the opportunity of seeing him at the same place next Friday night he is matches with Jack Smith a keen contender for the title and they will fight all in style. This event is the top of what should prove a very entertaining Bill, Strathcons the South African middleweight champion who highly delighted last Tuesdays spectators by his great display against Riley has accepted the challenge of the well known Burnley wrestler Peter Bannon, ex middleweight champion of the world.[28]

August

Another demonstration of the all in style of wrestling will be given in Burnley on Friday at Lowerhouse when Billy Riley the British champion will meet Jack Smith who is described as a keen contender for the title. In support of this bout will be several other wrestling encounters.[29]

Burnley wrestling enthusiasts had still another demonstration of the American style of fighting at the Lowerhouse football ground last night. The demonstration was provided by Billy Riley middleweight champion of the British Empire and Joe Straithcona the South African champion. Their contest was over three ten minute rounds and while their methods di not always meet with the approval of the large crowd they gave glimpses of the type of wrestling which is so popular on the continent and in America. Riley was the more scientific of the two but victory eluded him until the final round when the hammerlock forced Strathcons retirement. Riley first of all tried to secure the scissors hold and when his opponent bridged slightly he secured the supporting arm and twisted it unmercifully until Strathcona signaled his retirement. In the previous round Riley made many promising moved but the South Africans strength prevented a fall. Riley figured prominently with the scissors and half nelson holds and Strathcona's best method of attack was half nelson on the arms. On one occasion in the second round Riley was forced to the ground by this hold but he escaped by gouging. Strathcona had been billed to meet Peter Bannon of Burnley[30]

September

It is stated that the promoter of this bill who introduced Billy Riley to Burnley is anxious to find a local boy to meet the best of Riley's "stable" and as a first step is trying to bring together J.W.Walsh and J.W.Price junior[31]

Wrestling

The last open air wrestling bill of the season is announced will take place at Lowerhouse sports ground next Monday night beginning at 6 pm. The top line brings together ex middleweight champion Peter Bannon of Burnley and Jack Smith who challenges Billy Riley the British champion seen at Lower house not long ago when the latter returns from his south African tour. The bout is scheduled for three ten minute rounds and the style of course is catch as catch can[32]

1934

October

Plymouth promenade pier last night

Billy Riley described as the light heavyweight champion of Europe won his contest with Hans Lagren a German who was substituted for Tony Baer. Riley displayed exceptional skill and secured a fall in the second round with a clever throw and press down. Riley tried hard for the second fall and once he threw his opponent out of the ring but the German as soon as he regained the ring made an effort to return the compliment. Riley however was too clever to be taken unawares. Lagren used his weight to advantage and for a time dominated the bout being loudly cheered when he threw the Englishman for the equalizing fall Riley however won in the fifth round with a very good throw and press down.[33]

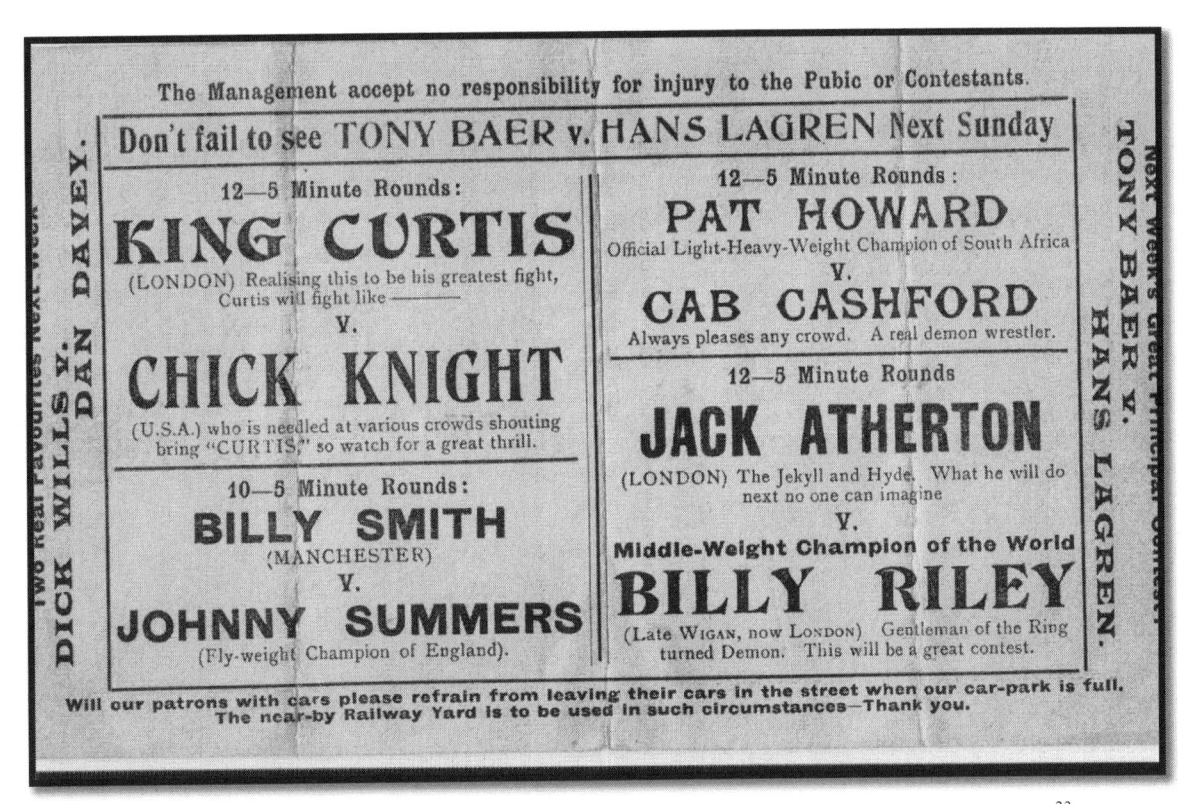

December

Plymouth pier pavilion last night

In his match with Al Barnes (Australia) Wigan wrestler Billy Riley gained a fall in the second round but Barnes who was substituted for Chopper Sims equalized with a pin hold. Riley swung his opponent, dropped him and fell upon him to hold his shoulders to the mat for victory in round four[34].

1935

February

Short arm scissors was the only real hold introduced in the match between Billy Riley (Wigan) and Dick Wills (Newbiggin) this was applied by Wills but was soon broken. During the third round

Riley shoulder pinned Wills after swinging him, but conceded a fall in the next session. Victory went to Riley when wills submitted to a legend.[35]

March

Wigan Wrestler

Willy Riley (Wigan) beat Frank Matcham by two falls two falls to one in the main contest during the free-style wrestling at the Majestic Rink, Preston last night. Matcham pinned Riley with a cradle then the Wigan man retaliated with two quick falls, a flying mare and an arm twist.[36]

May

Wild Jack Harrison (Wigan) lightweight champion of the world is now challenging Billy Riley for the middleweight championship of the world and £100 a side a real class wrestler.[37]

June

Billy Riley (Wigan) middleweight champion of the empire belt holder beat Fred Pirone USA by submission falls in the third and fifth of a 12 rounds contest. There were fireworks in the first round Pierone had a spread-eagle on Riley who was down on the mat. The referee was counting when Riley struck him and at one Mr. Walsh closed with the wrestler himself and the seconds had to part the two. Wilf Charnock (Newton) beat Paul Stirrup (London) ,Joe Robinson (Hudderfield) beat Paddy Kelly (Mayo)[38]

August

Another demonstration of the all in style

Burnley wrestling enthusiasts had still another demonstration of the American style of fighting at the Lowerhouse football ground last night.

The demonstration was provided by Billy Riley middleweight champion of the British Empire and Joe Strathcona the South African champion. Their contest was over three ten minute rounds and while their methods did not always meet with the approval of the large crowd they gave glimpses of the type of wrestling which is so popular on the continent and in America. Riley was the more scientific of the two but victory eluded him until the final round when the hammerlock hold forced Strathcona's retirement.

Riley first of all tried to secure the scissors hold and when his opponent bridged slightly he secured the supporting arm and twisted it unmercifully until Strathcoma signaled his retirement. In the previous round Riley made many promising moves but the South Africans strength prevented a fall. Riley figured prominently with the scissors and half nelson holds , and Strathcona's best method of attack was half nelson on the arm. On one occasion in the second round Riley was forced to the ground by this hold but he escaped by gouging[39].

1936

February

A free style wrestling tournament for the Middleweight championship of the North of England is the feature of a novel road show at Dewsbury Empire this week. Several champions and internationally known wrestlers have entered and last night there were some exciting and close bouts. The entrants include Billy Riley (Wigan) middleweight champion of the world; Jack Atherton (Lancaster); Ned Sparks (USA); Mike Howley (Batley Carr); Richard Wills (Northumberland) and Douglas, the Turk A programme apart from the wrestling is provided by several good turns including Doyle and Eileen comedy duo, the lane London cabaret girls a troupe of good dancers, Ann and Jayne Lee, Synch and Payne , Le Fre and Leopold , and Luigi and his continental band by permission of the international broadcasting company London..[40]

October

Tommy Rigby the former Padiham boxer and wrestler who has built up a reputation for himself in London wrestling circles is anxious to get a contest in Burnley or nelson in order as he says "to show my old followers that I have improved since I last wrestled in your town". Accordingly he challenges

Billy Riley of Wigan or any middleweight in Lancashire to a contest under all in rules for £25 aside.[41]

1937
January
Burnley All-In Wrestling

In all-in wrestling bouts at Burnley last night, Billy Riley (Wigan) beat Strangler Joe Warner (Manchester) by two falls to one.[42]

There was a peculiar end to the chief contest in an all in wrestling programme at the imperia ballroom nelson last Thursday. Dick wills (London) was matched against Jack Atherton (London) and each had secured a fall in the seventh session Wills secured the Indian death leg lock but unfortunately he fell back wards. Both men were in immediate agony and they each tapped for submission. Seconds and attendants rushed into the ring and some time elapsed before the locks could be released. Each wrestler had to be carried into his corner and as they were unable to resume the succeeding session the contest was declared to be a draw. Billy Riley (Wigan) beat Cab Cashford (USA) by two falls to one. After obtaining the first fall Bob Silcock Wigan was beaten by Vik Hessle Vienna.[43]

Preston Wrestling
Riley beaten in hard contest

Billy Riley the Wigan middle-weight gave Tony Baer, the Scottish light heavyweight, a hard fight in the main contest at the Majestic, Preston, last night. But had to acknowledge defeat.

Baer rarely had a chance to use his better physique, for Riley employed rough tactics which were not to the Scotsman's liking.

Riley used many body punches, and was usually on top in the early rounds gaining the first fall in the third session with a head lock and press. Baer put himself even in the fifth round with a bent press and won in the seventh with a similar hold.[44]

Billy Riley (Wigan) former middleweight champion of the world beat Ken Robertson of Hindley, by two falls to one. Robertson had gained a lead in the third round with a fall from a leg-lock and body press, but Riley soon gained the upper hand, and secured a fall with a crucifixion hold in the fifth second. Later Robertson failed to avoid a similar hold, and Riley gained the decision.[45]

February
Wrestling

A four 10 minute rounds contest between Billy Riley (Wigan) and the Masked Marvel ended in a draw. Each having secured a fall [46].

The four ten minute round contest between Billy Riley and the masked marvel ended in a draw each wrestler having secured a fall. The Masked Marvell had the better of the opening rounds[47].

In the principal contest at the free style wrestling at the Burnley Empress, last night Billy Riley (London) defeated Tommy Rigby (London) Riley obtained two falls without reply.[48]

March
Free-Style Tourney; Blackpool

Billy Riley of Wigan, beat Jack Owens of Leigh, by two falls to one.[49]

April
Blackpool wrestling

There was a sudden ending to a middle weight contest between Willie Riley (Wigan) and George French (Australia) when, in the sixth round, French had to be carried out of the ring owing to an injured knee.[50]

Dick Wills was defeated by Willie Riley (Wigan) in the fifth round by two falls to one.[51]

May

The other big contest between Jack Atherton (London) and Billy Riley (Wigan) middleweight champion of the world was a real three cornered affair for Atherton did as much wrestling with the referee as he did with Riley. The first fall went to Atherton in the third round but Riley gained an equalizing fall in the next round with a monkey climb and press. In the fifth round Riley gained the winning fall.[52]

Wrestling
Burnley Wrestling

In the chief contest at the all-in wrestling at Burnley last night Jack Wentworth (Canada) drew with Paddy Casey (Ireland) with a double submission fall after each had taken a fall. Jim Reid (Leigh) beat Stan Slade (Buxton) by two falls to one; Ginger Burke (Tyldesley) and Joe Reid (Leigh) wrestled a draw and Billy Riley (Wigan) beat Jack Atherton (London) by two falls to one.[53]

Empress ballroom.

The other big contest between Jack Atherton (London) and Billy Riley (Wigan) middleweight champion of the world was a real three cornered affair for Atherton did as much wrestling with the referee as he did with Riley. The first fall went to Atherton in the third round but Riley gained an equalizing fall in the next round with a monkey climb and press. In the fifth round Riley gained the winning fall.[54]

Preston Wrestling,
Skill Spills And Thrills but crowd displeased
....

Wild Tarzan (Canada) did not turn up for the contest with Jack Atherton (London), and Billy Riley (Wigan) acted as his substitute. Atherton won. There was nothing nice about the contest. Atherton began by saying Wild Tarzan was afraid of him, and at the opening of the first round tripped up the referee, whom he attacked on subsequent occasions. After getting the first fall with a body press in the third round. Atherton went as if to helped Riley to rise. Instead, he lifted him over his shoulders and threw him over the ropes Theatrically walking away as a protest against "barracking," Atherton was in the fifth round placed in a bent press from which there was no escape. In the next round Riley submitted to an arm and head lock.[55]

July

George de Relwyskows next all in wrestling bill takes place at the hull white city Albany road next Wednesday evening. Jack Atherton (Lancashire) vs. Billy Riley (Wigan)[56]

Jack Atherton (Lancashire) beat Billy Riley (Wigan) by two falls to one in a cleanly fought match (above)[57]

Billy near the end of his career

November

The meeting of Vic Hesselle, Austria and Billy Riley, London provided plenty of action both men receiving severe punishment before Riley won by two falls to one.

Jack Atherton, London defeated Eric Fisher, Dewsbury, who was substituting for Mario Majisti, Italy, and Tab Allen, Yorkshire on against Chris Taylor, Yorkshire.[58]

December

A thrilling money match as seen between Billy Riley formerly of Wigan and Vick Hesselle of Vienna. Riley secured the first fall and Hesselle equalized shortly afterwards. Both wrestlers adopted rough tactics and went down for counts. After Riley had met the boards for a short count, he rushed at

Hesselle and being wide open the latter connected with a blow on the chin and Riley was out for some time. The verdict went to Hesselle.[59]

.... rounds of light comedy. Wild .... (Canada) dived at his opponent Riley (Wigan), missed him and ended up outside the ring. He was .... and was carried to the dressing room like a sack of coal by Riley. Riley had .... obtained a double arm lock and ...... a body press.[60]

1938
January

Imperial ballroom last Thursday

There was a further disqualification in a supporting twelve five minute rounds contest between Billy Riley (London) and Wild Tarzan (Canada) the latter gained the first fall by a submission in the second round but Riley showed the superior ring craft and after the Canadian had been cautioned the referee had no alternative but to disqualify him. Riley twice threw his opponent our of the ring[61].

February

Imperial ballroom nelson.

Billy Riley (Wigan) undisputed worlds middleweight champion meets Bob Silcock (London) who gave Jack Atherton a great fight recently.[62]

Billy Riley beat Bob Silcock in the sixth round of a 12 round contest by a bent press gained in the third and a similar fall in the sixth to a body press in the fifth by Silcock[63]

March

Hull wrestling results

Madeley street baths hull last night

Billy Riley beat Pat Flannagan on a technical KO after each had gained a fall[64]

July

Preston wrestling

As was expected there were plenty of thrills very well put over too – in the fight between Jack Atherton(London) and Billy Riley (Wigan). It was nearly all rough and tumble and Atherton soon obtained a body press. The inevitable equalised followed when Riley punches Atherton about and then secured a double leg lock and press.

Riley was disqualified in the fifth round presumably for throwing Atherton by his hair. Atherton was thus declare the winner, seemed more disgusted than Riley and showed him by giving his opponent a few more strike to the face. Meanwhile the referee having fulfilled his part of the contract by announcing Atherton as the winner departed and left the wrestlers to it.

They kept up the show for a little while but soon gave up[65]

1939
March

Billy Riley (Wigan) beat Wild Tarzan (Canada) when he gained a Boston crab hold in the third round following which the towel was thrown in on behalf of Wild Tarzan[66].

It is from this point on that we see Billy becoming referee in a number of matches

1940
January

Billy Riley deputized for Joe Robinson of Springfield who had hurt his hand against the mercurial Mario Mageatti of Italy. Mario well known in Preston had the crowd howling from his entrance to the ring but found Riley too clever for him. The Italian lost on a knock out in the second round after taking much punishment[67]

April

Blackpool

The most scientific wrestling came in a bout between Bob McNab (Canada) and Billy Riley (Wigan) a fight which Riley won with a bent press and an arm lock and press. McNab in the second round scored bent press but was beaten by an obviously cleverer wrestler.[68]

Preston Wrestling

An opportunity seized by Wally Seddon (Bolton) won him his bout with Tom Blinkhorn (Lancashire)

at the Majestic, Preston last night. Each had gained a fall when Blinkhorn turned his back on his opponent. Seddon promptly scored with a bent press. The Bolton wrestler had previously been warned by referee Billy Riley for illegal tactics.[69]

November

Preston wrestling bouts

Billy Riley Wigan was laid out by his opponent, angel face Joe Batten, London, before the bout started at the majestic Preston last night. As the referee was giving the wrestlers instructions batten struck Riley across the temple and he had to be assisted back to his corner .he was till dazed when the first round began. And batten gained a fall with a body press. Riley recovered and gained falls with a bent press and a body press.

Joe Robinson Springfield easily defeated pat Kavanagh Ireland by two falls to one.

Jack Atherton Manchester forced the Red Devil France to submit to a leg lock in the first round of their contest. The Red Devil equalized with a body press and won the decisive fall when Atherton submitted to a leg lock[70]

1941

October

Madeley street baths hull last night – Dick Wills (Newcastle) defeated Billy Riley (Wigan) by a knock out in the fourth round after Riley had secured a fall in the second.[71]

1945

January

Madeley street baths last night – Billy Riley Wigan knocked out Glyn Evans Wales in fourth round[72].

Plymouth pier pavilion last night.

Bob Gregory pin held Billy Riley of Wigan for a fall in the second round, but in the next he had to retire in consequence of cramp and Riley was declared the victor[73].

February

Last night Madeley street baths . Billy Riley Wigan beat Cab Cashford by two falls to one in six rounds[74].

March

Hull wrestling. Madeley St. baths last night. Jack Atherton (Wigan) bt Billy Riley (Wigan) by two falls to one in eight rounds[75].

By 1947 Billy had moved more into promoting and frequently he would referee the bouts. However occasionally he would still would wrestle when for whatever reason wrestlers were ill or didn't turn up ,for example in February 1947 ,Billy Riley was due to referee a match at Doncaster. The match was between Wilf King and Seaman Willkie . Wilf King , was unable to attend and Riley stepped in, Riley won in the fourth round with two falls to one.[76]

---

[1] Blue Blood on the Mat – Sir Atholl Oakley – Summersdales Publishers (1996) Page 21.
[2] Blue Blood on the Mat – Sir Atholl Oakley Summersdales Publishers (1996) Page 26
[3] Blue Blood on the Mat – Sir Atholl Oakley Summersdales Publishers (1996) Page 28.
[4] Blue Blood on the Mat – Sir Atholl Oakley Summersdales Publishers (1996) page 29.
[5] http://manchesterhistory.net/bellevue/racing.html
[6] Machester guardian 16th dec 1930 ???
[7] Wrestling bouts:new style in Manchster, The Manchester guardian Dec 16th 1930
[8] Manchester guardian , March 7th 1931
[9] Nottingham evening post 8/12/31
[10] Nottingham evening post 13/11/31
[11] Daily mail 2/3/34
[12] Manchester Guardian March 10th 1932
[13] Manchester Guardian March 16th 1933
[14] Manchester Guardian – 16/3/33
[15] The citizen 21/3/33
[16] Manchester guardian 22/11/44
[17] Daily mail 11/1/37
[18] Yorkshire post 3/2/31
[19] Yorkshire post 4/10/32
[20] Yorkshire post 6/12/32
[21] Yorkshire post 21/1/33
[22] Yorkshire evening post 7/2/33
[23] Yorkshire post 21/2/33 p12.
[24] Yorkshire post 25/2/33 p.21
[25] Yorkshire evening post 21/2/33
[26] Express and advertiser 22/7/1933
[27] Yorkshire post 18th July 1933 p.10

[28] Express and advertiser 29/7/33
[29] Express and advertiser 2/8/33
[30] Express and advetisoer 5/8/33
[31] Express and advertiser 2/9/33
[32] express and advertiser 2/9/33
[33] The western morning news and daily gazette 13/10/34
[34] The Western morning news and daily gazette 22/12/34
[35] The Western morning news and daily gazette 2/2/35
[36] Lancashire daily post 30/3/35
[37] The daily mail 20/5/35
[38] Express and news 22/6/35
[39] Express and advertiser 5/8/1935
[40] Yorkshire post 25/2/36 p.5
[41] Express and news 10/10/36
[42] Lancashire daily post 15/1/37 p.3
[43] Express and news 23/1/37
[44] Lancashire daily post 23/1/37 p 3.
[45] Lancashire daily post 16/1/37 p.3
[46] Lancashire daily post 5/2/37 p.13
[47] Express and news 6/2/37
[48] Lancashire daily post 12/2/37 p.11
[49] Lancashire daily post 13/3/37 p.3
[50] Lancashire daily post 10/4/37 p 5
[51] Lancashire daily post 17/4/37
[52] Express and news 8/5/37
[53] Lancashire daily post $7^{5/37}$ p.13
[54] Express and news 8/5/37
[55] Lancashire dialy post 29/5/37 p6
[56] The Daily mail 17/7/37
[57] The Daily mail 22/7/37
[58] Lancashire daily post 5/11/37
[59] Express and news 4/12/37
[60] Th Lancashire daily post – 18/12/37 p.3
[61] Express and news 15/1/38
[62] Express and news 12/2/38
[63] Express and news 26/2/38
[64] The Daily mail 15/3/38
[65] Lancashire daily post30/7/38
[66] Lancashire evening post 17/3/39 - page 6
[67] Lancashire daily post 20/1/1940
[68] Lancashire daily post 27/4/1940
[69] The Lancashire Daily Post, 27th July 1940 p.3
[70] Lancashire dialy post 23/11/40
[71] The Daily mail 31/10/41
[72] The Daily mail 9/1/45
[73] The Western morning news and daily gazette 12/1/45
[74] The Daily mail 20/2/45
[75] The Daily mail 6/3/45
[76] Derby evening telegraphy February 14th 1947

Chapter 5

Riley's coaches

Over the length of his career, a number of people had an influence on Billy Riley and his wrestling. Arguably the man that had the most influence would have been Willie Charnock of Newton Wigan, who coached him over a number of years. However, one of the earliest influences was Waino Ketonen the Finnish wrestler who visited Wigan in the early 1900s and who in fact Riley would wrestle when he was in America.

Waino Ketonen

Waino was born on the 5th July 1888 in the city of Tampere Finland to Kustaa Ketonen and Matilda Ritala.

Waino began work in the cotton mill aged 12 years. The young Ketonen obviously drawn to athletic pursuits began gymnastics at the local club. He performed on the horizontal bar, the parallel bars rings and horse. However one day whilst working out in the gym he broke his thumb. Unfortunately it did not heal properly and ended his career as a gymnast[1]. So it was at the age of 17 after he had moved to Helsinki that he took up Greco-Roman wrestling. It was in 1908 whilst working in the town of Vaasa that he won the local wrestling championship. In 1909, he moved to Viipuri and the following year won the Finnish world championship representing the club of "Tarmo" of Viipuri.[2]

Believing the professional game in the United States held a brighter future for him rather than in his own native land, Waino decided to move to the USA[3]. Waino who had relatives in Massachusetts moved there to start is new life[4]. His first job in America was with a road construction gang in new Hampshire. Finish athletic clubs in new England soon learned of Ketonen's ability as a wrestler and tried to persuade him to retain his amateur standing [5]. In the fall of 1910 he wrestled fellow Fin John Mäki to a draw . They both received $20 purse for the match and he never looked back, he had begun his career in professional wrestling. He would never again take an amateur bought [6].

In the group-picture of 1909 Finnish championships you can see Ketonen seated on the floor second from the right and Tuominen third from the right. The group picture of Finish-championships, that was held in the city of Oulu 1909.[7]

From his early matches he was known for his double arm roll, a move "the like of which Jenkins, Gotch Roller or any other American grappler had never seen"[8]. One notable match was with Fritz Hanson. The match was stopped by the police for excessive roughness. The match had lasted 3 hours without a fall. However it should be noted that Ketonen had beaten Hanson before and after [9].

Harvey Parker sent to England to bring the best 150lbs wrestler of the isle. It was Peter Gotz, the trainer of Zybyzko who took up the challenge. Gotz was known for his scissors, and it was said that he had almost fractured the skull of an opponent with it. He managed to secure the scissors on Ketonen, but luckily for Ketonen it was too high and he was able to escape. Ketonen then rolled him for a fall in 8 minutes. Starting again Ketonen secured a second arm roll in 2 minutes. Peter Gotz went home defeated [10].

In 1911 he travelled to the UK. Whilst in the UK he wrestled a match with Jim foster. The match lasted over 90 minutes ,however Foster got the win [11].

The pictured letter was written by Ketonen to his brother, it is reproduced by historian Heikki Lehmusto in a book called " Mies sisun ja sitkeyden" (1943). Page 135.

Wigan 29. August 1911

Hello Brother,
I happened to win this (wrestling) so now there is one more "world" champion. First fall 6min 35sec, second 3min. With this test the next wrestling is the 9th of the next month. He is 8kg

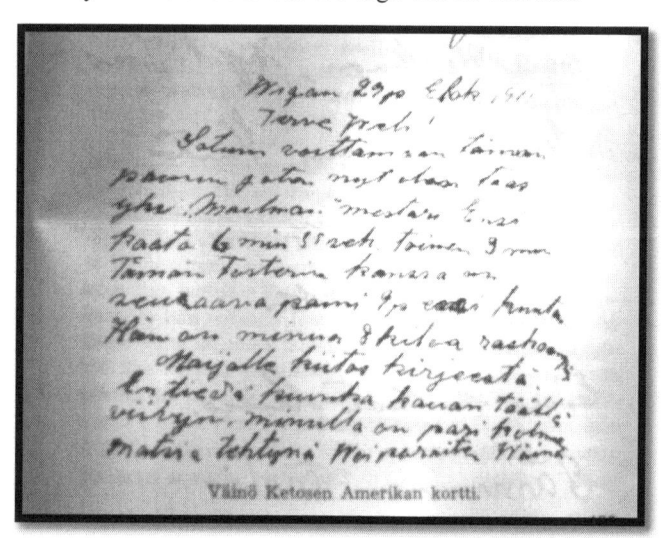

heavier than me. Thank Maija for her letter. I don't know how long will I stay here, I have couple of matches here done. Wäinö[12]

It was whilst in Wigan that Ketonen was to meet Billy Riley, a youngster, the older Ketonen was to take a liking to the young Riley and become his mentor [13].

He stayed in the UK for a total of 8 months, wrestling over 80 matches.[14]

Whilst in the UK Ketonen met with fellow Finn Nestori Tuominen, Finnish champion 1909 (beat Ketonen in the finals) and 1911. They both travelled back to the US together. Despite his poor grasp of English[15] Waino began to take his wrestling career more seriously and wrestled in many states totaling over 1000 bouts. Few of which he lost. He was wrestling up to 4 matches every week and had been given the nickname 'the terrible Finn'[16].

On his return to the US, armed with an improvement in his English, he decided to undertake a western tour on his own. Despite many matches, his only defeat was to Joe Carr in Minneapolis when he sustained a fractured leg. Not afraid to take on heavier opponents it was said that more than any other middleweight he defeated more heavyweights than any other grappler.[17]

Within five years of arriving he had adopted America as his home and gained citizenship of the country [18].

He bought a farm in Rutland, 10 miles from the city. Although not a large farm it was enough to give him a little outdoor exercise when he wanted, although wrestling tours to different parts of the country for the most part frequently interrupted his farming [19].

Ketonen fought many matches. In 1914 he had defeated Walter Miller of St Paul, formerly Calument, who had been welterweight champion for many years before losing to Mike Yokel. In the following year he would meet Yokel easily outclassing him and beating him in two straight falls "whirlwind fashion" [20].

It was in 1915 that Ketonen was to make his first bid for a championship title. However it was not at his usual weight of middleweight, rather, he trained down to 143 lbs. [21] to take on Fritz Hanson, the Swede who was title holder of the welterweight division and holder of the Lord Lonsdale belt. The match was held in January 1913 in Worcester Mass, He won the match gaining the title and the belt [22].

Next he turned his attention to his own natural weight class the middleweight. At the time Pete Brown of Texas held the title. His attention turned to Mike Yokel 'the rocky mountain lion', a Mormon and ex postmaster of Jackson Hole County, who previously had held the Middleweight championship title. The match was to be held in Duluth on the 9th March 1915. Yokel had underestimated the Finn and turned up for the match in a condition that was described as 'fat and flabby'. It was noted that Yokel refused to officially weigh in although he was noted to outweigh the fin by at least 15lbs the handicap did not bother Ketonen. Ketonen was noted to spend most of the portion of the first bout behind Yokel. Ketonen rode Yokel securing a succession of body scissors once turning him over with his shoulders nearly touching the mat for the fall but Yokel managed to fight out of the hold in what was commentated as one of the only real flashes of wrestling from him. Yokels weight was noted to be making him much slower than Ketonen who was said to be several moves ahead displaying a versatility of attack that kept the rocky mountain lion continually guessing where the match would turn next. Ketonen fastened a body scissors and then switching to a hammerlock slowly turned Yokel to gain the first fall after 37 minutes. It was shortly after the beginning of the next bout that Ketonen took Yokel to the mat and secured by the use of arm leverage the next fall. It was summed up by the Lincoln daily news as Ketonen winning with 'almost ridiculous ease'. Ketonen pocketed the 'long end' of a $3000 house as his reward for victory[23].

It was in May 1917 that Ketonen was to meet the Swede Fritz Hanson again, at the Columbia theatre on the 25th of the month. However this time Hanson was wrestling at the higher weight of 180 pounds which he was noted to be wrestling at regularly at that time. Unfortunately, as was becoming more the case the crowd was less than had been in previous years. Ketonen had been wrestling out of Chicago having a long string of victories over 'dangerous opponents'. The first fall came after 27 minutes of 'grueling wrestling', he secured a move favored by Joe Stecher, the body scissors and neck twist and it was said that was the first time it had been employed that season. The second round was a harder affair for both men, both applying and countering many holds. Hanson met with applause by reversing a hammerlock on two occasions both of which were nearly his undoing. It was Ketonen who was to secure the second and deciding fall using a cross body hold forcing Fritz shoulders down to gain the fall [24].

In 1917 he married Selma. [25]

In 1919 he was to defend his title at the Grand opera house Boston. His opponent was John Kilonis. The match was to be catch as catch can rules best 2 out of 3 falls. Kilonis gained the first fall with body hold in 1 hr. 11 min and 30 seconds. Ketonen came back with a fall in 16min 26 sec with a chancery, crutch and arm scissors. The match held in the balance. Ketonen made quick work of things securing a double arm lock to take the match in just 45 seconds, retaining his title[26].

It would appear that he had a rematch and lost as in the following October a match was held, Ketonen winning the world middleweight championship from Kilonis in one fall after 2hrs 15mins and 30 seconds utilising a toe grip and wrist lock[27]

In November the pair met for a re match. Kilonis this time defending his title implying a further loss to him by Ketonen. The match was held in the Grand opera house in Boston again on the 20th November 1919. This time the match was for best 2 out of three falls. The first fall went to Ketonen in 2minutes with a hammerlock and arm scissors. Next to score a fall was Kilonis with a crotch and body lift and body hold in 1 hr. 11min 30 sec. Ketonen was injured during the fall but insisted on continuing. After 11 minutes and 10s Kilonis secured a crotch hold and head chancery to win the match.[28]

Ketonen regained the title as in January 1920 he was due to meet mike Yokel again who was hoping to regain his title. The match was to take place in the mechanics building Boston on the 19th January. The match was originally to have been between Kilonis and Ketonen however, he had been taken ill and this gave Yokel his chance. The promoter Tuohey had hinted that because Yokel was in such good shape it had taken a lot of coaxing to get Ketonen to agree to the match. The weight stipulation was 160lbs and Yokel weighed in at 161. Ketonen argued that because he exceeded the limit the match therefore should not be for the title. However Ketonen eventually agreed to wave the extra weight. The match got under was, and after 42m 10s Yokel gained a double arm and body roll. Ketonon responded, on the offensive securing the second fall after 17min 30 seconds with a wristlock, body roll followed by double reverse arm lock with which he threw his opponent over his head and over the ropes. Yokel sustained a head injury from the edge of the platform. He returned to the ring, although he was still clearly groggy. Ketonen again on the offensive made short work of his gaining an arm scissors and hand lock in 2minutes 15 seconds.[29]

However Ketonen was to lose his title in a bout in Salt Lake City against Ira Dern. Ketonen secured the first fall in 8 minutes 30 secs using an elbow lock he used successfully whilst in England, however Dern was to secure the next two falls and the title.[30]

In February of 1921, Ketonen was noted to be the accredited titleholder of the Middleweight wrestling championship and was due to fight a bout with Pinky Gardner on the 17th day of that month against Pinky Gardner of Schenectady New York. They were required to weigh in to a limit of 160lbs before the match.[31]

The title passed to Pinky Gardner and Ketonen fought a match in March 1921 with Tony Ajax at the Grand opera house Boston to establish who would challenge Gardner for the title. The match was to be best 2 out of 3 falls. The previous night Ketonen had fought and defeated Adolphus Marshal in a match that saw a nearly full town hall in Brunswick. The first fall secured in 58 minutes with an Arm lock and a second in 10 minutes with hammerlock.[32].

The 7th April 1922 was to see Ketonen again to face Ira Dern, Dern having secured the championship once again. Ketonen at this point was regarded as one of the best middleweight wrestlers of the world. It was to take place at the salt lake theatre, best 2 out of three falls catch as catch can rules with no holds barred except the strangle. Ketonen had trained extensively for the contest and it was reported that his wrestling was easier and smoother than any other wrestler who had come to the city. Ketonen himself said he felt acclimatised and cold go 3 hours at top speed. He was to work a further 3 days in the gym and rest on the Thursday tapering his hard work off on the Wednesday. Dern left four days prior to the match for Logan to wrestle Tom Ray in a match. Commentators noted his gym work over the previous days showed him to be better than he had been for the previous months, He was to work in the day at the fire station on the Tuesday and Wednesday then rest [33]. Ketonen was to win , 2 out of three fails claiming the championship title[34].

A rematch was to be had as on the 18/4/22, it was reported that Ketonen and Dern were in negotiations with the Elks. The match was to be given for the benefit of the local lodge for charity and moved from Salt Lake City to the Orpheum. Ketonen wanted for his end of the purse more money than two wrestlers had received in one match before in Salt Lake City. The figure was so high it took a lot of planning on behalf of the elks o meet it. Ketonen also demanded that Dern weigh in at a limit of 160lbs. The elks relented to every request of Ketonen. And the match was to take place on the 28th April[35]. Unfortunately the result is lost to history.

In the July of 1922 Ketonen took on Joe turner who had beaten him in the intervening time gaining the title. The match was set to be best 2 out of three falls, however with the stipulation that if after 90 minutes no fall had been gained that one fall would decide the match. The match indeed passed the one-hour thirty marks, the next fall deciding the title. Ketonen after a further 12 minutes managed to gain a toehold on Turner gaining the fall and regaining his title[36].

The match had been a great success with fans and pressure was on turner for a rematch. It wasn't until the 22nd of august of 1922 that Joe Turner gave in accepting terms to meet Ketonen again. Ketonen posted a weight forfeit to ensure the match was a championship match. The weight was set at the usual 158lbs and both men agreed. Turner, still held the Police gazette belt which he won in the Boston tournament some years previously. Although he continued to claim the title his claims were not recognised. An interesting note here was the paper reporting the match noted Ketonen to be someone who 'doesn't go out of his way to wrestle for nothing', noting him to be a wealthy man , his farm in Vermont being valued at over $80000![37].

In October 1922 "Waino Ketonen defeated Charles Rentrop of little Rock on October 19th in a wrestling match in which it was claimed that the middleweight championship of the world was at stake. Renthrop surrendered a recently won belt to be emblematic of the title. The championship was long disputed"[38]

November 1922 was to see Ketonen take on and beet Utah wrestler Mark Howard of Salt Lake city in Beaumont Texas . Ketonen secured the first fall after 18minutes 13 seconds, and a second with a toehold, leg split and headlock[39].

In December 1922 Ketonen fought Heinie Engel. It was a six round match with the decision of the referee in Ketonen's favour. This was not popular with the local crows prompting John Doc'Krone, the promoter to send a telegram commenting " Waino Ketonen's decision over Heine Engle at the auditorium last night was not popular with Chicago fans. Heinie had the better of it and I thought the referee at least should have given Engle a draw "[40].

It was March of 1923 that Ketonen was to fight Carol 'Pinkie' Gardner again. The match had been hanging in the balance for some time. Talk had been that Pink had 'run out of matches with this man for some time claiming he was out of shape'[41]. The match was set for the 23rd of March at the Armory Athletic association. It was to be Ketonen's first appearance at the venue. This was not the first time that Pink and Ketonen had met, they had wrestled two matches in Boston. Each had won a match a piece. Although he agreed to meet Ketonen, Gardner still claimed he didn't feel in the best shape in order to meet the Finn. It was said that Ketonen had been after his scalp for some time. Pink had been in hard training for the match, Ketonen was said to have been in the best shape of his life. Ketonen was confident stating that he would "take Gardner and then match with Turner and any one else that thinks they may have a chance" [42]. The match was to be fought best 2 out of 3 falls catch as catch can style. Ketonen was recognised as one of the few grapplers who merited any serious consideration, and claimed him to be one of the most finished artists of the mat game at the time. It was said that he knew more inside stuff about the tricks of the game as needed for success than any other grappler. Pink weighted in at 156 and Ketonen at 157 lbs.[43].

It was Ketonen who was to secure the first fall, gaining an arm scissors and wrist lock, however Gardner didn't give in straight away, rolling shoulder to shoulder to prevent the fall but eventually both shoulders hit the mat and the fall given after 48 minutes and 8 seconds. Ketonen was given a standing ovation by the crowd. The men came out for the second round. The fall this time however caused some confusion amongst the observers. Gardner attempted pull Ketonen over his head whilst in a standing position, failing however he quickly reached under and grabbed Ketonen by his feet, there was a dull thud and some rolling and Ketonen's shoulders were pinned to the mat. Some dubbed it a Cornish back heel hold others a straight body hold, admitting heels had something to do with it also noting that it was a favorite of the Zbyszko family whatever it was Gardner had secured the equalising fall after 14 minutes and 51 seconds. It was obvious to all that Ketonen was stunned and had to be assisted for the mat. The men met again for the deciding fall however the effect of the last fall meant that Gardner was able to secure a cradle hold after the relatively short time of 2 minutes 43 with a cradle hold[44].

In 1922/23, Billy Riley during a tour in America fought pinkie Gardner in New York to gain the middleweight championship[45]. However Riley was to meet Ketonen his former mentor from Wigan all the years previously in 1911. Riley was to lose to Ketonen and was quoted a number of years later in the ringsider wrestling magazine " I have always looked up on this fight as the greatest contest of my career. I enjoyed every minute of it. It was a ding dong battle from the sound of the bell and I realized that I had lost my title I got consolation in the fact that I had passed it on to one well worthy of it" [46].

December 1923 and Ketonen defeated William O'Connel. He gained the first fall in 31 minutes with a hammerlock and body hold. O'Connel followed up in 5minutes with a front headlock gaining the fall. However, Ketonen was to gain victory after just 8 minutes with a body scissors to get the deciding fall[47].

In April 1924 he was to regain his title in a match with Charles gribble of South America. He took the first fall in 30 minutes, and lost the second in eight minutes gaining the third fall and match in 7minutes[48].

Joe Turner and Ketonen were to meet again in the February of 1925. It was a follow up match as the two had met in Greensboro in early February. Each man had gained a fall a piece, however Turner got thrown from the ring and was deemed unable to continue and the match was given to Ketonen[49].

In February of 1927 Ketonen was booked to grapple Joe Parelli of Chicago. The venue was the Van Curer theatre under the direction of the Sportsmen's Amateur Association. Ketonen was based at Chicago at this point, and was training for the match out of the local YMCA, opposing all comers. Ketonen was campaigning all around the country in a bid to regain his title. Parelli had previously fought Pink Gardner, and his unusual sensational actions in the match kept fans on the edge of their seats throughout, even when he was losing the fans were doubtful of it. Ketonen was noted to "Relies solely on his skill he is strong and scientific, fast but not furious and the ability to remain cool under the fire of his opponent's attacks. He is a wonderful wrestler and is rated by any a sport writer as the greatest middleweight that was ever developed"[50]

In 1928 he was to have a match with Henry Kolln, a student of the famous Farmer Burns, coach of Frank Gotch. At the time Waino was the American middleweight champion and Henry Kolln was the Canadian champion. The match was due to take place at the American Legion hall in Cameron[51]. However it was postponed until the Friday, February 24th. There had been a violent storm, which prevented fans from getting to the hall. The wrestlers agreed to re-arrange the match. Kolln left Cameron to attend a match elsewhere, Ketonen left for Dallas to make other arrangements but was due to return on the afternoon of the match itself[52]. The match was a two-fall match. Ketonen took the first two falls from Kolln winning the match. Although it was noted that Kolln was one of the best seen there[53].

In 1929, October he was to meet Dern again who was in a bid for Ketonen's title. Ketonen had regained the title from Yokel in the spring of that year. Dern at the time was being coached by Will Thornton, an English trainer who had previously taught both Ketonen and Yokel.[54]

Although usually known for his clean wrestling, Ketonen occasionally would consider 'rougher' tactics. In November of 1930 he was due to wrestle 'wildcat Pete' worlds junior middleweight titleholder. Ketonen was noted to comment that although he disliked rough tactics he said if forced to he would resort to such tactics against the youngster. An article by the Astorian budget had noted that this was a different Ketonen to the one that had wrestled there previously, throwing cleverness to the wind in favour of tactics used by rough artists. The match was to be 2 out of 3 falls with no set time limit.[55]

Towards the end of his career Ketonen wrestled Robin Reed of Reedsport. Waino took the first fall in 25 minutes but robin returned for a second and gave Ketonen a bad eye when he kicked him during the process of an arm stretch. He whip wrist locked him and took the fall. Ketonen returned for the third but the ye was getting worse and reed made short work of him Ketonen losing 2 falls to one

However in 1929 it is said that he sold his farm, moving himself his wife and son to Palo Alto in California. He was engaged in teaching students of Stanford university wrestling. An article at the time stated he was teaching wristlocks, nelsons, arm bars and other effective wrestling holds. It was thought that the wrestling in the 1932 Olympics would be held at the university and he was employed to teach the wrestlers going for the Greco roman titles.[56]

Ketonen vacated his title, giving it to the national boxing association. A tournament was held and it was fellow Finn Gus Kallio who won it.[57]

Ketonen also played the role of 'policeman' for his old friend Chris Jordan, another veteran wrestler and promoter. A young grappler by the name of Carl Brown, known for some excellent wrestling in Iowa, held Jordan to a two and a half hour draw. Brown also was threatening some of Jordan's territory. Jordan called on Ketonen to take on the much younger middleweight. Ketonen was outweighed by 15 lbs. Waino agreed to the match and after demonstrating some excellent holds beat his twice in 4 minutes with a double arm lock or back drop.[58]

In an interview in 1934 he was asked what his feelings were on the wrestlers of the day, his answer was as follows "Waino believes the present type of jumping kicking and tackling grapplers, Ketonen dismisses them with a shrug Most of them regardless of their weight can not even give him a good workout he declares."[59]. When asked the secret of wrestling "it is the ability to use your strength from any position as well as a real knowledge of holds and their blocks. A thorough grounding in Greco roman wrestling as well as the fundamentals of catch as catch can grappling is necessary for any one to become a great wrestler."[60]

He retired in 1934 as world champion at 73KG, He retired to a 'chicken farm' in Rutland Massachusetts.[61]

One interesting find, which I haven't been able to corroborate elsewhere is that Ketonen had a brother by the name of Andrew, also a wrestler. In March 1922 Andrew Ketonen "brother of middleweight champion of the world" held a show at the local theatre in Cook county, offering to throw any man and giving a demonstration of the holds used by the wrestlers of the day.[62]

Two Finnish newspapers report Waino's death; other informs that he died in the age of 86 and the other 87. He died at Massachusetts, US.

Willie Charnock

Willie Charnock of Hopwood street in Newton[63] was known to be a trainer of Billy Riley between the war years. He was known to be teaching Billy and a small group at the Crispin arms, which included Charlie Carroll. There is very little information about Charnock, even his own family have little knowledge of him.

I have presented here any references to Willie Charnock I could find in the newspapers of the time.

1905

On the 26th March 1905 Billy Charnock was recorded as being in the United States and beat George Brothmere for the worlds Lightweight championship title in New York.

1908

Burnly Wrestling tournament 1908
Wrestling tournament at Burnley

Though valuable prizes in cash and trophies are being offered by Mesars Cooke and Mitchel for a wrestling tournament at the Burnley athletic grounds there was not as large as attendance on the opening day as was confidently expected, though about 800 people were present. Several foremost wrestlers in the 6sc 14lb division failed to put in an appearance but ten of those who did turn out passed the scales, and eight passed for the 7sc competition. Every man was given the privilege of seeing the others weight in and the wrestlers themselves took part in the drawing which in addition to being something of an innovation is an assurance of the bona fides of the competition.

First Day
Charnock was in the 6sc 14lb division.
Billy Charnock was drawn against Jack Hodson who retired.

Second day – five left in the 6sc 14lb competition. Charnock was drawn against Peter Mangham of Burnley. Charnock was first at the back, but after a few minutes Mangham reversed the positions. Attacking with a three quarter nelson Charnock turned out and almost gained a throw by the muscle and elbow hold. After 20 minutes work he succeeded in throwing Mangham by a wrist and crutch hold. In the second bout Charnock gained the fall in 2 ½ minutes.

Jack Smith of Greenbeys was appointed referee by the editor of the sporting chronicle.

G. Weedall (Manchester) bt J Rimmer of Burnley (3min and 4 min)

Peter Mangham (Burnley) bt T Cunningham (Burnley) 11min and 30 sec

Hardy (Hull) bt Jack Milroy (Richton) 6 min, 15min

Peter Connor (Burnley) bt J Goodham

Charnock (Wigan) bt Peter Mangham (Burnley)

A Hardy bt G Weedhall (Manchester) 10min 4 min

W Charnock bt P Connor Burnley 3 ½ and 1 min[64]

The Burnley wrestling tournament came to a close on Saturday in the worst weather possible, rain falling all the time the men were in the ring. The enterprising proprietors Mesars Cook and Mitchel are to be sympethised with for although the wrestling through the preliminary bouts had been very good the attendance was poor. The ground was a huge puddle the wrestlers presenting pitiable sights as they floundered and splashed about I their endeavors to secure decent holds.

Singularly the 6sc 14 championships competition although being of ten times the value in prises as compared with the 7 score one did not furnish nearly so good wrestling. There was little interest in the final of the 6sc 14lb with Chanrock and Hardy. Although Hardy had not much chance he in spite of the disadvantage in weight put up a stout resistance. True, he never looked like a winner and possibly the wet helped him a deal but Charnock was working desperately for 8 minutes before he secured a fall. The Hull lad, nothing daunted, tried gamely in the second bout but had to retire in the end of six minutes owing to an injury. The bout for third and fourth prize between G. Weedall of Manchester and P Connor of Burnley was short duration

Weedall won in 2 and 4 min.

The winner of the 50-guinea cup is bound to defend it against any challenger who staked a deposit of £1 with the editor of the Sporting chronicle and who is willing to wager not less than £15 aside, and weigh in at 6sc 14bs. Should any man hold the cup for 18 months it becomes his own property. The holder is compelled to wrestle in 3 weeks from being challenged or forfeit.[65]

The Alhambra tournaments

1909

In 1909 Willy Charnock took part in the famous Alhambara tournament. He was in the lightweight division. His first match was on day two of the tournament, a Tuesday and was against G Schneider of Bloomsbury. Reports noted that although Charnock was continually on the attack he was not strong enough to secure the verdict until 16 minutes and 6 seconds.

The next round saw him against E.B Koch of Germany. Again Charnock went on the attack, however the German who was noted to be tremendously strong , and stood the onslaught. Charcock was cautioned for using the cradle, head and further shoulder, and well as other holds that were actually legitimate holds under the rules. It seems he gave up all further attempts to throw his man was noted to be contented to staying behind 'practically went to sleep for the last 10 minutes". The match went to the limit of 30 minutes and the win was awarded on points.

The next round on Saturday, day 6, saw him facing Job Smith of Aspull. The first minute seemed a pretty even match between the two wrestlers. Charnock was able to slip behind Smith and he managed to secure a leg and arm hold. Smith struggled desperately but ended up going down and Charnock won in 2 minutes 45 seconds.

His next match was on day 10 of the tournament, which was a Thursday and was against Alf Hardy of Hull. Charnock won with a crotch hold and half nelson in 2 minutes and 25 seconds.

Having got through to the semi final he was set to face Tom Rose of Barnsley. The match lasted 14 minutes and 9 seconds and was rolled and pinned.

Charnock and Rose

"The second contest between Tom Rose and W. Charnock furnished the prettiest wrestling seen in the tournament up to date. Both looked wonderfully fit and Charnock set the pace. He went first behind with a leg hold, and picking rose up by the crotch slammed him down. Rose got clear and got on top. Charnock twisted round secured another leg hold and got behind but lost his man. Rose forced the pace and almost got a fall by pulling up one of Charnock's legs and kicking the other way, but Charnock's twisted into a squatting position from which he forced himself up. Some very fast and brilliant work all over the mat, each man extricating himself from serious trouble time after time in really wonderful fashion. At last rose secured a leg and wrist turned Charnock and secured the reversed chest position. Charnock bridged out of this trouble in most marvelous fashion but a few seconds later succumbed to an exactly similar hold. Time 14 mins 9 secs.

Starting again the struggle was as beautiful as before. Rose was early in trouble following a head hold and pull down. He struggled desperately and only escaped by foiling a leg half nelson, which Charnock tried to get on. Charnock was behind again and in a few seconds and after smashing rose down allowed him to slip away in an extraordinary fashion.

Willy Charnock - Alhambra 1909

Rose was now banged about pretty badly for a time and the work got faster than ever. The Wigan lad hot behind and at once made a bad slip. Rose at once rolled him and was putting on a reversed chest hold when Charnock bridged and twisted out in a miraculous fashion. He again bot behind but was immediately arm rolled and pinned in 13 min 59 sec"[66]

Tom Rose went on to win the lightweight division in the final against Jack Broadbent of Accrington.[67]

Bolton tournament

A wrestling tournament for the 10st 6 1lb catch as catch can title was commenced at the Grand theatre Bolton on Saturday afternoon when there was a crowded house. The principle prize was a splendid gold and silver belt with a handsome silver cup for the runner up. 14 preliminary heats were decided – James Whittle (Ince), W. Woodcock (Ince), Jack Bentley (Accrington), W. Charnock (Wigan), Harry Tonge (West Houghton), Jack Milroy (Accrington), Percy Ellis (Tyldesley), Mc Ewans novice (Scotland), William Moores (Bolton), Alec Grant (London), Matt Seddon (Bolton), George Dootson (Rochadale), Jack Hart (Farnsworth) and Miles Sweeney (Atherton)[68].

1910

Charnock took part in the third tournament that was held in the Alhambra.

25/1/1910 – He beat Fred Altila
27/1/1910 – He beat James Webster
29/1/1910 – He beat Adolph Blady, Charnock beat Joe Smith from Aspull 2min 45 seconds third round.
31/1/1910 – He lost to Young Olsen in under 10 minutes via a half nelson and leg hold[69]

1911

Worlds championship at Bolton – 10st 2lb championship of world between Tom Rose of Bolton and Bob Somerville of America was decided at the Grand Theatre Bolton on Saturday. The men had signed articles to wrestle the best of three falls and failing a fall in the stipulated hour and a half the contest to be decided on points. The stakes at issue were £50 and the title of the world's champion. Preceding the match there were bouts between Job Shambley and Jimmy Taylor and between Teddy

Whittaker and Billy Charnock both of which resulted in draws.

Somerville won on points.

Peter Gotz the holder of Lord Lonsdale's lightweight championship belt challenged the winner at 10st 6lb immediately after the contest.[70]

In October 1914 Charnock enlisted in the Kings Regiment Liverpool. Initially he was stationed in the South of England. After a period of several months his regiment was deployed in France. He received a head injury on the 12th of July 1915, whilst near Ypres. After a period of recuperation at the base hospital he returned to his battalion. In the September, the 10th to be accurate he was wounded 'about the body' (possibly via shrapnel), and was sent back home to convalesce at a hospital in Eastbourne[71].

Jayne Byrne, Billy Riley's daughter, only has a few memories of seeing Willie Charnock at the House[72]. He was known to have taught Billy in the post war years [73]at least until the 1930s as he coached Billy for his match against Reginsky [74] although one newspaper source stated that Bill had ben training with Bill Duggan. In Billy Robinsons book Physical Chess he states that Charnock and Riley fell out although Bill Robinson did not discuss the reasons with Billy Riley[75]. Charnock was known to have a gym in which he or possibly 'Pop Saxton' taught the Belshaw brothers. Later one of the Belshaws would face Billy's protégé Billy Joyce in what was considered the last catch match in Wigan.

Peter Burns

It was Ernie Riley that stated Peter Burns was a coach of his father[76]. Unfortunately very little is known about Peter Burns, however I have included the one Newspaper report I was able to find.

At Lancaster hippodrome on Saturday Peter Burns Wigan bantamweight champion wrestled J. Winstanley Barnsley for £10 a side and a purse of £15. winstanley gained the first fall in 20 minutes. In the second bout burns got on level terms at the end of six minutes and won the match at the end of another seven minutes[77]

Bob Bootle

A coal miner, born in Whelley in 1902. He is pictured with Billy Riley holding a towel in the photograph, which was taken to celebrate the winning one of his championship belts, as such it was believed he was a trainer of Billy Riley. After getting in contact with his son, also named Bob Bootle, it turns out that he was not in fact a trainer of Billy Riley but rather a friend. He knew the Riley family as a youth and was later friendly with Billy's son Ernie Riley. He was with Billy on the day the newspaper photographer arrived. Billy stripped off to his trunks and since they were now 'creating a photo' they decided to place Bob in the photo alongside Billy holding a towel in order to make a 'professional looking shot' his son also comments it may have been there to also illustrate the considerable size of Billy.

In 1936 he married and rented a house from Jack Myers who was also the landlord of the Crispin arms, where he used to drink. Jack Myers lived in Plat lane Wigan earlier as did Bob and his family, he had also spent a short time living in Caroline street before he got married. Although he was interested in wrestling all his life and involved in with the Riley family, he was not a wrestler or trainer. He suffered from 'bronchial weakness' which the coal mining aggravated and from which he dies in 1972. He knew the local wrestlers but did not train them.[78]

---

[1] Evening independent Massillon ohio may 10 34
[2] Interview of Ketonen published by newspaper "Uusi suomi" Friday 14.12. 1962
[3] Evening independent Massillon ohio may 10 34
[4] Interview of Ketonen published by newspaper "Uusi suomi" Friday 14.12. 1962
[5] Interview of Ketonen published by newspaper "Uusi suomi" Friday 14.12. 1962
[6] Interview of Ketonen published by newspaper "Uusi suomi" Friday 14.12. 1962
[7] "Suomen urheilulehti 1909, XII vuosikerta, s. 718" = Sport magazine of finland or finnish sportmagazine 1909, XII vintage p.718
[8] Boston globe 31/3/29 daily
[9] Boston globe 31/3/29 daily

[10] Boston globe 31/3/29 daily
[11] Interview of Ketonen published by newspaper "Uusi suomi" Friday 14.12. 1962
[12] Translation – Jasse Junkari
[13] Ernie Riley interview
[14] Boston globe 31/3/29 daily
[15] Boston globe 31/3/29 daily
[16] Interview of Ketonen published by newspaper "Uusi suomi" Friday 14.12. 1962
[17] 1/3/29 daily Boston globe
[18] 1/3/29 daily Boston globe
[19] 1/3/29 daily Boston globe
[20] 22/10/15 milwaukee sentinell
[21] Lincoln daily news March 10 1915
[22] Lincoln daily newsJan 12 15
[23] Lincoln daily news March 10 1915, Loincoln daily news March 13 1915
[24] Morning star, Wilmington may 25 ,17
[25] Interview of Ketonen published by newspaper "Uusi suomi" Friday 14.12. 1962
[26] 11/4/19 daily Boston globe
[27] 10/10/10 borer cities star
[28] 22/11/19 – Boston daily globe
[29] 19-20/1/1920 Boston daily globe
[30] 9/3/20 Zeehan and dundas herald
[31] Rome NY daily sentinel feb 17 21
[32] 10/3/21 Boston daily globe
[33] 3/4/22 Desert news
[34] El paso herald 070422
[35] 18/4/22 deser news
[36] New york evening telegram July 1 22
[37] Washington herald 23/8/22
[38] The charlotte news fri oct 20 1922 page 10
[39] El paso herald 16/11/22
[40] 9/12/22Boston daily globe
[41] Schenactady NY Gazette March 19 23
[42] Schenectady Gazette 22/3/23
[43] Schenectady ny gazette March 23 1923
[44] Schenectady ny gazette March 24 23
[45] Wigan Observer 22-8-31
[46] Ringsider magazine
[47] 13/12/23 Boston daily globe
[48] 4/4/24 Boston daily globe
[49] The bee,dancille VA feb 23 1925
[50] Schenectady ny gazette feb 23 27
[51] Cameron herals 16/2/28
[52] Cameron Herlad 23/2/28
[53] Cameron herald 1/3/28
[54] 16/10/29 Boston daily globe
[55] 28/11/30 eugene register guard
[56] 1/3/29 daily Boston globe
[57] Evening independent Massillon Ohio May 10 34
[58] Evening independent Massillon Ohio May 10 34
[59] Evening independent Massillon Ohio May 10 34
[60] Evening independent Massillon Ohio May 10 34
[61] interview of Ketonen published by newspaper "Uusi suomi" Friday 14.12. 1962
[62] Cook county news herald 9/3/22
[63] Wigan Examiner Nov 20th 1915
[64] Express and advetser 10/6/1908
[65] Burnley gazette 17/6/08
[66] Health & strength Vol 17 no 7 Feb 1909 p7
[67] Health and strength Vol 17 no 7 Feb 1909
[68] Manchester courier March 1 1909
[69] Sheffield daily telegraph 1/2/10
[70] Manchester courier 30/10/11
[71] Wigan Examiner Nov 20th 1915
[72] Interview Jayne Byrne
[73] Tommy Heyes
[74] Tommy Heyes
[75] Physcial Chess , Billy Robinson ECW Press 2012 page 25
[76] Ernie Riley Interview
[77] The daily mail 17/2/1919
[78] Email correspondence with Bob Bootles son.

Chapter 6

Billy Riley – the coach

" Everyone one of us feels that my father bill is the man who put us where we are today. His coaching methods are exacting at times but they certainly get the results" – Ernie Riley

Billy Riley coached many people over his career and went on to be amongst the most well known and well respected wrestlers across the world. Although it was the gym in Whelley that Billy Riley was associated with as being a coach, Billy was a coach prior to opening the gym there. Training sessions took place in the number of pubs he lived at and ran as well as at rented venue such as that above a Haulage company depot[1].

Even after his retirement we would return to the gym to watch the proceedings and advise Roy Wood on how to improve a particular aspect of his coaching. One of the earlier wrestlers to be coached by Billy was George Gregory[2], when Billy Joyce, widely regarded as one of the best Lancashire catch as catch can wrestlers of the modern age was asked for who he looked up to, he named George Gregory. Billy Riley also coached Jimmy Nibblet, known as the man of granite. In an interview he told of how Riley approached him and told Jimmy that he was going to build a gym and that he should attend. Jimmy would call at the house and ask if the gym was open yet, he would be told no not yet but come in. Billy then would then get down on the floor of his living room to show some moves to him[3]. Jayne Byrne also recalls her father being in the living room down on the floor coaching wrestlers. "If you were talking in conversation and it got to about the gym the next thing is they'd be on the floor y'know. Wrestling or giving them holds saying this is the way you should be doing it. I mean that was a regular occurrence that was that."[4]

When asked about his thoughts on coaching Billy Riley replied, "there's no secret to success in my tactics. It's only a question of being conscientious. When they start learning a hold I make sure they do it properly – no stopping half way they must get it off to perfection or else try again until they do. The lads are keen enough to learn, and they are down most days. They don't grumble at half-crown a week because that's just to cover costs of heating and lighting .I don't charge for any tips given or coaching. I get my reward when I see a Wigan lad wearing a championship belt"[5].

Seamus Dunelavy had the following to say about Billy Riley as a coach "He was absolutely brilliant, he was an old man when I got there and he'd get on the mat with you sometimes and he'd be explaining the hold, and he'd watch us putting it on then he'd slip down on the mat as he was full of arthritis at this stage, he'd put it on and it was totally different, like he'd put a bar around you head, it would be like a steel bar, it would be like being in a square box and everything would be squeezing in on you, it was phenomenal really. He was very technical really, I learned a lot from him. He would say for example if you were opening a screw top on a bottle you could transfer all the energy from your arm into your fingers. And Billy would do this when putting a hold on you see, he would say if you putting a hold around your head he would say I'm going to make the ring that little bit smaller ', going to tighten the ring and you could feel it happening to you, he was technical and strong. Because what he was doing was dead right, not like you see with lads with their foot away from it should be, it was balance. He knew everything back to front, and he'd keep you at the one hold for weeks. You'd think there was nothing more he could show me but he'd keep on and on and on and on and eventually you could do it in your sleep. When I was courting my wife Mary, and she'd tell you this and I'd put holds on her we'd be talking or embracing and I'd put a hold on her, I'd say "if I put my hand up there or slip it around there" and she'd say "you're in the gym again", but you got that way that as soon as you touched someone you'd be moving all around the body with holds and things"[6]

It was not only the training aspects that he would advise his students on, he also advised them about their money and kept them on the straight and narrow, his grandson Patrick remembers his advice to the wrestlers "Yeah, you'd see lads I suppose they worked and they wrestled, so they were getting that money in and he was like 'y'know it doesn't last forever. Save it or put it into a business,' that was always his advice to them y'know. Look after your money; invest your money either in a house or a business or something like that because these times only last so long. And that was his thing to lads because he was trying to save y'know"[7]. Roy Wood remembers being told by Billy "get yourself straight home from the gym don't go stopping at the pub" and "gambling and drinking are a waste of hard earned money"

He treated the wrestlers like family this is how his daughter remembers it "'It's no good, coming and going, you have to stick at it.' And that was it, and apart from being a trainer to them as Roy will probably tell you, he was a father figure in some and that's how it was run it was like a family in a way wasn't it some of them were very close." [8]

Michael Moore said of Billy Riley "He was a very patient man, sometimes however be would swear, not bad language he would say 'you lazy ways wasn't he. If he thought some lads were going a bit astray he'd give them a talking too and take them under his wing y'know. Because he never had the love of a father." A lot of them used to come and I can remember some of the old ones; George Gregory used to come to our house like regularly, like one of the family, and a lot of them did they used to come like lads now that came up from Birmingham, the Dunleavy's they used to come up on the train, my mother, they put their feet under the table and my mother would give them something to eat before they went back she hadn't to do it but she made them well buggers get up' when he got frustrated with someone. However he took great lengths to show you things[9].

He also taught children "there was some guy in Liverpool he got to know my father through the wrestling, it was interesting wrestling but there was a school. I think somewhere near Salford for children which came from bad homes of had got into trouble and for ages my father went once a week just to teach them a bit of wrestling y'know. He did it just out of you know well these children haven't had a chance"[10]

The gym attracted people from all around the world from people such as Ricky Star, Ben Sherman and then others such as Karl Istaz (aka Karl Gotch).

Jayne remembers many from around the world attending the gym "I can remember Jean Morand he was French, he'd been in the French foreign legion, dropped behind enemy lines, I can remember him coming. He was a chef at the Mill in Manchester, and then he moved to London, I don't know whether he wrestled professionally or not, but he was his friend. There was some Czechoslovakians guys come and with Benny Englblom he was from Iceland, and Karl Istaz and I can't think of where, and Caribbean lads, I can't think of names but god knows, Indian lads of course"[11].

I asked Roy Wood what Billy Riley was like as a coach, he replied "When I was wrestling professional, I spent a lot of time with him. He loved talking about wrestling that's all we ever discussed, wrestling. He was a very nice person he was like a father figure to me. He put me on the straight and narrow; he was, he told you what to do with your money, he advised me to get an accountant when I turned pro. He was just giving me very good advice. He would tell me when I was away keep out of the pubs and out of the posh restaurants or I'd finish up wrestling for nothing. He told me how to look after myself in general."[12]

Always ready with advice and guidance for his wrestlers Billy would know the right thing to say to encourage them, Seamus Dunleavy recalls "Going through the rounds the day after the match Billy Riley said 'how did you get on jimmy?' I said 'alright but I was tired and had three or four rounds' hut he'd say 'when you're tired the other fella's tired as well' he stuck those things in our heads."[13]

Training at the gym

"We were from Wigan and once you were from Wigan you all stuck together"[14]

The gym was open on a Tuesday, Thursday and Sunday mornings. However the professionals worked out in the gym in the morning and there were some professionals that attended the gym that were never seen by those attending the regular classes. Seamus Dunleavy writes in his autobiography how the professional wrestlers would start training around 11 am leaving the gym around 1-2. The cost was half a crown, (2 shillings and six pence). However you could make arrangements with Billy, and some were given a key[15].

Being a newcomer to the gym was an intimidating prospect of for most. Roy Wood remembers his first time in the gym "I stumbled in the gym one Sunday morning and sat in the corner and hoped no one would notice me, and that happened for a long while I used to creep in at the back, watching all these men wrestling I was fascinated by them all, Billy Riley turned round to me and said if you want to keep coming bring some stuff and have a go. Instead of just keeping sitting there every Sunday morning bring a swimming costume, a pair of trainers and have a go at It."[16]. Billy Robinson had been training in the YMCA and done well in the amateurs. When he first attended the gym he was asked what his best hold was. To which he replied the crucifix. He was told to put the hold on Jack Dempsey (Tommy Moore) who he outweighed significantly. In the blink of an eye the hold was broken and a submission was applied. This happened each time it was tried. Eventually he was told 'That stuff if good for the amateurs but this is professional wrestling"[17]. Billy Robinson tells of how when he first went to the Gym how he was paired with Charlie Carroll, who managed to hurt Billy whatever he did. For 3 months he wasn't taught anything, they just 'beat the living shit' out of him. It was only when they could see that he wasn't going to quit that they began to teach him. Even after Billy Won the British Amateurs he was kept humble when he went to the gym the next day. This idea of being kept humble was something that was common in the gym, even when the wrestlers turned pro and won titles and belts, again Billy Robinson recounts "every time I won something or beat somebody, I hated going back to the gym the next day, because I knew what would happen. I wouldn't be sparring with somebody who should be able to beat me. I would be sparring with an old timer who I was a lot bigger than, a lot younger than a lot stronger than. And he'd beat the living shit out of me"[18]

'Give newcomers a good scuffing around the mat; put submission holds on hard and keep them on after the unsuspecting newcomer had shouted his submission; let knees fists and elbows stray accidentally into the new lads face and belly. If they come back a second time they are threated almost as roughly! It sorts the wheat from the chaff and when you eventually get into a professional ring you know that your opponent has suffered the same treatment and will be dependable and reliable' [19].Tom Billingotn a.k.a the Dynamite Kid had his own experience of Riley's Gym, and much like the others it was a common theme. He tells of the fact that he was taken down, and submissions such as front face locks, leg locks and double wristlock applied until he screamed. No quarter was given for the fact he was young or inexperienced[20]. He didn't return too often, but that was not the end of his association with Riley's gym. He later trained with Billy chambers (Jack Fallon) at a nearby Gym, his manager in the stampede wrestling was John Foley (known as J.R. Foley , a gimmick at the time Dallas was a well known TV show). Tom Billington's cousin Davey Boy Smith, who made up the British bulldogs had trained with Roy Wood also.

People would get on the mat and wrestle, a pair at a time with Billy watching on. There was no drilling as such; you started out doing your own thing, making your own mistakes. You learned by watching others and having the moves applied on you, you then sought to learn the counters. It was only after you had been there for a while, put your time in, maybe even up to a year, then Billy Would take you aside after and start to tell you where you had gone wrong. "Once people improved then Billy wouldn't let them get away with anything that wasn't perfect, you were made to do it inch perfect. Or you'd be cursed by, him , not in a bad way, bad language wasn't allowed in the gym"[21]. In an article for SWS Roy was interviewed and had the following to say about the training "Riley was very strict on technical points. He would never say "Do this!". You had to try something and he would then comment on what you did. From that you would learn something or you would see what effect of the advice he had given had on what you were trying."[22]. When Billy did find something wrong he would have you drill it until he saw it done right and then he would allow the wrestling to continue. He would concentrate on one move for anything up to a month having the wrestlers only being allowed to use that one move in wrestling, to onlookers it would look strange with one of the wrestlers going for just one move and the other trying multiple different ones, but that's how Billy wanted it. [23]

Roy tells of the way the training was organised "So if you went up to Tommy Moore, or Jimmy Hart ' I'll have a wrestle' they'd look at you as if thinking 'you're not good enough to wrestle me and knock hell out of you'. Then you knew you weren't good enough to wrestle them and you'd do the same the week after.' There were no rounds, you wrestled until someone got the 'knock' or submission.

If a wrestler did go to his back during sparring Billy would give them a few seconds to see if they could get themselves out and then would say "Go to your belly", they would then have to fight up from there, you weren't brought back to a standing position, you had to get yourself out, same with submissions, if someone gave a "knock" and submitted, the submission was let off and the person had to fight out of the position they were in.[24] "When you were wrestling, if you got submitted, if your opponent was in a funny position, when he let the move off you didn't take advantage you turned to your belly and give him the back. There was no getting up, once you were underneath you were underneath. You had to be very very clever to get out.". There were no rounds. You wrestled until you 'knocked' or submitted[25]

Billy Robinson had the following to say in his book about the training at the gym "In the old Wigan gym, the coach would get five or six good guys and you'd go on the mat for an hour and a half or two and a half hours non stop. He would send a new guy in every three to five minutes. If you were getting the better of the guy too easy he'd send somebody else in. Then you learn how to make your opponent do all the work"[26]

One of the things Billy Riley tried to instill into the wrestlers was to be "one move ahead". He used to say "If a move is half on then it is easy to counter" – so when you were wrestling you would have the counter in your mind and then when they had half achieved the move you had allowed them to get you would retaliate with your move. Roy Wood says that many old timers would let a submission hold on themselves in order to gain their own. Sometimes it wasn't the submission that won its who has the most guts.[27]

Seamus Dunleavy in an interview had the following to say on how he remembered the training at the gym "There would be 10-12 of us there we'd all pull with each other, Billy would be there, it was a small ramshackle place like all good gyms really. Billy would sit there and we'd all be sitting there, and he's say to me 'Jimmy' as Seamus is the Gaelic name for James, and he'd say get on with Ernie, and Ernie would do 5 10 minutes with me and if I was training for some championship at the time I'd be the principle one they would all want to wrestle with, so I'd have a pull with 3 or 4 or 5 of them and that's what went on all the time, and then if some man had a serious match that man would be picked out as having most of the training. And if you made a mistake you'd be the pit prop, the pit prop is the thing that holds up the pit, and is useless so Billy would say ' you're the bloody pit prop, I've showed you that move' and you'd feel bad as you like to get Billy's respect. And at the end of it you would know that whoever you met and wherever you met them you could put yourself right."[28]

It was usual for the Old timers to come to the gym and watch the training, sharing their knowledge. There were others in the Gym that would sometimes teach if Billy wasn't there. According to Ernie Riley Joe Robinson would teach when his dad wasn't there. Billy and Joe were great friends, Joe and Billy used to go to Ernie's house for a sauna after classes and have a cup of tea in the sauna whilst remising on wrestling, but they had a rivalry two. Billy Robinson recounted this rivalry in his book Physical chess, it was good-natured however. Roy tells of one particular old timer "There was another fellow that came, a friend of Billy's that just stood there, and he was coming a couple of years and it was only when Billy didn't turn up that I realized Charlie Carroll was a good coach and he started coaching me and telling me what to do and I couldn't believe how knowledgeable he was. He was just a nice fellow, in Ashton somewhere. But I didn't realize he knew anything about wrestling. I just thought he knew Billy".[29]

Billy used to say to Roy Wood "Roy you can do hours in the gym you want to go in have warm up good wrestle and be back on the bus how in half an hour"[30]

Sometimes Billy would be asked questions on his experiences of wrestling, one common question he was asked was "What's your favourite hold Billy?", the reply was always the same "The one I have on", another was "If I find myself in this position on the mat Billy ,how do I get out" again his reply would always be the same "Don't let yourself get in the position in the first place". Roy Wood has a similar philosophy, when talking about wrestling moves he passed on the following "There are many moves which aren't particularly good. However, you

Rileys wrestlers including Brian Burke with the cup from the interclub match they won against Bolton

can still be beaten by a bad move done well .All good wrestlers should have a full knowledge of all the moves and pay them the respect they deserve. The wrestler wouldn't necessarily use the poor moves but would know it firstly so he wasn't beaten by it but also they did have the choice of using it if necessary"[31]

Timing was another important factor. Roy said that when he was going to the gym 3-4 times per week, you would encounter wrestlers who were better than you , but if that wrestler took a couple of weeks of then when they returned it was possible to beat him as their timing would have slipped[32].

Although harsh at times, the gym produced results, its wrestlers read like a who's who of British wrestling 'Royalty'. They were respected and feared throughout the pro ranks for their ability and attitude. Eddie Rose stated 'they graduated from Riley's gym as fit, strong, technically accomplished and with a never say die approach to life, let alone fighting'[33]. Adrian street in his series of biography books talks about George Kid who went to Riley's gym 'Kidd spent a year and a half with morel before taking a trip to Billy Riley's Snakepit in Wigan where he claimed he learned more in a few weeks than he learned so far in his life'[34]

It wasn't uncommon for Police officers to train at the Gym including Ted Knipe, Jock Scott and Alan Cotton[35]

It was not only the British wrestlers that would seek out Riley's gym, in Billy's own words "It was like United nations. I've had French men here, Belgians,Italians,Finns,Spaniards,Indians,Pakistanis, Turks,Americand and Canadians. It must have been a shock for them at first. We've always had some tough ,classy local boys in here. And we usually start taking visitors down a peg or two. Names and reputations count for nothing here.. But when they left us they were usually better for it"

The gym was to become famous even abroad. Billy Robinson whilst on a tour in Bombay wrestled the local champion, the man outweighed him, and was tipped the scales at 25 stone. Robinson beat him in 50 seconds flat , when asked by the man where he learned to wrestle, Billy replied "Wigan". "Ah yes said the Indian "with Billy Riley"[36].

In his book with Alison Coleman the Dynamite kid recounts his visit to the gym "When I went to Riley's Gym in 1971, Billy Riley was still there with his son Ernie Riley, Billy Joyce, and Jack Dempsey; all grown men with years of experience but there were no young boys. It had never been a young boys gym. Anyway they said to me 'come on we'll teach you to shoot'. But they didn't make any allowances for the fact that I was just a young kid with no experience.

They kept taking me down to the mat, throwing me around and putting double wristlocks, front face locks and leg locks on me until I screamed. I thought they were going to break my legs. . . . I'll be honest with you, I was scared. By the time they'd finished with me, I could hardly stand up and I had burns all over my face and arms where they'd dragged me across the mat."[37]

The training produced a wrestler who was able to handle himself and was physically and mentally tough.

Despite being a hard training environment, a good sense of humour was kept by all and frequently practical jokes were played on each other. Jayne Riley remembers a joke played on John Foley "John came and he talked really slow what they'd done they'd got a plastic toy black cockroach and they put it on the soap in the gym and he went in to have his shower and he must have been naked in the shower and he went to grab this soap, 'hey Billy, there's a cockroach on the soap and it's a hard backed one.' But he used to do things like that do tricks and that, my dad would tell us about it when he came home."[38]

However Jayne Byrne said there were a number of rules observed at the gym, firstly No women" no women were allowed to go in the gym. He wouldn't have had girls no way. Oh no, that's not on. Just for men. I think there's just one comedian, used to be on coronation street , Jill Summers, her husband was a doctor and I forget who got to know her and they brought her and he allowed because she was off the telly he let her go in but she was the only woman that was allowed in the gym." Secondly Billy wouldn't stand for any bullying "Well he was like that, what I say about my dad. It didn't make any difference creed, colour he respected other people and he expected them to respect us, I mean him. He wouldn't stand for no bullying or anything like that, would he." [39]

Physical fitness

The gym apart from the wrestling mat, had exercise equipment too. But it was deemed very much up to the wrestlers to do their own physical fitness. The ethos of Billy Riley was very much that the best exercise for being a wrestler was in fact wrestling. His students echo this. Roy wood when asked about his feelings on what was required in terms of physical fitness for wrestling stated 'To wrestle you wrestle, best exercise for wrestling is wrestling. You don't need running, wrestling gets you fit enough, it gets you flexible enough. I don't think two much weight training is good. Too much running isn't any good for wrestling, I'm not saying don't go for any runs because its good for your stamina. I think the best exercise for wrestling is actual wrestling, by the time we come out of wrestling, we weren't fit for anything but bed.' However Billy did give him some direction in his physical training 'What Billy used to have me doing, as you went in through the main door, when there were 4 or 5 of us, and we knew no one else was coming we used to take a weight lifting bar and shove it through some metal hooks which were above the door, and I would do sit ups, maybe 20 or 30 then when I couldn't do any more I would hook my legs over and do sit ups hanging upside down until I couldn't do any more then I would do pull ups again and that were it more or less , we had skipping ropes and a few basic things, nothing special'[40]

Bob Robinson, in an article for the Mat Review said "If you want to be a wrestler you've got to wrestle and when you've wrestled wrestle again and when you are tired you wrestle some more and when you are so thoroughly tired that you feel you cant stand any more you take a hiding because you cant stand your ground. If you're going to be a wrestler you have got to wrestle. Billy says the muscle you build must be wresting muscle , 100% through, the lung power you develop is for wrestling not cross country running or fell racing. For my kind of wrestling I don't want any other agility other than what wrestling brings if you have time off for

Tommy Moore (Jack Dempsey) being watched over by Billy Riley

recreation then by all means for fun run jump heave weights ride a bike or do what you like but don't train for these sports."[41]

Billy Riley used to say 'if you want to be a weightlifter, lift weights. If you want to be a runner, go run. But if you want to wrestle, you've got to get on the mat and wrestle and spar. That will give you conditioning faster than any of the other things' [42]

Billy's grandson Patrick remembers what his grandfather had to say about weight training "He knew, it gave you like a false strength you know. It's more like endurance because like in them days it was a bit like the boxing matches as he grew up in them days, the boxing matches were like y'know a hundred rounds and if you went in carrying a load of muscle you wouldn't have last. The wrestling was a bit the same, it was constantly, like you know, strength against strength and it was always like resistance or a pull or a push so you just had to have that strength all the time whereas if you've very big muscles they're great for a little while but then you're carrying it and you'll tire yourself out. He was saying you don't do that like, he was like into going for a run and there would be a certain amount of, you'd have to lift weights but not terrifically huge weights, it was constantly yeah, you do lots of reps of them so small weight but loads of them and he was like that. A lot before more people came out with this training where people knew a lot and I suppose he could learn a lot even now of what they do but like in his day he was like way ahead of a lot of people. By saying right you don't do it like that way, you do lots of reps."

Billy would always take a walk everyday. Throughout his adult life he had always had a dog as a companion. Alan Latham once asked him "Why do you bother having a dog Billy?". He replied that whilst he had a dog, he never had an excuse not to go for a walk, rain or shine the dog would need a walk, and there so would he[43].

With regards to diet his daughter Jayne and grandson Patrick had the following to say

Jayne: He was the same weight all his life, he never varied, y'know, and it wasn't because he dieted or anything like that. He just used to have simple, good whole food but he didn't over eat, he was very plain in his life. He led a very healthy life, really, he used to walk a lot. That was how I think he became a, it was natural to him, y'know it was just natural to him. I mean even as an old man the gym wasn't it regular.

Michael: Oh yeah, every, I don't know what it was whether it was 4 o'clock or something. The older men I suppose used to go after work and he used to go at that time, not so much later at night as he got older you know. But, as my mother was saying, like back then the way he ate, well I suppose it was long before anybody in the dietary thing knew, his thing was eat often but little. He'd like probably 5 times a day but it would never be like he had a huge meal. It was always like you'd have something for breakfast.

Jayne: He wasn't a big meat eater, he liked fish, he liked chicken.

M: Something at teatime, dinner and maybe a cup of tea before bed, but he was never like have a big meal here or there. It was always have a small

meal, so that maybe the body knew it needed that energy

Jayne: I mean he liked a breakfast didn't he?

M: Yeah, it was always like a constant, it was never like a huge, huge, meal it was always like have a little bit here, little bit there. Throughout his life, he was like that, so he never

Jayne: Never varied, so he was very regimental with things like that with health. Very good and with the training. Very much so with the training."[44]

Matt Moran and the fairground

The fairground or carnival wrestling/boxing booth has a central history in the world of catch wrestling, in America it was what ensured the preservation of the art of Catch as Catch can with wrestlers such as Billy Wicks and Dick cardinal plying their trade against all comers. In Wigan it was also used as a proving ground for the Riley's wrestlers not only to earn some extra money but as a middle ground where they could learn the 'craft of show wrestling'. It was Matt Moran's booth that the Wigan wrestlers would usually wrestle in front of a crowd for the first time. It was Matt Moran that can be seen in the Granada black and white documentary 'The Wrestlers'.

Matt Moran, born Matthew Watson on the 10th of October 1913, fifth in a family of 5 boys and four girls. He left school at the young age of 14, not uncommon at that time, to follow his father's footsteps in becoming a miner at the Houghton Main colliery. His elder brother Robert however began to travel with Len Johnsons Boxing booth and he asking his brother Matt to join him. Len Johnson a black fighter was a victim of prejudice at the time and was widely regarded as the 'uncrowned' champion.

Len Johnson told Matt that he was too young and to come back when he was 16. Undaunted by the knock back Matt approached Charlie Hardcastle a Barnsely ex fighter and ex featherweight champion of England. . His first fight was behind one of the local pubs the Montagu Arms. He accepted his wages in pigeons in lieu of wages, which later flew back home.

In 1929 he started travelling with Len Johnson. Although he did box with other booths such as those run by Billy Woods, Spider Stewart and Professor Boscoe.

He knew he was never going to be a champion, and instead using the proceeds from a Show he ran in Chorley Town Hall, he bought his own booth. His first stand being at the Woodhouse feast in Leeds.

He later travelled as part of the Silcox family fair and it was here that the Riley's wrestlers would be employed. The fair would be at St Helens, Wigan and would be there between a few weeks and sometimes a few months.

The Silcox family had its routes in the fairground back to the beginning part of the 20th century. Edward Silcox started by running games stalls outside the Wigan mines as the miners returned home after work. Later Edward and his brothers Laurence Herbert and Arthur would begin touring the country just before the First World War, building up their catalogue of rides over the years[45].

Alan Latham in an interview recounted his memories of wrestling in the booth "You see, we started off wrestling to get experience from our amateur, from our days of straight wrestling eh, Lancashire Catch Can Style to show wrestling with entertainment, eh I started a bit, his dad said to us, you want to get used to wrestling in front of a crowd its very different wrestling in the gym, you need to be used to wrestling in front of a crowd so they don't effect ye so he sent us to a fella called Matt Moran, who I've heard around Boothe called the Shamrock Gardens And so we used to go on t'fairs and St Helens, Wigan all round Layle and in this area wrestling to get used to working in front of the crowd, and Matt Moran, because they're like travelling people their drinking, their eating pies in every town in Lancashire different week and drinking water in every town in Lancashire and it makes them like people and he used to say to us, What it's all about, he said, this business, he said everything in this wide world is bent apart from wall paper hanging he said, and that's a put up job."

But it was not only wrestling that the boys took part in, Roy Wood recounts his time boxing for Matt "When I had been going a few years and considered turning professional I started turning up at the fairground because they used to have wrestling at the fairground, I used to get the newspaper the world fair to see where the fair would be and turn up, a fellow called Matt Moran, and me and Tommy Heyes turned up at Bolton, and asked him could we wrestle. And he said he had enough wrestlers, it was boxers he wanted. I'd done a bit of boxing; my brother was a boxer.so I boxed for him. And I won and I think he gave me £1.50.

I was only 17 when I started. I stood on this platform and he shouted, 'who will fight my boy'. People were putting their hands up, half of them drunk, half of them you didn't know if they were world champion or what. I only boxed. He was a character. He had a guy wrestling for him, a big guy, and someone in the audience put their hand up and he said ' weight sinks battleships and he'll sink you' . He had the spiel, and he was on TV once and they asked him whether wrestling was a put up job, he said 'it's the same as anything else wallpapers a put up job , but its straight '"

Seamus Dunleavy in his book 'Finally meeting Princess Maud' said Billy Riley put in him in the booth with Matt. At the time there were three wrestlers and three boxers. The offer was for £5 to anyone who could last three rounds. Initially he found it difficult to adjust to the ring, which was smaller than the mat at Riley's gym. His first night he didn't get a match but second night he had two. There were no limits and if the crowd felt they had good value Matt used to encourage the crowd to throw money into the ring , this was called 'Nobbins'. Ernie Riley in an interview remembered Matt always tried to get a bit of extra money for the boys wrestling for him "I used to say back I remember when I wrestled and he's wrestled going round the fairground and they'd give you a couple of quid for wrestling and he used to have a collection, he'd say, go round with a cap, now go round we'll have a collection for these lads, he'd say don't you go yellow or you'll have a bit of jaundice."

Seamus said he was a 'Real Lancashire man' and had all the spiel. "One night a girl climbed in over the top rope was looking up her skirt and said 'I'll give you 24 hrs to climb down'"

After selling his boxing booth Matt and his wife Nellie Settled in the Southport area. They lived in the Birkdale area. Seemingly the 'fairground blood' still ran in his veins as he bought a stall on Pleasure Island and ran it during the 70s and 80s. [46]

Matt died aged 97 years old in a nursing home in Bolton on 31st May 2010[47]

---

[1] Ernie Riley interview A.Coleman
[2] Britain by Mass Observation – Harrisson,Madge,Jennings – Ebury Press 1986
[3] Catch the hold not taken – Riverhorse productions - 2005
[4] Jayne Byrne interview November 2013
[5] Mat Wrestling review issue 366 feb 1965
[6] Seamus Dunleavy interview July 2014
[7] Jayne Byrne interview November 2013
[8] Jayne Byrne interview November 2013
[9] Michael Moore interview 10/7/14
[10] Jayne Byrne interview November 2013
[11] Jayne Byrne interview November 2013
[12] Roy Wood interview November 2013
[13] Finally meeting princess maud – Shirley Thompson – Brewin Books – page 95
[14] Seamus Dunleavy interview July 2014
[15] Finally meeting princess maud – Shirley Thompson – Brewin Books –
[16] Catch the hold not taken
[17] WAR DVD series – Scientific Wrestling
[18] Physical chess ECW Press 2012
[19] Send in the Clowns – Kindle Edition – Eddie Rose – YonYonson – 2012
[20] Pure Dyanmite – Tom Billington,Alison Coleman – Winding Stair Press - 2001
[21] Roy Wood interview
[22] SWS article – translation Eric Shahan
[23] Roy Wood interview September 2014
[24] Roy Wood interview September 2014
[25] Finally meeting princess maud – Shirley Thompson – Brewin Books page 92
[26] Physical chess – B.Robinson ,J Shannon ECW Press 2012page
[27] Roy Wood interview September 2014
[28] Seamus Dunleavy interview July 2014
[29] Roy Wood interview

[30] Roy Wood interview
[31] Interview Roy Wood September 2014
[32] Roy Wood interview September 2014
[33] Send in the Clowns – Kindle Edition – Eddie Rose – YonYonson – 2012
[34] Adrian street –sadist in sequins 47.
[35] http://www.wiganworld.co.uk/album/photo.php?opt=7&id=23266&gallery=Wrestler&offset=0
[36] Town that put wrestling on the map – Graeme Kay
[37] Pure Dyanmite – Tom Billington, Alison Coleman – Winding Stair Press - 2001
[38] Jayne Byrne interview November 2013
[39] Jayne Byrne interview November 2013
[40] Interview roy wood
[41] Mat Review – no.
[42] Physical chess – B.Robinson ,J Shannon ECW Press 2012 page 84
[43] Jane Byrne interview September 2014
[44] Jayne Byrne interview November 2013
[45] http://www.silcocksfunfairs.com/behind.htm
[46] http://www.qlocal.co.uk/southport/news_list/R_I_P__Matt_Moran_(Boxing_Booth_Fighter)-50429677.htm
[47] http://www.qlocal.co.uk/southport/news_list/R_I_P__Matt_Moran_(Boxing_Booth_Fighter)-50429677.htm

Chapter 7

Billy – The promoter

Billy Riley had many roles, wrestler, coach, referee and also promoter. He once told Tommy Moore "You cant live off cups and medals, turn pro and make some real money"[1] a similar sentiment he shared with Billy Robinson[2] and the other wrestlers in the gym.

He formed Riley and Atherton Promotions with his old sparring partner Jack Atherton, a fellow wrestler from the 'Catch as catch can' and 'All in' eras. In many of the old all in era bills you would find Atherton and Riley pitched against each other in venues throughout the country[3]. A bill from the 'All in' era billed him as follows "Jack Atherton - - London . one of the most feared men in the game. Can be clean, but if the other man asks for trouble Jack will sure be there [4]".

Jack had won the William Bankier £50 challenge and gold medal at the Liverpool stadium in 1934, in the same year he wrestled Billy Riley at the Holborn stadium, which at that point was a Masonic Hall, in front of the Prince of Wales (later HRH Duke of Windsor)[5]. He also helped Billy Riley train Danno O'Mahoney before he set off for the USA[6].

Jack was universally loved by the wrestlers, he was straight helpful and friendly and as a promoter tended to pay better wages than most[7]. When Jack died his funeral took place at Manchester Southern cemetery and was well attended by the wrestling fraternity.[8]

His humour sometimes came across in interviews he gave to the press, in the Ringsider magazine was the following conversation between Jack Atherton and a reporter

Jack Atherton

Got your khaki yet?' said the friendly voice of Jack Atherton to me last weekend. "Why?" I asked. Well replied \\\jack "When war breaks out all the wrestlers will have to join up", "But I am not a wrestler" I replied. "Ah but watch me make some money when they have all gone to war", "how?" I asked. This is what he replied. "When all the wrestlers have gone to the front there will have to be a lot of substitutes and I shall be the only wrestler *left. Then I'll be a big attraction and wherever I go they will bill he match as Jack Atherton vs.Jack Atherton. Then I shall have to substitute for Jack Atherton and have to go on for Jack Atherton and Jack..."*

I stopped him by saying "Well if they changed your name you would go broke so stick to Jack Atherton the one and only and we will do our best to publicise it"[9]

It seems that Jack had been involved in promotion and management quite early on, even during the heyday of his own career as shown in the following newspaper article in 1933

Mr. Jack Atherton of 4 regent street Hindley near Wigan writes on behalf of Dan Kelly at present London that Kelly has not forgotten that he and Peter Bannon of Burnley have £5 each down and adds that he is quite willing to wrestle Bannon if he will make it to £20 ."Kelly will wrestle him at Burnley or at any place the stakeholder may appoint" he adds[10]

Jack was protective of his wrestlers and also knew how to handle himself, he was not averse to seeing the other wrestlers were ok ,Adrian street in his book Sadist in sequins tells of how one night Jack saved him "another night Jack Atherton leapt out of the crowd that I was trying to beat a pathway though and hyped a hooligan about 7 feet in the air a split second before he was about to smash a heavy wooden chair down on the back of my head"[11]

In latter years he lived in Manchester close to professional wrestler Eddie Rose who became friendly with him and would visit his house after being introduced by a mutual friend Grant Foderingham (the Black panther). He introduced Eddy Rose to the world of catch as catch can as practiced at the Wigan gym. Initially this was on the linoleum of his front office where he cleared away the furniture to make room. Initially showing him how to grip the opponent, breaking the balance, and the grobbit. He would help Eddie after each bout by going though the bout and pointing out anything he felt was a fault and praising the good points. Later he invited Eddie to attend Wryton stadium in Bolton on Sunday mornings. People such as Mark Wayne ,Ian Wilson, Johnny South Bobby Ryan, Hippy Anderson, Casanova, Paul Mitchell, Paul Duval, Mad-dog Wilson and Pete Lindeburg would attend. The first half of the training sessions consisted of Wigan wrestlers such as Alan Wood and Jack Fallon who would teach catch as catch can. Although painful Eddie felt this gave him a better understanding of wrestling and something that could protect them in the ring. The second half of the session were show

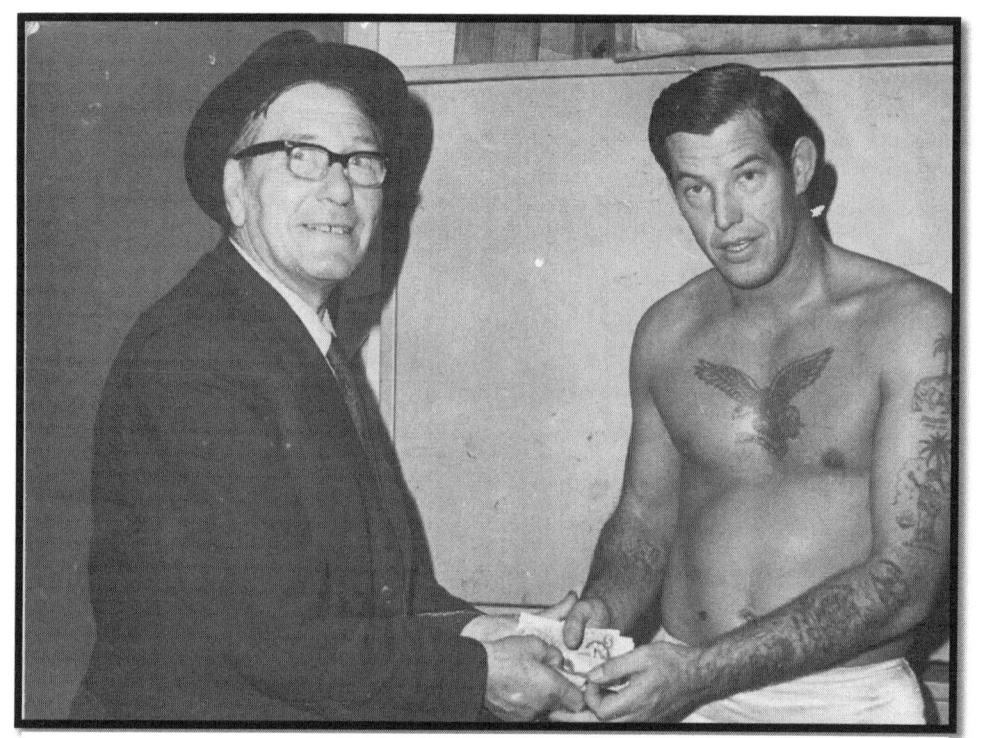

Jack Atherton and Johnny Eagles

moves for professional wrestling until Jack and Ken Cadman's direction[12]

At one point the wrestler Lord Bertie Topham was being considered by Joint promotions. It was Jacks job to get into shape however he only attended one session at Wryton and refused Jacks advice of weights. Jacks comment was "Topham always looks as if he's in an armchair when he wrestles"[13]

Jack Atherton was certainly a character. Always looking for a way to improve the shows. In the 1960s a wrestler from the US named Billy Rivers came over and was known for doing a wardance, and his signature tomahawk chop. In order to get in on the action Jack Atherton decided to make his own red Indian. In an interview Alan Latham, Ernie Riley and Roy wood they remembered the episode.

Alan: so that his dad's partner (Jack Atherton), they were only small promoters, they made a bloody Indian of their own, they went and got an Indian dress cause Two Rivers was booked every night, he went and made an Indian headdress in Manchester and got a fella called Harry Bennett, who worked in pits, up t'Barnsley, and he just looked like an Indian when he was dressed but when he stood topless he looked like a bloody bottle of milk. They put him on, they put him on, on the Isle of Man with a fellow called Milton Reeves, who he wrestled as Jungle boy in a terrific type of long hair and wrestled in his bare feet and we took this Harry Bennett to the Isle of Man, what did we call him, Son of Warclan or something like that

Ernie: Red Eagle

Alan: Red Eagle, they got him in Isle of Man and walked in him along the front from one end of Douglas Bay to the other, stopping and signing autographs and he had these feathers wrapped right around to his knees, he just looked like a bloody Indian then he stripped off in the dressing rooms and Jack Atherton said he looked like a bottle of milk, he said I can't bloody be an Indian he said, so he says to Jungle Boy, just try them feathers on, he put the bloody feathers on well he looked a million dollars the fellow said Right he said, You be Red Eagle and you Jungle Boy and nobody said a bloody dickie bird, and he'd been signing bloody autographs all day but that shows how bloody good the public are, you know

Also known for being careful with his money, there were a number of humorous stories about Jack and money

Alan: Well when he's, Jack Atherton this fella who made his own Indian, when he was promoting he said to us he said when you work for me, he said you can do anything he said, you can even cross buttock the promoter but don't batter the bloody ref

Roy Wood: He told me that!

Ernie: He said that we don't care if you call us names but don't ask us for a rise. We get very insulted he said when you ask us for money.

Alan: I bought a van it was a Trojan van, it had a 3 cylinder, diesel oil engine, it had windows then, but you had to put down the seats. They had to be sat on them and they used to call it Sullivan's flying birdcage, and I said why you call it Sullivan's flying birdcage because we're sat on bloody perches. Jack

Atherton booked me for a show, he were trying to get in at Cheltenham and Cheltenham at back then Is a very snooty place they didn't want wrestling to turn out Cheltenham, Jack was thinking about how we could get in and prove like that we weren't all like a load of morons so he took the football ground at Cheltenham and he said how many can get in that van, I said I've got 8 wrestlers and a referee in , right he said that's great get a tow bar on it he said and take it over, he said I've got a friend at just outside of Rochdale he said he makes chassis for Willoughby Caravans he said He'll lend ya an empty chassis he said, Bill R Reeds has a sectional ring which'll go on it, so we get this ring on this chassis, 8 wresters and a referee in the next seat and we all go down to Cheltenham, beautiful afternoon in Summer and we build a ring up in front of stand and we all go on

Alan: Yeah and we all go on and wrestle and when we finished we had John take the ring down, and put it back on t'trailer and coming back home and Jack has a bloody big towel on the floor with all the takings and he's counting it all, and him and Billy Howes were carrying all the ring sections and loading it up and Billy Howes stood up and trod on the towel and Jack Atherton quick as a flash said "Keep out of this bloody office with that ring "

Always known for his sense of humour and quick wit Alan Latham recalls an incident with one of the wrestlers who was also a strongman

Alan: Jimmy Inn whose a South African fella and he used to go out as a strong man and he was a strong fella he used to break horse shoes and you'd think how'd he do that, well how he'd do it was an easy way to do everything he used to get the horseshoe in the middle case hardened which means very hard so if you are strong enough to move it a fraction of an inch it'll break

Roy Wood: like cast iron

Alan: And so he used to get in the middle of the shoe he'd get 'em hardened and so he was strong enough to go like that and they'd break and he took it to Dumphries and he did his act in Dumphries and a fella, Yells out lets have a look at that horseshoe so he broke this bloody horseshoe and he went 'lets have a look at that bloody horseshoe and threw it at the little fella's forehead and knocked him out.

Roy: Jack Atherton went over and was saying he's split his head open he can have free seat next week

As for the money side of things many stories were told about the promotion especially Jack Atherton

Ernie: He said that we don't care if you call us names but don't ask us for a rise
Alan: I'll tell you something
Roy Wood: He's a character though ain't he Jack.
Ernie: We get very insulted he said when you ask us for money.

As a promoter, Billy Riley gained the friendship and respect of many wrestlers across the world, one in particular was Ricky Starr.

Alan: (Ricky was)only 13 stone, well in America at that time the only place he could wrestle was in Texas, the only state, they're the only state that employed fellas who looked like athletes at 13 and a half stone there. All rest of the country you had to start at 17 and a half stone to about 25 stone to get work Lou Thesz and all their top men were all from 17 stone and upwards, Zebra Kid, George, he was about 23 stone, Sky High Lee but Ricky Starr one day he was training in the gym and there was an old American boxer who'd always had a gimmick he was the best light heavy weight boxer ever of his era and he couldn't get work cause he was just a very good boxer he wasn't a showman a fella Archie Moore and Ricky Starr got talking to him and he said how's things and he said I can't break in anyway because of me size I can only get work in Texas, he said what you wanna do is get yourself a gimmick he said, they'll have to use you then so get a gimmick that can draw, If I go in ring with a big wide belt on with a Billy Buckle there'll be six of them next week, If I go in he said there, with me hooks and a parrot on me shoulder I'll be Long John Silver, but there'll be six of them next week by now he said have 12 months off he said and go and take half a dozen rudimentary ballet steps, like a pas de deux, a back somersault,

Ricky Starr

cartwheel so he did. He could stand up corner post and he could like drop kick ye from the top, back somersault off top rope, so then he was sorted when he went into wrestling with his gimmick. American promoters saw him, suddenly he was big enough to wrestle all these 17 and 18, 20 stone fellas even though he were still only 13 and a half stone and he had the record that fella, he packed the Yankee stadium, Madison Square Gardens in New York, 13 weeks running. Packed it out every week for 13 weeks and they all come to see him do this and he came over here and he was a big draw over here.

Ernie: He got, you remember the Mr. Ed show, he did a nice spell on that, he did quite a few weeks on that

Alan: I remember wrestling about the place, a fella come to me, in London, and he said he's a marvelous Ballet dancer ain't he, I said he knows about 6, I said he's hellava nice fella, I said but if you're interested in Ballet dancing, I'd go to bloody Covent gardens, but you've gone to watch the bloody wrestling, you know.

Ernie: But he was a good athlete

Alan: He was a good athlete, he was a good college wrestler

Ernie: He was very fond of me father, and he bought a caravan over here for his European tour, then they were only around for about 30

Alan: 40 shows

Ernie: 40 in a given time

Alan: In a year

Ernie: What it is he came, he split it up as we were doing going to Europe and going to the European Continent like France and Germany and they bought a Mercedes Benz, a brand new Mercedes Benz, Cause obviously a lot cheaper here than in the United States and at the time I'd got married and was living away, my dad had a garage and he said, he was friendly with my father, do you have anywhere Billy where I can garage this Mercedes Benz and pay rent for it and garage it and me Dad said you can garage it at my house he said, my son he's got married he said his car's gone with it and I've an empty garage and you could put it there, he said how much would you like, And he said you can have it there for nothing so he put this brand new Mercedes into my father's garage and it was there for 6 months and my father used to say come and have a look at my new car and when he was ready for going home he took it to Liverpool and shipped it home cause it saved them a lot of money and one of his things was, one of his favourite things as Ricky Star had, which he got from Wigan was Uncle Joe's Mintballs, he used to be mad on 'em which he used to take back to America with him. He'd take a bag ten pound of 'em and he'd take a whole bag with him.

Although considered one of the smaller promotions they held shows at a number of venues included Brierley hill, Derby, Worcester, Kidderminster, Nelson, Malvern, Sutton in Ashfield, Burton on Trent, Alfreton, Kirky in Ashifield, Isle of Man and Dumfries. Roy Wood remembers accompanying Billy to the Isle of Man on the

91

Hovercraft in order to attend some of the promotions, he remembers these journeys fondly, spending time with his mentor talking about wrestling.

In 1949 along with Tom Storr of Colne , Billy Riley organized what was said to be "the first catch as catch can wrestling tournament to be held in the town for many years". The venue was the Municipal Hall, Colne, Burnley.Over 100 people attended a number of matches headlined by Jack Atherton and Billy Joyce. The match ended in a draw. Other matches of the evening included Harry Chellor and Jim Lewis (Chellor won 2:1), Accra (India) vs. James Fay (Accra won 2:1) and Douglas the Turk who knocked out Lew Roseby.[14].

Ernie Riley in an interview best summed up the wresting at the time his father and Jack were running their promotion "they ran it purely, strictly, it were a set of rules where you weren't allowed to do certain things and like there was certain rules about it where you had to, if you, like if you were, if you wrestled for Dale Martin or you wrestled for my father or Jack Atherton, or you wrestled for Normal Morell you, you adhered to a certain set of rules. If you did anything out of the ordinary like, deliberate fouling or clowning, they suspended yer."[15].

---

[1] First Tuesday documentary
[2] Physical chess – B.Robinson ,J Shannon ECW Press 2012– Page 23
[3] Ernie Riley interview – A.Coleman
[4] Britain by Mass Observation – Harrisson,Madge,Jennings – Ebury Press 1986 p 121 exert from programme
[5] The Wrestler September 1962 page 34
[6] The Wrestler September 1962 page 34
[7] Eddie Rose letter
[8] Eddie rose letter
[9] Ringsider vol1 no 11 page 2
[10] Express and advertiser 23/9/33
[11] Sadist in sequins Adrian street Page 131
[12] Eddie Rose letter
[13] Eddie Rose letter
[14] Burnley express and news October 29 1949
[15] Ernie Riley interview A.Coleman

Chapter 8

To Ireland, in style

Billy Riley met Jack McGrath whilst he was in the United states. McGrath was from Worcester Massachusetts, where Riley and Jimmy Cox had visited in 1922/23[1]. McGrath, a former wrestler who in 1916 had wrestled a draw with Strangler Lewis at the Opera house in New York[2] worked for Paul Bowser of Boston. Boswer, a former middleweight wrestling champion was part of the 'Eastern wheel' trust which consisted of Jack Curley of New York, Tom Packs of St Louis, Ray Fabiani of Philadelphia, Joe Toots Mondt and Ed White of Chicago who was the manager of Londos[3].

The 'Eastern wheel' moguls had came to the realisation that wrestling was in a downturn and their gate receipts were dropping. Fearing the end was in sight they were on the look out for a new wrestler that would re-vitalise their fortunes. Due to the high Irish immigrant population on the East coast it was felt that an Irish wrestler would be the answer[4]. In an article in the Irish press in October 1934 Jack McGrath gave an interview to a reporter. It notes that he was staying in Ireland for 2 weeks after being on a tour of Europe. He noted that he had a fair working knowledge of the big men prominent in Irish Athletics of any kind. "I want a man who can be trained into a first class wrestler .I can put him into a camp where he will learn enough in three months and if he has any adaptability he can learn more about the game than will last him a lifetime.". In the same article he noted that "Willie Reilly an Irishman living in Wigan was the best middleweight wrestler in the world" and that Reilly was 'always assured of drawing a crowd in America'[5]. Jack McGrath was sent to Dublin by Paul Bowser in order to try and persuade Patrick O'Callaghan to come back to the USA in order to wrestle. O'Callaghan, a medical Doctor, was a two time Olympic gold medalist of the 1928 Olympiad in the Hammer throw. He refused offers from Paul Bowser enterprises who offered him $125,000 for four years with the option of accepting 7½ % of gross receipts should they amount to more than $125,000[6]. O'Callaghan stated that he 'had enough money' and refused to return to the USA with McGrath[7]. He also refused offers from Pittsburg ,Notre Dame and Southern California Universities as an athletic coach stating he did not wish to leave Ireland[8]

The accounts of what happened next differ slightly. In the book Milo to Londos it states that O'Callaghan pointed him in the direction of Danno O'Mahoney , whilst in the book Fall Guys it states that after his refusal by O'Callaghan McGrath retired to the local pub. There he got talking to O'Mahoney's uncle after seeing him put the shot on the grass outside the pub. Ernie Riley gives a different version of events again. He states in an interview that it was after hearing about a wrestler in Ireland with 'exceptional talent' that they came over to find him, this seems to be corroborated by some press reports form the time of O'Mahoney's death that report that is was Tim McCarthy who had played a part in bringing Jack Doyle to the public notice that had wired McGrath[9]. One American newspaper even stated it was Billy Riley 'a Boston middleweight' who had contacted Paul Bowser about Danno[10]. Whatever the true account it would seem that McGrath felt he had found his draw for the Irish crowds. O'Mahoney was 6ft 2 inches and 15st and 5lbs[11]. He was said to be a good around athlete and was known for being a hammer thrower – possibly how he was known to O'Callaghan as a newspaper account had stated that his 'greatest achievement with the weights was to defeat Dr. Patrick O'Callaghan, Irelands other great athlete in the 56lbs weight throw'[12]. McGrath bought O'Mahoney out of the free army[13].

O'Mahoney was born in 1912 and was from Balleydhob County Cork and was a farm worker and labourer. , the third of 6 brothers [14] At the age of 17 he started with hammer throwing of the 56 lb. weight soon beating local records[15]. He entered the Free Irish Army in 1933 [16]. Whilst in the army at the annual athletic championships at Croke park he won three Amy titles: 16 lb. hammer, 56 lb. over bar and 56 lb. without follow making records in all three events[17]. At best it seems he had a rudimentary knowledge of wrestling[18] if any. Unlike O'Callaghan, the money offered by McGrath tempted O'Mahoney. It was said that McGrath offered him a guaranteed £30,000 in the first 12 months. One newspaper account gave the offer as being $100,000 for six bouts[19]. According to Ernie Riley, Billy Riley was brought across to Ireland by Jack McGrath all expenses paid in order to give his opinion of O'Mahoney. His opinion was that 'yeah ,he's got great potential this kid like y'know', however he noted he was rough around the edges and needed them 'knocking off'. O'Mahoney was taken to London and according to Ernie Riley his father then was involved in coaching him over the next 3 months.

The following is the account given by Danno O'Mahoney on his first meeting with Riley:-

Unbeknown to me McGrath took Billy Reilly into his confidence. Billy you know was the middleweight champion of Europe at the time.

A few days later McGrath showed up at the camp with Reilly. He had one of the officers introduce him to me. "You do pretty well with the weights," says he. " Yes, " says I "my father was a great athlete in his day and he taught me"

"They tell me you're a wrestler," he continues

"Yes" says I. " I do pretty well among the boys in the army"

"Have you ever wrestled catch as catch can?" he asked, "I don't know what you mean I said. In the army we wrestled Greco Roman style

" Would you be meaning Lancashire style?" I asked him. That what we call catch as catch can over in Ireland and England. "That's it," says he

"I don't know"

"Will you try"?

I didn't suspect any trick at the time. I was young and a bit proud of my athlete ability

"Sure " I said" I'll try anything once"

McGrath who had already planned the whole thing soon had me and Reilly in the ring. I didn't know Reilly at all at that time. I thought he might be some American or maybe English man. I made up my mind to show McGrath what I could do. The match itself was short. I found my great strength was scarcely a match for Reilly's skill. I was a bit disappointed that I could not throw him like a sack of meal as I thought I could. But McGrath seemed satisfies. He saw all he wanted to see apparently.[20]

In December 1934 Danno met Ed Strangler Lewis in a match at the Albert hall. Whether due to his poor skills or as Fall guys would have it that he was just off the boat and 'swayed like a bent reed' Lewis made short work of him unable to carry the match, although by the time he got to the states the story had changed somewhat –"His most notable mat fray was with Ed. Lewis a few weeks ago in London, he scoring the first fall. Lewis refused to continue the match, evidently having got enough"[21]

On December 8th 1934 Danno left the British Isles on the SS.Bremen. Landing Early January 1935 he was met on docking by Paul Bowser, who as they had missed the regular plane chartered a flight to take them from Newark airfield to East Boston (it may have been an Airship). Bowser took him straight to a match at the 'Garden' featuring Ed Don George, the current champion at the time, ad Len Macaluso. He posed for photos and gave interviews[22].

SS.Bremen

O'Mahoney's first match was on the fourth of January, within days of arriving. The venue was the Boston Garden and was against Ernie Dusek of Nebraska. The venue was filled with 14,000 fans. O'Mahoney employed his signature 'Irish Whip' gaining a fall in 10 minutes 17 seconds and the second in 16 minutes and 50 s[23]. Ruby Dusek, Ernie's brother, jumped the ropes into the ring and attacked Danno with his fists, Danno in the confusion of defending himself managed to punch Referee Sam Smith to the left eye cutting him. McGrath got into the ring to join the party and clinched Ruby wrestling him and taking him to the canvas pinning him. The other wrestler, referee seconds and police rushed into the ring with Danno still throwing out fists landing blows wherever he could. This spectacle had the effect of driving the fans wild, surely the point of the exercise. Danno had won his first match and the 'event' established him as a fan favourite.[24]

A number of matches followed all of which he won, usually fairly easily utilising the 'Irish Whip'.

In Early 1935 he travelled to the states and was fed the best workers until 27th July where Ed Don George 'fell before O'Mahoney' and he became "undisputed champion of the world"[25]. Newspapers of the time noted his run of victories in the first few months of being inn America. Gate receipts were up to 20,000 [26]. He met Ed Lewis again in April 1935 where the Boston globe billed it as the Irish whip vs., the headlock, youth against a veteran (Lewis was noted to have 5000 bouts)[27]. The Irish whip was a move invented for Mahoney and consisted of a flying mare type maneuver off the ropes. The trustbusters appeared on the horizon and although Ed strangler Lewis was being utilised as a 'policeman ' for the trust, inevitably he was 'shot upon'.

The German wrestler Richard Shikat met Danno O'Mahoney on April 1st 1935 at Madison Square Garden. Shikat outweighed O'Mahoney 223 to 217lbs The match was a one fall affair. George Bothner the celebrated wrestler was to referee. Shikat who was recognised by the press as being one of the best men in the business had caught Danno with a few elbows, and one must of angered him as he let loose with an 'unscripted' punch to Shikat's Jaw. In connected well and drew blood. A few less well connecting punches were thrown by Danno enough to get Shikat's rise and he responded with a kick to the stomach, which earned him a disqualification and Danno the match[28].

On the 2nd March 1936 Shikat and O'Mahoney met again. The venue was Madison square Garden. The contest lasted 18 minutes and 57 seconds[29]. Shikat dominated the match applying headlocks am locks and leg holds that had Danno making for the ropes to escape. But after Shikat took Mahoney down for the last time Shikat emerged on top of his opponent and applied the hammerlock, Shikat was heard to taunt Mahoney "Now give up playboy, does it hurt champion?", his shoulders millimeters from the mat and from a pin Danno gave a nod to Bothner the referee that he submitted. Mahoney was a pitiful sight on the floor of the ring moaning, the hammerlock apparently causing dislocation to the shoulder, which was put back in place by first aiders in the ring. The crowd hissed at Danno and cheered for Shikat[30]. After the match in the dressing room Danno said "I'll fight him again and beat him, maybe in a fortnights time" but was said to be looking drawn, ill and crestfallen. McGrath stated that he was 'tired from he tough time he had with Yvon Robert and that "Danno has no immediate plans"[31].

In a 'damage limitation' exercise O'Mahoney gave an interview:-

"Nobody has been able to put my shoulders to the canvas for three seconds since I came to the United States. My bout with Shikat was not a championship affair. It was advertised merely as an exhibition. Shikat applies a hammerlock, which I could have broken easily. Referee George Bothner however got excited stepping in quickly and declared Shikat the winner. The referee later claimed I had given Shikat the fall but such was not the case"[32]

But it was not only the crowds at the match that would turn on Danno, but also the press. One journalist wrote "everybody who was surprised when Dick Shikat beat Danno O'Mahoney please stand up…ahh we thought so …not a standee. The Irishman wasn't only due to lose he was overdue"[33]. The 'Trust' didn't help matters it claimed that it had been double crossed by Shikat, however as a journalist pointed out at the time "It might be a splendid idea for the so called trust to explain what they mean when they say Shikat double crossed O'Mahoney, if that is what the claim he did. It would seem that the only way there could be a double cross in such an instance is for one of the athletes to refuse to obey orders and win when he was told not to. After all this sports business is supposed to be on the level and if the trust indicates that someone failed to obey an order a rigid investigation expose should be ordered at once"[34].

McGrath also stated "Danno was in no danger whatsoever when Bothner patted him. I was in Danno's corner and heard him tell Bothner he would not give up. I was the most surprised man in the world when Bothner patted Shikat and stopped the match"[35]

If an effort to control the situation the trust got one of their own men Joe Alvarez, who claimed to hold a contract to manage Shikat, to sign contracts with various promoters across the country for Shikat's service with the view that when he failed to show he would be suspended by the state commissions. However in the New York Mirror Dan Marker said

O'Mahoney just after being submitted by Shikat

that Shikat would not wrestle in any state where the trust controls wrestling as he knew that when he stepped in the ring he might as well kiss his title good bye.[36] Shikat notified Alvarez that he himself would be the only person to sign matches. It seemed inevitable it would end in court, and it did. Alvarez obtained a restraining order on Shikat preventing him taking part in matches arranged on his behalf by Columbus promoter Al Haft. Both Shikat and Haft were named as defendants in the case that took place in Columbus Ohio. Shikat claimed that the contract held by Alvarez was obtained by duress an fraud, and that he would "blow the lid off the manipulations of the wrestling trust"[37]. And that he did. Shikat claimed that wrestlers had to pay money to the trusts prior to matches in cash, this was then held by the trust to ensure that the match was wrestled in accord with the instructions from the 'higher ups'. Shikat claimed the trust held $18,000 of his money, which he wanted back[38] this money was a guarantee he would 'lie down' to O'Mahoney within 45 minutes[39]. Later in the case John Connor Shikat's counsel alleged that Shikat was offered return of the money plus a further $25,000 dollar (quoted as £5000 in the newspaper, conversion rates at time were $5 to £1) if he had rematch and lost[40]. This was clearly airing the 'dirty laundry' of wrestling in public and maybe in order to cut their losses the attorney Fred Rector for Joe Alvarez submitted an entry to John Connor asking for dismissal without prejudice, Connor refused asking for dismissal of the case with prejudice in order to prevent Alvarez from filing a new suit in equity[41]. Dismissal with prejudice was accepted. Another reason sited at the time was that Shikat had lost his title to Ali baba in matches in Detroit and New York[42] some papers suggesting the whole affair of the losses was engineered by Shikat and more ultimately Billy Sandow(including the shoot on O'Mahoney) to get one over on the trust and discourage their continuation of the court case[43]. What ever the reason, the case was dropped

Whilst the New York State Athletic commission upheld Dick Shikat as champion[44], the Boston authorities, American Wrestling association and St Louis Commission recognised O'Mahoney as the champion after protestations from Bowser. This led to a situation where Shikat ,O'Mahoney and Yvon Robert were all claiming the title, Robert claiming it after O'Mahoney refused to re meet him after the bout the previous week where he claimed he pinned O'Mahoney at least 15 times although the match was awarded to O'Mahoney[45]. Add onto this claims that were still being made by Ed Lewis and Ed Don George and it all left a very confusing situation[46].

Danno returned to Ireland and wrestled there. Ernie Riley recounts a match where his father was referee.

The match occurred in Dalymount park in Dublin on the 9th of August. The official crowd count was 15,000 (other accounts state 20,000 [47]). Billy's wife remarked 'we are never going to get out of here'. Billy Riley and his family (Ernie, his sister and his mother) had their hotel paid for the week. The match was against the American wrestler Ruby Wright. Before the match a couple of hundred men from the cheap seats 'crashed' the ringside seats fighting their way through the crowd for a better view and refused to be moved [48]The supporting matches were Charlie Stack of America vs. Anaconda of London (although some accounts state it to be Jan Gotch of Poland[49]) and Carl Hansen of Sweden vs. King Curtis of London. The main event was Danno O'Mahoney against Rube Wright of Texas and it was a title match. Wright outweighed Mahoney by 2 stone [50].The match was refereed by Billy Riley(paper notes it as Mr. W Reilly of Wigan [51]). Newspaper reports noted that Riley had to prevent Mahoney throwing Wright out of the ring in the beginning round. Next Mahoney applied a number of leg and arm locks which Wright expertly countered. The second round began with a 'punching match' of which Mahoney is said to have come off the better, this was followed by a number of occasions of Mahoney having to 'wriggle out of a number of awkward positions' and then turning his defense into an offence against his opponent applying arm locks and throwing Wright heavily but Mahoney not being quick enough to pin his opponent. The third round saw Wright taking a large amount of punishment with punches to face n body and ended crawling out of the ring on a three occasions. Wright dropped Mahoney with a kick to the stomach but countered with a punch that landed on the back of Wrights neck ending up with him hanging over the ropes. The fourth round saw Wright on the offensive applying arm and leg locks and Mahoney narrowly escaped getting pinned. He came back with punishment to Wright in the form of a nasty leg lock that had Wright making for the ropes and then Mahoney employed his signature move of the Irish whip a number of times with the crowd showing their pleasure with cheers. One of the whips connected to land Wright on the canvas and he narrowly missed being pinned. It was described by one journalist as follows "He caught Wright by the wrist, lifted the 18 stone lump of flesh over his shoulder as if he was handling a parcel of feathers and deposited him neatly on the mat his shoulders fairly and squarely pinned"[52] .It was the sixth round that saw the Irish whip applied for the last time with Mahoney pinning Wright for the count of three. O'Mahoney was carried out of the ring on the shoulders of his admirers[53] taking a full 10 minutes to get to his dressing room losing his characteristic green dressing gown on route. And was met in the dressing room by his wife who was accompanied by her sister Kathleen Burke[54]. Wright was said to have lost 6 teeth during the bout and 'a pint of blood', both his eyes were closed and he almost had to be carried from the ring and both men were noted to be smeared with blood from the waist up [55]. The match lasted 36 ½ minutes [56]. Stack challenged Mahoney for a £500 a side match but was booed by the crowd for doing so[57]. McGrath had nothing to say about the challenge; Danno's comment was "I'll wrestle only if I have to"[58]

However the display wasn't universally celebrated in a newspaper article in the Irish press it labeled the match as a disgusting display of brutality. They noted that people had travelled long distances to witness the match and even 'Women had ringside seats and yelled loudly and lustily as the men while the blood drenched wrestlers went 'all out' to tear each other to ribbons'.[59]

There was a second match with Rube Wright that occurred in the September on the 9th in the[60] Galway sports ground. Supporting matches were Cary Hansen from Sweden against Billy Jordan, and John Ross of London vs. Steve Casey from Kerry. The crowd was 5000 strong to witness Mahoney beat Rube Wright again[61]

Danno was to return again in to Ireland in 1938 and wrestled a series of matches, most notably with Steve Casey. Jayne, Billy Daughter remembered attending these "I remember the time when we went to Ireland, I was 7 and my father was refereeing between Danno Mahoney and somebody else and it was a German name on the bill in Dalamount park and my father said he was a very good wrestler and I remember Steve Casey coming, Danno Mahoney must have been wrestling Steve Casey cause I was about 7 and I can remember Steve Casey coming round to our house to be trained by my father and this Irishman coming you know, cause I was about 7 and we went, he went away, I think my dad had him in London as well. I can't remember the guy that brought him over (Jack McGrath) brought Steve Casey, he found this amateur wrestler, my father knew him well, my father must have met him in America and he'd heard about this Steve Casey, and they'd heard that he was good so they said well we'll bring him to England and let Billy Riley have a try with him and within 2 minutes he had him down, he'd had him well beaten so they had him training with my dad for a while. I think it was Steve Casey and we went over to Ireland and my father had to referee, I think it was Danno O'Mahoney and Steve Casey, and it was a German name on the bill and my father reckoned that that one was, he probably wasn't German but maybe ancestors but he said he was a very good wrestler, I can't remember his name."[62]

In an tribute article to Danno , Steve Casey wrote of the match 'The year was 1938 .Danno and I had both been wrestling all over America. But this time it wasn't only Danno and I who were to be in the ring. It was to be the fighting generations of Casey's and O'Mahoney's back to the days of when they fought together against the Normans and Cromwellians. And so the Sunday came when from all the Munster crowds converged on Mallow , the hub of the south. Bets were flung down on the counters of pubs from Caherciveen to Clommel on the night before. Bill Riley of Wigan once a middleweight Olympic champion and now in his fifties was to see that Danno and I didn't kick each other or gouge each others eyes out". Steve Casey won the fight by pin[63]

One of his last bouts was again Frank Sexton , the then world champion , at Boston arena. With over 20,000 spectators the match was a draw[64].

During the war he served in the US army. He returned to Ireland on holiday six weeks prior to November 1950.He was in his car with brothers Jack and Dermot and Miss Mary Hamilton of Sligo. Danno was driving. He collided with a stationary lorry in Kilminchy Portlaoise, the lorry was owned by Messrs Mahon of Castle St Roscrea which was in the charge of a Laurence O'Brien[65]. He underwent surgery but became weaker[66]. On the 3rd of November 1950 at 9.15 [67]aged 38 he died in Portlaoise county hospital following internal injuries and two broken legs [68]. The other passengers although detained in hospital were said to be comfortable.[69] He was left wife Kathleen and 5 children[70]. (Other accounts say 4[71])

---

[1] Irish Press 30/10/34 Page 12
[2] Irish Press 30/10/34 page 12
[3] Milo to Londos and Catch wrestling round 2 page 2
[4] From Milo to Londos. – The story of wrestling through the ages – N.Fleisscher - 1936
[5] Irish Pres 30/10/34 page 12 (original spellings from article given)
[6] Irish independent 15/11/34 page 7
[7] Fall guy:The Barnums of bounce he inside story of the wrestling business, America's most profitable and best organized professional sport Unknown Binding – 1 Jan 1937 page 156
[8] Irish independent 15/11/34 page 7
[9] Irish Press 4/11/50 page1
[10] Indiana Gazette (Indianna Pennsylvania) 23/7/34
[11] Irishi independent 16/11/34 page 14
[12] Southern Star 5.1.35 age 5
[13] Irish indepednent 16/11/34 page 14
[14] Irish press 4/11/50 page 1
[15] Irish press 4/11/50 page 1
[16] Irish independent 4/11/50 page 7
[17] Irish press 4/11/50 page 1
[18] Irish Independent 16/11/34 page 14
[19] Southern Sar 5/1/35 page 5
[20] Page129 Danno Mahoney- John Pollard,Litho Press Co.
[21] Sounthern star 5/1/35 page 5
[22] Southern Star 5/1/35 page 5
[23] Southern Star 9/2/35 page 1
[24] Southern Star 5/1/35 Page 5
[25] Fall guy:The Barnums of bounce he inside story of the wrestling business, America's most profitable and best organized professional sport Unknown Binding – 1 Jan 1937page 159
[26] Boston globe March 30 1935
[27] Boston Globe April 22 1935 pg 7
[28] The Brooklyn Daily Eagle (Brooklyn New york) page 23 2/4/35
[29] Irish Press 3/3/36 page 1
[30] Irish press 4/3/36 page 8
[31] Irish independent 4/3/36 page 14
[32] Southern star 11/4/36 page 11
[33] Clovis News Journal ,New Mexico – Page 7
[34] Irish press 16/4/36 page 10
[35] Irish Press 18/4/36 page 11
[36] Irish press 16/4/36 page 10
[37] Coshocton Tribune – 23/4/35
[38] The Lincoln star,Nebraska page 6 26/4/36
[39] Southern Star 2/5/36 page 3
[40] Southern Star 2/5/36 page 3
[41] Evening Independent – Massillon Ohio – page 8 – 9/5/36
[42] Reading times, Readin Pensylvannia – 13/5/36 page 15
[43] Lincoln Star (Lincoln,Nebraska)13/5/36
[44] Irish Press 13/3/36 page 12
[45] Daily Boston Globe, March 4th 1936
[46] Irish Press 16/4/36
[47] Irish press 10/8/36 page 1
[48] Irish press 10/8/36 page 1
[49] Irish independent 10/8/36 page 14
[50] Irish Press 10/8/36 page 16
[51] Irish independent 10/8/36 page 14
[52] Irish Press 10/8/36 page 16
[53] Kerryman 15/08/36 page 11
[54] Irish independent 10/8/36 page 9
[55] Irish press 10/8/36 Page 1
[56] Irish independent 10/8/36 page 14
[57] Irish independent 10/8/36 page 14
[58] Irish Press 10/8/36 page 16
[59] Irish Press 10/8/36 page 1
[60] Irish press 4/11/50 page 1
[61] Southern Star 12/09/1936 page 14
[62] Jayne Riley interview nov 2013
[63] Danno Mahony Polland,Lewis,O'Connel,Hickey – page 290
[64] Danno Mahony Polland,Lewis,O'Connel,Hickey – page 278
[65] Nenagh Guardian 18/11/50 page 5
[66] Irish independent 4/11/50 page 7
[67] Irish independent 4/11/50 page 7
[68] Irish press 4/5/11/50 page 1
[69] Irish independent 4/11/50 page 7
[70] Irish press 4/5/11/50 page 1
[71] Irish independent 4/11/50 page 7

Chapter 9

Building a legend

" It is the Oxford-Cambridge, Eton-Harrow educational centre of the wrestling world"- Kent Walton

The gym in the allotments at the bottom of Pyke Street has been known by a number of names. Karl Gotch who had trained there christened it 'The Snakepit'. Roy Wood was surprised to hear from the Japanese when he visited Japan it was known by this name as like the wrestlers that trained there, and the local residents it was known as 'Riley's gym' by the wrestlers and locals. Its full name was in fact 'Wigan wrestling and physical culture club'. Pyke Street wasn't the first venue that Billy Riley used for training. When the Riley's had lived in Wellington Street off Scholes in the White bear pub, one of the back rooms of the pub , and a hut outside the pub were used to practice wrestling. Later the family moved to the Crispin arms when Ernie was about 6-7 years old. In the Crispin arms there was a function room upstairs and it was this that was used as a practice venue. Later they had a room above the garage of a haulage company. However, Billy was never satisfied, always being worried at being at the mercy of others, he lamented the fact that they could be kicked out at any time and could not do anything about it. "What we should do is build our own gym, we could do what we want train as long as we want and no one would bother us". Whilst in America in the 1920's Billy had been impressed with the athletics facilities available in the

The Crispin arms public house

States. He commented to the wrestlers that the Americans were 50 years ahead of the British in terms of facilities. He told them about a place in America he had trained at. "There is a building there it looks like Eggersly factory" he said "they got a floor which has an indoor running track, they're another floor which is like for physiotherapy and then they have a gymnasium, and you want to see it , it looks like central park there every kind of equipment you could imagine". Most likely Billy was either talking about the Worcester academy at which he taught , or the Knights of Columbus gyms in Worcester and Boston. Billy approached Tom Winners, a friend of his who had built his house and enquired about buying a plot of land. The site was bought for a 'trifling sum' as the land was thought to be of no commercial value, and was quite large in size. Billy would lease out some of the land for allotments, or "pens" to enthusiasts and market gardeners[1]. In 1947/8 the wrestlers all worked together to build the Gym. There was Harold Winstanley who was a Joiner, Ernie and Alan Latham

Roy Wood's membership book for Rileys

were electricians. Together they built the gym.

The Building was small, but it had a raised matted area that touched three walls, there was a water boiler in one corner which "Noah had before us" according to Roy Wood, the copper pipes ran along the wall to feed the Shower in one corner and also to provide heat. The pipes got very hot and Billy Robinson tells a story in his book Physical Chess how when sparring with Bob Robinson one day he made him move in such a way as his backside hit the pipes and he screamed and jumped much to everyone's amusement [2]. There was Gym equipment that was stolen by 'Big burns' [3], One piece of equipment from the Gym was a kettle bell, it currently resides in the new Snakepit gym in Aspull, and Roy tells of the fact that "It came out of there, funnily enough they call them kettle bells that's the only one I saw for 50 years and all of a sudden all these kettle bells came out , Tommy Moore used to use that thing, swing it around his head and what have you."

There was a pull up bar, and a rope attached to the ceiling the wrestlers used to use. And there was also seating or about fifteen to twenty people[4].

There were no toilet facilities at the gym however later they expanded the facilities by putting in a shower, Karl Gotch recollects in his interview with Jake Shannon how he helped to dig the ditch.

. The matted area in the gym was elevated ,and was made form canvas stuffed with hoarse hair. There were seams in the mat that used to cut the knees and elbows of the wrestlers. There were two sheets that covered the mats and once a week the sheets were taken up and taken to the local hospital that disinfected them [5]

The gym had a pair of buffalo horns on the wall Billy Robinson sent them over from America[6] they were there for a number of years until they rotted away.

Although the gym wasn't the best facility around, although it didn't have the newest or best equipment, it became the mecca of professional wrestling in the UK and was to become a world famous gym, and held a special place in the heart of the wrestlers who trained there.

---

[1] http://www.wiganworld.co.uk/album/photo.php?opt=7&id=23276&gallery=Wrestler&offset=0
[2] Physical chess – B.Robinson ,J Shannon ECW Press 201page 38
[3] `Ernie Riley interview A.Coleman
[4] Finally meeting princess maud – Shirley Thompson – Brewin Books Page 91
[5] My cigar with Karl Gotch – J.Shannon- youtube
[6] Michael Moore Interview 10/7/14

Chapter 10

A change of focus

In the early 1970's when Roy Wood was in his 20s and working and wrestling full time, and had ceased going to the gym, the old timers such as Alan Latham, Tommy Moore, Ernie Riley and Bob Robinson had their businesses to run, attendance at the gym fell off. In an interview Bob Robinson stated, "the Snake pit became a lonely place". Michael Moore used to walk to the Gym with his dad, Tommy Moore(Jack Dempsey). Tommy turned to his son and said "Billy is talking about shutting the gym, but I want to keep it going". Michael said "you know dad I will help you", but his dad reminded him "You cant get on the mat anymore, you gotta get down on the mat and show them". Michaels wrestling career had been cut short after an operation on his lower spine and on the advice of Doctors had given up wresting. But Michael helped his father in any way he could. In the early 1970s there was a heavy snowfall which cause the roof of the gym to came in Tommy Bentham jacked up the roof and with the help of Michael , Tommy and Brian Connelly a local rugby league player they propped the roof up with a plank. However eventually the roof of the gym caved in and the gym closed.[1] Then around 1974, Roy Wood and Ernie Gradwell had sons who wanted to start wrestling. Along with Tommy Heyes they built the Gym back up. The materials to rebuild the gym were

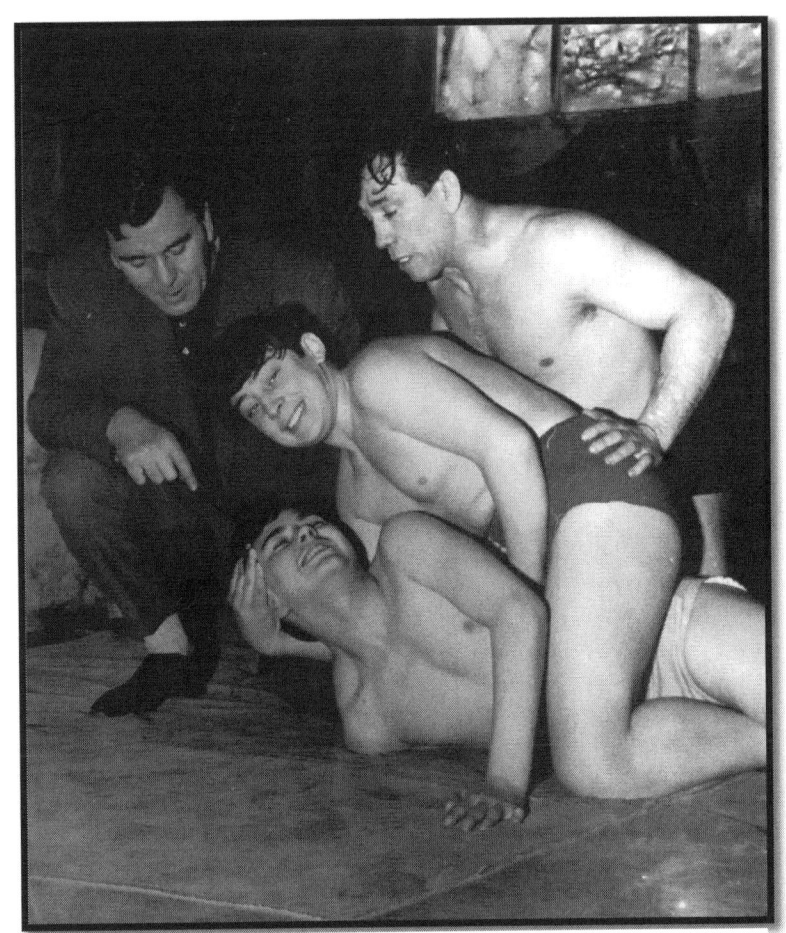

Alan Latham and Tommy Moore teaching their sons at the gym

obtained from a local farmer named Bill Swires who gave them the wood, bricks and hardcore were obtained by the men by using a wheelbarrow to more it from the site of a local pub that had been

103

demolished. Concrete came from a friend of Roy Wood who owned a concrete wagon and one Sunday morning after having the concrete dropped off they built a base and managed to double the size of the gym. With the help of Tommy Benthom who leant them some acrojacks. , the roof was acro jacked back up and the Gym was re-opened. Roy brought his son Darren, who was 7 years old at the time, to the new club, and Ernie brought his sons, and along with Tommy Heyes they began an amateur club, teaching children[2]

Billy Riley, who hadn't been near the gym since it fell down began coming around to the gym again and began watching. Billy Riley ran a strict club, and a dispute arose between Ernie Gradwell and Billy Riley because of the use of bad language, something that was unheard of and not tolerated in Riley's Gym , so Ernie Gradwell and his son were banned from the Gym. Ernie went on to open his own gym in Wigan.

Although Billy wasn't actively teaching at this time, he would come around for a chat and sit and watch , then later when everyone went home he would tell Roy where he had gone wrong and how he could improve and become a better coach.

In 1989 Roger Finnegan, a producer ,on the advice of Jack Atherton (Billy Riley's old Business partner and wrestling promoter) approached Roy wood and requested a meeting to discuss making a documentary on wrestling. The filming went ahead. Some of the old timers got involved with Ernie Riley, Tommy Moore and Bob Robinson appearing in the film.

The documentary came in two parts, the other part of the program containing a segment on

Tommy Heyes and Roy Wood with the second generation of wrestlers

Roy Wood standing at the site of the old gym

Debutants, a stark contrast between the two worlds of the haves and have not's.

The documentary raised the profile of the gym, however not all the attention was positive, Roy's Comments on Horse riding not being "a natural sport" in the film had him receiving phone calls from many people asking him what he had against horse riding and local papers were not happy with the way in which Wigan was portrayed. The Wigan observer commented, "Wrestling received a favorable airing. The same could not be said though of Wigan. If the programme makers had gone out of their way to find the least attractive parts of the town they could not have done a better job. Cobbled streets grimy canal banks rows of semi derelict terraced houses….in fact all the old hackneyed stereotypes of Wigan were wheeled out.". On a more serious note, the Sports council was concerned about the state of the Gym. Riley's Gym even in its heyday although a centre of excellence for training, was not well known for its luxury facilities, a number of wrestlers remarked on seeing it for the first time that they couldn't believe it was a tin shed. It was at a time where leisure centres were opening, people wanted and expected better facilities. So the sports council more or less had the building condemned, they did offer to fund demolition of the old gym and to rebuild new facilities on the site, although this appealed to Roy from the nostalgic point of view it transpired that the Riley family who owned the land had thoughts of developing houses on the land. The gym was once again in peril of coming to an end. Reports in the papers said that the gym burned down [3]

Aspull

Roy Wood, who hailed from Aspull, had helped some of his school friends raise money to establish a local Boys club in Aspull. He had arranged a couple of charity football matches. The first was against a police team, the second against some professional footballers. This included people from Wigan athletic, Bolton and Preston north end. The players all gave up their time free of charge.

Site of the old gym as it is now

Aspull gym / the Snakepit now

Later the boys club moved to new premises, and Roy bought the building from the club. However, things still weren't plain sailing and it took a further 12 months to negotiate with the local Church who owned the land. There were also negotiations with the Charity commission as the original boys club had been a charity bought building. Riley's Gym had a new home The sports council grant of £25,000 was put to good use in enlarging and improving the building and Aspull Olypmic wrestling club was born.

---

[1] Michael Moore Interview 10/7/14
[2] Interview Roy Wood
[3] Wigan Evening post Nov 5th 1990

Chapter 11

The Japanese and Wigan

The history of catch wrestling and the Japanese seem inexorably intertwined. One of the early encounters with catch wrestling and the Japanese was with Yukio Tani who visited Wigan in the early 1900s. However, much of the reason that catch wrestling survived is down to the Japanese love and respect for the Lancashire catch as catch can Wrestling. Following World War 2, it was an ex sumo Wrestler turned professional wrestler by the name of Rikidozan that helped lift the spirits of the Japanese people and became a symbol of hope of for the Japanese people decimated by the war.

People were striving to restore the country from the devastation of war. Rikidozan's fighting spirit inspired the whole nation. It was the dawn of the television in Japan. Thousands of people flocked around small televisions installed on high poles in streets of big cities. People were very exited by a Japanese sumo wrestler beating big American wrestlers one after another. Rikidozan became the hero that the nation had been longing to see even appearing on the cover of Japanese history textbooks next to presidents and olympic medalists, professional wrestling having a great influence on not only sport but also culture after the war.

One of his most famous matches was that against Judo Legend Masashiko Kimura, whose name is used in the BJJ community for the Double Wrist lock after Helio Gracie was beaten by Kimura with the lock,.

Inevitably the techniques shown in the ring were Japanese martial arts such as Sumo, Judo, Karate and also American style pro-wrestling. Karl Gotch first came to Japan in 1961; in 1968 he was hired to coach Japanese young pro-wrestlers including the wrestling legend Antonio Inoki who later fought the Boxing heavy weight champion, Muhammad Ali in Tokyo in 1976.

In 1968 Billy Robinson wrestled in Japan and showed wrestling moves that Japanese people had never seen. People were amazed and attracted by the catch wrestling moves shown. Billy Robinson soon became a star in Japan.

People were curious to know what kind of wrestling that had been shown. Soon the name of Billy Riley's Gym and Lancashire "catch-as-catch-can" wrestling became well known.

The bout with Ali and Inoki's way of thinking about pro-wrestling are believed to be the root of UWF, Shooto and MMA. Since Karl was a coach of Inoki, people started to call Gotch "Kamisama" or "God" of pro-wrestling".

While Karl became more famous as a coach than a wrestler, Billy Robinson kept fascinating Japanese fans with his fantastic skills which he learned from Billy Riley.

In the late 60's and early 70's he always appeared in the middle of pro-wrestling posters, magazines in Japan, and of course he always wrestled in the main event of the day.

Pro-wrestling magazines often wrote articles about Billy Robinson, Billy Riley's Gym and Lancashire "catch-as-catch-can" wrestling.

Roy teaching catch in Japan

But back then, flight tickets were very expensive and it was very difficult for Japanese journalists to fly all the way to Wigan to report Riley's gym. So no one was sure what the gym and catch were really like.

Bob Robinson (Billy Joyce) had wrestled in Japan during his career and obviously made an impression. He travelled to Japan in 1968 for the pro wrestling 'world elimination series' [1]The SWS promotion ((Super world of sports).was formed by Genricho Tenryu.Two Japanese gentleman,Mr Watamatzu and Mr Sakurada from SWS travelled to Wigan in 1990 . Wakamatsu went on a sightseeing tour from the 14th to the 25th June. Initially he travelled to Dallas to meet Sakuraba , then to Calgary to see Hito. He arrived in Manchester on the 22nd of June. He initially went to the Isle of Man to see Ted Bentley who had taught the Dynamite Kid, Steve Wright and Marty Jones. On the 23rd he travelled to Wigan and met with Billy Joyce seeking out the famous catch wrestler, widely regarded as one of the greatest wrestlers of his time by both his fellow wrestlers and commentators[2]. They were looking for Bob to travel back to Japan and coach. However, Bob Robinson's wife was unwell at the time and he had no want to leave her and travel to Japan. He recommended that they seek out Roy Wood. At the time Roy was on holiday with his family in the Lake District. Roy received a phone call from his son Darren asking him to come back to Wigan, as there were two visitors at the house to meet him. Roy drove back to Wigan. . The Japanese visitors requested to see the old Gym. Roy took them to see the gym, which was little more than rubble on the ground. Roy commented that he thought they were going to cry on seeing it and that one of them

Roy wrestling in Yokohama arena

even tried to lift the roof up. In the article 'Technician Wakamatsu visits UK' he states "leaving this place buried would be a waste. If they were to get on track with SWS then we would like to offer our support in rebuilding the Hebi no ana(the Snakepit)"

Bob recommended Roy go to Japan and they had him wrestle one of the Japanese . They obviously liked what they say of the 51 year old, and came back with a contract to sign to go back to Japan. Roy went to Japan and coached for SWS in Machida.

Roy travelled to Japan on October 5th at the invitation of SWS .In an article called SWS hot news, it recounts this first meeting. It states that Roy

Roy with the wrestlers at the MUGA event

was the 'Third generation head instructor at the Billy Riley gym or "Snakepit". In the article it says that Roy Wood has students in the UK, Germany and Belgium and that he has over 50 students between the ages of 5 and 23 in his gym. The purpose of the visit was at the request of Mr Wakamatsu to 'desire to have the essence of Lancashire wrestling transmitted to the young SWS wrestlers'. Roy commented 'I have heard about the high level of Japanese wrestlers from Billy Joyce and Bill Robinson'. Roy also stated that he has no favourite technique as he had tried to learn and master them all. He is shown putting a headlock on Akio Setsuhara. He was due to stay in Japan until the 21st.He finished his visit by wrestling in Yokohama arena. On returning to Wigan he gave an interview to the Wigan Evening post "I wrestled in front of 26000 people in an arena looking like central park with a roof on appeared on several TV programmes and in all the national newspapers. Had I gone 15 years ago I reckon I would be a millionaire by now. Everyone has heard of Whelleys Snakepit gym where I used to be based and taught by the great Billy Riley, in fact everyone heard of it apart from the English".

" I gave two hour classes every day and there were two video cameras trained on me at all times"[3]

Antonio Inoki, co-founder of the New Japan Pro wrestling had told Osamu Nishimura, one of his wrestlers, to go to England to pursue his dream of finding real Lancashire wrestling. He had heard stories from Inoki about Karl Gotch who had taught him the Wigan style and colleague Fujinami who had also trained under Karl Gotch. Karl Gotch had told Mr Fujinami about Roy Wood and advised he go to train with him in Wigan. So it was that he travelled to Wigan looking for Roy Wood. He found the local police station and asked for the Gym, they unfortunately directed him to the wrong gym, thankfully the people at the gym redirected him to Aspull. On meeting Roy he excitedly rang Fujinami telling him "I've found it, you have to come!". Fujinami jumped on a plane and with Nishimura met Roy at the Midland Hotel in Manchester. It was agreed that Roy and a team would fly to Japan in the October to form a role in the launch of MUGA. The first Muga event was to take place in the ATC centre in Osaka.

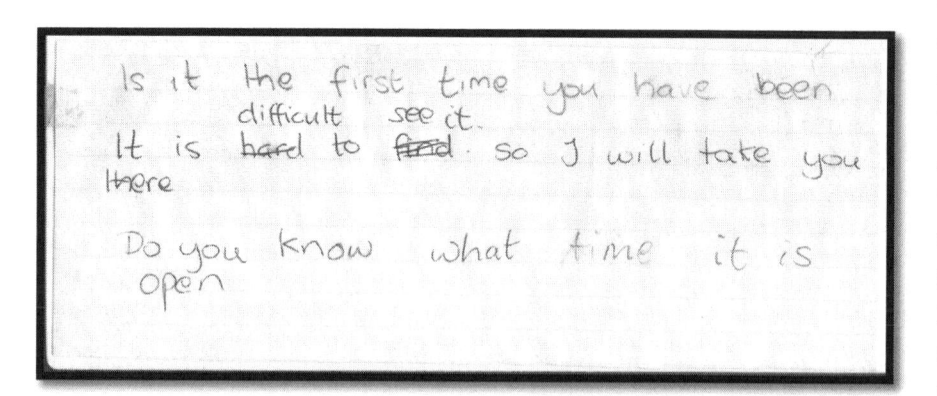

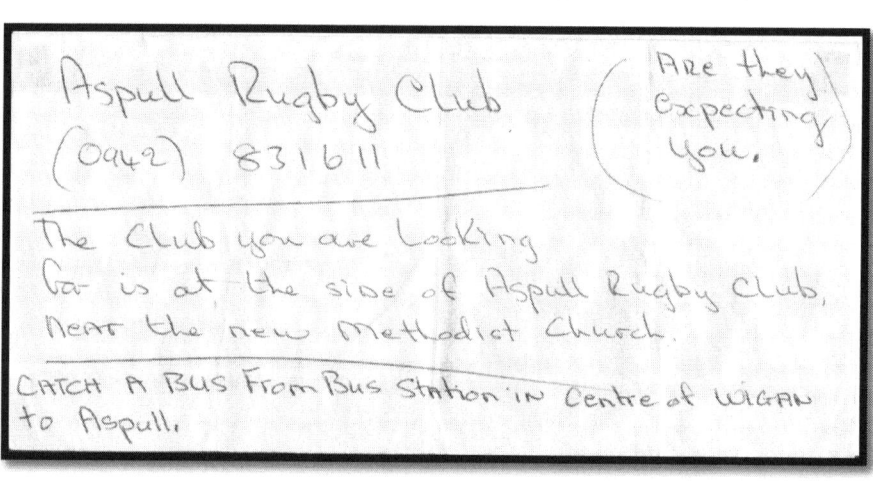

In 1994 the UWFi , formed by Anjo and Takada (union of wrestling force international) Miyato and Anjo came to Wigan to visit Roy again seeking out his skills. It was Shin, a senior member of the UWFi promotion that would enter into discussions regarding getting wrestlers contracted for his organization, unfortunately an agreement for a contract did not occur however it was agreed that two wrestlers Tony Leyland and Neil Maxwell to train in America with Billy Robinson in Nashville.

In February 1998 Roy would wrestle for the New Japan promotions.

A Musha Shugyo[4]

It was in 1989 that Osamu Matsunami , a young man of 18 first heard of Riley's Gym. The Pro-wrestling magazine, Weekly Gong, had an article about the visit of the Dynamite Kid Tom Billington accompanied by a Japanese Journalist to the gym. The article featured Billy Joyce and Roy Wood. It was this article that changed Osamus life. It was here the dream of travelling to Wigan was born. In September 1990 Roy Wood was in Japan with the SWS promotion. Interviews appeared in the pro wrestling magazines. Osamu now 19 decided that he was going to Wigan. He began training in a wrestling gym run by a former pro-wrestler, saving money and finding out as much as possible about the gym. His only clue from the articles was 'Billy Riley's Gym closed about 10 years ago now. Now Roy Wood teaches at Aspull Olympic Wrestling club. HE lives in Wigan'. His lake of skill in English caused him concern and doubt as to his decision, but he made his mind up and though "It's

> Nice to meet you My name is Osamu Matsunami from Japan. I'm a professional wrestling fan.
> I have come here to meet you
> I want to learn "Lancashire Wrestling"
> I want to be a real professional wrestler, not a circus wrestler
> I hope "Snake pit" will revival.
> I'd like to succeed to Lancashire Wrestling
> I have to go back Japan on May.14
> But if you teach me Lancashire Wrestling, I'll come here again after half year
> When I come here agan, I want to stay as long as possible.

ok if I can't meet Roy Wood. I will just go sightseeing in England. If I am lucky, I will meet him. Whatever happens there, I will learn something. If I can't meet him, I will learn that I wasn't prepared enough. This won't be the end of my life. Just go!". He booked his ticket.

In May 1993 he landed in Manchester airport. Tired from his trip he went straight to bed and slept like a log. The next morning he began his search. He set out; in his hand was a note in English saying 'Billy Riley's gym, Roy Wood, Wigan, Aspull Olympic wrestling club'. His search began by simply asking the hotel staff whether or not they had knowledge of Riley's gym or Aspull, to no avail.

Unlike Japan where Sunday is one of the busiest days of the week Osamu found the town centre shut, the only place being open being the tourist information centre. One of the staff had heard of Aspull and advised Osamu it may be near the Aspull Rugby Club. Because of his poor English, she wrote a note saying that he should go to the bus station and catch a bus to Aspull.

He decided to begin his search again on the Monday. He travelled to the bus station, but when there found the scene very confusing with so many buses there. A local approached him and asked where he was going. He showed the note from the tourist information centre the day before and she

Osamu and Roys daughter Andrea

advised him she knew where the gym was and as she was getting off the bus nearby she would take him to the gym. Unfortunately the language barrier proved difficult and he asked her to write down what she had said and looked it up in his dictionary. They got off the bus and she walked him to the door of Aspull Olympic wrestling club. He had succeeded, he had reached his goal. Unfortunately it was shut. He decided to sit down and wait. After about an hour a gentleman emerged from one of the sheds on the nearby allotment. It must have been a strange sight to see the young Japanese man sat outside the gym. The man approached Osamu and asked what he was

Pub where Osamu lived whilst in the UK

doing. Although he found it difficult Osamu tried to explain, "I am from Japan to meet Roy Wood. I have never met him and I don't have an appointment with him. I read about him in a Japanese wrestling magazine and I just came to England. In Wigan city centre I asked people if they knew where the gym was, and finally a kind lady took me here about an hour ago."

Osamu, Roy and Bob Robinson

He asked Osamu to stay in his shed a little while and he would help him. He came back about half an hour later and informed him he had rung Roy's office. Darren, Roy's son arrived shortly after and took him to the family business, Roy Wood bar Supplies. Roy was out but Darren said that he would be back later that afternoon. He sat in the office with regular cups of tea provided until Roy arrived later that afternoon.

Knowing his English was not very good, Osamu had prepared a letter of introduction in the hotel room the night before. Roy and his family were very welcoming to their unexpected Japanese guest and made him feel like part of the family.

That evening, Osamu was to get his first taste of training with Roy. The class was predominantly made up of children with only a few adult wrestlers. Osamu noticed that the style being practiced was Olympic wrestling rather than Lancashire Catch as catch can. The training was very hard, and although the session didn't last long he found it difficult to keep up with the others, however he was happy that he was working out there.

After the training Roy took Osamu back to his hotel and they shared drinks. Roy asked him to cancel his hotel and instead stay at his home until he left Wigan in five days. Osamu felt moved by the generous offer and the next morning relocated to Roy's home.

The same afternoon a journalist visited Roy's home to interview him because of the success the Aspurll wrestlers had achieved in a competition the week before. Osamu was asked to pose with Roy and photos were taken. It was a big surprise to Osamu to see his face in the local newspaper the next day.

Miyato, Osamu, Anju and Roy

Roy and Osamu at the Rileys gym Kyoto

The following day Osamu accompanied Roy to one of the local schools, Roy was teaching wrestling to the children there. Osamu helped Roy with the mats. Osamu was inspired by his dedication, passing on his skills, in his own time, to ensure that wrestling didn't die out in Wigan.

Roy and his wife Brenda left for Egypt the next day on holiday, their son Darren took care of Osamu for the rest of his stay. He visited the site of the old Riley's gym which at that time consisted of a few piles of bricks, even so, Osamu felt lucky to be standing on the site where the Wigan greats had once trained. He also got to meet the great Bob Robinson at his home; at the time he was 75. It was this 10-day trip that made him determined to pursue Lancashire catch as catch can wrestling for the rest of his life.

It was this determination that convinced Osamu he had to go back. In November of the same year he travelled to Wigan again for a six month stay. His entry to the country was not as smooth as his first visit and the immigration official seemed a little wary of his intentions and reason for visit, however a phone call to Roy convinced them and a few hours later Roy collected him from the airport.

This time he stayed at one of the local pubs near the gym. He studied English at a local school for two days of the week and worked out in the gym alone in the daytime. He wrestled the other gym members such as Shane Rigby, Richard Moore, and Tony Rowland when they were available. In the evenings he wrestled Paul Stridgeon, Neil Maxwell with Richard and Tony and some other guys from the gym.

The training was short but intense; he was kept on the move at all times. Their training began with circuits and after a short break they sparred until Roy declared 'Ok, finished' During the sparring if Roy saw one of the wrestlers doing

Rileys Gym Kyoto

something wrong, they wrestlers would be stopped, corrected and then they were made to drill it in the correct way over and over. Once Roy was happy, the sparring continued.

Osamu accompanied Roy as he taught the children at a local school near the gym twice a week. Roy exhibited a lot of patience and Osamu learned a lot watching how the children reacted naturally to the moves applied by the opponent.

Because of his tourist visa, Osamu could only stay six months. He travelled back and fore to Wigan over the years, November 1993, February 1995, April 1996, April 1997, and May 2003 staying 4-6 months at a time.

Back in Japan, Osamu didn't have many sparring partners. However, UWFi was popular at the time. The wrestlers in the UWFi having been taught by Karl Gotch, some wrestlers were interested in the material Osamu learned in Wigan and asked to train with him. He also learned freestyle, and Judo from other fighters. Towards the end of the 1990s with the UFC and Brazilian Jujutsu gaining popularity in Japan, a lot of the local fighters began to fight more from their backs, however Osamu continued to apply the techniques he learned from Roy in Wigan. He was asked to teach catch skills at a local Karate and MMA gym in Kyoto, and used the opportunity to learn how to wrestle against Jujutsu and MMA opponents with his catch skills.

Other wrestlers that visited included Katsaushi Taemura, who wrestled for Mr Fujinami He lived with Roy's son Darren for 6 months in 1997 and returned with Roy to Japan along with Patrick Govan. They were due to wrestle at Fukokua.

In 1999, a former UWF wrestler by the name of Yuko Miyato opened a wrestling gym in Tokyo. Osamu had met Miyato in Wigan when he had visited Roy. Miyato hired Billy Robinson as head coach of the gym. On the day the gym opened, Billy appeared

Fujinami, Roy Wood and Bob Robinson (Billy Joyce)

on a satellite TV program. Watching the program Osamu realised that he could learn Catch as catch can from Billy Robinson. He moved to Tokyo and made his way to the Gym. Osamu felt that maybe Billy was a little suspicious of him at first. He tested the young Osamu's knowledge of catch as catch can with questions about the great Billy Joyce. It was after demonstrating one of Billy Joyce's moves that had been taught to him by Roy that Billy Robinson got excited shouting for Miyato and his interpreter Koji to come over. He asked Osamu to demonstrate the over again for them. It seemed that Billy was happy to see the legacy of Wigan and the great Billy Joyce was alive and well in the young Japanese boy in front of him. Billy told Osamu to come back the next day and show him more of his wrestling skills. He helped at the gym by demonstrating some of the moves for Billy who had problems with his knees. He also remembered being shouted at too! Osamu described his teaching style at the time as being precise, and scientific. They was moves worked, the angle of the body the feet knees etc. were all part of the explanations. When a move didn't work for a wrestler, he would get the wrestler to think about what that move wasn't working for them and get them to discover and learn for themselves.

At the end of 2006, Osamu rented a small storage room near his house in Kyoto. He laid mats and began teaching pure Lancashire catch as catch can wrestling.

The gyms facilities were Spartan, no toilet, gas or water. However, Osamu was proud of his gym and its resemblance to that of Riley's original gym in Wigan were not lost on him. The number of students wasn't important, what was important was that he could continue to learn and teach catch wrestling.

In April 2007, Osamu received an email from Roy. He notified Osamu that he was coming to Japan for a holiday. They met in Kyoto and Osamu extended to Roy the hospitality shown to him in Wigan. He told Roy "Actually I have opened my own gym, but it is very small and I don't have many students". Roy asked to see the gym. He told Osamu that it was as large as the original Riley's gym. Roy taught there then after training they went back to the hotel and had a drink. He asked Roy to name his gym. "How about Riley's Gym Kyoto". Feeling unsure that he deserved to name his gym such he asked Roy a number of times if this was ok. Roy's reply was , "sure". Osamu recalls this memory as one of the happiest and proudest moments of his life.

I was lucky enough to meet Osamu ("Sam") in November 2012 and November 2013. I got to spend the week training with him, drilling, sparring, and sweating our way through the workouts. We lived in the same house, Roy's house, for the week and talked about my experiences of Japan and about catch wrestling, Riley's gym, his experiences etc. His wrestling was technical, fluid and more that anyone else I had wrestled before or after, his resistance to 'tap' was what I remember most. I outweighed him significantly, and managed to get him in a gorbbit, I though I had won the match, he didn't tap. Wanting to win against him I lifted him , from a grobbit until he was vertical, he didn't tap. I applied a shin lock with all my weight thought my elbow into his shin, he didn't tap. How did it end? I tapped! Osamu and Gregg Crompton made history by wrestling the first catch match in Wigan in 50 years since Bob Robinsons match with Arthur Belshaw. In a twist of fate Osamu won the match with the move that had been applied on Bob Robinson by Arthur Belshaw those 50 years prior.

---

[1] Dynamite kid – Japanese article – translation E.Shahan
[2] Wakamatsu visits uk – Japanese article – translation E.Shahan
[3] Wigan Evening post November 5th 1990
[4] Musha Shugyo is Japanese for a Warriors quest or pilgrimage

Chapter 12

Rebirth of the Snakepit

Andrea, Roy's daughter who runs the charity Heartlift, had long tried to get her father to teach Lancashire catch as catch wrestling. Roy thought that people no longer had any interest in the old style of wrestling in the UK. However, catch wrestling had begun to re-emerge as a grappling art. The likes of Kazushi Sakuraba, known as the Gracie hunter, and Josh Barnett, who had both trained with Billy Robinson at the 'Snakepit Japan' run by Miyato had raised the profile of catch wrestling. Billy Robinson and Jake Shannon had been keeping the 'catch flame' alive by putting on seminars and producing DVD training material.

In 2011 I once again met up with Jamie Phillips from Llanelli South Wales, who had previously been a student of mine in Japanese Martial arts, he told me that he had been training in BJJ but had been interested in Catch as Catch can wrestling and as such had began to seek out people to learn from. He had corresponded with a gentleman by the name of Kris Iatskevich from Canada and had travelled to Canada to train with him. At the same time he had been in contact with Tommy Heyes and also Roy Wood. Roy had begun to realize that there might be interest in the traditional Lancashire catch as catch can. In August 2011 Roy Wood held the first seminar in the Aspull Gym. I remember the four-hour journey to Wigan for the first seminar well. We all sat on the elevated seating in the gym as Roy spoke to us about Catch, Billy Riley and the Gym. Next we started with a 'Quick warm-up' which I think most people in the room found more challenging than any workout that we had ever done. Roy shouted encouragement "If you're not fit, you cant wrestle". Roy called us together on the mat and began demonstrating. The pace at which he showed us techniques was tremendous; we must have covered 20 or 30 techniques in the 3-hour seminar. Roy told us he was making things easy on us, as when he was at the gym techniques weren't shown to you like this, rather you had to learn them yourself from wrestling others. Roy demonstrated all the techniques including suplexes and most of us sat open mouthed at this man, who was nearing his seventieth year was throwing himself around the mat. Next we lined against the wall and were called up in pairs to wrestle, without fail every session finishes with wrestling, its one thing drilling techniques, another doing them. Drilling is not wrestling.

In the September Billy Robinson visited the UK with Scientific Wrestling, hosted by Andy Crittenden of Doncaster.

Roy held further seminars in Cardiff University facility in Tal A Bont ,and a seminar in a local gym in Cardiff.

In January 2012 the seminars moved back to the gym in Wigan, renamed the Snakepit. Monthly seminars were held throughout the year with a break in July for the 2012 Olympics in London at which Roy was attending with Maria Dunn of Guam whom he was coaching. Month on month attendance grew at the seminars, Later the gym attracted international visitors such as Jasse Junkari, from Finland who had a background in BJJ. This echoed the history of Waino Ketonen, visiting Wigan in the early part of the 20th century and training Billy Riley. It was November before we saw Jasse Again when he attended the first international seminar.

The seminar saw participants attend from all over the world. Osamu Matsunami attended form Japan

Raul Ramirez from USA

Kol – Thailand

Edward Makarus - Canada

Andy Crittenden, Jake Shannon, Sam Kressin, Leona Fujinami, Tatsumi Fujinami, Billy Robinson and Roy Wood

Wayne Tappin - England
Steve Greenfield - Wales
Heddi Karaoui - Denmark
Greg Crompton - England
Jasse Junkari - Finnland
Ian Bromley - England

A demanding week, the wrestlers trained 3 times a day. As demanding as ever, the conditioning sessions alone were enough to put strain on the wrestlers. The day began with 2 hrs of conditioning. Jogging, sprinting, squats, pressups, sit-ups, v sit-ups, partner drills, and burpees, plyo jumps, the pace was relentless. Roy didn't sit on the sidelines; he did the exercise with us. But it wasn't just a case of him keeping up, he bettered all of us, to see the pace at which he was able to exercise, and to see his strength and agility was inspiring to everyone in the room. We then would break followed by a 2 hr. afternoon session consisting of technique drills. All aspects of wrestling were covered from Stand up, takedowns, mat wrestling, pins and submissions all covered in detail and at a relentless pace. The evening sessions were there to catch up on technique from the afternoon session and also to wrestle. Each day we went home completely exhausted.

In the week Roy passed on techniques he had learned from Billy Riley those years before. As a participant it was physically demanding but a unique experience. We were living, breathing, eating sleeping catch wrestling. The evenings saw a number of us sitting round talking about catch whilst we all swapped pain medication to get through the next day. The thing that stands out most is how we were made to feel like family by Roy, Andrea and the rest of their family.

The Friday night saw us attend the Greater Manchester Sporting awards in Manchester. Roy had been nominated for Coach of the year and Apsull for Club of the Year. Not only did Roy win Coach of the year but was also awarded the 'Unsung hero award'. The week also produced two new coaches, Osamu Matsunami and Ian Bromley, both with over 20 years experience under Roy Wood.

The following day saw the first Catch Wrestling match in Wigan for fifty years. The first match saw Osamu Matsunami vs. Gregg Crompton, in a nod to history the match was won by the move that beat Bob Robinson in his match with Arthur Belshaw 50 years previously, catch had come full circle.

Seminars were to continue in 2013 with another international week and competition. In 2014 Roy Wood, Andrea Wood and Stephen Greenfield, along with Chris Crossan and Amin Nazeer travelled to Los Angeles to attend a catch competition organized by Raul Ramirez. This was an important time as not only did it see a great international event, Roy Wood giving his first seminar in the USA but also saw the Snakepit Wigan and the Billy Wicks foundation cement their relationship under the banner of the Catch Wrestling Alliance in order to promote traditional Catch as Catch Can wrestling.

The Wrestlers

The following pages contain chapters on the wrestlers from Riley's Gym. A number of professionals attended the gym on a small number of occasions but I have only included those wrestlers that trained in the gym on a regular basis. There will always be omissions and I apologise in advance if I have missed anybody, out, If there are further contributions to this section then please contact me via email at Stephen@snakepitwigan.com so that people can be included in later editions.

Chapter 13

Ernie Riley

Born in 1927 in the White Bear pub in Wellington street off Scholes, Ernie Riley was surrounded by wrestlers as far back as he could remember. Whether it was the wrestlers coming to train in the back room or upstairs room of the pub, or Americans such as Benny Sherman or Jack McGrath visiting his world famous father, wrestling was always a part of his life. Ernie was 7 when the family moved to the Crispin arms in Birkett bank. During the period when his father was away in South Africa (1932-1934 on two separate visits), the family moved into a house on Beech hill for six months prior to settling into the off license in Whelley that his father took over when he came home from touring permanently. [1]

Ernie didn't start wrestling until he was aged seventeen. Starting out as a fitness pursuit and hobby, he didn't think initially that he would cope professionally. But little by little the wrestling bug bit him. Although his father never forced him into wrestling, his father was proud to see him go into the profession that had shaped his life. However, much like he would to all the wrestlers he coached he advised his son not to rely on wrestling alone. He told his son 'you cant rely on wrestling y'know, you could get injured tomorrow, and once you finish having a place to train that no one could 'throw them out of' a reality by building the gym at the end of Pyke street. Ernie commented that "My father treated all the boys like his sons, and I suppose that's what binds us all together"[3]. He noted that his father had " the mind of a world chess champion"[4].

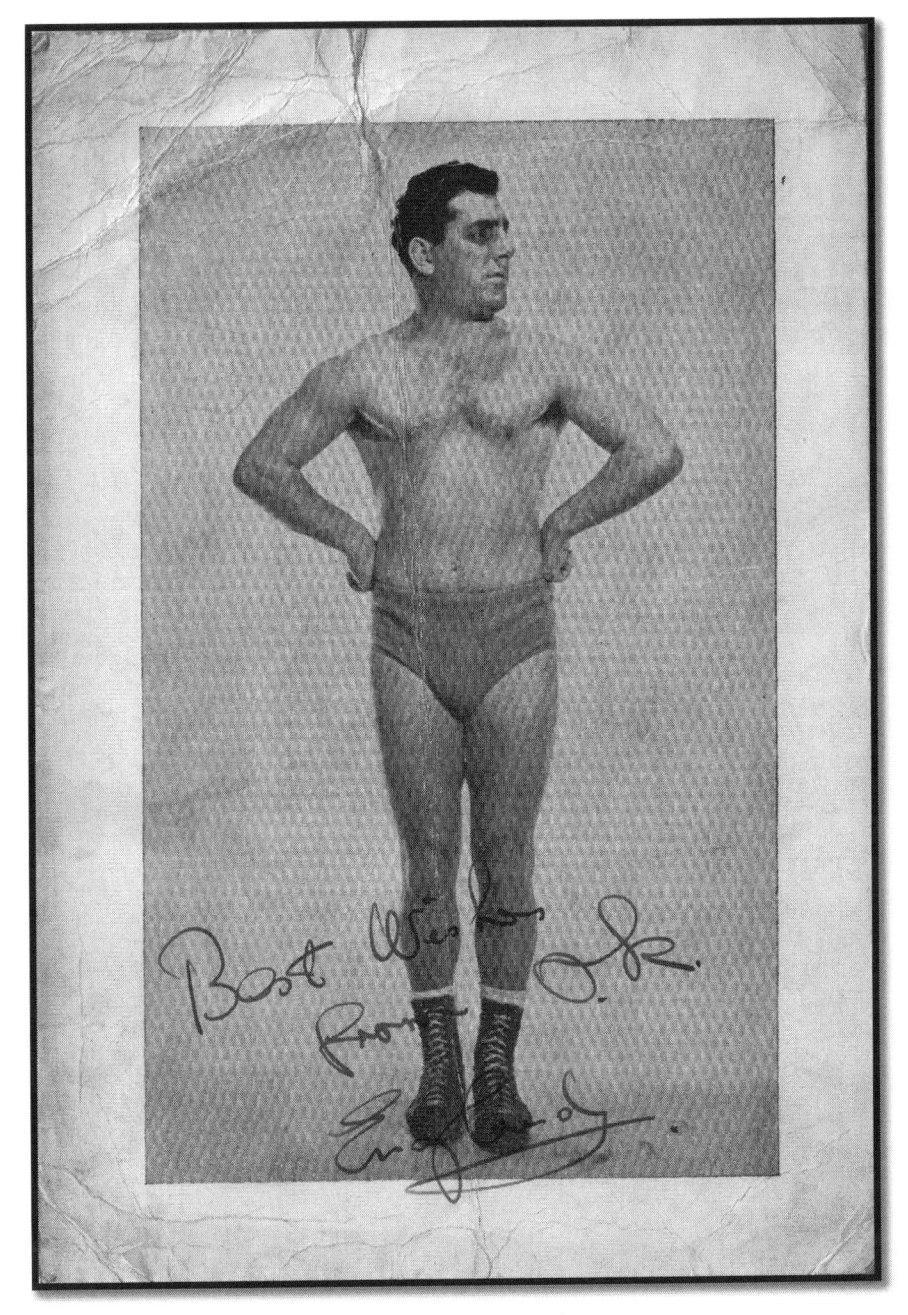

Initially be began doing the odd professional job for Dale martins promotions. Then one day Jackie Dale, asked him whether he would like to wrestle in Istanbul. At the time there was some anxiety amongst some of the professional wrestlers about wrestling the Turks as they had a reputation of being very capable wrestlers. However, he asked the advice of his father who told him "Listen, you go, it don't matter if you get beaten it's the experience you want". And with that advice he agreed to his first trip abroad wrestling. The year was 1953[5].

your career you'd be washed up so you want a trade behind you." Heeding his fathers words Ernie trained as an Electrician before he began his career in professional wrestling.[2]

Part of the 'class of 48' , Ernie would form friendships with his fellow wresters such as Tommy Moore and Alan Latham that would last the rest of their lives and was one of the wrestlers and tradesmen that helped make his fathers dream of

The trip was to begin in the October and would last a few months, meaning for the first time as a young lad of 23 he would miss Christmas at home. However, the tournament finished 2 days before Christmas and he flew home, initially to London, to report to Jack Dale and to get his pay. Everything had been paid for him during the trip and it was his first experience of living the professional wrestlers life.[6]

He had proven popular, and next came a contract for Germany in 1954. He wrestled there for a local promoter who obviously impressed by the Wigan boy asked if he could bring over a welterweight as well. Ernie sent for John Foley who at the time was working as a miner in the Parsonage pit. At the time John was 20 years old. Both of them were being treated to nice hotels all paid for, meals at nice restaurants, this turned the young Foley's head who vowed never to go down a pit again. They impressed the promoters and were asked to wrestle for Germany in a tournament in Helsinki, Finland. It was to be a 6-week contract, and once again they were treated to taxis everywhere. They wrestled in Linnanmaki Park. This was followed by a tournament in Berlin. Whilst there, his father sent him a telegram requesting him to go to India to wrestle.[7]

And so he travelled to India for a 12-month stay [8]. It was a culture shock to Ernie when he got there, he told Roy Wood that he remembered hearing a cart going down the road and when he looked there were dead bodies on them[9]. He found the poverty very depressing [10]. Whilst in India Bert Assarati who was there wrestling took Ernie under his wing and spent a lot of time with him[11]. Ernie wrestled in Calcutta, Bombay then Delhi. He was constantly moving around never in one place for more than a month at a time.

As part of his wrestling he had travelled to Finland, India, Turkey, France, Germany, Belgium, Spain and Italy. The Wrestler magazine at the time said that he learned the following from his travels

Ernie Riley and Tommy Moore

"From the Turks – when skill is equal strength tells. As quick as lightening flash – a lesson from the Finns, skill and strength brought to naught by speed in thinking and practice. From India the skill of counter moves and elusiveness. From his father the tricks of the trade and the balance without which none of the other assets would avail him. From himself the endurance and experience he has gained from regular training and match competition. A truly worthy champion"[12]. In his prime he was 5 feet 9 ½ inches tall and weighed 13stone 10lbs.

Jayne, Ernie's sister remembers her brother's travels abroad "Ernie, my brother took it up then you see. He started going and he did start taking it up and of course Ernie went to Turkey. He went to India, he went to Germany, he went to Iceland or somewhere like that and he had a good, I think France as well, had like a captain, well not a captain but a minder and it'd be that guy who was going to be the fella or the guy that was going to beat them all, they had to beat this other fella first and I remember when Ernie was in Germany, he was that guy. You had to beat Ernie, my brother before anyone else. So it was all,

Ernie Riley and Alan Latham at their business premises

but he enjoyed somewhere in India where I don't know if they have really good wrestlers there and they really admire the Wigan ones and I don't know if he was in Turkey and there was a famous wrestler there and there was a lad from London, this very good Turk lad even came with Ernie to see him off when he was coming back to England, he was there for a couple of weeks, because he admired the Wigan style for wrestling and knew they were well like to take care of themselves and when they used to do this, say when they used to go away and there'd be a set of wrestlers and one, one guy would be the champion but if he was ever challenged they always that was like when it was like professional but they really used to try it out on the gym didn't they."[13]

When Ernie came back to the UK in late 1954 early 1955 wrestling was starting to become a televised sport and it was around this period that he won the championship and the promoters didn't want him leaving the country as much.[14]

Despite being champions the wrestlers would still train in the gym, as Ernie noted "Sunday was a big day at the gym , from 2-6pm"[15] and even the wrestling magazines of the period knew this commenting that you could find "stars like Jack

Dempsey and Ernie Riley busy training and learning new holds and trying new escapes"[16].

The light heavyweight title fell vacant in the mid 1950s, and an elimination tournament was held. It was Steve Logan that Ernie beat for the title[17]. As holder of the light heavyweight title, it seems that he did not receive that many challenges to it, however it was noted that he was always more than happy to accommodate an established claim. Challengers included Bob Sweeney who lost to Ernie on the 17th March 1964[18].

Like his colleagues from the gym he liked to keep himself in good shape and tried to get to the gym every day. He trained frequently with friend and gym mate Jack Dempsey (Tommy Moore). His regime included gym work, weight training and cross-country running and sprints[19].

Sometimes members of the public would get carried away and on one such occasion was reported as follows

"Ernie Riley was the light heavyweight champion of Great Britain and an arrogant performer.

On more than one occasion he would argue with ringsiders. He annoyed one of them so much that the man jumped into the ring after the bout and said,

"You're useless. I could beat you, just give me a chance".

After lots of pushing and shoving, the promoter agreed to a three-round challenge contest in four weeks' time. The lad looked as though he could handle himself, so we knew to get a ticket early.

The excitement built that night and the spectator had some early success but then Ernie took him apart. The crowd started shouting for the fight to be stopped and it was."[20]

Ernie retired in 1966 undefeated [21] at the age of 37 in order to concentrate on his business [22] having spent 18 years in the game[23].

Ernie married Hilda who was originally from Staines. They had three children; Mark, who would later wrestle as an amateur for Roy Wood and indeed work for Roy in his bar supplies company, a daughter Jayne who for a period lived in the Middle East[24] and Paul.

Like many Riley's wrestlers, Ernie had a standalone business, not only relying on his wrestling to provide his income, and investing at the advice of his father in a business to provide for him in later life. He went into partnership with Alan Latham, a fellow Riley's wrestler. . They would purchase the Monaco ballroom with Silent partner Jack Isherwood [25] and the wrestlers from the gym would work on the doors there[26]. Whilst wrestling in the Isle of man and seeing the amusement arcades there Alan had come up with the idea of setting up their own business. The business was very successful and at one point they were supplying over 200 pubs and clubs with fruit machines. Although their personalities were the polar opposites, with Ernie being the quiet one and Alan a very jovial loud character they complemented each other Ernie and Alan both retired from the business about aged 60, as they were finding the late night call outs for the machines more and more difficult.

Ernie died 25th October 2000. Mass was held on the 30th October at St Mary's Standish with burial at Gridlow cemetery.

Titles

British Light Heavyweight title; **1952**; Defeats Steve Logans; **1955** again defeating Steve Logan; **1957-1960**; **May 1961**; Vacant December 1969 when Riley retires.

European Heavyweight title; **1950's**; Middlesborough; **1967**.

---

[1] Ernie Riley interview – A.Coleman
[2] Ernie Riley interview - – A.Coleman
[3] First Tuesday 1989
[4] Wrestler magazine November 1963 – page26
[5] Ernie Riley interview – A.Coleman
[6] Ernie Riley interview – A.Coleman
[7] Ernie Riley interview – A.Coleman
[8] Ernie Riley interview – A.Coleman
[9] Roy Wood interview – Andrea Wood2013
[10] Roy Wood interview – Andrea Wood 2013
[11] Roy Wood interview – Andrea Wood 2013
[12] Matt Review 205
[13] J Jayne Byrne interview November 2013
[14] Ernie Riley interview – A.Coleman
[15] First Tuesday 1989
[16] November 1961 Wrewtler magazine page 9
[17] Wrestler magazine – Novemeber 1963 – Page 26
[18] Wrestler magazine June 1964 – page 11
[19] Wrestler magazine November 1963 – page 26
[20] Read more: http://legacy.thisisderbyshire.co.uk/day-local-lad-jumped-ring-champ-Ernie/story-11623998-detail/story.html#ixzz2uBjpyuVm
[21] Wrestler magazine November 1970
[22] Ernie Riley interview – A.Coleman
[23] First Tuesday 1989
[24] Ernie Riley interview – A.Coleman / Roy wood interview Andrea 2013
[25] Roy Wood and Andrea Wood 2013
[26] Karen Lynch interview – S Greenfield Nov 2013

Chapter 14

Billy Joyce

"I've a good wife a good home and good business and when I'm no wrestling what better hobby than living where you are wanted?"[1]

In Billy's opinion the very best wrestler of his time- Billy Robinson[2]

Born September 22 1916, Bob Robinson started his working life like many of those in the gym, as a miner. He worked at the coalface with the father of his fellow gym colleague and friend Roy wood. Charlie Wood's job was to spade up all the coal, and then Bob, his haulage lad, would push the tub holding the coal. Although a hard, dirty unhealthy job the work made Bob and all those in the pit fit and strong. However, Bob wanted to have a better life for himself and started wrestling in order to get out of the pit.[3]

Bob married Edna, who later was to become a great friend of Roy Wood's wife Brenda. Edna during the war had driven a wagon. He had a daughter called Dorothy. He was a great family man and loved nothing better than taking his family to see shows in Blackpool[4]. He always endeavored to get home after a wrestling match even when wrestling further field in places such as Middleborough and London[5].Although never a heavy drinker or pub goer Bob owned the Grapes pub. The pub had previously been run by John Riley, Mayor and Alderman of Wigan, and Billy Riley's brother. The pub later closed. Later Edna and Bob would open a shop in Swann Street Wigan[6].

Tragedy struck the family in 1952. On Wednesday 8th of October 1952 . The Perth – Euston express impacted with the crowded local train transformed the Harrows and Wealdstone station into a scene of death and confusion[7]. On board the train were Bob, brother Joe and Jimmy and sister Vera. Jimmy was on the train on his way to Southampton to return home to America[8]. Three days following the event 87 were still in hospital injured, a further 64 had been discharged and there were 110 fatalities[9]. Included in that list was Bobs sister Vera[10]

Always a humble man, despite as being regarded as one of the greatest wrestlers of all time he was never heard to boast of his achievements. Roy Wood tells of an occasion where the wrestlers were out socialising "I remember once whilst wrestlers were out for a meal, one of the wrestlers loudly announced Bob as a champion. Bob was so embarrassed as he never told anyone. He was a very quiet man. He was one of the most humble men you would ever meet."[11]. Bob was widely regarded as the best wrestler of his generation., when asked who he regarded as the best his answer was George Gregory.[12]

In the early days of Professional wrestling he used to set off with his small bag containing a hot or cold drink, and training gear and cycle to his matches, sometimes having to rely on follow local wrestlers for lifts in cars until he saved enough to buy a second hand car[13].

His philosophy on wrestling training very much mirrored that of his mentor Billy Riley. If you wanted to be a wrestler, then wrestle and when you've wrestled wrestle again and when you're tired you wrestle some more and when you are so thoroughly tired you feel you cant stand any more you take a hiding because you cant stand your ground. The muscle that you build must be wrestling muscle, the lungpower and endurance should be for wrestling not for cross-country running or fell racing. You down want any other agility other than what wrestling brings you, If you want to pursue weights, running or jumping in your free time then that's fine but don't train for these sports[14]. Billy Robinson noted that Bob, like the other old timers in the gym didn't tire during matches, they knew how to make the other person work.[15]

Bob was not always the great wrestler that his known for. Billy Riley told Billy Robinson "For 12 years, Bob was the dumbest guy we ever had in the gym". For 12 years he worked out in the Gym after his shift in the coalmine with either Joe Robinson or Billy Riley. Then one day, overnight something changed and all the training he did over the years suddenly clicked into place[16]. Billy Joyce turned professional in 1944[17].Always a hard worker he took little rest between his engagements and he would honor his contracts to promoters even with injuries that would have made other wrestlers cry off[18]. Roy wood summed up the great mans style as follows "Bob was also a great technician. He would give you his leg and you would have a moment where you might think you had something but Bob would just being playing with you as he had endless techniques just waiting for you when you tried something."[19].This was echoed in an article on Bob in the Matt review magazine, it noted that Bob was "cat like, he is content to wait for an opponent to make a mistake and then pounce in for the kill .A master tactician he may often lure his opponents to believe the champion is in difficulties only to reverse the position with a quick counter move. Nothing flamboyant. Master of every hold in the wrestling textbook – for that matter master of many holds that have not yet appeared. From his vast experience can weigh up a wrestler and can often pace the fight with tactics specially suited to him against the man he faces in the ring.."[20]. Although widely regarded by his peers as the best, his particular wresting style and persona was not always as equally received by fans and commentators alike. Eddie Caldwell said 'many ringside critics and wrestling journalists underestimate Joyce and compare him in unfavorable light with past masters of the ring' and explains 'his ring manner upsets many in the audience. He is determined and grim faced and takes his wrestling very seriously. He has no time for fun and games' [21]. The mat review commented, "So unobtrusive is his style that the quality of his wrestling often goes unnoticed except by the more experienced spectators"[22]. An American promoter compared him to Lou Thesz "there you have a wrestler with all the mean ways of Lou Thesz, combined with his wrestling ability. Most likely this boy will like Lou Thesz be no colourful champion but the men who come forward to depose him will sure have to learn a thing or two"[23]. Seamus Dunleavy had the following to say about Billy Joyce "– soft looking to feel no muscles at all .He looked like farmer or a fisherman but he was absolutely dynamite you couldn't get near him. His technique was so good that you were always off balance he was a great mover always one step ahead of his opponent. He'd shift you into a position so that you couldn't move or you couldn't use your strength and he was always against your joints as well. There were no rounds you wrestled until you 'knocked' until you gave in and you always said that if you were behind someone he'd very rarely get away from you. Now Billy Joyce would always get behind you and you never saw him. Billy Robinson on the other hand was a young Manchester lad who came along and he was very good. He was big well built muscular man but he could never beat Billy Joyce. "Billy Joyce was the man he used to be all over me"[24].Patrick, Billy Riley's grandson remembers seeing Bob wrestling in the gym "Well I remember Bob being on the mat, literally he would look like a spider, he just used to seem to be all over them, he used to go on Sundays. I'd be dragged along. I'd probably run riot around the mat, but I always remember Bob being on and being very just seemed to be all over somebody really like they're not getting away"[25].

During the time he was the British heavyweight titleholder he had an open challenge, with a purse of £1000 to anyone who would come along and take his title[26]. This arose as for a period he had to wrestle with a knee injury, possibly the one gained from his shoot match with Arthur Belshaw. In an article in the wrestler magazine in 1965 it was noted that he had been dogged by knee problems since 1960, but had been wearing an elastic support bandage on his knee since the 1950s[27]. He was loath to take time off to have the knee operated on and for a time was worried that the surgery may be unsuccessful. A number of people challenged his abilities during this period 'from the safety of their own homes' however after having surgery, he gave them the opportunity to put their money where their mouth was and step into the ring with him, and he put up a £1000 side stake [28].

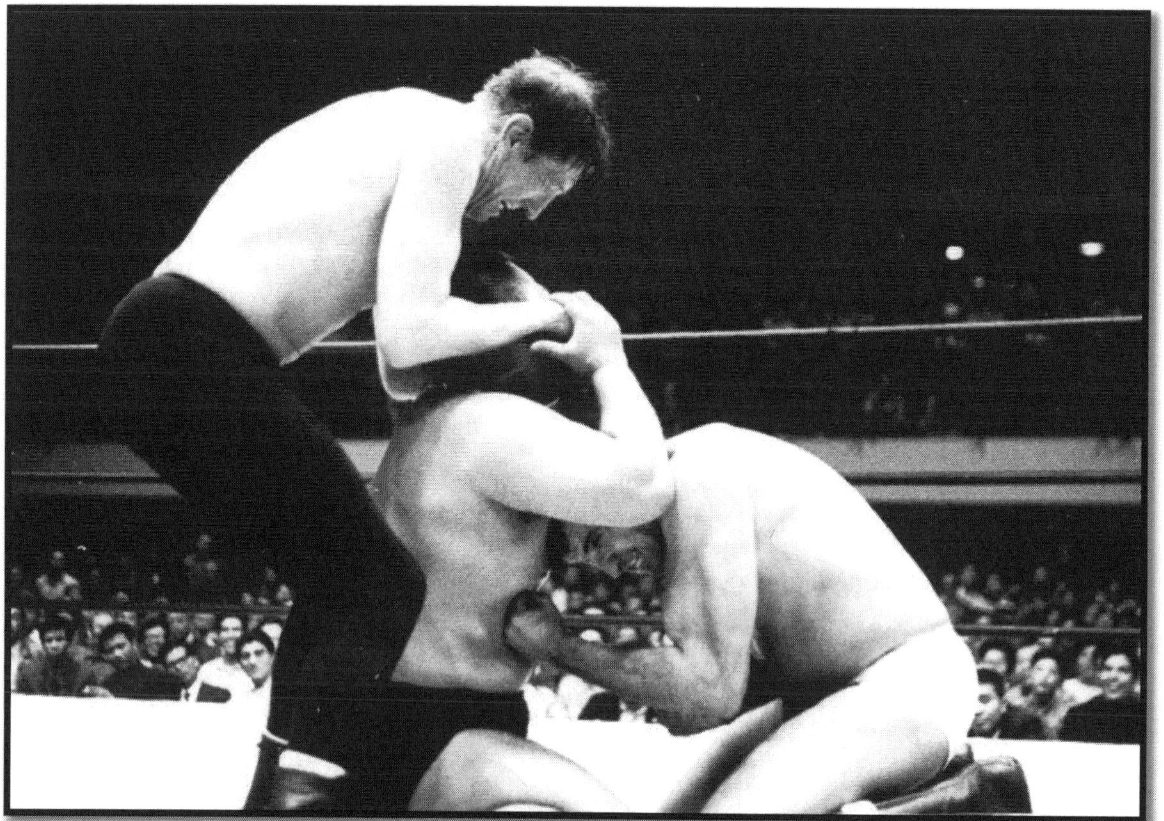

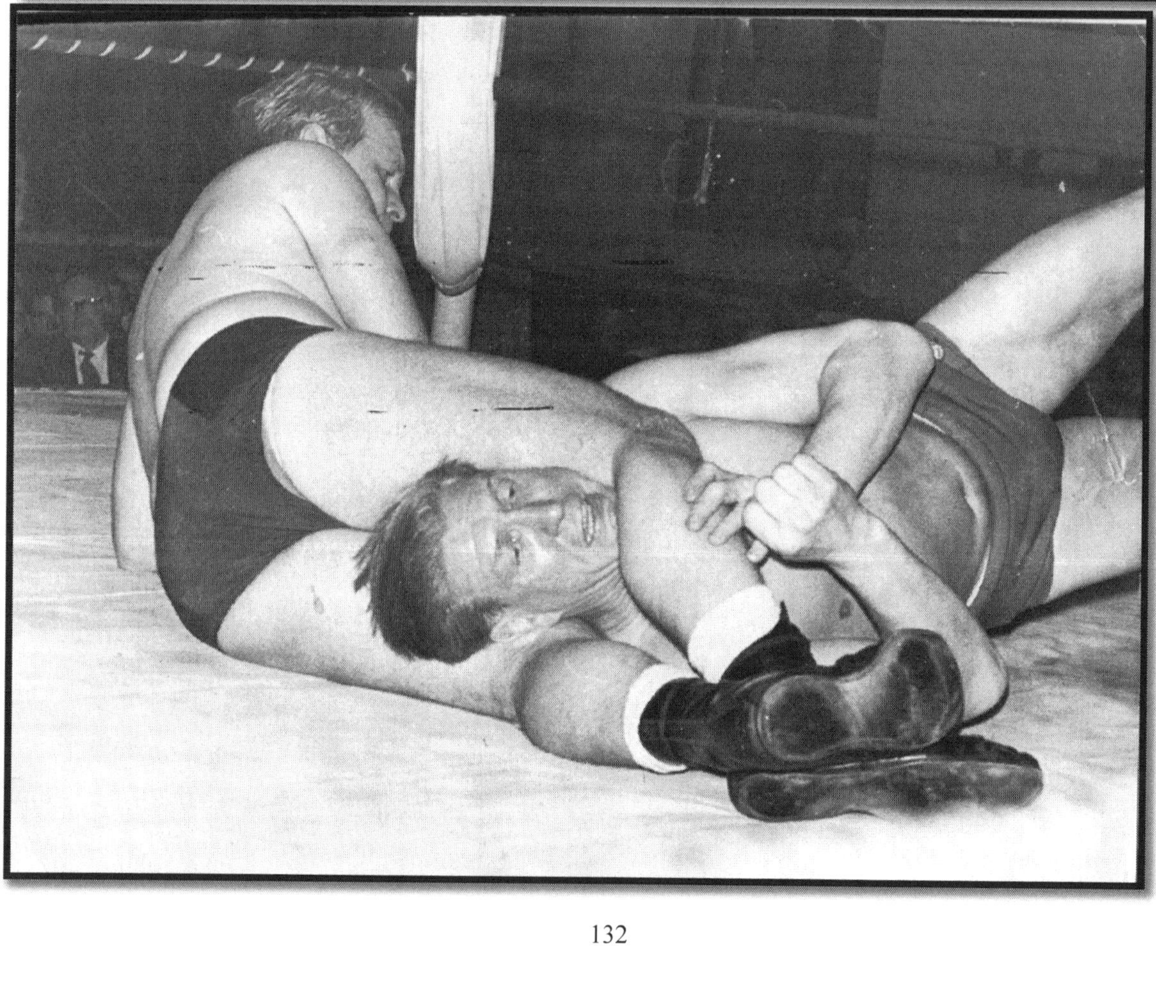

Another of Bob's roles was that of 'Policeman'. Bob would attend Rileys promotion shows, not to wrestle, but to be there is anyone 'jumped the ring'. Bob was there as a shooter to take care of business if necessary.

Although he was always keen to stay close to home as possible, he did wrestle abroad in Sweden, Belgium, France, Spain , Germany and Japan.[29]. He went to Japan in 1968 for the pro wrestling 'World elimination series'[30] His companions on the tour were Bill Robinson, John Lees, Tony Charles, John Foley, Colin Joynson, Barry Douglas, and Johnny Eagles. It seems he picked up an injury to one of his legs during the tournament[31]..He must have made an impression, as when the Japanese came to Wigan in 1994 it was Billy Joyce they were looking for. Mr Watamatzu and Mr Sakurada from SWS were the wrestlers and they met up with Billy Joyce who because of his age recommended they seek out Roy Wood.[32]

Although one of the best wrestlers ever, his skill didn't lay in coaching. As Roy Wood says, "He couldn't coach for toffee, he didn't have the patience". This was echoed by Michael Moore who said that Bob Robinson got easily frustrated when trying to coach "I've told thee, I've showed ya now and you still cant do it'[33]He did attend the gym every so often to watch the youngsters wrestling. He can be seen on the documentary on Riley's gym that was aired in the 1980s on the first Tuesday program and also in the Wrestlers documentary from Granada commenting on the match with the young Roy Wood. Osamu Matsunami tells of his first meeting with Bob Robinson "One day Roy Wood Sensei requested Billy Joyce to instruct him in training. Cold English

Roy said "That's it then. Just like always. He's gone home." Billy Joyce saw the aerobics and left. He came to see wrestling, if there wasn't any good wrestling going on he makes himself scarce."[34]

However that didn't mean he wasn't happy to lend his advice to those who asked it, in an interview Seamus Dunleavy spoke of Bob Robinson "my lad was a good amateur , and every time I came up to Wigan I'd make sure Bob Robinson was there and he'd give us the benefit of his knowledge"[35].On another occasions when Roy and Tommy were running the gym their wrestlers were getting beaten by another club week in week out with the same move, although Roy and Tommy tried to come up with a counter they couldn't find on. The move had the opponent pushing their head into the ribs in order to set up a cradle. One day Bob Robinson was in the Gym and they decided to ask him. Bob watched, shook his head, then laughed "You should never let him get near your ribs, just put your elbow in thier training. So in order to warm up I arrived 30 min early. At the gym there was some kind of aerobics class going on. The gym was large so other individuals and groups rented it out as well.

Billy Joyce appeared as I was warming up in one area. We greeted one another. After a while Coach Roy Wood appeared and said "Bob(Billy Joyce) show up yet?" "He was here a minute ago, didn't you see him" I answered beginning to look around for him.

face," they never lost against that move again. That was a skill he and many of the old timers had, they could watch something and come up with an instant counter because of their knowledge of wrestling and the fact it was so ingrained into their bodies.[36]

The last shoot in Wigan

"Arthur Belshaw was the one that had the last shoot with Bob. I was 10, my dad was in the pit, Bob was me dads apprentice, I remember my dad coming home and saying he was going to watch a wrestling match in a school. It was just in a school, Arthur Wright put £1000 up and the Wigan fellows matched it. All I know, Billy Riley's brother Charlie, fixed that match up, no Jimmy Riley. It was a silly match, the Belshaws would have wrestled Bob straight, but the match they fixed up was that Bob would beat him 3 or 4 times in 5 minutes or whatever it was. So if it had been the best of three falls it would have been a different matter, it was a funny match that Jimmy fixed up. When they wrestled, they said Bob was knocking hell out of him, Bob was behind him, and was playing with him, and he hooked in, and apparently the Bellshaws were waiting for Bob to hook in, one of the Bellshaws said 'its there now Arthur', and it's a move I had never seen until Ernie Riley showed it to me just before he died, and I never knew he beat him that way. He grabbed Bobs leg and he submitted, and he got up and could have continued but they had to carry Arthur off, so if it was the best of three Arthur wasn't in a state to continue"[37]. Billy Robinson confirmed this in a Facebook post in 2011. He also suggested that Billy Joyce might have had to lose weight for the match. The other terms were 3 pins submissions in a set time period compared to the one for Arthur Belshaw. He also noted that Arthur was carried off to the hospital and that the Belshaws would not accept a return match[38].

Bob retired in 1976, like the other wrestlers had ran his own business, firstly the Grapes pub and later a shop with his wife.

Unfortunately later in life his wife Edna became very unwell and Bob devoted his time to caring for her until she died in January 2000. Bob passed away in September 2000 two weeks before his 84 birthday. Roy Wood, who also lost his own wife to a terminal illness said of him "I have always respected Bob but towards the end of his life when his wife was poorly, the way he cared for her and the love he had was on a different level to what you often see. He died not long after, in my opinion of a broken heart. Fortunately, Bob, myself and many of the Riley's wrestlers have great faith so we have the comfort of knowing we go to a better place in the future. "[39]

Best summed up by his wrestling colleagues, Karl Gotch said of him "You were the crème de la crème Bob", and Roy Wood "The best wrestler I have ever seen in all of my life! He was also one of the nicest men I have ever had the pleasure to know! He was a very proud man, a family man and an extremely good friend."[40]

Titles

Joint Promotions British heavyweight title

Heavyweight title declared vacant after Assirati "carried on the pre war tradition of ignoring all the authorities" – tournament organized in London in 1955 which Bert Assirati was invited but did not participate. Winner was Billy Joyce. Joyce published an open challenge of £500 side stake to defend his title against Assirati it was agreed that they were to be matched at a hall in Leicester in April 1959 but a severe eye injury to Assirati put an end to the fight and an end to Bert's career

15/4/58 – Beat Gordie Nelson – London
December 1959 – Beat Ernie Baldwin – London
15/7/60 – Beat Dennis Mitchel – Bradford
29/6/64 – Beat Geoff Portz Middlesborough
17/3/66 – Beat Gwyn Davies – Nottingham
28/6/66 – Beat Jim Olivera – Manchester
October 1966 – Beat Albert Wall Lemington Spa
November 1966 – Beat Billy Robinson
December 1966 – Beat Billy Robinson in Bradford
8/2/67 – Beat Albert Wall
Billy Joyce 15/4/69 – London beat Gordon nelson for vacant title

Joint Promotions British light heavyweight title
1957 – Beat Ernie Riley
27/3/71 – Beat Tony Charles – Blackburn

Joint promotions European Heavyweight title
1961 – Beat Jim Olivera - Manchester

The Above titles were drawn from two main resources

---

[1] Mat review
[2] Physical chess – B.Robinson ,J Shannon ECW Press 201– page 24
[3] Roy Wood interview – Andrea Wood 2013
[4] Roy Wood interview – Andrea Wood 2013
[5] Shy Shoter of ther NOrth
[6] Shy Shooter of the north
[7] Dundee Courier and advertiser Uct 9 1952 – page 2
[8] Shy shooter of the north
[9] Courier and advertiser October 11 1952 page 3
[10] Shy shooter of the north
[11] Roy Wood interview – Andrea Wood 2013
[12] Physical chess – B.Robinson ,J Shannon ECW Press 201page 81
[13] Shy Shooter of the north
[14] Mat review
[15] Physical chess – B.Robinson ,J Shannon ECW Press 201– page 24

[16] Physical chess – B.Robinson ,J Shannon ECW Press 201– page 89 –
[17] Wrestler magazine June 1964 page 9
[18] Mat Review
[19] Roy Wood interview – Andrea Wood 2013
[20] Mat review
[21] Greeting grappling fans – location 576 – John Lister – Kindle edition
[22] Mat review
[23] Mat review
[24] Finally meeting princess maud – Shirley Thompson – Brewin Books – page 92
[25] Jayne Byrne interview November 2013
[26] Mat review
[27] Wrestler Magazine April 1965
[28] Mat review issue 203
[29] Wresling encyclopedia 1971
[30] Dynamite Kid – Japanese article – Translation E.Shahan
[31] The wrestler Magazine – October 1965
[32] Japanese article
[33] Michael Moore 10/7/14
[34] http://Rileygymkyoto.blog50.fc2.com/blog-entry-91.html
[35] Seamus Dunleavy interview July 2014
[36] Roy Wood interview September 2014
[37] Roy wood interview September 2014
[38] Billy Robinson post on Facebook on Matteo Boia Fadini wall 12 October 2011
[39] Roy Wood interview – Andrea Wood 2013
[40] Roy Wood interview – Andrea Wood 2013
[41] Mat review 523

Chapter 15

Joe Robinson

"Brilliant mind for wrestling, fantastic submission wrestler"

Older than his brother Bob, Joe was regarded as a great wrestler by those in the gym, although more naturally gifted, Joe was more laid back than his brother Bob who was more driven. A great friend of Billy Riley, there was still a rivalry that existed between them. Joe was known to coach in the gym on occasion if Billy was late or unable to attend. However he was very exacting. The following incident was recalled by Michael Moore "If you used to touch weights in the gym he would go mad. 'That's no good for thee is that' he would say. He came down to the gym when Billy was not so good. I used to see him in the working mans club 'I'll come down but if tha doesn't do as I tell thee I'm going home'. When I arrived some lads were on the mat so I went over to the weights by the big mirror to warm up. I picked up the barbell 'What's tha doing?' –.

[1]'I'm just warming up' 'I've told thee if tha touched those I'm doing one' he got up and walked out. I saw him few days later he said 'tha does it my way, tha knows nothing, I'm reet, I'm telling thee, tha's not telling me.'

Joe's personality was a contrast to that of his brother Bob. Joe had the natural talent but perhaps lacked the drive to apply it, it came naturally to him whereas Bob had to work for years before his genius locked into place, Joe liked socialising, and wasn't as focused on training.

Joe had, like his younger brother Bob worked down the mine. Jayne Byrne, Billy Riley's daughter

```
TO-NIGHT'S PROGRAMME
ENGLAND — v. — AMERICA
ATHOLL OAKELEY'S TEAM.                    HERBERT P. MORGAN'S TEAM.
              HEAVY-WEIGHTS. 2/3 Falls, K.O. or Points.
ATHOLL OAKELEY      v.    'Hard-boiled' Herbie Rosenberg
              RESULT_____
              LIGHT-HEAVY-WEIGHTS. 2/3 Falls, K.O. or Points.
ART. SPARKES        v.    CAB CASHFORD
              RESULT_____
              MIDDLE-WEIGHTS. 2/3 Falls, K.O. or Points.
LEN FISHER          v.    Amazing AMERSHAM
              RESULT_____
              WELTER-WEIGHTS. 2/3 Falls, K.O. or Points.
JOE ROBINSON        v.    RED ROSENTHALL
              RESULT_____
              LIGHT-WEIGHTS. 2/3 Falls, K.O. or Points.
LITTLE LARRY        v.    BUD BOWLEY
              RESULT_____
              BANTAM-WEIGHTS. 2/3 Falls, K.O. or Points.
JIMMIE GROGAN       v.    DWIGHT DENVERS
              RESULT_____
              FLY-WEIGHTS. 2/3 Falls, K.O. or Points.
JOHNNY SUMMERS      v.    HERMAN HEELE
              RESULT_____
```

remembered visiting the house of Joe and Bob's parents. She said that their father would stand at the foot of the stairs and squeeze an accordion loudy in order to wake up the boys for their work in the mornings. She also remembered that Joe had been involved in a collapse in the mine and had been trapped sustaining an injury to his chest, which affected his ability to wrestle.[2]

He had a business that traded in waste paper. He had a wagon with big tall sides collecting paper and cardboard selling it on[3].

Joe was a great friend of Billy Riley, although there was a friendly rivalry between them. The death of his friend had a terrible effect on him and he died a few months later.

---

[1] Michael Moore interview 10/7/14
[2] Jayne Byrne interview September 2014
[3] Roy wood interview 18/7/14

Chapter 16

Jack Dempsey

"One of the toughest little wrestlers ever to come out of the Wigan gym"

Born 25th November 1920[1], a face worker in the pit, Tommy Moore like a number of his contempories used wrestling as a means of escape from the hard grueling work, in his own words "It was actually to get away from the pit. It was bloody hard work down that pit" [2].

Tommy Moore started boxing at the age of 11 at the Wigan Boys club, which at the time was located on Clayton Street. As he grew he became more muscular which made him quite heavy for his height, which would have made matching him up for fights more difficult, he made the decision to change over to wrestling which seemed to suit his powerful physique better.[3]

He began work at the age of 15 in the Slipperworks in Wigan, however was soon to lose this position because he stood up for something he believed was right, he asked for a pay rise. His next job was in the Standish Bleachworks. The foreman put him on night shifts, when he approached the foreman to complain he was told, "either you go on nights or you go home". Years later his son was driving his father through Standish and his father told him to stop the car " I know him there". Michael stopped the car and his father got out, Michael could see and hear the conversation going on. "Hello,……(although Tommy remembered the mans name Michael has forgotten)", "do you remember me?". The man looked quizzically then it dawned on him " you're Tucker Moore". " My friends call me Tucker and you're not a friend of

Tommy Moore with son Michael

mine". He told him "do you remember what you said to me? Well I want to thank you , it was through you I was determined to make something of my life and I did , I became a professional wrestler made something of myself, I have wrestled around the world and appeared on Television and I did so I did not have rely on shithouses like you. I would like to thank you and shake your hand, I've been a somebody, you have been nothing but what you are, a shithouse"[4]

Living in in Vine Street [5] only a stone throw away from the gym, he started his apprenticeship under Riley.[6] He met Billy Riley through Charlie Carroll who was involved in sports ,predominantly boxing wrestling and Rugby. He put Tommy in touch with Billy Riley and he began training [7] aged 17[8] , like many other wrestlers thought about amateur competition. Norman Morell, a promoter, tried to persuade Tommy to enter the amateur ranks . He told Tommy "you'll clean them all up you'll beat them easy" however, on seeking advice from Billy Riley he was told what a number of other wrestlers were told about amateur wrestling "you cant live off cups and medals" and he decided to take his advice and turned professional [9].

He wrestled under the name of Dempsey, from his grandmothers side of the family, and took the

With the Lord Mountevans belt

name Jack because of his famous namesake in the Boxing world[10]. His grandmothers name was Mary Jayne Dempsey, not only did she contribute to his professional name, it was her who gave him the nickname of Tucker, something only his close friends were allowed to call him[11]

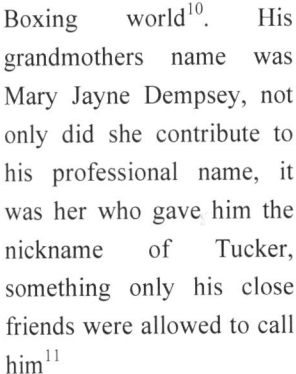

Tommy also helped the younger wrestlers at Riley's. Roy wood remembers training at Riley's gym "I learned a lot of submissions off Tommy. The only way you learned anything in Riley's gym was having them put on you and then if you were lucky someone may show you something. Tommy taught me a lot this way. I remember one day, he was helping me and my cousin Alan and he aid to me 'One day you two will know what this is worth'"[12]

The atmosphere of the gym can be summed up by Tommy's comments "all the lads in our gym looked on each other like a kind of brotherly love, we used to go on the mat pull each other to bits but we didn't bare each other any animosity"[13]

Not only a wrestler, Tommy was a good rugby league player, he was involved in a number of amateur teams as a scrum half also travelling to Bradford Northern several times to play for them[14]. He took part in the first competition for the Ken Gee cup[15]. He was also a "catcher", having great gymnastic skills and was often seen demonstrating his skills at the Wigan Hippodrome[16]. He was a keen swimmer, frequently swimming in the Westwood canal in his younger days [17]. He used his gymnastic skills to supplement his training and improve his flexibility. He would do hand springs, handstand walking, even up and down his stairs. Hand stand pressups were a staple of his routine, he didn't need weights, relying heavily on bodyweight exercises. His warm up consistsed of chins, dips, situps on the incline abdominal board, mat wrestling, pressups then he would put his legs over the chinning bar and do situps. He did use one weight in his warm up routine. Long before training with kettlebells became popular Rileys gym had one, in fact it is in the Snaekpit to this very day. It weighs an impressive 75lbs, and Tommy used to press it 12 times each arm as part of his warm up[18]

Tommy was part of the Rileys Rugby team known as the 'Baskeys', they were an amateur team made up from some very good players from the Riley's club. They won any trophies and there were moves to ban them from entering competitions due to their prowess.[19]

In 1948, the year he met lifelong friend Ernie Riley [20] he gained the British Lightweight title. Later gaining the British, European and World welterweight titles [21]. He was one of the first to wrestle on television, before wrestling was on ITV it was on the BBC and Tommy wrestled Ken Joyce. However Richard Dimbleby didn't approve of wrestling and it was taken off the air of the BBC and picked up by ITV[22]. Always happy to take on challenges to his titles his views are best summed up by his own statement on the matter "I don't mind putting my title up I know I can beat them all and each title shot is an extra pay day for me'"[23]. However, it was at the peak of his career in 1966 that he was dealt a cruel blow. He announced in October of that year he was retiring on ill health grounds[24]. He had seen his doctor and was diagnosed with a heart condition and had been ordered to rest[25]. This was a devastating blow to Tommy, "when I gave up wrestling due to my heart I was the British welterweight wrestling champion. I cancelled it. I came home and I burned all me training gear I was shattered, it was just like falling off the planet"[26]. On his announcement the Wrestler magazine commented "Rare combination of skill, Wigan type know how strength beyond his size and sheer courage"[27]. He had suffered a black out and had been diagnosed with a heart condition, fortunately this turned out to be incorrect[28]. In April/May 1967 he was passed by medical opinion as fighting fit. A columnist wrote, "I wrestled him ten years ago and today he's even better than he was then. Take my word for it he moves like a precision machine"[29]. One of his first bouts was at Belle Vue in Manchester against Bradford's Mike

Bennet and was noted to be looking fitter and faster than ever[30].

He was known for being a good show wrestler and being guaranteed to entertain the crowd [31] Although noted to be 'Smooth as silk' to work with, this seemed to be only the case if you did 'Tommy's show' ,Eddie Rose tells of the fact that during a match he tried to body slam Tommy, unfortunately he realized what he was doing , countered, lifted him up and slammed him into the ring whispering in his ear 'Tha doesn't slam t' fucking champion!!"[32] Like many of the wrestlers in Riley's he didn't suffer fools gladly. Eddie Rose in his book send in the clowns said "In Dempsey's opinion if you were not Wigan trained at Billy Riley's gym you were not a proper wrestler." Further exemplified by his comments on the Wryton Stadium gym, run by the Wryton promotions, "it was known as the "sausage factory" by Tommy Moore in that he felt it turned out "an endless supply of cheap poor quality workers for Wryton promotions"[33]. Michael Moore said that his father had the following thoughts on the Pro wrestling game at the time "Dad thought the pro game helped to kill "real" wrestling with too many

The 'Baskeys' Rileys gym Rugby team

clowns and gimmicks coming into it, and also people who could not wrestle. Dad challenged the likes of Mick McManus and Jackie Pallo in the 60's to real bouts as opposed to promoted pro bouts, but none would accept the challenge of wrestling him "on the level", as it was called."[34]

His favourite wrestling holds were hooking in and face bars. [35]

His son Michael also attended Riley's gym[36] and became a professional wrestler. However Tommy still kept a watchful eye on his son once admonishing Eddie Rose and Ian Wilson who had given Michael a lift back from a Pro bout in Birmingham. They had stopped in a motorway station on the way home for a cup of tea. Tommy wasn't amused and told them off for taking 'our Michael into expensive motorway cafes spending all his bloody wages when he's only five minutes from home".[37]

Also known for his great sense of humor Roy wood remembers a story about Tommy "I remember one time, there was a young family moved opposite Tommy. They asked me to have a word with Tommy saying that it upset his wife that Tommy would open his curtains naked. This young man seemingly afraid to approach Tommy himself asked me if I could have a quiet word. I agreed. When I mentioned it to Tommy he said " Well Roy you know, she doesn't have to be stood there waiting at half past eight every morning for me to do it tha' knows"[38]. In an interview Alan Latham recounted a incident that occurred with Tommy ", I'll tell you something funny, y'know, I would fly, I went through a period, I would fly to Belfast and going over the Isle of Man you always used to get turbulence and we were using

Michael Moore

those bloody Turbo props then. And I refused to fly for a long time, anyway I used to job for the hills and going to Paris, at this cirque d'éveil, when I had George Kidd here and another young wrestler Jack Dempsey there and three or four of them so we're in this hotel in Montpelier I think the fella who lived there before was bloody Toulouse Lautrec it were so old this bloody hotel well Dempsey says We're sharing rooms he said 'Do you mind sharing with me?', I said 'oh ok', he said 'I've had a funny experience today', I said 'have you righ?t', he said 'this old fella' he said when I come in he said' he were travelling I went in t'bathroom he said to have a shower he said, only he said there's a toilet bidet he said, I've used it he said I can't flush it', I said 'it's a bloody bidet', I said 'Well how's it gone down?' , he said 'I went and got an ice lollipop and I've pushed it round'.[39]

Dancing with Billy Riley's daughter Jayne

Stories told by his son Michael reveal a flavour of Tommy's character "Whilst playing a match for Bradford Northern, Dad kept using his skill and speed around the scrum. The opposition loose forward latched on to this and the next time Dad went around the blind side the Loose Forward stiff-armed him. The Loose Forward then tapped Dad on the head and said "you gotta be tough to play this game". He made the mistake of thinking that as he was bigger than Dad that he could get away with it. What a mistake! Dad took great exception to the lack of respect and he informed the Loose Forward that before the match was over he would stick the offending arm up his opponents arsee! When the Loose Forward took the ball up dad took his arm in a double wristlock and drove him into the pitch. The Loose Forward then realised what was going on and started to complain but it was too late for him, as Dad reminded him what he said he would do to him. This torture continued throughout the game. A foolish mistake to underestimate your opponent. Peter Rann the former wrestler from London, also noted on several occasions that the majority of the heavyweights were afraid of Dad because of his fitness, wrestling prowess and the fact he was a very hard man. Although Dad was always a straightforward honest gentleman, who did not like bullying or anything of that type. On another occasion driving around London, Dad saw man hitting his wife. Dad being the type of person he is got out of the car and got hold of the man to restrain him. The wife took exception to this and hit Dad with her hand bag, which had a rather large buckle on it that hit him in the mouth, knocking out two of his teeth."[40]

Like many of the wrestlers in Riley's, He took great comfort in his faith, he was a devout Catholic and would very often carry the banner for walking day for St Patrick's[41]

On his fellow wrestlers he talked of the mutual respect in the gym. With regards to Ernie Riley, Ernie stated that "we've become more or less like brothers", and Tommy recalled his chats with Ernie" we always have a good chat about wrestling, and sometimes about politics, although we have various views about politics, mines a bit left of Ernie's"[42]

He travelled, whilst being holder of the welterweight championship of Europe in 1949 in the summer he completed a tour of Spain[43]. He also toured France and Germany Belgium and Switzerland [44]. Whilst in France he - met Julian Maurice and travelled to the South of France. As a practicing Roman Catholic he tried to get to Lourdes, didn't manage to get there, got down to Le Mans and wrestled there. He liked French and German people.

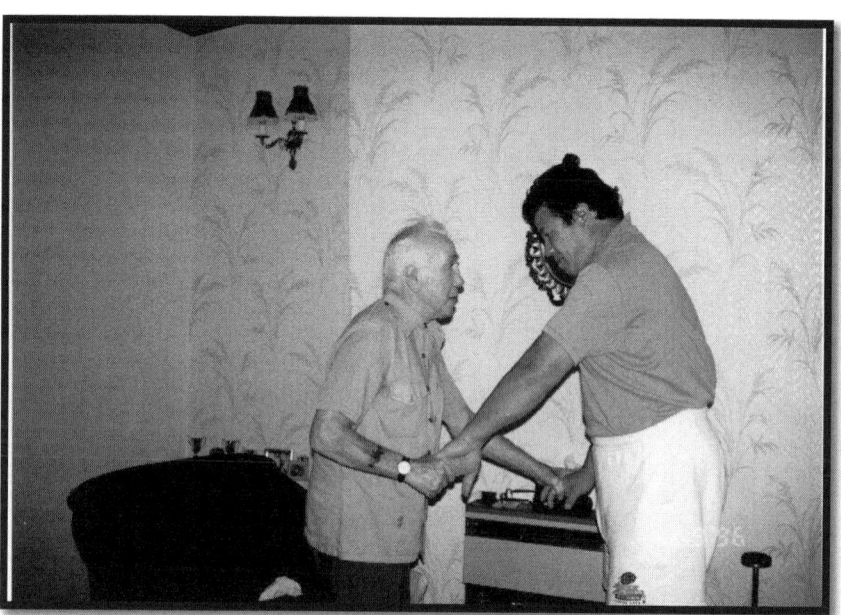

Tommy Moore demonstrating Lancashire catch to Fujinami

"people talk about the Germans this and Germans that , and French are funny . But people are people wherever you go". Although he travelled he didn't like it much preferring to stay near home.[45]

He retired aged 52 after 27 years in the ring, he had grown somewhat weary of the gimmicks being employed in the ring "in my time we were told to go in the ring and fight clean and to give the public some good entertainment not like the comedians you get now"[46]. In another interview he commented, "Wigan is the home of wrestling it used to be said you could stick your hand down any pit and drag out a top wrestler. I turned professional to get away from the pit. It was hard down there. The professional game is now an insult to people's intelligence. Today's professionals are overacting. I much prefer amateur wrestling. That's what got me excited as a young man as it does now"[47]

In 1974 in an interview with the Evening chronicle and post it was noted that he still wrestled privately with friends and was still a regular in the gym "we open as often as people want to come. What we really would like to do is teach youngsters how to wrestle. We'll teach anybody who wants to learn" this included his grandsons Paul and Mark , who although keen learners didn't want to enter the professional ring. He continued to work as an engineer at Gullick and Dobson of Ince [48].

Tommy ran a shop with his wife. Located on Vaughan street, around the corner from Wigan Rugby Leagues old central park stadium. It has since been demolished to make way for the new Tesco. The shop was a small mixed business. And was referred to as the original "open all hours"[49]. He had a son Michael and daughter Sheila.

Always well turned out Tommy became a well-recognised sight in his later years with his characteristic beret and bow tie.[50]

He was said to have a love of music especially Opera, his favourite composers being Mozart and Puccini. He was also a keen Ballroom dancer[51].

He spent his last years in Westwood Lodge Nursing Home in Poolstock. Just before his death his said to his son Michael "we've had our glory days us lad. If anyone ever tells you it couldn't be done, you tell them you've seen it could be done'"[52]. He died on 15th November 2007 at age 86[53]. His funeral held at St Mary's RC Church in Standishgate, he was later buried in Gidlow Cemetery on November 26 [54].

Titles

British Empire Welterweight title; 1954; Held until vacant in 1966 when Jack Dempsey temporary retires due to illness.

***British Lightweight title*; 1948;** Middlesborough

British Welterweight title; **1951, 1953, 1957, 1958**; vacant in 1966 when Jack Dempsey temporary retires due to illness

European Lightweight title; **1954**

European Welterweight title; **1954**; **25th Oct 1958**; Newcastle; **1959, 1960 & 1964** Dempsey regained title from Alan Colbeck.

World Welterweight title; **1956**; Leeds

Joint promotions Allstar Promotions British Welterweight title
1/1/53 – Beckenham – beat Mick McManus
23/4/58 – London beat Mick McManus
1959 –Joint promotions All star promotions European Welterweight title
1954
25/10/58 – Newcastle – beat Alan Colbeck
1969
1960

British empire Commonwealth Welterweight title
1964

BWA / Joint promotions British lightweight title
1954-
1948 – Middlesborough – Beat Joe Reid

Northern area Middleweight title Held in the 1960's

---

[1] Michael moore interview 10/7/14
[2] First Tuesday
[3] Michael moore interview
[4] Michael Moore interview 10/7/14
[5] Evening post and chronicle September 30th 1970
[6] Roy Wood interview – Andrea Wood 2013
[7] Michael Moore interview
[8] The Wrestler magazine March 1963
[9] First Tuesday
[10] Michael Moore interview 10/7/14
[11] Michael Moore 10/7/14
[12] Roy Wood interview – Andrea Wood 2013
[13] First Tuesday
[14] Michael Moore interview
[15] http://www.wigantoday.net/news/local/british-wrestling-champ-dies-1-179502British wrestling champ dies
[16] Roy Wood interview – Andrea Wood 2013
[17] First tuesday
[18] Michael Moore interview 10/7/14
[19] Michael Moore interview 10/7/14
[20] First tuesday
[21] Wrestling titles.com
[22] Michael Moore Interview 10/7/14
[23] The Wrestler October 1966
[24] The Wrestler October 1966
[25] The Wrestler November 1966
[26] First tuesday
[27] The Wrestler October 1966
[28] Micael Moore interview 10/7/14
[29] The Wrestler April 1967
[30] The Wrestler May 1967 Page 10
[31] Roy Wood interview – Nov 2013
[32] Send in the Clowns – Kindle Edition – Eddie Rose – YonYonson – 2012
[33] Send in the Clowns – Kindle Edition – Eddie Rose – YonYonson – 2012
[34] Michael moore interview 10/7/14
[35] Michael moore interview 10/7/14
[36] Wrestler magazine June 1967
[37] Send in the Clowns – Kindle Edition – Eddie Rose – YonYonson – 2012
[38] Roy Wood interview – Andrea Wood 2013
[39] Interview Alan latham
[40] Michae moore interview
[41] Roy Wood interview – Andrea Wood 2013
[42] First tuesday
[43] Castke feld wrestling programme August 1949
[44] The Wrestler March 1963
[45] Michael moore interview 10/7/14
[46] Evenig post and chronicle – September 30 1974
[47] Wigan Observer February 2nd 1989
[48] Evenig post and chronicle – September 30 1974
[49] Michael Moore 10/7/14
[50] Michael Moore 10/7/14
[51] The Wrestler March 1963
[52] Michael moore interview 10/7/14
[53] Michael moore interview 10/7/14
[54] http://www.wigantoday.net/news/local/british-wrestling-champ-dies-1-179502British wrestling champ dies

Chapter 17

George Gregory

Born in Bolton, George Gregory began wrestling not long after leaving school and having started work as a nursery man. The household was not far from the banks of the Rumworth lodge, where on a Sunday men known as the Sherwind gang would swim and wrestle. George took to it and excelled. At the age of 17 he was a member of the Lancashire wrestling amateur association and won the welterweight division 4 years in succession followed by further victories in the middleweight and heavyweight divisions.[1]

He travelled to Australia in 1929[2] predominantly to farm, but also did wrestle in matches and in booths and sideshows. He was said have won all of his matches[3]. Once he returned to England he knuckled down to his wrestling career and became one of the countries biggest draws. He also learned his trade from the great Billy Riley.

Like many of the wrestlers he didn't particularly advocate anything other than wrestling to keep fit, a smoker like many of the peers, he devoted his time to practicing grips, balance and muscle control. He felt the most important thing to be a good wrestler was to have 'that little bit of fire that makes you feel you can squeeze your man in two'. As for diet, although he did try being vegetarian for a period and indeed noted that whilst on the diet for six months he felt fitter than ever before ' didn't have that little bit of fire' and so returned to a meat laden diet, eating whenever he felt like it and not at any fixed times.

At the time period he was wrestling it was the 'All in style' that was in vogue. He had a dissatisfaction of the circumstances under which they worked and tried to organize a union for the sport on three occasions, running into problems where he lost money from a treasurer running away with the funds, the second suffered with too many people on the committee with too much talk and the third time the promoters said they would have nothing to do with it unless they had representatives on the committee, this was passed and they set about sabotaging the scheme.

Free Style WRESTLING
Broadway Palace, Chester, FRIDAY July 21st.
(OFF FOREGATE STREET)
(Licensed under the Wrestling Board of Control.) Doors open at 7 p.m. Commence at 8-15 p.m.
JACK CULLEN, the Premier Northern Wrestling Promotions presents--

Sensational Heavy-weight Challenge Contest. 12 - 5 min. Rounds.

GEORGE GREGORY
BOLTON. Known to all as "Gentleman George." Heavy-weight Tournament Winner Belle Vue, 1936. Has met all the best, including Sherry, Pojello, Clark, etc.
versus   CHALLENGER

BOB SILCOCK
WIGAN. (BLUE MASK.) This match has been brewing for months. Now made possible by Silcock's open challenge. It is understood that Silcock's connections wish to back him for any amount up to £30. This promises to be ... So here goes, and may the best man win.

Smashing Fly-weight Contest. 6 - 5 min. Rounds.

JOHNNY SUMMERS v **CURLY KENN**
CHORLEY. Official Fly-weight Champion.   BARNSLEY. A real good kid.

Special Middle-weight Contest. 8 - 5 min. Rounds.

CHICK MOORES v **JOE REID**
MANCHESTER. Pupil of Chick Elliott. A certain future champion.   LEIGH. 7 times Olympic Games man.

Great Cruiser-weight Contest. 10 - 5 min. Rounds.

TAFFY JONES
WALES. Claims to be Cruiser-weight Champion of Wales. versus

PAT MADDEN
MANCHESTER. A good genuine boy.

USUAL POPULAR PRICES:
Ringside 3/-   Outer Ring 2/-   STANDING & TEIRING 1/-
Ladies specially Invited :   1/- to all Parts   (including tax)
Seats may be booked at the Broadway Palace.   Telephone Chester 3080

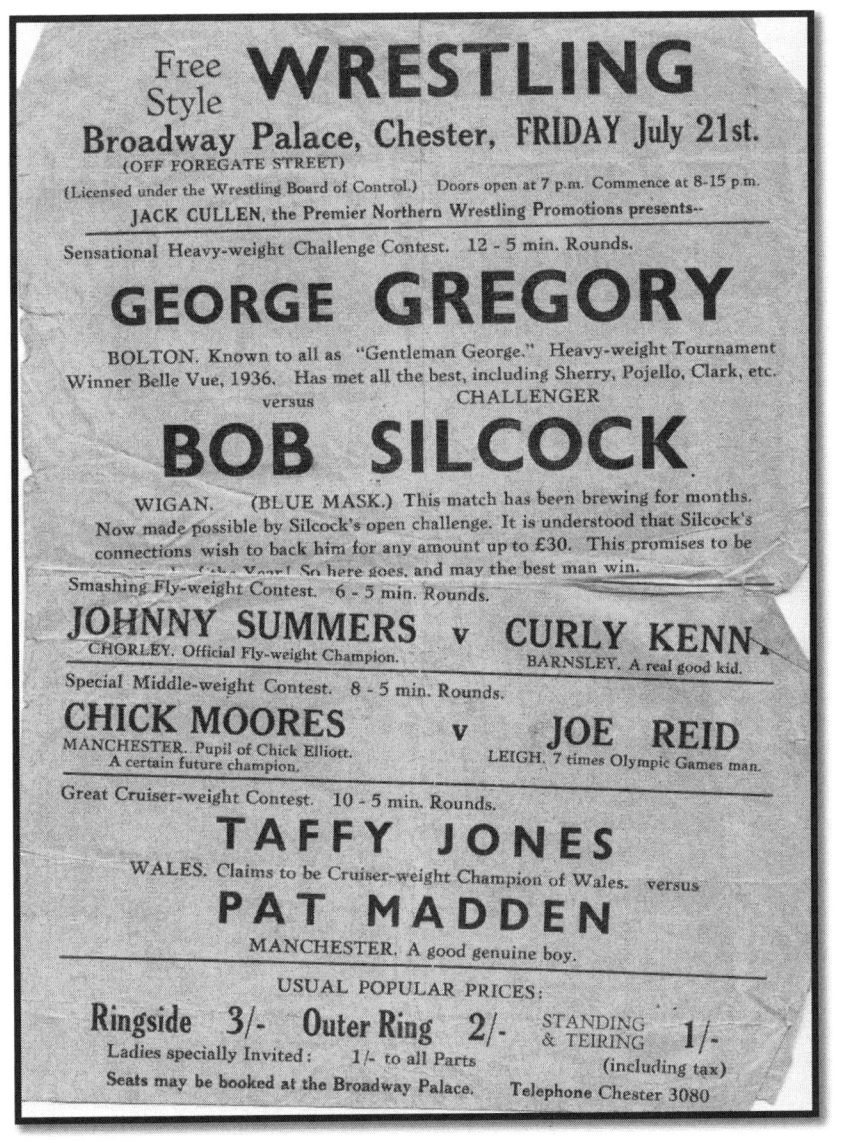

However he noted the most difficult thing was getting to organsie the wrestlers themselves, with so many across the country it meant wrestlers would work for a pittance, and than anyone that could put on an act was getting into the ring.

He suffered a number of injuries throughout his career including breaks and dislocations such as 3 shoulder injuries, one knee and two ankles.

He noted his toughest fight was at Belle Vue against De Groot for the European championship where he suffered a rib injury during the first round and continued through the match despite breathing being very painful. Footage of this match exists within the old newsreels.

He lost his title to Bert Assirati. He worked for the joint promotions, which his mentor Billy Riley was part of and was a star attraction during the early period.

One of his bouts in 1937 was reported as following

"George Gregory of Bolton the light heavyweight champion of England beat Jack Atherton of London who retired in the seventh round with a damaged shoulder on one of a number of free style wrestling contests at Blackpool tower circus last night.

Gregory gained a fall in the third round after the referee had intervened twice in the previous round to break the wrestlers. The contestants were a well-matched pain who each showed amazing strength and great agility. Atherton climbed out of the ring in the third round but Gregory was soon after him. He pulled him back and gained a fall with a flat body press. The Londoner continued but in the seventh round had the misfortune to damage a shoulder thus ending a thrilling contest.[4]

No higher accolade can be said than the fact the Bob Robinson rated him as the one he rated the highest.

---

[1] Portsmouth Evening News - Saturday 09 December 1933
[2] Portsmouth Evening News - Saturday 09 December 1933
[3] Portsmouth Evening News - Saturday 09 December 1933
[4] Lancashire Daily Post 16/1/37

Chapter 18

Charlie Carroll

Charlie Carroll was born at the turn of the 20th century, no relation of the famous Carroll family of wrestlers, started as part of Billy Riley's group of wrestlers at the Crispin arms, where Charnock had taught Billy. In fact, Charlie was Billy's main training partner for Riley's title defense match against Reginsky.

In 1933 Jack Carrol ("The Whistler") famous catch as catch can wrestler, tried reviving the sport in the Wigan district by organizing a tournament. He was to face the "Black Devil", a sparring partner of Battling Siki a London wrestler. However, on the day of the tournament the "Black Devil" did not turn up for the match and Charlie Carroll stepped in at the last moment. The account of the match in the Wigan Examiner is as follows:

"Jackie Carrol ("whistler") 11 stone world's champion and Lord Lonsdale belt holder, wrestled Charley Carrol ("Chuck"), Wigan. The veteran got a wonderful ovation and gave many interesting points, which were eagerly followed by the younger generation of wrestlers. "Chuck" Carroll, who deputized for a London wrestler who failed to turn up, was not dismayed, and put up a good fight. There will certainly be more heard of him in the near future. He possesses all the qualities that go to make a good wrestler. The champion ("Whistler") gained the verdict in this bout in 11 minutes and 8 seconds.[1]

I once had a conversation with Tommy Heyes in the Wigan museum of life where he told he story of Charlie Carroll telling him how to control a wrestler by controlling their hands and then proceeded to demonstrate on me much to the amusement of some and the annoyance of many others in the library.

Roy Wood remembers Charlie at the Gym. He remembered that he used to come to the gym regularly to se and have a chat with Billy, then one day Billy didn't turn up and Charlie started teaching it was only at that point that Roy realised he was a wrestler.

Charlie Carroll was one of the first wrestlers that Billy Robinson sparred with at Riley's, and despite the fact that he was in his early fifties and Billy out weighed him by a good thirty counts he beat Billy easily[2].

A similar story is told by Seamus Dunleavy "I was on the mat one morning, and I was in good nick, I was 22 or 23 and I was strong growing up and my mother was a strong woman. Charlie come in after a shift and I've never seen the like before, and he had the miners face and he stripped off and he was like a milk bottle and I though Christ almighty. I arrived on the mat with him and I couldn't do anything with him I couldn't bend his arms or his legs. But he was on of the old school wrestling up and down Lancashire for money in the old days. and I though to myself 'bloody hell' but then someone turned to me and said "that's Charlie carol he's been going for bloody years', but he never came that much as Charlie was pushing on. I had a lot of respect for him after that."[3]

Charlie had a daughter Alison who went to school with Michael Moore, Jack Dmepsey's son.

---

[1] Wigan Examiner, June 11th 1933
[2] Physical chess – B.Robinson ,J Shannon ECW Press 2012 page 17
[3] Seamus dunlevay interview July 2014

Chapter 19

Karl Gotch

'The truth only hurts a fool, I've been around a long time and I've found out the world is full of fools because nobody can stand the truth.'[1]

Karel Charles Istaz was born in Antwerp, Belgium 3rd August 1924, and was said to have been brought up in Hamburg, Germany. In wrestling magazines stories of Gotch's childhood vary with some asserting he was a German youth interred in Hamburg's concentration camp[2] What is clear is that like many other professional wrestlers, there is a substantial amount of myth and legend associated with the late Karl Gotch, but with few reputable sources to corroborate and separate myth from fact.

The embellishments of wrestling magazines and newspapers give a mythos of a young Karl Gotch destitute in Hamburg, Germany. One account says that Karl's father was executed by the Nazi's during World War II and Alphonse, and an older brother of Karl was killed in action on the Russian front. Karl, who shared his father's anti-Nazi beliefs was sent to a concentration near Hamburg, Germany known as Stalag Veddel. *'His captors decided it would be a waste to shoot a fine example of German manhood as Karl. He would work for the fatherland, so he laboured on the railroad with French prisoners of war.'*[3] However, another account of his youth was recounted by Karl in an interview in 'Official Wrestling', February 1964. *'I had 8 years of grade school, but after that I attended trade school. This is the custom in Europe. Children do not automatically go on to high school... Because I seemed physically able for it, I was put in Blacksmith school. This had nothing to do with shoeing horses, but was concerned with making anchors and chains for large ships.*

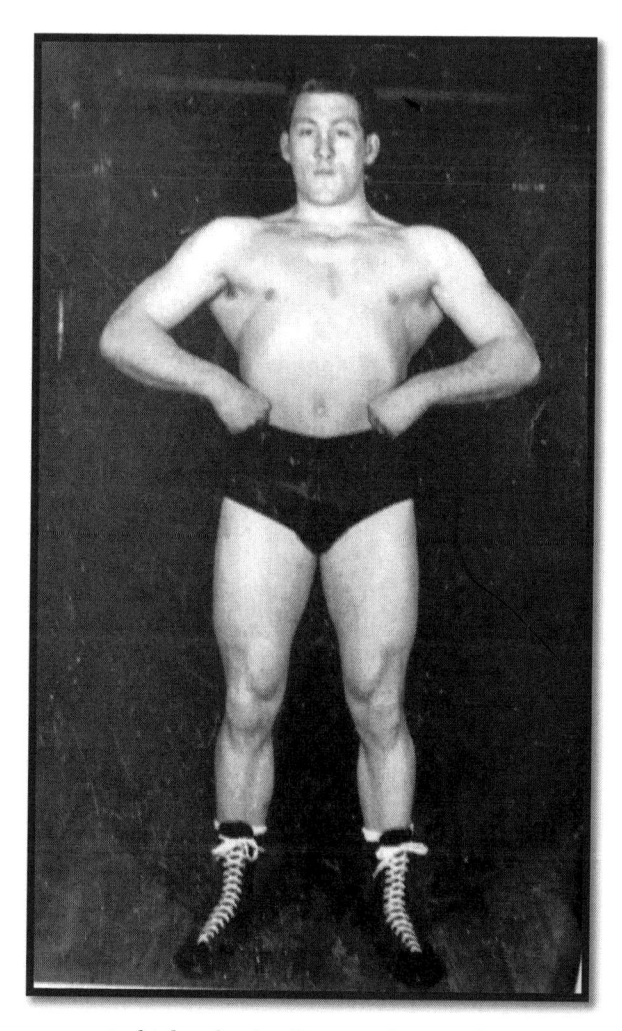

Before long I was swinging a great sledgehammer against an anvil. Then I would be employed as a long-shoreman loading and unloading ships.'[4]

In interviews Karl Gotch recounts stories of a successful amateur career in Germany in the Greco-Roman Style. Claims attributed to Karl Gotch are of *'being undefeated as a novice,' 'winning 17 national titles to become Landesmeister Heavyweight Champion of Germany,'*[5]. Whilst many keen amateur historians, including those whose native language is German, have endeavoured to confirm such achievements, the evidence to support these results has not yet been secured. Karl Gotch stated that as a young man he would learn to wrestle in German taverns which acted as equivalent to the British athletic clubs for the German youth. *'Fortunately for me, Hamburg was one of the centres of wrestling for Germany and I was able to, as you say in the U.S, 'fall in' when a chance came up to become a member of one of the many wrestling clubs in my city. Most of the larger taverns in Hamburg were in reality, athletic organisations, some devoted to duelling... Some of the taverns sponsored soccer clubs, other engaged in boating but a goodly number provided facilities for wrestling. These wrestling organisations built additions at the back of the tavern proper with usually excellent facilities for the would be aspirants of the grappling art...There were 35-40 tavern backed wrestling clubs in Hamburg, many of them with exceptional facilities which are available to youngsters and young men of all ages virtually free of charge. The tavern owners would arrange these facilities so that you could practice at any hour of the day when the tavern was open for trade and unusually provided a more experienced person who would give instruction in the sport.'*[6] However in the short film Kamisama; The Karl Gotch story, Karl said *'It was wartime, so when it came to my time to learn or while I was there, there was nobody there. They were in the war and they didn't come back so I had to think for myself and build myself up in every way that I could..... but what took me years to get, I could of learnt in months if I had somebody like me to help me.'*[7]

The earliest confirmed references to the early career of Karel Istaz relate to the 1948 Summer Olympics. Whilst some articles have claimed that Gotch won gold as an Olympian in 1952 Helsinki Games[8][9] this is false as Karel Istaz didn't compete in those games. Karl's Olympic record stands as; 1948 Summer Olympic Greco-Roman Light heavyweight competition, in his first match he was defeated by Kelpo Groendahl (Finland) in 3 min 54 secs[10]. He then defeated Athanase Kabaflis (Greece) but in the 3rd round lost to G. Kovacs (Hungary) by a fall in 4min 1 sec[11]. In both Freestyle and Greco Roman styles he had a couple of repechage matches. His Olympic wrestling career consisted of 1 win and 5 losses. Karel Istaz was eliminated out of both Wrestling competitions in the 3rd round after receiving a bye for the 2nd round in Freestyle wrestling[12].

Karl Gotch turned to professional wrestling in the early 1950's, however *'there was no such thing as professional wrestling in Germany on a grand scale. Everything was controlled by the state.'*[13]

Karl Gotch was said to be competing in France when some English wrestlers told Karl about Billy Riley's gym, Wigan. *'Riley is a former wrestler who fought in the United States many times in the 1930's* (note: he actually travelled in the 1920s with one confirmed 6 month tour). *He and his partner Joe Robinson were teaching other men how to become the best. It was explained to me that the training would be very hard and that it was unlikely that I would want to stay long, but I was welcome to try.*[14]' He recounted the time in the gym as follows *'during the sessions at the school that Gotch learned more fundamentals of wrestling than ever before. The relentless charges of the fearless breed who were his opponents gave Karl the added experience he was seeking. He further realised he would have to learn quickly how to cope with the Catch-as-Catch-can style the school instructors taught their recruits.'*[15] Karl Gotch relayed in another interview with Joe Tendler *'many of those wrestlers were tougher than most of the wrestlers I've met in America. They had no mercy in their hearts and if you made the mistake of pitying them you might as well leave town on the next bus!'*[16] Consistently, in interviews held with Karl Gotch during his career, he paid reference and respect to his mentors Billy Riley and Joe Robinson. *'I give credit for any and all success to Billy Riley, the old master at Wigan, England.'*[17] Karl expanded further *'Two Englishmen, Billy Riley & Joe Robinson, have been important factors in my career. When I first visited England years ago, they took me under their wing and taught me many of the tricks they used.... they were among the top European wrestlers of their time.'*[18] Karl had pride in the teachings of Riley's gym stating *'Billy and I have the same teacher; a former Irish middleweight champion named Bill Riley. I think that Riley's Rebels, as we students call ourselves, have more than proved we can hold our own in the wrestling world.'*[19] Karl is attributed as having said *'The young huskies that endured the Snake pit called themselves 'Riley's rebels' The tuition was the equivalent of just a few dollars a week to cover expenses and Riley and Robinson apparently took no salary.'*[20] In one of his interviews with Bob Leonard, Karl recounted *'When Riley trained you, you learned to wrestle in the strictest sense of the word.*[21]' Karl continued regarding the training methods *'You learned the basic moves first, really learned them, and then refined them. Nothing was*

With the Compliments of
KAREL ISTAZ
(BELGIUM)

neglected! When you left Wigan, you took with you the benefit of the knowledge that Billy has gained in thousands of matches; that knowledge of true wrestling let me work against any man, no matter what his background of training, and effectively combat him.... But basically I do all these things by applying the knowledge of Billy Riley.'[22]

Karl Gotch was a keen fan of conditioning exercises promoting the use of traditional routines involving 'Hindu squats and Hindu pushups.... supposing I were in the gymnasium, I'd do about 300 squats and maybe 75 or 100 pushups.... then I'd do some front and back bridges and abdominal exercises... to finish off I'd throw the medicine ball for a short while.'[23] Whilst other coaches promoted the use of weights and in some wrestling promotions steroids were widely used, Karl simply said 'Everybody wants to use weights, I don't. I use my own bodyweight'[24]. Karl Gotch was a man who impressed upon others the need for conditioning. His renowned workouts were challenges of the human condition. Frank Shamrock described Gotch as 'a freak about conditioning. His theory was that if you conditioned enough, no one could beat you.'[25]

A workout associated with Gotch was 'Gotch's Bible' simple and effective in its design. A deck of cards is shuffled, including two Jokers, the Black cards are squats and red cards are push-ups. The black cards when dealt are doubled i.e. a six becomes 12 squats, the red cards value is the number of push-ups i.e. 8 is 8 push-ups. Spades are Hindu squats, Clubs are jumping squats, Diamonds are Hindu push-ups, Hearts are ½ Moon push-ups. When the 1st Joker is drawn you do 40 Hindu squats consecutively, when the 2nd Joker is drawn you do 20 Hindu push-ups consecutively.

In his matches in the United States, Karl Gotch would be billed as European Heavyweight Champion *'In dynamic and spectacular fashion he faced six of the best heavyweight in Europe and emerged from the tournament as the European titleholder.'*[26] *'Karl Gotch, European heavyweight champion, defeated Bob Viking Morse.'*[27] The Professional wrestling records in Europe have Karel Istaz come first in a tournament-taking place in Monchen-Gladbach, Germany[28], however Karel Istaz lost to Gideon Gida during the course of the tournament.

Karl Gotch spent time in Western Canada with reports stating *'Karl has never been defeated, though scores of matches against the top competition that promoters Rod Fenton, Stu Hart and Cyclone McAlpine have thrown his way.'*[29] Karl bested the *'Mormon Mammoth'* Don Leo Jonathan in one of the few defeats of his career. In his spell in Canada, Karl proved the victor against Sandor Kovacs, Big Hansen of Denmark lasted 2 mins in a match against Gotch and the likes of Tiger Joe Tomasso were caught in a *'Boston crab'* after 5 minutes of wrestling[30]. Karl Gotch was popular amongst the Canadian populace and he performed in tandem with some of the wrestlers he faced in the ring. Tag team matches involved Karl teaming with the Mormon Mammoth, Don Leo Jonathan and Roy McClarty against the likes of the 'Fabulous Kangaroos'[31].

Karl Gotch had various Tag team partners including Mike Debiase, Alex Medina, Han Lee and Ron Romano to name a few. Karl Gotch & Mike Dibiase held the Worldwide Wrestling Associates Tag team championship title. In a contentious affair in 1967 *'Pedro Morales and Victor Rivera won the Worldwide Wrestling Association title last night at San Bernardino Arena from Mike DiBiase and Karl Gotch but don't have the belts to show for it. Just when Referee Hank Metheny was preparing to hand the WWA belts to Morales and Rivera, DiBiase and Gotch grabbed them, ran to the dressing room and refused to return them.'*[32] In response to this *'The latin sensations defeated the WWA champs last week, but Gotch and DiBiase refused to give up the belts. The purses were held up, and the WWA ordered a return match. It will be for 2-of-3 falls within one hour.'*[33]

Karl Gotch headed to Canada in 1959 and after making an initial impression, word travelled to Al Haft, who wanted to see Karl wrestle in Ohio. Karl Gotch bought a home in Reynoldsburg, Ohio and brought over his wife, Ella and daughter Janine[34]. According to Tim Hornbaker, *'Haft possessed a good eye for amateur talent, stemming from his true fascination with the fundamentals of wrestling, and a multitude of college athletes were lured into pro-wrestling and schooled at his famous gymnasium on third floor of 261 S. High Street. Some of the best wrestling matches occurred there, hidden away from the public, and Haft's gym was a place where reputations were made and destroyed. Silverstein,*

Bill Miller and Karl Gotch stretched young up-and-comers and a host of future legends gained instruction they would carry for their entire careers.'[35] It was Al Haft who had Karel Istaz adopt the name of 'Karl Gotch' to distance him from the previous moniker Karol Krauser which he felt sounded too German.

Karl Gotch found the stylistic difference between the wrestling he had been used to in Britain and Europe with America troublesome. '*Gotch was astonished by the rough-house tactics he encountered here after he 'scientifically' demolished the top stars in winning the Europe... It was difficult at first to believe an opponent would kick me, jab me in the eyes, use his elbows and fists.. In this country, wrestlers even shove referees around. You try that just once in Europe and the referee would disqualify you on the spot. Then you'd be suspended. In Europe they wrestle more and fight less. Over here you have to knock out a man to win most of the time. It does not seem to matter how you do it, just so you flatten him.*'[36] Karl said '*In Europe they wrestle more scientific and before one can become a professional he must have a wrestling background of at least 7 years as an amateur. One learns to wrestle Greco-Roman and free-style over there... In the Americas and Canada, the toughest obstacle to overcome is the rough and unruly style.*'[37] The wrestling magazines said '*Gotch headed for Canada, where he got his first taste of the free-wheeling, American style of rough house wrestling. He was jabbed, kicked, mauled, gouged and surprised... He never expected anything like this and it threw him off stride badly.*'[38] But given the level of training Karl Gotch had received at Riley's gym '*In Europe, against the club wrestlers I had been great and seldom knew defeat. But in the Snake pit I learned about submission holds; those not intended for a pin, but to inflict so much pain that your opponent submits; and this was something new to me. Such things as a wrist lock and a crooked head scissors gave me much trouble.*'[39] Verne Gagne said of Gotch '*You have to give him all the credit in the world. He had to learn a new style, and he did it in record time. Right now, I would say he's one of the top wrestler's in the world.*'[40] However, the wrestling press were quite positive of Karl Gotch's stint in America & Canada '*Gotch himself has been perhaps the biggest standout during the past few months, and his illustrious record speaks for itself. Karl has defeated virtually every wrestler of note campaigning in North America.*'[41] To Gannon in 1960 said '*Gannon states the new Karol is actually Karel Istaz who has a good reputation in Europe and is billed from Belgium, Istaz is a far better wrestler that is Edouard Carpentier who is known under the names of Eduardo Wieckorsky or Eddy Wiecz* '[42] Karl Gotch was growing disenfranchised with the state of wrestling and allegedly carried a photo of Pesek, whom he idolised '*I hope the style made popular by those men comes back some day.*'[43] Gotch remised.

Karl Gotch would face up against the late great Lou Thesz more than eight times over the course of his career. In the match for the 2nd May 1964, Detroit Michigan, Karl Gotch injured Lou Thesz in the midst of the bout. Allegedly, during the course of the bout when Lou Thesz attempted to perform a suplex (Greco-Roman drop), Karl Gotch took the opportunity to shoot on Lou. Lou Thesz suffered five broken ribs due to Gotch's double-cross. Publically concerning his injury Lou Thesz said "*I was back at it in 10 weeks. And you know, I always say I never pick my opponents, but I was careful not to go in there against anybody too good for a while.*"[44] However, comments made from those close to Thesz attribute the following to Lou "*I still had the resort in Tucson at the time, so I crawled back there and holed up in my room. I slept on a mattress on the floor and had food sent in from the kitchen; I saw nobody, because I didn't want to be around people, and I didn't want anyone to see me in that condition. Broken ribs are extremely painful, and I was a long time healing. Mike DiBiase came around a couple of times just to check on me, but that was it in terms of companionship.*" [45] Whilst another states '*Lou never indicated he thought Karl intentionally hurt him with the broken ribs, but he felt Karl was trying to show his skills as a shooter and by not telling Lou they were shooting, endangered them both.*'[46] Records of the match state it ended in a draw but Lou said '*When Karl blocked him, it hit Lou immediately that something was up, and he ended things immediately. "I made him howl," is how Lou put it.'* [47]

Karl was involved in an incident with a prominent wrestler in September 1962, Buddy Roger's was the World Champion, he and Karl Gotch had been scheduled to be on the same fight card at the Coliseum, Columbus, Ohio. In a renowned spat, the pair met in the dressing room and *'One word led to the other and then we were going at each other,'* [48] Gotch said. During the altercation *'everybody cleared out in seconds'* the fight allegedly lasted minutes but Buddy Rogers suffered an elbow injury. The article recollects that Buddy Rogers was unable to wrestle for some weeks post altercation leading to the cancellation of several bouts. Another account gives the event as *'he was in the locker room when Karl Gotch and Bill Miller, two tough but popular big men, smashed his hand in a door.'* [49] Buddy Rogers did file a charge with the sheriff's office which Gotch and Miller admitted to and paid a fine. This combined with the low draw for Gotch's matches served as the death knell for Gotch in the United states professional wrestling circuits.

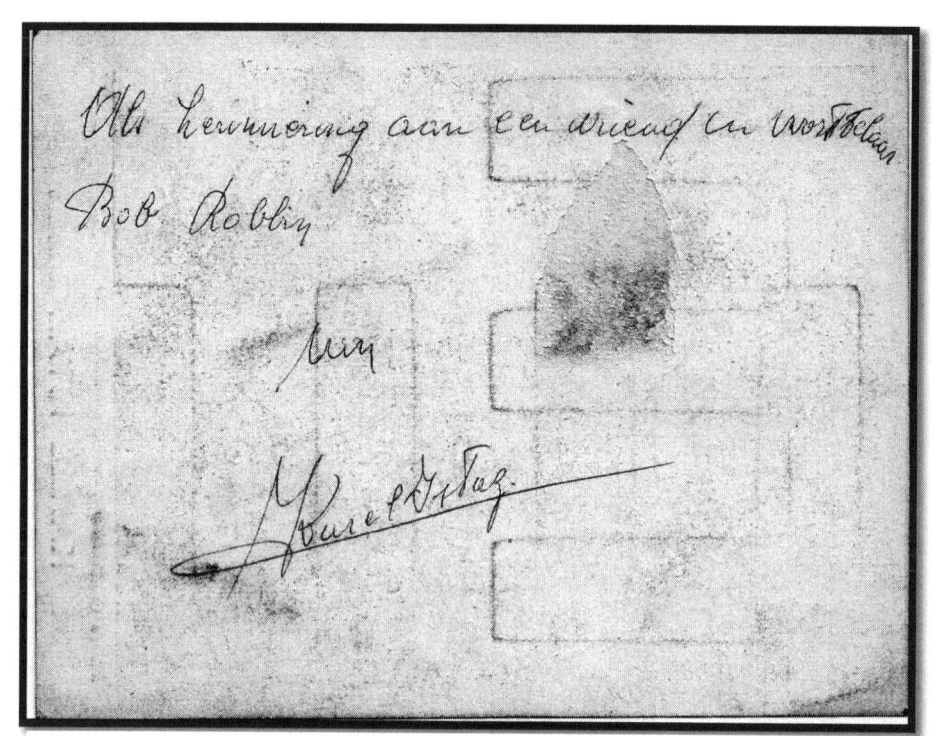

Note to Bob Robinson

Karl Gotch had toured in the Southern hemisphere and Japan during the 1960s, and following the incident in the Coliseum the Eastern market was one of the few circuits available to Gotch. It was during this time that he developed a relationship with Antonio Inoki, Antonio Inoki trained under Karl Gotch for 2 years in the United States[50] (1963-1965) so much so that when Inoki started his own promotion, the initial billing was between the two.

Karl Gotch wrestled for a number of promotions in his career, All Star Wrestling (ASW) in Vancouver, American Wrestling Alliance (AWA), Worldwide Wrestling Associates (WWA), New Japan Pro Wrestling (NJPW) and World Wide Wrestling Federation (WWWF).

It was with Rene Goulet that he reached the most famous achievement in wrestling with the WWWF Tag team World Championship title on December 6, 1971. *'One night in Madison Square Garden, Karl Gotch & Rene Goulet combined forces and defeated the deadly duo in straight falls.. A head butt, a forearm smash and a beautifully executed mule kick sent Graham reeling to the mat. Gotch seeing an opening came in close to Tyler, bounced off the ropes and quickly applied a reverse jack knife for the pin...He picked up Goulet and applied an airplane spin, knocking him first into Graham and then onto Tyler. As both men lay on the floor, Gotch hurled Goulet onto the fallen Graham, and ran over towards Tyler to prevent him from interfering. Referee Danny Bartfield counted to three and Gotch & Goulet were declared the new champions.'* [51] Whilst Gotch had been once associated with straight wrestling, Al Haft a promoter from Reynoldsburg, Ohio said *'he was that rare commodity in the mat world – a man without a gimmick, just science.'*[52] his greatest wrestling achievement would be won without the application of the straight wrestling art of Billy Riley *'catch-as-catch-can'* but with theatrical 'professional wrestling' moves. As the professional wrestling style was changing there were some that criticised the direction that the WWWF were taking. In relation to the criticisms levelled at the WWWF style of wrestling Gorilla Monsoon said *'If we gave people, collegiate or international or AAU type wrestling, the arenas would be empty. We add color.'*[53] During his time with the WWWF Karl Gotch was classed as one of the wrestling good guys for the promotion. Karl Gotch's time with the WWWF was limited for when Inoki proposed that Gotch become a booker he accepted. "He got an offer to become the booker in Japan for Inoki," says Rene Goulet. "We were wrestling in Philadelphia, and some of his guys came up there to make the offer to Karl. He accepted, and that was the end of our tag team. When McMahon (Vince Sr.) found out about it, he was really (ticked). We dropped the belts at the following TV to King Curtis (Iaukea) and (Baron) Mike Scicluna."[54]

The pro-wrestling circuit in Japan wasn't the up to the same standards as the western markets, the promotions acted as territories for the American promotions NWA, AWA. The bigger draws were for 'Japan Vs Foreign wrestlers'. When Inoki was fired from the Japan Pro-Wrestling promotion for planning a takeover he formed the New Japan Pro Wrestling promotion. The first bout was Antonio Inoki and Karl Gotch, held on the 3rd June 1972. Karl Gotch would compete with Inoki on a number of events, one such match included Karl Gotch and Lou Thesz against Antonio Inoki and Seiji Sakaguchi on the 14th October 1974. Inoki & Sakaguchi proved victorious in the bout.

Antonio Inoki was a promoter of *'strong style'* of professional wrestling rather than the popular gimmick lead style found internationally. Tom Billington (Dynamite kid) recollected *'Karl Gotch who trained at Riley's gym and was working as the top wrestling coach for Inoki. The promotion would send all its young boys to the NJPW dojo in Tokyo to be trained by him.'*[55] Tom Billington believed that Gotch had a high opinion of himself and his coaching ability, when talking about Joe & Dean Malenko he said *'I rated both of them. Karl Gotch had trained them and as usual, boasted to everybody about what a good job he'd done; so good he reckoned Joe was unbeatable on the floor.'*[56]

Following Inoki and Gotch's match the NJPW organisation attracted the likes of Satoru Sayama, Yoshiaki Fujiwara and Akira Maeda. Whilst these men were already proficient in their respective arts they would add the *'strong style'* of professional wrestling that Inoki favoured. Gotch is attributed at having trained these men with a blend of the wrestling and conditioning exercises accrued over his career. These men combined their fighting specialism with the submission wrestling promoted by Gotch to develop their own unique *'hybrid-fighting styles'*[57]. Tom Billington was impressed with the wrestler Satoru Sayama as he had combined the wrestling style of Mexico with his Japanese style, he recounted *'MaxCrabtree was watching Sayama get ready, shaking his head and saying 'What the fucking hell has Karl Gotch sent me?.. Sayama was fantastic'*[58]

During the 1980's and 90's the promotions fractured with the members splintering off to form the likes of the UWF (Universal Wrestling Federation), Newborn UWF, Japan Pro-Wrestling, UWFI, Fighting Network RINGs.

According to Frank Shamrock, Karl Gotch trained various Japanese fighters including Yoshiaki Fujiwara, who founded the Fujiwara Gumi, which trained the Pancrase fighters. Shamrock reminisced *'Gotch's and Fujiwara's pictures were on the wall at the entrance to the mats. Every morning we would have to line up and bow to them before beginning our workout.'*[59] The dojo head was Masaru Funaki, a man shamrock greatly respected. Shamrock attributed a large part of their training to conditioning exercises which he identified as *'the Gotch legacy.'*[60] Shamrock said *'Maybe that's why the Japanese loved him so much. It was all about repetition and ritual..We'd do three hundred squats in a row, all counting out loud, all together. Then we'd do the exact same number of sit-ups, and the exact same number of push-ups, and so on. We did that all day, six days a week.'*[61]

In time, as Fujiwara's promotion 'Fujiwara Gumi' began to co-operate with other promotions and favoured the showmanship element of wrestling key members of the organisation splintered. In 1993, Masakatsu Funaki, Minoru Suzuki, Takaku Fuke and Masami Ozaki established World Pancrase Create Inc. more commonly known as Pancrase, allegedly with a blessing from Karl Gotch, to focus on pure shoot-style wrestling[62].

The presence of fighters like Funaki[63], who were submission based, meant that action was based on technique with many matches decided on the ground, however with the presence of the ropes a wrestler had but to make their way to the edge to be stood up and escape defeat. Ken Shamrock was a key fighter who joined the organisation from the professional wrestling scene, as was Bas Rutten, a Dutch kick-boxer who would win the King of Pancrase tournament 3 times.

The new forms of 'Japanese professional wrestling' bore little resemblance to the wrestling art taught to Gotch in Riley's gym, Wigan but it was undoubtedly influenced by it. However, Gotch's outlook was *'Wrestling is like a language, it lives. I always try and put an improvement on it.'*[64]

Karl Gotch had been a resident of Florida for many years. Billy Robinson elected to tour there in 1975 so that he could allegedly be close to Gotch as he was going through a difficult time. According to *'The Pro Wrestling Hall of Fame: Heroes and Icons'* Karl Gotch's wife had cancer at the time and Billy Robinson wanted to be nearby for support.[65]

Karl with Ed 'Strangler' Lewis

Over the course of his career Karl would state that there were many men that he highly rated depending upon the promotion he was working with. *'Buddy Rogers 'Man! This guy is unstoppable. When you're in the ring with him you feel like you're wrestling a tank.'*[66] Karl said that *'I came to Vancouver and the rest of Western Canada is because some of the greatest wrestling talent on Earth is concentrated here,'* In another interview Karl Gotch spoke highly of Big Bill Miller. *' You know Big Bill Miller has not only a wonderful amateur wrestling background...Wrestling him is something like trying to wrestle a big snake, bear and a lion all combined into one man.'*[67] In the same piece Karl espouses *'I would rate Von Erich the best, by all means. Fritz is very much like Bill Miller but a more savage competitor, who doesn't use science when power will do.'*[68]

Karl stated that the best wrestler bar none was *'the old fox Lou Thesz. Lou knows every trick of the trade... Thesz best offense is a double wristlock. It's one thing you have to be alert for at all times, and be prepared to block it from any position.'*[69] Karl felt that the similarity between Lou Thesz and his wrestling stemmed from *'both Lou and I learned to wrestle by utilizing the experience of the old time greats.. Lou picked up many of the same theories and tricks that I did under Billy Riley and the other European wrestlers.'*[70] In the same article Karl said ' *I know from experience that with men like Billy Joyce, Bill Robinson and George Gordienko...an English team would give almost any of the Americans a tough night,*[71]*'* In a later article Karl would again give praise to Bill Robinson. *'When I wrestled Bill Robinson it was like wrestling my shadow because Bill has patterned his whole wrestling style after mine. I tried to duplicate the style of the great Bert Assirati in my early years, and now Bill is copying me. Verne Gagne is a fine athlete and I respect him and everything he stands for, but I feel that Billy Robinson will win the AWA World title from Gagne in the near future.'*[72] Karl said *'Billy is one of the top men in Europe today, and although I have not seen the boy for some time. I have been told that someday soon, he will be a contender for World honors.'*[73]

Karl Gotch being a graduate of the school of wrestling found in Billy Riley's gym wowed audiences with his brand of professional wrestling. *'Seldom have Canadian mat fans witnessed such an expert display of true wrestling as Gotch puts on,'* the interviewer continues *'He'll tie a man in knots, leave him gasping for breath and all this just with scientific holds, without the help of a well-placed punch.'*[74] Utilising moves such as the **'Boston crab'** and **'Atomic suplex'** Gotch entertained mat fans in his matches. *'dangerous and thrilling, 'Atomic Suplex,'...*

To carry out the suplex, Karl hooks his man around the waist from the rear, with a mighty heave backwards, Gotch smashes his opponent's head into the mat while coming to rest himself only on the top of his head and his toes, in a perfect bridge.'[75] Karl Gotch explained the origins of the Suplex as *'That was the suplex, it is an old Greco-Roman hold.'*[76] Karl said in another interview *'The suplex started about 150 years ago, actually, and was brought into being by the Finns. That's why in German you call it, to translate exactly "Finnish Overthrow,".*[77]*'* Whilst for a while Karl was renowned for his use of the **'Atomic suplex,'** he lambasted those wrestlers that were synonymous with a particular trick. *'Too often a wrestler will place his success on one special hold...To me you must use any and all holds that will end a match quickly as possible. For a wrestler to limit himself to a single hold, or try and manoeuvre an opponent into a situation where his special hold will appear foolish.'*[78] Karl's wrestling style developed out of his early days in Greco-Roman coupled with his training in Billy Riley's gym but he didn't stop there. Karl's approach to wrestling was to continue to learn and adapt, changing his core arts to the new context provided by 'Professional wrestling'. *'Wrestling is a sport of stresses, conditioning and speed. Many holds at many times are the best. I try to learn... to digest each opponent's moves and if they perfect a hold I feel I can use, I try to add it to my attack if possible.'*[79] Karl said that *'the best years of a man's wrestling life come between the ages 35-45, when he's amassed a lot of experience,'*[80]

Karl Gotch was a divisive figure in wrestling. Many disliked his attitude, lack of showmanship and gimmicks, finding him stubborn, uncompromising and curmudgeonly, an allegation made against some of his stablemates at Riley's gym, ultimately whilst these factors held him back in the western promotions they are the reasons for his success in the East. Tom Billington had this to say about Gotch *'Karl Gotch was, well, a nice enough man, but a big-headed bastard. Whatever you had, he had twice as many. Whatever you did, he'd already done it, only better.*[81] According to an article, Bob Cook said this about Gotch *"People say he was such a great wrestler. Sorry! As a pro wrestler, from a performance standpoint, he wasn't a great wrestler. Maybe he could rip your head off in a real fight, but this isn't a real fight. This is entertainment. He wasn't a good pro wrestler."*[82] In his later years Karl Gotch became further recluse[83], passing away in his hometown of Tampa Florida, 28th July 2007[84].

As stated, like soe of the other wrestlers to emerge from Riley's gym he divided opinion, however, one cannot argue with the impact he had on wrestling, certainly that in Japan where he is still held as 'Kamisana' or the 'God of professional wrestling'. In a nutshell Tom Billington summed up what many thought of Gotch in the wider professional wrestling community when he said *'I liked Karl, well not that much, but I have respect for what he'd done for wrestling'*[85]. Some argue, as he himself did as stated in the video interview 'My Cigar with Karl Gotch' by Jake Shannon that it was Karl that put Wigan on the map, but I think this undervalues the contribution made by others such as Billy Robinson, Billy Joyce and Roy Wood.

His legacy continues today in the many Japanese and Western wrestlers that were influenced by his wrestling style and conditioning practices.

Titles

- MWA Ohio Heavyweight Championship, defeating Magnificent Maurice 15th Oct 1960[86]

- American Wrestling Alliance (Ohio) World Heavyweight Championship defeating Don Leo Jonathan 14th Sep, 1962

- World Wrestling Association (Los Angeles) World Tag Team Championship with Mike Dibiase, 1967

- New Japan Pro Wrestling NJPW Real World Championship

- World Wide Wrestling Federation WWWF World Tag Team Championship with Rene Goulet, 6th Dec, 1971

References

[1] Kamisama: The Karl Gotch Story; Fumihiko Saito
[2] Karol Krauser; Wrestler's wrestler by Joe Tendler p.55
[3] Karol Krauser; Wrestler's wrestler by Joe Tendler p.55
[4] Official Wrestling, February 1964, p.65
[5] Master of 1,000 holds, Earle Yetter p.44
[6] Karl Gotch; A man to be reckoned with; Marty Blake p.28
[7] Kamisama: The Karl Gotch Story; Fumihiko Saito
[8] Master of 1,000 holds, Earle Yetter p.53
[9] Wrestling Review, April 1963 p.14
[10] Cairns Post 5th August 1948 p.1
[11] Cairns Post 7th August 1948 p.1
[12] http://www.sports-reference.com/olympics/athletes/is/karel-istaz-1.html
[13] Karl Gotch; A man to be reckoned with by Marty Blake p.28
[14] Official Wrestling, February 1964 p.65
[15] Master of 1,000 holds, Earle Yetter p.44
[16] Karol Krauser; Wrestler's wrestler by Joe Tendler p.55
[17] From Success to success; Bob Leonard interview p.20
[18] Karl Gotch; A man to be reckoned with by Marty Blake p.32
[19] Wrestler Monthly, February 1972 p.30
[20] Official Wrestling, February 1964 p.66
[21] From Success to success; Bob Leonard interview p.20
[22] From Success to success; Bob Leonard interview p.20
[23] From Success to success; Bob Leonard interview p.20
[24] Kamisama: The Karl Gotch Story; Fumihiko Saito
[25] Uncaged: My Life as a Champion MMA Fighter, Frank Shamrock, Charles Fleming p.69-70.
[26] Master of 1,000 holds, Earle Yetter p.45
[27] The Chilliwack Progress, 28th Oct 1964 p.7
[28] Tom Gannon's History of wrestling p.1596
[29] The Wrestler, January 1965 p.20
[30] The Wrestler, January 1965 p.20
[31] The Wrestler, March 1965 p.20
[32] The San Bernardino County Sun, 30th Jul 1967 p.49
[33] The San Bernardino County Sun, 5th Aug 1967

[34] Wrestling Review, April 1963 p.12
[35] National Wrestling Alliance: Untold story of the monopoly that strangled Pro-wrestling, p.274. Tim Hornbaker, ECW Press, 2007
[36] Wrestling Review, April 1963, P.12
[37] Wrestling Life, October 1960 p.6
[38] Wrestling Review, April 1963 p.13
[39] Official Wrestling, February 1964 p.66
[40] Wrestling Review, April 1963 p.14
[41] The Wrestler, January 1965 p.20
[42] Tom Gannon's International wrestling results 1960, Vol 6 p.5
[43] Offical Wrestling, February 1964 p.66
[44] The Kansas City Times, 13th Jan 1965 p15
[45] Kit Bauman; Lou Thesz Biographer; http://wrestlingclassics.com/cgi-bin/.ubbcgi/ultimatebb.cgi?ubb=get_topic;f=10;t=001327;p=0
[46] Charlie Thesz; http://wrestlingclassics.com/cgi-bin/.ubbcgi/ultimatebb.cgi?ubb=get_topic;f=10;t=001327;p=0
[47] Kit Bauman; Lou Thesz Biographer; http://wrestlingclassics.com/cgi-bin/.ubbcgi/ultimatebb.cgi?ubb=get_topic;f=10;t=001327;p=0
[48] Official Wrestling, February 1964 p.66
[49] Buddy Rogers, Ross Davies;p.71, 2001 The Rosen Publishing Group
[50] The Kingston Daily Freeman, 20th Jun 1976 p.35
[51] Wrestling Monthly, April 1972 p.43
[52] Wrestling Review, April 1963 p.14
[53] The Lincoln Star, 2nd Apr 1972 p.91
[54] http://www.mikemooneyham.com/2007/08/05/god-of-wrestling-gotch-dead/
[55] Pure Dynamite; The price you pay for wrestling stardom by Tom Billington, p.34
[56] Pure Dynamite; The price you pay for wrestling stardom by Tom Billington,p.166
[57] Brawl: A Behind the scenes look at Mixed Martial Arts Competition, Erich Krauss, Bret Aita
[58] Pure Dynamite; The price you pay for wrestling stardom by Tom Billington, p.24
[59] Uncaged: My Life as a Champion MMA Fighter, Frank Shamrock, Charles Fleming p.69-70.
[60] Uncaged: My Life as a Champion MMA Fighter, Frank Shamrock, Charles Fleming p.69-70.
[61] Uncaged: My Life as a Champion MMA Fighter, Frank Shamrock, Charles Fleming p.69-70.
[62] Brawl: A Behind the scenes look at Mixed Martial Arts Competition, Erich Krauss, Bret Aita
[63] Brawl: A Behind the scenes look at Mixed Martial Arts Competition, Erich Krauss, Bret Aita
[64] Kamisama: The Karl Gotch Story; Fumihiko Saito
[65] The Pro Wrestling Hall of Fame: Heroes and Icons, Steven Johnson, Greg Oliver, Mike Mooneyham, ECW Press, 1 Oct 2012
[66] Karol Krauser; Wrestler's wrestler by Joe Tendler p.55
[67] From Success to success; Bob Leonard interview p.20
[68] From Success to success; Bob Leonard interview p.20
[69] The Wrestler, August 1965 p.20
[70] The Wrestler, August 1965 p.20
[71] The Wrestler, August 1965 p.20
[72] Wrestler Monthly, February 1972 p.30
[73] Karl Gotch; A man to be reckoned with by Marty Blake p.32
[74] The Wrestler, December 1964 p.20
[75] The Wrestler, January 1965 p.20
[76] Official Wrestling, February 1964 p.65
[77] From Success to success; Bob Leonard interview p.20
[78] Karl Gotch; A man to be reckoned with by Marty Blake p.32
[79] Karl Gotch; A man to be reckoned with by Marty Blake p.32
[80] The Wrestler, August 1965 p.20
[81] Pure Dynamite; The price you pay for wrestling stardom by Tom Billington, p.7
[82] http://slam.canoe.ca/Slam/Wrestling/2007/07/30/pf-4381219.html
[83] http://slam.canoe.ca/Slam/Wrestling/2007/07/30/pf-4381219.html
[84] http://www.postandcourier.com/article/20070805/ARCHIVES/308059958
[85] Pure Dynamite; The price you pay for wrestling stardom by Tom Billington, p.35
[86] Tom Gannon's International wrestling results 1960, Vol.10 p.2

Chapter 20

Billy Robinson

Billy Robinson was born 18th September 1938[1] Colleyhurst Manchester[2]. He was born to a family with a distinguished fighting heritage. His great, great grandfather, Harry Robinson had held the bare-knuckle boxing championship of Great Britain [3]. Harry's obituary was as follows *"The death took place at South Shields last night of Mr. Harry Robinson the father of young Johnny Robinson the well known featherweight boxer who passed away just over a week before. Mr. Robinson's death like that of his son was due to pneumonia. The deceased who was 60 years of age was the proprietor of the Model house in Deer's lane .He was in his younger days a prominent bare knuckle fighter and was only once defeated in his career namely by Jimmy Johnson of Sunderland"[4]*

Billy's father, boxing under the name of Harry Robinson had been North of England champion, having victories over the American title holder 'Kid' Moose' [5] and had also fought Tiger Flowers. [6]. His Uncle Alf had been both a Boxer, boxing world champion Max Baer, and later a wrestler, wrestling Jack Sherry in Belgium.[7]. He also won the Lonsdale trophy in 1934, he had beaten Archie Normal, then George Downer to get to the final. An account of the final was as follows *"Alf Robinson a Manchester fruiterer who has been boxing for several years last night won the £1000 heavy weight tourney at the Wembley sports arena over six rounds in the final he beat on points Norman Baines of Neston, Cheshire formers a grocers assistant and an equally experienced fighter.*

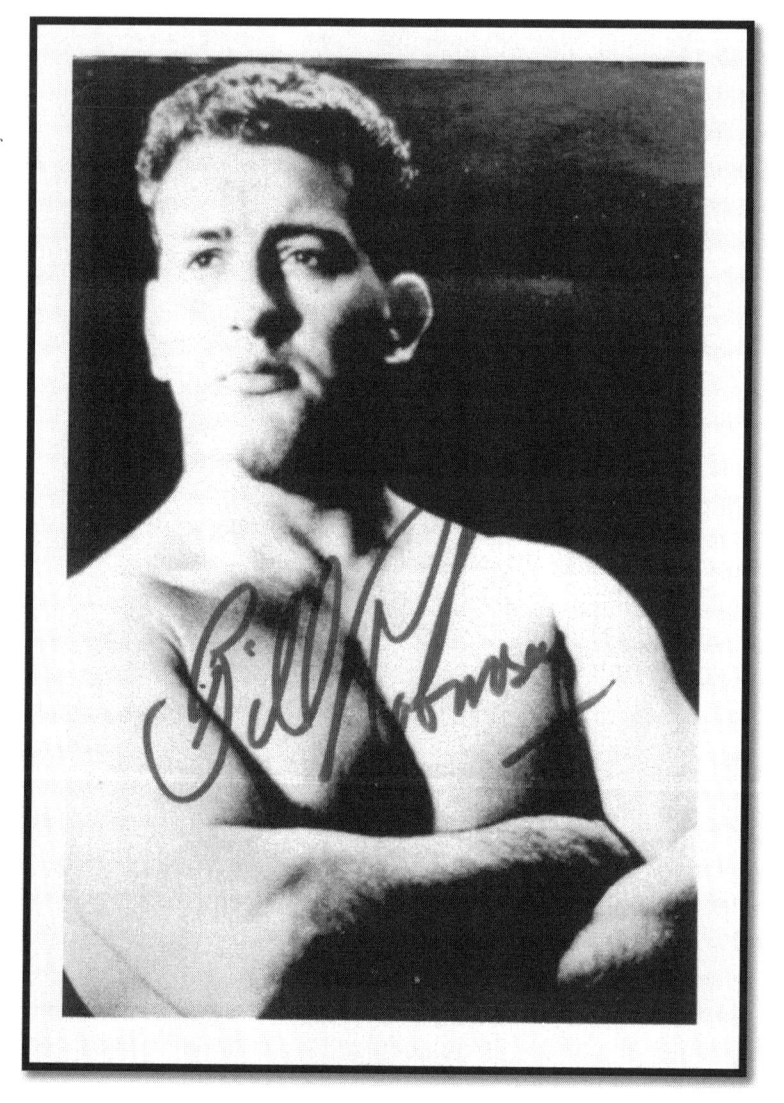

Robinson won £300 and a silver trophy which was presented to him by the donor Lord Lonsdale"[8]

Billy attended Heaton Moor College, then later Stafford Boys School in Ashton under Lyme. His forte was sports, and whilst a member of the Boy scouts 1st and 2nd Hurst troupe, was selected to swim for Ashton and Hyde Scouts[9]. His natural affinity for sports and his family heritage would seem to suggest Billy was destined to be a boxer, and indeed he wanted to follow in his father's footsteps. His father took him to a professional boxing gym; Billy loved Sparring in the gym. However, fate was to step in. In the book Physical chess, Billy states that whilst working at his fathers greengrocers shop he got caught in the right eye with a piece of a coca cola sign which had been thrown by another boy (another interview in 1966 states a piece of cardboard). This resulted in a retinal tear requiring 2 surgeries and a stay in hospital of 6 months. The result was that he was unable to get a boxing license.[10]

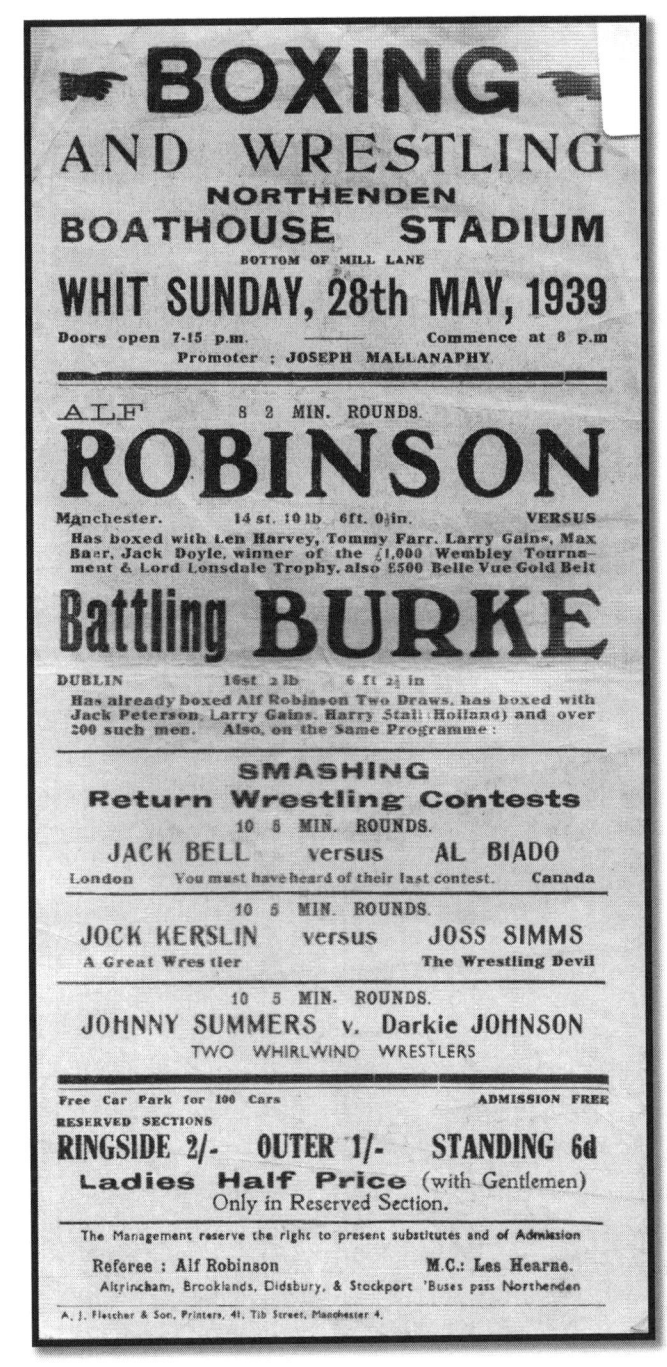

Jack Doyle vs. Alf Robinson January 1937

Like many of his generation Billy left school early aged 14 to work. Not only did he take over his fathers shop for a period when his father was ill, he also worked in Smithfield market in Manchester as a porter [11]. A mix of natural genetics, and also the heavy work manual work that he was doing, resulted in the fact that aged 14 Billy weighed an impressive 180bs. With the end of the hopes for a boxing career, his uncle Alf suggested a career in professional wrestling would be a natural outlet for his talents. However, his father wanted him to learn amateur wrestling first [12]. His uncle Alf suggested the YMCA in Manchester [13]. It would seem that a career in wrestling was fated, as even at this stage Bill recalled seeing Benny Sherman the American wrestler in the YMCA, Sherman would go to the YMCA with Billy's Father as he was interested in the street fighting aspect, he also recalls sitting on George Gregory's back whilst he was swimming laps [14]. Both these wrestlers were good friends of Billy Riley. It was a suggestion from his father however that would prove to be a turning point in Billy's life. His father wanted him to attend a gym in Wigan, run by the wrestling legend Billy Riley to learn with the "real wrestlers" [15]. It was whilst at Belle Vue, that he met a man that gave him a phone number to ring Billy Riley, that man was Billy Joyce.[16]

Riley's Gym

At age 15 Billy would start at Billy Riley's gym, an association that would go on for a total of 12 years [17]. In an article in the Wrester magazine Billy recalled his first experience of the gym " I went there feeling confident strong and fit and ready to show them just what I was made of the first man I went on the mat was Ernie Riley and he played cat and mouse game with me that I shall never forget." [18]. Later in his book Physical chess he tells of how Billy Riley asked him what his best hold was, "The crucifix" he replied. He was asked to put it on one of the wrestlers. But every time he put it on he ended up on the floor screaming. Billy Riley told him "Okay you can start, we'll teach you" [19]. And so began his apprenticeship at the gym which was to be christened "The Snake pit" for the nature of its training.

Billy used to catch the train from Manchester across to Wigan to train at the gym and it was Billy Riley who would meet him at the station and walk him to the gym. Ever the trainer Billy Riley would show holds to the eager youth, however the mix of grappling and Billy Riley singing songs would have got the pair stares from passers by, and perhaps even a red faced young Bill Robinson. In the early days, Billy recalls the punishment handed out by the older wrestlers such as Jimmy Hart who whilst hooked in would cross face and back elbow him repeatedly leaving his journey home a trial, causing him to have to stop many times on his way up the hill to his house to rest and support his neck. Jimmy Hart's justification of "never mind lad you'll have an 18

Alf Robinson

inch never before your 16 years old" didn't provide much solace[20].

Amateur days

Billy Robinson had a highly successful amateur career. His accomplishments included
- 3 Lancashire titles
- 2 Northern counties titles
- British Championship – He won the British light heavyweight title form Chris Sheady at the Royal Albert hall in 1957.
- Irish Championship. [21]
- 1956 first year at nationals placed 3rd
- 1957 – won, later that year European open championships in Ireland wrested 2 weight classes - light heavyweight beat 4th place finisher at 1956 Olympics Gerry Martina. Heavyweight Ken Richmond bronze medalist in 1952 Olympics beat him. Beat him 1 month later at YMCA [22]

However, Billy Riley wouldn't allow this success to go to the young mans head, "each time I won a title or did anything in competition to be proud of I was matched the following day with a smaller man in the gym and was fairly soundly beaten just to keep me in my place" he admitted in an article in the wrestler Magazine, "his system was shrewdly calculated to take me down a peg or two and ensure I did not overstep the mark and begin to think I was 'the greatest'. It was part of the mental conditioning that was all part of the thorough training which I got from Billy Riley" – his defeats coming from the likes of John Foley, Melvyn Riss, Jack Dempsey [23] and Joe Carroll were there to keep him humble [24]. It was a former colleague of Smithfield market, Arthur Eckersley who took him to many of his bouts in amateur days and was invaluable in spurring him on when things slowing. " I almost packed things up a couple of times when I felt I wasn't getting anywhere but Arthur was always there with help, advice and encouragement and I still owe him a lot. It still happens occasionally when you seem to reach a stage but cannot progress to the next one. Then you need some encouragement and eventually you are off again until you complete another invisible stage. Sometimes its staleness or overtraining that causes it but you need someone to encourage you and I have been fortunate in Arthur's company and advice" [25]

Seamus Dunleavy recalled training with Billy Robinson "Some mornings you'd go to gym and you'd be walking past the rugby ground there in front of you would be Bill and I'd think Christ, and I'd have a feeling in the pit of your stomach and you'd

Record of Billy Robinsons entrance music in Japan

know that day you'd be busy, and sometimes he wouldn't be there as he was wrestling. But you'd learn an awful lot as Billy really stuck at it seriously and he did it for years day in day out and he made it his life"[26]

However, it was a conversation from his trainer and mentor Billy Riley that would change the course of his career. "Listen, son, you've won all the cups and the medals. Why don't you take me out? I taught you how to wrestle, take me out and buy me a steak dinner?". He replied to his teacher that although he would love to, he couldn't afford to. His teacher replied "it just goes to show you, kid. You can't buy steaks with medals. It's time you turned pro" [27]

His own gym

In an effort to help support Billy's training, his father helped him put together a gym in a converted loft in Ashton. Initially it consisted of only a mat and boxing gear, however a number of local lads showed an interest and the gym was formed. They eventually moved to more suitable premises in Failsworth in a an old dancing school known as Valley house which consisted of two army huts put together, It was called Failsworth amateur wrestling club. Even when he turned professional he still found time to come back to the gym to train the keen bunch of amateurs that formed the club. Billys professional schedule was hectic ,however, in-between it was Arthur McNally who trained the amateurs at the gym when Billy was away. "Arthur does a great job keeping things going when I am away and his help in training is invaluable to me" " he is also partly responsible for any success I have had because he keeps me at it during training seasons and also helps me work out some of my ring moves". The club claimed a number of champions including Woods (mid) Steve Bolton (junior 9 st.) Brian Sellers (junior 6st) Brian O'Hara who won Scottish welterweight and Bills cousin Jack Robinson and Barry Deeme[28]. Another one of students was Dave Currie who went on to become chairman of the Manchester YMCA when Billy had learned his amateur wrestling[29].

Results from the club

Feb 66	7 stone class winner Brookdale championships
	M Jones (Failsworth) bt B.Dunning (Barton)[30]
April 66	Lancashire junior championships
	7 stone 3rd M.Jones
	9 stone 1st R. Greenhalgh
	Intermediate
	Flyweight 1st M Sellars
	Junior schoolboy
	Bury technical college Jan 29th
	7st 1st m jones
	9stone 3rd R Greenhalgh[31]
Feb 68	Bury junior championships
Apr 68	Senior
	Middleweight – 2nd Morris Failsworth
	Intermediate
	Lt featherweight 2nd M.jones Failsworth
	6 ½ stone 2nd J.Ainsworth
	Northern counties intermediate junior
	61/2 stone 3rd – J.Ainsworth (joint)
	Lancashire county championships
	Social hall Irlam
	6 ½ stone 1st J.Ainsworth
May 68	Northern counties senior
	Lancashire steel mfg co's social hall March 29th
	Featherweight
	3rd B.Sellars Failsworth[32]

Turning pro

In his book Physical chess Billy states he turned pro at the age of 19 [33], however in an earlier interview with the Wrestler magazine in 1966 it states he turned professional in 1958 aged 18 [34]. During his time at Riley's gym he went from 13st 9lbs when he started to 16/12 at a height of 6ft 1-½ inches. His first professional bout was a light heavy weight bout in Brierly Hill Birmingham where he defeated Bill Hargreaves in the 6th round. Despite turning pro, he still worked in the market during the day , travelling to Wigan three times a week to train. He did however take a break when his father was taken ill and he had to take over management of the family shop. However when his father recovered he went back to work in Smithfield, The heavy manual work helped keep him in shape between training sessions and help improve his physique. Still a scout at the time he enjoyed hiking and camping with them. He turned fully professional in 1960. He was still living at home with his parents at the time and didn't have a car and regularly hired a driver to take him to his bouts, the man in charge of the car hire became a fan and firm friend[35]. It was noted by wrestling journalists his thorough grounding in amateur wrestling in Manchester YMCA and then his time in

Riley's had made his style stand out. He was noted to be one of only a very few wrestlers who used hooking in with the leg and a far arm lever, or a figure four hook with the leg or the classic suplex[36].

1960

A school friend of Billy was friendly with Spanish Promoter Jesus Chausson. He offered Billy double the normal rate to do a tour in Spain. Joint promotions were not happy with Billy going to Spain and in the first disagreement with his mentor, Billy Riley who said that he could not go, Billy went against his wishes as had given his word and he went to Spain. When arrived there nobody was present at the airport to meet him. However, despite the shaky start, he got digs with an American English professor, and after a week got cheap lodgings at a local hotel[37]. Later he would live 5 months in a 12-roomed flat in Madrid. Initially he took out lease with 2 American soldiers who joined he joined as extras on film "King of Kings" and played a centurion. He met Sophia Loren and Charleston Hesston who visited set. He was also introduced to Ernest Hemingway. Various promoters gave him work, and he spent 1960 and 1961 in Spain.[38]. His companions in the flat were to move to another country after few weeks.

It was a 'feeling out' trip, he wrestled successfully in Madrid, and won the Barcelona tournament beating Jose Torres 'the man with the iron head' .He went to Palma, Majorca to fight Jim Olivera in the Balearics tournament, and won[39].

1961

Billy went to Spain again after establishing himself as firm favourite on British circuit this time he stayed in Barcelona in a hotel on famous tree lined Ramblas in the centre of city. He competed in and won the Barcelona tournament defeating Felix Lamban. In Palma he beat Jim Olivera. He stayed four months and came away with a reputation much enhanced having met men of the stature of Pedro Bengochea "the best wrestler in Spain undoubtedly next to Jose Arroyo"[40]

Next he travelled to Austria and Germany taking part in the tournaments. In Germany he took on all comers [41]. However despite his success he stated that he hated going back to gym as the old timers would "beat the shit" out of him to keep him grounded.[42]

He won the Albert hall tournament by defeating Joe Cornelius in the final of 61/62 season, having disposed of Gordon Nelson in semi final .1961 would see his first try at Billy Joyce for the British heavyweight title,he lost by 2-1 falls.

He said of Billy Joyce " he is really the master. At time he may appear to be doing no more than he has in order to in and with some people his methods may be unpopular. But when you re up there in the ring with him you have a very experienced and very wily character to deal with. I used to spar in the gymnasium with him but the times became fewer as I progressed because he was wily enough to know that the more I sparred the more of his style I took in. I have held his title for a short time and I want it back badly and while I know that at the moment he is not rushing to meet me again he will soon have to when opposition runs out and this time shall not make any mistakes"[43]

1962

New Zealand Maori Johnny da Silva recommended Billy to top Indian heavyweight Dara Singh. Not long after, a telegram arrived from India offering bill a tournament there. " I was on my way

St.Xaviers school and orphanage

within 3 days of receiving the telegram and found myself a little bewildered touching down in Calcutta at the start of what turned out to be a five month tour".

The tour would take in Delhi, Hyderabad, Calcutta Bombay and Nepal.

During the later part of the tour, Billy's ability came to the notice of the King of Nepal. He heard from the Kings third youngest brother known as the Third Prince, who had seen Bill wrestling in Delhi. Having reported back on his ability, Billy was summoned to Nepal along with Dara Singh. Billy was one of first to get into Nepal without a visa. He wrestled on 5 occasions in Katmandu in a sports arena before crowds of up to 10000 with the King present.

A garden party held in honor of the wresters at the palace gardens, and Billy was accorded the honour of dining at the palace.

Staying with the US economic advisor to Nepal, William Thweat, he was shown round a Catholic orphanage and school, and later the University of Katmandu. He stayed several weeks teaching 3 times weekly at St Xavier's Catholic orphanage and nearby at the University. Later, he was to establish amateur wrestling clubs at both institutions. The principal of the school at the time was Fr.Martin P.Coyne,S.J who served as Billy's sparring partner to demonstrate wrestling to the students. He also donated a dozen

Billy Robinson Seniors cup

silver cups for annual competition among the seniors and junior in the orphanages. The current Senior Vice Principal Mr.Laxman Gurung was also a participant in the Billy Robinson wrestling cup tournament. The tournament stopped in 1996 when the school became co-ed. He taught the students an exercise routine, which continues to be demonstrated by the boys at the school. "since then I have had letters from the orphanage boys telling me of their progress and it feels good to know that the little I did while I was there is enabling them to develop a new interesting their lives". He returned to the UK late august 1962[44]

Next he was to attend the German heavyweight tournament. India however had taken its toll on his health, he had caught a gastric infection in Bombay at the time 200 people died of cholera and Yellow fever in Churchgate area of Bombay, his eyes and skin turned yellow and he lost weight. His weight dropped from 17st to 12 st 12 lb. He presented himself to

Gustl Kaiser – promoter who said he did not want Billy to compete at that weight against some of the top men in Europe but agreed to give him one chance to prove himself. He was to draw the bout, but was an immediate success with the crowd. However, he was not at his best and after couple more bouts was to become ill once more. Unfortunately he developed a painful abscess to his armpit that needed surgery. Billy paid tribute to Scottish heavyweight Ian Campbell for the way he stuck by him during this trying time of sickness. "Ian really was the best at this time. I was really off it and he looked after me and bumped my spirits up tremendously and organised everything for me"

Lastly, he travelled to Krefeld where he won the tournament before returning to home in December 1962[45]

1963

Billy won Daily Mirror tournament in June 1963 beating Joseph Kovacs winning an inscribed gold watch.

In May 1963 Billy Robinson set off for a tour of the East starting with India[46] he spent the rest of the summer in Britain for the first time in 3 years. He managed a further 3 title bouts during the 63/64 season.

His amateurs did well in Lancashire northern counties and British gaining three firsts and two seconds [47]

Billy Robinson compiled an album of his tour of the east, which included pictures of himself with the King of Nepal and many of the Indian notabilities yet it was commented in the Wrestler magazine that he was strangely reticent to show or speak of them. He did however agree to make a take recording of some of the experiences he had in India and Arthur Green prompted him to release some of his album pictures for publication

In one incident 150,000 people turned up to watch wrestling in a large open-air stadium where a race riot broke out and where the stadium was virtually smashed to pieces by the rioting mob[48].

1964

He met Billy Joyce twice in early 1964 – the first

Teaching the students at St.Xaviers

occasion resulted in a draw over 15 rounds , the second, he was fall ahead when injured his neck.[49]

Students wrestling for the Billy Robinson cup

One again Billy travelled to India. He flew out in March to Bombay for a 4-month tour. During the tour Nizam Hyderabad world richest and took an interest in Billy, Billy told him of travel problems, he asked Billy if he would like to borrow a car for duration of trip "but what about you what will you do for transport if I take it", he replied "we have 170 cars in the garage, we will not miss one" – even so he declined. However he did get an invitation to Nizam's private museum, which contained such priceless items as the actual armour worn in the crusades by Richard the Lionheart and the sword of Saladin.

"I was not allowed to wrestle Sikhs because I had been accepted as the Muslim champion and there could have been trouble"- Bill became revered in wrestling circles appearing before crowds of 100,000 or more. Biggest crows was in Bombay 135,000 ringside seats were 4 guineas and others three pence much further back. Six hour program – 10 bouts of Indian style wrestling. Also wrestled in the pits, perspiration clogged fine sand to Billy's body as he wrestled making it a really painful proposition to remove after the bouts.

Whilst there he tried Kushti, Indian wrestling, he wrestled 350lb Tejer Singh, Billy weighed 15 st. at time. Billy beat him in 50 seconds.

Billy returned to the UK in September – via Lebanon wrestling in Beirut on way to Germany. Ray Appolon was also in Beirut at time and the pair were top attractions of an eight-week tour. With crowds of 5000 in an outdoor stadium. Billy took 8mm cine film of his travels

Billy arrived in Germany for the Nuremburg tournament of 1964 – he was introduced by a reporter to the European promotions manager for a large chain of bowling alleys in the Brunswick bowling corporation. It was a young woman by the name of Ulla, who was partnering world champion bowlers in an exhibition matches. Billy and Ulla began a relationship and Ulla came to UK in 1965 and in the June married Billy. "She is my greatest critic and never misses any of the major bouts I have. This, of course is a great source of encouragement to me and whatever conditioning my mind needed before I married all it needs now is to know that she is at the ringside and I am ready for anyone". Ulla helped look after Billy's grocery shop in Belgrave road, new Moston, Manchester with Billy's father looking in to help now and then he having retired some time previously. He listed his likes in an interview as swimming canoeing and water skiing. Like Ulla he had an interest in dogs, he owned English Bull Terrier and Ulla a German shepherd[50]. The honeymoon spent in Blackpool , before he sets out again for Germany.

Billy took part in Gustyl Kaisers Autumn all nations heavyweight tournament at Krefeld Germany. There were 13 other star wrestlers in the tournament including Gideon Gida, Fritz Muuller, Ricky Star, Josef Kovacs, Enrico Marques and Jose Arroyo[51]

Billy and Horst Hoffman, a German wrestler, each had won nine matches, with one defeat in the fortnight long competition (Robinson had lost one match to Ray Appollon who finished fourth.) but as Robinsons record included a victory over the German he was declared over all winner.

In December he defeated Billy Joyce to become the Euopean champion. In a previous bout he had lost out on the title by disqualification, from a low blow, having been ahead by one fall at the time. "By no stretch of the imagination was that blow deliberate but it counted and I lost the title" "I promised the crowd from the ring that I would bring that title back to Manchester, but Joyce doesn't want to know about it. He will eventually run out of opponents and be forced to meet me again although must be fair and say that in his place I might feel the same way but when that time comes there will be no mistakes."

" I am sick of the type of wrestler who is ridiculed for his gimmicks or ring methods and who does nothing to improve his own image. This way wrestling will never rise to the heights it out to as a top sport in this country. I am sometimes almost ashamed to be introduced as a professional wrestler because of what some promoters stoop to in finding men for their bouts who are figures of fun and not sportsmen or athletes"" I try to demolish these types as quickly as possible if I am matched with them but it is largely the bad element in the game the cheap promoters and showmen who give us this rotten tag with their cheapskate billing and standard of wrestling"

He was insensed at the treatment given to amateurs "instead of some of our youngsters ruining their bodies through smoking and drinking in early youth amateur wrestling is an ideal way of giving them a chance to prove themselves in the correct manner, but what encouragement do the authorities give them – none at all"[52].

1965

Billy went off on a long tour taking in India the Fareast Lebanon and Germany.He was to return Christmas eve after the 10 month tour.

He was unbeaten in India although he was unable to gain a match with Dara Singh. He wrestled the open air with boiling sun and a crowd of 80000 spectators. "wrestling men who weigh up to 25st , has taught me more than ever the value of submission holds" he was to comment on the experience.

After returning he said that he was hoping for some matches against lighter opponents such as Ernie Riley to quicken him up.

" I have the opportunity of a visit to America and I hope to go eventually and win the world heavyweight title. But when I go to the States I shall go as the official heavy weight champion of Britain"

" My ambition is to win the world and you can take it from me that I shall be after Billy Joyce or whoever happens to be holding the British belt, just as soon as I get acclimatized"

At this point he had been wrestling professionally for 5 years. He attributed his success to Billy Riley.

"Whenever I get the opportunity even now I off to Wigan to see Billy. I can honestly say and I'm now a much travelled man you know that nowhere have I met anyone who comes near Riley's standard as a coach"

He gained victory in Germany winning the all nations tournament in Germany.[53]

Billy was considered heir apparent to Joyce title above Geoff Portz, Dennis Mitchel etc.[54]

The following is an account of one of his matches against Billy Joyce for the European title:-

"Belle Vue's majestic Kings hall was packed to capacity with fanatical Robinson fans and they left no one in no doubt as to where their allegiance lay. Both men were rather over eager to come to grips, and it looked for a moment as if the fight would begin before the bell. The opening round was "spit and fire" as Joyce slammed right into Robinson. A good portion of the round was spent brawling on, or near the ropes. The second round was in the same vein , until referee Doug de Relwyskow issued a public warning to Joyce for an infringement on the ropes and immediately gave one to Robinson who stamped on Joyce head as he lay on the canvas . From that point on sanity was restored and thanks largely to the firm and fair refereeing the next four rounds saw as fine a showing of Wigan type submission wrestling as anyone could hope for.

During this part of the bout Robinson had the upper hand and several times the ex champion worried with vicious back drops to his knee, Joyce perhaps realizing that the initiative was slipping away attacked Robinsons legs and in the fifth round forced a submission after a long and savagely applied single leg Boston.

It looked as if the bout was over there and then but at the start of the sixth Robinson staggered upright as the referee began to count him out. He survived by employing Joyce's own tactics – of scrambling for the ropes as soon as danger threatened. This he had to do to stay in the fight, for if Joyce could have secured another such hold he would have won. Impatient angry and over confident Joyce stormed into Robinson and fell for the young Billy's favourite move, the suplex. Robinson took Joyce way over and his head thudded into the canvas nearly knocking him out as Robinson followed up with a body press to equalize.

Again at the start of the seventh round Robinson had great trouble with is leg, but this time Joyce was in similar trouble with a badly banged head, Joyce attacked all the time reaching for the champions leg and Robinson beat off the attacks with forearm foot knee and shoulder. Anything to save himself. Then again as Joyce rushed to attack he was taken off balance by a surprise move. Robinson took a crotch hold as for a body slam into a head pile driver. Joyce just beat the count only to be seized in a merciless front head chancery that almost ripped the head from the shoulders. He submitted at once.

Robinson danced in delight as his thousands of fans howled in triumph. He made a fabulous fight back when all seemed lost. Joyce as is his wont argued the toss with the referee Relwyskow but all the talk in the world would not reverse the decision. A really great four rounds after the unpleasantness of the first two. Again well handled by Doug De Relwyskow. Robinson has established his superiority over the veteran Joyce lets see now how he will deal with the rest of the top European heavyweights"[55]

1966

Billy was to start his year abroad wrestling on the continent in France and Germany[56]

In the June Billy took part in a football match as part of a 'TV all star wrestlers XI, the team contained Reg Williams, Jim Hussy, Abe Ginsburgh Johnny Eagles, Joe Keegan, Ken Cadman Hans Streiger. Peter Stewart, Alf Cadman, Vic Faulkner, Bert Royal and Billy Robinson the referee was superstar footballer George best[57]

Billy took part in a televised bout against Geoff Portz on World cup final day, the year England won the world cup[58]

In December, Billy told the Wrestler magazine that he was determined to make 1967 best year of his life. Whilst in London, he spent time in gym showing technical moves to Brian Maxine from Cheshire[59]

1967

In May it was commented in the wrestling press that Billy had been on "tremendous tours of India Pakistan and had entered German tournaments"

He was compared to Bert Assirati, in that he didn't employ gimmicks, but that he differed although he wasno dandy or villain but had a dashing style. There was speculation regarding him travelling to the US and Canada as a contender for the world heavyweight title[60].

In December a sports magazine editor from the USA requested information from Joint Promotions on Robinson.[61]

1969

1969 would be another globe trotting tour for Billy Robinson. In July he held Dory Funk Jr NWA world heavyweight wrestling champion to a draw, although he was said to have controlled 80% of the bout[62]. He also beat Verne Gagne who at the time held the American alliance world heavyweight championship, however, there was some question over whether this was a title bout though[63]

He travelled to Japan and wrestled as part of the IWE (International wrestling enterprise) who were in opposition to the JWA (japan pro wrestling alliance) who had Karl Gotch.[64]

In the September he became World Heavyweight champion. Next he captured World Wrestling Alliance belt and World Heavyweight championship in Japan. Next he travelled to Hawaii, the wrestlers and promoters however were not keen to welcome him. After 5 weeks he had "whipped all the local wrestlers" including Buddy Austen Hawaiian champ. Then went to North America where he wrestled Gordon Nelson in Florida[65].

In Canada he met Cowboy Jack Bence, Marcel Trudeae (lasted 4 ½ minutes), Prusovitch –(6 ½ minutes). Whilst in Canada took part in Calgary stampede. Stu Hart after seeing him wrestle Jack Bence said come to Calgary to wrestle for Stampede.

On arriving Billy underwent an interview with Ed Whalen, along with Stu Hart, Dory Funk Jr and Iron Dave Ruhl. Next onto a Stampede grounds for a bow in front of 25,000 cheering fans. Next into Calgary Press Club beef and beans barbecue, for reception with Mayor and Mrs. Jack Leslie Stampede Queen along with her 'Princesses' Carol Burns, Patty Johnston and Winifred Reid. Although Bill doesn't get to bed at midnight he's up again at six o'clock for a reception with 3000 guests at the sausages and eggs and potatoes breakfast tossed by Canadian Senator Harry Hys on his ranch. Robinson and Funk meeting with Canada's Governor General Roland Michener, as well as fames western singer-actor Rex Allen. Next onto a football game between the Calgary Stampeders v British Columbia Lions at the McMahon Stadium. All the grapplers on the huge card converge on downtown Calgary for a three mile ride in the kickoff parade before a ¼ million cheering watchers.

The card consisted of
Earl "Mr. Universe" Maynard v Jack "Killer" Kris
Sandor Kovacs v Marcel Trudeau
Stu Hart v "Chi-Chi" (a 36st Bengal tigress
Bud and Ray Osborne v Jack Pesek and Clem St. Louis
Dr.Olaf Simon's "Karate Spectacular"
Little Beaver and the Jamaica Kid v Sky Low and little Brutus
Klondike Bill v Darrell Cochran
Texas Jack Bence v Iron Dave Ruhl.
Dory Funk Jr. vs. Bill Robinson for the World Heavyweight Championship

The first fall came after thirty minutes when after suplexing Funk twice, Billy caught him with a one armed lift around the waist and dropped him over an outstretched knee. Then pressed him for a 3 count.

The second submission going to Dork Funk Jr. at the forty minute mark when Funk caught Bill with a perfect Drop toehold; instantly changing into a Boston Crab.

After 60 minutes when Stu Hart entered the ring with the Belt, Billy took the belt and fastened it around Funks waist lifting his arm aloft declaring him the winner[66]

He won the ring-wrestling trophy – for "outstanding wrester of the tournament". Stu Hart said " I've been wrestling for over thirty years and I've seen only one man I'd put in the same class with Bill. That's George Gordienko. Robinson has to be one of the greatest ring men ever to come to America" "I've taken a version of the world title, and I feel I qualify for a shot at Funk's title, or the claim of any other man to the world belt. I'll wrestle anyone, anytime anywhere if it will lead to a final solution to the championship tangle…. And I feel that I can, finally, become the undisputed World Heavyweight Champion". The NWA awarded North American Heavyweight Championship to Bill following his inconclusive bout against "The stomper' where the wrestler had walked out of the ring.[67]

Billy stated whilst he was happy to fly back to England to defend his European and British titles he didn't think anyone good enough to beat him.[68]

He also travelled to Singapore and Hong Kong then Australia and won world championship in Australia with Jim Barnett promoting[69]

1970

In February of 1970, the controlling body of British wrestling took the decision to strip Billy Robinson of his Heavyweight British title. The reason given was that the title had gone undefended for two years as Billy was pursuing his quest for world honors overseas[70]

In the March, Billy was back in Canada after finishing the Australian phase of the tour he was on. He lost the version of the world heavyweight title he gained in the Japanese tournament in 1967/68. He had successfully defended it on a number of occasions including one against Freddie Blaisse. King Curtis challenged him for the title,and beat him[71].

In April, Billy jetted into Manchester from America to see his wife and his young son Spencer and jetted out 3 days later to continue his tour.[72]

Billy travelled to Austria, Hong Kong and Canada. Whilst in Canada he wrestled in Calgary's Victoria Pavilion and Edmonton's sales Pavilion, Saskaoons Civic arena, Regina exhibition auditorium, Lethbridge municipal arena and dozen small arenas.

Billy received a here's welcome on his return to defend his NWA Heavyweight championship

The first challenge being against Wild Bill Dromo, with Billy winning was with an over the knee back breaker after Wild Bill had cut Robinson with a mule kick

Next was Angelo Mosca, a hard-hitting Canadian Football league lineman. His career included a dozen seasons with the Hamilton, Ontario Tiger Cats. Bill gained the victory after thirty-five minutes with a suplex and pin fall.

Alex the Butcher was the next man on the list aiming for the title. However Billy yet again gained victory after he dropped his opponent on his knee three times and secured the win.

His last match was with the 19 st. Sudanese wrestler Abdullah the Butcher. He was the holder of the Canadian Open Championship. The opening fall was to go to the Butcher, with Billy securing the next after a knee drop. It looked like Bill was to win after he suplexed the giant however in the course of the suplex the referee had been struck and he wasn't there to count the fall. After getting up the Butcher slipped his hand into his tights and some ringside spectators swore they saw more metal than flesh in the fist that struck Robinson allowing the butcher to get the fall. Hart convinced of the Sudanese' wrestlers guilt with regards to the contents of his fist insisted that he agree to a rematch.

The rematch came again and the butcher was disqualified after again using a metal implement in his hand as he slugged Billy full force in the throat. However, the title was not awarded on this disqualification, but another return match ordered.

The third match was to see blood spilled from the Butcher as Billy pummeled the skull of the Sudanese wrestler. Yet again the Butcher pulled out his metal tool however Billy wiser after his previous bouts intercepted and removed the object showing the crowd much to their pleasure. Robinson was to get his revenge as he drop kicked, elbowed, Judo chopped and knee dropped him at will finishing with a body press that gained him victory and the championship title.[73]

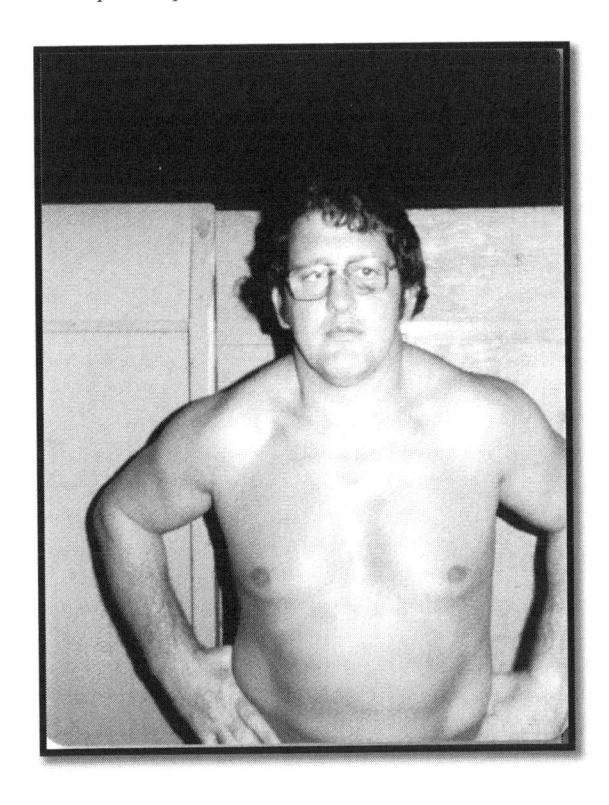

1971

Billy gained the IWE world championship and European heavyweight title. In an article it was noted that he had travelled further afield than any other British champ visiting Europe, Japan, India, Africa, Canada Malaya, USA, South America and Hong Kong to wrestle. He rated his hardest opponents as Billy Joyce, Karl Gotch George Gordienko and Dory Funk. It noted that senator Hatta minister of sport had invited him to Japan. His ambition was to win the Official world title away from the Americans. His weight at the time 17st 7lbs at the height of 6'1", he said his favourite food was German and favourite drink wine.[74]

1972

In May, Billy was said to be "going great guns after defeating Verne Gagne for a version of the world heavyweight. Bill, living in Minnesota has his own regular television shows giving instructional wrestling for young amateurs"[75].

Some of his accomplishments were listed in an article about him in this year. Including Special coach to Japanese Olympic mat team in Mexico games, four one hour long draws with world heavyweight Dory Funk Jr. He went on an oriental campaign until late 1971, and then went to Minneapolis for promoter Wally Karbo. Then through dozen states where he downed every top grappler in single and tag matches.. even against Gagne . " Gagne only saved himself by forcing his own disqualification in most bouts", "Robinson obviously outclassed him throughout the bouts". Also fought San Francisco's Ray Stevens, Russian Ivan Kolloff, Nick Bockwinkel and Blackjack Mulligan and Blackjack Lanza. Partnered with Dr.X, Wilbur Snyder, and Don Muraci against combos including Rampaging Blackjacks, Stevens and Bockwinkle, Larry Hennig and Lars Anderson and Hennig and Dirty Dusty Rhodes. He then travelled American west coast and Canada. Match in Calgary against Abdulla the butcher – ending double count out.

"I feel I've shown American and Canadian fans that pure wrestling can be just as exciting and just as victorious as the rough stuff" [76]

In October, whilst in Japan he competed in a tournament which he won the,later winning the World championship.[77]

Billy's professional career petered out during the 1980's and, despite his success in professional wrestling, and being involved in films such as 'The Wrestler' he ended up living in Minnesota a manager of store at gas station, Inoki called and asked him to come to Japan. Yukio Miyato had gotten in touch even earlier – when in he was working in Las Vegas as a security guard, coaching the other guards. He took part in an exhibition match with Nick Bockwinkel although he would later admit he was not in shape but did it on UWFi fight card. Miyato asked him to go to Nashville and coach UWFi guys from America who were sent there. He would fly to Japan 4-5 times a year to be at matches. Wrestlers such as Billy Scott, Gary Albright and Lydick would come to Tennessee to work out with him. In the Early 90s he became head a coach of UWFi and head coach of Snakepit gym Japan and would go on to live in Japan 15 years. In his book he admitted that he had started to drink too much and put on too much weight as result of divorce[78].

The following is an account of training in Japan with Billy Robinson, it is the account of Osamu Matsunami who trained extensively both with Billy Robinson and Roy Wood. It has been edited for ease of reading, as although Osamu has excellent English language skills it is not his first language. I believe it gives us a more personal view of the person behind the legend.

Miyato rented a flat for Billy right next to the gym, which was a big relief for Billy since he had bad knees, although only around sixty at the time his knees had suffered as the result of his long Professional-wrestling career.

Whilst teaching at the gym he taught from a chair, he had gained weight since he had finished wrestling professionally, I am not sure what his exact weight was then but it was around 120kg.

He taught and explained to us about numerous moves and counter attacks against them, but he himself couldn't show most of them. So he usually picked me to demonstrate to others because I had

Billy Robinson and Osamu Matsunami, Snakepit Gym Japan

learned catch-as-catch-can from Roy Wood in Wigan. Also, I could speak better English than any other people in the gym and I always translated what Billy said into Japanese so that all wrestlers there could understand what they should do not only by watching but also by listening to an explanation of how the moves worked.

However, sometimes, neither Miyato nor I understood what he wanted us to do, or we couldn't do it properly. That was when Billy had to show the moves himself. When he was watching me doing the move wrong in his chair, he shouted "No!" "I'll show you." Then he put his hands on the armrests of the chair trying to stand up. He had to do it very slowly and carefully. There was an unwritten rule then. When Billy put his hands on the arm rests, we had to get ready for his walk. First we would gather closer to Billy so that he did not have to walk as far. But if we got too close to him, it wasn't good either. There wasn't enough room for him to show the move he was going to do. We had to think how much room he would need for it.

Billy would reach where he wanted to stand. However if he was showing a ground-wrestling move he had to kneel. Whoever was standing the closest to him was supposed to make a defense position (to go down on hands and knees) so that Billy could put his hands on the guy's back. Then Billy could go down on his knees easily.

Again, we had to think about the place we should make a defense position, which decided where Billy would go and which way he would face. You needed to guess where he wanted to kneel down, which was also good training for wrestling. You had to read Billy's mind and anticipate what he was going to do next. After he showed a move, the same thing had to be done to help him stand up.

It was always nice to see a legendary wrestler Billy Robinson demonstrate his moves right in front of us although it wasn't easy for him. He often hurt himself, groaned and said, "Damn it! My knees are killing me!" as he was demonstrating.

We carefully watched him because we wanted to learn the moves properly and we were worried if his knees were okay. But there was something more – we were worried about the guy underneath Billy!

He put a move on one of his students, but sometimes he had little control of his own body because the pain of his bad knees. He had to lean against the guy he was putting a move on. The guy supporting Billy's weight, which was well over 120 kg, Billy would choose big guys for it, which was safer for both Billy and the guy he put his moves on.

When new members joined Billy's class, of course they didn't know this rule at first.

Anyone could learn it after they took part in a couple of classes. But when new members made a defense position for Billy for the first time, many of them collapsed as soon as Billy placed his hands on their back. That was not because they were weak, but because it felt a lot heavier than they expected! You literally had to support all of Billy's weight. Once again, that was good training to have a strong defense position.

I didn't know why, but Billy wasn't using a walking stick then though he definitely seemed to need one. Maybe he didn't want to admit that his knees were as bad as the idea that he couldn't walk without a support. Once I suggested to Miyato that we should buy him a cane for his birthday. But we decided not to do it, being afraid that he would be unhappy receiving that kind of present, which could have implied, "Now you are old enough to use a cane." He was only in his early 60s then.

Despite the fact that he suffered from knee pains, he actually liked going for walks. He walked very slowly and needed to have a rest every 100 meters or so. His flat was near Koenji station, and there were

Billy and Osamu at Ume's wedding

many shops around. He visited cafés, bars, restaurants, barbers, drycleaners, off-licences and so on and soon made friends with the shopkeepers and shop assistants. People were happy to meet a famous professional wrestler like Billy Robinson. Especially for men in their 40s and 50s, he was their hero in their youth.

I often went to dinner with him, and he told me all about his stories drinking large quantities of beer. He always taught me wrestling moves even at the dinner table, bar, in fact anywhere! Sometimes other customers gave us a strange look, but I enjoyed that time – that moment he was teaching only me, feeling I felt I was learning something special that no one else can learn.

He would also go for long walks from where he lived in Koenji to Ogikubo, which is about two miles away. His favourite sento (public bath) was there. It had many different types of saunas and baths and you could get a massage there. Billy liked to spend daytime relaxing there.

He knew it would be a sort of vicious cycle if he did not work out. His bad knees prevented him from exercising and he put on more weight, which made it even more difficult for him to work out.

To make matters worse, he liked ice cream and he was a big drinker, too.

Occassionally it would lead to disaggreements between Billy and Miyato.

Billy ate a lot of ice cream all the time. He always showed up in the gym in the early evening before wrestling class started. What we saw in his hand was an ice cream! Well, I didn't think it was a big problem, but it really was for Miyato. He didn't want Billy to eat a lot of ice cream. I understand Miyato was worried about Billy's health. This would sometimes lead to arguments about Billy's health between Billy and a concerned Miyato.

From the beginning of the gym, Billy and Miyato had many chances to appear in magazines, newspapers, and on TV because the legendary former *pro-wrestler Billy Robinson had started to live in Tokyo and coach. When Miyato talked about Billy in interviews, he always said, "Billy is like a family member. He is like my father." Sometimes I had difficulty being caught in the middle of a dilemma between them. Since I spoke the best English around Billy, I was like his interpreter. Billy often asked me to run errands, such as newspapers, bread, some groceries and of course, ice cream and beer! He called and asked me to get an ice cream on my way to the gym. When I got to the gym, he was sitting in the lobby, usually watching a video. I said, "Here's your ice cream."*

Miyato saw this, and he screamed at me saying, "What are you thinking? You shouldn't let him eat that! You are not thinking about his diet!"
Miyato asked me to tell Billy to stop eating a lot of ice cream saying, "He's like my father and I must take care of his health too! Tell him not to eat too much ice cream." When I tried to tell Billy, however, he would scream at me saying, "I'm not a child and he's not my mother, either! Tell him I decide what I eat!" In fact, there were many times I did not translate their words or I translated differently from what they meant in order to avoid trouble.

Although they argued, it was obvious a strong bond existed between them, Miyato had great respect for Billy as the greatest wrestler and coach . I would like people to know the fact that it was Miyato that made Billy famous as the great catch coach he was and to achieve success later in his life. Had it not been for Miyato, Billy wouldn't have come back to the wrestling world to coach world-class wrestlers and MMA fighters. Without him he would have been a security guard in Las Vegas for the rest of his life and his great catch skills would have been left buried forever.

Billy's coaching was great. As he was always saying wrestling is physical chess, it was very scientific and precise. He always watched for scrupulous details such as the angles of your feet, your power force, momentum, where your centre of gravity was, and so on. If your move didn't work, you had to think why it didn't work, what was wrong with it, and how you were going to fix it. You couldn't just say, "Oh, bad luck. I'll try it again. Maybe I can do it properly next time." No, that was not Billy's teaching. You had to understand what was wrong with what you had done.

Once we had a TV crew shoot a program about ancient wrestling. They brought old pictures of wrestling drawn on the wall, like ancient Olympics which might have been thousands of years old.

They wanted Billy to replicate the moves and explain them. Some of them were easy to explain and replicate the moves from the pictures since they were still popular moves in modern wrestling or other combat sports.

However, there was one indecipherable picture what move wrestlers were doing. We tried to imitate the poses of the wrestlers were doing in the picture, but it was so complicated that we couldn't imagine how they could end up in that position from the way we normally wrestled.

We were all puzzled. Billy had just one look at it and said, "You know how they came in this position? First, you are doing wrong. You tried to do the same, but the way you are holding your opponent's elbow is a little different from the man in the picture doing. He is grabbing them like this."

He noticed a very slight difference, saying that it is small but very important to know what they did before they came to the position in this picture. He told us to break up and stand face to face from a start position. Then, he told me to do this, my opponent to counter it, and me to react to it. We went on five or six serial moves and at last, we naturally ended up in exactly the same position as the two wrestlers in the picture were in, which all of us had never seen. The whole sequence of moves cannot be seen in modern wrestling.

All of us were amazed at Billy's encyclopedic knowledge. He kept talking, "Look, wrestling started when humans were born, and our body hasn't changed. Ancient people wrestled the same way as we wrestle today. There was no new move. Someone must have done it before in the past. If you think you invented a move, it is not new but has just been forgotten. Saying you invented a new move just proves that you do not know much about wrestling."

He also told us a similar story like this he learned from his teacher, Billy Riley.

When Billy Robinson was training at Riley's, Turks won a lot of medals in Olympics with a move that was new to everybody. It became known as the "Turkish ride" and many wrestlers tried to copy it.

Billy Riley heard people talk about it, and asked them to come to his house where he kept numerous wrestling books. He brought out and showed a print of an etching that was hundreds of years old. Wrestlers in it were doing the "Turkish ride." This kind of story should be handed down, and I hope I can tell this story the best that I can in the future, like Billy Riley and Billy Robinson.

I learned a lot of philosophies from Billy, and this is one of my favorite – "There's no new move.".

In Japan, we have summer holidays in the middle of August. UWF Snakepit Japan had an intensive summer camp during this season. I think it was the summer of 2001. We went to Kawaguchi-ko lakes, which are at the foot of the famous Mt. Fuji. The hotel we stayed at was specially designed for athletes. It had tennis courts, running tracks and a gymnasium. Many sport clubs used it for intensive training camps. Fortunately, no other groups were staying there while we were training for a couple of days. We didn't have to worry about other guests and enjoyed acting our own way in the hotel.

After a day's worth of training, we all had dinner together in the hotel restaurant which was the last item on our schedule for the day. Then some of us went back to their own room to have a good rest, while some went to have a bath in the hotel large spa to relax, and others stayed in the restaurant to drink.

Billy of course chose to drink there and started to open beer bottles. It was a really fun night. Billy was in a good mood surrounded by his students and a lot of alcohol. There were some other big drinkers and they went get bottles and cans of beer one after another!

I cannot drink alcohol at all, not even a sip. But I kept staying with Billy because I was his interpreter. He told us many exciting stories about his family, childhood, Billy Riley's gym, American pro-wrestling, his rivals, and everything! It was like the Billy Robinson's talk show.

I often went with him to go shopping, eat out, and so on. So listening to his stories was nothing unusual for me. However, for most of the guys in the gym, it was very special to hear Billy's stories directly from him. They hardly ever had a chance to talk to him in the gym although they attended his class where he talked about only wrestling moves. I think the guys were so happy to have such opportunities to ask Billy questions about his anecdotes. They were all big pro-wrestling fans, and some of them became members of the gym just because they wanted to talk to Billy, take photos of him, and get his autograph.

Billy kept telling stories of his eventful life as he opened another bottle. He had already been very drunk when he reached the stories of the 1970s, around the time he wrestled for IWE in Japan. He began to talk about a wrestler of the promotion. "He was definitely the toughest guy in Japan. He was not tall but his body strength was amazing. Well, he didn't have many wrestling skills, though."

Then it seemed like his own words pulled the line for another memory. Billy suddenly banged the table and shouted, "Damn it! I lent him a lot of money but he never paid me back! How much did he owe me?"

Billy got so furious as if it had happened recently. The guy was notorious for being a heavy gambler but it was more than 30 years before. The guy was already dead then. I think Billy had forgotten about it for ages, too.

Around this time Billy got very emotional as he was telling stories. Actually, I was getting tired of interpreting and felt like going to bed. I think it was around 3:00 in the morning and I was hoping that he would stop drinking soon. However, there was no sign of it. Instead, it looked like his anger fueled his desire to drink more and a sip fueled his desire to talk more.

In IWE, he often toured in Japan with Karl Gotch. He started to remember memories with him.

Then, out of the blue, tears began to roll down his cheeks. It amazed us all.

When he was about 15 years old, Karl Gotch came to Wigan to learn wrestling. It was Billy's uncle who brought him to Riley's gym. Karl was already the Belgium champion in Greco-Roman style. He was in his late 20s.

Once, many people including wrestling promoters got together at the gym to see how good Karl was. However, no adult wrestlers showed up and Billy had to spar him although there was a big age gap. Karl beat him very easily, of course, since Billy was just a young teenager. But no matter how many times he got beaten, he couldn't say, "I want to quit," in front of his father who was a professional boxer. He kept coming back until he got completely wiped out. The sparring finally finished when Billy Riley ordered them to stop. Billy had to stay in bed for the next couple of days due to the his body had taken.

He clearly remembered all about this story and his feelings although nearly fifty years had passed. Tears kept running down his cheeks as he showed how frustrated and mortified he was then. He shouted, "I never give up!" "Dad is watching me!" While translating all his words, I felt his emotion and it made me think I had to do the best translation I could do in order to tell this story and his feelings to other people. I was about to shed tears too and I found myself talking very emotionally. I was really moved by Billy's spirits that he learned from his father, and he never forgot it for the rest of his life. This sparring with Karl might have been the beginning of the indomitable Billy Robinson – "The British Lion".

It is clear from the above account that Billy in his time in Japan inspired affection and loyalty from his students in particular Osamu and Miyato. It was because of Miyato that Jake Shannon, founder of Scientific wrestling asked Billy to come back to the United States to do a seminar on catch as catch can. This event is preserved in the "War" DVD series [79].

Billy later moved to Little Rock Arkansas to be closer to his son Spencer. Whilst there he coached classes on a Thursday and Friday at Westside mixed martial arts gym. With Jake Shannon and scientific wrestling Billy spread the art of catch wrestling initially around America then The UK and Italy. In 2011 he travelled to the new home of the Snakepit in Aspull meeting up with fellow Gym Mate Roy Wood reminiscing about old times in a way only those from the gym would understand.

On the March the 3rd 2014, the world of Catch wrestling lost a legend, when at the age of 75, Billy passed away peacefully in his bed of natural causes. Coaching until the very end, his students continue to have his phrase "Do it again!" ringing in their ears, his legacy continues with those he trained, most notably Josh Barnett and Kazushi Sakuraba who continue to bring attention to the Catch as catch can wrestling that was passed onto them by the great man.

Titles

1961 – Royal albert Hall trophy winders – London – beat Joe Cornelius

6/12/65 – Joint Promotions European Heavyweight title – Manchester – Beat Billy Joyce

23/4/66 – Joint Promotions British Heavyweight title – Manchester – Beat Billy Joyce

18/1/67 – Joint promotions British Heavyweight title – Bradford – Beat Billy Joyce

31/8/68 – Germany IBV European heavyweight tournament – Munster

19/12/68 – Japan IWE International Wrestling alliance title – Okayama – tournament

June 1969 – Honolulu European Title

31/10/1969 – Australia World Championship Wrestling IWA title – Sydney – Beat Killer Karl Kox

24/11/69 - Australia World Championship Wrestling IWA title - Perth – Beat Killer Karl Kox

1969 Calgary Stampede North American Title – beat Archie Gouldie

1970 – Calgary Stampede North American title – Beat Abdullah the butcher

1/7/70 – Honolulu Hawaiian Tag team title – Honolulu – partner Johnny Barend

28/10/70 – Honolulu Hawaiian Tag team title – Honolulu – partner Ed Francis

16/12/70 – Honolulu US/North American title (Ed Francis) – Beat the Destroyer

15/11/1972 – AWA Tag Team Title – Honolulu, partner Ed Francis

30/12/72 – AWA Tag team title – Minneapolis – Partner Verne Gagne

6/6/73 – Honolulu US/North American title (Ed Francis) – beat Dust Rhodes

3/6/74 – Japan IWE International wrestling alliance title – Tokyo – beat Great Kusatsu in tournament

1976 – Louisiana US Tag Team title – Shreeveport, LA – with Bill Watts

5/3/77 – Japan All Japan united national title – Jumbo Tsuruta

18/5/78 – AWA British empire title – Winnipeg,MB

12/6/78 Japan all Japan pro wrestling PWF title – Ichinomiya beat Tor Kamata

12/11/79 - AWA British empire title – Winnipeg,MB

28/4/1980 – CWA Continental wrestling association world title – Memphis beat Bill Eadie

11/8/80 CWA Continental wrestling association title – Memphis,TN, beat Bill Dundee

1983 – Montreal Promotions Varoussac International Wrestling title.

---

[1] Wrestling review 195 August 1962
[2] The Wrestler October 1966 - 14
[3] Physical chess – B.Robinson ,J Shannon ECW Press 2012 - page1
[4] Newcastle daily journal 13/1/14
[5] The Wrestler October 1966 - 14
[6] Physical chess – B.Robinson ,J Shannon ECW Press 2012 - page113
[7] Physical chess – B.Robinson ,J Shannon ECW Press 2012 - page11
[8] The courier and advertiser dec 11 34
[9] The Wrestler October 1966 - 14
[10] Physical chess – B.Robinson ,J Shannon ECW Press 2012 - page113, Wrestler October 1966 - 14
[11] The Wrestler October 1966 - 14
[12] Physical chess – B.Robinson ,J Shannon ECW Press 2012 - page114
[13] The Wrestler October 1966 - 14
[14] Physical chess – B.Robinson ,J Shannon ECW Press 2012 - page114
[15] The Wrestler October 1966 - 14
[16] The Wrestler October 1966 - 14
[17] Physical chess – B.Robinson ,J Shannon ECW Press 2012 - page129
[18] The Wrestler October 1966 - 14
[19] Physical chess – B.Robinson ,J Shannon ECW Press 2012 - page129
[20] Physical chess – B.Robinson ,J Shannon ECW Press 2012 - page 33
[21] The Wrestler October 1966 - 14
[22] Physical chess – B.Robinson ,J Shannon ECW Press 2012 - page142
[23] The Wrestler October 1966 - 14
[24] Physical chess – B.Robinson ,J Shannon ECW Press 2012 - page129
[25] The Wrestler October 1966 - 14
[26] Interview Seamus Dunleavy July 2014 – S Greenfield
[27] Physical chess – B.Robinson ,J Shannon ECW Press 2012 - page142
[28] The Wrestler October 1966 - 14
[29] The Wrestler 1965 September page 34
[30] The Wrestler feb 66 page 27
[31] Magazine of the BAWA – dates as noted in table
[32] British amateur wrestling association newsletter 1966-1968
[33] Physical chess – B.Robinson ,J Shannon ECW Press 2012 - 45
[34] The Wrestler October 1966 - 14
[35] The Wrestler October 1966 - 14
[36] The Wrestler magazine June 1966 page 17
[37] Physical chess – B.Robinson ,J Shannon ECW Press 2012 - page145
[38] Physical chess – B.Robinson ,J Shannon ECW Press 2012 - page145
[39] The Wrester magazine
[40] The Wrestler October 1966 - 14
[41] Physical chess – B.Robinson ,J Shannon ECW Press 2012 - page150
[42] Physical chess – B.Robinson ,J Shannon ECW Press 2012 - page148
[43] The Wrestler NOvemver 1966
[44] The Wrestling review – no.199 sept 4h 1962
[45] The Wrestler NOvemver 1966
[46] The Wrestler magazine may 1963 page 15
[47] The Wrestler Novemver 1966
[48] The Wrestler magazine December 1963 page 8
[49] The Wrestler Novemver 1966
[50] The Wrestler Novemver 1966
[51] The Wrestler Nov 1964 page 25
[52] The Wrestler Novemver 1966
[53] The Wrestler March 1965 16
[54] The Wrestler May 1965 17
[55] The Wrestler September 1965
[56] The Wrestler February 1966 page 14
[57] The Wrestler June 1966 Page 10
[58] The Wrestler Sept 1966 – 10
[59] December 1966 - 8
[60] Wrestler May 1967 - 10
[61] The Wrestler December 1967
[62] The Wrestler 1969 – Page 7
[63] The Wrestler July 1969

[64] The Wrestler September 1969 page 7
[65] The Wrestler September 1969 page 7
[66] The Wrestler October 1969 page 4
[67] The Wrestler 1969 – page 6
[68] The Wrestler September 1969 page 7
[69] Physical chess – B.Robinson ,J Shannon ECW Press 2012 - page170
[70] The Wrestler April 1970
[71] The Wrestler March 1970
[72] The Wrestler May 1970 page 10
[73] The Wrestler May 1970 Page 10
[74] red wrestling book
[75] The Wrestler 1972 – May 9
[76] The Wrestler 1972 – August - 8
[77] Physical chess – B.Robinson ,J Shannon ECW Press 2012 - page1120
[78] Physical chess – B.Robinson ,J Shannon ECW Press 2012 - page1123
[79] Physical chess – B.Robinson ,J Shannon ECW Press 2012 - page1123

Chapter 21

Billy Howes

He was born in Bristol, his real name being Billy Howson. He was the son of George Howson former Bristol city professional footballer. He began work in a hairdressing salon in Bolton. He began wrestling at the age of 18 [1] at Bolton Harriers club and later at Riley's gym [2]. However, his career was to be cut short by his national service. He had become a miner in order to be in a protected role to avoid conscription so could continue wrestling but was sacked because of absenteeism because of the wrestling and was therefore signed up to be in the Kings regiment of Liverpool with the rank of corporal[3]. As part of his service he did a tour in Korea. He was said to have taken part in a number of major battles in that war.[4] Including the campaign at Imjim River where the "Glorious Glosters" won fame[5].

Michael Moore, who was a youngster at the time, and rather fascinated as young men can be with war once asked Billy Howes what war was like, was it exciting? Billy Howes replied "It was terrifying you imagine a big crowd of people rushing towards you wanting to kill you, no matter how many you killed there were always more behind picking up the guns to kill you"[6]

On completing his national service he based himself in Bolton well in reach of the famous Riley's Gym[7]. It was just after his return that the famous barbell practical joke took place as told by Bill Robinson in his book Physical chess.

Billy Howes like many of the Riley's wrestlers enjoyed his fitness training and he installed his own gymnasium at Farnsworth[8] not too far form his

Bolton home and there when wrestling engagements do not take him too far away he would indulge in several hours of rigorous exercise a day. Often adding a session of swimming[9]. He said "People pay to see me wrestle. Its up to me to make sure I'm in he right condition to give my best"[10].

Other wrestlers that used his gym included Dave Armstrong, Vic Faulkner, Keith Williamson and Jim Hussey.

Billy was also a policeman, he was a special attached to Bolton division of Lancashire constabulary with whom he patrolled and taught self-defense.[11]

At this time he was wrestling as a light heavyweight and was noted for his performances including those with fellow gym mate Ernie Riley. Whether it was acknowledgement of the domination of Riley at this weight or whether it was just a natural progression Billy moved into the mid heavyweight division. Although he was unable to gain the title in this division from Normal Walsh, he set his sights on the European title instead[12].

In 1962 he entered in a series of tournaments whose goal was to find a challenger for the European Mid heavyweight title. He fought a number of memorable matches including one in Wembley town hall on cup final day in 1962. After a hard fight he secured victory over the Frenchman Jacques Legeat of Paris.[13].

The stage was set for a thrilling match against Poland's Warina Zarzecki. The venue was the prestigious Albert hall, 1963. In the Audience was the Duke of Edinburgh, a wrestling fan. Howes went on to win by straight falls gaining the title[14].

Like many wrestlers of the day Billy amassed a number of fans that formed fan clubs. One club was run by a Miss Rose Cullen, 15d Queen Anne place Liverpool, a second club was run by Marie Rotehrham of Trowbridge street Liverpool[15].

Unfortunately Billy was to take part in a match that had serious consequences due to injury. The match was with Alf Cadman and unfortunately Alf broke sustained a neck injury resulting in a fracture requiring vertebral and disc surgery[16]

In 1963 Billy took part in the Wills Woodbine challenge tournament. The event sponsored by WD and HO Wills of Bristol was promoted by Conrad Davies. It took place in the Embassy Sportsdrome in Birmingham. A knockout tournament over 3 weeks. The first Set of matches took place on Monday 1st April.

Reg Williams vs. Emile Poilve
Eric Taylor vs. Bill Howes
John Lees vs. Monty Swan
Steve Veidor vs. Alf Cadman

On April 8th the matches were as follows:-
Billy Howes vs. Reg Williams
Alf Cadman vs. John Lees

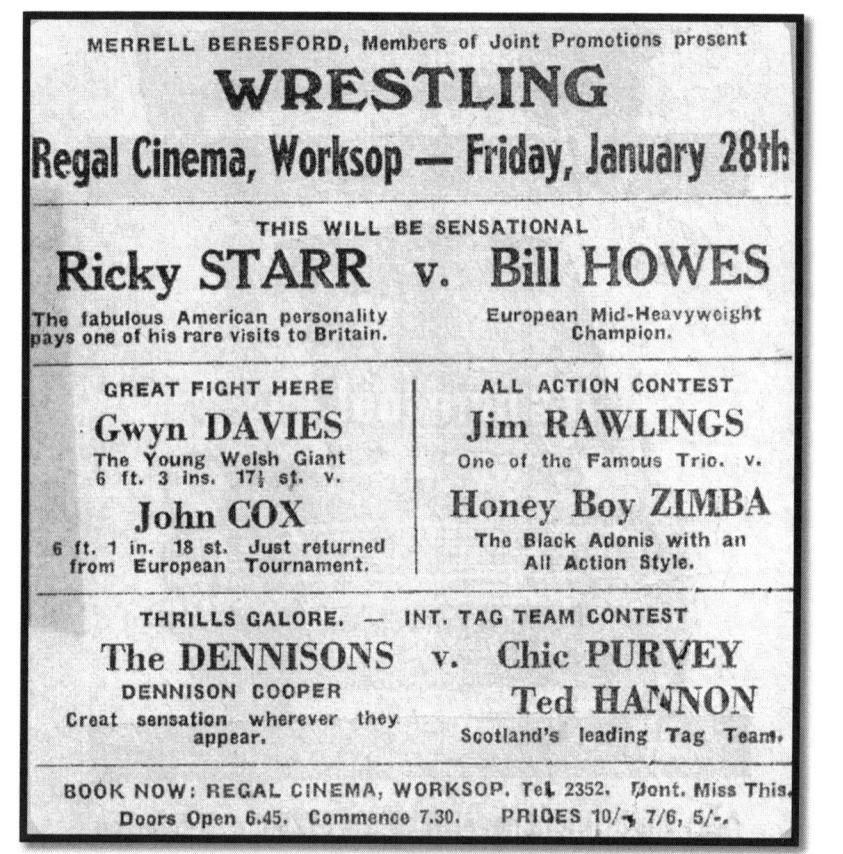

The final was held on the 15th of April and saw Bill Howes beat John Lees by 2 falls to one, the final fall coming in the 6th round[17].

Billy lived in Bolton with wife Marjorie; he had four daughters Susan Melanie, Jayne Elizabeth, Sally Ann and Louise. He had an extension built onto the house, being a handy man and amateur building he helped dig the foundations and did a lot of the hodd carrying and general laboring. He applied for the shop on the ground floor to become an off license[18].

Billy was an animal lover he had a Bull Mastiff called Bruise and a Cat from Jim Hussey, a professional wrestler, who owned a farm at Prestwich[19]

Roy Wood says of him " He had a lot of peoples respect. I wrestled for him in Isle of Man with my cousin Alan, He ended up there himself and he lived in the Isle of Man as steward of a golf course".[20]

Billy Howes can also make a claim to being the first wrestler to unmask kendo Nagasaki, no less than at the masked mans television debut![21]

Titles held

BWA/Joint Promotions – European mid heavyweight title 5/5/1962 – beat Jacques Lageat (held until he retired

Joint Promotions World Mid heavyweight title 1966.

---

[1] The Wrestler 1965 – page 31
[2] The Wrestler April 1964 page 17
[3] The Wrestler April 1964 page 17
[4] The Wrestler 1965 – page 31
[5] The Wrestler August 1962 page 5
[6] Michael Moore Interview 10/7/14
[7] The Wrestler 1965 – page 31
[8] The Wrestler August 1963
[9] The Wrestler June 1964 – page 12
[10] The Wrestler August 1963
[11] The Wrestler April 1964 page 11
[12] The Wrestler 1965 – page 31
[13] The Wrestler 1965 – page 31
[14] The Wrestler 1965 – page 31
[15] The Wrestler 1964 page 15
[16] Send in the Clowns – Kindle Edition – Eddie Rose – YonYonson – 2012 location 2030
[17] The Wrestler June 1963 page 29
[18] The Wrestler April 1964 page 17
[19] The Wrestler April 1964 page 17
[20] Roy wood interview November 2013
[21] Greetings Grapple fans – John Lister– location 1156

Chapter 22

Jimmy Hart

Born in Bryn, near Wigan Jimmy like many of his age entered the mines on leaving school. He decided he wanted to pursue a leisure pursuit that would make him not only fit for his job at the colliery but for life in general. At the age of 19 he approached Billy Riley who schooled him in the catch as catch can style of wrestling. After gaining a solid grounding under the Wigan master he turned professional[1]

His contemporaries in the gym were Ernie Riley, Karl Istaz, Billy Joyce and Jack Dempsey.

Eddie Rose, who worked on the doors of the Monaco Ballroom in Hindley with him remembered being told by the manager that he could be sure of minimum bother when Jimmy was on the door[2].

Roy Wood remembered him as "A big strong fellow, straight fellow, everything was black and white. When you wrestled him you knew you had had a wrestle". Jimmy was in his 30's whilst Roy was in his teens still.[3]

Billy Robinson in his book Physical chess noted that Jimmy had basic takedowns, was good at control and was an accomplished leg rider, he recounted how Jimmy would hook in and cross face and back elbow him until his neck ached telling him "never mind lad you'll have an 18 inch neck before your 16 years old"[4]

Jimmy enjoyed swimming and gym work as well as wrestling which helped to keep him fit[5].

He only went on one trip abroad as a professional that was to the German tournament in Hamburg[6]

Turning professional allowed Jimmy to leave the mines behind and instead he opened a grocery shop with his Wife Margaret, the shop was located on the same road that Bob Robinson (Billy Joyce) lived[7].

---

[1] The Wrestler 1963 page 10
[2] Send in the Clowns – Kindle Edition – Eddie Rose – YonYonson – 2012– location 854
[3] Roy wood interview November 2012
[4] Physical chess – B.Robinson ,J Shannon ECW Press 2012
[5] The Wrestler magazine 1963 page 10
[6] The Wrestler magazine 1963 page 10
[7] The Wrestler magazine 1963 page 10

Chapter 23

Melvyn Riss

Born 19 February 1931 Melvyn Riss[1], real name Harold Winstanley, came from the Upholland/Orrell area of Wigan. He began work as a joiner for Gaffney's building in New Springs. Mel was a very well respected wrestler both as show wrestler and a straight wrestler in the gym having a great command of the art of Lancashire catch as catch can wrestling[2].

He was described by Eddie Rose as "Old fashioned lad from Wigan. Wore a long overcoat, a flat cap carried his wrestling gear in his wife's home made shopping bag" [3]

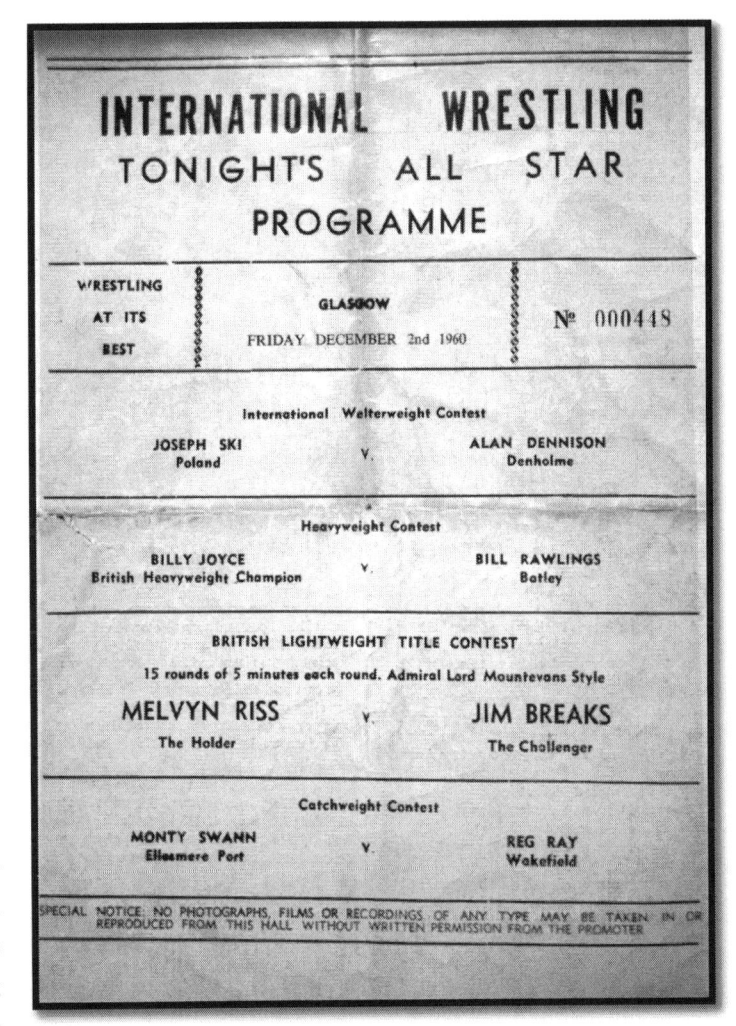

He was a man full of energy, and was able to turn his hand to most sports. He enjoyed playing golf but also played on the wing for Wigan Athletic football team. As a child he used to draw a line on a wall and spent hours kicking the ball at the line. He was a talented athlete but was always willing to put the time in to nurture that talent. He could never sit still, always moving. Roy Wood recounts when they attended Billy Riley's wedding anniversary at what was then called the Wigan tree on the top of Parbold Hill. He sat next to Mel for the evening. Roy remembers him constantly drumming his fingers on the table all the way through the evening and, when he wasn't he was rolling coins around his fingers; he was unable to keep still[4]. Like most of the Wigan wrestlers he was fierce and would stand his ground, but had a softer side, for his gym mates especially. An example of this is when Roy Wood and Mel had a bout in Blackpool tower. It was one of the only times that Roy's mum had come to watch. Afterwards, when Mel realised this, he said "If I'd have known your mother was here Roy you could have won" [5]. But as stated, Mel like the rest of the Wigan guys was fiercely proud of his wrestling. Eddy Rose in his book Send in the clowns recounts a story of when Mel, defending his British championship at the Royal Albert hall. He, arrived at 6.30pm to be greeted "hello sunshine what do you want here?" demanded the uniformed commissionaire looking down on the Wigan lad from his 6'3'' topped by guardsman's style military cap " my names Melvin Riss the British champion and I'm top of the bill here tonight" "if you're effin wrestling champion I'm a bleeding China man, the salvation army's down the end of the road mate". Up came the shopping bag followed by Mel's knee and down went the spit and polish commissionaire with a yelp and a groan " see you later Charlie bleeding Chan' as he stepping over the writhing body into the hall to defend his championship[6]

Melvyn Riss won the British Lightweight title and the Mountevans belt in December 1958. He lost the belt on the 16th October 1963. At the Royal Albert hall, Jimmy breaks the 22-year-old Bradford lad , was said to have shocked the wrestling world by defeating Mel , taking the title. Jimmy breaks, who had only had 4 years experience as a pro. Mel took the first fall , but Breaks replied with two falls to achieve was reported as "impossible for a lad of his age and experience"[7].

Mel died early 1983.

Mel Riss and Tommy Moore (Jack Dempsey)

---

[1] During my research I have seen a number of alternative spellings of his name including Melwyn and Ryss as well as less common others

[2] Interview Roy and Andrea Wood 2013
[3] Send in the Clowns – Kindle Edition – Eddie Rose – YonYonson – 2012
[4] Interview Roy and Andrea Wood 2013
[5] Interview Roy and Andrea Wood 2013
[6] Send in the Clowns – Kindle Edition – Eddie Rose – YonYonson – 2012
[7] The Wrestler– June 1964 – page 10

Chapter 24

Francis Sullivan

"Saunter through life and enjoy it. Too many people do a hundred yard sprint through life, they don't know what they are running from, and they don't know where they are running too"

Alan was born in 1925 in Ireland[1] later moving to Ince. Wrestling was always a part of his life. He recalled, "I remember as a lad, 8 years old, I lived in Ince. In Parkview, near Petticoat lane and there's a pub there, the Park Hotel, a bowling green behind there and they used to have quite a few wrestlers in Ince. A fellow called Jack Hawker who lived at the top of Eldrin lane, another fella called Alan Peat who lived in Fox street, there was a load of 'em, all like local lads who wrestled. I remember nearly every Sunday they'd either be wrestling on Ince common or else they'd make matches amongst themselves. Wrestling on the bowling green behind Park Hotel and I remember us climbing over t'fence to watch 'em this match. There's a fella who been a good amateur wrestler from Doncaster a fellow called Harold Angus came"[2].

He was an intelligent boy, passing his 11+ exams and gaining a place at Hindley Grammar School. However, being headstrong, a trait that would be a lifelong characteristic he decided after 2 weeks that it wasn't for him and transferred to a technical college[3] and qualified as an electrical engineer[4]. His father died when Alan was aged 16 and he inherited the small terraced house in Ince.[5]

A member of the Boys Brigade Alan would attend the Marches taking pride of place at the front throwing the baton. The family had a shop in Cale lane. Alan began to play rugby semi-professionally for Warrington[6] leaving "wires and currents" to take up rugby league full time[7] .He began attending Riley's Gym to learn wrestling[8]. After learning straight wrestling of the Lancashire Catch as catch can style and wrestling for 5 years in the amateur world where he didn't find much in the way of success " I never managed to win any titles they were all too good for me"[9]Billy Riley suggested that in order to learn Show wrestling that he should get used to wrestling in front of a crowd so that it wouldn't affect him. So like many others in the gym he was sent to see Matt Moran, he had a booth at the Shamrock gardens. He began wrestling at the fairs in St Helens, Wigan and Layle getting used to wrestling in front of a crowd.[10]

In order to supplement his income from the Shop in Top Lock Wigan, he began to wrestle professionally. Still playing for Warrington he used to receive £3 for a draw and £5 for a win , whereas he would earn £5 for a nights wrestling and so he began to wrestle professionally[11].

Unlike some of his counterparts at the gym such as Ernie Riley he preferred not to travel abroad and instead tended to wrestle across the UK including the Isle of Man. He didn't enjoy flying being put off by the single propeller planes, so instead would travel thousands of miles up and down the country in a Beatle car[12]. Always a man with a great sense of humour he would play jokes on his fellow wrestlers. On one occasion whilst driving to a wrestling venue they were travelling up a hill and the radio lost signal, one of the other wrestlers in the car asked "what's happened to the radio Alan" , "The signal cant keep up with us as we are going to fast" so when the signal came back he slowed a little and said "there you go I've slowed down , its back now" [13].

In the 1950s he worked a lot for Dale Martins promotions in London staying at a boarding house in Brixton run by a lady called Mary. The house was in Angel Row, and used to remark to his daughter that the bed would be still warm getting into them as the previous occupants had cleared out moments before. A lot of the houses were filled by Caribbean immigrants who had come to the UK in the 1950s and Alan remembers coming home after wrestling locally, at around 11pm to be greeted by the residents sat on the pavement drinking the rum and coke greeting him with 'you been wrestling tonight boss?'.[14][15]

One by-product of his wrestling was that he attracted the attention of the ladies. His tag line on programs was "The working girls Rock Hudson", later when news came out that Rock Hudson was gay

Alan never quite lived it down[16]. However the attention didn't go down too well with his wife. He would receive letters from all around the country from women wanting to meet him for more than his grappling skills in the ring. He recalled coming home one day at about 2 in the morning. He left a note for his wife to get him up as he had to travel to Middleborough. The note was on the back of a programme that he used to bring home for his children, in one of these was a write up by Charles Mascall, saying "Alan Latham returns from the South of France with a tan". On waking him with his still half asleep his wife said "come on bloody golden boy, if them women could see you now!"[17]

Always a showman, his signature move was the flying dropkick. His daughter Karen recalls seeing him on television when she was a child "when I was a little girl I can remember they always used to have wrestling on television on Saturday afternoon and this particularly Saturday he got knocked out of the ring and he was saying 'Turn the lights on, turn the lights on, he's turned the lights off' and I asked my mum, is dad alright'[18]. The match had been against

Alan Latham doing his signature move the dropkick

Frikki Alberta [19]He always wanted to please the crowd and his daughter said "and he always used to say when he was on, in the ring it was like having four audiences so she said, he'd get somebody in a hold or something, a headlock or something and he'd go like that and then he'd go, and then he'd go and turn round and repeat so everybody got a view in like in the wrestling auditorium"[20]

He would form a business partnership with Ernie Riley and purchased the Monaco ballroom with Silent partner Jack Isherwood [21]. The wrestlers from the gym would work on the doors there [22]. The company promoted dances there. The Monaco had been shut because of hooliganism " we were told it would be on trial for a month, and if there were any further outbreaks of rowdyism it would be closed. I brought down a few lads from the gymnasium and the first few days it was like coroners creek. However familiarity bred contempt and soon a couple of the local big men wanted to play it rough"

Sullivan drew them to one side and talked to them he explained if they behaved they could have

The building that was the Monaco ballroom

the best bands in Brittan to play at the dances, it worked

" All these kids need is to have the advantages of good behavior explained to them and they usually take the advice" he said[23].

Roy Wood remembers Alan's sense of humour would mean he would sometimes play practical jokes in the Monaco "I remember one New Years Eve when everyone had gone home and we went into the office upstairs at the Monaco ballroom where everyone was having a pint. There was a doorman from Westhoughton called Stan. Alan told Stan that they'd promised the church next door that every New Years Eve that they would put their clock right for them via the outside grid. Everyone knew Alan's sense of humour and watched as Stan took over this mission to fix the clock. As he lifted the grid, water shot everywhere and drenched him and he soon realized that Alan had been having a joke with him

unfortunately on this occasion for him, at his expense!". It was whilst in the Isle of Man wrestling that he saw the amusement arcades and came up with the idea of setting up a business. Along with his fellow wrestler Ernie Riley then set up 'Riley and Sullivan's' supplying pubs and clubs with fruit machines. At one point the business was supplying over 200 pubs and clubs. They were opposites in terms of their personality with one totally different from the other. Alan was loud and would call 'a spade a spade', Ernie tended to be very quiet, but they backed each other up 100%.[24] He retired from the ring in 1966 [25] aged 40[26] to concentrate fully on the business.

They would help set Roy Wood up in his business supplying bars with glasses and cigarette machines a business he continues to this day.[27]

Although they were fair they didn't take any messing, his son in law Mark remembers a time when he had to go to a pub to mend a pool table "So I went to these new springs and I'd been taught by Mark,

Alan Latham and Ernie Rileys business

who was Ernie's son how to put this cloth on top of the pool tables and they said they want a new change of slate, which is a big slate decking out the pool table so I goes down there and there's a lip in it and I thought this is cracked, and one of the stewards came out and said such a body's cracked that so I said well is he gonna pay for it right y'know, well he was like a local thug, big local thug so I said I'll change it and took it back to this workshop which is in the photograph there, and her dad comes in and he's come in a little red, it was a Volkswagen Beetle, Golf or something like that ' what are you doing?' I said changing the slate, such a body has done this, and he said 'Has he paid for it?' Well apparently not, 'Oh, is he not,' then Ernie rolls up. So I goes down, and they both go down where he lived 'Where does he live? Is it in that house there?' next thing their carrying out the TV. 'Oh he'll pay for it,' they said. So he ended up paying for it apparently but then they give him his stuff back like. They made sure they covered themselves like y'know. So he was like the local thug that picked on the wrong people, type of thing."[28]

Aged 45 he was met with tragedy as he lost his son, his daughter Karen felt it was something he never really recovered from. "He would never show it but you knew that it was killing him".[29]

Ernie and Alan were around 60 years old when they retired from their business, but always kept in close touch with each other. Part of the reason that they retired is that as they were getting older they didn't want to be out at night on call for the fruit machines.[30]

He took a keen interest in many subjects not that just of his business or wrestling but was well read on many subjects and always willing to pass his knowledge onto others so that he didn't make the same mistakes he did.

Even after selling the business and having become comfortably off, living in a wonderful large house that he renovated himself he didn't change. He typically carried on wearing his jeans and denim jacket even into his 70s, sometimes even sporting a 'builders bum'. His sense of humour was always forefront. One day whilst mowing the lawn of his large house somebody stopped parked their car and got the pram out of the car and put it on the lawn, they then got the kid and put it into it, pram, so he said 'I don't want you doing that, can you take that

Alan next to his pride and joy, his Mercedes

pram off the lawn.' She said ' I'll do what I fucking please, I'm gonna report you, whose your boss.' 'He said, just wait a minute, I'll go get him.' So he went in round the back and walked through the door and said 'yes? What is it? Now move that pram off me lawn.' He bought his Mercedes, his pride and joy in his denims and his daughter Karen dreaded to think what the garage owners though when he walked in. But he loved the Mercedes and would take out his dog, a Staffordshire Bull Terrier in his, he would wind the window down and shout 'Come on you little bastard' and it would jump right through the window.[31]

What was less known about Alan Latham was the work he did for charities. An example of this was that he had a love for horses and rode them himself. At the stable he used he bought riding saddles for children with disabilities so that they were able to ride as well.[32]

He developed Oral Cancer around the age of 80 and went through painful and difficult treatment, throughout which he remained very pragmatic about what was happening to him, he came home and told his wife 'Well, I've had a good life and done everything'.

---

[1] Wrestler magazine July1964
[2] Interview Ernie Riley and Alan Latham – A.Coleman
[3] Karen Lynch interview Nov 2013 S.Greenfield
[4] The Wrestler July 1964
[5] Karen Lynch interview Nov 2013 S.Greenfield
[6] Roy Wood interview – Andrea Wood 2013
[7] The Wrestler July 1964
[8] Interview Ernie Riley and Alan Latham – A.Coleman
[9] The Wrestler July 1964
[10] Interview Ernie Riley and Alan Latham – A.Coleman
[11] Karen Lynch interview Nov 2013 S.Greenfield
[12] Karen Lynch interview Nov 2013 S.Greenfield
[13] Karen Lynch interview Nov 2013 S.Greenfield
[14] Karen Lynch interview Nov 2013 S.Greenfield
[15] Interview Ernie Riley and Alan Latham – A.Coleman
[16] Karen Lynch interview Nov 2013 S.Greenfield
[17] Interview Ernie Riley and Alan Latham – A.Coleman
[18] Karen Lynch interview Nov 2013 S.Greenfield
[19] www.wrestlingheritage.co.uk
[20] Karen Lynch interview
[21] Roy Wood interview – Andrea Wood 2013
[22] Karen Lynch interview Nov 2013 S.Greenfield
[23] The Wrestler July 1964
[24] Karen Lynch interview Nov 2013 S.Greenfield
[25] www.wrestlingheritage.co.uk
[26] Karen Lynch interview Nov 2013 S.Greenfield
[27] Karen Lynch interview Nov 2013 S.Greenfield
[28] Karen Lynch interview Nov 2013 S.Greenfield
[29] Karen Lynch interview Nov 2013 S.Greenfield
[30] Karen Lynch interview Nov 2013 S.Greenfield
[31] Karen Lynch interview Nov 2013 S.Greenfield
[32] Roy Wood interview – Andrea Wood 2013

Chapter 25

Jimmy Niblett

Born in 1922, in Hallowell a suburb of Bolton. His father died serving in the First World War leaving his mother to bring up Jimmy and his two sisters[1]. He left St Thomas's school at the age of 14 to go down the pit for 16s (8p) a week[2]. In 1942 Jimmy Niblett at the age of 20 volunteered for the marines commanding a landing craft in the Normandy landings[3]. After the war he worked in the mines and later in the stone Quarry at Montcliffe stone quarry[4]. He was breaking rock of 50-60 tonnes per day in gangs of 4 or 5 people for 5p a tonne[5]. Jimmy became a keen footballer and began wrestling at Bolton Wrestling Club under John Nelson[6]. As an amateur he gained some success in the Northern and Lancashire welterweight division and Northwest Olympic trial for 1948 Olympics. He was due to travel to London to Slough for the trials on the weekend but sustained an injury to his ankle resulting in infection, which prevented him from entering the trials thus, missing his Olympic place[7]. In 1952 he won the Lancashire middleweight championship, despite the fact he was a welterweight and was wrestling with a rib injury[8]

It was following an exhibition bout with Bert Royal that Billy Riley approached him. "I'm Billy Riley from Wigan, I would like you to come, and I am going to open a gymnasium". Jimmy replied that yes he would definitely be there. He would call at the Riley household straight from the pit and ask if the gym was open yet. Billy would tell him the gym hadn't opened yet but invited him in and got down on the carpet to demonstrate moves[9]. He told Roy Wood about his first experiences at Wigan. He remembered thinking he would go and show the Wigan boys a thing or two, as he was an accomplished amateur wrestler however. His opponent was Billy Joyce (Bob Robinson); he told Roy "I cried on the bus all the way home"[10]

In 1952[11] as it meant a tremendous difference in his income, Jimmy decided to take up professional wrestling[12].

He toured many countries throughout Europe and further afield such as Malaya Saudi Arabia wrestling as "Killer James" and Bob Sherry having a career spanning over 20 years[13]. Not known for suffering fools gladly he was more than happy to show the young cocky TV wrestlers who was boss in the ring and wasn't averse to enacting revenge on those who he felt had slighted him as recounted by Eddie Rose in his book on his good friend Ian Wilson who had made a good hearted remark about Jimmy. Jimmy took the opportunity of their meeting in the ring to punish him with being repeatedly thrown finishing with the admonishment "you'll think twice about having another joke at my expense"[14]

He sponsored a cup called the Purple cup at Bolton wrestling club[15].

He married Ruth, A Swiss girl in 1952. She sadly passed away in 1985. He built up a successful scrap business. He Joined Horwich RMI Harriers in 1979 competing in many racing nationally and internationally at fell running. He stopped running around 1999[16] but continued to walk the hills and moors near his home throughout his life. Unfortunately he developed prostate carcinoma, and passed away on 25th November 2008. His funeral was held 3rd December The old parsonage Bolton, with internment at St Mary's, Deane [17].

---

[1] Bolton News – Wednesday Feb 28th 2001
[2] Bolton News – Wednesday Feb 28th 2001
[3] http://www.horwichrmiharriers.co.uk/articles/?p=221
[4] http://www.horwichrmiharriers.co.uk/articles/?p=221
[5] Catch the hold not taken Riverhorse Productions 2005
[6] http://www.horwichrmiharriers.co.uk/articles/?p=221
[7] Catch the hold not taken Riverhorse Productions 2005
[8] http://www.wrestlingheritage.co.uk/themanofgranite.htm
[9] Catch the hold not taken Riverhorse Productions 2005
[10] Roy Wood interview 23/7/14
[11] http://www.wrestlingheritage.co.uk/themanofgranite.htm
[12] Catch the hold not taken Riverhorse Productions 2005
[13] http://www.wrestlingheritage.co.uk/themanofgranite.htm
[14] Location 861 – eddie rose – send in the clowns
[15] Roy Wood interview 23/7/14
[16] http://www.wrestlingheritage.co.uk/themanofgranite.htm
[17] http://www.horwichrmiharriers.co.uk/articles/?p=221

Chapter 26

John Foley

John Foley was born on April 9th [1] in the 1930s in Wigan and lived in Leigh, he attended the Catholic school of the Sacred Heart[2]. He was a member of the schools rugby league team.[3] On leaving school John Foley began work as a Miner in Snapes Pit as a face worker[4][5]. It was around this time he began at Riley's gym as an amateur, and as an amateur defeated the Mewis brothers from Antwerp. Joseph Mewis won silver at the Olympic games in Melbourne in 1956 in freestyle in the featherweight category (57-62kg)[6]. In his book Physical chess Bill Robinson states that one of the toughest matches he ever saw was a 'friendly' workout between John Foley and Jack Dempsey. 'It was unbelievable – great technique, great moves and hard. They got black eyes, their noses were bent there was blood coming out of their ears and mouth and they were still the best of friends afterwards. But neither would give up; nobody was going to bow down to anybody"[7] One source says that he turned pro just after his 16th birthday[8] his first professional bout being against Tommy Mile[9]. Whilst searching through the archives in the Snakepit I found an interesting article, it dates from the 1950s unfortunately there is no source given however as it provides an interesting insight into both John and his wrestling I reproduce it here.

John Foley – courage abounding

Many experts believe John Foley the greatest natural wrestler of this century.

Three grueling ghost matches in an empty stadium in Lancashire raised the curtain seven years ago on the phenomenal career of John Foley the Leigh wrestler

Manchester, Leigh, Bolton and Wigan were the centres of wrestling in Lancashire when Lancashire was the centre of world catch as catch can wrestling.

From his home town have sprung many stalwart wrestlers and thinking away from heavyweight for a time all who follow wrestling will know of the inimitable Joe Reid several times amateur bantamweight champion of great Britain third in the European championships at Budapest and Britain's bantamweight Olympic representative in the 1932 Olympic games in LA. And empire games medalist in Canada in 1930.

Following in the footsteps of famous Leigh wrestlers. John Foley is emerging as one of the all time greats of wrestling history.

Then a youngster just settled in his trade the Lancashire lad brought up to grapple was making his first bid for recognition in the sport that was to become his living and a craft that was to replace a mundane trade.

Little more than a schoolboy he was pitting the enthusiasm of youth and the thorough training of a Lancashire lad against the wiles and experience of seasoned grapplers who combined wrestling strength with the deadly techniques and grim determination that befitted the craftiest veterans in wrestling.

The only witnesses to these three contests were a handful of enthusiasts and maestro Billy Riley. The empty stadium echoed to their voices. The advice their comments even their hushed silence seemed to have a voice of its own as the gleaming ring lights sent a parade of weird shadows flitting over the empty seats.

No raucous voiced announcer introduced the slightly built rather gangling frame of dark haired John Foley as he clambered through the ropes to meet his first opponent a seasoned veteran of the Wigan school of wrestling with experience gathered around the world.

The bell sounded and the wrestlers came to grips. In spit of lightning speed and suppleness Foley was having a bad time but somehow he succeeded in sharing off or wriggling out of near falls or damaging submissions. Eight minutes came nine followed by more until as the veteran began to tire Foley began to dominate the contest. Just as he was pressing for a fall a voice snapped out of the ringside "that'll do stop in Foley, in you go……." mentioning a Yorkshire man with a household name.

14 minutes 58 sec of hard fighting and with scarcely a minute breather, Foley was again locked to grips in another titanic struggle. Open mouthed the handful at ringside watched as the youth form Leigh ripped himself from punishing holds and catapulted his more experienced opponent across the ring. Confidence was taking the place of youthful fire and in 20 min 32 sec shooting

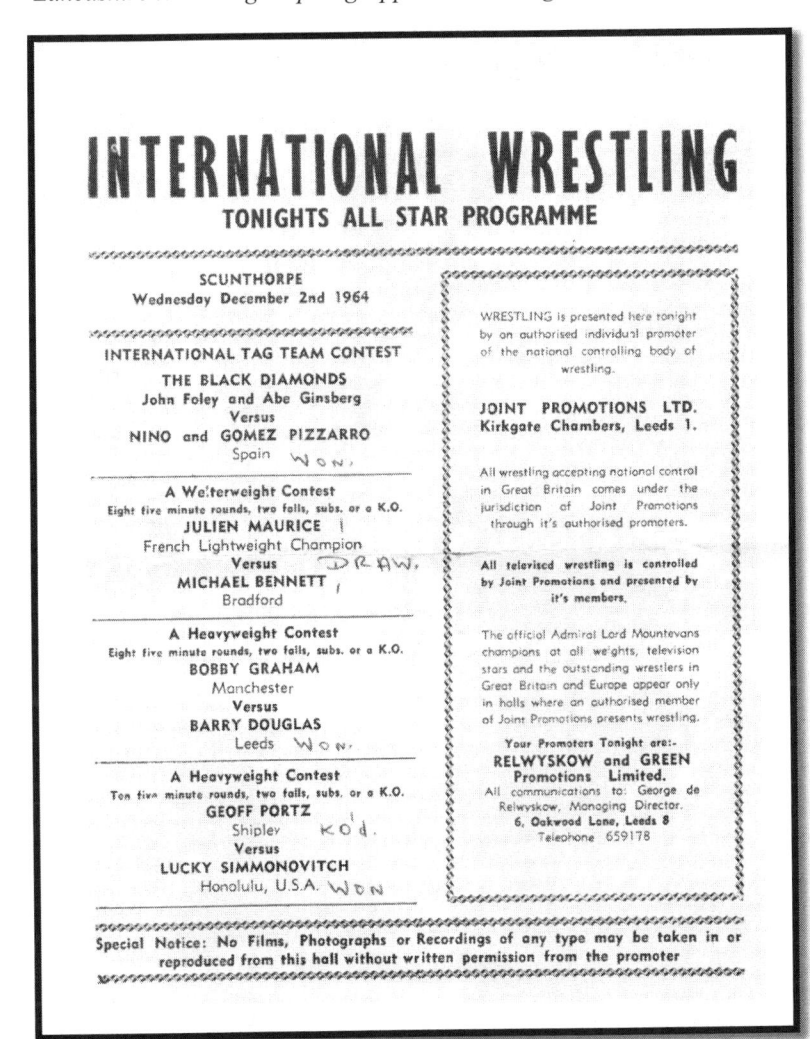

for a grommet he was caught by the wily veteran and spun flat on his back.

Almost before he had risen to his feet he saw his opponent disappearing out of the ring and his place being taken by another master craftsman of the ring.

Sweat glistening on his youthful body John Foley turned to meet his new opponent. Once again the viewers fell under the spell of the amazingly dexterous performance of the slim built youth. Disbelief registered on their faces as 37 minutes showed up on the clock and the slightly built lad was still in there battling. They watched his explosive attacks, darting foot work and eel like escape moves until a tiring veteran securing a headlock braced himself with might and main for a final effort. Cruelly his knuckles bit into Foleys cheekbone just underneath the eye, relentlessly the arm pressure tightened across Foleys ear, remorselessly the head was levered back on to his shoulders as simultaneously the veterans weight bore on Foleys spine.

Gradually Foley was borne to the floor with the grip still unmercifully held. A tap for submission would have relieved the pain. Grimly the youth held out. To be defeated twice would have put paid to the end of his ambition for a ring career. He must hold out……..he must hold out……..he must hol……he mus…..he…..finally oblivion.

We he came round the only faintly heard the hum of conversation and he showered and dressed it was a despondent John Foley who tried to hear the people around him through the bells ringing in his ears.

A few days later medical advice informed him that he had lost the hearing of that ear and there was nothing that could be done to restore it.

A sore head and disgrace all that had come out of his venture into professional circles?

Later he learned with glee that he had not been expected to win, not even last a few minutes with any of the three experiences wrestlers .To battle against the odds for 37 minutes was what was sought in the youth who would become a wrestler. Many mediocre men set off on the road to fame to be flung ruthlessly from the road as their footsteps fail and maestro Billy Riley was not the one to devote his talent to encouraging mediocrity. What he sought he had found in John Foley , a natural skill and wrestling frame allied to stark courage and grim determination the stuff of which champions are made.

Now on the threshold of all honours that wrestling can bring, John Foley stands out among the lighter men who may wrest the mantle of champion from the shoulders of Tommy Mann. In John Foley there stands a man who can battle his way through Europe to the coveted European title. Courage exists in him that will not let him stop short of the vista of a world crown. Such is the skill and courage of the Leigh grappler but withal there is a quiet shyness of manner and personality that belies the raging driving fury that simmers below the surface

The damage to his ear tends to make him seem a little aloof when failing to hear someone speak he may ignore them in a seeming supercilious way . to have such an impression of the warm hearted Lancastrian is an utter delusion. First to the help of those who need it , thoughtful and encouraging outside of the ring, John Foley is a man to be met. Inside the ropes his is better avoided by those whose ambitions lie in the same direction as his.

Billy Riley

For more years than I care to remember the name of Riley has been respected all over the world. Billy Riley was born in Leigh Lancashire in 1896.

In 1919 he won the middleweight championship of the world. In 1923 he defeated Jack Robinson in Johannesburg for the British Empire Middleweight crown with which he retired undefeated.

In 1953, whilst Ernie Riley was in Germany, the promoter he was working for asked Ernie whether or not he could get Welterweight John Foley across to wrestle. Ernie rang John who at that time was still working down the pits. John came across to Germany and entered a tournament in Hamburg where he met Karl Von Chenok, the Muller brothers and Eric Koltschak.[10]. John was suddenly catapulted into full professional life, staying in nice hotels, eating at nice restaurants. Ernie tells the story

" 'I'm never going back down t'pit' he said y'know and he was like wherever you went you were adored like, like you go in a restaurant and somebody would send a drink over and John couldn't get over all this and then while we were there, he'd only been there a month and this fella the promoter there, I can't think of his name he said 'What do you think about going to Finland, Helsinki?' that was 1953, because it was the year after the Olympic games they had the Olympic games in '52 Helsinki, y'know and we said oh, and we went to Finland to Helsinki and we were there about 6 weeks well that was the place where we were y'know, everything was found for us, we had a an hotel, taxi's everywhere and everywhere we went there was a place called Linnanmaki park where we wrestled like built of the style, do you remember up Belle Vue when it was an amusement place? Well it was like that but they also had a big stadium and we used to wrestle there and then after we'd wrestle there was a big dance hall there and we could go there and we'd used to get invited and all the girls were coming to ask for a dance all these lovely Finnish girls and John said 'Can't beat this life,' he never went back in the pit, John. He never went back after that"[11]

However he didn't quite always get it right when taking to the high life. Whilst at the opening night at Linnanmaki Gardens a banquet was put on. At the end of the evening liqueurs was served in small little shot glasses. On seeing them John was heard to say "Are we having boiled eggs now?"[12].

John also wrestled as masked wrestler named 'The Kat' although it's unclear why he had to conceal his identity.[13]

During his wrestling career he travelled abroad extensively to wrestle, not only Germany and Finland but also Japan, India and Hong Kong[14].

The Mechanics arms

In 1957 he received an injury to one of his legs and developed septicaemia, this meant he was in plaster for 12 months.[15]

He married his wife Vera in 1962 and had a daughter Michelle in 1967. Apart from his wrestling he enjoyed Rugby league, walking fishing and he bred poodles. He was also fluent in Spanish[16]

In his prime he was 13st 11 lbs. and stood at 5 feet 8 ½ inches.[17]. In 1956 he was one of the first wrestlers to be televised wrestling the likes of Johnny Eagles and Al Brown. He was known for his figure 4 submissions. He met Jack Dempsey on a number of occasions for the welterweight title and also met middleweights McManus, Pallo, Alan Colbeck and Chick Purser on a number of occasions. He also fought Galion Gaspini for the European middleweight at the Belle Vue Manchester, the result was a draw[18]. Respected by his fellow wrestlers Al Brown said of him "Foley is a real hard man. It is impossible to hurt him"[19]

Although rated by Charles Mascall, the renowned wresting writer as one of the 10 best middleweights of all time, at one point in his career he was better known on the continent, with the likes of Pallo and McManus avoiding him. In 1963 he formed a partnership with Abe Ginsberg and formed the tag team the Black Diamonds after becoming disenchanted by championship wrestling[20]. They wore black capes and sported beards and a black leather hats with earflaps. In 1964 they travelled to Paris in the November and 'created a sensation' with their stormy shock tactics. They were quoted at the time as saying "we'd like nothing better that to wrestle mick McManus and his longhaired partner Steve Logan. They could name the terms and we'd back the side stakes, anything they care to put up'[21]. However shorty after this John was involved in a car accident. He was asleep in the back of the car when it hit the back of a lorry and he was out of action for 14 week, however did reform with Abe Ginsberg when he had recovered.[22] In 1966 he took over the license of a public house in Wigan. Known as the Mechanics the pub still operates today. He decided to take time out from his wrestling career in order to try and build up a clientele for the pub. Eric Cutler replaced him in the black diamonds [23]. Later he would form a partnership with Ted Heath and became the original British Bulldogs.

John Foley also ran his own wrestling gym in Leigh[24]

After a five year break in tag wrestling and cutting back on his solo bouts to concentrate on his business in 1971 he decided to build himself up to qualify for the heavyweight division, however he felt that there was no one in Britain to challenge him. So after being impressed with the success of Billy Robinson who had travelled abroad. He initially wrestled for promoter Angelo Poffo in Kentucky and later, in 1976 he decided to go to Canada to wrestle in Vancouver.[25]

He wrestled in the Stampede wrestling for Stu Hart. He played the villain to Stu Hart white night filling the role of nemesis. Dressed in Khaki pants a WW2 helmet and a Hitler moustache he infuriated the fans. Later known as J.R.Foley playing up to the J R Ewing character from Dallas, popular at the time he wore a black Stetson, one occasion he got into the ring in tag matches against Stu Hart et al. He 'managed' the likes of The Dynamite kid, Duke Myers, Kerry Brown, Honky Tonk Wayne, The Viet Cong Express, and The Cobra[26].

He died from lung (throat[27]) cancer 24.06.1988[28].

Titles

Joint Promotions Northern area Middleweight champion – 1960s

---

[1] The Who's who of wrestling – J.D'Orazio – S.Paul 1971
[2] The Wrestler Oct 1965
[3] Wrestler oct 1965
[4] Ernie Riley interview A.Coleman
[5] The Wrestler 1965 oct
[6] The Wrestler 1965 October
[7] P Physical chess – B.Robinson ,J Shannon ECW Press 201page 37
[8] The Who's who of wrestling – J.D'Orazio – S.Paul 1971
[9] Wrestling hertigae.co.uk
[10] The Wrestler 1965 October
[11] Ernie Riley interview
[12] Alan latham , Ernie Riley interview – A.Coleman
[13] Wrestling hertigae.co.uk
[14] The Who's who of wrestling – J.D'Orazio – S.Paul 1971
[15] The Wrestler magazine 1965
[16] he Who's who of wrestling – J.D'Orazio – S.Paul 1971
[17] wrestling encyclopedia
[18] The Wrestler October 1965
[19] The Wrestler JJune 1964
[20] The Wrestler 1971 October
[21] The Wrestler December 1964

[22] The Wrestler Oct 1965
[23] The Wrestler 1966 September
[24] Physical chess – B.Robinson ,J Shannon ECW Press 2012 page 26
[25] The Wrestler October1971
[26] http://www.kayfabememories.com/Regions/stampede/stampede2.htm
[27] Pain and Passion – the history of Stampede wrestling – location 2759 – kindle edition – Heath McCoy
[28] http://www.cagematch.net/?id=2&nr=1485

Chapter 27

Seamus Dunleavy

Seamus Dunleavy was born in a three-bedroom house in Barrack Street, Charleston, near the County Mayo/Cligo border on November 28th 1934 to Mary Kate and Michael Dunleavy. He was one of eight children, Paddy, Luke Tommy, Mickey, Seamus Angela Kathleen and Monica. Seamus' father was a carpenter and they owned a Public house come Shop called Dunleavy's.

Seamus attended Lowpark national school and stayed until the sixth grade. Much like his mother and father's siblings who had left Ireland to settle in America, Seamus wanted to get out into the world. Like many of his countrymen he decided to leave Ireland. In 1953[1] He got on the bus to Dublin with £6 in his pocket with his worldly goods in his cardboard suitcase. His travelling companion was Jimmy Joe Mulligan who was on his way to Wigan to visit friends. However it was Liverpool that was to be their first destination and they arrived there one morning at 6 am.

He settled down, and began work as a carpenter[2]. After being in England six months came across Duffy's boxing club in Litherlands, however in the same venue for 3 nights of the week was the Pegasus wrestling club which he jointed with his brother Mike who had also joined him in England by that time

Seamus found that his body was more suited to wrestling than boxing and concentrated his efforts in this area. After working for 8 to 9 months he had become sufficiently proficient to be entered for the Northern Counties championship 1954[3]. This was to be held in Bark Street in Bolton. His trainer was Gerry Grat from Liverpool. He won his matches gaining a place in the final. He was to meet Bert

Seamus Dunleavy Eire

Mike Dunleavy, Jack Atherton and Seamus Dunleavy

Owen; unfortunately he lost after 8 minutes but did qualify for the All England Championships.

The Championships were held 3-4 months later and the venue was the Empress Hall in London. At the time he was a middleweight weighing 12 ½ stones. The prestigious event had a special guest, George Hackenschmidt the famous wrestler. Once again Seamus did well winning his matches and gaining a place in the final against Harry Kendal. He gained a fall in the 9th minute however, he later lost the bout achieving runner up.

He later moved to Birmingham and found work in the Shamrock Dance hall and the Rist Irish Ballroom in Birmingham. He worked a Saturday night and Sunday afternoon and evening. The Owner was Mat Byrne who was married to Billy Riley's daughter Jayne.

Matt Byrne made it ok for Seamus to train at Riley's Gym. His first trip to the Wigan gym in Pyke street however was to prove fruitless as it was shut. However his next visit was on a Monday morning and he found many of the Wigan boys to be present including Ernie Riley, Jack Dempsey, Mel Riss, Brian Burke, Frank Sullivan, Gerry Hogan, Jimmy Hart, Billy Joyce and Billy Robinson.

He trained regularly with Billy Robinson, noting that he was 'Absolutely hard as Iron'. He trained hard at the gym. The session started at 11 and finished around 2 but Seamus would hang back practicing how to fall so that no matter how he was thrown he always landed safely. He also practiced a move against the hanging punch bag that he would later excel at, the drop kick. His brother also attended the gym and although of similar height, couldn't manage the head high drop kicks that Seamus could.

Like many of the wrestlers, before he was allowed to start professional shows he was put through the booth at Matt Moran's wrestling and boxing booth. He would take on all comers with a prize of £5 being offered to anybody who could last 3 rounds. Matt had the gift of the gab and once introduced Seamus with the following story " This is

dropped when he saw a large man over a foot taller than him walk through the door, however he was terrified and visibly trembling and he beat him under 2 minutes.

Seamus on occasion whether due to business became the target of people out to hurt him and on once occasion was attacked and shot. Following this whilst at the Kings Hall in Derby Jack Atherton approached him " Seamus, I don't know what's happened but I have some 'material' here for you" – it was a .38 and a .22 caliber pistol and a machete.

He finished wrestling at the age of 36.

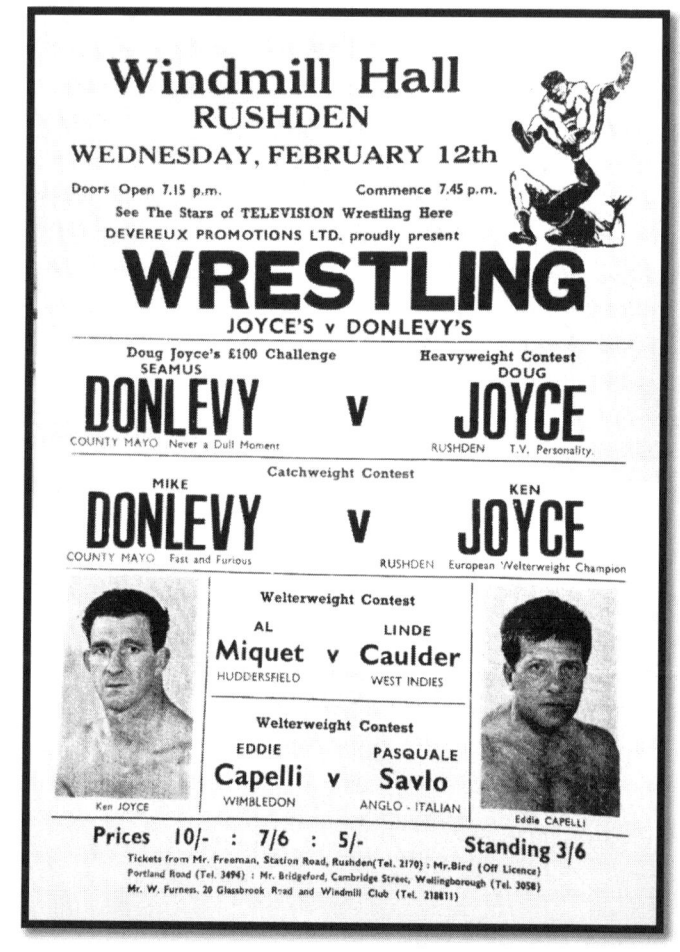

Seamus Dunleavy. I was down in the west of Ireland one day a very nice area and I saw this lad ploughing the field it was Seamus. I said 'Which way to Dublin?' Seamus picked up the plough and said 'That way!' At the end of the night Matt would call for 'nobbins' from the crowd, money thrown into the ring for appreciation of the wrestlers.

He turned professional in 1957 [4]. In an interview he talked about the reasons behind this "I just wanted to get in and get in the pro game, I won the northern championships then came runner up in nationals, so I thought I could do this again next year and I may win and I may not but the pro gym was on fire there was wrestling in every town so I got into the pro game to get a few quid together"[5]. His first professional match was in Colne against Alec Bray, a Wigan lad but not from the same gym. It was for R&A promotions, run by Billy Riley and Jack Atherton. Billy Riley would frequently referee the matches. That first match went well and he was on his way in his professional career. However it wasn't always plane sailing and one night in Derry Jack Atherton said to him " Seamus there's a fellow here who reckons that wrestling isn't what it's supposed to be that its mostly a put up job, so when the show is over I want you to wrestle him". Seamus didn't know what to expect and his heart

He met his wife Mary in 1960 in a Birmingham dance hall and married in April 1963 [6]

He developed his business interests including nightclubs (one called the 'Liffey') ,later forming a family business called Corncrake properties which rented commercial properties all over the country including Yorkshire, Lincolnshire Norfolk Nottinghamshire Buckinghamshire Staffordshire Lancashire Warwickshire London Somerset Wells Dorset and Wiltshire

He runs the business with his children Shamus, Tracey and Russell. Russell himself was a wrestler. He became Irish amateur light middleweight champion, captained the Irish team from 1996, wrestled in the European and world championships and became 3-time winner of the World States wrestling tournament. He also trained in the USA at a naval academy. He stopped wrestling in 1998 to concentrate on the family business.

His hobbies included handball, piano accordion and saxophone as well as dancing[7].

An account of his life was recorded in the book 'Finally meeting Princess Maud' authored by Shirley Thompson.

[1] The Wrestler November 1963
[2] The Wrestler November 1963
[3] The Wrestler November 1963
[4] The Wrestler November 1963
[5] Seamus Dunleavy Interview July 2014
[6] The Wrestler November 1963
[7] The Wrestler November 1963

Chapter 28

Tony Zale

Ken Baldwin wrestled under the name of Tony Zale, a name he had taken from a former boxing champion. Early on he had an accident lifting weights where some of the discs slipped of the barbell, he lost control and the bar struck him in the chin causing him to sustain a nasty cut which left him with a large scar. It was for this reason that he began to sport his characteristic beard and hence his moniker of the 'Bearded marvel'.[1]

He was known to his friends as 'Fluff Fleming'[2] or 'fluff' for short and was described my many as a 'likeable Rogue'[3].

His career spanned the 1950s and 1960s and although more a Showman than a straight wrestler put his time in at the Riley's gym. When Karl Istaz was in Wigan serving his apprenticeship under Billy Riley he stayed for 2 years with Tony Zale at his launderette[4].

He wrestled for the Paul Lincoln management and did some tag work with Max Crabtree (brother of Shirley Crabtree 'Big Daddy').[5] Later he would enter the promoting side of things with fellow Riley's wrestler Brian Burke[6]

He owned a number of businesses, including a Launderette then later a night club/Disco in Wigan called 'A room at the top/Top of the town' which was above the Alrods building – which had been a wholesale distributor. Later when he moved to Stockport he owned a nightclub there also.[7]

He developed a problem with a pilonidal abscess

Tony Zale the boxer

at the base of his spine but did go back to wrestling. Later in life he developed Spinal cancer[8].

---

[1] Roy Wood interview July 2014

[2] Michael Moore interview 9/7/14
[3] Roy Wood interview July 2014
[4] Roy Wood interview July 2014
[5] Wrestling heritage
[6] Roy Wood interview Nov 2013
[7] Roy wood interview July 2014
[8] Michael Moore interview 9/7/14

Chapter 29

Joe Critchley

"The man the ladies love."

Romeo Joe was a real character. Loved by the ladies and christened the Jackie Pallo of the north by the wrestling journalists, Joe Critchley was one of the biggest draws in the northern ring. In the early 1950s he won the NCB amateur wrestling championship and attended Riley's gym. He gave up his job in the mines to wrestle professionally. Outside of the ring he was a quietly spoken dapper man, however when it came to his wrestling he was one of those men who send you away from the hall feeling that you have had good value for your money. As soon as the dressing room door opened the show began, from his sauntering stroll into the hall, to inspecting the ring and distributing photographs to the adoring female fans he gave the fans what they wanted. Although popular in the north he was generally unknown in the south, as he tended to wrestle outside of the north when asked why he simply replied "I'm happy as I am". His only serious injury was in October 1963 when he fell out of the ring and received a gash to his forehead in a match against Ivan Pennrekoff. It required 17 stitches[1].

Joe Critchley

N.C.B.
AMATEUR CHAMPION

also of
Television appearances

9 WINDERMERE ROAD
ORRELL . WIGAN

Telephone Wigan 83451

Roy Wood remembers Joe fondly "he couldn't wrestle to keep warm but he was a great showman, Billy wouldn't use him. I used to do Butlins with him. I would get him in full nelson lift him and throw him forwards and his false teeth would fall out, well I would do it again and again every time nearer his false teeth until he picked them up and put them back in. then I would hit him on the back of his head and knock them out again. The crowd would be wild. I would hit the rope with him between them and then he would walk around like that. Then I would look at where there was a woman, throw him through the rope and he would say 'look at that missus'. Billy Riley would have gone mad, because it killed the game, but that's what the crowd wanted "[2].

Joe Critchley had a chip

Roy Wood wrestling Joe Critchley

shop off Beech Hill; it looked like an old farmhouse[3]

Joe was a favorite of fellow wrestler Eddie Rose. Eddie worked and travelled with Joe quite a bit and noted at how surprised he was that he would slip technique into his show moves. He was certainly one of the Wigan lads that were more comfortable with the professional side of the game. One of Eddies last memories of Joe was at the Monaco Ballroom when Joe, at that point long retired put on a great show of ring comedy with fellow old timer Kevin Connealy[4].

---

[1] The Wrestler November 1964 – page 22
[2] Roy Wood and Joan Burke interview 2014
S.Greenfied – M.D'Courcy
[3] Roy Wood and Joan Burke interview 2014
S.Greenfied – M.D'Courcy
[4] Eddie Rose letter

Chapter 30

Brian Burke

"He was very quiet spoken and calm natured. He was a very good living man and a devout Catholic man." – Roy Wood

Brian Burke was born on the 28th December 1932, he one of the many wrestlers at Riley's gym that found success in both amateur and professional arenas. As a child his introduction to wrestling was via the Boys Club. He was to have taken up Boxing but didn't take to it, so tried wrestling at which he excelled and loved. [1]

He got married to his sweetheart Joan, but even then wrestlers were involved. It was Cliff Belshaw, one of the three Belshaw brothers who were from the Charnock gym, who also owned an undertaking business that took Joan to her wedding " I remember knocking my headdress on the taxi, I was a nervous wreck anyway, I remember saying I feel sick I feel sick and he said 'you be sick where you want love and I'll mop it up'[2].

Brian entered many amateur championships. His wife recalled one in particular in the Albert Hall in 1956. This took place on Friday 1st June. He is listed in the programme as being from 'Wheeley A.W.C.' the only other wrestler being E.J.Knipe. This appears to be a typo, the correct name being 'Whelley'. Brian took part in the lightweight division (67Kg, 10st 1 ½ lbs.). He later attended the award ceremony, a large dinner in Soho, with his wife[3]. Roy wood remembers him wrestling and beating 3 British amateur champions in a row[4].

Brian was member of the infamous Baskeys, the Riley's Rugby team.

Joan would see Brian returning home from the gym "We used to go over the fields at camels hump and

I'd see him going home on his bike from the wrestling, and I'd be waiting for him and he'd be going home to get ready to meet me." [5]

Later he joined with fellow Wiganer Tony Zale to start promoting[6], and he would also help out at the Wryton gym " Brian used to train the guys in Bolton along with Alan Wood and Billy Chambers. Many wrestlers wouldn't go on with Brian, he didn't look it but he was tough"[7]. He turned professional at the age of 23 wrestling under the name of Dave Newman. According to the wrestling heritage site, he mostly wrestled on the independent circuit during the 1960s, mostly in the North and the Midlands. Some of his best matches were those against fellow Wiganer Jack Dempsey (Tommy Moore)[8]. Joan his wife, remembers attending the Victoria Hall to watch him wrestle "I can remember his mother was in the front row, I only got there towards the end of this fight and there was blood everywhere, and I thought oh god, but he was winning, it wasn't his blood."[9].

One part of the professional wrestling Joan didn't like was the amount of travelling Brian did "He gave up his job to do it. I didn't go to many matches. I was a teacher so I was working. Later I was a medical secretary, they would be in Redruth in Cornwall one day Scotland the next."[10] . "When Brian first started he would get trains and buses as he had no car before we married, he got his first Ford 6-9 nine months after we got married, he came back on the milk train." Joan used to go to her friends on a Saturday as Brian was away. When they got married the house wasn't ready so they lived near the Crispin arms on Birkett Street for 2 years (the pub previously run by Billy Riley). "He travelled a lot, he did a lot of time in London, he used to come back with stories about where he stayed in Brixton. They stayed in Martinis, and he used to come back and tell me about the different foods he would sample, we were still on roast beef and Yorkshire pudding"[11]

His career continued until he retired at the age of 64.

He always felt that wrestling was a 'natural activity', one that could be witnessed when watching young animals playing; he felt it was a normal stage of development. He was known for encouraging a healthy lifestyle, especially amongst the younger generation. His wife, Joan, recalls the family being on holiday in Abersoch and meeting up with Brian from a wrestling trip. Brian was carrying a hold all that was full of Muesli, nuts and raisins, from on the family was on a strict healthy eating regime that was until they went to the Pub. .[12]

Like many of the Riley's wrestlers Brian didn't rely on wresting as his sole income, instead taking the advice of his mentor Billy Riley he also had a number of Business' including a carpet shop known as 'Newman's carpets'[13]

Brian Burke passed away a few years ago.

---

[1] Roy Wood and Joan Burke interview 2014
S.Greenfied – M.D'Courcy
[2] Roy Wood and Joan Burke interview 2014
S.Greenfied – M.D'Courcy

Brians medal from 1956

[3] Roy Wood and Joan Burke interview 2014 S.Greenfied – M.D'Courcy
[4] Roy Wood interview Nov 2013 S.Greenfield
[5] Roy Wood and Joan Burke interview 2014 S.Greenfied – M.D'Courcy
[6] Roy Wood interview Nov 2013 S.Greenfield
[7] Roy Wood interview Feb 2014
[8] Roy Wood interview Nov 2013 S.Greenfield
[9] Roy Wood and Joan Burke interview 2014 S.Greenfied – M.D'Courcy
[10] Roy Wood and Joan Burke interview 2014 S.Greenfied – M.D'Courcy
[11] Roy Wood and Joan Burke interview 2014 S.Greenfied – M.D'Courcy
[12] Roy Wood and Joan Burke interview 2014 S.Greenfied – M.D'Courcy
[13] Roy Wood Interview Nov 2013 S.Greenfield

Chapter 31

Harry Litherland

Wrestling under the name of Harry Hall, he was a great character. He was known for being very strong. He worked with Michael Moore at a local molding works in Horwhich, and one day they were casting an item for a bogey for a train. The item really needed an overhead crane to lift it up – "me and thee could lift it up" he said to Michael; "we can, but I don't think I want to its bloody heavy" Michael replied. " we'll have to wait all day for that crane"– being Wiganer's working in Horwhich there is that little bit of tribalism between the two areas and so the Horwhich guys would help their mates first.

"Come on" he said and they lifted it. Later when the workers from Horwich asked what had happened one of fellow would believe he'd lift it 'ya saying we telling lies' ' he'd look at them and follow them slowly, he was like a panther'

Harry is in his 70s and living in Aspull[1]

---

[1] Michael Moore interview 10/7/14

Chapter 32

Len Weatherby

Len Weatherby was from the Hindley area of Wigan. A strong aggressive wrestler he wrestled under the name of Gerry Hogan. He was employed at Leyland Motor Company at the same time Roy Wood was serving his apprenticeship there. He also worked as a doorman at the Casino in Wigan and Bluto's nightclub. Michael Moore remembers going to the casino in Wigan with his friends and seeing Len stood like the Godfather with all the other bouncers stood in front of him[1].

He began his wrestling and boxing at amateur level whilst in the merchant navy, sailing out of Liverpool on the vessels of pacific lines to the pacific coast of South America[2].

Starting in the amateurs, Len turned professional in 1959 after being at Riley's gym for 18 months. His first professional bout was for Jack Atherton at Brierly Hill against Alec Bray of Wigan. Most of his professional bouts were in the north and in the Butlins camps. He was to compete successfully at both middle and lightweight divisions and also took part in a number of tag matches, although he had no set partner he paired with Joe Keegan of Rockdale for a number of them[3].

Len had a well-developed physique and was said to look like he had been chiseled from rock. However, as with some of the Wigan guys he didn't make the transition to pro so well. Roy Wood comments "Len was not the best showman as he was too straight. Not all of the best wrestlers made the best pros as you have to have a different mindset and in a competitive gym environment you then had to switch for shows as it was all about putting on a good spectator bout. Roy went on to say to do shows you have to put all the basic things out of your mind, such as competitiveness. Sometimes you would wrestle to make your opponent look good, you would throw yourself as high as you could, take the bangs for your opponent. Some Riley wrestlers like Len and Jimmy Hart just couldn't convert. "He was at the gym when I was and I used to wrestle him. He did shows all over the country and I did a Butlins show at Pwllheli with him. Trying to put on a good show was very difficult though. The only way it would work was by letting Len throw me all round the ring as that's all you could do." said Roy[4]

However sometimes it was useful to have wrestlers of Lens type around. Everyone struggled with Len in the Gym sparring even the likes of the great Billy Robinson. "It was good that they were like that sometimes as we would get people with a chip on their shoulder or people who thought they were great and had attitude about it. They would then try and go rough and would soon find out. Where the likes of Tommy Moore would hold their own and hold back but still get the message across, the likes of Len and Jimmy would just go 100% and really drive the point home and hurt them. That's why Len and Jimmy never made it to the top. " said Roy[5].

Another factor which seems to have hampered his career according to Roy Wood that he gave a 'knock back' to a promoter who had invited him onto his yacht.

Len died in early 2014

---

[1] Michael Moore interview 10/7/14
[2] The Wrestler January 1965 page 16
[3] The Wrestler January 1965 page 16
[4] Roy Wood interview – Andrea Wood 2013
[5] R Roy Wood interview – Andrea Wood 2013

Chapter 33

Alan Wood

Alan Wood was born 17th March 1939 in Coppull. His father Tommy was the brother of Charlie, father of Roy Wood who currently runs the Snakepit gym. [1]. His trade was a boilermaker and worked in Horwich. Always a keen sportsman and keep fit fanatic Alan would frequently run to work with a bag on his back loaded with weights [2]. He was a keen runner and boxer. He boxed for Chorley and later at the Mechanics institute. His cousin Roy Wood summed his style up as following "he smiled a great big smile, and they'd hit him again and he'd smile wider. And they used to think what am I boxing here now and they'd give up. They'd give up in the end, they'd hit him with everything they'd got and then in the end Alan would batter them in the last round". This was at a time he was working at the Orange works with Harry Litherland a wrestler who also boxed who attended Riley's gym. Unfortunately due to a history of epilepsy in the family Alan was banned from boxing and so Harry Litherland had him start going to Riley's Gym with him.[3]

Training at Riley's gym, his partners included his cousins Tommy Heyes and Roy Wood, they were close. There was always a competitive edge to Alan and that extended to his relationship with Roy. Roy said "Me and Alan used to go for runs and he'd try run faster then me, and I'd try and run faster then him but we were just knackered and when we were wrestling we'd knock hell out of one another y'know what I mean, but that's just. It was just competitiveness weren't it. If we were walking to a rugby match, he'd start off walking and he'd walk a little bit in front of you, and you'd catch him up and

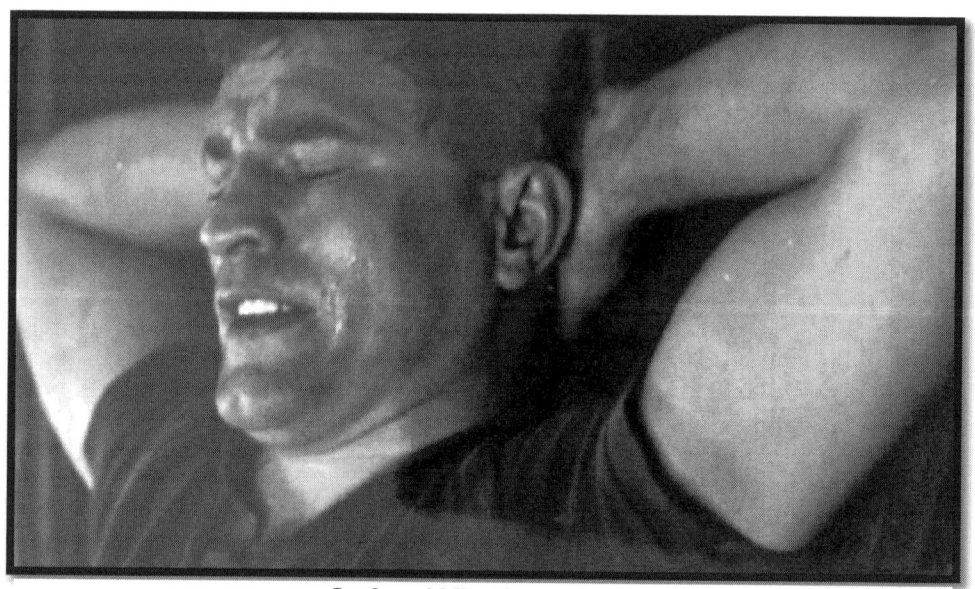

In the middle of a workout

With his parents

I'd walk in front and we'd finish up running to the blooming rugby match you couldn't even walk with him he were that way, it were a challenge even walking with him. Well in Riley's, he used to say 'C'mon Alan, we'll go for a bit of a jog,' so it should be about 5 or 6 mile and it'll be like having a race, the last mile was always a race."[4]. The competitive spirit even extended to his wife. She tells of his methods of convalescence after her back surgery "unfortunately I needed to have a back operation. But saying that, I came out of the hospital and it was my turn to convalesce cause I'd always done the looking after and he said 'Oi, don't think you are sitting there, y'know' and before I knew, I'd come out of the hospital and out of my own bed and he had me walking 15 miles and all the way I was saying 'I'm not supposed to be doing this, y'know.'"[5]. On another occasion "one particular year, y'know, we went to Pontins, umm Butlins. And you know the flagpoles outside, he said ' I'll have ye a race to the next flagpole.' Hey and I beat him, and he said 'That's a fluke,' so I did another one, beat him again, I were breathing like [panting] but on the sprint I beat him, and he didn't like that. No, he didn't, well unknown to me, you know the Butlins games? Paul and Andrew had entered and he'd had a go and I'm watching, he shoved me forward 'It's your turn now,' and I was in a race with the other women, and I won that and all. So he said 'You're going to Chorley athletics,'"[6]

Aged 16 he won an inter county amateur wrestling championship and elected to represent his country at the preliminary Olympic trials, unfortunately he was involved in a car accident which meant he was hospitalized with a fractured pelvis and had to withdraw. However, using weight and remedial exercises found previous

At the gym

form and aged 18 his prowess reached the ears of promoters and was placed under contract.[7]

He was known to favour the use of the body scissors but was also admired for his speed the 'sinuous ease' in which he was able to counter holds placed on him.[8]

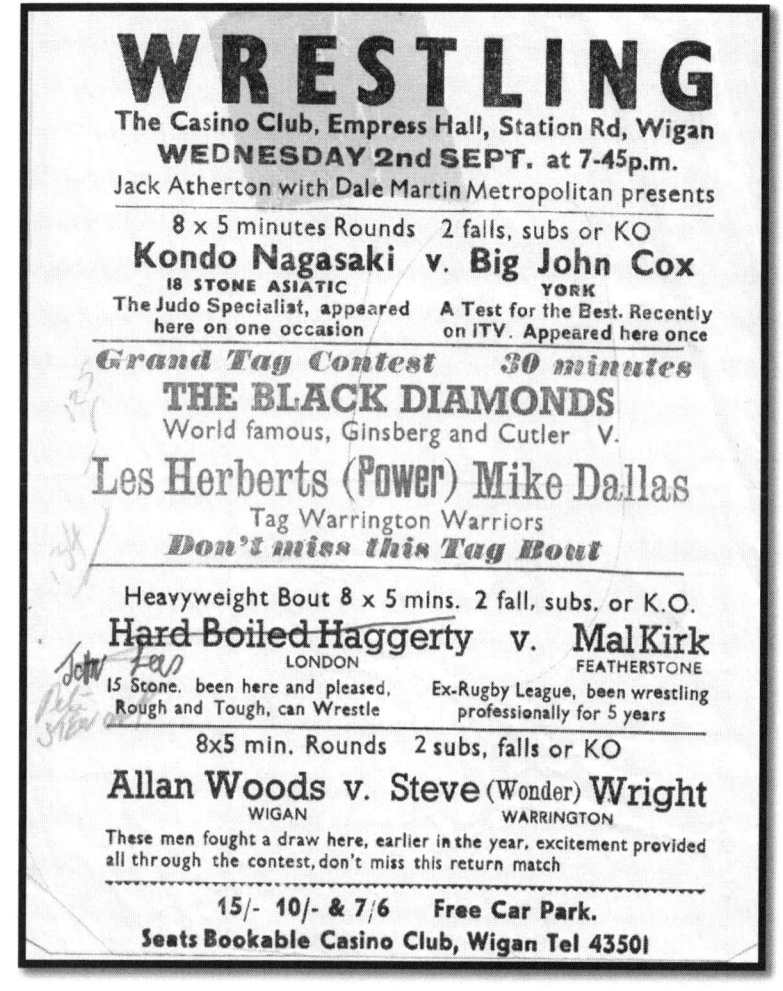

His professional debut was in the Isle of Man again Dennis Rothwell[9]. A welterweight wrestler he was 5'8" and 11st 7lbs at his peak. His style of wrestling was described as 'Textbook stylist' and was noted to spurn the gimmicky wrestling, and was noted in the Wrestler magazine that during his early years had to endure 'nerve wracking barracking from the northern audiences ' because his style was straight and they tended to enjoy more showmanship. Although he never gave into gimmicks, his only slight nod being brightly coloured striped shorts, he did learn showmanship and became a firm favorite in the ring [10] [11] although never gaining the recognition he deserved.[12]

His appearance was deceptive, although extremely fit and strong he didn't necessarily look it. Roy Wood said "You'd never thought he were tough. I bet if you, I'll tell you what I noticed about Alan. It deceived everybody, we were walking to a wrestling hall and Alan, and he'd have a coat on. You'd think he doesn't look much y'know what I mean, then when he took his coat off, you'd think blooming heck he's a bit bigger then he looks. And when he took his shirt off he went bigger as he went undressed didn't he. And when he was undressed and ready it were like blooming heck he's fit but if you'd have seen him walking around as he like slouched a little bit didn't he" on another occasion whilst travelling with Billy Riley "I remember we were wrestling in Burton on Trent and we stopped at a café called Salt Box. It were a couple of miles from the wrestling hall. Billy Riley and me were sat in the car and Alan wandered out eating an ice-lolly. Billy Riley says, 'Look would you believe he were a wrestler?' 'He's licking that ice-lolly' 'what if any punters see him wrestling tonight,' but it didn't bother Alan. '[13].

The fact he didn't look tough sometimes played to his advantage as an episode recalled by his son Andrew "I mean, one day Paul was coming home from school, and he were only about 14 then our Paul. This lad who was about 23 at the time, and he were a big black lad, 6ft black lad, he just came out walking at Paul cause I was short this one particularly lad set on him so I rushed home and told me dad now I always looked at me dad as being me dad, nothing else. People used to tell stories how he was a man and everything but he were just me dad and then I was scared cause he made me get in the car 'take me to these lads,' so we shot down the road, and Paul wasn't there when we were coming down the road. I were crying my eyes out me cause I was only about 12, anyway these two lads were there like. Me dad got out of the car, I thought these two lads were gonna flatten him y'know what I mean. He said 'Oi, lad,' a little stocky fella he was 'Have you just given a lad a good hiding, you?' and he said 'yeah, and what the f- are you gonna do about it?' he said 'I'll show you what I'll do about it,' and he just knocked them out. Banged him down, well he didn't knock him out, he banged him down. And he were all over the place, and the big black lad who you'd have thought would have done something was like puff, he was running off. Y'know what I mean. "[14]

His closest brush with a championship title came in 1966 . There was an open tournament held in the beginning of November for Jack Dempsey's vacated British welterweight title. The preliminary rounds were held on the 5th of November. * contenders initially entered. Alan won his match against Bradford's Mike Bennet and got through to the semifinals. The final was held on the 26th November and was between Alan Wood's and Alan Sergeant. Sergeant won by a cross over toehold to become the British welterweight champion and lord Mountevans gold belt holder.[15]

Like many of the others in the gym, Alan gave no quarter to anyone outside of the Riley's gym. Eddie Rose in his book 'Send in the clowns' tells of the fact that on a Sunday morning he would collect Jack Atherton and give him a lift to Bolton for a wrestling session. The first hour was taken up with wrestling catch as catch can Lancashire style with Alan wood and Jack Fallon from Riley's gym. Treatment was rough, but this was intentional, if you wanted to be able to wrestle you learned the hard way, holds on a little too long, the odd elbow or fist separated the wheat from the chaff producing wrestlers who when they got in the professional ring were dependable and reliable.[16]

Alan had a heart attack aged 46 . Despite this he didn't seem to slow down . However, despite wanting to help Roy coach the kids at Aspull, he told Roy ' I want to but Jacqueline would kill me back home", Jacqueline would later explain in an interview that it was because he had already suffered a heart attack and that she felt he was still doing too much that she would put her foot down[17]. He later collapsed at a swimming pool and died after that [18]

As summed up by Roy Wood "Alan was my training partner, my family and my friend and I will never forget him. "[19]

---

[1] Roy Wood interview – Andrea Wood 2013
[2] Roy Wood interview – Andrea Wood 2013, Jaqueline Wood and Roy Wood interview Nov 2013 S Greenfield
[3] Jaqueline Wood and Roy Wood interview Nov 2013 S Greenfield
[4] Jaqueline Wood and Roy Wood interview Nov 2013 S Greenfield
[5] Jaqueline Wood and Roy Wood interview Nov 2013 S Greenfield
[6] Jaqueline Wood and Roy Wood interview Nov 2013 S Greenfield
[7] The Wrestler Feb 1972
[8] The Wrestler Feb 1968
[9] www.wrestlingheritage.com
[10] The Wrestler February 1968
[11] The Wrestler February 1972
[12] www.wrestlingheritage.com
[13] Jaqueline Wood and Roy Wood interview Nov 2013 S Greenfield
[14] Jaqueline Wood, Andrew Wood and Roy Wood interview Nov 2013 S Greenfield
[15] The Wrester December 1966, Janurary 1967
[16] Send in the clowns eddie rose position 363
[17] Jaqueline Wood and Roy Wood interview Nov 2013 S Greenfield
[18] Roy Wood interview – Andrea Wood 2013
[19] Roy Wood interview – Andrea Wood 2013

Chapter 34

Jack Fallon

Wrestling under the moniker of 'The Destroyer' Jack Fallon, real name Billy Chambers was a light/Mid heavyweight of the 1960s and 70s. Standing at 5 feet and 8 inches he weighed in at 14st 2lbs. Jack was deaf.[1]

He was a typical product of Riley's gym, and in 1971 was said to be training there up to 15 hrs. a week.[2] He started in the Gym in the 1960s just after Roy and Alan wood.

Although he ran his own gym Jack Fallon along with Alan Wood would also take sessions in Bolton for Ken Cadman and Jack Atherton. They would teach the genuine Lancashire catch as catch can wrestling to the pro wrestlers frequently giving them a hard time, Eddie Rose in his book noted that sometimes Jacks hearing preventing him from releasing a submission hold when his opponent was screaming.[3] .Tom BIllington a.k.a the Dynamite Kid also trained at Jack's gym.

Roy Wood had fond memories of working with Jack "A good tough lad, a good submission wrestler. We was once wresting in the Isle of man, and Jack Atherton paid a man, Terry O'Neil, to take us back to Wigan. He was a giant of a fellow. He left his car in Liverpool, and he lived in Southport, he got to Haydock and dropped us off in the pouring rain and we had 7-8 miles to walk, we objected and it made no difference. What he didn't realize was that in a months time he was wrestling Jack and Jack knocked every colour out of him. He pasted him. There was once we was wrestling somewhere, I was wrestling Billy, it was like having a straight fight, more straight than show. I threw Billy into the ropes and timed my dropkick right so that he couldn't get out of the way; I broke his nose and blacked his eye. We was in the dressing room after, and there was a fellow there taking the mickey out of Billy, the

Trencherfield Mill WRESTLING
FRIDAY, JANUARY 24th
Commence 8-0 p.m.

Keith Martinelli v. *Bo Bo Matu*
BOLTON — The friendly man from the Friendly Isles

Dave Finch v Mark Wain
PRESTON. Knows all the tricks — STOCKPORT. Fast and Clever

DOCTOR DEATH v **JACK FALON**
Never been unmasked, says if he loses he will take his mask off — WIGAN

RIPPER WILSON v. **TOMMY WALSH**
No holds barred with this man — WIGAN

Referee: JACK DEMPSEY (Ex-World Champion)
Admission £1.70 Children & O.A.P 75p

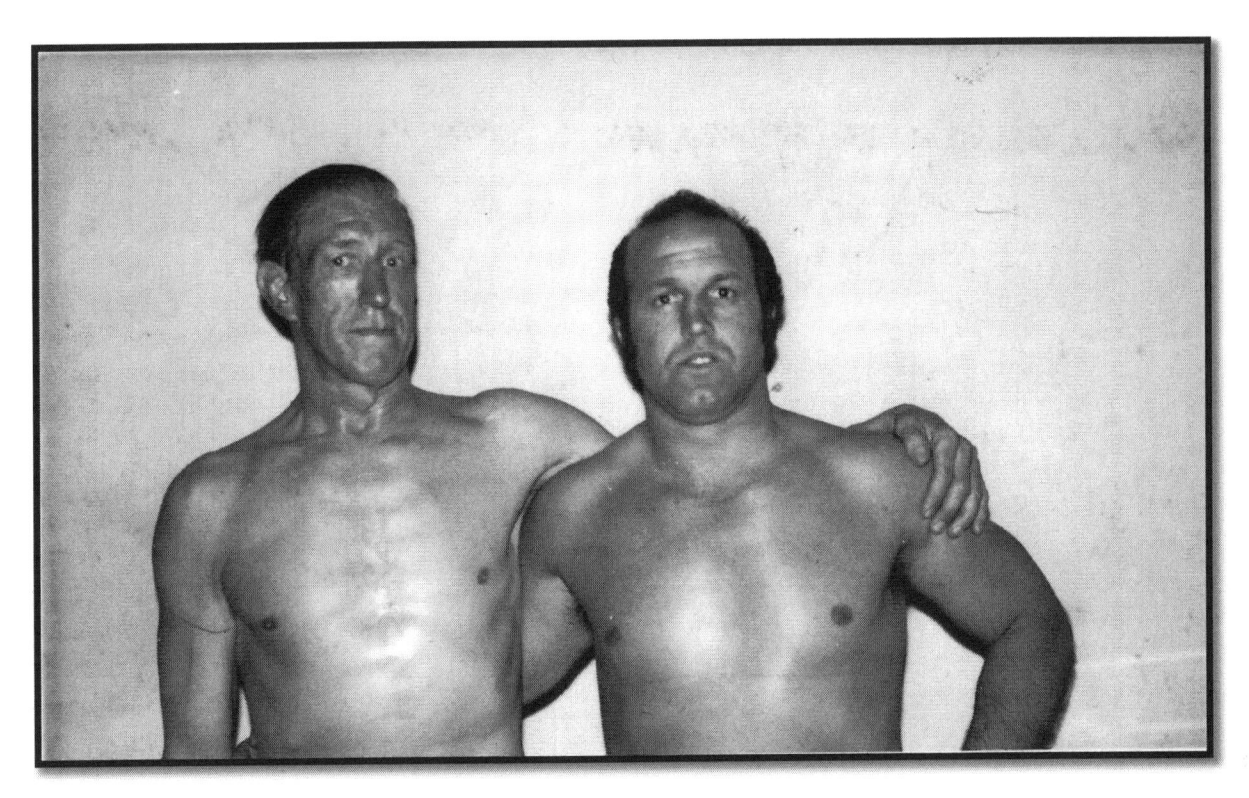

Jack Fallon and Bob Robinson (Billy Joyce)

Turk or something, he was a big fellow, he was a doorman, Billy was deaf and couldn't hear him, so I told Billy that he was taking the mick out of him so Billy turned around and hammered him. We had more and better fights in the dressing room than we did in the hall.[4]

Michael Moore remembers the son of a famous wrestler attending the gym "Ted Shambley, Joe Shambley's son, came to gym he was a PTI in the parachute regiment knew Tommy Moore's younger brother who was in the parachute regiment (Norman). Billy says, "Are you Shambley's lad?" "yeah I am" he replied, "he's a tough fellow your father, I broke his arm in the first round, it took me three rounds to submit" replied Billy.

Billy Riley's last words to Jack were " this lad hasn't done this before take your time, don't hurt him"

Jack kept taking him down and then would let him up again, to be taken down again. Ted turned to Billy to

Jack Fallon wrestling with Jack Dempsey as ref.

229

say "hard work this", Billy replied "It will do you good"

However, Jack didn't take to people who turned away from him and talking. Jack applied a three quarter Nelson, pinning him and rolling into a ball. Ted cried out in pain as his ribs broke. Billy got onto the mat to tell him to stop. They carried Ted out of the gym on a stretcher and put him in the back of an ambulance. It wasn't done in malice he just didn't hear the screams"[5]

One time Jack Atherton put Jack Fallon on with a guy who was due to wrestle on TV the following week and he wanted Jack to let him win 2:1 to make him look good. Whether it was selective deafness or his actual hearing problem but Jack didn't quite get the message. On the way to the ring he told the wrestler " I'm going to win 2:1" at which the other wrestler who had already been told by Jack Atherton that he was to win went and spoke to Jack Atherton again. Jack Atherton once again told Jack Fallon, "let him win", Jack shook his head. As the bout went on Jack Atherton stood at the side of the ring mouthing to Jack unless he let him win he was going to cancel all his engagements. Still Fallon shook his head, and took the match . As Roy Wood said ,whilst recounting the story "That was Jack!"[6]

He also wrestled in Germany in 1974 as a single wrestler against Jack Rowlands, Marty Jones, Josef Molnar, and Dave Morgan and also as a take team partner with Josef Molnar, Jack Rowlands and Steve Wright.[7]

His mascot was said to be a 1917 Guinea piece.[8]

Married to wife Dorothy he had 5 children, William, Kevin, Marie, Anthony and Bernadette[9]
He was a keen swimmer and golf player he also enjoyed chess[10]

In early 1971 he made an attempt for the British light heavyweight title against fellow gym member Billy Joyce, the champion at the time, however Joyce retained his title [11]

Jack Fallon passed away 26th August 2010 aged 74[12] of cancer.

---

[1] The Who's who of wrestling – J.D'Orazio – S.Paul 1971
[2] The Who's who of wrestling – J.D'Orazio – S.Paul 1971
[3] Send in the Clowns – Kindle Edition – Eddie Rose – YonYonson – 2012– location 391 Kindle edition
[4] Roy wood interview Nov 2013
[5] Michael Moore interview July 2014
[6] Roy wood interview Feb 2014
[7] http://wrestlingdata.com/index.php?befehl=bios&wrestler=11038&bild=1&details=11
[8] The Who's who of wrestling – J.D'Orazio – S.Paul 1971
[9] The Who's who of wrestling – J.D'Orazio – S.Paul 1971
[10] The Who's who of wrestling – J.D'Orazio – S.Paul 1971
[11] The Wrestler May 1972 page 9
[12] http://www.wrestlingheritage.co.uk/wrestlersf.htm

Chapter 35

Jack Cheers

Jack Cheers started wrestling in his late 20's or early thirties [1]. His trade was a stoker on the railways. His responsibility was to keep the fires full of fuel, which meant continually shoveling heavy loads of coal into the fires. Roy Wood believes that it is this tough work that helped contribute to Jack being so strong[2].

Jacks daughter Pauline recalls that they used to live across the road from the old gym. "It was only a little shack". The house had an old brick boiler in the kitchen and she remembers one day her mother telling her father " The coalman hasn't been today so I burnt your old wrestling boots". Pauline says he father "Went mad" telling her mother "They cost £15", that being a large sum of money in those days[3].

Jack also used to teach his daughters how to take care of themselves. Of the two sisters who were twins it was Kathleen who was the more athletic of the two. "Our Kathleen was a bugger, if you came from behind she would throw you and didn't care where you landed", she once threw Pauline in the back kitchen and there was a hole in the wall where her heel went through then our grandmother came in and shouted 'who made this hole in wall?' ".

Kathleen didn't think nothing of it and she threw a lad in the middle of the road, although the roads weren't as busy as they were today"[4].

Kathleen also remembers the other wrestlers visiting their home. She recalls Billy Riley, Ernie Riley, Jimmy Hart and Tommy Moore coming to see her father, as they were all local, and all friends. Roy Wood would visit her father when he was young and would ask his advice on wrestling "What would tha do Jack?"[5]

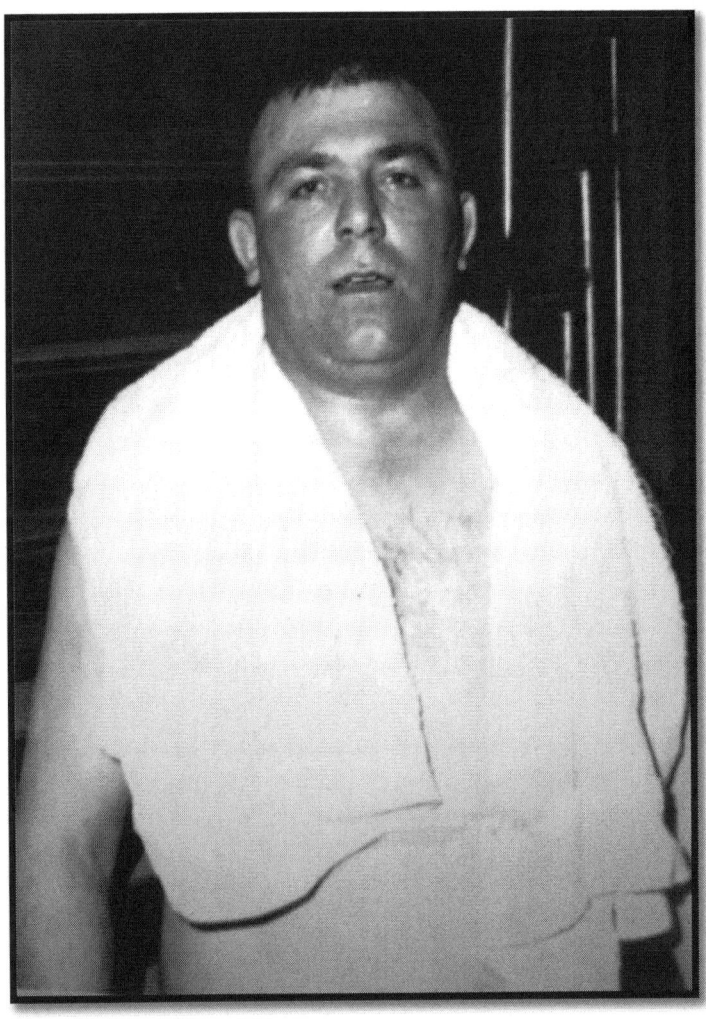

Roy's memories of him were that he was full of character and was great fun to be around, however in the gym, Jack didn't pull any punches. Like many of the Riley's wrestlers their ability in the gym didn't always translate to being well received as a pro because of their great wrestling skills and the fact they could be 'too stiff'. Roy joked that they used to say in the gym " I don't think anyone has told him it's fixed".

Riley's gym used to have a competition with Bolton wrestling club and they used to wrestle for a cup. The Riley's gym was the last ones to win the cup. The team consisted of Jack, Alan Latham, Ernie Gradwell, Brian Burke, Ernie Riley, Harold Winstanley, Tommy Moore, Gordon Rushton and Jimmy Hart. The cup is in possession of the Cheers family.[6]

In his professional career he wrestled a lot in the Isle of Man and was used as a fill in frequently and therefore wrestled under a number of different names. Roy Wood recalls wrestling against him in a Tag match. The match was at Brierley Hill near Birmingham He was partnered with a wrestler from Bolton. Jack was partnered with Tommy Heyes (aka. Gene Riscoe or Tall Tommy) Roy started the round against Jack and whilst on the floor took a kick to the ribs leaving him in pain. On seeing this his partner from Bolton refused to get in the ring saying " I'm not wrestling him!" and Roy was left to wrestle both of them for the rest of the match [7].

Like many of the other wrestlers he also wrestled in the fairground. The fair was the Silcox fair and he wrestled for Matt Moran taking on all comers.[8]

He retired as a pro wrestler in 1968 aged 46. Although Pauline and her sister never used to go and watch her dad when he was wrestling, her husband recalled attending a Gala in Scholles with Jack where there was a wrestling match with Les Kellet. Les Kellet picked out Jack straight away and came over to speak to them. He told Pauline's husband that whenever they wrestled Les always had to lose to jack.[9]

He was always a fit man, and continued going to swim at the local baths into his 80s. He also had a little dog he used to walk for miles every day. He suffered from diabetes and began having issues with falling, which unfortunately meant that his exercise became curtailed on safety grounds. He died seven years ago. On the day he died one of his great grandchildren was born. [10] The family maintains its connections with wrestling. His grandson Roy, who is friends with Roy Wood's son Darren, wrestled at the Gym with Roy when he was younger, although his mother Pauline says he stopped once girls came along but she recalls with a smile some of the stories he told of his time Wrestling in Belgium. [11]

Roy Wood and Jacky Cheers

---

[1] Interview Pauline Cheers – Novemeber 2013/11/23
[2] Interview Roy and Andrea Wood - 2013

[3] Interview Pauline Cheers – Novemeber 2013/11/23 – S.Greenfield
[4] Interview Pauline Cheers – Novemeber 2013/11/23 S.Greenfield
[5] Interview Pauline Cheers – Novemeber 2013/11/23 S.Greenfield
[6] Interview Roy and Andrea Wood - 2013
[7] Interview Roy and Andrea Wood - 2013
[8] Interview Pauline Cheers – Novemeber 2013/11/23 S.Greenfield
[9] Interview Pauline Cheers – Novemeber 2013/11/23 S.Greenfield
[10] Interview Pauline Cheers – Novemeber 2013/11/23 S.Greenfield
[11] Interview Pauline Cheers – Novemeber 2013/11/23 S.Greenfield

Chapter 36

Paul Duval

Born on the 2nd of May his real name Harry Preston. Originally from Montserrat, West Indies Harry came over to the UK and settled in the town of Preston.

He was said to have said to have started using the name Paul Duval when a wrestler hadn't turned up for Jack Taylor one night at Leicester[1]

Harry was a heavyweight; in 1971 his measurements were 18st at a height of 6 feet one inch.[2]. Strong and muscular he was able to blow up and explode hot water bottles with lungpower alone.

He trained at the Riley's gym and was affectionately known as 'Black Harry'. Bill Squires brought him to the Gym [3]. At the time of training he was around the age of 26, he weighted 19st. At the time Roy Wood weighed 10st and Alan Wood 12 ½, they were all around 20 years old at the time and despite this advantage the Wigan guys were able to easily hold their own wrestling him, [4], and helped coach him[5].

The Wrestler magazine predicted he was the man most likely to succeed Billy Robinson, however it was not to be, for whatever reason it did not convince the promoters. That however did not deter Harry himself from striving for the title, in fact he once challenged Billy Robinson, Billy was having a sauna in Preston, and it was one of the models where you sit in them. And Harry went in and said 'I hear you think you're a bit of a wrestler, we'll I'm not afraid of you". By the time Billy got out Harry had gone, and they never crossed paths in the gym either[6],[7].

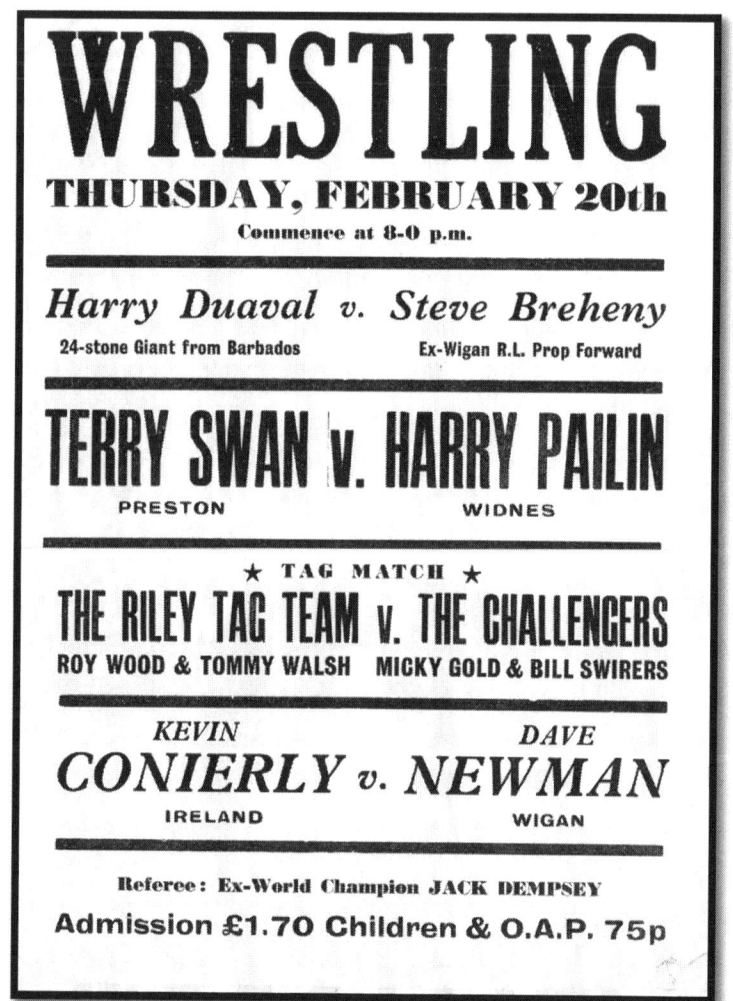

Predominantly a showman rather than a shooter Roy Wood remembers his first show. It was against Prince Curtis Laukea. Harry got in the ring, the match only lasted 2-3 minutes, with Harry taking the match Roy's comment was "Harry was that stiff, and harry didn't know it was fixed, I don't think anyone ever told him" he laughed[8]

In 1969, he began wrestling in a promotion by Max Crabtree. Max had come up with the idea of a 6 man 'Battle Royal' .It was a six mag tag team event, although there were supposed to be only 2 in the ring at any one time, frequently it ended up with all six. He was part of a team with Mike Pritchard and Larry Coulton[9].

Memorable wins included Pat Roach, Gwyn Davies and Albert Wall[10]

An ex soldier, he was married to Jayne and had two sons Robert and Phillip.[11]. He was a singer, a doorman and a compare[12] and was known as the "singing wrestler"[13]

He passed away in 2013.

---

[1] Wrestlingheritage
[2] The Who's who of wrestling – J.D'Orazio – S.Paul 1971
[3] Roy interview 22/2/14
[4] Roy Wood interview Nov 2013 S Greenfield
[5] Roy interview 22/2/14 S Greenfield
[6] Roy Wood interview Nov 2013 S Greenfield
[7] Roy Wood interview 22/2/14
[8] Roy wood interview Nov 2013 S Greenfield
[9] The Wrestler – June 1969 page 15
[10] Wrestling heritage
[11] 1971 encyclopedia
[12] Ro Wood interview 22/2/14 S Greenfield
[13] The Wrestler November 1968 Page 13

Chapter 37

John Naylor

John Naylor was born in 1944 and was one of the latter wrestlers to emerge from Riley's Gym, none the less is credited by some as being a force for change in the wrestling style of the 1970s although somewhat lesser known and forgotten amongst the wrestlers of that era such as Tom Billington 'The dynamite kid' (with whom he was friendly), Steve Wright and Mark 'Rollerball' Rocco[1]. . He became known as 'The golden ace'.

An article in the 'Wrestler' magazine in February 1972 had a quote from Jack Atherton stating, "John Naylor, a young wrestler from Wigan is going to be one of the best young wrestlers to emerge this year"[2]. At the time he was 26 years of age and had been wrestling since the age of 19. He spent several years in the amateur ranks and eventually decided to turn Pro in 1970[3]. Like many of the other wrestlers he had other business commitments outside of wrestling. This unfortunately had the effect of limiting his booking availability to weekends only and many of the promoters at the time were unwilling to give a newcomer the premium Saturday Bookings. It was Emil Poilve, an Anglo French referee and ex wrestler who on seeing him and noting his promise decided to take him to Paris to give him a chance. However, in order to get over the same worries as the English promoters he introduced him to them as an established English wrestler. During his first weekend in Paris a substitute was required. The match was at the Cirque d.Hiver in Paris and John got his first job there as a pro. He lost to former world champion Rene Ben Chemoul in two straight falls. However, Chemoul was so impressed that he persuaded other promoters to give John a chance and book him.[4]

During the next four years John would work 5 days a week in Wigan and at the weekend would commute to France to wrestle in Paris, Rheimes, Lille Lyons and even Belgium. This resulted in his fame and popularity spreading throughout Europe. Off the back of this John changed his job and decided to take a gamble on wrestling in Britain. He took a number of bookings for promoters, which saw him beating some of the better-known wrestlers such as Alan Wood and Steve Wright.[5] He also went on to face Jim Breaks, and Vic Faulkner and won the World of Sport Trophy, later dutifully losing to Mick McManus.[6]

Another notable part of his history was his involvement with the program 'The Big Time'. The program was devised and narrated by Esther Rantzen initially and then later by John Pitman and ran from 1976 to 1980. The premise of the show was to place an amateur in the limelight and follow them seeing how they faired [7]. On the 26th March 1980 an amateur, given the stage name of 'Rip Rawlinson' was placed on a bill at the Royal Albert Hall against John Naylor. Also on the bill were 16 wrestlers including Johnny Saint, Roller Ball Rocco and Big Daddy. Keith Rawlinson was the name of the member of the public. The show opened with him playing the organ in the local Methodist church. He was shown as running a local wrestling club for kids, although it noted he had never wrestled himself. His initial exposure to wrestling was with Cyanide Syd Cooper for the benefit of Max Crabtree, promoter, to see if he exhibited enough 'bottle' for him to promote his fight. Unfortunately it became painfully obvious that he is ill equipped and after a couple of minutes trying to get his opponent down and then trying some drop kicks first time, it ends with him being sick .It was wrestler 'Tally ho Kay' that was tasked with turning this complete novice into a pro wrestler. Real name Peter Kaye, he was a Lancashire lad who donned the moniker of Tally Ho after his love of horses and the link with his feud with Show Jumper Harvey Smith who made a foray into the world of Pro wrestling.[8] After a 'real' match with his trainer in the gym Max Crabtree agrees for him to go on the bill, and John Naylor is chosen for him to wrestle as someone who 'wouldn't over awe Keith'. According to Roy Wood it was Esther that chose John from a photo album, as he looked a nice guy. As for the main event, although obviously a pro match one gets the impression that John Naylor didn't 'suffer fools gladly' and taught Rip Rawlinson a lesson. He attacked his left leg in the first round with a 'single leg Boston crab with bar', which looked more like a step over toe hold/calf crusher, and it was obvious that Rip was experiencing very real pain leaving him to limp out of the first round. The next two rounds continued in the same vein with John going for his left leg time and time again and combining it with a cross face neck crank, the ref stepping in at one point to place Rips hand on the rope to facilitate release of the hold. Rip, somewhat living up to the initials that made up his stage name, remained in his corner on the floor at the start of round four, and retired. How much was stage, how much was John Naylor teaching him a lesson, its difficult to tell. However, for all those that watch the match, you can see the Riley wrestler characteristics in evidence, he took his craft seriously, and didn't take well to gimmicks and didn't suffer fools gladly![9]

Titles

TV trophy Winners – Walthanstow – Beat Leon Fortuna 1975 –

---

[1] http://www.wrestlingheritage.co.uk/WEBPROTECT-evolutionoftvsfinestint.htm
[2] Wrestler magazine – page 22 February 1972
[3] World of Sport annual - 1975
[4] Wrestler magazine – page 22 February 1972
[5] Wrestler magazine – page 22 February 1972
[6] http://www.wrestlingheritage.co.uk/WEBPROTECT-evolutionoftvsfinestint.htm
[7] http://en.wikipedia.org/wiki/The_Big_Time_(TV_series)
[8] http://www.wrestlingheritage.co.uk/kkaye.htm
[9] The Big Time - 1980, BBC TV

Chapter 38

Tommy Heyes

Also known as Tall Tommy in the gym to differentiate him from Tommy Moore, he wrestled under the name of Gene Riscoe. Eddie Rose in his book send in the clowns tells of an encounter with Tall Tommy " Jack rang me up, said Ginsy, and gave his imitation of a Jack Atherton phone call. Ginsy, can you do Hindley on Friday night? You're on with Tall Tommy. Make your own way for eight o'clock. Bye! – and the phone was slammed down On the Friday night in the changing rooms Ginsy is introduced to Tall Tommy who turned out to be just that – six feet three inches and twelve stone. Jack told them to sort it out between them 'ok' said Ginsy, 'I'll take the first three rounds and get a fall then you come back and do your bits and pieces. The bout went to plan. Ginsy steamed in with throws head butts forearms slams and took his fall in round three this thought Abe is too easy t o be true

The bell went for round four and tall Tommy took over. Ginsy told me for the next three round my feet never touched. He did everything to me, bang bang. I couldn't do a thing about it. My head was spinning. Round six Tommy took the equalising fall for a draw. Tall Tommy shook hands and jumped out the ring leaving Ginsy to milk the audience. When he got back to the changing room Tall Tommy had collected his wages and gone home. ' Who the hell was that' Ginsy asked Jack Atherton 'that were Tall Tommy. Everyone at Riley's gym knows Tommy'. But Ginsy never heard of him before and neither had anyone else. More to the point he never to my knowledge appeared in the

Teaching a new generation of Rileys gym wrestlers

professional ring again."[1]

His shoulder was damaged in the gym whilst wrestling with Billy Robinson.

On the reopening of the Gym he helped re establish the gym and train the youngsters.

Currently Tommy Heyes teaches at Bolton Olympic Wrestling club. Tommy is a Keen historian and I met him in the Library in Wigan where we spent two hours talking about the history of Catch as Catch can wrestling, Billy Riley and much to the amusement and annoyance of some of the library members he began showing me some of the wrestling grips taught to him form Riley's gym by Joe Carroll, I'm sure it looked somewhat of a spectacle.

Some of his writing on wrestling can be found on the

Bolton web page and in the library in Wigan.

---

[1] Send in the Clowns – Kindle Edition – Eddie Rose – YonYonson – 2012 – location 1129

Chapter 39

Roy Wood

"When you are no longer in your teens or early 20s and don't have the energy you used to, you ten to depend more on your experience and technique which is just as important as being able to run around a field

Roy was born on the 10th June 1943. It was boxing; not wrestling that Roy began his lifelong association with the combat sports. His father as well as brothers Jack, Alan and Colin were boxers as was his cousin Alan. Every weekend from aged 8 onwards they would box in the back garden with people coming from all over the local area in order to spar. At aged 14 he was boxing for Chorley boys club and Horwich RMI. Like many of that era he left school early in 1959 to become an apprentice molder at Leyland motors. It was school friend Tommy Heyes, who had started attending Riley's a few months prior with Roy's cousin Alan Wood who convinced Roy to go along and have a look and so it was at aged 15 that Roy started wrestling at Riley's gym.

He went to the gym and sat at the back. Then after a few occasions of this Billy Riley turned to him and said if you want to come and wrestle you will have to bring kit with you and his long career started from there. He remembered the atmosphere, where every match was a challenge. You would walk up to someone and ask him for a wrestle and it would be as if you had challenged him to a gunfight. Roy took his knocks learning from Billy as well as others in the Gym such as Tommy Moore, who one day whilst teaching Roy and his Cousin Alan submissions said to them "one day you will know the value of this". He remembered those early sessions "I got murdered. I used to wonder to myself why I was doing it, but I kept going". He was attending the gym three to four times a week and gradually he began winning matches.

At the age of 17 Roy and Tommy Heyes went to Matt Moran's fairground booth like many of the wrestlers form the gym before them. Matt told them he had enough wrestlers but could do with a Boxer. Roy, whose father had taught him to box, and indeed there was boxing ring in his garden as a child, took him up on the offer. Roy talked of his memories ". I stood on this platform and he shouted, 'who will fight my boy'. People were putting their hands up, half of them drunk, half of them you didn't know if they were world champion or what. I only boxed. He was a character. He had a guy wrestling for him, a big guy, and someone in the audience put they're had up and he said ' weight sinks battleships and he'll sink you'. He had the spiel, and he was on TV once and they asked him whether wrestling was a put up job, he said 'it's the same as anything else wallpapers a put up job, but its straight '"[1].

His first professional match was at the age of 17 for the promotion run by his fellow gym mates Tony Zale and Brian Burke. The match was in Haslingdon and was with Riley's wrestler Harry Hall The next one was in a Labour club in Newtown in Wigan. It was full of smoke, I did 7-8 rounds with Tommy Heyes, we were panting for our breath with all the smoke".[2] About a year later, when he had "cut his teeth" Billy Riley began using him in his own promotions. He recalled how he would be put on with new wrestlers coming into the professional game to help them ease into the professional bouts. Jack Atherton said of him "Roy would have been an international class amateur, and I expect him to reach similar heights in the professional world"[3]

Roy enjoyed a long professional career, but still kept up his day job as a molder in British Leyland. He would finish his day's work and then go to wrestle in the evening. He Wrestled under many names, Roy Wood, Ray Wood, etc. etc. sometimes even returning to the same venue the following week with a different name and from a different place according to the posters!

The highlight of his career was topping the bill at the Blackpool tower as part of the White Eagles with Johnny Eagles; the Eagles originally consisted of Johnny and Terry Jowett with Roy replacing Terry. Their opponents on that night were Less Kellet and Brian Glover.

Roy spent a lot of time with Billy Riley travelling to the Isle of Man accompanying him over on the ferry on the Isle of Man Steam Packet line, in which Billy owned shares. Wrestling was obviously discussed but Billy also gave him advice on being sensible with his money, getting an accountant, making provision for the future.

Later when in his 20s when he was wrestling full time and working, the gym fell into disuse and closed. It was later when his son Darren wanted to

Ernie Riley and Roy Wood

Bob Robinson and Roy Wood

wrestle that he and Tommy Heyes rebuilt the gym. Roy Wood coached at the Gym and Billy Riley started coming again, he didn't coach but watched Roy coaching the youngsters. After the classes he would tell Roy what to do differently how to improve his coaching.

There were some issues however with Roy having been a professional coaching amateurs "when I first started coaching, they all tried to get me banned saying I was a professional. In the streets behind me I had five British champions. Govans, three Govan's, Darren, Maxwell's, Woolley Tony Leyland. I put in a paper saying wrestling needs me more than I need wrestling."[4]

After the First Tuesday documentary and the intervention of the Sports council the club in Aspull established.

Roy coached many British and international champions. With wrestlers entering the commonwealth games. In 2012 he realized his ambition of going to the Olympics as coach for Guam and Maria Dunn.

It's not just wrestling that Roy has contributed his coaching expertise. In 2004 he helped coach the players of St. Helens Rugby team, showing them how wrestling could improve their tackling and St. Helens went on to win the Challenge cup against rivals Wigan.

Andrea his daughter persuaded Roy that if he didn't teach the catch as catch can wrestling then it would die. So, he started offering seminars at the gym in Aspull, which was re-christened 'The Snakepit' the name given to the gym by Karl Gotch and the Japanese. He also provided some seminars in Cardiff. The monthly seminars were established in Wigan and the first International seminar week occurred in 2012. In 2014 he travelled to LA for the Catch Wrestling Alliance event and gave a seminar at the Los Angeles Gym of Raul Ramirez who had trained at the international week events in Wigan.

On a personal level, I met Roy in 2011, and from day one he has been a kind generous man. He is a hard taskmaster, a wonderful coach who not only gets on the mat, but also frequently puts his students to shame with his fitness and ability. He has an encyclopedic knowledge of wrestling. Nothing is too much effort for him. You only have to see the fierce loyalty he inspires in his students to see what a great man he truly is.

Achievements and accolades

Roy has coached amateur wrestling for over 40 years producing many champions many of which went on to be successful themselves in other sports such as Paul Stridgeon who competed at the Commonwealth games in Manchester 2002. Paul went on to become the fitness coach at Wasps Rugby union club then England Rugby union, and more recently as a coach at Toulon Rugby union club.

Several wrestlers from the northwest competed at the most recent commonwealth games in Scotland, three of whom Roy coached in the past. Two of them won bronze medals.

Roy took a team to South Africa to train and compete. Andrew Pendlebury won a gold medal in the Greco-Roman section.

Trophy cabinet at Aspull

He also took a team to Bulgaria to train. A team was taken to Germany to compete at Greco-roman. Five competitors went, and 4 gold and 1 silver medal was won.

Every year in June for over 30 years, a team has been taken to the international wrestling competition in Krubeke Belgium.

Because Aspull won the team award 3 years running, they were allowed to bring the trophy back to the club.

Roy was nominated by the BBC North West to carry the Olympic torch in Abram, Wigan for the London 2012 Olympic games – carried the Olympic torch. They nominated him because he had won the sports unsung hero

Receiving the Be Inspired award from para-olympian David Weir

award for the North West. .
Aspull Community Awards 2003. Award presented for his services to the community.
Wigan Borough Sports Awards Coach of the Year 2008.
Roy was the national coach for the junior Commonwealth Games in 2005-
In 2011 Roy Won the **BBC North West Unsung Sport Hero Award**
2012 Greater Manchester sports awards – coach of the year, Be inspired award, Aspull club of the year
2012 Wigan borough awards – coach of the year, Aspull club of the year
2012 – Olympic games- Olympic coach to Guam.
Wigan sports council presented him with a **lifetime achievement award, 2000 coach of the year award.** work for charity.
Wish FM Local Hero Awards. Roy won Man of the Year.
12th annual Wigan Borough sports awards Coach of the Year 2012 and Club of the Year for Aspull wrestling club.

---

[1] Roy Wood interview Nov 2013 S.Greenfield
[2] Roy Wood interview 18/7/14 S.Greenifeld
[3] The Wrestler October 1967
[4] Roy Wood and Joan Burke interview S.Greenfield M.D'Courcy

Results

The following section records the matches of Billy Riley and his wrestlers from a number of sources including Tom Gannon's book, the World of sporting wrestling archives as well as hand bills. This section would not have been possible without the healp of Raymond Rlunkett.

Billy Riley

Date	Match	Outcome	Venue
1919	Billy Riley Vs Jack Moores	Billy won	Springfield Park, England
1932	Billy Riley Vs Bob Myers	Bob won	South Africa
1934	Billy Riley Vs Jack Garner	Billy won	Blackpool, England
1934	Billy Riley Vs Jack Wentworth	Draw	London, England
1939	Billy Riley Vs Sam Radnor	Draw	Liverpool, England
01/11/1932	Billy Riley Vs Leo Lightbody	Draw	Huddersfield, England
01/12/1932	Billy Riley Vs Jack Garner	Billy won	Blackpool, England
06/02/1933	Billy Riley Vs Harry Brooks	Billy won, HB DQ	Leeds, England
20/02/1933	Billy Riley Vs Harry Brooks	Billy won, HB DQ	Leeds, England
24/02/1933	Billy Riley Vs Fighting Ferguson	Riley won	Leigh, Lancashire
25/03/1933	Billy Riley Vs Moonraker Kid	Riley won	Shrewsbury, England
02/05/1933	Billy Riley Vs Ricky Royal	Riley won	Dewsbury, England
22/05/1933	Billy Riley Vs Harry Brooks	Draw	Leeds, West yorkshire
17/07/1933	Billy Riley Vs Jack Pye	Riley won	Wigan, England
24/09/1933	Billy Riley Vs Moonraker Kid	Riley won	Swansea, Wales
28/11/1933	Billy Riley Vs White Owl	Draw	West Ham, England
25/03/1934	Billy Riley Vs Tony Mancelli	Not Known (NK)	Smethwick
01/04/1934	Billy Riley Vs Zebra	Zebra won	Catford, England
16/04/1934	Billy Riley Vs Manson	Riley won	Poplar, England
22/06/1934	Billy Riley Vs Sam Radnor	NK	Liverpool, England
27/07/1934	Billy Riley Vs Atholl Oakley	Atholl won	West Ham, England
28/07/1934	Billy Riley Vs Atholl Oakley	Riley won	Acton, England
15/08/1934	Billy Riley Vs Society Boy	Riley won	West Ham, England
15/08/1934	Billy Riley Vs Lampard	Riley won	West Ham, England
15/08/1934	Billy Riley Vs Chalky White	Riley won	West Ham, England
16/08/1934	Billy Riley Vs Chalky White	White won	Blackfriars, London
28/08/1934	Billy Riley Vs Dutch Holland	Riley won	Acton, England
28/08/1934	Billy Riley Vs Chalky White	Riley won	Acton, England
06/09/1934	Billy Riley Vs Lampard	Riley won	Tooting, England
06/09/1934	Billy Riley Vs Chalky White	Riley won	Tooting, England
07/09/1934	Billy Riley Vs Society Boy	Riley won	Harrow, Hill, England
08/09/1934	Billy Riley Vs Top Hat	Riley won	Baker St, London
08/09/1934	Billy Riley Vs Society Boy	Riley won	Baker St, London
08/09/1934	Billy Riley Vs Chalky White	Riley won	Baker St, London
14/09/1934	Billy Riley Vs Society Boy	Riley won	Poplar, England
22/09/1934	Billy Riley Vs Half Nelson Keyes	Nelson won	Poplar, England
12/10/1934	Billy Riley Vs Hans Lagren	Riley won	Plymouth, England
14/11/1934	Billy Riley Vs Hans Lagren	Riley won	London, England
24/11/1934	Billy Riley Vs Society Boy	Riley won	St. Pancras, England
01/02/1935	Bilyl Riley Vs Dick Wills	Riley won	Plymouth, England

Date	Match	Result	Location
11/01/1936	Billy Riley Vs Battling Swede	NK	Newcastle, England
18/11/1936	Billy Riley Vs Pat Stewart	NK	Newcastle, England
20/12/1936	Billy Riley Vs Jack Wentworth	NK	Manchester, England
22/01/1937	Billy Riley Vs Tony Baer	Baer won	Preston, England
10/02/1937	Billy Riley Vs Johnny Owens	NK	Newcastle, England
12/03/1937	Billy Riley Vs Jack Owens	Riley won	Blackpool, England
24/03/1937	Billy Riley Vs Dick Wills	NK	Newcastle, England
26/03/1937	Billy Riley Vs Jack Atherton	NK	Preston, England
09/04/1937	Billy Riley Vs George French	NK	Blackpool, England
21/04/1937	Billy Riley Vs Bob Fife	NK	Newcastle, England
13/05/1937	Billy Riley Vs Jim Anderson	Jim won	Edinburgh, Scotland
13/05/1937	Bilyl Riley Vs Jim Anderson	Anderson won	Edinburgh, Scotland
28/05/1937	Billy Riley Vs Jack Atherton	Atherton won	Preston, England
12/08/1937	Billy Riley Vs Jack Robinson	Billy won	Edinburgh, Scotland
16/09/1937	Billy Riley Vs White Owl	Riley won	Morecambe, Lancashire
04/11/1937	Billy Riley Vs Vic Hessell	NK	Nelson, England
04/11/1937	Billy Riley Vs Vic Hessle	Riley won	Nelson
05/11/1937	Billy Riley Vs Masked Marvel	NK	Preston, England
02/12/1937	Billy Riley Vs Vic Hessell	Hessell won	Nelson, England
17/12/1937	Billy Riley Vs Wild Tarzan	Riley won	Preston, England
13/01/1938	Billy Riley Vs Wild Tarzam	Riley won WTDQ	Nelson, England
27/01/1938	Billy Riley Vs Jack Owens	Owens won	Douglas, Isle of Man
17/06/1938	Billy Riley Vs Vic Hessell	NK	Preston, Lancashire
30/07/1938	Billy Riley Vs Costa Astreos	NK	Newcastle, England
20/08/1938	Billy Riley Vs Jack Atherton	Riley won	Newcastle, England
24/08/1938	Billy Riley Vs Hal Leonard	Riley won	Birmingham, England
08/10/1938	Billy Riley Vs Terry Van	Riley won	Newcastle, England
14/04/1939	George Gregory Vs Ric DeGroote	Draw	Belle Vue, Manchester
17/04/1939	Billy Riley Vs Jim DeLisle	Billy won	Doncaster, South Yorkshire
17/04/1939	Billy Riley Vs Tiger Delisle	Riley won	Doncaster, South Yorkshire
27/06/1939	Billy Riley Vs Lew Roseby	NK	Whitley Bay, England
22/08/1939	Billy Riley Vs Joe Batten	NK	Whitley Bay, England
11/12/1939	Billy Riley Vs Jack Hunter	NK	Bolton, Lancashire
11/01/1941	Billy Riley Vs Joe Batten	NK	Newcastle, England
12/05/1941	Billy Riley Vs Jimmy Doran	NK	Blackpool, England
05/07/1941	Billy Riley Vs Dick Wills	NK	Newcastle, England
20/10/1941	Billy Riley Vs Jack Atherton	Riley won	Edinburgh, Scotland
01/12/1941	Billy Riley Vs Joe Robinson	Riley won	Edinburgh, Scotland
08/12/1941	Billy Riley Vs Tiger Tasker	NK	Blackpool, England
22/12/1941	Billy Riley Vs Al Gardiner	Riley won	Edinburgh, Scotland
26/01/1942	Billy Riley Vs Jim Williams	NK	Blackpool, England
26/01/1942	Billy Riley Vs Jim Williams	NK	Blackpool, England
23/02/1942	Billy Riley Vs Mick Doran	NK	Blackpool, England
23/02/1942	Billy Riley Vs Mike Doran	NK	Blackpool, England
07/04/1942	Billy Riley Vs Joe Hill	NK	Ossett, England

Date	Match	Result	Location
14/05/1942	Billy Riley Vs Bob McDonald	NK	Morecambe, Lancashire
14/05/1942	Billy Riley Vs Bob McDonald	NK	Morecambe, Lancashire
29/10/1942	Billy Riley Vs Dick Wills	NK	Morecambe, Lancashire
29/10/1942	Billy Riley Vs Dick Wills	NK	Morecambe, Lancashire
31/10/1942	Billy Riley Vs Joe Robinson	NK	Belle Vue, Manchester
04/11/1942	Billy Riley Vs Billy Joyce	NK	Belle Vue, Manchester
07/11/1942	Billy Riley Vs Red Brokau	NK	Belle Vue, Manchester
01/12/1942	Billy Riley Vs Black Panther (John Grant)	NK	Liverpool, England
08/02/1943	Billy Riley Vs Ross McNeill	NK	Blackpool, England
08/02/1943	Billy Riley Vs Ross McNeill	NK	Blackpool, England
19/03/1943	Billy Riley Vs Joe Hill	NK	Heckmondwicke, England
21/07/1943	Billy Riley Vs Carl Van Wurden	NK	Belle Vue, Manchester
15/11/1943	Billy Riley Vs Ross McNeill	NK	Blackpool, England
15/11/1943	Billy Riley Vs Ross McNeill	NK	Blackpool, England
13/12/1943	Billy Riley Vs Tony Baer	NK	Blackpool, England
13/12/1943	Billy Riley Vs Tony Baer	NK	Blackpool, England
03/01/1944	Billy Riley Vs J. Beaumont	NK	Blackpool, England
21/02/1944	Billy Riley Vs Jackie Robinson	NK	Blackpool, England
13/03/1944	Billy Riley Vs Joe Robinson	NK	Blackpool, England
05/06/1944	Billy Riley Vs Douglas the Turk	NK	Doncaster, South Yorkshire
24/07/1944	Billy Riley Vs Jack Atherton	Draw	Doncaster, South Yorkshire
18/09/1944	Billy Riley Vs Herbie Rose	NK	Lincoln, Lincolnshire
19/09/1944	Billy Riley Vs Jacquerez	NK	Warrington, England
20/11/1944	Billy Riley Vs Val Cerino	Riley won	Hull, England
08/01/1945	Billy Riley Vs Glynn Evans	Riley won	Hull, England
29/01/1945	Billy Riley Vs Eric Haskins	NK	Hull, England
19/02/1945	Billy Riley Vs Cab Cashford	Riley won	Hull, England
05/03/1945	Billy Riley Vs Jack Atherton	Atherton won	Hull, England
05/06/1945	Billy Riley Vs Douglas the Turk	NK	Doncaster
26/11/1945	Billy Riley Vs Ron Jackson	NK	Hull, England
31/01/1946	Billy Riley Vs Sid Askins	Riley won	Norwich, England
08/02/1946	Billy Riley Vs Frank Manto	NK	Hull, England
11/02/1946	Billy Riley Vs Eric Fisher	NK	Hull, England
14/02/1946	Billy Riley Vs Bully Pye	NK	Norwich, England
25/02/1946	Billy Riley Vs Pat Kavanagh	NK	Tipton, England
04/03/1946	Billy Riley Vs Rex Maxine	NK	Hull, England
13/02/1947	Billy Riley Vs Seaman Wilkie	Riley won	Derby, Derbyshire
11/06/1947	Billy Riley Vs Iron Duke	Riely won	Folkestone, England
11/06/1947	Billy Riley Vs Jeff Conda	Conda won	Folkestone, England
03/11/1947	Billy Riley Vs Tom Rigby	NK	Blackpool, England
11/12/1947	Billy Riley Vs Jeff Conda	Riley won	Crewe, England
23/06/1948	Billy Riley Vs Jim Holden	NK	Bury
22/11/1950	Billy Riley Vs Joe Batten	Riley won	Preston
09/07/1955	Billy Riley Vs Bill McDonald	Riley won	Douglas, Isle of Man
18/11/1958	Billy Riley Vs Emil Foy	NK	Wakefield, England

Jack Atherton

Date	Match	Outcome	Venue
1937	Jack Atherton Vs Brown Masked Marvel	Marvel won	Preston, England
27/10/1933	Jack Atherton Vs Leo Lightbody	Leo won	Chelmsford, England
29/07/1935	Jack Atherton Vs Percy Smart	Percy won	Charlton, England
01/08/1935	Jack Atherton Vs Tony Demarte	Jack won	Gillingham, England
08/08/1935	Jack Atherton Vs George Gregory	George Won	Rochester, England
08/08/1935	Jack Atherton Vs George Gregory	Gregory won	Rochester, England
09/08/1935	Jack Atherton Vs George Baker	Jack won	Deptford, England
06/10/1935	Jack Atherton Vs Roy Carver	Roy won	South London, England
17/10/1935	Jack Atherton Vs Cab Cashford	Jack won	Hackney, England
18/10/1935	Jack Atherton Vs Chick Holfe	Jack won	Edmunton, England
03/11/1935	Jack Atherton Vs Jack Owens	Owens won, JA DQ	Whitechapel, England
08/11/1935	Jack Atherton Vs Tony Mancelli	NK	Deptford, England
15/11/1935	Jack Atherton Vs Cab Cashford	Jack won	Deptford, England
17/11/1935	Jack Atherton Vs Guy Falls	Guy won	Whitechapel, England
29/11/1935	Jack Atherton Vs The Iron Duke	Duke won	Deptford, England
01/01/1936	Jack Atherton Vs Aussie the Butch	Jack won	South London, England
03/01/1936	Jack Atherton Vs John Player	John won	Edmonton, England
30/01/1936	Jack Atherton Vs Slasher Jack Owens	Owens won	Edinburgh, Scotland
12/03/1936	Jack Atherton Vs Jack Dale	Dale won	Edinburgh, Scotland
14/05/1936	Jack Atherton Vs Horace Taylor	Horace won	Edinburgh, Scotland
25/06/1936	Jack Atherton Vs Jim Anderson	Jim won	Edinburgh, Scotland
19/11/1936	Jack Atherton Vs Harry Pye	Jack won	Edinburgh, Scotland
15/01/1937	Jack Atherton Vs George Gregory	Gregory won	Blackpool, England
27/01/1937	Jack Atherton Vs Chick Holfe	Jack won	Edinburgh, Scotland
26/03/1937	Jack Atherton Vs Billy Riley	NK	Preston, England
22/04/1937	Jack Atherton Vs Whipper Watson	Watson won	Edinburgh, Scotland
27/05/1937	Jack Atherton Vs George Baker	Jack won	Edinburgh, Scotland
28/05/1937	Jack Atherton Vs Billy Riley	Atherton won	Preston, England
24/06/1937	Jack Atherton Vs George Baker	George won	Edinburgh, Scotland
01/07/1937	Jack Atherton Vs Bob Fyfe	Bob won	Edinburgh, Scotland
16/07/1937	Jack Atherton Vs George Gregory	Gregory won	Preston, England
23/09/1937	Jack Atherton Vs Chris Christophedes	Jack won	Edinburgh, Scotland
02/06/1938	Jack Atherton Vs Jim Anderson	Jim won	Edinburgh, Scotland
16/06/1938	Jack Atherton Vs Ronnie Marshall	Ronnie won	Edinburgh, Scotland
11/08/1938	Jack Atherton Vs George Gregory	George won	Edinburgh, Scotland
10/11/1938	Jack Atherton Vs Vic Hesselle	Vic won	Edinburgh, Scotland
29/12/1938	Jack Atherton Vs Farmer's Boy	Jack won	Edinburgh, Scotland
09/02/1939	Jack Atherton Vs Young Madrali	Jack won	Edinburgh, Scotland
01/03/1939	Jack Atherton Vs Iron Duke	Duke won	Preston, England
11/12/1939	Jack Atherton Vs Lew Faulkner	NK	Bolton, Lancashire

Date	Match	Result	Location
20/10/1941	Jack Atherton Vs Billy Riley	Riley won	Edinburgh, Scotland
29/11/1941	Jack Atherton Vs George Gregory	NK	Belle Vue, Manchester
25/02/1943	Jack Atherton Vs Van Wurden	NK	Morecambe, Lancashire
08/11/1943	Jack Atherton Vs Wills	NK	Blackpool, England
23/12/1943	Jack Atherton Vs Van Wurden	NK	Morecambe, Lancashire
05/03/1945	Jack Atherton Vs Billy Riley	Atherton won	Hull, England
15/04/1946	Jack Atherton Vs Tony Baer	Jack won	Newcastle, England
06/05/1946	Jack Atherton Vs The Farmer	The farmer won	Edinburgh, Scotland
06/07/1946	Jack Atherton Vs Billy Joyce	NK	Belle Vue, Manchester
20/07/1946	Jack Atherton Vs Sam Crossley	Jack won	Newcastle, England
12/08/1946	Jack Atherton Vs Vic Hesselle	Vic won	Edinburgh, Scotland
17/08/1946	Jack Atherton Vs Billy Joyce	NK	Belle Vue, Manchester
14/10/1946	Jack Atherton Vs Carl Van Wurden	Jack won	Edinburgh, Scotland
06/01/1947	Jack Atherton Vs Robert McDonald	Rob won	Edinburgh, Scotland
08/02/1947	Jack Atherton Vs Jack Pye	Pye won	Edinburgh, Scotland
10/03/1947	Jack Atherton Vs Tony Baer	Tony won	Edinburgh, Scotland
18/08/1947	Jack Atherton Vs Ken Davies	Jack won	Edinburgh, Scotland
19/09/1947	Jack Atherton Vs Billy Joyce	NK	Hale, England
03/11/1947	Jack Atherton Vs Ernest Baldwin	Ernest won	Edinburgh, Scotland
01/12/1947	Jack Atherton Vs Izzy Van Dutz	Jack won, IVD DQ	Edinburgh, Scotland
06/01/1948	Jack Atherton Vs Cliff Parks	Jack won	Aberdeen, Scotland
19/01/1948	Jack Atherton Vs Henry Wilkie	Draw	Edinburgh, Scotland
26/01/1948	Jack Atherton Vs Billy Joyce	NK	Derby, England
22/03/1948	Jack Atherton Vs Bill Benny	Bill won	Edinburgh, Scotland
27/05/1949	Jack Atherton & Louis Loew Vs Albert Callens & Joschi Stefanovich	Draw	Vienna, Austria
29/05/1949	Jack Atherton Vs Leon Marciniak	Draw	Vienna, Austria
30/05/1949	Jack Atherton & Louis Loew Vs Fernard Roussel & Gaston Woignez	Draw	Vienna, Austria
01/06/1949	Jack Atherton Vs Arthur Cheveart	Arthur won	Vienna, Austria
06/01/1950	Jack Atherton Vs Josef Linski	Jack won	Dumfries, Scotland
04/04/1950	Jack Atherton Vs Francis Sullivan	NK	Rhyl, Wales
14/08/1950	Jack Atherton Vs Bill Warner	NK	Hastings, England
18/10/1950	Jack Atherton Vs don Steadman	Don won	Worthing, England
21/10/1950	Jack Atherton Vs Chick Elliott	Chick won	Manchester, England
08/11/1950	Jack Atherton Vs Kiwi Kingston	Kiwi won	Manchester, England
25/11/1950	Jack Atherton Vs Les Herberts	Les won, JA DQ	Manchester, England
01/12/1950	Jack Atherton Vs Ron Johnson	Ron won	Lime Grove, London
08/12/1950	Jack Atherton Vs Bill Malloy	Bill won	Glasgow, Scotland
09/12/1950	Jack Atherton Vs Tony Baer	Tony won	Manchester, England
09/12/1950	Jack Atherton Vs Tony Baer	Tony won	Manchester, England
13/01/1951	Jack Atherton Vs Kiwi Kingston	Kiwi won	Manchester, England
15/01/1951	Jack Atherton Vs Jack Hunter	Jack H won	Edinburgh, Scotland
15/01/1951	Jack Atherton Vs Jack Hunter	Jack H won	Edinburgh, Scotland
09/02/1951	Jack Atherton Vs Ron Johnson	Jack won	Glasgow, Scotland
20/04/1951	Jack Atherton Vs Sandy Orford	Sandy won	Glasgow, Scotland

Date	Match	Result	Location
23/07/1951	Jack Atherton Vs Dai Sullivan	Dai won	Edinburgh, Scotland
25/08/1951	Jack Atherton Vs Tony Baer	Tony won	Manchester, England
20/10/1951	Jack Atherton Vs Johnny Doulas	Jack won	Manchester, England
14/03/1952	Jack Atherton Vs Bill Malloy	Bill won	Glasgow, Scotland
29/03/1952	Jack Atherton Vs Bob McMaster	Bob won	Newcastle, England
09/05/1952	Jack Atherton Vs Les Kellet	Les won, JA DQ	Glasgow, Scotland
17/05/1952	Jack Atherton Vs Ron Harrison	Jack won	Newcastle, England
20/06/1952	Jack Atherton Vs Tony Mansi	Jack won, TM DQ	Portsmouth, England
17/07/1952	Jack Atherton Vs Cyril Morris	Jack won	Morecambe, Lancashire
26/07/1952	Jack Atherton Vs Jack Wilkinson	Jack A won	Middlesborough, North Yorkshire
22/08/1952	Jack Atherton Vs Ernie Robertson	Ernie won	Glasgow, Scotland
08/09/1952	Jack Atherton Vs Angelo Papini	Angelo won	Edinburgh, Scotland
31/10/1952	Jack Atherton Vs Don Mendoza	Don won	Glasgow, Scotland
13/11/1952	Jack Atherton Vs Mike Demitre	Mike won	Morecambe, Lancashire
01/12/1952	Jack Atherton Vs Tommy Pye	Jack won	Derby, England
06/12/1952	Jack Atherton Vs Chick Booth	Jack won	Newcastle, England
05/01/1953	Jack Atherton Vs Emile Poilve	Emile won	Middlesborough, North Yorkshire
08/01/1953	Jack Atherton Vs Gerry De Jager	Gerry won	Bristol, England
19/01/1953	Jack Atherton Vs Masambula	Masambula won	Leeds, England
18/02/1953	Jack Atherton Vs Dave Valentine	dave won	Hawick, Scotland
20/02/1953	Jack Atherton Vs Ron Johnson	Ron won	Glasgow, Scotland
19/08/1953	Jack Atherton & Leonhard Marciniak Vs Tommy Mann & OK 11	NK	Vienna, Austria
02/04/1954	Jack Atherton Vs Mr Universe (Arnold Dyson)	Jack won	Glasgow, Scotland
23/04/1954	Jack Atherton Vs Billy Howes	Jack won	Glasgow, Scotland
27/12/1954	Jack Atherton Vs Jack Stevenson	Jack A won	Edinburgh, Scotland
21/01/1955	Jack Atherton Vs Reg Williams	Reg won	Leicester, England

Ernie Riley

Date	Match	Outcome	Venue
13/05/1952	Ernie Riley Vs Jack Dale	Draw	Swindon, England
14/05/1952	Ernie Riley Vs Harry Fields	Harry won	Cardiff, Wales
19/07/1952	Ernie Riley Vs Harry Yardley	NK	Costa Green, Birmingham
13/09/1952	Ernie Riley Vs Billy Joyce	Billy won	Newcastle, England
01/12/1952	Ernie Riley Vs Kid Pittman	Ernie won	Bath, England
17/12/1952	Ernie Riley Vs Ed Capelli	Ed won	Paddington, England
01/01/1953	Competed in Germany	NK	Miscellaneous
01/01/1953	Ernie Riley Vs Gene Styzchi	Ernie won	Miscellaneous
05/01/1953	Ernie Riley Vs Francis Sullivan	Ernie won	Blackpool, England
12/01/1953	Ernie Riley Vs Jimmy Munlack	Ernie won	West Ham, England
14/01/1953	Ernie Riley Vs Tommy Mann	Ernie won	Cardiff, Wales
11/02/1953	Ernie Riley Vs Johnny Allan	Ernie won	Cardiff, Wales
24/04/1953	Ernie Rilay Vs Jack Beaumont	Ernie won	Liverpool, England
7 Aug- 1 Sep 1953	Ernie Riley Vs Bob McDonald	Ernie won	Berlin, Germany
7 Aug- 1 Sep 1953	Ernie Riley Vs Hans Richard Beherne	Ernie won	Berlin, Germany
7 Aug- 1 Sep 1953	Ernie Riley Vs Jimmy Dula	Jimmy won	Berlin, Germany
7 Aug- 1 Sep 1953	Ernie Riley Vs Jean Groajean	Ernie won	Berlin, Germany
7 Aug- 1 Sep 1953	Ernie Riley Vs Martin Chenok	Martin won	Berlin, Germany
7 Aug- 1 Sep 1953	Ernie Riley Vs Erich Ecker	Ernie won	Berlin, Germany
7 Aug- 1 Sep 1953	Ernie Riley Vs Erick Koltschak	Ernie won	Berlin, Germany
7 Aug- 1 Sep 1953	Ernie Riley Vs Gideon Gida	Gideon won	Berlin, Germany
7 Aug- 1 Sep 1953	Ernie Riley Vs Gideon Gida	Gideon won	Berlin, Germany
7 Aug- 1 Sep 1953	Ernie Riley Vs Oskar Mueller	Ernie won	Berlin, Germany
7 Aug- 1 Sep 1953	Ernie Riley Vs Nicolai Selenkowitsch	Ernie won	Berlin, Germany
7 Aug- 1 Sep 1953	Ernie Riley Vs Josef Vavra	Josef won	Berlin, Germany
7 Aug- 1 Sep 1953	Ernie Riley Vs Riedel Vogt	Riedel won	Berlin, Germany
22/10/1953	Ernie Riley Vs Hermann Vollhofer	Hermann won	Berlin, Germany
24/03/1954	Ernie Riley Vs Seye Saif Shah	NK	New Delhi, India
03/04/1954	Ernie Riley Vs Vaeant Singh	NK	Jodhpur, India
08/04/1954	Ernie Riley Vs Saudagar Singh	NK	New Delhi, India
01/05/1954	Ernie Riley Vs Vasant Singh	NK	Bombay, India
20/09/1954	Ernie Riley Vs Eugeniosz Stezycki	Ernie won	High Wycombe, England
02/10/1954	Ernie Riley (Jack Fay) Vs Johnny Allan	Johnny won	Middlesborough, North Yorkshire
14/02/1955	Ernie Riley Vs Count Bartelli	Draw	Glasgow, Scotland
11/03/1955	Ernie Riley Vs Geoff Portz	Geoff won	Glasgow, Scotland
30/04/1955	Ernie Riley Vs Les Kellett	Ernie won	Middlesborough, North Yorkshire
28/05/1955	Ernie Riley Vs Les Kellett	Les won	Middlesborough, North Yorkshire
25/06/1955	Ernie Riley Vs Johnny Allan	Johnny won	Middlesborough, North Yorkshire

Date	Match	Result	Location
13/08/1955	Ernie Riley Vs Marty Jacobs	Marty won	Middlesborough, North Yorkshire
27/08/1955	Ernie Riley Vs Eric Taylor	Ernie won	Middlesborough, North Yorkshire
01/09/1955	Ernie Riley Vs Charlie Cae	Ernie won	Torquay, England
01/09/1955	Ernie Riley Vs Bert Royal	Ernie won	Torquay, England
01/09/1955	Ernie Riley Vs Steve Logan	Ernie won	Torquay, England
06/09/1955	Ernie Riley Vs Jack Dempsey	Jack won	Swindon
07/09/1955	Ernie Riley Vs Arthur Beaumont	arthur won	Douglas, Isle of Man
15/09/1955	Ernie Riley Vs Garhardt de Jager	Ernie won	Bristol, England
04/10/1955	Ernie Riley Vs Gerhardt de Jager	Draw	Swindon, England
10/10/1955	Ernie Riley Vs Billy Howes	Ernie won	Edinburgh, Scotland
17/10/1955	Ernie Riley Vs Charro Montes	Ernie won, CM DQ	Edinburgh, Scotland
28/10/1955	Ernie Riley Vs Jim Ralwings	Ernie won	Glasgow, Scotland
29/10/1955	Ernie Riley Vs Johnny Allan	Johnny won	Middlesborough, North Yorkshire
04/11/1955	Ernie Riley Vs Johnny Yearsley	Ernie won	Ipswich, England
07/11/1955	Ernie Riley Vs Eric Taylor	Draw	Edinburgh, Scotland
10/11/1955	Ernie Riley Vs Charro Montes	Ernie won	Bristol, England
23/11/1955	Ernie Riley Vs Steve Logan	Draw	Cardiff, Wales
24/11/1955	Ernie Riley Vs Black Kwango	Ernie won	Bristol, England
01/12/1955	Ernie Riley Vs Wolfgang Ehrl	Ernie won	Morecambe, Lancashire
09/12/1955	Ernie Riley Vs Masambula	Masambula won	Glasgow, Scotland
10/12/1955	Ernie Riley Vs Johnny Allan	Draw	Middlesborough, North Yorkshire
13/12/1955	Ernie Riley Vs Ron Johnson	Ernie won	Dundee, Scotland
19/12/1955	Ernie Riley Vs Les Kellett	Les won	Edinburgh, Scotland
20/12/1955	Ernie Riley Vs Billy Howes	Ernie won	Aberdeen, Scotland
06/01/1956	Ernie Riley Vs Billy Howes	NK	Ramsgate
03/02/1956	Ernie Riley Vs Masambula	Ernie Won, Mas DQ	Glasgow, Scotland
11/02/1956	Ernie Riley Vs Wolfgang Ehrl	Ernie won	Newcastle, England
16/02/1956	Ernie Riley Vs Steve Logan	Ernie won	Bristol, England
18/02/1956	Ernie Riley Vs Baron Von Hoffman	Baron won	Middlesborough, North Yorkshire
29/03/1956	Ernie Riley Vs Bob McDonald	Bob won	Morecambe, Lancashire
17/04/1956	Ernie Riley Vs Ray Hunter	Draw	Lime Grove, England
20/04/1956	Ernie Riley Vs Doug Joyce	Ernie won	Coventry, England
05/05/1956	Ernie Riley & Francis Sullivan Vs John Grant & Masambula	Ernie & Francis won	Middlesborough, North Yorkshire
24/05/1956	Ernie Riley Vs Tomy Mann	Tommy won	Morecambe, Lancashire
11/06/1956	Ernie Riley Vs Mike Marino	mike won	Edinburgh, Scotland
14/06/1956	Ernie Riley Vs Tommy Mann	Tommy won	Morecambe, Lancashire
23/06/1956	Ernie Riley Vs Johnny Allan	Johnny won	Middlesborough, North Yorkshire
30/07/1956	Ernie Riley Vs Don Mendoza	Don won	Edinburgh, Scotland
31/07/1956	Ernie Riley Vs Alf Cadman	Ernie won	Aberdeen, Scotland
04/09/1956	Ernie Riley Vs Steve Logan	NK	Wimbledon, England
18/09/1956	Ernie Riley Vs Doug Joyce	Ernie won	Swindon, England
27/09/1956	Ernie Riley Vs Johnny allen	Ernie won	Morecambe, Lancashire
03/10/1956	Ernie Riley Vs Norman Walsh	Norman won	Lincoln, Lincolnshire
01/11/1956	Ernie Riley Vs Steve Logan	Ernie won	Aylesbury, Buckinghamshire

Date	Match	Result	Location
01/11/1956	Ernie Riley Vs Charlie Fisher	Charlie won	Aylesbury, Buckinghamshire
28/11/1956	Ernie Riley Vs Martin Conroy	Ernie won	Belfast, Ireland
03/12/1956	Ernie Riley Vs Billy Howes	NK	Altrincham
08/12/1956	Ernie Riley Vs Grant Foderingham	Ernie won	Shrewsbury, England
01/01/1957	Ernie Riley Vs Charlie Fisher	Ernie won	Lime Grove, England
02/01/1957	Ernie Riley Vs Billy Howes	Ernie won	Lincoln, Lincolnshire
15/01/1957	Ernie Riley Vs Knowles Peters	Ernie won	Hamilton, Scotland
15/01/1957	Ernie Riley Vs Oskar Mueller	Draw	Edinburgh, Scotland
18/01/1957	Ernie Riley Vs Ray DuBarry	Ernie won	Belfast, Ireland
31/01/1957	Ernie Riley Vs Billy Howes	Draw	Bristol, England
02/02/1957	Ernie Riley Vs Jack Beaumont	NC	Middlesborough, North Yorkshire
08/02/1957	Ernie Riley Vs Masambula	Ernie won	Liverpool, England
12/02/1957	Ernie Riley Vs Eric taylor	Ernie won	Lime Grove, England
16/02/1957	Ernie Riley Vs Oskar Mueller	Ernie won	Middlesborough, North Yorkshire
22/02/1957	Ernie Riley Vs Vittorio Ochoa	Vittoirio won	Liverpool, England
27/02/1957	Ernie Riley Vs Eric taylor	Eric won	Glasgow, Scotland
08/03/1957	Ernie Riley Vs Judo Al Hayes	Judo won	Ipswich, England
14/03/1957	Ernie Riley Vs Gordon Nelson	Gordon won	Bristol, England
21/03/1957	Ernie Riley Vs Johnny Allan	NK	Wimbledon, England
22/03/1957	Ernie Riley Vs Steve Logan	Ernie won	Ipswich, England
22/03/1957	Ernie Riley Vs Eric Taylor	Ernie won	Ipswich, England
22/03/1957	Ernie Rily Vs Tibor Szakacs	Tibor won	Ipswich, England
27/03/1957	Ernie Riley Vs Billy Howes	Billy won	Belfast, Ireland
10/04/1957	Ernie Riley Vs Masambula	Masambula won	Lincoln, Lincolnshire
12/04/1957	Ernie Riley Vs Eric taylor	Ernie won	Willenhall, England
24/04/1957	Ernie Riley Vs Don Mendoza	NC	Lincoln, Lincolnshire
01/07/1957	Ernie Riley Vs Tibor Szakacs	Draw	Leeds, England
06/07/1957	Ernie Riley Vs Billy Howes	Riley won	Blackpool, England
13/07/1957	Ernie Riley Vs Milo Popocopolis	Ernie won	Middlesborough, North Yorkshire
10/08/1957	Ernie Riley Vs Masambula	NC	Newcastle, England
30/08/1957	Ernie Riley Vs Johnny Peters	NK	Liverpool, England
31/08/1957	Ernie Riley Vs Milo Popocopolis	NC	Middlesborough, North Yorkshire
16/09/1957	Ernie Riley Vs Lew Roseby	Draw	Leeds, England
19/09/1957	Ernie Riley Vs Billy Howes	NK	Crewe, England
21/09/1957	Ernie Riley Vs Roger Trigeaud	Ernie won	Middlesborough, North Yorkshire
26/09/1957	Ernie Riley Vs Steve Logan	NK	Liverpool, England
03/10/1957	Ernie Riley Vs Billy Howes	NK	Southampton
05/10/1957	Ernie Riley Vs Billy Howes	NK	Luton, London
12/10/1957	Ernie Riley Vs Doug joyce	Ernie won	Coventry, England
13/12/1957	Ernie Riley Vs Jim Hussey	Draw	Willenhall, England
16/12/1957	Ernie Riley Vs Max Schnabel	Ernie won	Leeds, England
14/02/1958	Ernie Riley Vs Francis Gregory	Ernie won	Willenhall, England
15/02/1958	Ernie Riley Vs Steve Logan	(Draw 1 each)	Hanley
23/03/1958	Ernie Riley Vs Reg Williams	NK	NK
27/03/1958	Ernie Riley Vs Steve Logan	Ernie won	Beckenham, England

Date	Match	Result	Location
05/04/1958	Ernie Riley Vs Reg Williams	Ernie won	Manchester, England
08/04/1958	Ernie Riley Vs Arthur Ricardo	Ernie won	Lime Grove, England
15/04/1958	Ernie Riley Vs Ron Johnson	Ernie won	Lime Grove, England
15/04/1958	Ernie Riley Vs Gordon Nelson	Gordon won	Lime Grove, England
23/04/1958	Ernie Riley Vs Ivan Zaranoff	Ernie won	Lincoln, Lincolnshire
03/05/1958	Ernie Riley Vs Masambula	Ernie won	Wolverhampton, West Midlands
06/05/1958	Ernie Riley Vs Tony Vallon	Ernie won	Birmingham, England
10/05/1958	Ernie Riley Vs Eric taylor	Draw	Middlesborough, North Yorkshire
16/05/1958	Ernie Riley & Johnny Allan Vs Alf Cadman & Steve Logan	Ernie won	Liverpool, England
16/05/1958	Ernie Riley Vs Count Bartelli	Count won	Crewe, England
19/05/1958	Ernie Riley Vs Harry Fields	Ernie won	Tunbridge Wells, England
30/05/1958	Ernie Riley Vs Billy Howes	Billy won	Liverpool, England
31/05/1958	Ernie Riley Vs Eric Taylor	Ernie won	Middlesborough, North Yorkshire
03/07/1958	Ernie Riley Vs Les Kellett	Ernie won	Morecambe, Lancashire
04/07/1958	Ernie Riley Vs Steve Logan	Ernie won	Liverpool, England
05/07/1958	Ernie Riley Vs Johnny Czeslaw	Ernie won	Newcastle, England
12/07/1958	Ernie Riley Vs Gordon Nelson	Ernie won	Middlesborough, North Yorkshire
15/07/1958	Ernie Riley Vs Eddie Saxon	Ernie won	Purley, England
17/07/1958	Ernie Riley Vs Ivor Barratt	Ernie won	Bristol, England
20/07/1958	Ernie Riley Vs Billy Howes	Billy won	Birmingham, England
07/08/1958	Ernie Riley Vs Eric taylor	Draw	Liverpool, England
23/08/1958	Ernie Riley Vs Don Mendoza*	Ernie won	Newcastle, England
23/08/1958	Ernie Riley Vs Tibor Szakacs	Ernie won	Newcastle, England
23/08/1958	Ernie Riley Vs Don Mendoza	Don won	Newcastle, England
24/08/1958	Ernie Riley Vs Alf Cadman	Alf won	Birmingham, England
01/09/1958	Ernie Riley Vs Billy Howes	NK	Bridlington
07/09/1958	Ernie Riley Vs Alf Cadman	Alf won	Birmingham, England
13/09/1958	Ernie Riley Vs Vincent Nicolini	Ernie won	Newcastle, England
20/09/1958	Ernie Riley Vs Judo Al Hayes	Ernie won	Middlesborough, North Yorkshire
21/09/1958	Ernie Riley Vs Josef Zaranoff	Ernie won	Birmingham, England
03/10/1958	Ernie Riley Vs Billy Joyce	Billy won	Glasgow, Scotland
04/10/1958	Ernie Riley Vs Mike Marino	Ernie won	Middlesborough, North Yorkshire
08/10/1958	Ernie Riley Vs Charlie Fisher	Draw	Cardiff, Wales
12/10/1958	Ernie Riley Vs Billy Howes	Ernie won	Birmingham, England
18/10/1958	Ernie Riley Vs Francis Sullivan	Ernie won	Shrewsbury, England
29/10/1958	Ernie Riley Vs Francis Sullivan	NK	Dudley, England
30/10/1958	Ernie Riley Vs Bill Robinson	NC	Nottingham, England
02/11/1958	Ernie Riley Vs Alf Cadman	Ernie won	Birmingham, England
15/11/1958	Ernie Riley Vs Billy Howes	Ernie won	Middlesborough, North Yorkshire
20/11/1958	Ernie Riley Vs Knowles Peters	Ernie won	Morecambe, Lancashire
21/11/1958	Ernie Riley Vs Billy Joyce	Billy won	Glasgow, Scotland
05/12/1958	Ernie Riley Vs Tony Vallon	Ernie won	Liverpool, England
17/12/1958	Ernie Riley Vs Eric taylor	Ernie won	Lincoln, Lincolnshire
20/12/1958	Ernie Riley Vs Alec Bray	Ernie won	Middlesborough, North Yorkshire
02/01/1959	Ernie Riley Vs Billy Joyce	Ernie won	Glasgow, Scotland

Date	Match	Result	Location
03/01/1959	Ernie Riley Vs Vic Stewart	Ernie won	Newcastle, England
08/01/1959	Ernie Riley Vs Spencer Churchill	Ernie won	Nottingham, England
16/01/1959	Ernie Riley Vs Axel Dieter	Ernie won	Willenhall, England
17/01/1959	Ernie Riley Vs Eric Taylor	Ernie won	Lincoln, Lincolnshire
17/01/1959	Ernie Riley Vs Hans Behrens	Ernie won	Shrewsbury, England
24/01/1959	Ernie Riley Vs Daula Singh	Draw	Middlesborough, North Yorkshire
27/01/1959	Ernie Riley Vs Bill Robinson	Draw	Wolverhampton, West Midlands
30/01/1959	Ernie Riley Vs Billy Howes	NK	Bolton, Lancashire
01/02/1959	Ernie Riley Vs Tony Vallon	Ernie won	Birmingham, England
06/02/1959	Ernie Riley Vs Bill Robinson	Draw	Willenhall, England
13/02/1959	Ernie Riley Vs Billy Joyce	Billy won	Glasgow, Scotland
21/02/1959	Ernie Riley Vs Don Mendoza	Ernie won	Newcastle, England
28/02/1959	Ernie Riley Vs Don Mendoza	Ernie won	Middlesborough, North Yorkshire
13/03/1959	Ernie Riley Vs Billy Howes	NK	Bolton, Lancashire
14/03/1959	Ernie Riley Vs Albert Wall	Ernie won	Middlesborough, North Yorkshire
17/03/1959	Ernie Riley Vs Billy Howes	NK	Wakefield, England
19/03/1959	Ernie Riley Vs Bob McDonald	Ernie won	Beckenham, England
20/03/1959	Ernie Riley Vs Tony Vallon	Ernie won	Willenhall, England
03/04/1959	Ernie Riley Vs Alf Cadman	Ernie won	Glasgow, Scotland
25/04/1959	Ernie Riley Vs Billy Joyce	Billy won	Middlesborough, North Yorkshire
04/05/1959	Ernie Riley Vs Billy Howes	Riley won	Blackpool, England
08/05/1959	Ernie Riley & Bert Royal Vs Billy Howes & Tommy Mann	NK	Liverpool, England
15/05/1959	Ernie Riley Vs Bill Robinson	NK	Dudley, England
23/05/1959	Ernie Riley Vs Billy Joyce	Nk	Grantham, England
16/07/1959	Ernie Riley Vs Francis Sullivan	NK	Hulme
25/09/1959	Ernie Riley Vs Billy howes	Nk	Dudley, England
26/12/1959	Ernie Riley Vs Billy Howes	NK	Bolton, Lancashire
12/01/1960	Ernie Riley Vs Billy Howes	NK	Lime Grove, London
26/01/1960	Ernie Riley Vs Billy Howes	Howes won	Lime Grove, London
12/02/1960	Erniie Riley Vs Billy Joyce	NK	Bradford, England
24/02/1960	Ernie Riley Vs Vittorio Ochoa	Ernie won	Lincoln, England
08/03/1960	Ernie Riley Vs Billy Howes	NK	Wolverhampton, England
12/03/1960	Ernie Riley Vs Billy Howes	Riley won	Hanley
26/03/1960	Ernie Riley Vs Johnny allen	NK	Canteen of Joseph Sankey & Sons Ltd, Hadley Castle, Wellington
26/03/1960	Ernie Riley Vs Johnny Allan	Ernie won	Wellington, England
02/04/1960	Ernie Riley Vs Bill Robinson	NK	Doncaster, England
09/04/1960	Ernie Riley Vs Billy Howes	NK	Middlesborough, England
12/04/1960	Ernie Riley Vs Billy Howes	NK	Lime Grove, London
14/04/1960	Ernie Riley Vs Francis Sullivan	NK	Bradford, England
16/04/1960	Ernie Riley Vs Francis Sullivan	Riley won	Newcastle, England
07/05/1960	Ernie Riley (LHWC) Vs Remy Bale (ELHWC)	NK	Leeds, West Yorkshire
11/05/1960	Ernie Riley Vs Eric Taylor	Draw	Lincoln, England
22/06/1960	Ernie Riley Vs Billy Howes	NK	Southend
23/06/1960	Ernie Riley Vs Billy Howes	Draw	Bath, England
27/07/1960	Ernie Riley Vs Billy Howes	NK	Withernsea

Date	Match	Result	Location
06/08/1960	Ernie Riley Vs Bill Robinson	NK	Middlesborough, North Yorkshire
13/09/1960	Ernie Riley Vs Francis Sullivan	NK	Wakefield, England
21/09/1960	Ernie Riley Vs Eric Taylor	Eric won	Lincoln, England
26/11/1960	Ernie Riley Vs Don Branch	NK	Chesterfield
25/02/1961	Ernie Riley Vs ?	N/A	Ellesmere Port
08/03/1961	Ernie Riley Vs Francis Sullivan	NK	Preston, England
23/03/1961	Ernie Riley Vs Bill Robinson	NK	Smethwick
12/05/1961	Ernie Riley Vs Francis Sullivan	NK	Bradford, England
25/05/1961	Ernie Riley Vs Billy Howes	NK	Birkenhead
21/08/1961	Ernie Riley Vs Francis Sullivan	Draw	Hamilton, Scotland
25/08/1961	Ernie Riley Vs Francis Sullivan	Riley won	Belfast, Ireland
09/09/1961	Ernie Riley Vs Arjit Singh	E/R1-1/A/S	Bolton, Lancashire
06/10/1961	Ernie Riley Vs Billy Howes	NK	Wellington
03/11/1961	Ernie Riley Vs Billy Howes	Howes won	Glasgow, Scotland
04/11/1961	Ernie Riley Vs Billy Joyce	NK	Grantham,
13/11/1961	Ernie Riley Vs Francis Sullivan	Sullivan won	Hamilton, Scotland
25/11/1961	Ernie Riley (replaced Portz)Vs Albert Wall	NK	Portchester Hall, London
23/12/1961	Ernie Riley Vs Billy Howes	E/R 1-B/H 2	Trowell, Nottinghamshire
27/01/1962	Ernie Riley Vs Bert Royal	E/R (W)	Wolverhampton, West Midlands
13/03/1962	Ernie Riley Vs Francis Sullivan	Riley won	Kidderminster
24/03/1962	Ernie Riley Vs Tony Charles	NK	Leeds, West Yorkshire
12/05/1962	Ernie Riley Vs Francis Sullivan	Sullivan won	Belle Vue, Manchester
04/06/1962	Ernie Riley Vs Billy Howes	NK	Buxton, England
27/10/1962	Ernie Riley Vs Francis Sullivan	NK	Middlesborough, England
17/11/1962	Ernire Riley (LHWC) Vs Eric Liederman	NK	Lime Grove, Shepherd's Bush, London
08/12/1962	Ernire Riley Vs Bob Sweeney	NK	York
22/12/1962	Ernie Riley Vs Steve Bell	NK	Lime Grove, Shepherd's Bush, London
27/04/1963	Ernie Riley Vs Vic Stewart	E/R 1-1 V/S	Wolverhampton, West Midlands
09/05/1963	Ernie Riley Vs Bill Robinson	NK	Brierly Hill
13/06/1963	Ernie Riley Vs Billy Howes	NK	Crewe
15/06/1963	Ernie Riley Vs Billy Joyce	NK	Bromsgrove
07/08/1963	Ernie Riley Vs Billy Howes	Draw (DKO)	Douglas, Isle of Man
14/09/1963	Ernie Riley Vs Alf Cadman	NK	Wolverhampton, West Midlands
17/10/1963	Ernie Riley Vs Bill Robinson	NK	Crewe
04/01/1964	Ernie Riley Vs Reg Williams	E/R (W)	Wolverhampton, West Midlands
18/01/1964	Ernire Riley (LHWC) Vs Brian Trevors	NK	Bradford, West Yorkshire
21/03/1964	Ernie Riley Vs Gordon Nelson	draw (1 each)	Lime Grove, Shepherd's Bush, London
06/05/1964	Ernie Riley Vs Eric taylor	NK	Wolverhampton, West Midlands
09/05/1964	Ernie Riley Vs Johnny Czeslaw	NK	Bolton, Lancashire
22/08/1964	Ernie Riley Vs Ajit Singh	E/r 2-1 A/s	Wembley, London
29/08/1964	Ernie Riley Vs Jim Rawlings	NK	Bradford, West Yorkshire
07/05/1965	Ernie Riley Vs Billy Howes	Howes won	Bolton
08/05/1965	Ernie Riley Vs Francis Sullivan	NK	Doncaster
25/05/1965	Ernie Riley Vs Billy Howes (F)	Howes won	Wolverhampton, West Midlands
28/05/1965	Ernie Riley Vs Billy Howes (F)	Riley won	Bolton

29/05/1965	Ernie Riley Vs Billy Howes (F)	Howes won	Hanley
19/06/1965	Ernie Riley Vs Vic Stewart	NK	Solihull, West Midlands
17/07/1965	Ernie Riley Vs Billy Howes	Howes won	Newcastle, England
18/07/1965	Ernie Riley Vs Francis Sullivan	NK	Douglas, Isle of Man
03/06/1966	Ernie Riley Vs Bill Robinson	NK	Dumfries

Billy Joyce (Bob Robinson)

Date	Match	Outcome	Venue
25/08/1939	Billy Joyce Vs Reg Bell	Joyce won	Preston
24/05/1940	Billy Joyce Vs Joe Reid	Reid won	Preston
29/11/1940	Billy Joyce Vs Fred Norman	Norman won	Preston
13/12/1940	Billy Joyce Vs Cliff Bodo	NK	Preston
13/12/1940	Billy Joyce Vs Cliff Bodo	NK	Preston
31/01/1941	Billy Joyce Vs Pat Kavannagh	Joyce won	Preston
14/02/1941	Billy Joyce Vs Pat Kavannagh	Joyce won	Preston
28/02/1941	Billy Joyce Vs Jack Stevens	Joyce won	Preston
21/03/1941	Billy Joyce Vs Eric Askins	Joyce won	Preston
04/11/1942	Billy Joyce Vs Billy Riley	NK	Belle Vue, Manchester
15/11/1943	Billy Joyce Vs Rod McNeill	Joyce won	Hull, England
27/11/1943	Billy Joyce Vs Pat Kavanagh	NK	Chorley
27/11/1943	Billy Joyce Vs Pat Kavanagh	NK	Chorley
06/12/1943	Billy Joyce Vs George Gregory	Gregory won	Edinburgh, Scotland
11/03/1944	Billy joyce Vs Pat Kavanagh	NK	Belle Vue, Manchester
01/04/1944	Billy Joyce Vs Taffy Jones	NK	Belle Vue, Manchester
13/05/1944	Billy Joyce Vs Andre Nicole	NK	Belle Vue, Manchester
24/05/1944	Billy Joyce Vs Taffy Jones	NK	Belle Vue, Manchester
03/06/1944	Billy Joyce Vs Taffy Jones	NK	Belle Vue, Manchester
01/07/1944	Billy Joyce Vs Joe Batten	NK	Belle Vue, Manchester
26/05/1945	Billy Joyce Vs Ernie Vasey	Joyce won	Newcastle, England
09/08/1945	Billy Joyce Vs Val Cerino	NK	Morecambe, Lancashire
10/10/1945	Billy Joyce Vs Charlie Green	NK	Belle Vue, Manchester
14/01/1946	Billy Joyce Vs Terry Ricardo	Joyce won	Edinburgh, Scotland
28/01/1946	Billy Joyce Vs Frank Manto	NK	Kidderminster, England
29/01/1946	Billy Joyce Vs Hec Trudeau	NK	Lime Grove, England
23/02/1946	Billy Joyce Vs Padvo Peltonin	NK	Belle Vue, Manchester
20/03/1946	Billy Joyce Vs College Boy	NK	Caledonian Road, London
30/03/1946	Billy Joyce Vs Charlie Fisher	NK	Belle Vue, Manchester
24/04/1946	Billy Joyce Vs Jan Blears	NK	Belle Vue, Manchester
29/05/1946	Billy Joyce Vs Sonny Wallis	NK	Belle Vue, Manchester
12/06/1946	Billy Joyce Vs Bob Silcock	NK	Belle Vue, Manchester
22/06/1946	Billy Joyce Vs Sonny Wallis	NK	Belle Vue, Manchester
06/07/1946	Billy Joyce Vs Jack Atherton	NK	Belle Vue, Manchester
17/07/1946	Billy Joyce Vs Padvo Peltonin	NK	Belle Vue, Manchester
07/08/1946	Billy Joyce Vs Padvo Peltonin	NK	Belle Vue, Manchester
17/08/1946	Billy Joyce Vs Jack Atherton	NK	Belle Vue, Manchester
16/10/1946	Billy Joyce Vs Andre Drapp	NK	Belle Vue, Manchester
09/11/1946	Billy Joyce Vs Jim Anderson	NK	Belle Vue, Manchester
29/11/1946	Billy Joyce Vs Cab Cashford	NK	Hale
30/11/1946	Billy Joyce Vs Charlie Case	NK	Belle Vue, Manchester
13/02/1947	Billy Joyce Vs Freddi Rex	Joyce won	Derby, Derbyshire

Date	Match	Result	Venue
22/03/1947	Billy Joyce Vs Charlie Fisher	NK	Belle Vue, Manchester
04/04/1947	Billy Joyce Vs Ted Davey	NK	Belle Vue, Manchester
09/04/1947	Billy Joyce Vs Harry Brooks	NK	Belle Vue, Manchester
23/04/1947	Billy Joyce Vs Jack Dale	NK	Belle Vue, Manchester
10/05/1947	Billy Joyce Vs Jack Dale	NK	Belle Vue, Manchester
15/05/1947	Billy Joyce Vs Dick Wills	NK	Redruth, England
26/05/1947	Billy Joyce Vs Danno Davey	NK	Belle Vue, Manchester
14/06/1947	Billy Joyce Vs Jack Dale	NK	Belle Vue, Manchester
16/06/1947	Billy Joyce Vs George Finnie	George won	Edinburgh, Scotland
16/06/1947	Billy Joyce Vs George Finnie	Finnie won	Edinburgh, Scotland
17/06/1947	Billy Joyce Vs Jeff Conda	Draw	Poplar, England
26/06/1947	Billy Joyce Vs Young Mazurki	NK	Redruth, England
28/06/1947	Billy Joyce Vs Dick Wills	NK	Belle Vue, Manchester
16/08/1947	Billy Joyce Vs College Boy	NK	Belle Vue, Manchester
27/08/1947	Billy Joyce Vs Dick Wills	NK	Belle Vue, Manchester
19/09/1947	Billy Joyce Vs Jack Atherton	NK	Hale, England
27/09/1947	Billy Joyce Vs Jack Dale	NK	Belle Vue, Manchester
08/12/1947	Billy Joyce Vs Jack Dale	NK	Derby, England
12/12/1947	Billy Joyce Vs Lew Roseby	NK	Hale, England
26/01/1948	Billy Joyce Vs Jack Atherton	NK	Derby, England
12/03/1948	Billy Joyce Vs Lew Roseby	NK	Hale, England
26/04/1948	Billy Joyce Vs Can Cashford	NK	Hamilton, Scotland
23/06/1948	Billy Joyve Vs Jim Anderson	NK	Belle Vue, Manchester
10/07/1948	Billy Joyce Vs Lew Roseby	NK	Belle Vue, Manchester
21/07/1948	Billy Joyce Vs Stan Garside	NK	Belle Vue, Manchester
27/07/1948	Billy Joyce Vs Joe Fletcher	Fletcher won	Aberdeen, Scotland
28/07/1948	Billy Joyce Vs Joe Fletcher	Draw	Arbroath
07/08/1948	Billy Joyce Vs Lew Roseby	NK	Belle Vue, Manchester
18/08/1948	Billy Joyce Vs Mike Demitre	NK	Belle Vue, Manchester
04/09/1948	Billy Joyce Vs Jim Anderson	NK	Belle Vue, Manchester
13/09/1948	Billy Joyce Vs Frank Flash Hammond	NK	Hamilton, Scotland
13/09/1948	Billy Joyce Vs Flash Hammond	NK	Hamilton, Scotland
29/09/1948	Billy Joyce Vs Sid Askins	NK	Belle Vue, Manchester
06/10/1948	Billy Joyce Vs Taffy Jones	NK	Belle Vue, Manchester
15/10/1948	Billy Joyce Vs Cab Cashford	NK	Bradford, West Yorkshire
08/11/1948	Billy Joyce Vs Emile Poilve	NK	Derby, England
12/11/1948	Billy Joyce Vs Jack Cunningham	NK	Hale, England
24/11/1948	Billy Joyce Vs Cab Cashford	NK	Belle Vue, Manchester
04/02/1949	Billy Joyce Vs Sid Askins	Joyce won	Hale, England
19/03/1949	Billy Joyce Vs Amedi Peters	NK	Belle Vue, Manchester
07/05/1949	Billy Joyce Vs Emile Poilve	NK	Belle Vue, Manchester
27/08/1949	Billy Joyce Vs Lew Roseby	NK	Belle Vue, Manchester
08/10/1949	Billy Joyce Vs Gil Leduc	NK	Belle Vue, Manchester
09/11/1949	Billy Joyce Vs Mike Demitre	NK	Belle Vue, Manchester
26/11/1949	Billy Joyce Vs Tim McCoy	NK	Belle Vue, Manchester
28/11/1949	Billy Joyce Vs Dick Wills	Billy won	Leeds, West yorkshire

Date	Match	Result	Venue
27/12/1949	Billy Joyce Vs Milo Popocopolis	Milo won	Chelmsford, England
27/02/1950	Billy Joyce Vs Frank Pollard	NK	Derby, England
13/03/1950	Billy Joyce Vs Vardi	NK	Derby, England
28/03/1950	Billy Joyce Vs Bill Ogden	NK	Rhyl, Wales
08/04/1950	Billy Joyce Vs Tim McCoy	NK	Rhyl, Wales
22/04/1950	Billy Joyce Vs Carl Van Wurden	Carl won	Manchester, England
22/04/1950	Billy Joyce Vs Carl Van Wurden	Wurden won	Belle Vue, Manchester
06/05/1950	Billy Joyce Vs Billy Howes	NK	Belle Vue, Manchester
09/05/1950	Billy Joyce Vs Louis Loew	Loew won	Rhyl, Wales
29/05/1950	Billy Joyce Vs Cab Cashford	NK	Belle Vue, Manchester
01/06/1950	Billy Joyce Vs Ted Beckley	NK	Rhyl, Wales
20/06/1950	Billy Joyce Vs Gustav Haens	NK	Rhyl, Wales
21/06/1950	Billy Joyce Vs Ray Bukovac	Joyce won	Belle Vue, Manchester
04/10/1950	Billy Joyce Vs Fighting Malone	Joyce won FMDQ	Preston
27/10/1950	Billy Joyce Vs Henry Wilkie	Draw	Caley Baths, England
10/11/1950	Billy Joyce Vs Dominic Pye	Billy won	North London, England
22/11/1950	Billy Joyce Vs Dominic Pye	NK	Belle Vue, Manchester
24/11/1950	Billy Joyce Vs Tommy Mann	Billy won	North London, England
30/11/1950	Billy Joyce Vs Ron Harrison	Ron won	Morecambe, Lancashire
30/12/1950	Billy Joyce Vs Tony Baer	Tony Baer	Manchester, England
19/05/1951	Billy Joyce Vs Ron Jackson	Ron won	Manchester, England
07/07/1951	Billy Joyce Vs Lew Roseby	NK	Belle Vue, Manchester
24/07/1951	Billy Joyce Vs Emile Poilve	NK	Rhyl, Wales
18/08/1951	Billy Joyce Vs Freddie Rex	Joyce won	Belle Vue, Manchester
24/08/1951	Billy Joyce Vs Tony Baer	Baer won BJ DQ	Plymouth, England
24/11/1951	Billy Joyce Vs Norman Walsh	Billy won	Manchester, England
05/03/1952	Billy Joyce Vs Emil Foy	NK	Belle Vue, Manchester
10/05/1952	Billy Joyce Vs Lew Roseby	Lew won	Manchester, England
28/05/1952	Billy Joyce Vs Norman Walsh	NK	Belle Vue, Manchester
14/06/1952	Billy Joyce Vs Tony Baer	Billy won	Manchester, England
09/07/1952	Billy Joyce Vs Emile Poilve	NK	Belle Vue, Manchester
19/07/1952	Billy Joyce Vs Carl Van Wurden	Bill won	Manchester, England
19/07/1952	Billy Joyce Vs Francis Sullivan	NK	Costa Green, Birmingham
02/08/1952	Billy Joyce Vs Tony Baer	Billy won	Manchester, England
11/09/1952	Billy Joyce Vs Count Bartelli	Count won	Morecambe, Lancashire
13/09/1952	Billy Joyce Vs Ernie Riley	Billy won	Newcastle, England
26/11/1952	Billy Joyce Vs Lew Roseby	NK	Belle Vue, Manchester
02/03/1953	Billy Joyce Vs Gerry De Jager	Billy won	Leeds, England
13/04/1953	Billy Joyce Vs Rex Cable	Rex won	Leeds, England
24/04/1953	Billy Joyce Vs Karel Istaz	Joyce won	Hanover, Germany
07/05/1953	Billy Joyce Vs Salvatore Font	Bilyl won	Berlin, Germany
11/05/1953	Billy Joyce Vs Hans Lerche	Billy won	Berlin, Germany
13/05/1953	Jimmy Dula Vs Billy Joyce	Jimmy won	Berlin, Germany
19/05/1953	Billy Joyce Vs Francesco Tabola	Billy won	Berlin, Germany
20/05/1953	Billy Joyce Vs Martyn Chenok	Billy won	Berlin, Germany
23/05/1953	Billy Joyce Vs Ivar Martinson	NK	Berlin, Germany

Date	Match	Result	Location
24/05/1953	Billy Joyce Vs Conny Rux	Conny won	Berlin, Germany
25/05/1953	Billy Joyce Vs Michael Chaisne	Michael won	Berlin, Germany
30/07/1953	Billy Joyce Vs Jim Anderson	Jim won	Morecambe, Lancashire
17/09/1953	Billy Joyce Vs Lloyd Barnett	Billy won	Morecambe, Lancashire
26/09/1953	Billy Joyce Vs Johnny Douglas	Billy won	Manchester, England
31/10/1953	Billy Joyce Vs Bill McDonald	Billy won	Manchester, England
08/01/1954	Billy Joyce Vs Dave Valentine	Billy won	Edinburgh, Scotland
01/03/1954	Billy Joyce Vs Black Kwango	Billy won	Edinburgh, Scotland
13/03/1954	Billy Joyce Vs Dans Brouwers	Dans won	Manchester, England
27/03/1954	Billy Joyce Vs Baptiste Benoy	Draw	Manchester, England
14/04/1954	Billy Joyce Vs Emil Foy	NK	Belle Vue, Manchester
19/04/1954	Billy Joyce Vs Joe Cornelius	NK	Belle Vue, Manchester
16/06/1954	Billy Joyce Vs Gwyn Davies	NK	Belle Vue, Manchester
19/06/1954	Billy Joyce Vs Emile Poilve	NK	Belle Vue, Manchester
17/07/1954	Billy Joyce Vs Bob McNab	NK	Belle Vue, Manchester
31/07/1954	Billy Joyce Vs Jan Walkiss	NK	Belle Vue, Manchester
11/08/1954	Billy Joyce Vs Neil McBride	NK	Belle Vue, Manchester
13/10/1954	Billy Joyce Vs Baptiste Benoy	Joyce won	Belle Vue, Manchester
23/10/1954	Billy Joyce Vs Mister Universe	Joyce won	Belle Vue, Manchester
01/12/1954	Billy Joyce Vs Bill McDonald	Billy won	Manchester, England
01/12/1954	Billy Joyce Vs Karel Istaz	Billy won	Manchester, England
04/12/1954	Billy Joyce Vs Bill McDonald	Joyce won	Belle Vue, Manchester
12/03/1955	Billy Joyce Vs Baptiste Benoy	NK	Belle Vue, Manchester
26/03/1955	Billy Joyce Vs Baptiste Benoy	NK	Belle Vue, Manchester
30/05/1955	Billy Joyce Vs Joe Cornelius	NK	Belle Vue, Manchester
11/06/1955	Billy Joyce Vs Bill McDonald	Joyce won	New Brighton
01/08/1955	Billy Joyce Vs Gwyn Davies	NK	Belle Vue, Manchester
27/08/1955	Billy Joyce Vs Stan Furness	NK	Belle Vue, Manchester
08/10/1955	Billy Joyce Vs George Dulaye	Joyce won	Belle Vue, Manchester
03/11/1955	Billy Joyce Vs Cubano Badu	Billy won	Morecambe, Lancashire
13/12/1955	Billy Joyce Vs Francis Gregory	Billy won, FG DQ	Dundee, Scotland
06/01/1956	Billy Joyce Vs Bill McDonald	McDonald won	Glasgow, Scotland
30/01/1956	Billy Joyce Vs Mike Demitre	Mike won, BJ DQ	Leeds, West yorkshire
10/02/1956	Billy Joyce Vs Geoff Portz	Geoff won	Glasgow, Scotland
21/02/1956	Billy Joyce Vs Emile Poilve	NK	Hull, England
27/02/1956	Billy Joyce Vs Judo Al Hayes	Judo won	Edinburgh, Scotland
28/02/1956	Bilyl Joyce Vs Terence Ricardo	Terence won, Billy DQ	Aberdeen, Scotland
03/03/1956	Billy Joyce Vs Gwyn Davies	Billy won	Middlesborough, North Yorkshire
09/03/1956	Billy Joyce Vs Geoff Portz	NK	Ipswich, England
19/03/1956	Billy Joyce Vs Ray Hunter	Ray won	Edinburgh, Scotland
20/03/1956	Billy Joyce Vs Francis Sullivan	Billy Won	Hamilton, Scotland
24/03/1956	Billy Joyce Vs Jim Hussey	Billy won	Newcastle, England
24/03/1956	Billy Joyce Vs Jim Hussey	Joyce won	Newcastle, England
14/04/1956	Billy joyce Vs Masambula	Masambula won	Newcastle, England
17/04/1956	Billy Joyce Vs Don Mendoza	NK	Lime Grove, London

Date	Match	Result	Location
28/04/1956	Billy Joyce Vs Gwyn Davies	Davies won	Hanley
01/05/1956	Billy Joyce Vs Ray Hunter	Draw	Tunbridge Wells, England
11/06/1956	Billy Joyce Vs Tony Mancelli	Tony won	Leeds, West yorkshire
16/06/1956	Billy Joyce Vs Don Mendoza	Don won	Middlesborough, North Yorkshire
09/07/1956	Billy Joyce Vs Mike Marino	Mike won, Billy DQ	Edinburgh, Scotland
28/07/1956	Billy Joyce Vs Francis Gregory	Francis won	Newcastle, England
23/08/1956	Billy Joyce Vs Norman Walsh	Norman won	Morecambe, Lancashire
27/08/1956	Billy Joyce Vs Don Mendoza	Mendoza won	Edinburgh, Scotland
06/09/1956	Billy Joyce Vs Doug Joyce	Billy won	Morecambe, Lancashire
08/09/1956	Billy Joyce Vs Ernest Baldwin	Ernest won	Newcastle, England
17/09/1956	Billy Joyce Vs Rex Gable	Billy won	Leeds, West yorkshire
01/10/1956	Billy Joyce Vs Reg Williams	Draw	Edinburgh, Scotland
12/10/1956	Billy Joyce Vs Francis Sullivan	Sullivan won	Glasgow, Scotland
23/10/1956	Billy Joyce Vs Dave Armstrong	Dave won	Hamilton, Scotland
26/10/1956	Billy Joyce Vs Black Panther	NK	Dumfries, Scotland
27/10/1956	Billy Joyce Vs Tony Mancelli	Billy won	Middlesborough, North Yorkshire
29/10/1956	Billy Joyce Vs Steve Logan	Billy won	Edinburgh, Scotland
31/10/1956	Billy Joyce Vs Jim Hussey	Billy won JHDQ	Aberdeen, Scotland
01/11/1956	Billy Joyce Vs Antone Vargas	Billy won	Morecambe, Lancashire
09/11/1956	Billy joyce Vs Masambula	Masambula won	Belfast, Ireland
17/11/1956	Billy Joyce Vs Gwyn Davies	Gwyn won	Shrewsbury, England
17/11/1956	Billy Joyce Vs Alf Cadman	Cadman won	Shrewsbury, England
19/11/1956	Billy Joyce Vs Charlie Green	Billy won	Edinburgh, Scotland
30/11/1956	Billy Joyce Vs Francis Sullivan	Francis won	Glasgow, Scotland
10/12/1956	Billy Joyce Vs Emile Poilve	Emile Poilve won	Edinburgh, Scotland
11/12/1956	Billy Joyce Vs Dai Sullivan	Dai won	Dundee, Scotland
18/12/1956	Billy Joyce Vs Gipsy Fernando Herdia	Gypsy Fernando Heredia won, Billy Joyce DQ	Leeds, England
01/01/1957	Billy Joyce Vs Judo Al Hayes	Billy won	Lime Grove, England
06/01/1957	Billy Joyce Vs Reg Williams	Reg won	Shrewsbury, England
12/01/1957	Billy Joyce Vs Gordon Nelson	Billy won	Middlesborough, North Yorkshire
19/01/1957	Billy Joyce Vs Shirley Crabtree	Shirley won	Newcastle, England
31/01/1957	Billy Joyce Vs Francis Sullivan	NK	Nottingham, England
02/02/1957	Billy Joyce Vs Masambula	Masambula won BJDQ	Doncaster, England
05/02/1957	Billy Joyce Vs Ernest Baldwin	Ernest won	Huddersfield, England
11/02/1957	Billy Joyce Vs Rudi Schumacher	Billy Won	Edinburgh, Scotland
11/02/1957	Billy Joyce Vs Jim Hussey	Jim won	Hamilton, Scotland
12/02/1957	Billy Joyce Vs Jim Hussey	Hussey won	Hamilton, Scotland
13/02/1957	Billy Joyce Vs Gordon Kilmartin	Billy won	Belfast, Ireland
18/02/1957	Billy Joyce Vs Reg Williams	NK	Altrincham
21/02/1957	Billy Joyce Vs Dai Sullivan	NK	Blackburn, England
04/03/1957	Billy Joyce Vs Dennis Mitchell	Dennis won	Edinburgh, Scotland
06/03/1957	Billy Joyce Vs Tamaru Radak	Radak won, BJ DQ	Glasgow, Scotland
15/03/1957	Billy Joyce Vs Tony Mancelli	Tony won	Belfast, Ireland

Date	Match	Result	Location
16/03/1957	Billy Joyce Vs Reg Williams	Joyce won	Hanley
20/03/1957	Billy Joyce Vs Tommy Kilmartin	Billy won	Glasgow, Scotland
23/03/1957	Billy Joyce Vs Jim Hussey	Billy won	Middlesborough, North Yorkshire
23/03/1957	Billy Joyce Vs Don Mendoza	Billy won	Newcastle, England
27/04/1957	Billy Joyce Vs Dave Armstrong	Armstrong won	Newcastle, England
20/05/1957	Billy Joyce Vs Ernie Kingston	Ernie won	Edinburgh, Scotland
01/06/1957	Billy Joyce Vs Charlie Fisher	NK	Belle Vue, Manchester
05/06/1957	Billy Joyce Vs Masambula	Joyce won	Royal Albert Hall, London
07/06/1957	Billy Joyce Vs Tibor Szakacs	NK	Dudley, England
18/06/1957	Billy Joyce Vs Dennis Mitchell	Dennis won	Leeds, England
22/06/1957	Billy Joyce Vs Bert Craddock	NK	Belle Vue, Manchester
13/07/1957	Billy Joyce Vs Bill McDonald	McDonald won	Middlesborough, England
15/07/1957	Billy Joyce vs Johnny Allan	Draw	Edinburgh, Scotland
18/07/1957	Billy Joyce vs Johnny Allan	Billy won	Morecambe, Lancashire
20/07/1957	Billy Joyce Vs Francis Sullivan	Billy Won	Middlesborough, North Yorkshire
02/08/1957	Billy Joyce Vs Alf Cadman	NK	Dudley, England
03/08/1957	Billy Joyce Vs Francis St Clair Gregory	Joyce won	Middlesborough, England
08/08/1957	Billy Joyce Vs Bob McDonald	Billy won	Morecambe, Lancashire
24/08/1957	Billy Joyce Vs Vic Hesselle	Billy won	Newcastle, England
26/08/1957	Billy Joyce Vs Tibor Szakacs	Billy won	Edinburgh, Scotland
29/08/1957	Billy Joyce Vs Gwyn Davies	Billy won	Morecambe, Lancashire
30/08/1957	Billy Joyce Vs Vic Hesselle	Vic won	Hadley, England
06/09/1957	Billy Joyce Vs Hassan Ali Bey	NK	Blackburn, England
07/09/1957	Billy Joyce Vs Francis Sullivan	Francis won	Newcastle, England
13/09/1957	Billy Joyce Vs Tibor Szakacs	NK	Dudley, England
28/09/1957	Billy Joyce Vs Tibor Szakacs	Joyce won	Newcastle, England
05/10/1957	Billy Joyce Vs Bill Coverdale	Billy won	Manchester, England
13/11/1957	Billy Joyce Vs Tibor Szakacs	Billy won	Lincoln, Lincolnshire
27/11/1957	Billy Joyce Vs Bill Robinson	Billy J won	Lincoln, Lincolnshire
07/12/1957	Billy Joyce Vs Tibor Szakacs	NK	Shrewsbury, England
14/12/1957	Billy Joyce Vs Anton Vargas	Joyce won	Doncaster, England
18/12/1957	Billy Joyce Vs Kiwi Kingston	Joyce inj	Cardiff, Wales
01/01/1958	Billy Joyce Vs Ray Apollon	Ray won	Lincoln, Lincolnshire
09/01/1958	Billy Joyce Vs Reg Williams	NK	Blackburn, England
29/01/1958	Billy Joyce Vs Bill Robinson	Billy J won	Lincoln, Lincolnshire
14/02/1958	Billy Joyce Vs Masambula	NK	Chesterfield, England
01/03/1958	Bilyl Joyce Vs Brian Malloy	Joyce won	Newcastle, England
04/03/1958	Billy Joyce Vs Alan Garfield	Garfield won	Hull, England
13/03/1958	Billy Joyce Vs Don Mendoza	Draw	Gainsborough, England
21/03/1958	Billy Joyce Vs Kiwi Kingston	Draw	Glasgow, Scotland
25/03/1958	Billy Joyce Vs Bill Robinson	NK	Wakefield
26/03/1958	Billy Joyce Vs Tony Mancelli	Tony Won, BJ DQ	Lincoln, Lincolnshire
04/04/1958	Billy Joyce Vs Johnny Allan	NK	Chesterfield, England
05/04/1958	Billy Joye Vs Bill Malloy	NK	Wimbledon Palace
05/04/1958	Billy Joyce Vs Bill Malloy	Billy won	Wimbledon, England

Date	Match	Result	Venue
08/04/1958	Billy Joyce Vs Eric Taylor	Billy won	Lime Grove, England
12/04/1958	Billy Joyce Vs Sandy Orford	Sandy won	Middlesborough, North Yorkshire
15/04/1958	Billy Joyce Vs Dai Sullivan	Billy won	Lime Grove, England
15/04/1958	Billy Joyce Vs Sandy Orford	Billy won	Lime Grove, England
15/04/1958	Billy Joyce Vs Gordon Nelson	Billy Won	Lime Grove, England
19/04/1958	Billy Joyce Vs Joe Cornelius	NK	Belle Vue, Manchester
25/04/1958	Billy Joyce Vs Francis Sullivan	NK	Brierley
28/04/1958	Billy joyce Vs Masambula	Billy won	Leeds, England
01/05/1958	Billy Joyce Vs Geoff Portz	Geoff won	Morecambe, Lancashire
02/05/1958	Billy Joyce vs Johnny Allan	Billy won	Belfast, Ireland
10/05/1958	Billy Joyce Vs Gwyn Davies	Billy won	Newcastle, England
10/05/1958	Billy Joyce Vs Gwyn Davies	Joyce won	Newcastle, England
15/05/1958	Billy Joyce Vs Bill Coverdale	Billy won	Morecambe, Lancashire
15/05/1958	Billy Joyce Vs Mario Matassa	Billy won	Belfast, Ireland
16/05/1958	Billy Joyce Vs Mario Matassa	Joyce won	Belfast, Ireland
17/05/1958	Billy Joyce Vs Gwyn Davies	NK	Belle Vue, Manchester
20/05/1958	Billy joyce Vs Masambula	Billy won	Purley, England
21/05/1958	Billy Joyce Vs Roberts	Billy won	Albert Hall, London
21/05/1958	Billy Joyce Vs Big Bill Verna	Big Bill won	Albert Hall, London
07/06/1958	Billy Joyce Vs Norman Walsh	Draw	Middlesborough, North Yorkshire
14/06/1958	Billy Joyce Vs Bill Verna	Billy won	Coventry, England
28/06/1958	Billy Joyce Vs Norman Walsh	Billy won	Newcastle, England
30/06/1958	Billy joyce Vs Jim Malloy	Billy won	Leeds, England
03/07/1958	Billy Joyce Vs Dave Armstrong	Billy won	Bristol, England
19/07/1958	Billy Joyce Vs Geoff Portz	Billy won	Newcastle, England
24/07/1958	Billy Joyce Vs Tibor Szakacs	Billy won	Morecambe, Lancashire
26/07/1958	Billy Joyce Vs Dennis Mitchell	NK	Middlesborough, England
29/07/1958	Billy Joyce Vs Bud Cody	Bilyl won	Purley, England
05/08/1958	Billy Joyce Vs Josef Zaranoff	NK	Scarborough
14/08/1958	Billy Joyce Vs Vincent Nicolini	Billy won	Morecambe, Lancashire
16/08/1958	Billy Joyce Vs Dennis Mitchell	Billy won	Middlesborough, North Yorkshire
18/08/1958	Billy Joyce Vs Bert Royal	Joyce won	Edinburgh, Scotland
23/08/1958	Billy Joyce Vs Johnny Yearsley	Billy won	Maidstone, England
28/08/1958	Billy Joyce Vs Vic Hesselle	Billy won	Morecambe, Lancashire
29/08/1958	Billy Joyce Vs Cyril Morris	Joyce won	Blackburn, England
29/08/1958	Billy Joyce Vs Don Mendoza	Joyce won	Blackburn, England
29/08/1958	Billy Joyce Vs Alf Rawlings (F)	Joyce won	Blackburn, England
30/08/1958	Billy Joyce Vs Bill McDonald	NK	Belle Vue, Manchester
01/09/1958	Billy Joyce Vs Gordon Nelson	NK	Bridlington
03/09/1958	Billy Joyce Vs Tibor Szakacs	Joyce won	Withernsea
06/09/1958	Billy Joyce Vs Arthur Ricardo	Arthur won	Middlesborough, North Yorkshire
11/09/1958	Billy Joyce Vs Norman Walsh	NK	Blackburn, England
13/09/1958	Billy Joyce Vs Sandy Orford	Billy won	Newcastle, England
15/09/1958	Billy Joyce Vs Bill Coverdale	Billy J won	Leeds, England

Date	Match	Result	Location
18/09/1958	Billy Joyce Vs El Said Arabet	NK	Morecambe, Lancashire
20/09/1958	Billy Joyce Vs Geoff Portz	NC	Middlesborough, North Yorkshire
23/09/1958	Billy Joyce Vs Charlie Fisher	Billy won	Purley, England
24/09/1958	Billy Joyce Vs Alan Garfield	Billy won, alan DQ	Cardiff, Wales
25/09/1958	Billy Joyce Vs El Said Arabet	Billy won	Bristol, England
01/10/1958	Billy Joyce Vs Gwyn Davies	NK	Sheffield, England
03/10/1958	Billy Joyce Vs Ernie Riley	Billy won	Glasgow, Scotland
04/10/1958	Billy Howes Vs Jack Beaumont	Jack won	Middlesborough, North Yorkshire
09/10/1958	Billy Joyce Vs Norman Walsh	NC	Morecambe, Lancashire
11/10/1958	Heavyweight Tournament- Bill Verna, John Yearsley, John Da Silva, Billy Joyce	N/A	Lime Grove, Shepherd's Bush, London
11/10/1958	Billy Joyce Vs Bill Verna	Billy won	Lime Grove, England
11/10/1958	Billy Joyce Vs Johnny Da Silva (F)	Bilyl won	Lime Grove, England
18/10/1958	Billy Joyce Vs Kurt Rakowski	Billy won	Newcastle, England
23/10/1958	Billy Joyce Vs John DaSilva	NK	Blackburn, England
25/10/1958	Billy Joyce Vs Tibor Szakacs	Billy won	Middlesborough, North Yorkshire
31/10/1958	Billy Joyce Vs Johnny Yearsley	NK	Barnehurst
02/11/1958	Billy Jocye Vs Johnny DaSilva	NK	Nottingham, England
03/11/1958	Billy Joyce Vs Eric Koltschak	NK	Blackpool, England
04/11/1958	Billy Joyce Vs Jose Calderon	NK	Bridlington
10/11/1958	Billy Joyce Vs Brian Malloy	NK	Bradford, England
11/11/1958	Billy Joyce Vs Ernie Baldwin	NK	Wakefield, England
13/11/1958	Billy Joyce Vs Don Mendoza	NK	Blackburn, England
15/11/1958	Billy Joyce Vs Tibor Szakacs	Billy won	Newcastle, England
18/11/1958	Billy Joyce Vs Ken Davies	Joyce won	Bridlington
20/11/1958	Billy Joyce Vs John DaSilva	NK	Nottingham, England
21/11/1958	Billy Joyce Vs Ernie Riley	Billy won	Glasgow, Scotland
22/11/1958	Billy Joyce Vs Mike Marino	NK	Belle Vue, Manchester
25/11/1958	Billy Joyce Vs Dai Sullivan	NK	Chelmsford, England
26/11/1958	Billy Joyce Vs Sandy Orford	Billy won	Albert Hall, London
28/11/1958	Billy Joyce Vs Charlie Fisher	Billy won	Ipswich, England
29/11/1958	Billy Joyce Vs Gwyn Davies	Billy won	Purley, England
01/12/1958	Billy Joyce Vs Josef Zaranoff	NK	Great Yarmouth, England
02/12/1958	Billy Joyce Vs Johnny Allan	NK	Lime Grove, London
05/12/1958	Billy Joyce Vs Jim Hart	Billy won	Glasgow, Scotland
06/12/1958	Billy Joyce Vs Bill Robinson	Billy won	Middlesborough, North Yorkshire
08/12/1958	Billy Joyce Vs Ernie Baldwin	NK	Kirkby, Ashfield
16/12/1958	Billy Joyce Vs Tibor Szakacs	Joyce won	Lime Grove, London
20/12/1958	Billy Joyce Vs Albert Wall	Billy won	Middlesborough, North Yorkshire
27/12/1958	Billy Joyce Vs Gwyn Davies	Billy won	Newcastle, England
02/01/1959	Billy Joyce Vs Ernie Riley	Ernie won	Glasgow, Scotland
03/01/1959	Billy Joyce Vs Bill Robinson	Billy J won	Middlesborough, North Yorkshire
03/01/1959	Billy Joyce Vs Bill Robinson	Joyce won	Middlesborough, North Yorkshire
05/01/1959	Billy Joyce Vs Buddy Cody	NK	Folkestone

Date	Match	Result	Location
06/01/1959	Billy Joyce Vs Ray Apollon	Billy won	Swindon, England
10/01/1959	Billy Joyce Vs Axel Dieter	NK	Eastbourne
12/01/1959	Billy Joyce Vs Judo Al Hayes	Billy won	Leeds, England
13/01/1959	Billy Joyce Vs Gwyn Davies	NC	Hull, England
16/01/1959	Billy Joyce Vs Hans Dillinger	Joyce won	Rotherham
22/01/1959	Billy Joyce Vs Geoff Portz	NK	Nottingham, England
26/01/1959	Billy Joyce Vs Judo Al Hayes	Judo won	Leeds, England
31/01/1959	Billy Jocye Vs Dai Sullivan	Billy won	Newcastle, England
06/02/1959	Billy Joyce Vs Johann Dillinger	Billy won	Glasgow, Scotland
10/02/1959	Billy Joyce Vs Joe Cornelius	Billy won	Purley, England
13/02/1959	Billy Joyce Vs Ernie Riley	Billy won	Glasgow, Scotland
13/02/1959	Billy Joyce Vs Bill Verna	NK	Brighton, England
18/02/1959	Billy Joyce Vs Daula Singh	NK	Grimsby, England
21/02/1959	Billy Joyce Vs Jim Hussey	Billy won	Newcastle, England
23/02/1959	Billy Joyce Vs Horst Hoffman	NK	Hamilton, Scotland
25/02/1959	Billy Joyce Vs Horst Hoffman	NK	Scunthorpe, England
26/02/1959	Billy Joyce Vs Horst Hoffman	NK	Bridlington
28/02/1959	Billy Joyce Vs Dave Armstrong	Billy won	Middlesborough, North Yorkshire
09/03/1959	Billy Joyce Vs Norman Walsh	NK	Bradford, England
12/03/1959	Billy Joyce Vs Don Mendoza	Billy won	Nottingham, England
13/03/1959	Billy Joyce Vs Cyril Morris	Billy won	Glasgow, Scotland
19/03/1959	Billy Joyce Vs Dennis Mitchell	NC	Morecambe, Lancashire
23/03/1959	Billy Joyce Vs Jim Hussey	NK	Seymour Hall, London
24/03/1959	Billy Joyce Vs Tibor Szakacs	NK	Wakefield, England
03/04/1959	Billy Joyce Vs Felix Kerschitz	Billy won	Glasgow, Scotland
08/04/1959	Billy Joyce Vs Ernie Baldwin	NK	Sheffield, England
11/04/1959	Billy Joyce Vs Dai Sullivan	Joyce won	Newcastle, England
13/04/1959	Billy Joyce Vs Kiwi Kingston	NK	Hamilton, Scotland
15/04/1959	Billy Joyce Vs Sandy Orford	NK	Grimsby, England
18/04/1959	Billy Joyce Vs Peter Deakin	NK	Belle Vue, Manchester
25/04/1959	Billy Joyce Vs Ernie Riley	Billy won	Middlesborough, North Yorkshire
29/04/1959	Billy Joyce Vs Ernie Baldwin	NK	Sheffield, England
30/04/1959	Billy Joyce Vs Dennis Mitchell	Bill won	Morecambe, Lancashire
02/05/1959	Billy Joyce Vs Mike Marino	Joyce won	Newcastle, England
04/05/1959	Billy Joyce Vs Rudi Schumacher	NK	Aylesbury, England
16/05/1959	Billy Joyce Vs Bill Robinson	Joyce won	Middlesborough, North Yorkshire
21/05/1959	Billy Joyce Vs Ernie Baldwin	Joyce won	Morecambe, Lancashire
23/05/1959	Billy Joyce Vs Ernie Riley	Nk	Grantham, England
29/05/1959	Billy Joyce Vs Piet Slabbett	NK	Dumfries, Scotland
02/06/1959	Billy Joyce Vs Bill Verna	Joyce won	Hinckley, England
06/06/1959	Billy Joyce Vs John DaSilva	NK	Luton, London
23/06/1959	Billy Joyce Vs Carl Dane	NK	Wakefield, England
15/08/1959	Billy Joyce Vs Joe Cornelius	NK	Belle Vue, Manchester
15/10/1959	Billy Joyce Vs Norman Walsh	NK	Morecambe, Lancashire
31/10/1959	Billy Joyce Vs Rik DeGroote	NK	Belle Vue, Manchester

Date	Match	Result	Location
04/11/1959	Billy Joyce Vs Jose Calderon	Joyce won	Bridlington
06/11/1959	Billy Joyce Vs Ernie Baldwin	Baldwin won	Glasgow, Scotland
10/11/1959	Billy Joyce Vs Ramon Napolitano	Joyce won RNDQ	Welling
11/11/1959	Billy Joyce Vs Geoff Portz	NK	Grimsby, England
20/11/1959	Billy Joyce Vs Digger Rowell	NK	Rotherham
24/11/1959	Billy Joyce Vs Geoff Portz	Nk	Bridlington
02/12/1959	Billy Joyce Vs Billy Two Rivers	Rivers won	Lincoln, England
09/12/1959	Billy Joyce Vs Francis St Clair Gregory	NK	Scunthorpe
15/12/1959	Billy Joyce Vs Don Mendoza	NK	Welling
17/12/1959	Bilyl Joyce Vs John DaSilva	DaSilva won	Bristol, England
02/01/1960	Billy Joyce Vs Dennis Mitchell	Joyce won	Newcastle, England
09/01/1960	Billy Joyce Vs Al Hayes	NK	Middlesborough, North Yorkshire
12/01/1960	Billy Joyce Vs Alan Garfield	NK	Welling
18/01/1960	Billy Joyce Vs Rocky Wall	Joyce won	Loughborough, England
20/01/1960	Billy Joyce Vs Seamus Dunleavy	NK	Grimsby, England
21/01/1960	Billy Joyce Vs Seamus Dunleavy	NK	Kirkcaldy
22/01/1960	Billy Joyce Vs Dai Sullivan	NK	Bradford, England
23/01/1960	Billy Joyce Vs Dai Sullivan	Joyce won	Newcastle, England
29/01/1960	Billy Joyce Vs Geoff Portz	NK	Leicester, England
30/01/1960	Billy Joyce Vs Don Mendoza	NK	Grantham,
01/02/1960	Billy Joyce Vs Zebra Kid	NK	Leeds, England
06/02/1960	Billy Joyce Vs Vittorio Ochoa	Joyce won	Newcastle, England
12/02/1960	Billy Joyce Vs Ernie Riley	NK	Bradford, England
20/02/1960	Billy Joyce Vs Bill Coverdale	Joyce won	Coventry, England
22/02/1960	Billy Joyce Vs Emile Poilve	NK	Sutton, Ashfield
26/02/1960	Billy Joyce Vs Pedro Bengochea	NK	Leicester, England
27/02/1960	Billy Joyce Vs Pedro Bengochea	Joyce won	Newcastle, England
01/03/1960	Billy Joyce Vs Johnny Yearsley	NK	Seymour Hall, London
02/03/1960	Billy joyce Vs Sandy Orford	NK	Preston, England
05/03/1960	Billy Joyce Vs Eric Koltschak	Draw	Coventry, England
07/03/1960	Billy Joyce Vs Billy Two Rivers	NK	Leeds, England
08/03/1960	Billy Joyce Vs Ian Campbell	NK	Wakefield, England
15/03/1960	Billy Joyce Vs Billy Howes	NK	Scarborough, England
16/03/1960	Billy Joyce Vs Carnera	NK	Grimsby, England
18/03/1960	Billy Joyce Vs Bill Robinson	NK	Glasgow, Scotland
19/03/1960	Billy Joyce Vs Digger Rowell	NK	Huddersfield, England
22/03/1960	Billy Joyce Vs Pedro Bengochea	NK	Lime Grove, London
24/03/1960	Billy Joyce Vs Johnny Yearsley	Joyce won	Beckenham, England
26/03/1960	Billy Joyce Vs Ray Hunter	Joyce won	Portsmouth, England
28/03/1960	Billy Joyce Vs Frank Hurley	NK	Seymour Hall, London
02/04/1960	Billy Joyce Vs Geoff Portz	NK	Huddersfield, England
07/04/1960	Billy Joyce Vs Dennis Mitchell	NK	Bradford, England
11/04/1960	Billy Joyce Vs Bill Verna	NK	Wembley, England
15/04/1960	Billy Joyce Vs Dai Sullivan	NK	Chesterfield, England
18/04/1960	Billy Joyce Vs Dennis Mitchell	NK	Kirkby, Ashfield

Date	Match	Result	Location
19/04/1960	Billy Joyce Vs Geoff Portz	NK	Middlesborough, England
21/04/1960	Billy Joyce Vs Norman Walsh	Joyce won	Morecambe, Lancashire
26/04/1960	Billy Joyce Vs Jim Rawlings	NK	Wakefield, England
29/04/1960	Billy Joyce Vs Bill Robinson	NK	Glasgow, Scotland
03/05/1960	Billy Joyce Vs Geoff Portz	NK	Wakefield, England
06/05/1960	Billy Joyce Vs Tibor Szakacs	NK	Liverpool, England
07/05/1960	Billy Joyce Vs Gordon Nelson	NK	Leeds, England
11/05/1960	Billy Joyce Vs Eric Liederman	NK	Watford
12/05/1960	Billy Joyce Vs Ian Campbell	Campbell won	Morecambe, Lancashire
14/05/1960	Billy joyce Vs Sandy Orford	Orford won BJDQ	Newcastle, England
16/05/1960	Billy Joyce Vs Gwynn Davies	NK	Halifax, England
18/05/1960	Billy Joyce Vs Geoff Portz	NK	Sheffield, England
19/05/1960	Billy Joyce Vs Joe Cornelius	Joyce won	Morecambe, Lancashire
04/06/1960	Billy joyce Vs Sandy Orford	Orford won	Newcastle, England
07/06/1960	Billy Joyce Vs Norman Walsh	NK	Trowell
11/06/1960	Billy Joyce Vs Norman Walsh	NK	Middlesborough, England
13/06/1960	Billy Joyce Vs Arthur Ricardo	NK	Preston, England
14/06/1960	Billy Joyce Vs Eric Taylor	Joyce won	Welling
14/06/1960	Billy Joyce Vs Mike Marino	Joyce won	Welling
14/06/1960	Billy Joyce Vs Ray Hunter (F)	Hunter won	Welling
15/06/1960	Billy Joyce Vs Al Hayes	Hayes won	Banbury
17/06/1960	Billy Joyce Vs Geoff Portz	Joyce won	Bradford, England
18/06/1960	Billy joyce Vs Sandy Orford	Joyce won	Newcastle, England
24/06/1960	Billy Joyce Vs Dennis Mitchell	NK	Bradford, England
27/06/1960	Billy Joyce Vs Norman Walsh	NK	Leeds, England
15/07/1960	Billy Joyce Vs Dennis Mitchell	Joyce won	Bradford, England
27/07/1960	Billy Joyce Vs Norman Walsh	NK	Grimsby, England
28/07/1960	Billy Joyce Vs John Lees	NK	Scarborough, England
30/07/1960	Billy Joyce Vs Dennis Mitchell	NK	Middlesborough, England
05/08/1960	In KO Tournament	NK	Barnehurst
07/08/1960	Billy Joyce Vs Alan Garfield	Joyce won AGDQ	Brighton, England
09/08/1960	Billy Joyce Vs Bill McDonald	NK	Aberdeen, Scotland
13/08/1960	Billy Joyce Vs Robert Duranton	NK	Middlesborough, England
15/08/1960	Billy Joyce Vs Reg Williams	NK	York, England
16/08/1960	Billy Joyce Vs John lees	NK	Aberdeen, Scotland
18/08/1960	Billy Joyce Vs Reg Williams	NK	Scarborough, England
20/08/1960	Billy Joyce Vs Gwynn Davies	NK	Newcastle, England
25/08/1960	Billy Joyce Vs The Mask	The mask won	Morecambe, Lancashire
27/08/1960	Billy Joyce Vs Ramon Napolitano	NK	Belle Vue, Manchester
01/09/1960	Billy Joyce Vs Ernie Baldwin	NK	Scarborough, England
03/09/1960	Billy Joyce (HWC)Vs Albert Wall	NK	Blackburn, Lancashire
03/09/1960	Billy joyce Vs Sandy Orford	NK	Middlesborough, England
05/09/1960	Billy Joyce Vs Masambula	Joyce won	Leeds, England
12/09/1960	Billy Joyce Vs Joe Cornelius	NK	Preston, England
13/09/1960	Billy Joyce Vs Tony Mancelli	NK	Wakefield, England
16/09/1960	Billy Joyce Vs David Nenic	NK	Glasgow, Scotland

Date	Match	Result	Venue
19/09/1960	Billy Joyce Vs Masambula	NK	Matlock
22/09/1960	Billy Joyce Vs Norman Walsh	Walsh won	Morecambe, Lancashire
24/09/1960	Billy Joyce Vs Josef Zaranoff	NK	Belle Vue, Manchester
27/09/1960	Billy Joyce Vs Reg Williams	NK	Swindon, England
30/09/1960	Billy Joyce Vs Ernie Baldwin	NK	Bolton, England
01/10/1960	Billy Joyce Vs Kurt Stein	Joyce won	Newcastle, England
03/10/1960	Billy Joyce Vs Roman Wanniek	NK	Leeds, England
04/10/1960	Billy Joyce Vs The Mask	NK	Hull
17/10/1960	Billy Joyce Vs Colin Williamson	NK	Preston, England
20/10/1960	Billy Joyce Vs Ray Apollon	NK	Bradford, England
24/10/1960	Billy Joyce Vs John Lees	NK	Sutton, Ashfield
26/10/1960	Billy Joyce Vs Emile Poilve	NK	Cardiff, Wales
27/10/1960	Billy Joyce Vs Ramon Napolitano	Joyce won	Beckenham, England
30/10/1960	Billy Joyce Vs Gwynn Davies	NK	Huddersfield, England
01/11/1960	Billy Joyce Vs Roger Gueret	Joyce won	Wakefield, England
05/11/1960	Billy Joyce Vs Bill Robinson	NK	Belle Vue, Manchester
12/11/1960	Billy Joyce (HWC) vs Yves Amor	NK	Leicester, Leicestershire
12/11/1960	Billy Joyce Vs Roger Gueret	NK	Leicester, England
19/11/1960	Billy Joyce Vs Jamie Olivera	NK	Belle Vue, Manchester
21/11/1960	Billy Joyce Vs Josef Zaranoff	Joyce won	Eltham
24/11/1960	Billy Joyce Vs Doug Joyce	Joyce won	Morecambe, Lancashire
26/11/1960	Billy Joyce Vs Masambula	NC	Newcastle, England
28/11/1960	Billy Joyce Vs Bill Rawlings	NK	Huddersfield, England
29/11/1960	Billy Joyce Vs Zebra Kid	NK	Scarborough, England
30/11/1960	Billy Joyce Vs Norman Walsh	NK	Lincoln, England
01/12/1960	Billy Joyce Vs Dennis Mitchell	NK	Nottingham, England
02/12/1960	Billy Joyce Vs Bill Rawlings	Joyce won	Glasgow, Scotland
03/12/1960	Billy Joyce Vs Johnny Allan	NK	Halifax, England
05/12/1960	Billy Joyce Vs Eric Taylor	NK	Bradford, England
10/12/1960	Billy Joyce Vs Bill Robinson	NK	Belle Vue, Manchester
16/12/1960	Billy Joyce Vs Bill McDonald	NK	Liverpool, England
20/12/1960	Billy Joyce Vs Gordon Nelson	Joyce won	Hull, England
02/01/1961	Billy Joyce Vs Colin Williamson	NK	Loughborough, England
10/01/1961	Billy Joyce Vs Buddy Cody	NK	Newbury
11/01/1961	Billy Joyce Vs Josef Zaranoff	Joyce won	Cardiff, Wales
13/01/1961	Billy Joyce Vs Joe Cornelius	NK	Bermondsey
16/01/1961	Billy Joyce Vs Ian Campbell	NK	York, England
17/01/1961	Billy Joyce Vs Pat Barrett	NK	Lime Grove, London
18/01/1961	Billy Joyce Vs Ian Campbell	NK	Grimsby, England
19/01/1961	Billy Joyce Vs Ian Campbell	NK	Kirkcaldy
24/01/1961	Billy Joyce Vs Francis Sullivan	NK	Lime Grove, London
25/01/1961	Billy Joyce Vs Ian Campbell	NK	Scunthorpe
27/01/1961	Billy Joyce Vs Jose Arroyo	NK	Rotherham, England
28/01/1961	Billy Joyce Vs Ernie Baldwin	NK	Grantham,
30/01/1961	Billy Joyce Vs The Mask	NK	West Ham, England
30/01/1961	Billy Joyce Vs Masambula	Draw	Loughborough, England

Date	Match	Result	Venue
31/01/1961	Billy Joyce Vs Jim Hussey	NK	Trowell
01/02/1961	Billy Joyce Vs Jamie Dula	NK	Purley
02/02/1961	Billy Joyce Vs Geoff Portz	NK	Nottingham, England
04/02/1961	Billy Joyce Vs Ray Apollon	NK	Halifax, England
06/02/1961	Billy Joyce Vs Franz Orlik	Joyce won	Seymour Hall, London
07/02/1961	Billy Joyce Vs Frank Hurley	NK	Welling
08/02/1961	Billy Joyce Vs Gordon Nelson	NK	Cardiff, Wales
13/02/1961	Billy Joyce Vs Gwyn Davies	Joyce won	Eltham
14/02/1961	Billy Joyce Vs Ray Hunter	Draw	Lime Grove, London
15/02/1961	Billy Joyce Vs Ernie Baldwin	NK	Newcastle, England
16/02/1961	Billy Joyce Vs Kiwi Kingston	NK	Goole
17/02/1961	Billy Joyce Vs Gwyn Davies	NK	Bradford, England
20/02/1961	Billy Joyce Vs Bill Robinson	NK	Leeds, West yorkshire
21/02/1961	In KO Tournament	NK	Hinckley
22/02/1961	Billy Joyce Vs Frank Hurley	Joyce won FH DQ	Shoreditch
27/02/1961	Billy Joyce Vs Jim Olivera	NK	Harrogate
04/03/1961	Billy Joyce Vs Ernie Baldwin	Baldwin won	Newcastle, England
06/03/1961	Billy Joyce Vs Alf Rawlings	NK	Huddersfield, England
07/03/1961	Billy Joyce Vs Francis Sullivan	NK	Wakefield, England
08/03/1961	Billy Joyce Vs Horst Hoffman	Draw	Lincoln, England
09/03/1961	Billy Joyce Vs Horst Hoffman	NK	Nottingham, England
10/03/1961	Billy Joyce Vs Jose Arroyo	NK	Glasgow, Scotland
11/03/1961	Billy Joyce Vs John Lees	NK	Buxton
14/03/1961	Billy Joyce Vs Norman Walsh	Joyce won	Lime Grove, London
17/03/1961	Billy Joyce Vs Dennis Mitchell	NK	Leicester, England
18/03/1961	Billy Joyce Vs Masambula	NK	Halifax, England
20/03/1961	Billy Joyce Vs Buddy Cody	NK	West Ham, England
22/03/1961	Billy Joyce Vs Sheik Wadih Ayoub	Sheik won, BJDQ	Lincoln, England
23/03/1961	Billy Joyce Vs Tibor Szakacs	NK	Kirkcaldy
24/03/1961	Billy Joyce Vs Ian Campbell	Joyce won	Glasgow, Scotland
27/03/1961	Billy Joyce Vs Francis Sullivan	Joyce won	Eltham
28/03/1961	Billy joyce Vs Sandy Orford	NK	Wakefield, England
29/03/1961	Billy Joyce Vs Ernie Baldwin	NK	Newark
01/04/1961	Billy Joyce Vs Sheik Wadih Ayoub	Joyce won	Newcastle, England
07/04/1961	Billy Joyce Vs Sheik Wadih Ayoub	Joyce won	Bradford, England
11/04/1961	Billy Joyce Vs Jamie Olivera	NK	Lime Grove, London
13/04/1961	Billy joyce Vs Sandy Orford	NK	Malvern
14/04/1961	Billy Joyce Vs Francis Sullivan	NK	Bradford, England
15/04/1961	Billy Joyce Vs Norman Walsh	Walsh won, BJ Inj	Middlesborough, England
17/04/1961	Billy Joyce Vs Sheik Wadih Ayoub	NK	Preston, England
18/04/1961	In KO Tournament	NK	Hinckley
20/04/1961	Billy Joyce Vs Jim Hussey	NK	Worksop
25/04/1961	Billy Joyce Vs Rocky Wall	NK	Wakefield, England
28/04/1961	Billy Joyce Vs Dennis Mitchell	NK	Bradford, England
09/05/1961	Billy Joyce Vs Dennis Mitchell	NK	Trowell
10/05/1961	Billy Joyce Vs Colin Williamson	Joyce won	Lincoln, England

Date	Match	Result	Location
12/05/1961	Billy Joyce Vs Dennis Mitchell	Billy Joyce walked out	Glasgow, Scotland
15/05/1961	Billy Joyce Vs Pat Barrett	NK	Preston, England
18/05/1961	Billy Joyce Vs Tibor Szakacs	NK	Hayes
20/05/1961	Billy Joyce Vs Tibor Szakacs	NK	Middlesborough, England
22/05/1961	Billy Joyce Vs Josef Zaranoff	Joyce won	Belle Vue, Manchester
23/05/1961	Billy Joyce Vs Ian Campbell	NK	Bridlington, England
25/05/1961	Billy Joyce Vs Ian Campbell	Joyce won ICDQ	Morecambe, Lancashire
29/05/1961	Billy Joyce Vs Gerry DeJaegar	Joyce won	Shoreditch
31/05/1961	Billy Joyce Vs Bill Robinson	Joyce won	Cardiff, Wales
31/05/1961	Billy Joyce Vs Buddy Cody	Joyce won	Cardiff, Wales
31/05/1961	Billy Joyce Vs Mike Marino (F)	Joyce won	Cardiff, Wales
01/06/1961	Billy Joyce Vs Alan Garfield	NK	Dunstable
05/06/1961	Billy Joyce Vs Ian Campbell	Campbell won, Joyve inj	Leeds, England
08/06/1961	Billy joyce Vs Sandy Orford	NK	Malvern
10/06/1961	Billy Joyce Vs Norman Walsh	NK	Middlesborough, England
19/06/1961	Billy Joyce Vs Hans Streiger	NK	York, England
24/06/1961	Billy Joyce Vs Dennis Mitchell	NK	Glasgow, Scotland
27/06/1961	Billy Joyce Vs Ian Campbell	NK	Aberdeen, Scotland
30/06/1961	Billy Joyce Vs Ray Apollon	NK	Fleetwood
01/07/1961	Billy Joyce Vs Geoff Portz	NK	Middlesborough, England
03/07/1961	Billy Joyce Vs Rocky Wall	NK	Skegness
06/07/1961	Billy Joyce Vs Ian Campbell	NK	Scarborough, England
25/07/1961	Billy Joyce Vs Bill Verna	NK	Weston Super Mare
31/07/1961	Billy Joye Vs Rocky Wall	NK	Scarborough, England
08/08/1961	Billy Joyce Vs Bill McDonald	NK	Aberdeen, Scotland
09/08/1961	Billy Joyce Vs Masambula	NK	Liverpool, England
10/08/1961	Billy Joyce Vs Jim Armstrong	NK	Hornsea
11/08/1961	Billy Joyce Vs Jack Pye	NK	Fleetwood
12/08/1961	Billy Joyce Vs Rocky Wall	NK	Middlesborough, England
16/08/1961	Billy Joyce Vs Johnny Czeslaw	NK	Great Yarmouth, England
23/08/1961	Billy Joyce Vs Sheik Wadih Ayoub	NK	Douglas, Isle of Man
24/08/1961	Billy Joyce Vs Rocky Wall	NK	Scarborough, England
25/08/1961	Billy Joyce Vs Ramon Napolitano	Joyce won RNDQ	Glasgow, Scotland
26/08/1961	Billy Joyce Vs Dai Sullivan	Joyce won	Belle Vue, Manchester
28/08/1961	Billy Joyce Vs Norman Walsh	NK	Scarborough, England
02/09/1961	Billy Joyce Vs Norman Walsh	Draw	Middlesborough, England
05/09/1961	Billy Joyce Vs Rocky Wall	Joyce won	Welling
09/09/1961	Billy Joyce Vs Dennis Mitchell	Joyce won	Newcastle, England
16/09/1961	Billy Joyce Vs Ron Johnson	Joyce won	Belle Vue, Manchester
18/09/1961	Billy Joyce Vs Norman Walsh	NK	Carlisle, England
19/09/1961	Billy Joyce Vs Roy Bull Davis	NK	Wakefield, England
23/09/1961	Billy Joyce Vs Gwyn Davies	Joyce won	Newcastle, England
27/09/1961	Billy Joyce Vs Johnny Allan	NK	Grimsby, England
29/09/1961	Billy Joyce Vs Johnny Allan	Allan won	Glasgow, Scotland
30/09/1961	Billy Joyce Vs Sheik Wadih Ayoub	NK	Falkirk

Date	Match	Result	Location
02/10/1961	Billy Joyce Vs Josef Zaranoff	NK	Bradford, England
05/10/1961	Billy Joyce Vs Rocky Wall	NK	Hayes
07/10/1961	Billy Joyce Vs Rocky Wall	Joyce won	Middlesborough, England
09/10/1961	Billy Joyce Vs Masambula	NK	Preston, England
13/10/1961	Billy Joyce Vs Hassan Ali Bey	NK	Rotherham
16/10/1961	Billy Joyce Vs Tibor Szakacs	NK	Bradford, England
19/10/1961	Billy joyce Vs Bob Sweeney	NK	Hayes
20/10/1961	Billy Joyce Vs Billy Howes	NK	Leicester, England
21/10/1961	Billy Joyce Vs Dino Bravo	NK	Middlesborough, England
23/10/1961	Billy Joyce Vs Charlie Fisher	NK	Seymour Hall, London
24/10/1961	Billy Joyce Vs Geoff Portz	NK	Lime Grove, London
25/10/1961	Billy Joyce Vs Billy Howes	NK	Scunthorpe
27/10/1961	Billy Joyce Vs Rocky Wall	NK	Chesterfield, England
01/11/1961	Billy Joyce Vs Dennis Mitchell	Mitchell won	Lincoln, England
02/11/1961	Billy Joyce Vs Geoff Portz	NK	Nottingham, England
03/11/1961	Billy joyce Vs Ricky Waldo	Joyce won RWDQ	Glasgow, Scotland
04/11/1961	Billy Joyce Vs Ernie Riley	NK	Grantham,
06/11/1961	Billy Joyce Vs Bruno Elrington	NK	Derby, England
07/11/1961	Billy Joyce Vs Jim Hussey	Joyce won JHDQ	Kidderminster
14/11/1961	Billy Joyce Vs Billy Howes	NK	Harrogate
17/11/1961	Billy Joyce Vs Bill Rawlings	NK	Eltham
18/11/1961	Billy Joyce Vs Dai Sullivan	Joyce won	Belle Vue, Manchester
20/11/1961	Billy Joyce Vs Ian Campbell	NK	Kilmarnock
21/11/1961	Billy Joyce Vs Frankie Townsend	Joyce won	Hull
23/11/1961	Billy Joyce Vs Joe Cornelius	NK	Rotherham
25/11/1961	Billy Joyce Vs Dennis Mitchell	NK	Middlesborough, England
29/11/1961	Billy Joyce Vs Frankie Townsend	Nk	Sheffield, England
30/11/1961	Billy Joyce Vs Mario Matassa	NK	Goole
02/12/1961	Billy Joyce Vs Dino Bravo	NK	Middlesborough, England
04/12/1961	Billy Joyce Vs Earl Maynard	NK	Bradford, England
06/12/1961	Billy Joyce Vs Gwyn Davies	NK	Grimsby, England
09/12/1961	In KO Tournament	NK	Middlesborough, England
11/12/1961	Billy Joyce Vs Geoff Portz	NK	Carlisle, England
14/12/1961	Billy Joyce Vs Ian Campbell	NK	Kirkcaldy
21/12/1961	Billy Joyce Vs Bill Robinson	v	Nottingham
01/01/1962	Billy Joyce Vs Francis St Clair Gregory	NK	Sutton, Ashfield
13/01/1962	Billy Joyce Vs Bruno Elrington	B/J 2-1 B/E	Leicester, Leicestershire
16/01/1962	Billy Joyce Vs Willem Hall	NK	Leicester, England
18/01/1962	Billy Joyce Vs Pat Barrett	NK	Southampton, England
19/01/1962	Billy Joyce Vs Gomez Maximilliano	NK	Bermondsey
23/01/1962	Billy Joyce Vs Joe Cornelius	NK	Lime Grove, London
25/01/1962	Billy Joyce Vs Geoff Portz	NK	Hayes
27/01/1962	Billy Joyce Vs Ray Apollon	NK	Portsmouth, England
01/02/1962	Billy Joyce Vs Dennis Mitchell	NK	Cradley Heath
02/02/1962	Billy Joyce Vs Geoff Portz	NK	Rotherham
05/02/1962	Billy Joyce Vs Rocky Wall	NK	Warrington

Date	Match	Result	Location
09/02/1962	Billy Joyce Vs Masambula	Draw	Glasgow, Scotland
10/02/1962	Billy joyce Vs Sandy Orford	Joyce won	Newcastle, England
12/02/1962	Billy Joyce Vs Ian Campbell	NK	Kilmarnock
14/02/1962	Billy Joyce Vs Rocky Wall	Wall won	Lincoln, England
15/02/1962	Billy Joyce Vs Earl Maynard	NK	Barrow, England
16/02/1962	Billy Joyce Vs Ian Campbell	NK	Rotherham
17/02/1962	Billy Joyce Vs Billy Howes	Howes won	Middlesborough, England
19/02/1962	Billy joyce Vs El Grande Apachee	NK	Aylesbury
21/02/1962	Billy Joyce Vs Iskha Khan	Khan won	Dorking
22/02/1962	Billy joyce Vs El Grande Apachee	NK	Walthamstow
23/02/1962	Billy Joyce Vs Iskha Khan	NK	Bermondsey
24/02/1962	Billy Joyce Vs Joe Cornelius	Cornelius won	Luton, England
26/02/1962	Billy Joyce Vs Josef Kovacs	NK	West Ham, England
08/03/1962	Billy Joyce Vs Geoff Portz	NK	Nottingham, England
09/03/1962	Billy Joyce Vs Ian Campbell	NK	Dumfries
10/03/1962	Billy Joyce Vs Jan Brouwers	Joyce won	Middlesborough, England
12/03/1962	Billy Joyce Vs Ian Campbell	NK	Kilmarnock
13/03/1962	Billy joyce Vs The Monster	NK	Trowell
15/03/1962	Billy joyce Vs The Monster	NK	Cradley Heath
15/03/1962	Billy Joyce Vs Billy Howes	NK	Blackburn, England
16/03/1962	Billy Joyce Vs Dennis Mitchell	NC	Glasgow, Scotland
17/03/1962	Billy Joyce Vs Rocky Wall	NK	Falkirk
26/03/1962	Billy Joyce Vs Dennis Mitchell	NK	Nelson
02/04/1962	Billy Joyce Vs Dai Sullivan	Joyce won	Bradford, England
14/04/1962	Billy Joyce Vs Billy Howes	Joyce won	Middlesborough, England
16/04/1962	Billy Joyce Vs Tibor Szakacs	NK	Leeds, England
17/04/1962	Billy Joyce Vs Horst Hoffman	NK	Purley
23/04/1962	Billy Joyce Vs Yure Borienko	Joyce won	Bradford, England
24/04/1962	Billy Joyce Vs George Gordienko	NK	Purley
26/04/1962	Billy Joyce Vs George Gordienko	Gordienko won	Dunstable
28/04/1962	Billy Joyce Vs Dennis Mitchell	Mitchell won	Middlesborough, England
01/05/1962	Billy Joyce Vs Dennis Mitchell	Joyce won	Huddersfield, England
19/05/1962	Billy Joyce Vs Billy Howes	Howes won	Middlesborough, England
04/06/1962	Billy Joyce Vs Bill McDonald	NK	Buxton, England
05/06/1962	In KO Tournament	NK	Purley
09/06/1962	Billy Joyce Vs Bill Rawlings	Draw	Middlesborough, England
18/06/1962	Billy Joyce Vs Frank Hurley	Joyce won	Catford
20/06/1962	Billy Joyce Vs Seamus Dunleavy	Joyce won	Cardiff, Wales
21/06/1962	Billy Joyce Vs Navarro Moyans	NK	Dunstable
24/06/1962	Billy Joyce Vs Gerry DeJaegar	Joyce won	Brighton
27/06/1962	Billy Joyce Vs Bob Taylor	Joyce won	Great Yarmouth, England
28/06/1962	Billy Joyce Vs Ezzard Hart	NK	Scarborough, England
29/06/1962	Billy Joyce Vs Ian Campbell	NK	Glasgow, Scotland
30/06/1962	Billy Joyce Vs Josef Zaranoff	Joyce won	Middlesborough, England
03/07/1962	Billy Joyce Vs Norman Walsh	NK	Trowell
17/07/1962	Billy Joyce Vs Max Crabtree	NK	Leicester, England

Date	Match	Result	Venue
21/07/1962	Billy Joyce Vs Ian Campbell	Joyce won	Belle Vue, Manchester
26/07/1962	Billy Joyce Vs Rocky Wall	NK	Scarborough, England
30/07/1962	Billy Joyce Vs Colin Williamson	NK	Hamilton, Scotland
31/07/1962	Billy Joyce Vs Dave Armstrong	NK	Aberdeen, Scotland
03/08/1962	Billy joyce Vs Reg Williams	NK	Withernsea
13/09/1962	Billy Joyce Vs Josef Zaranoff	NK	Scarborough, England
29/09/1962	Billy Joyce Vs Rocky Wall	Joyce won	Newcastle, England
01/10/1962	Billy Joyce Vs Willem Hall	Joyce won	Leeds, England
02/10/1962	Billy Joyce Vs Norman Walsh	NK	Harrogate
13/10/1962	Billy Joyce Vs Bruno Elrington	NK	Grantham,
15/10/1962	Billy Joyce Vs John DaSilva	Joyce won	Bradford, England
19/10/1962	Billy Joyce Vs John DaSilva	Joyce won	Leicester, England
20/10/1962	Billy Joyce Vs Tibor Szakacs	NC	Newcastle, England
22/10/1962	Billy Joyce Vs Leon Arras	NK	Derby, England
23/10/1962	Billy Joyce Vs Fineschi	Joyce won	Kidderminster
29/10/1962	Billy Joyce Vs Frikki Alberta	NK	West Ham, England
30/10/1962	Billy Joyce Vs Angelo Romeiro	Joyce won	Swindon, England
31/10/1962	Billy Joyce Vs Johnny Yearsley	Joyce won	Great Yarmouth, England
31/10/1962	Billy Joyce Vs John DaSilva	NC	Lincoln, England
01/11/1962	Billy Joyce Vs Willem Hall	Hall won BJDQ	Wimbledon
05/11/1962	Billy Joyce Vs Rocky Wall	NK	Bradford, England
07/11/1962	Billy Joyce Vs Pierre Bernhardt	NK	Preston, Lancashire
09/11/1962	Billy Joyce Vs Rocky Wall	NK	Leicester, England
10/11/1962	Billy Joyce Vs Bruno Elrington	Joyce won	Newcastle, England
17/11/1962	Billy Joyce Vs Masambula	NC	Belle Vue, Manchester
23/11/1962	Billy Joyce Vs Ray Apollon	NK	Leicester, England
30/11/1962	Billy Joyce Vs Jim Rawlings	Draw	Glasgow, Scotland
03/12/1962	Billy Joyce Vs Rocky Wall	NK	Bradford, England
04/12/1962	Billy Joyce Vs Rocky Wall	NK	Leicester, England
05/12/1962	Billy Joyce Vs Syed Saif Shah	NK	Preston, Lancashire
10/12/1962	Billy Joyce Vs Bill Robinson	Joyce won	Loughborough, England
13/12/1962	Billy Joyce Vs Norman Walsh	NK	Kirkcaldy
14/12/1962	Billy Joyce Vs Johnny Allan	Joyce won JADQ	Glasgow, Scotland
17/12/1962	Billy Joyce Vs Jacquerez	NK	Colwyn Bay, Wales
22/12/1962	Billy joyce Vs John Peters	NK	Lime Grove, Shepherd's Bush, London
26/12/1962	Billy Joyce Vs Gwyn Davies	Joyce won	Blackpool, England
27/12/1962	Billy Joyce Vs Johnny Allan	NK	Nottingham, England
07/01/1963	Billy Joyce Vs Ian Campbell	Campbell won	Belle Vue, Manchester
09/01/1963	Billy Joyce Vs Dennis Mitchell	NK	Preston, Lancashire
10/01/1963	Billy Joyce Vs Dennis Mitchell	NK	Nelson
11/01/1963	Billy Joyce Vs Ian Campbell	Campbell won	Glasgow, Scotland
12/01/1963	Billy Joyce Vs Rocky Wall	NK	Falkirk
14/01/1963	Billy Joyce Vs Johnny Allan	NK	York
21/01/1963	Billy Joyce Vs Norman Walsh	Joyce won	Bradford, England
26/01/1963	Billy Joyce Vs Dai Sullivan	Draw	Newcastle, England

Date	Match	Result	Venue
28/01/1963	Billy Joyce Vs Bruno Elrington	Joyce won	Belle Vue, Manchester
29/01/1963	Billy Joyce Vs Colin Williamson	Joyce won	Leicester, England
01/02/1963	Billy Joyce Vs Tibor Szakacs	Szakacs won BJ Inj	Liverpool, England
01/02/1963	Billy Joyce Vs Yure Borienko	Joyce won YBDQ	Farnham
04/02/1963	Billy Joyce Vs Syed Saif Shah	NK	Derby, England
08/02/1963	Billy Joyce Vs Ian Campbell	Campbell won	Glasgow, Scotland
09/02/1963	Billy joyce Vs Pietro Capello	NK	Grantham,
11/02/1963	Billy Joyce Vs Billy Howes	NK	York
13/02/1963	Billy joyce Vs Pietro Capello	NK	Preston, Lancashire
14/02/1963	Billy Joyce Vs Rocky Wall	NK	Kirkcaldy
21/02/1963	Billy Joyce Vs Gwyn Davies	NK	Nottingham, England
23/02/1963	Billy Joyce Vs Dai Sullivan	NC	Newcastle, England
25/02/1963	Billy Joyce Vs Gomez Maximilliano	NK	Aylesbury
26/02/1963	Billy Joyce Vs Jim Hussey	NK	Wolverhampton, England
01/03/1963	Billy Joyce Vs John Lees	NK	Bolton, England
02/03/1963	Billy Joyce Vs John Lees	NK	Sutton, Ashfield
05/03/1963	Billy joyce Vs Pietro Capello	Joyce won	Huddersfield, England
07/03/1963	Billy Joyce Vs Norman Walsh	NK	Nottingham, England
11/03/1963	Billy Joyce Vs Ian Campbell	NK	Derby, England
12/03/1963	Billy Joyce Vs Henri Pierlot	NK	Wellington
13/03/1963	Billy Joyce Vs John DaSilva	NK	Sheffield, England
14/03/1963	Billy Joyce Vs Dennis Mitchell	NK	Kirkcaldy
18/03/1963	Billy Joyce Vs Gordon Kilmartin	NK	Bradford, England
19/03/1963	Billy Joyce Vs Joe Cornelius	NK	Lime Grove, London
20/03/1963	Billy Joyce Vs Rocky Wall	Draw	Leicester, England
21/03/1963	Billy Joyce Vs Dennis Mitchell	NK	Kirkcaldy
22/03/1963	Billy Joyce Vs Peter Maivia	Joyce won	Glasgow, Scotland
23/03/1963	Billy Joyce Vs Joe Keegan	Joyce won	Middlesborough, England
26/03/1963	Billy Joyce Vs Johnny Allan	NK	Lime Grove, London
27/03/1963	Billy Joyce Vs Jim Hussey	Joyce won	Wallasey
29/03/1963	Billy Joyce Vs Jim Hussey	NK	Willenhall
30/03/1963	Billy Joyce Vs Rocky Wall	Draw	Newcastle, England
04/04/1963	Billy Joyce Vs Count Bartelli	NK	Brierly Hill
05/04/1963	Billy Joyce Vs Ian Campbell	Joyce won	Glasgow, Scotland
06/04/1963	Billy Joyce Vs Dennis Mitchell	Mitchell Won BJDQ	Middlesbrough
08/04/1963	Billy Joyce Vs Geoff Portz	NK	York
09/04/1963	Billy joyce Vs Pietro Capello	NK	Wolverhampton
10/04/1963	Billy Joyce Vs Geoff Portz	NK	Grimsby
11/04/1963	Billy Joyce Vs Bill McDonald	Joyce won	Bridgend
12/04/1963	Billy Joyce Vs Geoff Portz	NK	Chesterfield, England
13/04/1963	Billy Joyce Vs Bill McDonald	Joyce won	Newcastle, England
15/04/1963	Billy Joyce Vs Bill McDonald	NK	Dumfries
16/04/1963	Billy Joyce Vs Tibor Szakacs	NK	Solihull
18/04/1963	Billy Joyce Vs Rocky Wall	NK	Malvern
19/04/1963	Billy Joyce Vs Rocky Wall	Joyce won	Bolton
25/04/1963	Billy Joyce Vs Dennis Mitchell	NK	Nelson

Date	Match	Result	Venue
27/04/1963	Billy Joyce Vs Bill Robinson	Joyce won	Belle Vue, Manchester
29/04/1963	Billy Joyce Vs Zebra Kid	Kid won	Bradford
03/05/1963	Billy Joyce Vs Gwyn Davies	NK	Bolton
04/05/1963	Billy Joyce Vs Eric Taylor	Joyce won	Middlesbrough
07/05/1963	Billy Joyce Vs Prince Kumali	NK	Preston
08/05/1963	Billy Joyce Vs Geoff Portz	Draw	Lincoln
10/05/1963	Billy Joyce Vs Johnny Allan	NK	Leicester, England
11/05/1963	Billy Joyce Vs Johnny Allan	Joyce won	Newcastle, England
14/05/1963	Billy Joyce Vs Dave Armstrong	NK	Wellington
17/05/1963	Billy Joyce Vs Roy Bull Davis	Joyce won	Bolton
18/05/1963	Billy Joyce Vs Bill Robinson	Draw	Belle Vue, Manchester
20/05/1963	Billy Joyce Vs Josef Zaranoff	Joyce won	Hamilton, Scotland
25/05/1963	Billy Joyce Vs Rocky Wall	Joyce won	Newcastle, England
27/05/1963	Billy Joyce Vs Bill Robinson	Robinson won	Bradford
01/06/1963	Billy Joyce Vs Bill Robinson	Draw	Middlesborough, North Yorkshire
01/06/1963	Billy Joyce Vs Bill Robinson	Draw	Middlesbrough
08/06/1963	Billy Joyce Vs Peter Maivia	NK	Portsmouth
11/06/1963	Billy Joyce Vs John DaSilva	NK	Solihull
13/06/1963	Billy Joyce Vs Bill Robinson	NK	Morecambe, Lancashire
13/06/1963	Billy Joyce Vs Bill Robinson	NK	Morecambe
14/06/1963	Billy Joyce Vs John DaSilva	Joyce won	Bolton
15/06/1963	Billy Joyce Vs Ernie Riley	NK	Bromsgrove
18/06/1963	Billy Joyce Vs Dai Sullivan	Joyce won DSDQ	Wolverhampton
21/06/1963	Billy Joyce Vs Johnny Allan	Joyce won	Leicester, England
22/06/1963	Billy Joyce Vs Masambula	Joyce won	Middlesbrough
25/06/1963	Billy Joyce Vs Norman Walsh	NK	Bridlington, England
29/06/1963	Billy Joyce Vs Norman Walsh	NK	Belle Vue, Manchester
01/07/1963	Billy Joyce Vs Prince Kumali	NK	Margate
02/07/1963	Billy Joyce Vs Prince Kumali	NK	Weymouth
03/07/1963	Billy Joyce Vs Syed Saif Shah	Joyce won	Great Yarmouth, England
23/07/1963	Billy Joyce Vs Norman Walsh	NK	Bridlington, England
25/07/1963	Billy Joyce Vs Seamus Dunleavy	NK	Wimbledon
26/07/1963	Billy Joyce Vs Bill Robinson	NK	Glasgow, Scotland
26/07/1963	Billy Joyce Vs Bill Robinson	NK	Glasgow, Scotland
27/07/1963	Billy Joyce Vs Bill Rawlings	NK	Cleethorpes
29/07/1963	Billy Joyce Vs Geoff Portz	NK	York
30/07/1963	Billy Joyce Vs Ian Campbell	NC	Aberdeen, Scotland
01/08/1963	Billy Joyce Vs Dennis Mitchell	NK	Morecambe
05/08/1963	Billy Joyce Vs Rocky Wall	NK	Belle Vue, Manchester
07/08/1963	Billy Joyce Vs Marjid Ackra	NK	Felixstowe
13/08/1963	Billy Joyce Vs Dave Armstrong	NK	Bridlington, England
31/08/1963	Billy Joyce Vs Rocky Wall	Wall won	Newcastle, England
02/09/1963	Billy Joyce Vs Bill Robinson	Draw	Bradford
06/09/1963	Billy Joyce Vs Masambula	Joyce won	Bolton
07/09/1963	Billy Joyce Vs John DaSilva	Joyce inj	Middlesbrough

Date	Match	Result	Location
10/09/1963	Billy Joyce Vs Majid Ackra	NK	Wolverhampton
17/09/1963	Billy joyce Vs Pietro Capello	NK	Huddersfield
19/09/1963	Billy Joyce Vs Bill Robinson	NK	Morecambe, Lancashire
20/09/1963	Billy Joyce Vs Norman Walsh	Draw (DKO)	Glasgow, Scotland
28/09/1963	Billy Joyce Vs Bill Robinson	Robinson won	Middlesborough, North Yorkshire
28/09/1963	Billy Joyce Vs Bill Robinson	Robinson won	Middlesbrough
30/09/1963	Billy Joyce Vs Jamie Dula	NK	Folkestone
01/10/1963	Billy Joyce Vs Bill Robinson	Robinson won	Huddersfield, England
01/10/1963	Billy Joyce Vs Bill Robinson	Robinson won	Huddersfield
02/10/1963	Billy Joyce Vs Gerry DeJaegar	Joyce won	Cardiff, Wales
03/10/1963	Billy Joyce Vs Ezzard Hart	NK	East Grinstead
04/10/1963	Billy Joyce Vs Jamie Dula	NK	Herne bay
05/10/1963	Billy Joyce Vs Eric Froelich	Joyce won	Coventry, England
06/10/1963	Billy Joyce Vs Roy Bull Davis	NK	Blackpool, England
07/10/1963	Billy Joyce Vs Bill Robinson	Draw	Bradford
12/10/1963	Billy Joyce Vs Bilyl Howes	Joyce won	Newcastle, England
15/10/1963	Billy Joyce Vs Count Bartelli	NK	Warrington
16/10/1963	Billy Joyce Vs Bruno Elrington	Elrington won	Sheffield, England
17/10/1963	Billy Joyce Vs Bruno Elrington	NK	Barrow
19/10/1963	Billy Joyce Vs Bruno Elrington	NK	Portsmouth
23/10/1963	Billy Joyce Vs The Mask	NK	York
25/10/1963	Billy Joyce Vs Dennis Mitchell	Joyce won	Sheffield, England
25/10/1963	Billy Joyce Vs Rocky Wall	NK	Horncastle
26/10/1963	Billy Joyce Vs Bill Robinson	NK	Middlesborough, North Yorkshire
26/10/1963	Billy Joyce Vs Bill Robinson	NK	Middlesbrough
27/10/1963	Billy Joyce Vs Masambula	NK	Chesterfield, England
29/10/1963	Billy Joyce Vs Norman Walsh	NK	Lime Grove, London
31/10/1963	Billy Joyce Vs Rocky Wall	NK	Nottingham, England
04/11/1963	Billy Joyce Vs John Lees	NK	Birmingham
12/11/1963	Billy Joyce Vs Rocky Wall	NK	Solihull
15/11/1963	Billy Joyce Vs Dennis Mitchell	NK	Halifax
18/11/1963	Billy Joyce Vs Ian Campbell	NK	Kilmarnock
21/11/1963	Billy Joyce Vs Bill Robinson	NK	Morecambe, Lancashire
21/11/1963	Billy Joyce Vs Bill Robinson	NK	Morecambe
25/11/1963	Billy Joyce Vs John Lees	NK	Hamilton, Scotland
28/11/1963	Billy Joyce Vs Tibor Szakacs	NK	Barrow
29/11/1963	Billy Joyce Vs Norman Walsh	NK	Willenhall
30/11/1963	Billy Joyce Vs Eric Taylor	NK	Middlesbrough
14/12/1963	Billy Joyce (HWC) vs Ernest Baldwin	NK	Lime Grove, Shepherd's Bush, London
14/01/1964	Billy Joyce Vs Bill Robinson	NK	Wellington
01/02/1964	Billy Joyce Vs Dennis Mitchell	B/J 1- D/M1	Preston, Lancashire
10/02/1964	Billy Joyce Vs Bill Robinson	Robinson won	Cheltenham, England
23/06/1964	Billy Joyce vs Johnny Allan	NK	Scarborough
01/07/1964	Billy Joyce (European HWC) Vs Jan Kovacs	NK	Belle Vue
12/08/1964	Billy Joyce Vs Jans Kovacs	B/J (w)	Belle Vue

Date	Match	Result	Location
04/01/1965	Billy Joyce Vs Gordon Nelson	Joyce inj	Leeds
08/01/1965	Billy Joyce Vs Ian Campbell	NK	Dumfries
13/01/1965	Billy Joyce Vs Jim Rawlings	NK	Rugby
14/01/1965	Billy Joyce Vs Earl Maynard	NK	Kirkcaldy
15/01/1965	Billy Joyce Vs Ricky Starr	NK	Glasgow, Scotland
16/01/1965	Billy Joyce Vs Earl Maynard	NK	Falkirk
18/01/1965	Billy Joyce Vs John Lees	NK	Kilmarnock
18/01/1965	Billy Joyce Vs Dennis Mitchell	Joyce won	Huddersfield
19/01/1965	Billy Joyce Vs John Lees	Joyce won	Aberdeen, Scotland
20/01/1965	Billy Joyce Vs Lucky Simonovich	NK	Perth
21/01/1965	Billy Joyce Vs Rocky Wall	NK	Airdrie
25/01/1965	Billy Joyce Vs Francis Sullivan	NK	Worcester, England
26/01/1965	Billy Joyce Vs Rocky Wall	NK	Lime Grove, London
29/01/1965	Billy Joyce Vs Rocky Wall	Joyce won	Bolton
30/01/1965	Billy Joyce Vs Gordon Nelson	Joyce won	Hanley
01/02/1965	Billy Joyce Vs Ramon Napolitano	NK	Aylesbury
02/02/1965	Billy Joyce Vs Johnny Yearlsey	Joyce won JYDQ	Finsbury Park
04/02/1965	Billy Joyce Vs Joe Cornelius	NK	Weymouth
06/02/1965	Billy Joyce Vs Warnia Zarzecki	NK	Seymour Hall, Marylebone, London
08/02/1965	Billy Joyce Vs Francis Sullivan	NK	Worcester, England
09/02/1965	Billy Joyce Vs Dennis Mitchell	NK	Lime Grove, London
13/02/1965	Billy Joyce Vs John Lees	Joyce won	Newcastle, England
19/02/1965	Billy Joyce Vs Bill Robinson	Robinson won	Liverpool
19/02/1965	Billy Joyce Vs Bill Robinson	Robinson won	Liverpool
24/02/1965	Billy Joyce Vs Enrique Marquess	NK	Scarborough, England
01/03/1965	Billy Joyce Vs Young Apollo	NK	Kilmarnock
02/03/1965	Billy Joyce Vs Josef Zaranoff	NK	Aberdeen, Scotland
04/03/1965	Billy Joyce Vs Young Apollo	NK	Alloa
05/03/1965	Billy Joyce Vs Ian Campbell	NK	Dumfries
06/03/1965	Billy Joyce Vs John Lees	Lees won	Belle Vue, Manchester
13/03/1965	Billy Joyce Vs Hassan Ali Bey	Joyce won	Doncaster
16/03/1965	Billy Joyce Vs Kiwi Kingston	NK	Bournemouth
19/03/1965	Billy Joyce Vs John Cox	Joyce won	Rochester
22/03/1965	Billy Joyce Vs Francis Sullivan	NK	Bradford
24/03/1965	Billy Joyce Vs Norman Walsh	NK	Middlesbrough
27/03/1965	Billy Joyce Vs Francis Sullivan	Joyce won	Newcastle, England
03/04/1965	Billy Joyce Vs Hans Dillinger	Joyce won	Hanley
09/04/1965	Billy Joyce Vs Henri Pierlot	NK	Bolton
10/04/1965	Billy Joyce Vs Rocky Wall	NK	Grantham,
12/04/1965	Billy Joyce Vs Ricky Starr	Starr won	Leeds
17/04/1965	Billy Joyce Vs Rocky Wall	Draw	Barnsley
19/04/1965	Billy Joyce Vs Hans Streiger	Joyce won HSDQ	Blackpool, England
23/04/1965	Billy Joyce Vs Roy Bull Davis	Joyce won RD DQ	Bolton
26/04/1965	Billy Joyce Vs Johnny Yearsley	NK	Aylesbury
27/04/1965	Billy Joyce Vs Danny Lynch	Joyce won	Finsbury Park

Date	Match	Result	Location
05/05/1965	Billy Joyce Vs Rocky Wall	NK	Middlesbrough
06/05/1965	Billy Joyce Vs Norman Walsh	Draw	Edinburgh
13/05/1965	Billy Joyce Vs Bill Robinson	NK	Nottingham
13/05/1965	Billy Joyce Vs Bill Robinson	NK	Nottingham, England
14/05/1965	Billy Joyce Vs Bill Robinson	Robinson won	Glasgow, Scotland
14/05/1965	Billy Joyce Vs Bill Robinson	Robinson won	Glasgow, Scotland
15/05/1965	Billy Joyce Vs Bill Robinson	Robinson won	Belle Vue, Manchester
15/05/1965	Billy Joyce Vs Bill Robinson	Robinson won	Belle Vue, Manchester
18/05/1965	Billy Joyce Vs Tibor Szakacs	NK	Leicester
19/05/1965	Billy Joyce Vs Norman Walsh	Walsh won	Middlesbrough
22/05/1965	Billy Joyce Vs Dennis Mitchell	Joyce won	Newcastle, England
24/05/1965	Billy Jocye Vs Gordon Kilmartin	Joyce won	Leeds
05/06/1965	Billy Joyce Vs Geoff Portz	Joyce won	Newcastle, England
08/06/1965	Billy Joyce Vs Pietro Capello	NK	Croydon
09/06/1965	Billy Joyce Vs Gerry DeJaegar	NK	Cliftonville
11/06/1965	Billy Joyce Vs Alan Garfield	Joyce won	Northampton
12/06/1965	Billy Joyce Vs Bill Robinson	Robinson won	Belle Vue, Manchester
14/06/1965	Billy Joyce Vs john Lees	NK	Bradford
15/06/1965	Billy Joyce Vs Bill Robinson	Draw	Trowell
15/06/1965	Billy Joyce Vs Bill Robinson	Draw	Trowell
19/06/1965	Billy Joyce Vs Gwyn Davies	NK	Newcastle, England
25/06/1965	Billy Joyce Vs Gordon Nelson	Joyce won	Liverpool
27/06/1965	Billy Joyce Vs Emile Poilve	Joyce won	Blackpool, England
28/06/1965	Billy Joyce Vs Norman Walsh	NK	York
29/06/1965	Billy Joyce Vs Bill Robinson	NK	Scarborough
29/06/1965	Billy Joyce Vs Bill Robinson	NK	Scarborough, England
02/07/1965	Billy Joyce Vs Bill Robinson	Joyce won	Glasgow, Scotland
03/07/1965	Billy Joyce Vs Hans Streiger	NK	Lincoln
07/07/1965	Billy Joyce Vs Pietro Capello	NK	Arbroath
17/07/1965	Billy Joyce Vs Hans Streiger	NK	Rhyl, Wales
26/07/1965	Billy Joyce Vs Hans Streiger	Joyce won	Birmingham
30/07/1965	Billy Joyce Vs Johnny Allan	NK	Skegness
31/07/1965	Billy Joyce Vs Johnny Allan	Joyce won	Newcastle, England
07/08/1965	Billy Joyce Vs Bill Robinson	Robinson won	Belle Vue, Manchester
07/08/1965	Billy Joyce Vs Bill Robinson	Robinson won	Belle Vue, Manchester
09/08/1965	Billy Joyce Vs Josef Zaranoff	NK	York
13/08/1965	Billy Joyce Vs John Cox	Joyce won	Glasgow, Scotland
20/08/1965	Billy Joyce Vs Steve Veidor	Joyce won	Liverpool
22/08/1965	Billy Joyce Vs john Lees	Joyce won	Blackpool, England
30/08/1965	Billy Joyce Vs John DaSilva	NK	Weston Super Mare
04/09/1965	Billy Joyce Vs Rocky Wall	Joyce won	Newcastle, England
06/09/1965	Billy Joyce Vs Rocky Wall	Nk	Bradford
08/09/1965	Billy Joyce Vs John Lees	Joyce won	Middlesbrough
11/09/1965	Billy Joyce Vs Rocky Wall	Joyce won	Newcastle, England
14/09/1965	Billy Joyce Vs Dennis Mitchell	Joyce won	Wolverhampton, West Midlands

Date	Match	Result	Location
18/09/1965	Billy Joyce Vs Johnny Allan	Joyce won	Bridlington
24/09/1965	Billy Joyce Vs Dennis Mitchell	Mitchell won BJDQ	Glasgow, Scotland
27/09/1965	Billy Joyce Vs Jim Rawlings	Joyce	Hamilton, Scotland
30/09/1965	Billy Joyce Vs Timmy Geoghegan	NK	Morecambe, Lancashire
04/10/1965	Billy Joyce Vs John Lees	NK	St Ives, Cornwall
05/10/1965	Billy Joyce Vs Josef Kovacs	NK	Solihull
07/10/1965	Billy Joyce Vs Billy Howes	NK	Nelson
12/10/1965	Billy Joyce Vs Ezzard hart	NK	Croydon
13/10/1965	Billy Joyce Vs Josef Zaranoff	Joyce won	Cromer
15/10/1965	Billy Joyce Vs Paul Vachon	Joyce won PVDQ	Northampton
16/10/1965	Billy Joyce Vs Johnny Yearsley	NK	Camberwell
18/10/1965	Billy Joyce Vs Bruno Elrington	NK	Bradford
21/10/1965	Billy Joyce Vs Gabrielle Kane	Joyce won	Paisley
21/10/1965	Billy Joyce Vs Prince Kumali	Joyce won	Paisley
21/10/1965	Billy Joyce Vs Gwyn Davies (F)	Davies won	Paisley
25/10/1965	Billy Joyce Vs Joe Cornelius	NK	Derby
26/10/1965	Billy Joyce Vs Henri Pierlot	NK	Wellington
27/10/1965	Billy Joyce Vs Peter Maivia	Joyce won	Hindley
03/11/1965	Billy Joyce Vs Arne Saari	NK	Lincoln
06/11/1965	Billy Joyce Vs Gwyn Davies	Joyce won	Belle Vue, Manchester
06/11/1965	Billy Joyce Vs John Cox	Joyce won	Belle Vue, Manchester
08/11/1965	Billy Joyce & John Lees Vs Doug Joyce & Hans Streiger	NK	Blackpool, England
09/11/1965	Billy Joyce Vs Kangaroo kennedy	Joyce won	Hull
10/11/1965	Billy Joyce Vs Roy St Clair	Joyce won	Scunthorpe
12/11/1965	Billy Joyce Vs Arne Saari	Joyce won	Rotherham
15/11/1965	Billy Joyce Vs Hans Streiger	NK	Leeds
19/11/1965	Billy Joyce Vs Count Bartelli	NK	Willenhall
20/11/1965	Billy Joyce Vs Masambula	NK	Shrewsbury
22/11/1965	Billy Joyce Vs Yure Borienko	Joyce won	Seymour Hall, London
22/11/1965	Billy Joyce & Jim Hussey Vs Doug Joyce & Hans Streiger	NK	Blackpool, England
24/11/1965	Billy Joyce Vs Johnny Czeslaw	Joyce won	Shoreditch
26/11/1965	Billy Joyce Vs Paul Vachon	NK	Ilford
27/11/1965	Billy Joyce Vs Gwyn Davies	Davies won	Belle Vue, Manchester
29/11/1965	Billy Joyce Vs Aene Saari	NK	Bradford
30/11/1965	Billy Joyce Vs Tibor Szakacs	Joyce won	Leicester
04/12/1965	Billy Joyce Vs Dennis Mitchell	Joyce won	Newcastle, England
07/12/1965	Billy Jocye Vs Joe Cornelius	NK	Kidderminster
08/12/1965	Billy Joyce Vs Billy Howes	NC	Hindley
09/12/1965	Billy Joyce Vs Joe Cornelius	NK	Nelson
11/12/1965	Billy Joyce Vs John DaSilva	NK	Sutton, Ashfield
13/12/1965	Billy Joyce Vs Bill Robinson	NK	Leeds, West yorkshire
05/01/1966	Billy Joyce Vs Paul Duval	NK	Leicester, Leicestershire
06/01/1966	Billy joyce Vs Masambula	NK	Preston, Lancashire
07/01/1966	Billy joyce Vs Masambula	NK	Glasgow
08/01/1966	Billy Joyce Vs Dennis Mitchell	Mitchell won BJDQ	Newcastle, England
10/01/1966	Billy Joyce Vs Syed Saif Shah	NK	Loughborough

Date	Match	Result	Venue
11/01/1966	Billy Joyce & Hans Streiger Vs Ian Campbell & Josef Zaranoff	Joyce et al DQ, Campbell won	Hull
15/01/1966	Billy Joyce Vs Earl Maynard	NK	Horncastle
17/01/1966	Billy Joyce Vs Leon Arras	NK	Derby, Derbyshire
21/01/1966	Billy Joyce Vs Pat Roach	NK	Dumfries
24/01/1966	Billy Joyce Vs Dennis Mitchell	NK	Bradford
27/01/1966	Billy Joyce Vs Paul Duval	NK	Kirkcaldy
28/01/1966	Billy Joyce Vs Earl Maynard	Joyce won	Glasgow
29/01/1966	Billy Joyce Vs Dennis Mitchell	Joyce won	Newcastle, England
31/01/1966	Billy Joyce Vs Kendo Nagasaki	NK	Derby, Derbyshire
04/02/1966	Billy Joyce Vs Pat Roach	Roach won	Dumfries
07/02/1966	Billy Joyce Vs Gwyn Davies	Joyce won	Blackpool, England
12/02/1966	Billy Joyce Vs John Allan	NK	Festival inn, Trwell, Nottinghamshire
12/02/1966	Billy Joyce Vs Johnny Allan	Joyce won	Trowell
14/02/1966	Billy Joyce Vs John Cox	NK	Derby, Derbyshire
15/02/1966	Billy Joyce Vs Bill Robinson	NK	Harrogate
15/02/1966	Billy Joyce Vs Bill Robinson	NK	Harrogate, north Yorkshire
17/02/1966	Billy Joyce Vs Pat Roach	NK	Malvern
21/02/1966	Billy Joyce Vs Wildman of Borneo	NK	Bradford
24/02/1966	Billy Joyce Vs Billy Howes	NK	Nelson
25/02/1966	Billy Joyce Vs Steve Veidor	Joyce won	Middlesborough, North Yorkshire
28/02/1966	Billy Joyce Vs Alex Gaul	Joyce won	Hamilton, Scotland
01/03/1966	Billy Joyce Vs Gwyn Davies	Wolverhampton	Wolverhampton, West Midlands
04/03/1966	Billy joyce Vs Rocky Wall	Wall won	Glasgow
05/03/1966	Billy Joyce Vs Dennis Mitchell	Mitchell won	Falkirk
07/03/1966	Billy Joyce Vs Dennis Mitchell	Joyce won	Bradford
09/03/1966	Billy Joyce Vs Ian Campbell	Campbell won	Perth
10/03/1966	Billy Joyce Vs Ian Campbell	Campbell won	Morecambe, Lancashire
12/03/1966	Billy Joyce Vs Dennis Mitchell	Draw	Newcastle, England
14/03/1966	Billy Joyce Vs Kendo Nagasaki	NK	Derby, Derbyshire
15/03/1966	Billy Joyce Vs Dennis Mitchell	Mitchell won	Huddersfield
01/04/1966	Billy Joyce Vs Pat Roach	NK	Dumfries
04/04/1966	Billy Joyce Vs Johnny Allan	NK	Bradford
06/04/1966	Billy Joyce Vs Dennis Mitchell	Joyce won	Liverpool
13/04/1966	Billy Joyce Vs Billy Robinson	NK	Lincoln, England
13/04/1966	Billy Joyce Vs Bill Robinson	NK	Lincoln, Lincolnshire
14/04/1966	Billy Joyce Vs Kendo Nagasaki	NK	Brierly Hill
25/04/1966	Billy Joyce Vs Billy Robinson	Robinson won	Belle Vue, Manchester
30/04/1966	Billy Joyce Vs Mike Marino	Joyce won	Newcastle, England
02/05/1966	Billy Joyce Vs Ian Campbell	Joyce won	Bradford
04/05/1966	Billy Joyce Vs Ian Campbell	Campbell won	Perth
07/05/1966	Billy Joyce Vs Geoff Portz	NK	St. George's Hall, Bradford, West yorkshire
07/05/1966	Billy Joyce Vs Geoff Portz	Portz won BJDQ	Bradford
13/05/1966	Billy Joyce Vs Billy Robinson	Robinson won	Glasgow, Scotland
13/05/1966	Billy Joyce Vs Bill Robinson	Robinson won	Glasgow

Date	Match	Result	Venue
14/05/1966	Billy Joyce Vs Billy Robinson	Joyce won	Belle Vue, Manchester
18/05/1966	Billy Joyce Vs Jim Hussey	Joyce won	Sheffield, South Yorkshire
20/05/1966	Billy Joyce Vs Bruno Elrington	Elrington won	Liverpool
26/05/1966	Billy Joyce Vs Billy Robinson	NK	Nelson
26/05/1966	Billy Joyce Vs Bill Robinson	NK	Nelson
28/05/1966	Billy Joyce Vs 'Dazzler' Joe Conrelius	NK	The Pavillion, Hemel Hempstead, Hertfordshire
28/05/1966	Billy Joyce Vs Joe Cornelius	Joyce won	Hemel Hempstead, Hertfordshire
30/05/1966	Billy Joyce Vs Geoff Portz	NK	Bradford
12/06/1966	Billy Joyce Vs Kendo Nagasaki	NK	Douglas, Isle of Man
18/06/1966	Billy Joyce Vs Pat Roach	NK	Watford Town Hall, Hertfordshire
21/06/1966	Billy Joyce Vs Pat Roach	NK	Wolverhampton, West Midlands
22/06/1966	Billy Joyce Vs Billy Robinson	Robinson won	Glasgow, Scotland
23/06/1966	Billy Joyce Vs Bill Robinson	NK	Glasgow
25/06/1966	Billy Joyce Vs The Outlaw	NC	Newcastle, England
27/06/1966	Billy Joyce Vs Dennis Mitchell	NK	York
29/06/1966	Billy Joyce Vs Billy Robinson	Robinson won	Sheffield, England
29/06/1966	Billy Joyce Vs Bill Robinson	Robinson won	Sheffield, South Yorkshire
19/07/1966	Billy Joyce Vs Geoff Portz	NK	Bridlington
23/07/1966	Billy Joyce Vs John Lees	NC	Hanley
04/08/1966	Billy Joyce Vs Lee Sharron	Sharron won BJDQ	Morecambe, Lancashire
05/08/1966	Billy Joyce Vs Bill Robinson	Robinson won	Hindley
05/08/1966	Billy Joyce Vs Bill Robinson	Joyce won	Hindley
06/08/1966	Billy Joyce Vs Charlie Fisher	NK	Brent Town Hall, Wembley
06/08/1966	Billy Joyce Vs Charlie Fisher	NK	Wembley
10/08/1966	Billy Joyce Vs Gwyn Davies	NK	Cliftonville
25/08/1966	Billy Joyce Vs Peter Maivia	Joyce won	Wimbledon
03/09/1966	Billy Joyce Vs Bill Robinson	Joyce won	Newcastle, England
03/09/1966	Billy Joyce Vs Bill Robinson	Joyce won	Newcastle, England
04/09/1966	Billy Joyce Vs Tibor Szakacs	Draw	Blackpool, England
10/09/1966	Billy Joyce Vs Johnny Yearsley	NK	Catford
12/09/1966	Billy Joyce Vs The Outlaw	NK	Bradford
14/09/1966	Billy Joyce Vs john Yearsly	NK	Lewisham, London
18/09/1966	Billy Joyce Vs Jim Hussey	Joyce won	Blackpool, England
24/09/1966	Billy Joyce Vs Bill Robinson	Robinson won	Newcastle, England
24/09/1966	Billy Joyce Vs Bill Robinson	Robinson won	Newcastle, England
01/10/1966	Billy Joyce Vs Pat Roach	Joyce won	Hanley
02/10/1966	Billy Joyce Vs Gwyn Davies	NK	Blackpool, England
05/10/1966	Billy Joyce Vs Bill Robinson	NK	Glasgow, Scotland
05/10/1966	Billy Joyce Vs Bill Robinson	Robinson won	Glasgow
07/10/1966	Billy Joyce Vs Andy Robbins	NK	Dumfries
09/10/1966	Billy Joyce Vs Masambula	NK	Longwith
10/10/1966	Billy Joyce Vs Johnny Allan	Allan won BJDQ	Bradford
12/10/1966	Billy Joyce Vs Wildman of Borneo	Joyce won	Leicester, Leicestershire
15/10/1966	Billy Joyce Vs Pat Roach	NK	The Miner's Welfare Scheme, Coalville,

Date	Match	Result	Venue
			Leicestershire
15/10/1966	Billy Joyce Vs Pat Roach	Joyce won	Coalville
17/10/1966	Billy Joyce Vs Steve Veidor	NK	York
21/10/1966	Billy Joyce Vs Barry Douglas	Joyce won	Liverpool
24/10/1966	Billy Joyce Vs Dennis Mitchell	NK	Loughborough
29/10/1966	Billy joyce Vs Masambula	NK	St. George's Hall, Bradford, West yorkshire
29/10/1966	Billy Joyce Vs Masambula	Joyce won	Bradford
31/10/1966	Billy Joyce Vs Steve Veidor	NK	Derby, Derbyshire
05/11/1966	Billy Joyce Vs Jim Hussey	Joyce won JHDQ	Belle Vue, Manchester
07/11/1966	Billy Joyce Vs Bill Rawlings	Joyce won	Bradford
10/11/1966	Billy Joyce Vs Dennis Mitchell	Joyce won	Preston, Lancashire
19/11/1966	Billy Joyce Vs Bill Robinson	Joyce won	Newcastle, England
02/12/1966	Billy Joyce Vs Roy Bull Davies	Joyce won	Bolton, Lancashire
03/12/1966	Billy Joyce Vs Masambula	NK	Shrewsbury
05/12/1966	Billy Joyce Vs John Lees	Joyce won	Cheltenham
08/12/1966	In KO tournament	NK	Southampton, England
12/12/1966	Billy Joyce Vs Bill Robinson	Joyce won	Bradford
12/12/1966	Billy Joyce Vs Bill Robinson	Joyce won	Bradford
14/12/1966	Billy Joyce Vs Mike Marino	Joyce won	Sheffield, South Yorkshire
17/12/1966	Billy Joyce Vs John Cox	Joyce won	Newcastle, England
19/12/1966	Billy Joyce Vs John Cox	NK	Blackpool, England
11/01/1967	Billy Joyce Vs Bill Robinson	NC	Leicester
18/01/1967	Billy Joyce Vs Bill Robinson	Robinson won	Manchester
23/01/1967	Billy Joyce Vs Bill Robinson	Robinson won	Bradford
13/03/1967	Billy Joyce Vs Bill Robinson	NK	Derby, England
06/05/1967	Billy Joyce Vs John Lees	NK	St. George's Hall, Bradford, West yorkshire
06/01/1968	Billy Joyce Vs Tony Charles	NK	Rotherham, South Yorkshire
06/01/1968	Billy Joyce Vs Tony Charles	NK	Rotherham, South Yorkshire
22/01/1968	Billy Joyce Vd Bobby Graham	Joyce won	Birmingham
27/01/1968	Billy Joyce Vs Josef Mulnar	NK	Shrewsbury
01/02/1968	Billy Joyce Vs Sean Regan	Regan won	Ilford
02/02/1968	Billy Joyce Vs Johnny Czeslaw	Draw	Rochester
05/02/1968	Billy Joyce Vs Geoff Portz	Joyce won	Bradford
09/02/1968	Billy Joyce & Dennis Mitchell Vs Ian Campbell & Wild Angus	Joyce et al won IC WA DQ	Carlisle
17/02/1968	Billy joyce Vs Rocky Wall	NK	Morecambe, Lancashire
17/02/1968	Billy joyce Vs Rocky Wall	NK	Morecambe, Lancashire
19/02/1968	Billy Joyce Vs Josef Mulnar	NK	Derby, Derbyshire
22/02/1968	Billy Joyce Vs Johnny Allan	NK	Nelson
26/02/1968	Billy Joyce Vs Billy Robinson	Robinson won	Leeds
26/02/1968	Billy Joyce Vs Bill Robinson	Robinson won	Leeds
29/02/1968	Billy Joyce Vs Kendo Nagasaki	NK	Brierly Hill
01/03/1968	Billy Joyce Vs Gwyn Davies	Davies won BJDQ	Newcastle, England
06/03/1968	Billy Joyce Vs Bob Kirkwood	NK	Sheffield, South Yorkshire
12/03/1968	Billy Joyce Vs Wayne Bridges	Draw DKO	Hastings

Date	Match	Result	Location
13/03/1968	Billy Joyce Vs Roy Bull Davies	NK	Banbury
25/03/1968	Billy Joyce Vs Alf Cadman	Joyce won	Blackpool, England
02/04/1968	Billy Joyce Vs Bruno Elrington	Joyce won BEDQ	Worcester
04/04/1968	Billy joyce Vs Rocky Wall	NK	Nelson
05/04/1968	Billy Joyce Vs Roy St Clair	NK	Dumfries
20/04/1968	Billy Joyce Vs Wildman of Borneo	Joyce won	Hanley
22/04/1968	Billy Joyce Vs Johnny Czeslaw	Draw	Cheltenham
23/04/1968	Billy Joyce Vs Bob Kirkwood	Draw	Croydon, London
26/04/1968	Billy Joyce Vs Johnny Yearsley	Joyce won	Northampton
21/05/1968	Billy Joyce & Enriqu Edo Juan Vs Great Kusatsu & Thunder Sugiyama	Kusatsu et al won	Hanno
22/05/1968	Billy Joyce Vs Tadaharu Tanaka	Tanaka won	Tokyo
25/05/1968	Billy Joyce Vs Thunder Sugiyama	Thunder won	Sapporo
26/05/1968	Billy Joyce Vs Masao Kimura	Joyce won MKDQ	Sapporo
27/05/1968	Billy Joyce & John Cox & Colin Joynson Vs Great Kusatsu & Thunder Sugiyama & Toyonobori	Kusatsu et al won	Wakkana
28/05/1968	Billy Joyce & Colin Joynson & John Cox Vs Tadahara Tanaka & Thunder Sugiyama & Toyonobori	Thunder et al won	Asahikawa
29/05/1968	Billy Joyce & Colin Joynson & John Cox Vs Great Kusatsu & Thunder Sugiyama & Toyonobori	Thunder et al won	Obihiro
30/05/1968	Billy Joyce & Colin Joynson & Rocky Wall Vs Thunder Sugiyama & Mammoth Suzuki & Toyonobori	Thunder et al won	Kushiro
31/05/1968	Billy Joyce & Colin Joynson & Rocky Wall Vs Thunder Sugiyama & Great Kusatsu & Toyonobori	Thunder et al won	Abashiri
01/06/1968	Billy Joyce & Colin Joynson & Rocky Wall Vs Thunder Sugiyama & Tadaharu Tanaka & Toyonobori	Thunder et al won	Tomakomai
03/06/1968	Billy Joyce & Colin Joynson & Rocky Wall Vs Thunder Sugiyama & Great Kusatsu & Toyonobori	Thunder et al won	Kakodate
05/06/1968	Billy Joyce & Colin Joynson & Rocky Wall Vs Thunder Sugiyama & Tadaharu Tanaka & Toyonobori	Thunder et al won	Akita
08/06/1968	Billy Joyce & Rocky Wall & Enrique Edo Juan Vs Thunder Sugiyama & Tadaharu Tanaka & Tetsunosuke Daigo	Thunder et al won	Yokohama
09/06/1968	Billy Joyce & Rocky Wall & John Cox Vs Thunder Sugiyama & Tadaharu Tanaka & Yoyonobori	Thunder et al won	Owase
15/06/1968	Billy Joyce Vs Enzo Inoue	Joyce won	Tokyo
15/08/1968	Billy Joyce Vs John Cox	NK	Morecambe, Lancashire
07/04/1969	Billy Joyce Vs Kendo Nagasaki	Nagasaki won	Bradford
17/04/1969	Billy Joyce Vs Honeyboy Zimba	Joyce won	Malvern
18/04/1969	Billy Joyce Vs Henri Pierlot	Draw	Dumfries
18/06/1969	Billy Joyce Vs Pete Roberts	Joyce won	Wigan, Lancashire
11/09/1969	Billy Joyce Vs Peter Stewart	NK	Morecambe, Lancashire
06/10/1969	Billy Joyce Vs Don Vines	Joyce won DVDQ	Bradford
03/11/1969	Billy Joyce Vs Jack Fallon	NK	Derby, Derbyshire
05/11/1969	Billy Joyce Vs Tony Orford	NK	Loughborough
06/02/1971	Billy Joyce Vs Bobo Matu	NK	Derby, Derbyshire
17/05/1965	Billy Joyce Vs John Cox	NK	York

Joe Robinson

Date	Match	Outcome	Venue
1937	All England Champion Welterweight	N/A	Manchester, England
01/06/1939	Joe Robinson Vs Jose Sims	Joe won	Crewe, England
18/12/1939	Joe Robinson Vs Hercules Boyne	NK	Bolton, Lancashire
13/12/1943	Joe Robinson Vs Wentworth	NK	Blackpool, England
20/10/1952	Joe Robinson Vs Ken Davies	Joe won	Leeds, England
01/12/1952	Joe Robinson Vs Dai Sullivan	Joe won	Edinburgh, Scotland
01/12/1952	Joe Robinson Vs The Farmer	Joe won	Carlisle, England
01/12/1952	Joe Robinson Vs The Farmer	Joe won	Hull, England
01/12/1952	Joe Robinson Vs The Farmer	Joe won	Rotherham, England
04/12/1952	Joe Robinson Vs Ernest Baldwin	Joe won	Morecambe, Lancashire
18/12/1952	Joe Robinson Vs Eugenio Gonzales	Joe won	Albert Hall, London
02/02/1953	Joe Robinson Vs Dave Armstrong	draw	Leeds, England
05/02/1953	Joe Robinson Vs Merie Matassa	Joe won	Albert Hall, London
29/01/1956	Joe Robinson Vs Gedeon Gida	Joe won	Berlin, Germany
30/01/1956	Joe Robinson Vs Rene Lasartesse	Rene won	Berlin, Germany
30/10/1956	Joe Robinson Vs Rudi Schmacher	Rudi won	Berlin, Germany

Jack Dempsey(Tommy Moore)

Date	Match	Outcome	Venue
12/01/1946	Jack Dempsey Vs Ernie Vasey	Vasey won	Newcastle, England
25/02/1946	Jack Dempsey Vs Reg Maxwell	Reg won	Edinburgh, Scotland
25/02/1946	Jack Dempsey Vs Reg Naxwell	Naxwell won	Edinburgh, Scotland
04/03/1946	Jack Dempsey Vs Carlton Smith	Smith won	Edinburgh, Scotland
05/03/1946	Jack Dempsey Vs Snaky Allan	Draw	Dundee, Scotland
08/03/1946	Jack Dempsey Vs Jackie Harries	NK	Belfast, Ireland
30/03/1946	Jack Dempsey Vs Johnny Nelson	NK	Newcastle, England
11/05/1946	Jack Dempsey Vs Pat Brennan	Dempsey won	Newcastle, England
19/07/1946	Jack Dempsey Vs Alf Jenkins	NK	Belfast, Ireland
05/08/1946	Jack Dmepsey Vs Archer O'Brien	Archer won	Edinburgh, Scotland
16/08/1946	Jack Dempsey Vs Carlton Smith	NK	Belfast, Ireland
31/08/1946	Jack Dempsey Vs Johnny Nelson	Dempsey won	Newcastle, England
28/10/1946	Jack Dempsey Vs George Kidd	George Won	Edinburgh, Scotland
28/10/1946	Jack Dempsey Vs George Kidd	Kidd won	Edinburgh, Scotland
10/01/1947	Jack Dempsey Vs Johnny King	NK	Belfast, Ireland
20/01/1947	Jack Dempsey Vs Pat Brennan	Jack won	Edinburgh, Scotland
02/05/1947	Jack Dempsey Vs Les Stent	Stent won	Goole, England
19/05/1947	Jack Dempsey Vs George Kidd	Kidd won	Edinburgh, Scotland
28/06/1947	Jack Dempsey Vs Hal Fuller	NK	Newcastle, England
14/07/1947	Jack Dempsey Vs Granville Lawrence	Jack won	Edinburgh, Scotland
14/07/1947	Jack Dempsey Vs Granville Lawrence	Dempsey won	Edinburgh, Scotland
15/07/1947	Jack Dempsey Vs Andy Anderson	Dempsey won	Aberdeen, Scotland
26/07/1947	Jack Dempsey & Harry Fields Vs Mike Howley & Al Fuller	NK	Newcastle, England
01/09/1947	Jack Dempsey Vs Alan Colbeck	Jack won	Edinburgh, Scotland
01/09/1947	Jack Dempsey Vs Alan Colbeck	NK	Edinburgh, Scotland
20/10/1947	Jack Dempsey Vs Andy Anderson	Dempsey won	Edinburgh, Scotland
21/10/1947	Jack Dempsey Vs Andy Anderson	Dempsey won	Dundee, Scotland
17/11/1947	Jack Dempsey Vs Wal Trdoff	Jack won	Edinburgh, Scotland
01/12/1947	Jack Dempsey Vs Alec Anderson	Jack won	Aberdeen, Scotland
10/01/1948	Jack Dempsey Vs Danny Flynn	NK	Hanley, England
23/02/1948	Jack Dempsey Vs Joe Reid	Draw	Edinburgh, Scotland
23/02/1948	Jack Dempsey Vs Joe Reid	Draw	Edinburgh, Scotland
04/06/1948	Jack Dempsey & George Kidd Vs Tiger Wood & Cordite Conroy	NK	Levenshulme
05/06/1948	Jack Dempsey Vs Martin Conroy	NK	Belle Vue, Manchester
18/06/1948	Jack Dempsey Vs Frank Manto	NK	Levenshulme
02/07/1948	Jack Dempsey Vs Cliff Beaumont	NK	Levenshulme
05/07/1948	Jack Dempsey Vs Bernard Murray	Bernard won	Edinburgh, Scotland
05/07/1948	Jack Dempsey Vs Bernard Murray	Murray won	Edinburgh, Scotland
17/07/1948	Jack Dempsey Vs Tiger Wood	NK	Bury, England
19/07/1948	Jack Dempsey Vs George Kidd	NC	Aberdeen, Scotland
14/08/1948	Jack Dempsey Vs Cordite Conroy	NK	Bury, England
27/08/1948	Jack Dempsey Vs Tiger Wood	NK	Levenshulme

Date	Match	Result	Location
24/09/1948	Jack Dempsey Vs Bill Brennan	NK	Fleetwood, England
09/10/1948	Jack Dempsey Vs Tommy Mann	NK	Bury, England
15/10/1948	Jack Dempsey Vs Tiger Wood	NK	Levenshulme
29/10/1948	Jack Dempsey Vs Fred Murray	NK	Levenshulme
01/11/1948	Jack Dempsey Vs George Kidd	George Won	Edinburgh, Scotland
01/11/1948	Jack Dempsey Vs George Kidd	Kidd won	Edinburgh, Scotland
01/01/1949	Jack Dempsey Vs Bernard Murray	Bernard won	Aberdeen, Scotland
08/01/1949	Jack Dempsey Vs George Goldie	NK	Hanley, England
12/01/1949	Jack Dempsey Vs George Twinn	NK	Lincoln
12/01/1949	Jack Dempsey Vs George Twinn	NK	Lincoln
15/01/1949	Jack Dempsey Vs Young Atlas	NK	Kings Lynn, England
24/01/1949	Jack Dempsey Vs Tommy Mann	Mann won	Edinburgh, Scotland
25/01/1949	Jack Dempsey Vs Tommy Mann	Mann won, JD DQ	Dundee, Scotland
04/02/1949	Jack Dempsey Vs Ginger Nicholls	NK	Folkestone, England
09/02/1949	Jack Dempsey Vs George Kidd	NK	Lincoln
09/02/1949	Jack Dempsey Vs George Kidd	NK	Lincoln
14/02/1949	Jack Dempsey Vs Jackie Harries	NK	Hull, England
22/02/1949	Jack Dempsey Vs Tommy Mann	NK	Dundee, Scotland
04/08/1949	Jack Dempsey Vs Danny Flynn	Dempsey won	Gloucester, England
09/08/1949	Jack Dempsey Vs Granville Lawrence	Dempsey won	Aberdeen, Scotland
05/10/1949	Jack Dempsey Vs Bernard Murray	NK	Lincoln
05/10/1949	Jack Dempsey Vs Bernard Murray	NK	Lincoln
17/10/1949	Jack Dempsey Vs Young Atlas	Dempsey won	Hamilton, Scotland
18/10/1949	Jack Dempsey Vs Young Atlas	Jack won	Hamilton, Scotland
28/10/1949	Jack Dempsey Vs Al Lipman	Dempsey won	Ipswich, England
01/11/1949	Jack Dempsey Vs Ed Capelli	Ed won	NK
02/11/1949	Jack Dempsey Vs Eddie Capelli	NK	Ramsgate
18/11/1949	Jack Dempsey Vs Bernard Murray	Jack won	Glasgow, Scotland
18/11/1949	Jack Dempsey Vs Bernard Murray	Dempsey won	Glasgow, Scotland
29/11/1949	Jack Dempsey Vs Vic Coleman	Coleman won	Chelmsford, England
30/11/1949	Jack Dempsey Vs Mick McManus	NK	Cardiff, Wales
01/12/1949	Jack Dempsey Vs George Kidd	George Won	Aberdeen, Scotland
01/12/1949	Jack Dempsey Vs Johnny Peters	Johnny won	Portsmouth, England
01/12/1949	Jack Dmepsey Vs Les Stent	Draw	Rotherham, South Yorkshire
09/12/1949	Jack Dempsey Vs George Kidd	NK	Chesterfield, England
16/12/1949	Jack Dempsey Vs Johnny Nelson	Johnny won	Glasgow, Scotland
16/12/1949	Jack Dempsey Vs Johnny Nelson	Nelson won	Glasgow, Scotland
21/12/1949	Jack Dempsey Vs Harry Fields	NK	Lincoln
21/12/1949	Jack Dempsey Vs Harry Fields	NK	Lincoln
24/12/1949	Jack Dempsey Vs Bernard Murray	Murray won	Newcastle, England
28/12/1949	Jack Dempsey Vs Arthur Fisher	Dempsey won	Peterborough, England
29/12/1949	Jack Dempsey Vs Jackie Harris	Jackie won	Morecambe, Lancashire
29/12/1949	Jack Dempsey Vs Jackie Harries	Harries won	Morecambe, Lancashire
14/01/1950	Jack Dempsey Vs Rab Hannah	Dempsey won	Newcastle, England
16/01/1950	Jack Dempsey Vs Jackie Harries	NK	Derby, England

Date	Match	Result	Location
18/01/1950	Jack Dempsey Vs George Kidd	NK	Burnley, England
27/01/1950	Jack Dempsey Vs Gypsy Benito	NK	Chesterfield, England
28/01/1950	Jack Dempsey Vs Danny Flynn	Dempsey won	Newcastle, England
04/02/1950	Jack Dempsey Vs Danny Flynn	Dempsey won	Newcastle, England
06/02/1950	Jack Dempsey Vs Jimmy Rudd	Dempsey won	Aberdeen, Scotland
07/02/1950	Jack Dempsey Vs Tommy Mann	Tommy won	Hamilton, Scotland
20/02/1950	Jack Dempsey Vs Les Stent	NK	Cardiff, Wales
21/02/1950	Jack Dempsey Vs George Kidd	Kidd won	Aberdeen, Scotland
01/03/1950	Jack Dempsey Vs Vic Coleman	NK	Caledonian Road, London
02/03/1950	Jack Dempsey Vs Johnny Peters	NK	Southampton, England
09/03/1950	Jack Dempsey Vs Carlton Smith	Jack won	Beckenham, England
10/03/1950	Jack Dempsey Vs George Kidd	Kidd won	Glasgow, Scotland
13/03/1950	Jack Dempsey Vs Johnny Stead	Dempsey won	Edinburgh, Scotland
14/03/1950	Jack Dempsey Vs Alan Colbeck	Colbeck won	Dundee, Scotland
18/03/1950	Jack Dempsey Vs Tony Lawrence	Dempsey won	Newcastle, England
24/03/1950	Jack Dempsey Vs Rab Hannon	Jack won	Glasgow, Scotland
13/04/1950	Jack Dempsey Vs Eddie Capelli	NK	Southampton, England
17/04/1950	Jack Dempsey Vs Vic Coleman	NK	Caledonian Road, London
17/04/1950	Jack Dempsey Vs Bob Russell	Dempsey won	Peterborough, England
18/04/1950	Jack Dempsey Vs Alan Colbeck	Colbeck won	Chelmsford, England
20/04/1950	Jack Dempsey Vs Eddie Capelli	NK	Bath
22/04/1950	Jack Dempsey Vs Gypsy Benito	Dempsey won, GBDQ	Newcastle, England
01/05/1950	Jack Dempsey Vs Sanky Allan	Allan won	Hamilton, Scotland
08/05/1950	Jack Dempsey Vs Tony Lawrence	NC	Edinburgh, Scotland
15/05/1950	Jack Dempsey Vs Archer O'Brien	Jack won	Leeds, England
18/05/1950	Jack Dempsey Vs Mick McManus	NK	Southampton, England
15/06/1950	Jack Dempsey Vs Johnny Williams	NK	Southampton, England
17/06/1950	Jack Dempsey Vs Granville Lawrence	Dempsey won	Newcastle, England
21/06/1950	Jack Dempsey Vs George Kidd	NK	Mile End, London
22/06/1950	Jack Dempsey Vs George Kidd	NK	Bristol, England
12/07/1950	Jack Dempsey Vs Glyn Jones	NK	Cardiff, Wales
13/07/1950	Jack Dempsey Vs Fred Unwin	Draw	Bristol
07/08/1950	Jack Dempsey Vs George Kidd	George won	Edinburgh, Scotland
14/08/1950	Jack Dempsey Vs Steve Kilroy	NK	Hastings, England
29/08/1950	Jack Dempsey Vs Chris Londis	Draw	Plymouth, England
30/08/1950	Jack Dempsey Vs Chris Londis	NK	Cardiff, Wales
31/08/1950	Jack Dempsey Vs Carlton Smith	NK	Bristol, England
31/08/1950	Jack Dempsey Vs Carlton Smith	NK	Bristol
11/09/1950	Jack Dempsey Vs Alf Jenkins	NK	Derby, England
12/09/1950	Jack Dempsey Vs Kid Pitman	Pitman won	Chelmsford, England
20/09/1950	Jack Dempsey Vs Jack Harrington	NK	Hereford, England
21/09/1950	Jack Dempsey Vs Jack Cunningham	Dempsey won	Burnley, England
25/09/1950	Jack Dempsey Vs George Kidd	George won	Edinburgh, Scotland
25/09/1950	Jack Dempsey Vs George Kidd	George won	Edinburgh, Scotland
25/09/1950	Jack Dempsey Vs George Kidd	Kidd won	Edinburgh, Scotland

Date	Match	Result	Location
28/09/1950	Jack Dempsey Vs Jackie Harris	Draw	Bristol
28/09/1950	Jack Dempsey Vs Jackie Harris	Draw	Bristol
29/09/1950	Jack Dempsey Vs Jim Boyle	Jim won, JD DQ	Glasgow, Scotland
30/09/1950	Jack Dempsey Vs George Kidd	Kidd won	Newcastle, England
05/10/1950	Jack Dempsey Vs Carlton Smith	NK	Southampton, England
06/10/1950	Jack Dempsey Vs Carlton Smith	Smith won	Ipswich, England
25/10/1950	Jack Dempsey Vs George Kidd	NK	St. Albans, Hertfordshire
26/10/1950	Jack Dempsey Vs George Kidd	NK	Southampton, England
01/11/1950	Jack Dempsey Vs Ed Capelli	Draw	Washington DC
03/11/1950	Jack Dempsey Vs Tony Vallon	Dempsey won	Glasgow, Scotland
13/11/1950	Jack Dempsey Vs Johnny Peters	Johnny won	West Ham, England
25/11/1950	Jack Dempsey Vs Prince Banu	Draw	Shrewsbury, England
01/12/1950	Jack Dempsey Vs Johnny Peters	Draw	NK
01/12/1950	Jack Dmepsey Vs Johnny Peters	Draw	NK
01/12/1950	Jack Dempsey Vs Bob Sherry	Jack won	Glasgow, Scotland
11/12/1950	Jack Dempsey Vs Carlton Smith	Carlton won	Battersea, England
18/12/1950	Jack Dempsey Vs Alan Colbeck	Draw	Edinburgh, Scotland
18/12/1950	Jack Dempsey Vs Alan Colbeck	Jack won	Edinburgh, Scotland
21/12/1950	Jack Dempsey Vs Carlton Smith	Draw	Beckenham, England
06/01/1951	Jack Dempsey Vs Bernard Murray	NK	Chesterfield, England
09/01/1951	Jack Dempsey Vs Vic Coleman	Vic won	South London, England
09/01/1951	Jack Dempsey Vs Vic Coleman	Vic won	South London, England
16/01/1951	Jack Dempsey Vs Bob Archer O'Brien	NK	Colchester, England
17/01/1951	Jack Dempsey Vs Johnny Peters	NK	St. Albans, Hertfordshire
19/01/1951	Jack Dempsey Vs Johnny Williams	NK	Southampton, England
24/01/1951	Jack Dempsey Vs Granville Lawrence	NK	Halifax, England
26/01/1951	Jack Dempsey Vs Tony Lawrence	Jack won	Glasgow, Scotland
26/01/1951	Jack Dempsey Vs Tony Lawrence	Jack won	Glasgow, Scotland
31/01/1951	Jack Dempsey Vs George Kidd	NK	St. Albans, Hertfordshire
01/02/1951	Jack Dempsey Vs Mick McManus	NK	Southampton, England
08/02/1951	Jack Dempsey Vs Jackie Harries	NK	Southampton, England
18/02/1951	Jack Dempsey Vs Mick McManus	McManus won	West Ham, England
27/02/1951	Jack Dempsey Vs Mick McManus	NK	Kingston, England
01/03/1951	Jack Dempsey Vs Eddie Capelli	Jack won	Bury, England
13/03/1951	Jack Dempsey Vs Johnny Stead	Stead won	Dundee, Scotland
19/03/1951	Jack Dempsey Vs Johnny Maxwell	Jack won	Edinburgh, Scotland
02/04/1951	Jack Dempsey Vs Cliff Beaumont	Beaumont won	Aberdeen, Scotland
03/04/1951	Jack Dempsey Vs Sanky Allan	Sanky won	Hamilton, Scotland
03/04/1951	Jack Dempsey Vs Sanky Allan	Sanky won	Hamilton, Scotland
30/04/1951	Jack Dempsey Vs Sanky Allan	Jack won	Leeds, England
10/05/1951	Competed in Tournament	NK	Southampton, England
24/05/1951	Jack Dempsey Vs Carlton Smith	NK	Southampton, England
04/06/1951	Jack Dempsey Vs Mick McManus	Mick won	Edinburgh, Scotland
06/06/1951	Jack Dempsey Vs Johnny Peters	Draw	Cardiff, Wales
19/06/1951	Jack Dempsey Vs Joe Queseck	NK	Brighton, England

Date	Match	Result	Location
20/06/1951	Jack Dempsey Vs Al Lipman	Al won	Mile End, England
22/06/1951	Jack Dempsey Vs Joe Queseck	NK	Ramsgate
02/07/1951	Jack Dempsey Vs Fred Woolley	Jack won	Edinburgh, Scotland
07/07/1951	Jack Dempsey Vs Jim Boyle	Dempsey won	Newcastle, England
18/07/1951	Jack Dempsey Vs Bob Archer O'Brien	Draw	Mile End, London
23/07/1951	Jack Dempsey Vs Tony Lawrence	Tony won	Edinburgh, Scotland
25/07/1951	Jack Dempsey Vs Danny Flynn	Dempsey won	Newcastle, England
02/08/1951	Jack Dempsey Vs George Kidd	NK	Bristol, England
03/09/1951	Jack Dempsey Vs Bernard Murray	Jack won	Edinburgh, Scotland
03/09/1951	Jack Dempsey Vs Bernard Murray	Jack won	Edinburgh, Scotland
07/09/1951	Jack Dempsey Vs Johnny Stead	Stead win	Glasgow, Scotland
08/09/1951	Jack Dempsey Vs Johnny Stead	Johnny won	Glasgow, Scotland
13/09/1951	Jack Dempsey Vs Chic Purvey	NK	Southampton, England
19/09/1951	Jack Dempsey Vs Mick McManus	Draw	Cambridge, England
24/09/1951	Jack Dempsey Vs Joe Queseck	NK	Bury, England
02/10/1951	Jack Dempsey Vs Gipsy Guy Laroche	Draw	Swindon, England
03/10/1951	Jack Dempsey Vs George Kidd	NK	Cambridge, England
19/10/1951	Jack Dempsey Vs Granville Lawrence	NK	Halifax, England
23/10/1951	Jack Dempsey Vs Roger LaRoache	LaRoache	Beckenham, England
25/10/1951	Jack Dempsey Vs Gipsy Guy Laroche	Gipsy won	Beckenham, England
02/11/1951	Jack Dempsey Vs Les Stent	NK	Chesterfield, England
05/11/1951	Jack Dempsey Vs Chris London	Chris won	Edinburgh, Scotland
13/11/1951	Jack Dempsey Vs Carlton Smith	Jack won	Swindon, England
14/11/1951	Jack Dempsey Vs Pat Kloke	Dempsey won	Watford, England
15/11/1951	Jack Dempsey Vs Mick McManus	NK	Southampton, England
15/11/1951	Jack Dempsey Vs Mick McManus	NK	Southampton, England
26/11/1951	Jack Dempsey Vs Mick McManus	Jack won	Croyden, England
29/11/1951	Jack Dempsey Vs Johnny Williams	NK	Bury, England
03/12/1951	Jack Dempsey Vs Laurie Bailey	NK	Hull, England
04/12/1951	Jack Dempsey Vs Johnny Peters	Johnny won	Kings Hall, South London
08/12/1951	Jack Dempsey Vs Alan Colbeck	Alan won	Middlesborough, North Yorkshire
13/12/1951	Jack Dempsey Vs Pat Kloke	NK	Rusholme, England
19/12/1951	Jack Dempsey Vs Eddie Capelli	Draw	Cardiff, Wales
03/01/1952	Jack Dempsey Vs Tommy Mann	Mann won	Morecambe, Lancashire
08/01/1952	Jack Dempsey Vs Mick McManus	Draw	Swindon, England
15/01/1952	Jack Dempsey Vs Eddie Capelli	NK	Colchester, England
17/01/1952	Jack Dempsey Vs Carlton Smith	Carlton won	Bristol, England
24/01/1952	Jack Dempsey Vs Joe Queseck	NK	Southampton, England
30/01/1952	Jack Dempsey Vs Carlton Smith	Dempsey won	High Wycombe, England
07/02/1952	Jack Dempsey Vs Carlton Smith	Draw	Wimbledon, England
08/02/1952	Jack Dempsey Vs Arthur Fisher	NK	Ramsgate
12/02/1952	Jack Dempsey Vs George Kidd	NK	Hove, England
14/02/1952	Jack Dempsey Vs Ken Joyce	NK	Bristol, England
18/02/1952	Jack Dempsey Vs Ken Joyce	Jack won	Croyden, England
28/02/1952	Jack Dempsey Vs Carlton Smith	Jack won	Bristol, England
07/03/1952	Jack Dempsey Vs Granville Lawrence	Dempsey won	Ipswich, England

Date	Match	Result	Location
10/03/1952	Jack Dempsey Vs Arthur Fisher	NK	Peterborough, England
11/03/1952	Jack Dempsey Vs George Kidd	NK	Hove, England
12/03/1952	Jack Dempsey Vs Arthur Fisher	Jack won	Cardiff, Wales
13/03/1952	Jack Dempsey Vs George Kidd	NK	Bristol, England
18/03/1952	Jack Dempsey Vs Steve Logan	NK	Swindon, England
20/03/1952	Jack Dempsey Vs Johnny Williams	Jack won	Beckenham, England
24/03/1952	Jack Dempsey Vs Fred Unwin	Jack won	Croyden, England
25/03/1952	In Tournament	NK	Hove, England
26/03/1952	Jack Dempsey Vs Vic Coleman	NK	Hastings, England
07/04/1952	Jack Dempsey Vs Bob Archer O'Brien	O'Brien won	Peterborough, England
08/04/1952	Jack Dempsey Vs Archer O'Brien	Jack won	South London, England
15/04/1952	Jack Dempsey Vs Ed Capelli	Draw	Swindon, England
24/04/1952	Jack Dempsey Vs Ken Joyce	NK	Bristol, England
29/04/1952	Jack Dempsey Vs Jack Cunningham	Jack won	Swindon, England
29/04/1952	Jack Dempsey Vs Mick McManus	Jack won	Swindon, England
29/04/1952	Jack Dempsey Vs Archer O'Brien	Jack won	Swindon, England
05/05/1952	Jack Dempsey Vs Bob Archer O'Brien	Dempsey won	Peterborough, England
06/05/1952	Jack Dempsey Vs Mick McManus	Jack won	South London, England
07/05/1952	Jack Dempsey Vs Fred Unwin	Draw	Cardiff, Wales
21st May-8th Jul 1952	Jack Dempsey Vs Rene Ben Chemoul	Rene won	Berlin, Germany
21st May-8th Jul 1952	Jack Dempsey Vs Pat Kloke	Pat won	Berlin, Germany
21st May-8th Jul 1952	Jack Dempsey Vs Rudi Schumacher	Rudi won	Berlin, Germany
21/05/1952	Jack Dempsey Vs Mick McManus	Jack won	Cardiff, Wales
23/06/1952	Jack Dempsey Vs Johnny Williams	Jack won	Edinburgh, Scotland
24/06/1952	Jack Dempsey Vs Johnny Williams	Jack won	South London, England
25/06/1952	Jack Dempsey Vs Johnny Williams	Draw	Cardiff, Wales
26/06/1952	Jack Dempsey Vs Steve Logan	Logan won	Bristol, England
11/07/1952	Jack Dempsey Vs Mick McManus	NK	Ramsgate
18/07/1952	Jack Dempsey Vs Eddie Capelli	NK	Mile End, London
06/08/1952	Jack Dempsey Vs Mick McManus	Draw	Bournemouth, England
07/08/1952	Jack Dempsey Vs Archer O'Brien	Draw	Bristol, England
19/08/1952	Jack Dempsey Vs Johnny Maxwell	NK	Aberdeen, Scotland
25/08/1952	Jack Dempsey Vs Chris Londos	Draw	Becontree, England
28/08/1952	Jack Dempsey Vs Ken Joyce	Draw	Wimbledon, England
29/08/1952	Jack Dempsey Vs Bob Archer O'Brien	NK	Ramsgate
24/09/1952	Jack Dempsey Vs Johnny Peters	Draw	High Wycombe, England
25/09/1952	Jack Dempsey Vs Johnny Williams	NK	Bury, England
03/10/1952	Jack Dempsey Vs Jim Lewis	Draw	Glasgow, Scotland
07/10/1952	Jack Dempsey Vs Chris Londis	NK	Colchester, England
08/10/1952	Jack Dempsey Vs Arthur Fisher	NK	Cardiff, Wales
09/10/1952	Jack Dempsey Vs Chris Londos	Draw	Bristol, England
15/10/1952	Jack Dempsey Vs Jack Quesick	Jack won	Cardiff, Wales
16/10/1952	Jack Dempsey Vs Carlton Smith	Jack won	Swindon, England
20/10/1952	Jack Dempsey Vs Young Vulcan	Draw	Leeds, England
23/10/1952	Jack Dempsey Vs Reg Ray	Jack won	Morecambe, Lancashire

Date	Match	Result	Location
24/10/1952	Jack Dempsey Vs Jim Lewis	NK	Altrincham
29/10/1952	Jack Dempsey Vs Jack Queseck	Dempsey won	Hastings, England
30/10/1952	Jack Dempsey Vs Archer O'Brien	Draw	Bristol, England
31/10/1952	Jack Dempsey Vs Eddie Capelli	NK	Ramsgate
12/11/1952	Jack Dempsey Vs Raymond Andrew	Jack won	Bath, England
13/11/1952	Jack Dempsey Vs Chic Purvey	Jack won	Swindon, England
27/11/1952	Jack Dempsey Vs Martin Conroy	Jack won	Morecambe, Lancashire
02/12/1952	Jack Dempsey Vs George Kidd	NK	Colchester, England
09/12/1952	Jack Dempsey Vs Bernard Murray	NK	Lime Grove, England
22/12/1952	Jack Dempsey Vs Mick McManus	Mick won	West Ham, England
01/01/1953	Jack Dempsey Vs Lucien Guillod	Jack won	Miscellaneous
01/01/1953	Jack Dempsey Vs Mich McManus	Jack won	Beckenham, England
14/01/1953	Jack Dempsey Vs Bert Royal	Jack won	Cardiff, Wales
05/02/1953	Jack Dempsey Vs Bert Royal	Draw	Swindon, England
10/02/1953	Jack Dempsey Vs Chic Purvey	Chic won	Scarborough, England
04/03/1953	Jack Dempsey Vs Chic Purvey	Jack won	High Wycombe, England
13/04/1953	Jack Dempsey Vs Jim Lewis	Jim won	Leeds, England
15/04/1953	Jack Dempsey Vs Ken Joyce	Jack won, KJ DQ	Cardiff, Wales
16/04/1953	Jack Dempsey Vs Danny Flynn	Jack won	Bristol, England
01/05/1953	Jack Dempsey Vs Tony Lawrence	Jack won	Glasgow, Scotland
13/05/1953	Jack Dempsey Vs George Kidd	Jack won	Cardiff, Wales
08/06/1953	Jack Dempsey Vs Bernard Murray	Jack won	Leeds, England
06/08/1953	Jack Dempsey Vs Alan Colbeck	Jack won	Morecambe, Lancashire
13/08/1953	Jack Dempsey Vs Jackie Pallo	Jack D won	Wimbledon, England
07/09/1953	Jack Dempsey Vs Sanky Allan	Sanky won	Edinburgh, Scotland
10/09/1953	Jack Dempsey Vs Sanky Allan	Sanky won	Morecambe, Lancashire
12/09/1953	Jack Dempsey Vs Chic Purvey	Jack won	Bristol, England
14/09/1953	Jack Dempsey Vs Jim Lewis	Draw	Leeds, England
17/09/1953	Jack Dempsey Vs Chic Purvey	Jack won	Bristol, England
28/09/1953	Jack Dempsey Vs Sanky Allan	Jack won	Edinburgh, Scotland
01/10/1953	Jack Dempsey Vs Arthur Fisher	Jack won	Bristol, England
20/10/1953	Jack Dempsey Vs Andre DuBarry	Jack won	Swindon, England
26/10/1953	Jack Dempsey Vs Jim Lewis	Jack won	Leeds, England
12/11/1953	Jack Dempsey Vs Jack Cunningham	Jack C won	Bristol, England
17/11/1953	Jack Dempsey Vs Cliff Beaumont	Cliff won	Swindon, England
27/11/1953	Jack Dempsey Vs Archer O'Brien	Draw	Wimbledon, England
01/01/1954	Jack Dempsey Vs Eric Sands	Draw	Cardiff, Wales
07/01/1954	Jack Dempsey Vs Archer O'Brien	Draw	Wimbledon, England
08/01/1954	Jack Dempsey Vs Jim Lewis	Jim won	Glasgow, Scotland
11/01/1954	Jack Dempsey Vs Carlton Smith	NK	Bedford
20/01/1954	Jack Dempsey Vs Jack Cunningham	Dempsey Won	Cardiff, Wales
21/01/1954	Jack Dempsey Vs Jack Cunningham	NK	Bristol, England
22/01/1954	Jack Dempsey Vs Jack Cunningham	NK	Rochester
23/01/1954	Jack Dempsey Vs Pat Kloke	NK	Norwich, England
25/01/1954	Jack Dempsey Vs Harry Fields	NK	Blackpool, England

Date	Match	Result	Location
27/01/1954	Jack Dempsey Vs Eric Sands	Draw	Cardiff, Wales
28/01/1954	Jack Dempsey Vs Chris Londis	Londis won	Royal Albert Hall, London
29/01/1954	Jack Dempsey Vs Cyril Knowles Peters	NK	Liverpool, England
02/02/1954	Jack Dmepsey Vs Jim Lewis	NK	Hull
06/02/1954	Jack Dempsey Vs Frankie Hughes	Dempsey won	Middlesborough
09/02/1954	Jack Dempsey Vs Jack Cunningham	Jack D won	Wimbledon, England
15/02/1954	Jack Dempsey Vs Tony McDonald	NK	Blackpool, England
18/02/1954	Jack Dempsey Vs Pat Kloke	NK	Beckenham
19/02/1954	Jack Dempsey Vs Bert Royal	Royal won	Ipswich
20/02/1954	Jack Dempsey Vs George Kidd	NK	Norwich, England
22/02/1954	Jack Dempsey Vs Jim Lewis	Jack won	Edinburgh, Scotland
25/02/1954	Jack Dempsey Vs Tommy Milo	NK	Wimbledon, England
27/02/1954	Jack Dempsey Vs Alan Colbeck	Jack won	Middlesborough, North Yorkshire
02/03/1954	Jack Dempsey Vs Jim Lewis	Jack won	Lime Grove, England
05/03/1954	Jack Dempsey Vs Jim Lewis	Jim won	Glasgow, Scotland
08/03/1954	Jack Dempsey Vs Jim Lewis	Jim won	Edinburgh, Scotland
16/03/1954	Jack Dempsey Vs Johnny Stead	NK	Scarborough
18/03/1954	Jack Dempsey Vs Ken Joyce	Ken won, JD DQ	Wimbledon, England
21/03/1954	Jack Dempsey Vs Tony McDonald	NK	Blackpool, England
24/03/1954	Jack Dempsey Vs George Kidd	NK	Scunthorpe
25/03/1954	Jack Dempsey Vs Joe Hill	Joe won	Morecambe, Lancashire
26/03/1954	Jack Dempsey Vs Bert Royal	Royal won	Ipswich
01/04/1954	Jack Dempsey Vs Stefan Milla	NK	Bristol, England
02/04/1954	Jack Dempsey Vs Pat Kloke	Kloke won	Ramsgate
03/04/1954	Jack Dempsey Vs Eric Sands	Jack won	Newcastle, England
03/04/1954	Jack Dempsey Vs Bert Royal	Royal won	Norwich, England
05/04/1954	Jack Dmepsey Vs Ken Joyce	NK	High Wycombe
09/04/1954	Jack Dempsey Vs Stefan Milla	Jack won	Glasgow, Scotland
22/04/1954	Jack Dempsey Vs Sanky Allan	Sanky won	Morecambe, Lancashire
24/04/1954	Jack Dempsey Vs Sanky Allan	Sanky won	Middlesborough, North Yorkshire
26/04/1954	Jack Dempsey Vs Jim Lewis	NC	Edinburgh, Scotland
29/04/1954	Jack Dempsey Vs Archer O'Brien	Archer won	Wimbledon, England
06/05/1954	Jack Dempsey Vs Archer O'Brien	Archer won	Wimbledon, England
07/05/1954	Jack Dempsey Vs Stefan Milla	Jack won	Glasgow, Scotland
31/05/1954	Jack Dempsey Vs Bert Royal	Jack won	Edinburgh, Scotland
04/06/1954	Jack Dempsey Vs Tommy Mann	NK	Liverpool, England
09/06/1954	Jack Dempsey Vs Andre Dubarry	Jack won	Cardiff, Wales
10/06/1954	Jack Dempsey Vs Bob Archer O'Brien	Archer won	Wimbledon, England
11/06/1954	Jack Dempsey Vs Jimmy Johnson	Jack won	Ramsgate, England
12/06/1954	Jack Dempsey Vs Vic Coleman	NK	Norwich, England
26/06/1954	Jack Dempsey Vs Frank O'Donnell	Jack won, FD DQ	Edinburgh, Scotland
03/07/1954	Jack Dempsey Vs Eddie Capelli	Jack won	Newcastle, England
05/07/1954	Jack Dempsey Vs Tony Lawrence	draw	Leeds, England
23/07/1954	Jack Dempsey Vs Alan Colbeck	Alan won	Liverpool, England
27/07/1954	Jack Dempsey Vs Cliff Beaumont	NK	Douglas, Isle of Man

Date	Match	Result	Location
10/08/1954	Jack Dempsey Vs Don Dolas	NK	Douglas, Isle of Man
20/08/1954	Jack Dempsey Vs Tony Lawrence	NK	Ramsgate
02/09/1954	Jack Dempsey Vs Eddie Capelli	NK	Wimbledon, England
03/09/1954	Jack Dempsey Vs Peter Rann	Dempsey Won	Ramsgate
06/09/1954	Jack Dempsey Vs Alan Colbeck	Alan won	Edinburgh, Scotland
14/09/1954	Jack Dempsey Vs Bert Royal	NK	Colchester
16/09/1954	Jack Dempsey Vs Gipsy Guy Laroche	Draw	Bristol, England
16/09/1954	Jack Dempsey Vs Guy LaRoache	Draw	Bristol, England
23/09/1954	Jack Dempsey Vs Alan Colbeck	Alan won	Morecambe, Lancashire
01/10/1954	Jack Dempsey Vs Danny Flynn	NK	Manchester
08/10/1954	Jack Dempsey Vs Cliff Belshaw	Cliff won	Glasgow, Scotland
08/10/1954	Jack Dempsey Vs Cliff Beaumont	Beaumont won	Glasgow, Scotland
09/10/1954	Jack Dempsey Vs Chic Purvey	NK	Hanley
15/10/1954	Jack Dempsey Vs Chris Londis	NK	Ramsgate
18/10/1954	Jack Dempsey Vs Tiger Woods	Jack won	Edinburgh, Scotland
18/10/1954	Jack Dempsey Vs Alan Wood	Dempsey won	Edinburgh, Scotland
19/10/1954	Jack Dempsey Vs Alan Colbeck	NC	Hamilton, Scotland
19/10/1954	Jack Dempsey Vs Alan Colbeck	NC	Hamilton, Scotland
20/10/1954	Jack Dempsey Vs Jack Cunningham	Jack D Won	Cardiff, Wales
26/10/1954	Jack Dempsey Vs Jack Cunningham	Dempsey Won	Colchester
29/10/1954	Jack Dempsey Vs Stefan Milla	NK	Manchester
30/10/1954	Jack Dempsey Vs Guy Laroaxhe	NK	Hanley
04/11/1954	Jack Dempsey Vs Bob Archer O'Brien	NK	Southampton
10/11/1954	Jack Dempsey Vs Tommy Mann	Man won	Cardiff, Wales
11/11/1954	Jack Dempsey Vs Pat Kloke	Dempsey Won	Beckenham
12/11/1954	Jack Dempsey Vs Reg Ray	NK	Willenhall
19/11/1954	Jack Dempsey Vs Young Vulcan	NK	Manchester
23/11/1954	Jack Dempsey Vs Arthur Fisher	NK	Colchester
26/11/1954	Jack Dempsey Vs Jim Lewis	Jim won	Glasgow, Scotland
01/12/1954	Jack Dempsey Vs Stefan Milla	Draw	Eastbourne, England
01/12/1954	Jack Dempsey Vs Ken Joyce	NK	Scunthorpe
02/12/1954	Jack Dempsey Vs Bob Archer O'Brien	NK	Wimbledon, England
06/12/1954	Jack Dempsey Vs Jack Cunningham	Jack won	Leeds, England
10/12/1954	Jack Dempsey Vs Jim Lewis	NC	Glasgow, Scotland
13/12/1954	Jack Dempsey Vs Bobby Orlando	NK	Blackpool, England
16/12/1954	Jack Dempsey Vs Mick McManus	NK	Wimbledon, England
07/01/1955	Jack Dempsey Vs Stefan Milla	NK	Willenhall
11/01/1955	Jack Dempsey Vs Eric Sands	Dempsey Won	Swindon
12/01/1955	Jack Dempsey Vs Steve Logan	NK	Hove
14/01/1955	Jack Dempsey Vs Mick McManus	Jack won	Coventry, England
15/01/1955	Jack Dempsey Vs Pat Kloke	NK	Luton
19/01/1955	Jack Dempsey Vs Judah Israel	Jack won	Albert Hall, London
28/01/1955	Jack Dempsey Vs Tommy Mann	NK	Willenhall
29/01/1955	Jack Dempsey Vs Jim Lewis	NK	Hanley
02/02/1955	In KO Tournament	NK	Worthing
04/02/1955	Jack Dempsey Vs Reg Ray	Jack won	Belfast, Ireland

Date	Match	Result	Location
05/02/1955	Jack Dempsey Vs Tony Lawrence	Jack won	Newcastle, England
25/02/1955	Jack Dempsey Vs Stefan Milla	Jack won	Glasgow, Scotland
28/02/1955	Jack Dempsey Vs Bernard Murray	Murray won	Leeds, England
02/03/1955	Jack Dempsey Vs Jim Lewis	NK	Hove
03/03/1955	Jack Dempsey Vs Brian Trevors	NK	Colne
12/03/1955	Jack Dempsey Vs Mick McManus	NK	Camberwell, England
14/03/1955	Jack Dempsey Vs Bernard Murray	Draw	Leeds, England
14/03/1955	Jack Dempsey Vs Bernard Murray	Draw	Leeds, England
24/03/1955	Jack Dempsey Vs Zilha Romanos	NK	Southampton
25/03/1955	Jack Dempsey Vs Carlton Smith	Draw	Ipswich
29/03/1955	Jack Dempsey Vs Bert Royal	NK	Colchester
30/03/1955	Jack Dempsey Vs Ishca Israel	Jack won	Cardiff, Wales
30/03/1955	Jack Dempsey Vs Juda Ischa Israel	Israel won	Cardiff, Wales
02/04/1955	Jack Dempsey Vs Frank O'Donnell	NK	Coventry, England
04/04/1955	Jack Dempsey Vs Bert Royal	Bert won	Edinburgh, Scotland
05/04/1955	Jack Dempsey Vs Eric Sands	Eric won	Aberdeen, Scotland
06/04/1955	Jack Dempsey Vs Jim Lewis	NK	Hove
07/04/1955	Jack Dempsey Vs Mick McManus	Draw	Wimbledon, England
07/04/1955	Jack Dempsey Vs Mick McManus	NK	Wimbledon, England
09/04/1955	Jack Dempsey Vs Tony Vallon	NK	Newcastle, England
13/04/1955	Jack Dempsey Vs George Kidd	Kidd won	Royal Albert Hall, London
14/04/1955	Jack Dempsey Vs Arthur Fisher	NK	Bristol, England
15/04/1955	Jack Dempsey Vs George Kidd	George won	Albert Hall, London
18/04/1955	Jack Dempsey Vs Jim Lewis	NK	Bedford, England
19/04/1955	Jack Dempsey Vs Jim Lewis	Jack won	Chelmsford, England
25/04/1955	Jack Demsey Vs Jackie Pallo	Jack won	High Wycombe, England
26/04/1955	Jack Dempsey Vs Bob Archer O'Brien	NK	Colchester
29/04/1955	Jack Dempsey Vs Stefan Milla	Jack won	Bristol, England
02/05/1955	Jack Dempsey Vs Bernard Murray	Jack won	Leeds, England
09/05/1955	Jack Dempsey Vs Bert Royal	Bert won	Edinburgh, Scotland
10/05/1955	Jack Dempsey Vs Eric Sands	Eric won	Aberdeen, Scotland
14/05/1955	Jack Dempsey Vs Eric Sands	Jack won	Middlesborough, North Yorkshire
17/05/1955	Jack Dempsey Vs Jim Lewis	NK	Hove
25/05/1955	Jack Dempsey Vs Ken Joyce	Draw	Cardiff, Wales
26/05/1955	Jack Dempsey Vs Eric Sands	NK	Bury St. Edmunds
02/06/1955	Jack Dempsey Vs Black Kwango	Jack won	Wimbledon, England
04/06/1955	Jack Dempsey Vs Eric Sands	Eric won	Middlesborough, North Yorkshire
11/06/1955	Jack Dempsey Vs Arjit Singh	Jack won	New Brighton, England
11/06/1955	Jack Dempsey Vs Arjit Singh	Dempsey won	New Brighton
13/06/1955	Jack Dempsey Vs Bert Royal	Jack won	Edinburgh, Scotland
16/06/1955	Jack Dempsey Vs Jim Lewis	Jack won	Morecambe, Lancashire
04/07/1955	Jack Dempsey Vs Alan Colbeck	Jack won	Edinburgh, Scotland
05/07/1955	Jack Dempsey Vs Eric Sands	Eric won	Aberdeen, Scotland
09/07/1955	Jack Dempsey Vs Tommy Mann	Dempsey won	New Brighton
14/07/1955	Jack Dempsey Vs Ken Joyce	Draw	Wimbledon, England
18/07/1955	Jack Dempsey Vs Alan Colbeck	Alan won	Leeds, England

Date	Match	Result	Location
19/07/1955	Jack Dempsey Vs Arthur Beaumont	Draw	Douglas, Isle of Man
21/07/1955	Jack Dempsey Vs Eric Sands	Eric won	Morecambe, Lancashire
29/07/1955	Jack Dempsey Vs Eric Taylor	NK	Liverpool, England
26/08/1955	Jack Dempsey Vs Kid Pitman	NK	Ramsgate
31/08/1955	Jack Dempsey Vs Jim Lewis	NK	Douglas, Isle of Man
06/09/1955	Jack Dempsey Vs Ed Capelli	Jack won	Swindon, England
06/09/1955	Jack Dempsey Vs Ernie Riley	Jack won	Swindon
09/09/1955	Jack Dempsey Vs George Kidd	NK	Ramsgate
13/09/1955	Jack Dempsey Vs Eddie Capelli	NK	Colchester
14/09/1955	Jack Dempsey Vs Ken Joyce	Ken won	Cardiff, Wales
15/09/1955	Jack Dempsey Vs Pat Kloke	Jack won	Bristol, England
17/09/1955	Jack Dempsey Vs Jim Lewis	NK	Hanley
19/09/1955	Jack Dempsey Vs Stefan Milla	Jack won	Edinburgh, Scotland
23/09/1955	Jack Dempsey Vs Alan Colbeck	Dempsey won	Liverpool, England
04/10/1955	Jack Dempsey Vs Frank O'Donnell	Jack won	Hamilton, Scotland
14/10/1955	Jack Dempsey Vs Red Callaghan	Jack won	Glasgow, Scotland
18/10/1955	Jack Dempsey Vs Reg Ray	Jack won	Dundee, Scotland
22/10/1955	Jack Dempsey Vs George Kidd	George won	Newcastle, England
31/10/1955	Jack Dempsey Vs Mick McManus	Mick won	Edinburgh, Scotland
01/11/1955	Jack Dempsey Vs Jim Mellor	Jim won	Aberdeen, Scotland
01/11/1955	Jack Dempsey Vs Ken Joyce	Ken won	West Ham, England
11/11/1955	Jack Dempsey Vs Jim Lewis	NK	Willenhall
15/11/1955	Jack Dempsey Vs George Kidd	George won	Swindon, England
02/12/1955	Jack Dempsey Vs Red Callaghan	Jack won	Glasgow, Scotland
07/12/1955	Jack Dempsey Vs Peter Rann	Jack won	Cardiff, Wales
16/12/1955	Jack Dempsey Vs Alan Colbeck	Alan won	Glasgow, Scotland
16/12/1955	Jack Dempsey Vs Alan Colbeck	Colbeck won	Glasgow, Scotland
09/01/1956	Jack Dempsey Vs Eddie Capelli	Dempsey won	Bedford, England
11/01/1956	Jack Dempsey Vs Carlton Smith	NK	Hove
12/01/1956	Jack Dempsey Vs Billy Howes	NK	Wimbledon, England
13/01/1956	Jack Dempsey Vs Tommy Mann	Mann won	Glasgow, Scotland
16/01/1956	Jack Dempsey Vs Mick McManus	McManus won	Leeds, England
17/01/1956	Jack Dempsey Vs Tony Lawrence	NK	Hull, England
21/01/1956	Jack Dempsey Vs Eddie Capelli	NK	Norwich, England
26/01/1956	Jack Dempsey Vs Ken Joyce	NK	Southampton
28/01/1956	Jack Dempsey Vs Bert Royal	Royal won	Edinburgh, Scotland
30/01/1956	Jack Dempsey Vs Bert Royal	Bert won	Edinburgh, Scotland
25/02/1956	Jack Dempsey Vs Cliff Beaumont	NK	Hove
05/03/1956	Jack Dempsey Vs George Kidd	Draw	High Wycombe, England
08/03/1956	Jack Dempsey Vs Frank O'Donnell	NK	Southampton
09/03/1956	Jack Dempsey Vs Dennis Winn	Jack won	Ipswich, England
12/03/1956	Jack Dempsey Vs Mick McManus	Draw	Leeds, West yorkshire
15/03/1956	Jack Dempsey Vs Eric Sands	Eric won	Morecambe, Lancashire
20/03/1956	Jack Dempsey Vs Jim Lewis	Draw	Swindon, England
27/03/1956	Jack Dempsey Vs Harry Fields	NK	Lime Grove, London
28/03/1956	Jack Dempsey Vs Brian Trevors	NK	Scunthorpe, England

Date	Match	Result	Location
29/03/1956	Jack Dempsey Vs Ken Joyce	NK	Beckenham, England
09/04/1956	Jack Dempsey Vs Bert Royal	Bert won	Shoreditch, London
11/04/1956	Jack Dempsey Vs Jim Lewis	Draw	South End, England
12/04/1956	Jack Dempsey Vs Eddie Capelli	NK	Bury St. Edmunds
13/04/1956	Jack Dempsey Vs Tony Lawrence	Jack won	Ipswich, England
16/04/1956	Jack Dempsey Vs Stefan Milla	Jack won	Edinburgh, Scotland
17/04/1956	Jack Dempsey Vs Jim Lewis	Jack won	Swindon, England
17/04/1956	Jack Dempsey Vs Archer O'Brien	Archer won	Wimbledon, England
27/04/1956	Jack Dempsey Vs Brian Trevors	Jack won	Belfast Ireland
07/05/1956	Jack Dempsey Vs Bert Royal	Bert won JDDQ	Leeds, West yorkshire
10/05/1956	Jack Dempsey Vs George Kidd	Draw	Bristol, England
17/05/1956	Jack Dempsey Vs Ken Joyce	NK	Southampton
19/05/1956	Jack Dempsey Vs Bert Royal	NK	Luton, London
24/05/1956	Jack Dempsey Vs Harry Fields	Jack won	Morecambe, Lancashire
07/06/1956	Jack Dempsey Vs Eric Sands	Jack won	Morecambe, Lancashire
11/06/1956	Jack Dempsey Vs Bert Royal	Bert won	Edinburgh, Scotland
16/06/1956	Jack Dempsey Vs Bert Royal	Royal won	New Brighton
25/06/1956	Jack Dempsey Vs Bert Royal	Draw	Leeds, West yorkshire
29/06/1956	Jack Dempsey Vs Tommy Mann	NK	Coventry, England
12/07/1956	Jack Dempsey Vs Harry Fields	Jack won	Aberdeen, Scotland
16/07/1956	Jack Dempsey Vs Bert Royal	Draw	Edinburgh, Scotland
19/07/1956	Jack Dempsey Vs Bert Royal	Draw	Wimbledon, England
01/08/1956	Jack Dempsey Vs Jim Lewis	NK	Hove
09/08/1956	Jack Dempsey Vs Bob Archer O'Brien	NK	Wimbledon, England
21/08/1956	Jack Dempsey Vs Ken Joyce	NK	Wimbledon
21/08/1956	Jack Dempsey Vs Ken Joyce	NK	Wimbledon, England
27/08/1956	Jack Dempsey Vs Cyril Knowles	NK	Edinburgh, Scotland
30/08/1956	Jack Dempsey Vs Harry Fields	Harry won	Morecambe, Lancashire
31/08/1956	Jack Dempsey Vs Brian Trevors	Brian won	Belfast, Ireland
03/09/1956	Jack Dempsey Vs Bernard Murray	Bernard won	Edinburgh, Scotland
04/09/1956	Jack Dempsey Vs Brian Trevors	Trevors won JDDQ	Aberdeen, Scotland
11/09/1956	Jack Dempsey Vs Vic Coleman	NK	Colchester
13/09/1956	Jack Dempsey Vs Ken Joyce	Ken won	Bristol, England
27/09/1956	Jack Dempsey Vs George Kidd	NK	Wimbledon, England
08/10/1956	Jack Dempsey Vs Knowles Peters	NK	Edinburgh, Scotland
08/10/1956	Jack Dempsey & Cyril Knowles Vs Harry Fields & Bert Royal	Fields & Royal won	Edinburgh, Scotland
09/10/1956	Jack Dempsey Vs Archer O'Brien	Jack won	Lime Grove, England
12/10/1956	Jack Dempsey Vs Bert Royal	NK	Willenhall
13/10/1956	Jack Dempsey Vs Bernard Murray	Murray won	Middlesborough, England
20/10/1956	Jack Dempsey Vs Jack Cunningham	Jack D. Won	Newcastle, England
23/10/1956	Jack Dempsey Vs Ted Hannon	Dempsey won	Hull, England
03/11/1956	Jack Dempsey Vs Jim Lewis	Draw	Shrewsbury, England
08/11/1956	Jack Dempsey Vs Mick McManus	NK	Wimbledon, England
16/11/1956	Jack Dempsey Vs Jack Cunningham	Jack. C won	Belfast, Ireland
10/12/1956	Jack Dempsey Vs Chic Purvey	Purvey won	Leeds, England

Date	Match	Result	Location
21/12/1956	Jack Dempsey Vs Harry Hall	NK	Willenhall
02/01/1957	Jack Dempsey Vs Mick McManus	Drew	Cardiff, Wales
03/01/1957	Jack Dempsey Vs Ed Capelli	Jack won	Bristol, England
04/01/1957	Jack Dempsey Vs Guy Robin	Draw	Coventry, England
05/01/1957	Jack Dempsey Vs Mick McManus	McManus won	Norwich, England
09/01/1957	Jack Dempsey Vs Bobby Steele	Jack won	Albert Hall, London
10/01/1957	Jack Dempsey Vs Jim Lewis	Jack won	Morecambe, Lancashire
16/01/1957	Jack Dempsey Vs Jim Lewis	NK	Dorking, England
17/01/1957	Jack Dempsey Vs Jack Cunningham	Jack D. Won	Beckenham, England
18/01/1957	Jack Dempsey Vs Carlton Smith	Draw	Ipswich, England
21/01/1957	Jack Dempsey Vs Jackie Pallo	NK	Peterborough, England
24/01/1957	Jack Dempsey Vs Jack Cunningham	NK	Southampton
30/01/1957	Jack Dempsey Vs Harry Fields	Harry won	Lincoln, Lincolnshire
01/02/1957	Jack Dempsey Vs Mick McManus	Draw	Coventry, England
02/02/1957	Jack Dempsey Vs Jim Lewis	Jack won	Shrewsbury, England
04/02/1957	Jack Dempsey Vs Carlton Smith	Smith won	Bedford, England
05/02/1957	Jack Dempsey Vs Ken Shaw	Jack won	Swindon, England
08/02/1957	Jack Dempsey Vs Carlton Smith	Carlton won	Ipswich, England
18/02/1957	Jack Dempsey Vs julien Morice	Julien won	Edinburgh, Scotland
18/02/1957	Jack Dempsey Vs Sanky Allan	Sanky won	Aberdeen, Scotland
22/02/1957	Jack Dempsey Vs Black Kwango	Jack won	Northampton, England
27/02/1957	Jack Dempsey Vs Chic Purvey	Jack won	Cardiff, Wales
28/02/1957	Jack Dempsey Vs Jim Lewis	NK	Bristol, England
02/03/1957	Jack Dempsey Vs Stefan Milla	NK	Shrewsbury, England
06/03/1957	Jack Dempsey Vs Tony Quarnby	Dempsey won	Grimsby, England
07/03/1957	Jack Dempsey Vs Chic Purvey	NK	Wimbledon, England
09/03/1957	Jack Dempsey Vs Jim Lewis	Lewis won	Doncaster, England
14/03/1957	Jack Dempsey Vs Mick McManus	Draw	Peterborough, England
15/03/1957	Jack Dempsey Vs Arthur Fisher	Draw	Coventry, England
16/03/1957	Jack Dempsey Vs Fred Woolley	Fred Won	Shrewsbury, England
18/03/1957	Jack Dempsey Vs Reg Ray	Jack won	Edinburgh, Scotland
19/03/1957	Jack Dempsey Vs Jack Cunningham	Jack C. won	Hamilton, Scotland
20/03/1957	Jack Dempsey Vs George Kidd	George Won	Aberdeen, Scotland
23/03/1957	Jack Dempsey Vs Tommy Mann	Tommy won	Newcastle, England
28/03/1957	Jack Dempsey Vs Spencer Churchill	Draw	Bristol, England
29/03/1957	Jack Dempsey Vs Carlton Smith	Dempsey won	Ipswich, England
30/03/1957	Jack Dempsey Vs Tommy Mann	Mann won	Newcastle, England
04/04/1957	Jack Dempsey Vs Paul Debusne	NK	Blackburn, England
05/04/1957	Jack Dempsey Vs Marcel Manneveau	Jack Won	Willenhall, England
06/04/1957	Jack Dempsey Vs Stefan Milla	NK	Belle Vue, Manchester
10/04/1957	Jack Dempsey Vs Jim Lewis	Jack Wond	Cardiff, Wales
11/04/1957	Jack Dempsey Vs Ken Joyce	Dempsey won	Peterborough, England
15/04/1957	Jack Dempsey Vs John Foley	NK	Altrincham
16/04/1957	Jack Dempsey Vs Frankie Hughes	NK	Chelmsford, England
23/04/1957	Jack Dempsey Vs Tony Lawrence	NK	Colchester
26/04/1957	Jack Dempey Vs Stefan Milla	NK	Liverpool, England

Date	Match	Result	Venue
01/05/1957	Jack Dempsey Vs Mick McManus	McManus won	Royal Albert Hall, London
13/05/1957	Jack Dempsey Vs Mick McManus	NK	Carlisle, England
14/05/1957	Jack Dempsey Vs Carlton Smith	Dempsey won	Swindon, England
17/05/1957	Jack Dempsey Vs Carlton Smith	NK	Ramsgate
18/05/1957	Jack Dempsey Vs Carlton Smith	Draw	Peterborough, England
21/05/1957	Jack Dempsey Vs Tommy Mann	NK	Hamilton, Scotland
23/05/1957	Jack Dempsey Vs Carlton Smith	NK	Peterborough, England
25/05/1957	Jack Dempsey Vs Tommy Mann	Mann won	Hanley
05/06/1957	Jack Dempsey Vs Mick McManus	McManus won	Royal Albert Hall, London
08/06/1957	Jack Dempsey Vs Jim Lewis	Jack won	Newcastle, England
10/06/1957	Jack Dempsey Vs Alan Colbeck	Jack won	Edinburgh, Scotland
22/06/1957	Jack Dempsey Vs George Kidd	NK	Norwich, England
29/06/1957	Jack Dempsey Vs Inca Peruano	NK	Belle Vue, Manchester
30/06/1957	Jack Dempsey Vs Peter Rann	Dempsey won	Peterborough, England
04/07/1957	Jack Dempsey Vs George Kidd	NK	Morecambe, Lancashire
15/07/1957	Jack Dempsey Vs Harry Fields	Draw	Edinburgh, Scotland
25/07/1957	Jack Dempsey Vs Chic Purvey	NK	Wimbledon, England
29/07/1957	Jack Dempsey Vs Harry Fields	Jack won	Edinburgh, Scotland
30/07/1957	Jack Dempsey Vs Mick McManus	Mick won	Aberdeen, Scotland
02/08/1957	Jack Dempsey Vs Jackie Pallo	NK	Ramsgate
10/08/1957	Jack Dempsey Vs Al Nicol	Jack won	Middlesborough, North Yorkshire
17/08/1957	Jack Dempsey Vs Ken Joyce	NK	Belle Vue, Manchester
22/08/1957	Jack Dempsey Vs Mick McManus	NK	Wimbledon, England
26/08/1957	Jack Dempsey Vs Ken Joyce	Jack won	Edinburgh, Scotland
31/08/1957	Jack Dempsey Vs Mick McManus	Mick won	Newcastle, England
03/09/1957	Jack Dempsey Vs Cliff Beaumont	Cliff won	Swindon, England
07/09/1957	Jack Dempsey Vs Eric Sands	Jack won	Middlesborough, North Yorkshire
09/09/1957	Jack Dempsey Vs Alan Colbeck	Alan won	Edinburgh, Scotland
11/09/1957	Jack Dempsey Vs Ken Joyce	NK	Sheffield, England
12/09/1957	Jack Dempsey Vs Alan Colbeck	Jack won	Morecambe, Lancashire
14/09/1957	Jack Dempsey Vs Jim Mellor	NK	Hanley
21/09/1957	Jack Dempsey Vs Ken Joyce	NK	Leeds Town Hall, Leeds
21/09/1957	Jack Dempsey Vs Ken Joyce	Draw Jack won RT	Leeds, England
26/09/1957	Jack Dempsey Vs Roger Trigeaud	DQ	Morecambe, Lancashire
11/10/1957	Jack Dempsey Vs Reg Ray	NK	Rotherham
19/10/1957	Jack Dempsey Vs Ken Shaw	Dempsey won	Coventry, England
24/10/1957	Jack Dempsey Vs Bob Archer O'Brien	NK	Wimbledon, England
04/11/1957	Jack Dempsey Vs Pat Kloke	NK	Leeds, England
08/11/1957	Jack Dempsey Vs Joe Murphy	NK	Chesterfield, England
14/11/1957	Jack Dempsey Vs Peter Rann	NK	Southampton
15/11/1957	Jack Dempsey Vs George Kidd	Draw	Barnehurst
26/11/1957	Jack Dempsey Vs Johnny Kwango	NK	Walthamstow
27/11/1957	Jack Dempsey Vs George Kidd	NK	Brighton, England
28/11/1957	Jack Dempsey Vs Jim Lewis	NK	Beckenham, England
02/12/1957	Jack Dempsey Vs Alan Colbeck	NK	Bradford, England

Date	Match	Result	Location
04/12/1957	Jack Dempsey Vs Al Nicol	Draw	Lincoln, Lincolnshire
06/12/1957	Jack Dempsey Vs Stefan Milla	NK	Chesterfield, England
17/12/1957	Jack Dempsey Vs Stefan Milla	Jack won	Reading, Berkshire
20/12/1957	Jack Dempsey Vs Jack Cunningham	NK	Ramsgate
21/12/1957	Jack Dempsey Vs Jackie Pallo	NK	Norwich, England
26/12/1957	Jack Dempsey Vs Jackie Pallo	Dempsey won	Wimbledon, England
28/12/1957	Jack Dempsey Vs John Foley	Dempsey won	Newcastle, England
03/01/1958	Jack Dempsey Vs Alan Colbeck	NK	Rotherham
13/01/1958	Jack Dempsey Vs Ischa Israel	Jack won	Leeds, England
23/01/1958	Jack Dempsey Vs Jack Cunningham	NK	Wimbledon, England
31/01/1958	Jack Dempsey Vs Vic Coleman	NK	Horsham
03/02/1958	Jack Dempsey Vs Cliff Beaumont	NK	Bradford, England
04/02/1958	Jack Dempsey Vs Bert Royal	NK	Lime Grove, London
06/02/1958	Jack Dempsey Vs Bert Royal	NK	Nottingham, England
11/02/1958	Jack Dempsey Vs Ken Joyce	NK	Reading, England
12/02/1958	Jack Dempsey Vs Modesto Aledo	Dempsey won	Royal Albert Hall, London
13/02/1958	Jack Dempsey Vs Pat Kloke	NK	Peterborough, England
14/02/1958	Jack Dempsey Vs George Kidd	Draw	Rochester, England
15/02/1958	Jack Dempsey Vs George Kidd	Kidd won	Norwich, England
24/02/1958	Jack Dempsey Vs George Kidd	NK	Seymour Hall, Marylebone, London
27/02/1958	Jack Dempsey Vs Tommy Mann	NK	Nottingham, England
03/03/1958	Jack Dempsey Vs Mick McManus	NK	Leeds, England
07/03/1958	Jack Dempsey Vs Enrico Marques	Jack won	Belfast, Ireland
11/03/1958	Jack Dempsey Vs Jim Lewis	Lewis won	Hull, England
13/03/1958	Jack Dempsey Vs Jackie Pallo	Jack Won	Bristol, England
13/03/1958	Jack Dempsey Vs Jackie Pallo	Dempsey won	Bristol, England
17/03/1958	Jack Dempsey Vs George Kidd	NK	Seymour Hall, London
18/03/1958	Jack Dempsey Vs Mick McManus	NK	Chelmsford, England
20/03/1958	Jack Dempsey Vs Stefan Milla	NK	Southampton
22/03/1958	Jack Dempsey Vs Jackie Pallo	NK	Eastbourne
24/03/1958	Jack Dempsey Vs Chic Purvy	Chic won	Leeds, England
25/03/1958	Jack Dempsey Vs Jim Lewis	NK	Scarborough
31/03/1958	Jack Dempsey Vs Josef Ski	Josef won JD DQ	Edinburgh, Scotland
01/04/1958	Jack Dempsey Vs Al Nicol	Jack won	Edinburgh, Scotland
03/04/1958	Jack Dempsey Vs Tommy Mann	Tommy won	Morecambe, Lancashire
12/04/1958	Jack Dempsey Vs Tommy Mann	Tommy won	Portsmouth, England
14/04/1958	Jack Dempsey Vs Ben Chemoul	Ben won	Leeds, England
23/04/1958	Jack Dempsey Vs Mick McManus	Dempsey won	Royal Albert Hall, London
29/04/1958	Jack Dempsey Vs Tony Charles	NK	Swindon, England
30/04/1958	Jack Dempsey Vs Mich McManus	Jack won	Albert Hall, London
30/04/1958	Jack Dempsey Vs Bob Archer O'Brien	NK	Brighton, England
02/05/1958	Jack Dempsey Vs Jim Lewis	Dempsey won	Liverpool, England
03/05/1958	Jack Dempsey Vs Al Nicol	Jack won	Manchester, England
03/05/1958	Jack Dempsey Vs Jim Lewis	Jack won	Liverpool, England
05/05/1958	Jack Dempsey Vs Tommy Mann	Tommy won	Edinburgh, Scotland

Date	Match	Result	Location
08/05/1958	Jack Dempsey Vs Bert Royal	Bert won	Morecambe, Lancashire
10/05/1958	Jack Dempsey Vs Alan Colbeck	NK	Grantham, England
12/05/1958	Jack Dempsey Vs Alan Colbeck	Jack won	Leeds, England
17/05/1958	Jack Dempsey Vs Tommy Mann	Jack won	Newcastle, England
20/05/1958	Jack Dempsey Vs Jack Cunningham	Draw	Aylesbury, Buckinghamshire
23/05/1958	Jack Dempsey Vs Al Nicol	NK	Chesterfield, England
24/05/1958	Jack Dempsey Vs Alan Colbeck	NK	Grantham, England
29/05/1958	Jack Dempsey Vs Cliff Beaumont	Cliff won	Morecambe, Lancashire
31/05/1958	Jack Dempsey in KO tournament	NK	Wisbech
07/06/1958	Jack Dempsey Vs Eric Sands	Jack won	Middlesborough, North Yorkshire
09/06/1958	Jack Dempsey Vs Cliff Beaumont	NK	Bridlington
21/06/1958	Jack Dempsey Vs Josef Ski	Dempsey won	Newcastle, England
23/06/1958	Jack Dempsey Vs Alan Colbeck	Jack won	Leeds, England
26/06/1958	Jack Dempsey Vs Eric Sands	NK	Southampton
28/06/1958	Jack Dempsey Vs Bob Archer O'Brien	Dempsey won	Maidstone, England
08/07/1958	Jack Dempsey Vs Ted Hannon	Draw	Birmingham, England
12/07/1958	Jack Dempsey Vs Reg Ray	Jack won, RR DQ	Newcastle, England
16/07/1958	Jack Dempsey Vs Tony Charles	NK	Torquay, England
28/07/1958	Jack Dempsey Vs Harry Fields	Harry won	Edinburgh, Scotland
31/07/1958	Jack Dempsey Vs Alan Colbeck	Colbeck won	Morecambe, Lancashire
02/08/1958	Jack Dempsey Vs Cliff Beaumont	NK	Belle Vue, Manchester
06/08/1958	Jack Dempsey Vs Cliff Beaumont	Beaumont won	Withernsea
12/08/1958	Jack Dempsey Vs Arthur Fisher	Jack won	Purley, England
19/08/1958	Jack Dempsey Vs Brian Burke	NK	Scarborough
23/08/1958	Jack Dempsey Vs Bert Royal	Jack won	Newcastle, England
28/08/1958	Jack Dempsey Vs Fred Woolley	Dempsey won	Morecambe, Lancashire
30/08/1958	Jack Dempsey Vs Howard Morgan	NK	Grantham, England
01/09/1958	Jack Dempsey Vs Jano Horvath	Jack won	High Wycombe, England
01/09/1958	Jack Dempsey Vs Stefan Milla	Jack won	High Wycombe, England
01/09/1958	Jack Dempsey Vs Jack Cunningham	Jack C won	High Wycombe, England
01/09/1958	In KO tournament	NK	High Wycombe, England
02/09/1958	Jack Dempsey Vs Stefan Milla	NK	Chelmsford, England
06/09/1958	Jack Dempsey Vs Peter Szakacs	Jack won	Maidstone, England
12/09/1958	Jack Dempsey Vs Cliff Belshaw	Jack won	Liverpool, England
15/09/1958	Jack Dempsey Vs Fred Woolley	Draw	Leeds, England
17/09/1958	Jack Dempsey Vs Bert Royal	NK	Sheffield, England
19/09/1958	Jack Dempsey Vs Brian burke	Jack won	Belfast, Ireland
20/09/1958	Jack Dempsey Vs Bobby Steele	NK	Belle Vue, Manchester
23/09/1958	Jack Dempsey Vs Bobby Steele	Jack won	Purley, England
24/09/1958	Jack Dempsey Vs Peter Szakacs	Jack won	Cardiff, Wales
25/09/1958	Jack Dempsey Vs Stefan Milla	Jack won	Bristol, England
27/09/1958	Jack Dempsey Vs Frank O'Donnell	NK	Luton, London
02/10/1958	Jack Dempsey Vs Jim Hart	NK	Blackburn, England
03/10/1958	Jack Dempsey Vs Alan Dennison	Jack Won	Glasgow, Scotland
04/10/1958	Jack Dempsey Vs Brian Burke	Jack won	Newcastle, England

Date	Match	Result	Location
09/10/1958	Jack Dempsey Vs Eric Sands	Jack won	Nottingham, England
11/10/1958	Jack Dempsey Vs Chic Purvey	Jack won	Maidstone, England
13/10/1958	Jack Dempsey Vs Peter Szakacs	Dempsey won	Bedford, England
14/10/1958	Jack Dempsey Vs Peter Szakacs	Jack won	Swindon, England
17/10/1958	Jack Dempsey Vs Jack Cunningham	Draw	Ipswich, England
22/10/1958	Jack Dempsey Vs Fred Woolley	NK	Dudley, England
24/10/1958	Jack Dempsey Vs John Foley	NK	Bolton, Lancashire
25/10/1958	Jack Dempsey Vs Alan Colbeck	Jack won	Newcastle, England
29/10/1958	Jack Dempsey Vs Cliff Beaumont	NK	Sheffield, England
30/10/1958	Jack Dempsey Vs Lazlo Bajko	NK	Scarborough
04/11/1958	Jack Dempsey Vs Peter Szakacs	NK	Colchester
13/11/1958	Jack Dempsey Vs Al Nicol	Jack won	Nottingham, England
14/11/1958	Jack Dempsey Vs Karl Van Kramm	NK	Bolton, Lancashire
15/11/1958	Jack Dempsey Vs Brian Burke	Jack won	Middlesborough, North Yorkshire
22/11/1958	Jack Dempsey Vs Eric Sands	Eric won	Newcastle, England
25/11/1958	Jack Dempsey Vs Johnny Czeslaw	NK	Chelmsford, England
26/11/1958	Jack Dempsey Vs Brian Burke	Jack won	Albert Hall, London
01/12/1958	Jack Dempsey Vs Bob Archer O'Brien	NK	Bradford, England
02/12/1958	Jack Dempsey Vs Alan Colbeck	NK	Wakefield, England
03/12/1958	Jack Dempsey Vs Alan Dennison	NK	Preston, England
04/12/1958	Jack Dempsey Vs Bob Archer O'Brien	NK	Blackburn, England
06/12/1958	Jack Dempsey Vs Al Nicol	Al won, JD DQ	Nottingham, England
09/12/1958	Jack Dempsey Vs Brian Burke	Draw	Wolverhampton, West Midlands
12/12/1958	Jack Dempsey Vs Arturo Martinelli	NK	Liverpool, England
20/12/1958	Jack Dempsey Vs Alan Colbeck	Alan won	Newcastle, England
27/12/1958	Jack Dempsey Vs Bert Royal	Jack won	Newcastle, England
30/12/1958	Jack Dempsey Vs John Foley	Jack won	Birmingham, England
02/01/1959	Jack Dempsey Vs Chic Purvey	Draw	Willenhall, England
03/01/1959	Jack Dempsey Vs Tony Zale	NK	Doncaster, England
12/01/1959	Jack Dempsey Vs Ben Chemoul	Ben won	Leeds, England
13/01/1959	Jack Dempsey Vs John Foley	Foley won JD DQ	Hull, England
21/01/1959	Jack Dempsey Vs Sergei Reggiori	NK	Scunthorpe, England
23/01/1959	Jack Dempsey Vs Tony Charles	Jack won	Willenhall, England
24/01/1959	Jack Dempsey Vs Arturo Martinelli	Jack won	Shrewsbury, England
25/01/1959	Jack Dempsey Vs Danny Flynn	Jack won	Birmingham, England
26/01/1959	Jack Dempsey Vs Archer O'Brien	Jack won	Tunbridge Wells, England
29/01/1959	Jack Dempsey Vs Fred Woolley	NK	Bristol, England
30/01/1959	Jack Dempsey Vs Fred Woolley	Jack won	Ipswich, England
31/01/1959	Jack Dempsey Vs Mick McManus	Draw	Coventry, England
07/02/1959	Jack Dempsey Vs Tommy Mann	Tommy man	Newcastle, England
10/02/1959	Jack Dempsey Vs Al Nicol	NK	Wakefield, England
13/02/1959	Jack Dempsey Vs Alan Colbeck	Alan won	Glasgow, Scotland
13/02/1959	Jack Dempsey Vs Bob Anthony	NK	Bolton, Lancashire
14/02/1959	Jack Dempsey Vs Fred Woolley	Jack won	Shrewsbury, England
18/02/1959	Jack Dempsey Vs Alan Colbeck	NK	Grimsby, England

Date	Match	Result	Location
21/02/1959	Jack Dempsey Vs Alf Cadman	Alf won	Middlesborough, North Yorkshire
25/02/1959	Jack Dempsey Vs Chic Purvey	NK	Sheffield, England
28/02/1959	Jack Dempsey Vs Alan Colbeck	NK	Belle Vue, Manchester
05/03/1959	Jack Dempsey Vs Stefan Milla	NK	Cambridge, England
07/03/1959	Jack Dempsey Vs Arthur Fisher	Jack won	Maidstone, England
13/03/1959	Jack Dempsey Vs Chic Purvey	NK	Chesterfield, England
14/03/1959	Jack Dempsey Vs Tony Charles	NK	Dudley, England
16/03/1959	Jack Dempsey Vs Jack Cunningham	Draw	High Wycombe, England
17/03/1959	Jack Dempsey Vs Mick McManus	Jack won	Lime Grove, England
18/03/1959	Jack Dempsey Vs Alan Colbeck	Draw	Lincoln, Lincolnshire
19/03/1959	Jack Dempsey Vs Mick McManus	Draw	Nottingham, England
20/03/1959	Jack Dempsey Vs Alan Colbeck	Colbeck won	Glasgow, Scotland
21/03/1959	Jack Dempsey Vs Alan Colbeck	Alan won, JD Inj	Newcastle, England
28/03/1959	Jack Dempsey Vs Cliff Beaumont	NK	Grantham, England
31/03/1959	Jack Dempsey Vs Al Nicol	NK	Wakefield, England
03/04/1959	Jack Dempsey Vs Alan Colbeck	Jack won	Glasgow, Scotland
04/04/1959	Jack Dempsey Vs Alan Colbeck	Alan won	Newcastle, England
07/04/1959	Jack Dempsey Vs Keith Williams	Jack won	Birmingham, England
08/04/1959	Jack Dempsey Vs Fred Woolley	NK	Scunthorpe, England
09/04/1959	Jack Dempsey Vs Don Branch	Jack won	Morecambe, Lancashire
13/04/1959	Jack Dempsey Vs Melwyn Riss	NK	Folkestone
14/04/1959	Jack Dempsey Vs Jack Cunningham	NK	Swindon, England
16/04/1959	Jack Dempsey Vs Eddie Saxon	NK	Southampton
18/04/1959	Jack Dempsey Vs Danny Flynn	Jack won	Maidstone, England
21/04/1959	Jack Dempsey Vs Danny Flynn	Jack won	Birmingham, England
24/04/1959	Jack Dempsey Vs Ted Hannon	NK	Dumfries, Scotland
29/04/1959	Jack Dempsey Vs Tony Charles	draw	Swindon, England
09/05/1959	Jack Dempsey Vs Kenny Hogan	NK	Dudley, England
10/05/1959	Jack Dempsey Vs Jack Cunningham	NK	Brighton, England
12/05/1959	Jack Dempsey Vs Al Nicol	NK	Wakefield, England
20/05/1959	Jack Dempsey Vs Doug joyce	NK	Cardiff, Wales
21/05/1959	Jack Dempsey Vs Mick McManus	Draw	Peterborough, England
23/05/1959	Jack Dempsey Vs Mick McManus	Nk	Luton, London
29/05/1959	Jack Dempsey Vs Ted Hannon	NK	Dumfries, Scotland
04/06/1959	Jack Dempsey Vs Tony Charles	NK	Bristol, England
11/06/1959	Jack Dempsey Vs Bob Archer O'Brien	NK	Southampton
14/06/1959	Jack Dempsey Vs Rapghael Garcia	NK	Brighton, England
19/06/1959	Jack Dempsey Vs Tommy Mann	NK	Bolton, Lancashire
20/06/1959	Jack Dempsey Vs Etienne Gobi	NK	Hanley
21/06/1959	Jack Dempsey Vs George Kidd	Kidd won	Mile End, london
27/06/1959	Jack Dempsey Vs Alan Colbeck	Dempsey won	Coventry, England
16/07/1959	Jack Dempsey Vs Tony Charles	NK	Torquay, England
25/07/1959	Jack Dempsey Vs Alan Miquet	Nk	Grantham, England
09/08/1959	Jack Dempsey Vs Keith Williams	NK	Brighton, England
13/08/1959	Jack Dempsey Vs Eric Sands	Dempsey won	Morecambe, Lancashire

Date	Match	Result	Location
22/08/1959	Jack Dempsey Vs Alan Colbeck	Colbeck won	Newcastle, England
23/08/1959	Jack Dempsey Vs Stefan Milla	Nk	Brighton, England
24/08/1959	Jack Dempsey Vs Jack Cunningham	Nk	Folkestone
01/09/1959	Jack Dempsey Vs Tommy Mann	Dempsey won	Birmingham, England
04/09/1959	Jack Dempsey Vs Chic Purvey	NK	Bolton, Lancashire
07/09/1959	Jack Dempsey Vs Mick McManus	Nk	Folkestone
08/09/1959	Jack Dempsey Vs tomym Mann	Nk	Wolverhampton, England
19/09/1959	Jack Dempsey Vs Cliff Beaumont	Nk	Belle Vue, Manchester
22/09/1959	Jack Dempsey Vs Bob Anthony	Nk	Welling
24/09/1959	Jack Dempsey Vs Jackie Pallo	Draw	Peterborough, England
26/09/1959	Jack Dempsey Vs Cyril knowles	Nk	Grantham, England
30/09/1959	Jack Dempsey Vs Ted Hannon	Nk	Grimsby, England
05/10/1959	Jack Dempsey Vs Dick Conlon	NK	Shoreditch, England
06/10/1959	Jack Dempsey Vs Peter Szakacs	Dempsey won	Colchester
07/10/1959	Jack Dempsey Vs jackie pallo	NK	Ashford
08/10/1959	Jack Dempsey Vs Melwyn Riss	Dempsey won	Bristol, England
09/10/1959	Jack Dempsey Vs Arthur Fisher	Dempsey won	Brighton, England
12/10/1959	Jack Dempsey Vs Arturo Martinelli	NK	Kirkby, Ashfield
16/10/1959	Jack Dempsey Vs Tommy Mann	NK	Willenhall
17/10/1959	jack Dempsey Vs Jim Hart	Dempsey won	hanley
22/10/1959	Jack Dempsey Vs Stefan Milla	Dempsey won	Bristol, England
24/10/1959	Jack Dempsey Vs Bobby Graham	Nk	Luton, London
25/10/1959	Jack Dempsey Vs Tiger Ryan	NK	Kirkby, Ashfield
02/11/1959	Jack Dempsey Vs Eric Sands	NK	Aylesbury, England
03/11/1959	Jack Dempsey Vs Arthur Fisher	Dempsey won	Welling
04/11/1959	Jack Dempsey Vs Ronald Daumal	Dempsey won	Royal Albert Hall, London
06/11/1959	Jack Dempsey Carlo Valdez	Dempsey won	Ipswich, England
09/11/1959	Jack Dempsey Vs Tommy Mann	NK	Loughborough, England
21/11/1959	Jack Dempsey vs Alan Colbeck	NK	Norwich, England
24/11/1959	Jack Dempsey Vs jackie Pallo	NK	Swindon, England
25/11/1959	Jack Dempsey Vs Fernanrad Bawin	Nk	Shoreditch, England
28/11/1959	Jack Dempsey Vs Keith Williams	Nk	Hanley
05/12/1959	Jack Dempsey Vs jackie Pallo	NK	Norwich, England
09/12/1959	Jack Dempsey Vs Chic Purvey	NK	Grimsby, England
11/12/1959	Jack Dempsey Vs Cliff Beaumont	NK	Bolton, Lancashire
12/12/1959	Jack Dempsey Vs Cliff Beaumont	NK	hanley
15/12/1959	Jack Dempsey Vs Stefan Milla	NK	Welling
21/12/1959	Jack Dempsey Vs Cliff Beaumont	NK	Blackpool, England
22/12/1959	Jack Dempsey Vs Cliff Beaumont	Draw	Birmingham, England
26/12/1959	Jack Dempsey Vs Al Nicol	NK	Doncaster, England
29/12/1959	Jack Dempsey Vs julien Morice	NK	Welling
01/01/1960	Jack Dempsey Vs Tony Lawrence	Dempsey won	Ipswich, England
04/01/1960	Jack Dempsey Vs Eric Sands	NK	York, England
07/01/1960	Jack Dempsey Vs Alan Colbeck	NK	Nottingham, England
08/01/1960	Jack Dempsey Vs Brian Burke	NK	Glasgow, Scotland
09/01/1960	Jack Dempsey Vs Alan Colbeck	NK	Falkirk

Date	Match	Result	Location
14/01/1960	Jack Dempsey Vs Cliff Beaumont	NK	Barrow, England
15/01/1960	Jack Dempsey Vs John Foley	NK	Ipswich, England
18/01/1960	Jack Dempsey Vs Jackie Pallo	NK	Southampton, England
19/01/1960	Jack Dempsey Vs Jackie Pallo	NK	Swindon, England
20/01/1960	Jack Dempsey Vs Gomez Pizzaro	Dempsey won	Royal Albert Hall, London
22/01/1960	Jack Dempsey (BEWWC) Vs Bob Archer	NK	Wembley, London
23/01/1960	Jack Dempsey Vs Tony Charles	Dempsey won	Coventry, England
25/01/1960	Jack Dempsey Vs Jim Breaks	NK	Halifax, England
26/01/1960	Jack Dempsey Vs Don Branch	NK	Trowell
27/01/1960	Jack Dempsey Vs Alan Dennison	Jack won	Lincoln, England
28/01/1960	Jack Dempsey Vs Mike Donlevy	Dempsey won	Bristol, England
30/01/1960	Jack Dempsey Vs Bernard Murray	NK	Grantham,
01/02/1960	Jack Dempsey Vs Pasquale Salvo	Dempsey won	Bedford, England
02/02/1960	Jack Dempsey Vs Jackie Pallo	NK	Welling
10/02/1960	Jack Dempsey Vs Tony CHarles	Draw	Coventry, England
16/02/1960	Jack Dempsey Vs Bob Anthony	Draw	Chelmsford, England
17/02/1960	Jack Dempsey Vs Clayton Thomson	NK	Shoreditch
19/02/1960	Jack Dempsey Vs Dennis Dean	NK	Barnehurst
20/02/1960	Jack Dempsey Vs Peter Szakacs	NK	Camberwell
23/02/1960	Jack Dempsey Vs Mick McManus	Dempsey won	Bournemouth, England
27/02/1960	Jack Dempsey Vs Chic Purvey	NK	Grantham,
03/03/1960	Jack Dempsey Vs Al Nicol	Dempsey won	Beckenham, England
05/03/1960	Jack Dempsey Vs Gil Cesca	NK	Norwich, England
07/03/1960	Jack Dempsey Vs Tony Charles	NK	Warrington, England
08/03/1960	Jack Dempsey Vs Tony Charles	Dempsey won	Birmingham, England
09/03/1960	Jack Dempsey Vs Alan Colbeck	NK	Newcastle, England
12/03/1960	Jack Dempsey Vs Tony CHarles	NK	Doncaster, England
14/03/1960	Jack Dempsey Vs Alan Miquet	NK	Sutton, Ashfield
16/03/1960	Jack Dempsey Vs Bernard Murray	Dempsey won	Cardiff, Wales
18/03/1960	Jack Dempsey Vs Jim Mellor	NK	Alfreton
22/03/1960	Jack Dempsey Vs Alan Colbeck	Colbeck won	Colchester, England
24/03/1960	Jack Dempsey Vs Bob Archer O'Brien	Draw	Bristol, England
25/03/1960	Jack Dempsey Vs Monty Swann	Dempsey won	Ipswich, England
29/03/1960	Jack Dempsey Vs Jack Cunningham	NK	Huddersfield, England
02/04/1960	Jack Dempsey Vs Jackie Pallo	NK	Kings Lynn, London
09/04/1960	Jack Dempsey Vs Chic Purvey	NK	Huddersfield, England
13/04/1960	Jack Dempsey Vs Don Branch	NK	Scunthorpe
15/04/1960	Jack Dempsey Vs Keith Williams	Dempsey won	Brighton, England
16/04/1960	Jack Dempsey Vs Bob Archer O'Brien	NK	Norwich, England
20/04/1960	Jack Dempsey Vs Cliff Beaumont	NK	Sheffield, England
29/04/1960	Jack Dempsey Vs Chic Purvey	NK	Chesterfield, England
02/05/1960	Jack Dempsey Vs Jackie Pallo	NK	Tunbridge Wells
03/05/1960	Jack Dempsey Vs Julien Morice	Dempsey won	Purley
04/05/1960	Jack Dempsey Vs Jackie Pallo	Dempsey won	Banbury
07/05/1960	Jack Dempsey Vs Cliff Beaumont	NK	Leeds, England
12/05/1960	Jack Dempsey Vs John Foley	Draw	Barrow, England

Date	Match	Result	Location
13/05/1960	Jack Dempsey Vs Alan Colbeck	Dempsey won	Bradford, England
17/05/1960	Jack Dempsey Vs Alan Colbeck	Dempsey won	Colchester, England
23/05/1960	Jack Dempsey Vs Tiger Ryan	NK	Worcester, England
24/05/1960	Jack Dempsey Vs Brian Burke	NK	Nelson
01/06/1960	Jack Dempsey Vs Inca Peruano	Dempsey won	Cardiff, Wales
02/06/1960	Jack Dempsey Vs Jackie Pallo	NK	Walthamstow
04/06/1960	Jack Dempsey Vs Stefan Milla	Jack won	Coventry, England
05/06/1960	Jack Dempsey Vs Jack Cunningham	Dempsey won	Brighton, England
10/06/1960	Jack Dempsey Vs Brian Burke	NK	Bolton, England
14/06/1960	Jack Dempsey Vs Arthur Fisher	Dempsey won	Purley
16/06/1960	Jack Dempsey Vs Pasquale Salvo	Dempsey won	Peterborough, England
18/06/1960	Jack Dempsey Vs Alan Colbeck	Draw	Coventry, England
24/06/1960	Jack Dempsey Vs Alan Colbeck	NK	Bradford, England
25/06/1960	Jack Dempsey Vs Alan Colbeck	NK	Middlesborough, England
30/06/1960	Jack Dempsey Vs Jackie Pallo	NK	Walthamstow
01/07/1960	Jack Dempsey Vs Mel Riss	NK	Fleetwood
04/07/1960	Jack Dempsey Vs Alan Colbeck	NK	Shoreditch
23/07/1960	Jack Dempsey Vs Bernard Murray	NK	Middlesborough, England
26/07/1960	Jack Dempsey Vs Pasquale Salvo	NK	Welling
27/07/1960	Jack Dempsey Vs Bernard Murray	Dempsey won	Kettering
31/07/1960	Jack Dempsey Vs Bob Archer O'Brien	NK	Brighton, England
06/08/1960	Jack Dempsey Vs Bert Royal	Royal won	Newcastle, England
08/08/1960	Jack Dempsey Vs Cliff Beaumont	Draw	Douglas, Isle of Man
11/08/1960	Jack Dempsey Vs Alan Colbeck	NK	Scarborough, England
13/08/1960	Jack Dempsey Vs Reg Ray	NK	Middlesborough, England
15/08/1960	Jack Dempsey Vs Alan Colbeck	NK	York, England
17/08/1960	Jack Dempsey Vs tommy Mann	NK	Withernsea
19/08/1960	Jack Dempsey Vs Alan Miquet	NK	Fleetwood
26/08/1960	Jack Dempsey Vs Keith Williams	NK	Bolton, England
27/08/1960	Jack Dempsey Vs Brian Burke	NK	Doncaster, England
03/09/1960	Jack Dempsey Vs Bobby Steele	NK	Belle Vue, Manchester
06/09/1960	Jack Dempsey Vs Bobby Steele	NK	Welling
07/09/1960	Jack Dempsey Vs Tony Charles	NK	Southend
08/09/1960	Jack Dempsey Vs Mel Riss	NK	Walthamstow
10/09/1960	Jack Dempsey Vs Jackie Pallo	NK	Luton, England
11/09/1960	Jack Dempsey Vs Jack Cunningham	NK	Brighton, England
17/09/1960	Jack Dempsey Vs Ted Hannon	NK	Blackburn, England
19/09/1960	Jack Dempsey Vs Chic Purvey	NK	Carlisle
19/09/1960	Jack Dempsey Vs Tony Charles	Charles won	Devizes
22/09/1960	Jack Dempsey Vs Mel Riss	Dempsey won	Morecambe, Lancashire
26/09/1960	Jack Dempsey Vs Bob Anthony	NK	Bedford, England
28/09/1960	Jack Dempsey Vs Gil Cesca	NK	Hove
01/10/1960	Jack Dempsey Vs Julien Morice	NK	Norwich, England
06/10/1960	Jack Dempsey Vs Al Nicol	Dempsey won	Peterborough, England
07/10/1960	Jack Dempsey Vs Bobby Steele	Dempsey won	Ipswich, England
08/10/1960	Jack Dempsey Vs Lucon	NK	Belle Vue, Manchester

Date	Match	Result	Location
10/10/1960	Jack Dempsey Vs Alan Dennison	NK	Worksop
11/10/1960	Jack Dempsey Vs Julien Morice	NK	Welling
18/10/1960	Jack Dempsey Vs Len Wilding	Jack won	Reading, England
19/10/1960	Jack Dempsey Vs Jackie Pallo	NK	Banbury
20/10/1960	Jack Dempsey Vs Stefan Milla	Dempsey won	Beckenham, England
21/10/1960	Jack Dempsey Vs Stefan Milla	NK	Taunton, England
22/10/1960	Jack Dempsey Vs Bob Anthony	Dempsey won	Wembley, England
24/10/1960	Jack Dempsey Vs Jim Mellor	NK	Sutton, Ashfield
27/10/1960	Jack Dempsey Vs Jim Breaks	Dempsey won	Morecambe, Lancashire
29/10/1960	In KO Tournament	NK	Brighton, England
01/11/1960	Jack Dempsey Vs Bernard Murray	Draw	Colchester, England
02/11/1960	Jack Dempsey Vs Stefan Milla	Jack won	Cardiff, Wales
02/11/1960	Jack Dempsey Vs Mick McManus	Draw	Cardiff, Wales
03/11/1960	Jack Dempsey Vs Alan Colbeck	Draw	Bristol, England
04/11/1960	Jack Dempsey Vs Al Nicol	NK	Bermondsey
05/11/1960	Jack Dempsey Vs John Foley	NK	Grantham,
07/11/1960	Jack Dempsey Vs Tommy Mann	NK	Walsall
12/11/1960	Jack Dempsey Vs Cliff Beaumont	NK	Doncaster, England
14/11/1960	Jack Dempsey Vs Don Branch	Dempsey won	Hamilton, Scotland
15/11/1960	Jack Dempsey Vs Mick McMichael	NK	Hull
17/11/1960	Jack Dempsey Vs Julien Morice	Dempsey won	Barrow, England
19/11/1960	Jack Dempsey Vs Mick McMichael	Dempsey won	Huddersfield, England
21/11/1960	Jack Dempsey Vs Bob Anthony	Dempsey won	Wisbech
26/11/1960	Jack Dempsey Vs Keith Martinelli	NK	Halifax, England
28/11/1960	Jack Dempsey & Jim Breaks Vs Bobby Steele & Ted Hannon	NK	Leeds, England
30/11/1960	Jack Dempsey Vs Stefan Milla	NK	Winchester
01/12/1960	Jack Dempsey Vs Bob Anthony	NK	Walthamstow
03/12/1960	Jack Dempsey Vs Bob Archer O'Brien	NK	Kings Lynn, London
04/12/1960	Jack Dempsey Vs Brian Trevors	NK	Folkestone
06/12/1960	Jack Dempsey Vs Tony Charles	Dempsey won	Watford
07/12/1960	Jack Dempsey Vs Julien Morice	Jack won	Cardiff, Wales
07/12/1960	Jack Dempsey Vs Julien Morice	Dempsey won	Cardiff, Wales
10/12/1960	Jack Dempsey Vs Jack Cunningham	NK	Norwich, England
15/12/1960	Jack Dempsey Vs Jack Cunningham	Dempsey won	Beckenham, England
15/12/1960	Jack Dempsey Vs John Foley	Foley won	Beckenham, England
16/12/1960	Jack Dempsey Vs Jean Fryziuck	Dempsey won	Ipswich, England
17/12/1960	Jack Dempsey Vs John Foley	Foley won	Brighton, England
19/12/1960	Jack Dempsey Vs Reg Ray	NK	York, England
20/12/1960	Jack Dempsey Vs Ron Oakley	NK	Trowell
22/12/1960	Jack Dempsey Vs Josef Ski	NK	Nottingham, England
02/01/1961	Jack Dempsey Vs Peter Szakacs	Dempsey won	High Wycombe, England
02/01/1961	Jack Dempsey Vs Bob Archer O'Brien	Dempsey won	High Wycombe, England
02/01/1961	Jack Dempsey Vs Tony Charles	Charles won	High Wycombe, England
05/01/1961	Jack Dempsey Vs Peter Szakacs	Dempsey won	Dagenham
06/01/1961	Jack Dempsey Vs Inca Peruano	Inca won	Glasgow, Scotland

Date	Match	Result	Location
07/01/1961	Jack Dempsey Vs Brian Burke	NK	Falkirk
09/01/1961	Jack Dempsey Vs Jean Morandi	Draw	Aylesbury
11/01/1961	Jack Dempsey Vs Peter Szakacs	NK	Walthamstow
12/01/1961	Jack Dempsey Vs Pasquale Salvo	NK	Peterborough, England
16/01/1961	Jack Dempsey Vs Alan Colbeck	NK	Loughborough, England
21/01/1961	Jack Dempsey Vs Alan Colbeck	NK	Coventry, England
24/01/1961	Jack Dempsey Vs Mel Riss	NK	Hull, England
25/01/1961	Jack Dempsey Vs Ted Hannon	NK	Sheffield, England
26/01/1961	Jack Dempsey Vs Mike Donlevy	Dempsey won	Bristol, England
27/01/1961	Jack Dempsey Vs Mick McManus	Draw	Ipswich, England
27/01/1961	Jack Dempsey Vs Ron Oakley	NK	Leicester, England
30/01/1961	Jack Dempsey Vs Stefan Milla	NK	Wembley, England
31/01/1961	Jack Dempsey Vs Mick McManus	NK	Wakefield, England
01/02/1961	Jack Dempsey Vs Bernard Murray	NK	Grimsby, England
02/02/1961	Jack Dempsey Vs Bernard Murray	NK	Nottingham, England
03/02/1961	Jack Dempsey Vs Joe Critchley	Dempsey won	Glasgow, Scotland
07/02/1961	Jack Dempsey Vs Felix Bawin	Dempsey won	Colchester, England
09/02/1961	Jack Dempsey Vs Alan Colbeck	Draw	Beckenham, England
10/02/1961	Jack Dempsey Vs Julien Morice	NK	Eastbourne
11/02/1961	Jack Dempsey (BWWC) Vs Mike Donlevy	NK	Kinston Upon Thames
13/02/1961	Jack Dempsey Vs Jackie Pallo	Pallo won	Wisbech
15/02/1961	Jack Dempsey Vs Alan Dennison	Dempsey won	Royal Albert Hall, London
16/02/1961	Jack Dempsey Vs Fernan Bawin	NK	Dunstable
17/02/1961	Jack Dempsey Vs Jackie Pallo	Dempsey won	Streatham
18/02/1961	Jack Dempsey Vs Fernand	NK	Norwich, England
20/02/1961	Jack Dempsey Vs Bobby Steele	NK	Leeds, England
22/02/1961	Jack Dempsey Vs Brian Burke	NK	Scunthorpe
25/02/1961	Jack Dempsey Vs John Foley	NK	Middlesborough, England
28/02/1961	Jack Dempsey Vs Peter Szakacs	NK	Welling
01/03/1961	Jack Dempsey Vs Jean Fryziak	NK	Kingston
03/03/1961	Jack Dempsey Vs Mick McManus	McManus won	Ipswich, England
09/03/1961	In KO Tournament	NK	Wembley, England
11/03/1961	Jack Dempsey Vs Brian Burke	NK	Buxton
13/03/1961	Jack Dempsey Vs Inca Peruano	NK	Loughborough, England
14/03/1961	Jack Dempsey Vs Chic Purvey	NK	Trowell
15/03/1961	Jack Dempsey Vs Jackie Pallo	Draw	Royal Albert Hall, London
20/03/1961	Jack Dempsey Vs Brian Trevors	Draw	Tunbridge Wells
22/03/1961	Jack Dempsey Vs Jackie Pallo	Dempsey won	Royal Albert Hall, London
25/03/1961	Jack Dempsey Vs Bobby Steele	NK	Belle Vue, Manchester
27/03/1961	Jack Dempsey Vs Tommy Mann	NK	Worksop
28/03/1961	Jack Dempsey Vs Mike Donlevy	Dempsey won	Purley
29/03/1961	Jack Dempsey Vs Tony Charles	Dempsey won	Cardiff, Wales
04/04/1961	Jack Dempsey Vs Bob Archer O'Brien	NK	Welling
05/04/1961	Jack Dempsey Vs Mick McManus	NK	Winchester
06/04/1961	Jack Dempsey Vs Gil Cesca	Draw	Bristol, England
08/04/1961	Jack Dempsey Vs Alan Colbeck	NK	Belle Vue, Manchester

Date	Match	Result	Location
10/04/1961	Jack Dempsey Vs Jackie Pallo	NK	Wisbech
13/04/1961	Jack Dempsey Vs Fernand Bawin	Dempsey won	Dagenham
15/04/1961	Jack Dempsey Vs Jackie Pallo	NK	Eastbourne
19/04/1961	Jack Dempsey Vs Fernand Bawin	Bawin won	Cardiff, Wales
21/04/1961	Jack Dempsey Vs Gil Cesca	NK	Caledonian Road, London
27/04/1961	Jack Dempsey Vs Pasquale Salvo	NK	Southampton, England
29/04/1961	Jack Dempsey Vs John Foley	Draw	Coventry, England
03/05/1961	Jack Dempsey Vs Bob Archer O'Brien	Dempsey won	Cardiff, Wales
04/05/1961	Jack Dempsey Vs Ted Hannon	Dempsey won	Peterborough, England
06/05/1961	Jack Dempsey Vs John Foley	Draw	Coventry, England
12/05/1961	Jack Dempsey Vs Julien Morice	NK	Northampton, England
13/05/1961	Jack Dempsey Vs Modesto Aledo	NK	Eastbourne
15/05/1961	Jack Dempsey Vs Tommy Mann	NK	Buxton
19/05/1961	Jack Dempsey Vs Chic Purvey	Draw	Glasgow, Scotland
24/05/1961	Jack Dempsey Vs Jackie Pallo	Dempsey won	Royal Albert Hall, London
05/06/1961	Jack Dempsey Vs Alan Colbeck	Colbeck won	Bradford, England
06/06/1961	Jack Dempsey Vs Bob Anthony	Dempsey won	Swindon, England
07/06/1961	Jack Dempsey Vs Jack Cunningham	Draw	Banbury
08/06/1961	Jack Dempsey Vs Mick McManus	Draw	Dagenham
10/06/1961	Jack Dempsey Vs Tony Charles	NK	Kings Lynn, London
15/06/1961	Jack Dempsey Vs Julien Morice	NK	Southampton, England
17/06/1961	Jack Dempsey Vs Bernard Murray	NK	Dorking
20/06/1961	Jack Dempsey Vs Alan Colbeck	Draw	Swindon, England
21/06/1961	Jack Dempsey Vs Alan Colbeck	NK	Deal
22/06/1961	Jack Dempsey Vs Pasquale Salvo	NK	Dunstable
23/06/1961	Jack Dempsey Vs Cliff Beaumont	NK	Northampton, England
26/06/1961	Jack Dempsey Vs Ted Hannon	Dempsey won	Hamilton, Scotland
29/06/1961	Jack Dempsey Vs Ted Hannon	NK	Barrow, England
30/06/1961	Jack Dempsey Vs Alan Dennison	NK	Fleetwood
03/07/1961	Jack Dempsey Vs Chic Purvey	NK	York, England
11/07/1961	Jack Dempsey Vs Mick McManus	Dempsey won	Purley
11/07/1961	Jack Dempsey Vs Bernard Murray (F)	Dempsey won	Purley
13/07/1961	Jack Dempsey Vs Julien Morice	NK	Walthamstow
15/07/1961	Jack Dempsey Vs Tommy Mann	NK	Middlesborough, England
01/08/1961	Jack Dempsey Vs Stefan Milla	Nk	Weston Super Mare
02/08/1961	Jack Dempsey Vs Mel Riss	Dempsey won	Watford, England
02/08/1961	Jack Dempsey Vs Bernard Murray (F)	Dempsey won	Watford, England
04/08/1961	Jack Dempsey Vs Jack Cunningham	Dempsey won	Barking
10/08/1961	Jack Dempsey Vs Alan Colbeck	NK	Scarborough, England
12/08/1961	Jack Dempsey Vs Alan Colbeck	NK	Belle Vue, Manchester
15/08/1961	Jack Dempsey Vs Tommy Mann	NK	Aberdeen, Scotland
17/08/1961	Jack Dempsey Vs Brian Burke	Dempsey won	Morecambe, Lancashire
18/08/1961	Jack Dempsey Vs Al Nicol	NK	Fleetwood
21/08/1961	Jack Dempsey Vs Eric Wasburg	NK	Wembley, England
26/08/1961	Jack Dempsey Vs Mick McManus	NK	Portsmouth, England
01/09/1961	Jack Dempsey Vs Keith Williams	NK	Liverpool, England

Date	Match	Result	Venue
02/09/1961	Jack Dempsey Vs Alan Colbeck	Dempsey won	Belle Vue, Manchester
06/09/1961	Jack Dempsey Vs Pasquale Salvo	NK	Felixstowe
07/09/1961	Jack Dempsey Vs Melwyn Riss	NK	Torquay
09/09/1961	Jack Dempsey Vs Jean Rabutt	NK	Norwich, England
11/09/1961	Jack Dempsey Vs John Foley	NK	Leeds, England
20/09/1961	Jack Dempsey Vs Gil Cesca	NK	Winchester
21/09/1961	Jack Dempsey Vs Pasquale Salvo	NK	Hove
25/09/1961	Jack Dempsey Vs Mike Donlevy	NK	Worcester, England
30/09/1961	Jack Dempsey Vs Chich Purvey	NK	Wembley, London
05/10/1961	Jack Dempsey Vs Mick McMichael	Dempsey won	Peterborough, England
06/10/1961	Jack Dempsey Vs Bobby Steele	Dempsey won	Ipswich, England
09/10/1961	Jack Dempsey Vs Jim Elder	NK	Kilmarnocj
12/10/1961	Jack Dempsey Vs Keith Martinelli	NK	Malvern
13/10/1961	Jack Dempsey Vs Alan Dennison	NK	Dumfries
16/10/1961	Jack Dempsey Vs Alan Dennison	NK	Preston, England
17/10/1961	Jack Dempsey Vs Alan Colbeck	NK	Scarborough, England
21/10/1961	Jack Dempsey Vs Ted Hannon	Dempsey won	Newcastle, England
23/10/1961	Jack Dempsey Vs Jack Cunningham	NK	Derby, England
24/10/1961	Jack Dempsey Vs Jack Cunningham	NK	Kidderminster
25/10/1961	Jack Dempsey Vs Tiger Ryan	NK	Dorking
26/10/1961	Jack Dempsey Vs Etienne Gobi	NK	Dunstable
28/10/1961	Jack Dempsey Vs Bob Anthony	NK	Norwich, England
30/10/1961	In KO Tournament	NK	Kettering
01/11/1961	Jack Dempsey Vs Mick McManus	Draw	Shoreditch
03/11/1961	Jack Dempsey Vs Eddie Saxon	Dempsey won	Barking
06/11/1961	Jack Dempsey Vs Jack Cunningham	NK	Margate
07/11/1961	Jack Dempsey Vs Bob Archer O'Brien	NK	Chelmsford, England
08/11/1961	Jack Dempsey Vs Joachim LaBarba	Dempsey won	Cardiff, Wales
09/11/1961	Jack Dempsey Vs Mick McManus	NK	Cambridge, England
10/11/1961	Jack Dempsey Vs Joachim LaBarba	NK	Northampton, England
11/11/1961	Jack Dempsey Vs Brian Trevors	NK	Kings Lynn, London
14/11/1961	Jack Dempsey Vs Len Wilding	Dempsey won	Colchester, England
16/11/1961	Jack Dempsey Vs Len Wilding	NK	Dagenham
17/11/1961	Jack Dempsey Vs Tony Charles	Draw	Ipswich, England
18/11/1961	Jack Dempsey Vs Bernard Murray	Draw	Luton, England
18/11/1961	Jack Dempsey Vs Al Nicol	Dempsey won	Reading, England
21/11/1961	Jack Dempsey Vs Bob Archer O'Brien	Draw	Plymouth
22/11/1961	Jack Dempsey Vs Pasquale Salvo	NK	Banbury
23/11/1961	Jack Dempsey Vs Stefan Milla	NK	Dunstable
27/11/1961	Jack Dempsey Vs Billy Howes	NK	Kettering
28/11/1961	Jack Dempsey Vs Ray Leslie	Dempsey won	Folkestone
01/12/1961	Jack Dempsey Vs Jean Morandi	NK	Bermondsey
02/12/1961	Jack Dempsey (BEWWC) Vs Bernard Murray	NK	Lewisham, London
04/12/1961	Jack Dempsey Vs Tommy Mann	NK	Derby, England
05/12/1961	Jack Dempsey Vs Ken Cadman	Dempsey won	Kidderminster
07/12/1961	Jack Dempsey Vs Keith Martinelli	NK	Malvern

Date	Match	Result	Venue
09/12/1961	Jack Dempsey Vs Alan Colbeck	Colbeck won	Belle Vue, Manchester
13/12/1961	Jack Dempsey Vs Keith Martinelli	NK	Cradley Heath
14/12/1961	Jack Dempsey Vs Bob Anthony	NK	Peterborough, England
14/12/1961	Jack Dempsey Vs Bob Anthony	Draw	Peterborough
16/12/1961	Jack Dempsey Vs Mike Donlevy	Dempsey won	Camberwell
18/12/1961	Jack Dempsey Vs Johnny Kwange	NK	Bedford, England
19/12/1961	Jack Dempsey Vs Jack Cunningham	Dempsey won	Plymouth, England
20/12/1961	Jack Dempsey Vs Dennis Dean	Draw	Cardiff, Wales
28/12/1961	Jack Dempsey Vs Jackie Pallo	Pallo won	Yeovil
01/01/1962	Jack Dempsey Vs Tommy Mann	NK	Derby, England
02/01/1962	Jack Dempsey Vs Pasquale Salvo	Dempsey won	Swindon, England
03/01/1962	Jack Dempsey Vs Julien Morice	NK	Ashford
04/01/1962	Jack Dempsey Vs Bernard Murray	NK	Ilford
06/01/1962	Jack Dempsey Vs Alan Miquet	NK	Brighton, England
08/01/1962	Jack Dempsey Vs Young Vulcan	NK	Derby, England
15/01/1962	Jack Dempsey Vs Gil Cesca	NK	Cheltenham, England
18/01/1962	Jack Dempsey Vs Joe Murphy	NK	Poplar
24/01/1962	Jack Dempsey Vs Billy Stock	NK	Acton
26/01/1962	Jack Dempsey Vs Mick McManus	NK	Rochester
27/01/1962	Jack Dempsey Vs Julien Morice	NK	Camberwell
29/01/1962	Jack Dempsey Vs Joe Murphy	NK	Catford
30/01/1962	Jack Dempsey Vs Vassilios Mantopolous	NK	Swindon, England
31/01/1962	Jack Dempsey Vs Bob Anthony	Dempsey won	Bath
01/02/1962	Jack Dempsey Vs Julien Morice	NK	Southampton, England
03/02/1962	Jack Dempsey Vs Melwyn Riss	NK	Coventry, England
06/02/1962	Jack Dempsey Vs Keith Willams	NK	Kidderminster
07/02/1962	Jack Dempsey Vs Julien Morice	NK	Beckenham, England
09/02/1962	Jack Dempsey Vs Alan Miquet	NK	Leicester, England
10/02/1962	Jack Dempsey Vs Ted Hannon	Dempsey won	Belle Vue, Manchester
13/02/1962	Jack Dempsey Vs Cliff Beaumont	Draw	Chelmsford, England
14/02/1962	Jack Dempsey Vs Bob Archer O'Brien	Dempsey won	Cardiff, Wales
15/02/1962	Jack Dempsey Vs Jackie Pallo	NK	Poplar
16/02/1962	Jack Dempsey Vs Peter Szakacs	Dempsey won	Taunton, England
21/02/1962	Jack Dempsey Vs Eddie Capelli	Dempsey won	Royal Albert Hall, London
22/02/1962	Jack Dempsey Vs Julien Morice	Dempsey won	Peterborough, England
24/02/1962	Jack Dempsey Vs Alan Colbeck	Colbeck won	Newcastle, England
26/02/1962	Jack Dempsey Vs Keith Williams	NK	Derby, England
27/02/1962	Jack Dempsey Vs Jack Cunningham	NK	Kidderminster
28/02/1962	Jack Dempsey Vs Bobby Steele	NK	Kingston
01/03/1962	Jack Dempsey Vs Joe Critchley	Dempsey won	Bristol, England
05/03/1962	Jack Dempsey Vs Keith Martinelli	NK	Derby, England
08/03/1962	Jack Dempsey Vs Chic Purvey	NK	Cradley Heath
09/03/1962	Jack Dempsey Vs Keith Martinelli	NK	Dumfries
12/03/1962	Jack Dempsey Vs Ted Hannon	NK	Kilmarnock
13/03/1962	Jack Dempsye Vs Terry Nylands	Dempsey won	Kidderminster
15/03/1962	Jack Dempsey Vs Keith Williams	NK	Barrow, England

Date	Match	Result	Location
20/03/1962	Jack Dempsey Vs Julien Morice	NK	Dagenham
21/03/1962	Jack Dempsey Vs Pasquale Salvo	NK	Winchester
24/03/1962	Jack Dempsey Vs Mick McMichael	NK	Coventry, England
26/03/1962	Jack Dempsey Vs Alan Miquet	NK	Cheltenham
27/03/1962	Jack Dempseu Vs Bob Anthony	NK	Bournemouth, England
31/03/1962	Jack Dempsey Vs Keith Williams	Jack won	Tottenham
31/03/1962	Jack Dempsey Vs Joe Murphy	Dempsey won	Newcastle, England
05/04/1962	Jack Dempsey Vs Dean Stockton	Draw	Rotherham
07/04/1962	Jack Dempsey Vs Otto Accron	Dempsey won	Luton, England
09/04/1962	Jack Dempsey Vs Tiger Ryan	NK	Worcester, England
11/04/1962	Jack Dempsey Vs Chic Purvey	NK	Cradley Heath
13/04/1962	Jack Dempsey Vs Ted Hannon	NK	Dumfries
19/04/1962	Jack Dempsey Vs Bob Archer O'Brien	Dempsey won	Peterborough
20/04/1962	Jack Dempsey Vs Roger LaRoaches	Draw	Brighton
21/04/1962	Jack Dempsey Vs Jim Breaks	NK	Coventry, England
24/04/1962	Jack Dempsey Vs Roger LaRoaches	Draw	Swindon, England
27/04/1962	Jack Dempsey Vs Roger LaRoaches	NK	Rochester
28/04/1962	Jack Dempsey Vs Mike Donlevy	NK	Brighton
30/04/1962	Jack Dempsey Vs Brian Burke	NK	Kilmarnock
10/05/1962	Jack Dempsey Vs Bob Archer O'Brien	NK	Southampton, England
14/05/1962	Jack Dempsey Vs Bob Archer O'Brien	NK	Cheltenham
16/05/1962	Jack Dempsey Vs Eric Sands	NK	Winchester
29/05/1962	Jack Dempsey Vs Bob Anthony	NK	Bournemouth, England
04/06/1962	Jack Dempsey Vs Mick McMichael	NK	Worcester, England
05/06/1962	Jack Dempsey Vs John Foley	Foley won	Hove
13/06/1962	Jack Dempsey Vs Ted Hannon	NK	Malvern
16/06/1962	Jack Dempsey Vs Dean Stockton	Stockton won	Belle Vue, Manchester
18/06/1962	Jack Dempsey Vs Vic Faulkner	NK	Buxton, England
19/06/1962	Jack Dempsey Vs Bobby Steele	Draw	Aberdeen, Scotland
21/06/1962	Jack Dempsey Vs John Foley	NK	Barrow, England
02/07/1962	In KO Tournament	NK	Weston Super Mare
03/07/1962	In KO Tournament	NK	Walthamstow
05/07/1962	Jack Dempsey Vs Jackie Pallo	NK	Dunstable
06/07/1962	Jack Dempsey Vs Julien Morice	NK	Rochester
24/07/1962	Jack Dempsey Vs Bobby Steele	NK	Bridlington, England
26/07/1962	Jack Dempsey Vs Keith Williams	NK	Morecambe, Lancashire
27/07/1962	Jack Dempsey Vs Keith Martinelli	NK	Withernsea
29/07/1962	Jack Dempsey Vs Joe Murphy	NK	Brighton, England
01/08/1962	Jack Dempsey Vs Alan Colbeck	Dempsey won	Great Yarmouth, England
02/08/1962	Jack Dempsey Vs Alan Colbeck	Colbeck won	Wimbledon
03/08/1962	Jack Dempsey Vs Jack Cunningham	Dempsey won	Barking
04/08/1962	Jack Dempsey Vs John Foley	Foley won	Maidstone
13/08/1962	Jack Dempsey Vs Keith Williams	NK	Ramsgate
14/08/1962	Jack Dempsey Vs John Foley	Draw	Plymouth, England
16/08/1962	Jack Dempsey Vs Bob Archer O'Brien	Dempsey won	Southampton, England
17/08/1962	Jack Dempsey Vs Keith Williams	NK	Bridgewater

Date	Match	Result	Location
18/08/1962	Jack Dempsey Vs Mike Donlevy	Dempsey won	Great Yarmouth, England
20/08/1962	Jack Dempsey Vs Jim Breaks	NK	Hamilton, Scotland
21/08/1962	Jack Dempsey Vs Ken Joyce	NK	Hastings
25/08/1962	Jack Dempsey Vs Jim Breaks	NK	Great Yarmouth, England
27/08/1962	Jack Dempsey Vs Joe Murphy	NK	Cheltenham
30/08/1962	Jack Dempsey Vs Mick McManus	NK	Hounslow
31/08/1962	Jack Dempsey Vs Mike Donlevy	Dempsey won	Wembley
03/09/1962	Jack Dempsey Vs Eddie Capelli	NK	Folkestone
06/09/1962	Jack Dempsey Vs Mike Donlevy	NK	Torquay, England
09/09/1962	Jack Dempsey Vs Joe Murphy	Dempsey won	Brighton
11/09/1962	Jack Dempsey Vs Ken Shaw	Dempsey won	Plymouth, England
14/09/1962	Jack Dempsey Vs Bob Sherry	NK	Burton on trent, England
17/09/1962	Jack Dempsey Vs Pasquale Salvo	Dempsey won	High Wycombe, England
22/09/1962	Jack Dempsey Vs Jack Cunningham	NK	Southall
27/09/1962	Jack Dempsey Vs Manuel Lopez	NK	Bury, St Edmunds
28/09/1962	Jack Dempsey Vs Alan Colbeck	NK	Rochester
29/09/1962	Jack Dempsey Vs Jackie Pallo	Pallo won	Coventry, England
02/10/1962	Jack Dempsey Vs Peter Szakacs	NK	Colchester, England
03/10/1962	Jack Dempsey Vs Julien Morice	Draw	Great Yarmouth, England
12/10/1962	Jack Dempsey Vs Micky Gold	NK	Dumfries
17/10/1962	Jack Dempsey Vs Bobby Steele	NK	Ashford
18/10/1962	Jack Dempsey Vs Ken Shaw	Dempsey won	Wimbledon
24/10/1962	Jack Dempsey Vs Manuel Lopez	NK	Dorking
27/10/1962	Jack Dempsey Vs Modesto Aledo	NK	Tottenham
27/10/1962	Jack Dempsey Vs Modesto Aledo	NK	Tottenham
01/11/1962	Jack Dempsey Vs Bob Archer O'Brien	Dempsey won	Wimbledon
02/11/1962	Jack Dempsey Vs Julien Morice	Dempsey won	Ipswich
03/11/1962	Jack Dempsey Vs Ken Joyce	NK	Luton, England
05/11/1962	Jack Dempsey Vs Joe Critchley	NK	Derby, England
12/11/1962	Jack Dempsey Vs Marcel Manneveau	NK	Cheltenham
13/11/1962	Jack Dempsey Vs Linde Caulder	NK	Swindon, England
19/11/1962	Jack Dempsey Vs Jackie Pallo	Dempsey won JPDQ	Westbury
19/11/1962	Jack Dempsey Vs Peter Rann	NK	Aylesbury
20/11/1962	Jack Dempsey Vs Bobby Steele	Dempsey won	Croydon
21/11/1962	Jack Dempsey Vs Alan Miquet	Dempsey won	Great Yarmouth, England
24/11/1962	Jack Dempsey Vs Julien Morice	NK	Norwich
28/11/1962	Jack Dempsey Vs Mike Donlevy	Dempsey won	Banbury
29/11/1962	Jack Dempsey Vs Jackie Pallo	Dempsey won JPDQ	Peterborough, England
30/11/1962	Jack Dempsey Vs Eric Sands	NK	Rochester
01/12/1962	Jack Dempsey Vs Stefan Milla	Dempsey won	Camberwell
05/12/1962	Jack Dempsey Vs Peter Szakacs	NK	Dorking
06/12/1962	Jack Dempsey Vs Julien Morice	NK	Gloucester
11/12/1962	Jack Dempsey Vs John Foley	NK	Kidderminster
15/12/1962	Jack Dempsey Vs Terry Nylands	NK	Sutton, Ashfield
17/12/1962	Jack Dempsey Vs Eric Sands	Draw	Eltham

Date	Match	Result	Location
18/12/1962	Jack Dempsey Vs Joe Murphy	NK	Croydon
20/12/1962	Jack Dempsey Vs Ted Hannon	Draw	Bristol, England
21/12/1962	Jack Dempsey Vs Keith Williams	Dempsey won	Barking
28/12/1962	Jack Dempsey Vs John Foley	Dempsey won	Ipswich
29/12/1962	Jack Dempsey Vs Julien Morice	NK	Luton, England
03/01/1963	Jack Dempsey Vs Linde Caulder	NK	Southampton, England
05/01/1963	Jack Dempsey Vs Pasquale Salvo	NK	Norwich
07/01/1963	Jack Dempsey Vs Peter Rann	Dempsey won	Tunbridge Wells
08/01/1963	Jack Dempsey Vs Eric Sands	NK	Colchester, England
09/01/1963	Jack Dempsey Vs Julien Morice	Draw	Shoreditch
11/01/1963	Jack Dempsey Vs Mike Donlevy	Dempsey won	Rochester
12/01/1963	Jack Dempsey Vs Julien Morice	NK	Southall
14/01/1963	Jack Dempsey Vs Mike Donlevy	NK	Worcester, England
17/01/1963	Jack Dempsey Vs Terry Nylands	NK	Hertford, England
18/01/1963	Jack Dempsey Vs Jack Cunningham	Dempsey won	Farnham
22/01/1963	Jack Dempsey Vs Vassilios Mantopolous	NK	Reading, England
23/01/1963	Jack Dempsey Vs Alan Miquet	NK	Winchester
24/01/1963	Jack Dempsey Vs Vassilios Mantopolous	NK	Beckenham
25/01/1963	Jack Dempsey Vs Pasquale Salvo	NK	Bermondsey
01/02/1963	Jack Dempsey Vs Ted Hannon	NK	Dumfries
04/02/1963	Jack Dempsey Vs Joe Murphy	Draw	West Ham, England
05/02/1963	Jack Dempsey Vs Mike Donlevy	Dempsey won	Plymouth, England
07/02/1963	Jack Dempsey Vs Julien Morice	Morice won	Beckenham
11/02/1963	Jack Dempsey Vs Alan Miquet	Dempsey won	Bedford, England
14/02/1963	Jack Dempsey Vs Ted Hannon	NK	Malvern
15/02/1963	Jack Dempsey Vs Ted Hannon	NK	Dumfries
16/02/1963	Jack Dempsey Vs Ted Hannon	NK	Sutton, Ashfield
18/02/1963	Jack Dempsey Vs Ivan Penzekoff	Dempsey won	Hamilton, Scotland
25/02/1963	Jack Dempsey Vs Colin Joynson	Dempsey won	Leeds, England
26/02/1963	Jack Dempsey Vs George Kidd	NK	Croydon
27/02/1963	Jack Dempsey Vs George Kidd	Kidd won	Cardiff, Wales
01/03/1963	Jack Dempsey Vs Al Nicol	NK	Belfast
04/03/1963	Jack Dempsey Vs Ted Hannon	Dempsey won	Weston Super Mare
06/03/1963	Jack Dempsey Vs Peter Rann	NK	Hastings
08/03/1963	Jack Dempsey Vs Pasquale Salvo	NK	Bermondsey
11/03/1963	Jack Dempsey Vs Alan Dennison	NK	Carlisle
14/03/1963	Jack Dempsey Vs Abe Ginsberg	NK	Nelson
18/03/1963	Jack Dempsey Vs Jean Corne	Dempsey won	High Wycombe, England
19/03/1963	Jack Dempsey Vs Jean Corne	Dempsey won	Plymouth, England
20/03/1963	Jack Dempsey Vs Terry Nylands	NK	East Grinstead
23/03/1963	Jack Dempsey Vs Julien Morice	Draw	Kings Lynn, London
25/03/1963	Jack Dempsey Vs Jack Cunningham	Cunningham won	Leeds, England
28/03/1963	Jack Dempsey Vs John Foley	NK	Brierly Hill
29/03/1963	Jack Dempsey Vs Terry Downs	NK	Dumfries
30/03/1963	Jack Dempsey & Terry O'Neill Vs Alf Cadman & Cadman	Cadmans won	Belle Vue, Manchester

Date	Match	Result	Location
08/04/1963	Jack Dempsey Vs Eddie Capelli	Draw	Catford
11/04/1963	Jack Dempsey Vs Bob Archer O'Brien	NK	Southampton, England
12/04/1963	Jack Dempsey Vs Terry Nylands	Nylands won	Brighton
16/04/1963	Jack Dempsey Vs Ted Hannon	NK	Bridlington, England
17/04/1963	Jack Dempsey Vs Jackie Pallo	Dempsey won	Sheffield, England
19/04/1963	Jack Dempsey Vs Jim Breaks	NK	Burton on trent, England
25/04/1963	Jack Dempsey Vs Joe Keegan	NK	Nelson
30/04/1963	Jack Dempsey Vs Claude Gessatte	NK	Croydon
01/05/1963	In KO tournament	NK	Guildford
03/05/1963	Jack Dempsey Vs Julien Morice	NK	Ventnor, Isle of Wight
06/05/1963	Jack Dempsey Vs Jackie Pallo	NC	Carlisle
09/05/1963	Jack Dempsey Vs John Foley	NK	Brierly Hill
11/05/1963	Jack Dempsey Vs Ted Hannon	NK	Kirkby, Ashfield
13/05/1963	Jack Dempsey Vs Jim Breaks	NK	Worcester, England
17/05/1963	Jack Dempsey Vs Jack Cunningham	NK	Bridlington, England
20/05/1963	Jack Dempsey Vs Ted Hannon	Hannon won	Hamilton, Scotland
22/05/1963	Jack Dempsey Vs Chic Purvey	NK	Dunfermline
25/05/1963	Jack Dempsey Vs Mal Sample	Dempsey won	Belle Vue, Manchester
30/05/1963	Jack Dempsey Vs Ted Hannon	NK	Exeter
04/06/1963	Jack Dempsey Vs Ken Joyce	NK	Croydon
05/06/1963	Jack Dempsey Vs Mick McManus	NK	Watford
06/06/1963	Jack Dempsey Vs John Foley	Dempsey won	Wimbledon
07/06/1963	Jack Dempsey Vs linde Caulder	NK	Barking
08/06/1963	Jack Dempsey Vs Eddie Capelli	NK	Salisbury
11/06/1963	Jack Dempsey Vs Jackie Pallo	NK	Bridlington, England
15/06/1963	Jack Dempsey Vs Tommy Mann	NK	Belle Vue, Manchester
17/06/1963	In KO Tournament	NK	Bedford
18/06/1963	Jack Dempsey Vs Eddie Capelli	NK	Newbury
19/06/1963	Jack Dempsey Vs linde Caulder	Dempsey won	Cardiff, Wales
22/06/1963	Jack Dempsey Vs Pasquale Salvo	NK	Norwich
25/06/1963	Jack Dempsey Vs Barry Cannon	NK	Bridlington, England
27/06/1963	Jack Dempsey Vs Monty Swann	NK	Morecambe
01/07/1963	Jack Dempsey Vs Ted Hannon	Hannon won	Hamilton, Scotland
02/07/1963	Jack Dempsey Vs Bobby Steele	Steele won	Aberdeen, Scotland
23/07/1963	Jack Dempsey Vs Tommy Mann	NK	Bridlington, England
25/07/1963	Jack Dempsey Vs Linde Caulder	Dempsey won	Brighton
26/07/1963	Jack Dempsey Vs Jack Cunningham	Cunningham won	High Wycombe, England
29/07/1963	Jack Dempsey Vs Bob Archer O'Brien	NK	Margate
29/07/1963	Jack Dempsey Vs Reg Trood	Trood won	Wimbledon
30/07/1963	Jack Dempsey Vs Ron Oakley	Dempsey won	Plymouth, England
31/07/1963	Jack Dempsey Vs Ken Joyce	Draw	Great Yarmouth, England
01/08/1963	Jack Dempsey Vs Peter Rann	NK	Wimbledon
03/08/1963	Jack Dempsey Vs Ken Joyce	NK	Salisbury
05/08/1963	Jack Dempsey Vs Barry Sherman	Dempsey won	Douglas, Isle of Man
12/08/1963	Jack Dempsey Vs Joe Murphy	Draw	Great Yarmouth, England

Date	Match	Result	Location
14/08/1963	Jack Dempsey Vs Ken Joyce	Draw	Great Yarmouth, England
15/08/1963	Jack Dempsey Vs Peter Rann	NK	Torquay
16/08/1963	Jack Dempsey Vs Joe Murphy		Bognor Regis
17/08/1963	Jack Dempsey Vs Joe Murphy		Maidstone
09/09/1963	Jack Dempsey Vs Mike Donlevy	NK	Worcester, England
10/09/1963	Jack Dempsey Vs Mike Donlevy	NK	Weymouth
19/09/1963	Jack Dempsey Vs Alan Colbeck	NK	Walthamstow
20/09/1963	Jack Dempsey Vs Mick McMichael	Dempsey won	Rochester
21/09/1963	Jack Dempsey Vs Mike Donlevy	NK	Luton, England
23/09/1963	Jack Dempsey Vs Peter Szakacs	NK	Weston Super Mare
25/09/1963	Jack Dempsey Vs Mick McManus	NK	Dorking
27/09/1963	Jack Dempsey Vs Julien Morice	NK	Barking
28/09/1963	Jack Dempsey Vs Johnny Kwango	Kwango won	Coventry, England
29/09/1963	Jack Dempsey Vs Ted Hannon	NK	Kirkby, Ashfield
07/10/1963	Jack Dempsey Vs Ted Hannon	Dempsey won	Hamilton, Scotland
08/10/1963	Jack Dempsey Vs Bernard Murray	Murray won	Aberdeen, Scotland
10/10/1963	Jack Dempsey Vs Jack Fallon	NK	Nelson
11/10/1963	Jack Dempsey Vs John Foley	NK	Rotherham
12/10/1963	Jack Dempsey Vs Mike Donlevy	Jack won	Tottenham
17/10/1963	Jack Dempsey Vs Bert Royal	NK	Malvern
21/10/1963	Jack Dempsey Vs Joe Murphy	Draw	Eltham
22/10/1963	Jack Dempsey Vs Arthur Fisher	NK	Bournemouth, England
23/10/1963	Jack Dempsey Vs Joe Murphy	NK	Rushden
28/10/1963	Jack Dempsey Vs linde Caulder	NK	Birmingham
05/11/1963	Jack Dempsey Vs Mike Donlevy	NK	Croydon
06/11/1963	Jack Dempsey Vs Joe Murphy	Draw	Shoreditch
11/11/1963	Jack Dempsey Vs Alan Colbeck	Draw	Bradford
12/11/1963	Jack Dempsey Vs Vic Faulkner	NK	Kidderminster
19/11/1963	Jack Dempsey Vs Julien Morice	Dempsey won	Hove
22/11/1963	Jack Dempsey Vs Keith Martinelli	NK	Farnham
23/11/1963	Jack Dempsey Vs Linde Caulder	NK	Norwich
26/11/1963	Jack Dempsey Vs Billy Catanzaro	NK	Newbury
27/11/1963	Jack Dempsey Vs Joe Murphy	Draw	Brighton
28/11/1963	Jack Dempsey Vs Michael Saulnier	NK	Gloucester
03/12/1963	Jack Dempsey Vs Eddie Capelli	NK	Kidderminster
06/12/1963	Jack Dempsey Vs Terry Downs	NK	Willenhall
07/12/1963	Jack Dempsey Vs Ted Hannon	NK	Barrow
09/12/1963	Jack Dempsey Vs Melwyn Riss	NK	Derby
10/12/1963	Jack Dempsey Vs Rev Michael Brooks	NK	Kidderminster
12/12/1963	Jack Dempsey Vs John Foley	NK	Nelson
14/12/1963	Jack Dempsey Vs Colin Joynson	Dempsey won	Doncaster
16/12/1963	Jack Dempsey Vs Jim McKenzie	Dempsey won	Hamilton, Scotland
17/12/1963	Jack Dempsey Vs Jim Elder	Dempsey won	Aberdeen, Scotland
18/12/1963	Jack Dempsey Vs Terry Downs	NK	Welshpool
21/12/1963	Jack Dempsey Vs Rev Michael Brooks	NK	Hanley
23/12/1963	Jack Dempsey Vs Mike Donlevy	NK	Birmingham

Date	Match	Result	Location
27/12/1963	Jack Dempsey Vs Cliff Beaumont	Draw	Bolton
30/12/1963	Jack Dempsey Vs Cliff Beaumont	Dempsey won	Cheltenham
30/12/1963	Jack Dempsey Vs Julien Morice (F)	Morice won	Cheltenham
22/02/1964	Jack Dempsey (KO) Vs Michael Saulnier	NK	Leeds, West yorkshire
13/05/1964	Jack Dempsey (WWC) Vs Eddie Capelli	NK	Wembley, London
20/06/1964	Jack Dempsey (WWC) Vs Jim Breaks (LWC)	NK	Bridlington
29/07/1964	Jack Dempsey Vs Alan Dennison	NK	Belle Vue
01/08/1964	Jack Dempsey Vs Chich Purvey	NK	Wryton Stadium, Bolton
16/09/1964	Jack Dempsey Vs Bob Steele	NK	Wembley Town Hall, London
31/10/1964	Jack Dempsey Vs Eric Sands	Eric won	Bradford, West Yorkshire
22/12/1964	Jack Dempsey (WWC) Gil Cesca	NK	Croydon, London
02/01/1965	Jack Dempsey Vs Keith Williams	NK	Grantham,
04/01/1965	Jack Dempsey Vs Monty Swann	Dempsey won	Leeds
05/01/1965	Jack Dempsey Vs Jackie Pallo	Pallo won	Hull
06/01/1965	Jack Dempsey Vs Ted Hannon	NK	Perth
11/01/1965	Jack Dempsey Vs Josef Ski	Draw	Birmingham
13/01/1965	Jack Dempsey Vs Ian Gilmour	Dempsey won	Scunthorpe
15/01/1965	Jack Dempsey Vs Josef Ski	NK	Horncastle
16/01/1965	Jack Dempsey Vs Josef Ski	Dempsey won	Hanley
18/01/1965	Jack Dempsey Vs Alan Wood	Dempsey won	Cheltenham
18/01/1965	Jack dempsey Vs Keith Williams	NK	Wolverhampton, West Midlands
19/01/1965	Jack Dempsey Vs Mike Bennett	NK	Colchester, England
20/01/1965	Jack Dempsey Vs Billy Catanzaro	NK	Kingston
21/01/1965	Jack Dempsey Vs Linde Caulder	NK	Beckenham
22/01/1965	Jack Dempsey Vs Mick McManus	NK	Eltham
23/01/1965	Jack Dempsey Vs Peter Szakacs	NK	Wembley, London
23/01/1965	Jack Dempsey Vs Peter Szakacs	Dempsey won	Wembley
25/01/1965	Jack Dempsey Vs Johnny Eagles	NK	Derby
28/01/1965	Jack Dempsey Vs Terry Nylands	Draw	Barnsley
02/02/1965	Jack Dempsey Vs Jeff Kaye	Dempsey won	Wellington
03/02/1965	Jack Dempsey Vs Barry Cannon	Dempsey won	Pontypool, Wales
05/02/1965	Jack Dempsey Vs Barry Cannon	Dempsey won	Bolton
06/02/1965	Jack Dempsey Vs Barry Cannon	Dempsey won	Shrewsbury
09/02/1965	Jack Dempsey Vs Jim Lewis	Dempsey won	Finsbury Park
13/02/1965	Jack Dempsey Vs Peter Rann	Dempsey won	Eastbourne
17/02/1965	Jack Dempsey Vs Terry Nylands	NK	Rugby
18/02/1965	Jack Dempsey Vs Jim McKenzie	NK	Airdrie
20/02/1965	Jack Dempsey Vs Keith Williams	Dempsey won	Belle Vue, Manchester
22/02/1965	Jack Dempsey Vs Stefan Milla	Dempsey won	Birmingham
23/02/1965	Jack Dempsey Vs Melwyn Riss	NK	Kidderminster
25/02/1965	Jack Dempsey Vs Stefan Milla	NK	Corwen
26/02/1965	Jack Dempsey Vs Stefan Milla	Dempsey won	Bolton
27/02/1965	Jack Dempsey Vs Alan Wood	Dempsey won	Shrewsbury
01/03/1965	Jack Dempsey Vs Peter Cortez	NK	Aylesbury
02/03/1965	Jack Dempsey Vs Mike Donlevy	NK	Reading, England
04/03/1965	Jack Dempsey Vs Jackie Pallo	NK	Exeter

Date	Match	Result	Location
05/03/1965	Jack Dempsey Vs Alan Dennison	Dennison won	Northampton
06/03/1965	Jack Dempsey Vs Ken Joyce	Draw	Coventry
08/03/1965	Jack Dempsey Vs Sid Cooper	NK	Bradford
09/03/1965	Jack Dempsey Vs Terry Nylands	NK	Leicester, Leicestershire
10/03/1965	Jack Dempsey Vs Terry Nylands	Dempsey won	Middlesbrough
11/03/1965	Jack Dempsey Vs Alan Colbeck	Dempsey won	Blackburn
13/03/1965	Jack Dempsey Vs Alan Colbeck	Colbeck won	Newcastle, England
16/03/1965	Jack Dempsey Vs Jeff Kaye	Draw	Oswestry
19/03/1965	Jack Dempsey Vs Alan Dennison	NK	Liverpool
20/03/1965	Jack Dempsey Vs Jack Fallon	Dempsey won	Doncaster
22/03/1965	Jack Dempsey Vs Peter Szakacs	NK	Seymour Hall, London
23/03/1965	Jack Dempsey Vs Vic Faulkner	NK	Bournemouth
24/03/1965	Jack Dempsey Vs Peter Szakacs	Dempsey won	Shoreditch
25/03/1965	Jack Dempsey Vs Juda Ischa Israel	NK	Bury St Edmunds
29/03/1965	Jack Dempsey Vs Eric Cutler	NK	Warrington
01/04/1965	Jack Dempsey Vs Alan Dennison	NK	Malvern
03/04/1965	Jack Dempsey Vs Al Nicol	Dempsey won	Belle Vue, Manchester
13/04/1965	Jack Dempsey Vs Mick McManus	NK	Croydon
15/04/1965	Jack Dempsey Vs Braulio Veliz	Dempsey won	Peterborough, England
16/04/1965	Jack Dempsey Vs George Kidd	NK	Dumfries
17/04/1965	Jack Dempsey Vs Mick McManus	McManus won	Belle Vue, Manchester
19/04/1965	Jack Dempsey Vs Bernard Murray	NK	Bradford
20/04/1965	Jack Dempsey Vs Bernard Murray	NK	Leicester, England
21/04/1965	Jack Dempsey Vs Terry Downs	Draw	Middlesbrough
22/04/1965	Jack Dempsey Vs Keith Martinelli	NK	Nelson
24/04/1965	Jack Dempsey Vs Alan Colbeck	Colbeck won	Newcastle, England
27/04/1965	Jack Dempsey Vs Al Brown	NK	Caernarvon, Wales
28/04/1965	Jack Dempsey Vs Al Brown	Dempsey won	Ellesmere Port
29/04/1965	Jack Dempsey Vs Stefan Milla	NK	Aberystwyth, Wales
01/05/1965	Jack Dempsey Vs Melwyn Riss	Dempsey won	Doncaster
03/05/1965	Jack Dempsey Vs Joe Murphy	Dempsey won	Bedford
05/05/1965	Jack Dempsey Vs Georges Cohen	NK	Felixstowe
06/05/1965	Jack Dempsey Vs Eric Sands	NK	Southampton, England
10/05/1965	Jack Dempsey Vs Colin Joynson	NK	Leeds
12/05/1965	Jack Dempsey Vs Jackie Pallo	Dempsey won JPDQ	Sheffield, South Yorkshire
15/05/1965	Jack Dempsey Vs Mick McManus	Dempsey won	Belle Vue, Manchester
17/05/1965	Jack Dempsey Vs Barry Cannon	Dempsey won	Birmingham
18/05/1965	Jack Dempsey Vs Al Brown	Dempsey won	Rochdale
20/05/1965	Jack Dempsey Vs Barry Cannon	Dempsey won	Chester
22/05/1965	Jack Dempsey Vs Joe Critchley	Dempsey won	Doncaster
24/05/1965	Jack Dempsey Vs Jim Lewis	NK	Catford
30/05/1965	Jack Dempsey Vs Jackie Pallo	Draw	Brighton
31/05/1965	Jack Dempsey Vs Terry Downs	NK	Bradford
02/06/1965	Jack Dempsey Vs Terry Downs	Dempsey won	Middlesbrough
05/06/1965	Jack Dempsey Vs Chic Purvey	Dempsey won CPDQ	Newcastle, England

Date	Match	Result	Location
07/06/1965	Jack Dempsey Vs Mike Donlevy	Dempsey won	Birmingham
10/06/1965	Jack Dempsey Vs Al Brown	NK	Ross on Wye
11/06/1965	Jack Dempsey Vs Jackie Pallo	Pallo won	Liverpool
12/06/1965	Jack Dempsey Vs Joe Critchley	Dempsey won	Doncaster
14/06/1965	Jack Dempsey Vs Jim Lewis	Dempsey won	Wembley
15/06/1965	Jack Dempsey Vs Linde Caulder	NK	Reading, England
16/06/1965	Jack Dempsey Vs Eddie Saxon	NK	Felixstowe
17/06/1965	Jack Dempsey Vs Linde Caulder	Dempsey won	Bristol
24/06/1965	Jack Dempsey Vs Mick McMichael	NK	Morecambe, Lancashire
26/06/1965	Jack Dempsey Vs Alan Colbeck	NK	Leeds
28/06/1965	Jack Dempsey Vs Jim Breaks	Breaks won	Hamilton, Scotland
29/06/1965	Jack Dempsey Vs Jim Breaks	Breaks won	Aberdeen, Scotland
19/07/1965	Jack Dempsey Vs Ken Cadman	Dempsey won	Birmingham
20/07/1965	Jack Dempsey Vs Reg Ray	NK	Skegness
24/07/1965	Jack Dempsey Vs Terry Downs	Draw	Doncaster
26/07/1965	Jack Dempsey Vs Ray Leslie	NK	Paignton
28/07/1965	Jack Dempsey Vs Stefan Milla	NK	Carlyon Bay
29/07/1965	Jack Dempsey Vs Tiger Ryan	NK	Torquay
30/07/1965	Jack Dempsey Vs Brian Maxine	Dempsey won	Weymouth
31/07/1965	Jack Dempsey Vs Brian Maxine	NK	Salisbury
01/08/1965	Jack Dempsey Vs Jackie Pallo	Draw	Brighton
02/08/1965	Jack Dempsey Vs Bobby Bierne	NK	Arbroath
03/08/1965	Jack Dempsey Vs Alan Colbeck	NK	Aberdeen, Scotland
04/08/1965	Jack Dempsey Vs Bobby Bierne	NK	Dunbar
05/08/1965	Jack Dempsey Vs Bobby Steele	NK	Morecambe, Lancashire
06/08/1965	Jack Dempsey Vs Johnny Eagles	NK	Skegness
10/08/1965	Jack Dempsey Vs Joel De Noirbruell	Dempsey won	Weymouth
11/08/1965	Jack Dempsey Vs Peter Rann	NK	Eastbourne
12/08/1965	Jack Dempsey Vs Musa the Turk	NK	Wimbledon
17/08/1965	Jack Dempsey Vs Joel De Noirbruell	NK	Newbury
18/08/1965	Jack Dempsey Vs Ray Leslie	Dempsey won	Great Yarmouth
19/08/1965	Jack Dempsey Vs Peter Szakacs	NK	Walthamstow
21/08/1965	Jack Dempsey Vs Joe Murphy	NK	Wembley, London
21/08/1965	Jack Dempsey Vs Joe Murphy	Draw	Wembley
26/08/1965	Jack Dempsey Vs Alan Dennison	NK	Carlisle
28/08/1965	Jack Dempsey Vs Chic Purvey	Dempsey won	Newcastle, England
30/08/1965	Jack Dempsey Vs Alan Dennison	NK	Epworth show
31/08/1965	Jack Dempsey Vs Joe Keegan	NK	Skegness
01/09/1965	Jack Dempsey Vs Barry Cannon	NK	Hinckley
11/09/1965	Jack Dempsey Vs Alan Miquet	NK	Barking Assembly Hall
11/09/1965	Jack Dempsey Vs Alan Miquet	NK	Barking
13/09/1965	Jack Dempsey Vs Jim McKenzie	Dempsey won	Hamilton, Scotland
14/09/1965	Jack Dempsey Vs Jim Lewis	NK	Aberdeen, Scotland
16/09/1965	Jack Dempsey Vs Jim Lewis	Dempsey won	Morecambe, Lancashire
20/09/1965	Jack Dempsey Vs Barry Cannon	Dempsey won	Birmingham
21/09/1965	Jack Dempsey Vs Ian Gilmour	NK	Wellington

Date	Match	Result	Location
23/09/1965	Jack Dempsey Vs Alan Colbeck	NK	Paisley
25/09/1965	Jack Dempsey Vs Linde Caulder	Caulder won	Doncaster
27/09/1965	Jack Dempsey Vs Jackie Pallo	Pallo won	Cheltenham
28/09/1965	Jack Dempsey Vs Julien Morice	NK	Croydon
30/09/1965	Jack Dempsey Vs Bernard Murray	Draw	Westbury
02/10/1965	Jack Dempsey Vs Linde Caulder	NK	Wembley, London
04/10/1965	Jack Dempsey Vs Mick McMichael	NK	Bradford
05/10/1965	Jack Dempsey Vs Honeyboy Zimba	NK	Leicester
06/10/1965	Jack Dempsey Vs Chic Purvey	NK	Middlesbrough
09/10/1965	In KO Tournament	NK	Newcastle, England
11/10/1965	Jack Dempsey Vs Johnny Eagles	Eagles won	Birmingham
13/10/1965	Jack Dempsey Vs Terry Jowett	NK	Uttoxeter
16/10/1965	Jack Dempsey Vs Terry Jowett	Draw	Doncaster
20/10/1965	Jack Dempsey Vs Dick Conlon	Dempsey won	Bath
21/10/1965	Jack Dempsey Vs Eddie Capelli	Dempsey won	Bristol
22/10/1965	Jack Dempsey Vs Jeff Kaye	NK	Barking
25/10/1965	Jack Dempsey Vs Jeff Kaye	Dempsey won	Hamilton, Scotland
26/10/1965	Jack Dempsey Vs Linde Caulder	NK	Swindon
28/10/1965	Jack Dempsey Vs Jeff Kaye	Jack Dempsey	Morecambe, Lancashire
29/10/1965	Jack Dempsey Vs Billy Catanzaro	Dempsey won	Rotherham
02/11/1965	Jack Dempsey Vs Barry Cannon	NK	Solihull
03/11/1965	Jack Dempsey Vs Al Brown	NK	Caernarvon, Wales
04/11/1965	Jack Dempsey Vs Ken Cadman	NK	Southport
05/11/1965	Jack Dempsey Vs Al Brown	NK	Willenhall
06/11/1965	Jack Dempsey Vs Barry Cannon	Dempsey won	Doncaster
07/11/1965	Jack Dempsey Vs Jackie Pallo	Dempsey won	Cheltenham
09/11/1965	Jack Dempsey Vs Julien Morice	Draw	Croydon
10/11/1965	Jack Dempsey Vs Jon Cortez	NK	Dorking
12/11/1965	Jack Dempsey Vs Julien Morice	NK	Southampton, England
13/11/1965	Jack Dempsey Vs Joe Murphy	NK	Kings Lynn
15/11/1965	Jack Dempsey Vs Peter Preston	NK	Bradford
18/11/1965	Jack Dempsey Vs Alan Colbeck	NK	Morecambe, Lancashire
22/11/1965	Jack Dempsey Vs Johnny Eagles	Dempsey won	Birmingham
24/11/1965	Jack Dempsey Vs Colin Joynson	NK	Buckley
25/11/1965	Jack Dempsey Vs Barry Cannon	NK	Northwich
29/11/1965	Jack Dempsey Vs Mick McMichael	NK	York
01/12/1965	Jack Dempsey Vs Ted Heath	NK	Lincoln
02/12/1965	Jack Dempsey Vs Ken Cadman	NK	Crewe
04/12/1965	Jack Dempsey Vs Colin Joynson	Draw	Hanley
09/12/1965	Jack Dempsey Vs Peter Rann	NK	Cambridge
10/12/1965	Jack Dempsey Vs Ken Joyce	Draw	Rochester
14/12/1965	Jack Dempsey Vs Julien Morice	NK	Bournemouth
15/12/1965	Jack Dempsey Vs George Cohen	NK	Southend
19/12/1965	Jack Dempsey Vs Al Brown	Dempsey won	Bromsgrove
28/12/1965	Jack Dempsey Vs Bernard Murray	NK	Chelmsford
30/12/1965	Jack Dempsey Vs Peter Rann	Rann won	Bristol

Date	Match	Result	Location
03/01/1966	Jack Dempsey Vs Melwyn Riss	NK	Derby, Derbyshire
04/01/1966	Jack Dempsey Vs Mick McMichael	Dempsey won	Huddersfield
05/01/1966	Jack Dempsey Vs Mick McMichael	NK	Perth
07/01/1966	Jack Dempsey Vs George Kidd	NK	Glasgow
12/01/1966	Jack Dempsey Vs Jackie Pallo	Pallo won	Hastings
13/01/1966	Jack Dempsey Vs Peter Rann	Dempsey won	Southampton, England
15/01/1966	Jack Dempsey Vs Joe Murphy	Dempsey won	Kings Lynn, London
17/01/1966	Jack Dempsey Vs Terry Nylands	Dempsey won	Birmingham
20/01/1966	Jack Dempsey Vs Bobby Steele	Draw	Malvern
22/01/1966	Jack Dempsey Vs Micky Gold	Dempsey won	Hanley
24/01/1966	Jack Dempsey Vs Bernard Murray	Dempsey won	Seymour Hall, London
25/01/1966	Jack Dempsey Vs Mick McManus	McManus won	Bournemouth, England
26/01/1966	Jack Dempsey Vs Jean Menard	Dempsey won	Great Yarmouth
26/01/1966	Jack Dempsey Vs Ray Fury	Fury won	Great Yarmouth
27/01/1966	Jack Dempsey Vs Eddie Capelli	Dempsey won	Dunstable, Bedfordshire
28/01/1966	Jack Dempsey Vs Peter Rann	Rann won	Bermondsey
29/01/1966	Jack Dempsey Vs Joe Murphy	Dempsey won	Brixton
01/02/1966	Jack Dempsey Vs Monty Swann	Swann won	Edinburgh, Scotland
02/02/1966	Jack Dempsey Vs Mir Zaffar Ealam	Dempsey won	Scunthorpe
04/02/1966	Jack Dempsey Vs Terry Nylands	NK	Dumfries
07/02/1966	Jack Dempsey Vs Melwyn Riss	NK	Derby, Derbyshire
10/02/1966	Jack Dempsey Vs Mir Zaffar Ealam	NK	Nelson
12/02/1966	Jack Dempsey Vs Barry Cannon	NK	Shrewsbury
14/02/1966	Jack Dempsey Vs Julien Morice	NK	Epsom
16/02/1966	Jack Dempsey Vs Linde Caulder	Draw	Banbury
18/02/1966	Jack Dempsey Vs Peter Rann	NK	Ipswich
21/02/1966	Jack Dempsey Vs Melwyn Riss	Dempsey won	Derby, Derbyshire
22/02/1966	Jack Dempsey Vs Mike Dallas	Dempsey won	Worsley
01/03/1966	Jack Dempsey Vs Alan Miquet	Dempsey won	Croydon, London
03/03/1966	Jack Dempsey Vs Jackie Pallo	Dempsey inj	Walthamstow, London
04/03/1966	Jack Dempsey Vs Jackie Pallo	NK	Barnstaple
05/03/1966	Jack Dempsey Vs Peter Rann	Rann won	Coventry
07/03/1966	Jack Dempsey Vs Melwyn Riss	NK	Derby, Derbyshire
08/03/1966	Jack Dempsey Vs Colin Joynson	NK	Solihull, West Midlands
10/03/1966	Jack Dempsey Vs Melwyn Riss	NK	Nelson
12/03/1966	Jack Dempsey Vs Mick McManus	NK	Kidderminster
16/03/1966	Jack Dempsey Vs Al Brown	NK	Welshpool
17/03/1966	Jack Dempsey Vs Al Brown	Brown won JDDQ	Crewe
19/03/1966	Jack Dempsey Vs Alan Wood	Draw	Doncaster, South Yorkshire
21/03/1966	Jack Dempsey Vs Kalmen Gaston	NK	High Wycombe
22/03/1966	Jack Dempsey Vs Peter Rann	Dempsey won	Croydon, London
23/03/1966	Jack Dempsey Vs Ron Oakley	NK	Canterbury
24/03/1966	Jack Dempsey Vs Peter Szakacs	Dempsey won	Dunstable, Bedfordshire
25/03/1966	Jack Dempsey Vs Peter Rann	Dempsey won	Ipswich
26/03/1966	Jack Dempsey Vs Julien Morice	Morice won	Maidstone

Date	Match	Result	Location
28/03/1966	Jack Dempsey Vs Melwyn Riss	Dempsey won	Derby, Derbyshire
01/04/1966	Jack Dempsey Vs Melwyn Riss	NK	Dumfries
02/04/1966	Jack Dempsey Vs Johnny Eagles	NK	Doncaster, South Yorkshire
05/04/1966	Jack Dempsey Vs Linde Caulder	NK	Swindon
06/04/1966	Jack Dempsey Vs Bernard Murray	Dempsey won	Shoreditch
12/04/1966	Jack Dempsey Vs Al Brown	NK	Solihull, West Midlands
13/04/1966	Jack Dempsey Vs Mike Eagers	NK	Lincoln, Lincolnshire
15/04/1966	Jack Dempsey Vs Jim McKenzie	Dempsey won	Glasgow
16/04/1966	Jack Dempsey Vs Alan Colbeck	Colbeck won	Belle Vue, Manchester
18/04/1966	Jack Dempsey Vs Ken Cadman	Dempsey won	Birmingham
19/04/1966	Jack Dempsey Vs Al Nicol	NK	Trowell
20/04/1966	Jack Dempsey Vs Melwyn Riss	NK	Nelson
27/04/1966	Jack Dempsey Vs Alan Sergeant	NK	Rushden
03/05/1966	Jack Dempsey Vs Mick McManus	NK	Croydon, London
05/05/1966	Jack Dempsey Vs Jon Cortez	Draw	Dunstable, Bedfordshire
14/05/1966	Jack Dempsey Vs Sid Cooper	Dempsey won SCDQ	Wembley
18/05/1966	Jack Dempsey Vs Sid Cooper	NK	Brent Town Hall, Wembley
18/05/1966	Jack Dempsey Vs Alan Miquet	NK	Watford
19/05/1966	Jack Dempsey Vs Alan Miquet	NK	Westbury
21/05/1966	Jack Dempsey Vs Jackie Pallo	NK	Kings Lynn, London
26/05/1966	Jack Dempsey Vs Melwyn Riss	Draw	Malvern
30/05/1966	Jack Dempsey Vs Peter Szakacs	NK	Weston Super Mare
31/05/1966	Jack Dempsey Vs Mick McManus	NK	Reading, Berkshire
02/06/1966	Jack Dempsey Vs Eddie Capelli	NK	Wimbledon
04/06/1966	Jack Dempsey Vs Bernard Murray	NK	Bedford
07/06/1966	Jack Dempsey Vs Linde Caulder	Draw	Worthing
08/06/1966	Jack Dempsey Vs Bernard Murphy	NK	Corn Exchange, Bedford
08/06/1966	Jack Dempsey Vs Peter Rann	Draw	Eastbourne
11/06/1966	Jack Dempsey Vs ken Joyce	NK	Horsham
14/06/1966	Jack Dempsey Vs Stefan Milla	Dempsey won	Solihull, West Midlands
15/06/1966	Jack Dempsey Vs Mir Zaffar Ealam	NK	Glasgow
18/06/1966	Jack Dempsey Vs Jeff Kaye	Dempsey won	Belle Vue, Manchester
20/06/1966	Jack Dempsey Vs Brian Maxine	NK	Cheltenham
21/06/1966	Jack Dempsey Vs Peter Rann	NK	Paignton
24/06/1966	Jack Dempsey Vs Peter Szakacs	Draw	Rochester
29/06/1966	Jack Dempsey Vs Mick McManus	McManus won	Sheffield, South Yorkshire
30/06/1966	Jack Dempsey Vs Alan Colbeck	NK	Morecambe, Lancashire
02/07/1966	Jack Dempsey Vs Steve Clements	Dempsey won	Belle Vue, Manchester
11/07/1966	Jack Dempsey Vs Peter Szakacs	Dempsey won	Wembley
14/07/1966	Jack Dempsey Vs Jackie Pallo	Pallo won	Bristol
19/07/1966	Jack Dempsey Vs Peter Rann	Rann won	Croydon, London
20/07/1966	Jack Dempsey Vs Ken Joyce	NK	Felixstowe
21/07/1966	Jack Dempsey Vs Vic Faulkner	NK	Morecambe, Lancashire
26/07/1966	Jack Dempsey Vs Bernard Murray	Draw	Worthing
27/07/1966	Jack Dempsey Vs Vic Faulkner	NK	The Winter Gardens, Morecambe, Lancashire

Date	Match	Result	Venue
30/07/1966	Jack Dempsey Vs Alan Miquet	NK	Wembley
03/08/1966	Jack Dempsey Vs Alan Miquet	NK	Brent Town Hall, Wembley
04/08/1966	Jack Dempsey Vs Micky Gold	Draw	Morecambe, Lancashire
09/08/1966	Jack Dempsey Vs Brian Maxine	NK	Bridlington
16/08/1966	Jack Dempsey Vs Alan Dennison	NK	Bridlington
18/08/1966	Jack Dempsey Vs Jim Breaks	NK	Morecambe, Lancashire
23/08/1966	Jack Dempsey Vs Mick McManus	NK	Reading, Berkshire
03/09/1966	Jack Dempsey Vs Ken Joyce	NK	Horsham
17/09/1966	Jack Dempsey Vs Ken Joyce	NK	Horsham
06/10/1966	Jack Dempsey Vs Adrian Street	NK	Morecambe, Lancashire
05/12/1966	Jack Dempsey Vs Barry Cannon	NK	Blackpool, England
29/04/1967	Jack Dempsey Vs Ian Gilmour	Draw	Belle Vue, Manchester
15/01/1968	Jack Dempsey Vs Jim Mellor	Dempsey won	Birmingham
18/04/1968	Jack Dempsey Vs Fred Woolley	Dempsey won	Bromsgrove
15/07/1968	Jack Dempsey Vs Butcher Goodman	NK	Morecambe, Lancashire
11/08/1968	Jack Dempsey Vs Eric Sands	NK	Morecambe, Lancashire
01/10/1968	Jack Dempsey Vs Roy LaRue	Dempsey won	Digbeth
10/10/1968	Jack Dempsey Vs Bill Blackfoot	Dempsey won	Widnes
26/11/1968	Jack Dempsey Vs Reg Yates	Dempsey won	Digbeth
06/12/1968	Jack Dempsey Vs johnny Saint	Dempsey won	Stockport
16/05/1969	Jack Dempsey Vs Bobby Steele	Dempsey won	Newcastle, England

George Gregory

Date	Match	Outcome	Venue
1929	George Gregory Vs George de Relwyskow	Relwyskow won	NK
1934	George Gregory Vs Eric Fisher	George Won	London, England
1934	George Gregory Vs Bert Assirati	Bert won	Manchester, England
1935	George Gregory Vs Eric Fisher	George Won	Holborn, England
1936	George Gregory Vs Jack Pye	George won	Portsmouth, England
1937	George Gregory Vs Bert Mansfield	George won, BM DQ	Edmonton, England
1937	All England Champion Heavyweight	N/A	Manchester, England
1938	George Gregory Vs Douglas Clark	Clark won	Manchester, England
1938	George Gregory Vs Jack Sherry	Jack won	Manchester, England
1938	George Gregory Vs Harry Brooks	Harry won	London, England
1939	George Gregory Vs Golden Phantom	George won	England
1939	George Gregory Vs Padvo Peltonin	George won	Morecambe, Lancashire
1940	George Gregory Vs Harry Brooks	Harry won, GGDQ	Morecambe, Lancashire
1948	George Gregory Vs Francis St Clair	Francis won, GG DQ	Aberdeen, Scotland
08/02/1933	George Gregory Vs Black Eagle	Gregory won	Shipley,
11/03/1933	George Gregory Vs Red Jacques	Gregory won	Dewsbury, England
27/03/1933	George Gregory Vs Mitchell Gill	Draw	Leeds, West yorkshire
07/04/1933	George Gregory Vs The Mask	Gregory won	St. Helens, England
10/06/1933	George Gregory Vs The Mask	Gregory won	Dewsbury, England
08/07/1933	George Gregory Vs Spider Webb	Gregory won	Manchester, England
17/07/1933	George Gregory Vs Wlater Magnee	Gregory won	Nottingham, England
27/07/1933	George Gregory Vs The Angel	NK	Blackpool, England
15/08/1933	George Gregory Vs Karl Ketchinsky	Gregory won	Blackpool, England
15/08/1933	George Gregory Vs The Cat	Gregory won	Blackpool, England
24/08/1933	George Gregory in 4 man tournament with Spider Webb, The Mask, The Angel	N/A	Blackpool, England
09/11/1933	George Gregory Vs Rudi Barbua	Gregory won	Nelson, England
26/01/1934	George Gregory Vs Young Apollo	NK	London, England
23/02/1934	George Gregory Vs Karl Pojello	NK	Liverpool, England
14/03/1934	George Gregory Vs Black Eagle	Gregory won	Swansea, Wales
24/03/1934	George Gregory Vs Humpback	Gregory won	Shrewsbury, England
04/04/1934	George Gregory Vs Humpback	Gregory won	Swansea, Wales
07/04/1934	George Gregory Vs Karl Pojello	Gregory won	Manchester, England
01/06/1934	George Gregory Vs Len Franklin	Franklin won	Plymouth, England
08/06/1934	George Gregory Vs Great Scot.	Gregory won	Crewe, England
14/06/1934	George Gregory Vs Dave Armstrong	NK	Blackfriars, London
31/08/1934	George Gregory Vs Henry Wilkinson	Gregory won	Plymouth, England
07/12/1934	George Gregory Vs Henry Wilkie	Gregory won	Plymouth, England
09/12/1934	George Gregory Vs Black Butcher Johnson	NK	Islington, England
14/02/1935	George Gregory Vs Hall	NK	Blackfriars, London
14/03/1935	George Gregory Vs Chich Rolfe	Gregory won CR DQ	Elephant & Castle, London

Date	Match	Result	Location
08/08/1935	George Gregory Vs Jack Atherton	George Won	Rochester, England
08/08/1935	George Gregory Vs jack Atherton	Gregory won	Rochester, England
16/08/1935	George Gregory Vs Stoker Smith	Gregory won	Plymouth, England
28/08/1935	George Gregory Vs King Curtis	Gregory won	Camborne, England
02/10/1935	George Gregory Vs Tony Best	Gregory won	Plymouth, England
16/10/1935	George Gregory Vs Eric Fisher	Gregory won	Plymouth, England
23/10/1935	George Gregory Vs Cab Cashford	Gregory won	Plymouth, England
14/11/1935	George Gregory Vs Dubarry	Gregory won	Wolverhampton, England
20/11/1935	George Gregory Vs Guy Falla	Draw	Plymouth, England
22/01/1936	George Gregory Vs Francis St Clair Gregory	Draw	Plymouth, England
02/03/1936	George Gregory Vs Black Eagle	Draw	Wolverhampton
04/03/1936	George Gregory Vs Sam Rabin	Gregory won	Plymouth, England
26/03/1936	George Gregory Vs Mystery Mask	Draw	Portsmouth
02/04/1936	George Gregory Vs Stan Estelles	Draw	Nelson, England
02/05/1936	George Gregory Vs Black Arrow	NK	Newcastle, England
22/08/1936	George Gregory Vs Jack atherton	NK	Newcastle, England
03/09/1936	George Gregory Vs Mike Sullivan	George won, MS DQ	Edinburgh, Scotland
03/09/1936	George Gregory Vs Micky Sullivan	Gregory won, MS DQ	Edinburgh, Scotland
14/10/1936	George Gregory Vs Francis St Clair Gregory	NK	Newcastle, England
17/10/1936	George Gregory Vs Gentleman Jim	NK	Bristol, England
30/10/1936	George Gregory Vs Bob Fife	NK	Liverpool, England
31/10/1936	George Gregory Vs Garry Currie	NK	Blackburn, Lancashire
07/11/1936	George Gregory Vs Tony Baer	NK	Newcastle, England
13/11/1936	George Gregory Vs Jack Pye	NK	Liverpool, England
14/11/1936	George Gregory Vs Tony Baer	NK	Newcastle, England
28/11/1936	George Gregory Vs Douglas Clark	NK	Newcastle, England
12/12/1936	George Gregory Vs Bill Garnon	NK	Newcastle, England
15/01/1937	George Gregory Vs Jack Atherton	Gregory won	Blackpool, England
21/01/1937	George Gregory Vs Charlie Green	Gregory won	Portsmouth
30/01/1937	George Gregory Vs Anaconda	NK	Newcastle, England
12/02/1937	George Gregory Vs Jim Armstrong	Gregory won	Preston, England
13/02/1937	George Gregory Vs Mike Demitre	NK	Newcastle, England
27/02/1937	George Gregory Vs Anaconda	Gregory won	Newcastle, England
06/03/1937	George Gregory Vs Vic Hessell	Gregory won	Newcastle, England
07/03/1937	George Gregory Vs King Curtis	George won	Blackfriars, England
27/03/1937	George Gregory Vs Al Hamilton	NK	Newcastle, England
17/04/1937	George Gregory Vs Tony Baer	NK	Newcastle, England
29/04/1937	George Gregory Vs Charlie Green	NK	Morecambe, Lancashire
15/05/1937	George Gregory Vs Vic Hessell	Gregory won	Newcastle, England
21/05/1937	George Gregory Vs King Curtis	Gregory won, KCDQ	Preston, England
27/05/1937	George Gregory Vs Bob Fyfe	Draw	Edinburgh, Scotland
27/05/1937	George Gregory Vs Bob Fife	Fife won	Edinburgh, Scotland
11/06/1937	George Gregory Vs Jack Pettifer	Gregory won	Preston, England
15/07/1937	George Gregory Vs Choc Clayton	George won	Edinburgh, Scotland
16/07/1937	George Gregory Vs Jack Atherton	Gregory won	Preston, England

Date	Match	Result	Location
28/08/1937	George Gregory Vs Dave Armstrong	Draw	Newcastle, England
18/09/1937	George Gregory Vs Johnny Demchuck	Gregory won	Newcastle, England
02/10/1937	George Gregory Vs Johnny Demchuck	NK	Newcastle, England
15/10/1937	George Gregory Vs Wild Tarzan	Gregory won	Preston, England
23/10/1937	George Gregory Vs Black Arrow	NK	Newcastle, England
17/11/1937	George Gregory Vs Vic Hessell	NK	Newcastle, England
09/01/1938	George Gregory Vs Wally Seddon	Gregory won	West Bromwich, England
22/01/1938	George Gregory Vs Sam Radnor	Gregory won	Newcastle, England
07/03/1938	George Gregory Vs Blue Mask	Draw	Douglas, Isle of Man
12/03/1938	George Gregory Vs Blue Mask	Mask won	Newcastle, England
21/03/1938	Geroge Gregory Vs Cordite Conroy	Gregory won	Douglas, Isle of Man
09/04/1938	George Gregory Vs Blue Mask	Gregory won	Newcastle, England
30/04/1938	George Gregory Vs Tony Baer	Baer won	Newcastle, England
14/05/1938	George Gregory Vs Joe Devalto	Gregory won	Newcastle, England
14/07/1938	George Gregory Vs Cab Cashford	George won	Edinburgh, Scotland
14/07/1938	George Gregory Vs Cab Cashford	Gregory won	Edinburgh, Scotland
25/07/1938	George Gregory Vs Dave Armstrong	Dave won	Blackfriars, England
11/08/1938	George Gregory Vs Jack Atherton	George won	Edinburgh, Scotland
25/08/1938	George Gregory Vs Johnny Dallas	George won JD DQ	Edinburgh, Scotland
01/10/1938	George Gregory Vs Gil Knutson	NK	Newcastle, England
07/10/1938	George Gregory Vs Jack Sherry	Sherry won	Belle Vue, Manchester
22/10/1938	George Gregory Vs Basner Cunningham	Gregory won	Newcastle, England
28/10/1938	George Gregory Vs Dave Armstrong	NK	Belle Vue, Manchester
19/11/1938	George Gregory Vs Rex Gable	NK	Newcastle, England
24/11/1938	George Gregory Vs George Clark	Draw	Nelson, England
03/12/1938	George Gregory Vs Paul Lortie	NK	Newcastle, England
16/02/1939	George Gregory Vs Vic Hessle	Gregory won	Morecambe, Lancashire
04/04/1939	George Gregory Vs Ali Alaba	NK	Whitely, England
06/04/1939	George Gregory Vs Douglas Clark	Draw	Preston
12/04/1939	George Gregory Vs Johnny Demchuk	George won	Chester, Cheshire
13/04/1939	George Gregory Vs Johnny Demchuck	Gregory won	Chester, Cheshire
14/04/1939	George Gregory Vs Rik De Groot	Draw	Manchester, England
25/04/1939	George Gregory Vs Bill Silcock	NK	Chesterfield
01/06/1939	George Gregory Vs Alf Robinson	George won	Crewe, England
22/06/1939	George Gregory Vs Wild Tarzan	Gregory won	Morecambe, Lancashire
03/08/1939	George Gregory Vs Norman Stewart	Gregory won	Morecambe, Lancashire
19/08/1939	George Gregory Vs Chic Knight	Gregory won	Newcastle, England
07/10/1939	George Gregory Vs Bert Mansfield	Gregory won	Newcastle, England
11/12/1939	George Gregory Vs Jim Atlas	NK	Bolton, Lancashire
15/12/1939	George Gregory Vs Jim Atlas	Gregory won	Blackpool, England
19/01/1940	George Gregory Vs Harry Pye	NK	Middlesborough, North Yorkshire
03/02/1940	George Gregory Vs Alf Robinson	NK	Newcastle, England
13/03/1940	George Gregory Vs Wally Seddon	Gregory won	Edinburgh, Scotland
27/04/1940	George Gregory Vs Harry Pye	Gregory won	Hull, England
01/05/1940	George Gregory Vs Harry Pye	Gregory won	Edinburgh, Scotland

Date	Match	Result	Location
12/05/1940	George Gregory Vs Harry Brooks	NK	Merseyside, Liverpool
26/06/1940	George Gregory Vs Chic Knight	Gregory won, CK DQ	Edinburgh, Scotland
10/07/1940	George Gregory Vs Charlie Green	Gregory won	Edinburgh, Scotland
11/09/1940	George Gregory Vs Chic Knight	Gregory won	Edinburgh, Scotland
30/10/1940	George Gregory Vs Chic Knight	Gregory won, CK DQ	Edinburgh, Scotland
17/01/1941	George Gregory Vs Padvo Peltonin	Gregory won	Preston
27/01/1941	George Gregory Vs Padvo Peltonin	NK	Blackpool, England
30/01/1941	George Gregory Vs Chic Knight	NK	Morecambe, Lancashire
31/01/1941	George Gregory Vs Ray St Bernard	Gregory won	Preston
28/02/1941	George Gregory Vs Dave Armstrong	Gregory won	Preston
01/03/1941	George Gregory Vs Charlie Green	NK	Newcastle, England
22/03/1941	George Gregory Vs Padvo Peltonin	NK	Newcastle, England
27/03/1941	George Gregory Vs Carl Van Wurden	NK	Morecambe, Lancashire
31/03/1941	George Gregory Vs Carl Van Wurden	NK	Blackpool, England
01/05/1941	George Gregory Vs Farmers Boy	NK	Morecambe, Lancashire
24/05/1941	George Gregory Vs Douglas Clark	NK	Headingley, England
19/06/1941	George Gregory Vs Jan Gotch	NK	Morecambe, Lancashire
04/09/1941	George Gregory Vs Dave Armstrong	NK	Morecambe, Lancashire
29/09/1941	George Gregory Vs Vic Hessell	Gregory won	Edinburgh, Scotland
16/10/1941	George Gregory Vs Dave Armstrong	NK	Morecambe, Lancashire
10/11/1941	George Gregory Vs Jack Pye	Gregory won, JPDQ	Edinburgh, Scotland
11/11/1941	George Gregory Vs Wild Tarzan	Gregory won	Aberdeen, Scotland
15/11/1941	Geroge Gregory Vs Jock Murdoch	NK	Belle Vue, Manchester
29/11/1941	George Gregory Vs jack Atherton	NK	Belle Vue, Manchester
13/12/1941	George Gregory Vs Bill McDonald	NK	Belle Vue, Manchester
08/01/1942	George Gregory Vs Chic Knight	NK	Morecambe, Lancashire
08/01/1942	George Gregory Vs Chic Knight	NK	Morecambe, Lancashire
12/01/1942	George Gregory Vs Jack Pye	Gregory won	Edinburgh, Scotland
26/01/1942	George Gregory Vs Wally Seddon	NK	Blackpool, England
26/01/1942	George Gregory Vs Wally Seddon	NK	Blackpool, England
07/02/1942	George Gregory Vs Tony Baer	NK	Belle Vue, Manchester
23/02/1942	George Gregory Vs Jack Pye	NK	Edinburgh, Scotland
28/02/1942	George Gregory Vs George Finnie	NK	Belle Vue, Manchester
23/03/1942	George Gregory Vs Dave Armstrong	Draw	Edinburgh, Scotland
09/04/1942	George Gregory Vs Wally Seddon	NK	Morecambe, Lancashire
09/04/1942	George Gregory Vs Wally Seddon	NK	Morecambe, Lancashire
13/04/1942	George Gregory Alf Rawlings	Gregory won, ARDQ	Edinburgh, Scotland
20/04/1942	George Gregory Vs Bill McDonald	NK	Blackpool, England
20/04/1942	George Gregory Vs Jack Pye	NK	Blackpool, England
04/05/1942	George Gregory Cs Phil Siki	Gregory won	Edinburgh, Scotland
14/05/1942	George Gregory Vs Farmers Boy	NK	Morecambe, Lancashire
14/05/1942	George Gregory Vs Farmers Boy	NK	Morecambe, Lancashire
01/06/1942	George Gregory Vs Dave Armstrong	Gregory won	Edinburgh, Scotland
15/06/1942	George Gregory	Knight won GGDQ	Edinburgh, Scotland

Date	Match	Result	Location
11/07/1942	George Gregory Vs George Clark	NK	Belle Vue, Manchester
20/07/1942	George Gregory Vs Bert Mansfield	Gregory won	Edinburgh, Scotland
23/07/1942	George Gregory Vs Jack Pye	NK	Morecambe, Lancashire
23/07/1942	George Gregory Vs Jack Pye	NK	Morecambe, Lancashire
29/07/1942	George Gregory Vs Francis St Clair Gregory	NK	Bolton, Lancashire
06/08/1942	George Gregory Vs Phil Siki	NK	Morecambe, Lancashire
06/08/1942	George Gregory Vs Phil Siki	NK	Morecambe, Lancashire
10/08/1942	George Gregory Vs Bill McDonald	Gregory won	Edinburgh, Scotland
27/08/1942	George Gregory Vs Phil Siki	NK	Morecambe, Lancashire
27/08/1942	George Gregory Vs Phil Siki	NK	Morecambe, Lancashire
30/08/1942	George Gregory Vs Bill McDonald	NK	Edinburgh, Scotland
30/08/1942	George Gregory Vs Bill McDonald	NK	Edinburgh, Scotland
10/09/1942	George Gregory Vs Chic Knight	NK	Morecambe, Lancashire
10/09/1942	George Gregory Vs Chic Knight	NK	Morecambe, Lancashire
07/10/1942	George Gregory Vs Dave Armstrong	NK	Belle Vue, Manchester
17/10/1942	George Gregory Vs Farmers boy	NK	Belle Vue, Manchester
14/11/1942	George Gregory Vs Farmers boy	NK	Belle Vue, Manchester
25/11/1942	George Gregory Vs Farmers boy	NK	Belle Vue, Manchester
03/12/1942	George Gregory Vs Bill McDonald	NK	Morecambe, Lancashire
03/12/1942	George Gregory Vs Bill McDonald	NK	Morecambe, Lancashire
05/12/1942	George Gregory Vs Charlie Green	NK	Belle Vue, Manchester
11/01/1943	George Gregory Vs George Clarke	NK	Blackpool, England
11/01/1943	George Gregory Vs George Clarke	NK	Blackpool, England
25/01/1943	George Gregory Vs George Clark	Gregory won GCDQ	Edinburgh, Scotland
26/01/1943	George Gregory Vs Dave Armstrong	Gregory won	Dundee, Scotland
28/01/1943	George Gregory Vs Farmers Boy	NK	Morecambe, Lancashire
28/01/1943	George Gregory Vs Farmers Boy	NK	Morecambe, Lancashire
08/02/1943	George Gregory Vs Padvo Peltonin	Gregory won	Edinburgh, Scotland
11/02/1943	George Gregory Vs Padvo Peltonin	NK	Morecambe, Lancashire
11/02/1943	George Gregory Vs Peltonin	NK	Morecambe, Lancashire
22/02/1943	George Gregory Vs Flash Barker	NK	Blackpool, England
22/02/1943	George Gregory Vs Barker	NK	Blackpool, England
15/03/1943	George Gregory Vs Mike Byrne	NK	Blackpool, England
15/03/1943	George Gregory Vs Byrnes	NK	Blackpool, England
12/04/1943	George Gregory Vs St Clair Gregory	NK	Blackpool, England
12/04/1943	George Gregory Vs St Clair Gregory	NK	Blackpool, England
06/05/1943	George Gregory Vs Ed Gordon	NK	Morecambe, Lancashire
24/05/1943	George Gregory Vs Padvo Peltonin	Gregory won	Edinburgh, Scotland
14/06/1943	George Gregory Vs Flash Gordon	Gregory won	Edinburgh, Scotland
15/06/1943	George Gregory Vs Chic Knight	Knight won GGDQ	Dundee, Scotland
17/06/1943	George Gregory Vs Chic Knight	NK	Morecambe, Lancashire
17/06/1943	George Gregory Vs Chic Knight	NK	Morecambe, Lancashire
12/07/1943	George Gregory Vs Iron Duke	Gregory won	Edinburgh, Scotland
13/07/1943	George Gregory Vs Jack Pye	Pye won	Dundee, Scotland
17/07/1943	George Gregory Vs George Clarke	NK	Belle Vue, Manchester

Date	Match	Result	Venue
02/08/1943	George Gregory Vs Tom Blenkhorn	NK	Belle Vue, Manchester
07/08/1943	George Gregory Vs Padvo Peltonin	NK	Belle Vue, Manchester
12/08/1943	George Gregory Vs Jack Pye	NK	Morecambe, Lancashire
12/08/1943	George Gregory Vs Jack Pye	NK	Morecambe, Lancashire
28/08/1943	George Gregory Vs Sonny Wallis	NK	Belle Vue, Manchester
30/08/1943	George Gregory Vs Bill McDonald	Gregory won	Edinburgh, Scotland
31/08/1943	George Gregory Vs Charlie Green	Green won	Dundee, Scotland
13/09/1943	George Gregory Vs Flash Gordon	Gregory won	Edinburgh, Scotland
18/09/1943	George Gregory Vs Golden Ace	NK	Belle Vue, Manchester
23/09/1943	George Gregory Vs Dave Armstrong	NK	Morecambe, Lancashire
23/09/1943	George Gregory Vs Dave Armstrong	NK	Morecambe, Lancashire
26/10/1943	George Gregory Vs Jim Anderson	Anderson won, GGDQ	Dundee, Scotland
04/11/1943	George Gregory Vs Tony Baer	NK	Morecambe, Lancashire
04/11/1943	George Gregory Vs Tony Baer	NK	Morecambe, Lancashire
08/11/1943	George Gregory Vs Carl Van Wurden	NC	Edinburgh, Scotland
11/11/1943	George Gregory Vs Dave Armstrong	NK	Morecambe, Lancashire
11/11/1943	George Gregory Vs Dave Armstrong	NK	Morecambe, Lancashire
22/11/1943	George Gregory Vs The Farmer	NK	Blackpool, England
06/12/1943	George Gregory Vs Billy Joyce	Gregory won	Edinburgh, Scotland
20/12/1943	George Gregory Vs Bill McDonald	McDonald won GGDQ	Edinburgh, Scotland
21/12/1943	George Gregory Vs Jack Pye	Gregory won	Dundee, Scotland
22/12/1943	George Gregory Vs The Farmer	NK	Blackpool, England
23/12/1943	George Gregory Vs Sandy McLaren	NK	Morecambe, Lancashire
23/12/1943	George Gregory Vs McLaren	NK	Morecambe, Lancashire
30/12/1943	George Gregory Vs Ed Gordon	NK	Morecambe, Lancashire
03/01/1944	George Gregory Vs The Farmer	NK	Blackpool, England
05/02/1944	George Gregory Vs Bill Garnon	NK	Belle Vue, Manchester
12/02/1944	George Gregory Vs George Clark	NK	Belle Vue, Manchester
16/02/1944	George Gregory Vs Francis St Clair Gregory	NK	Belle Vue, Manchester
21/02/1944	George Gregory Vs Wally Seddon	NK	Blackpool, England
26/02/1944	George Gregory Vs Iron Duke	NK	Belle Vue, Manchester
01/03/1944	George Gregory Vs Chic Knight	NK	Belle Vue, Manchester
06/03/1944	George Gregory Vs Wally Seddon	NK	Blackpool, England
10/04/1944	George Gregory Vs Chic Knight	NK	Belle Vue, Manchester
15/04/1944	George Gregory Vs Anaconda	NK	Belle Vue, Manchester
19/04/1944	George Gregory Vs Bill Garnon	NK	Belle Vue, Manchester
24/04/1944	George Gregory Vs Jack Pye	NK	Blackpool, England
29/04/1944	George Gregory Vs Charlie Green	NK	Belle Vue, Manchester
06/05/1944	George Gregory Vs Farmers boy	NK	Belle Vue, Manchester
08/05/1944	George Gregory Vs Flash Barker	NK	Blackpool, England
17/05/1944	George Gregory Vs Farmers boy	NK	Belle Vue, Manchester
31/05/1944	George Gregory Vs Montiverdi	NK	Belle Vue, Manchester
07/06/1944	George Gregory Vs Farmers Boy	NK	Belle Vue, Manchester
14/06/1944	George Gregory Vs Iron Duke	NK	Belle Vue, Manchester
17/06/1944	George Gregory Vs Francis St Clair Gregory	NK	Newcastle, England

Date	Match	Result	Venue
01/07/1944	George Gregory Vs Vic Hessell	NK	Belle Vue, Manchester
08/07/1944	George Gregory Vs Iron Duke	NK	Newcastle, England
15/07/1944	George Gregory Vs Vic Hessell	NK	Belle Vue, Manchester
22/07/1944	George Gregory Vs Farmers Boy	NK	Newcastle, England
29/07/1944	George Gregory Vs Alf Robinson	NK	Belle Vue, Manchester
07/08/1944	George Gregory Vs Flash Barker	NK	Belle Vue, Manchester
12/08/1944	George Gregory Vs Farmers Boy	NK	Newcastle, England
02/09/1944	George Gregory Vs Tony Baer	NK	Newcastle, England
09/09/1944	George Gregory Vs Vic Hessell	NK	Belle Vue, Manchester
16/09/1944	George Gregory Vs Anaconda	NK	Belle Vue, Manchester
18/09/1944	George Gregory Vs The Farmer	NK	Edinburgh, Scotland
27/09/1944	George Gregory Vs Farmers Boy	NK	Belle Vue, Manchester
07/10/1944	George Gregory Vs Ben Sharpe	NK	Newcastle, England
09/10/1944	George Gregory Vs Tony Baer	Draw	Edinburgh, Scotland
14/10/1944	George Gregory Vs Big Ben	NK	Belle Vue, Manchester
25/10/1944	George Gregory Vs Selmer Jackson	NK	Belle Vue, Manchester
28/10/1944	George Gregory Vs Bill Garnon	NK	Newcastle, England
11/11/1944	George Gregory Vs Alf Robinson	NK	Belle Vue, Manchester
22/11/1944	George Gregory Vs Farmers boy	NK	Belle Vue, Manchester
27/11/1944	George Gregory Vs Tony Baer	NK	Edinburgh, Scotland
02/12/1944	George Gregory Vs Vic Hessell	NK	Belle Vue, Manchester
09/12/1944	George Gregory Vs Francis St Clair Gregory	NK	Belle Vue, Manchester
30/12/1944	George Gregory Vs Rocky Brannigan	NK	Newcastle, England
20/01/1945	George Gregory Vs Ernie Baldwin	NK	Newcastle, England
27/01/1945	George Gregory Vs Bert Assirati	Assirati won	Belle Vue, Manchester
17/02/1945	George Gregory Vs Alf Robinson	NK	Belle Vue, Manchester
28/02/1945	George Gregory Vs Farmers boy	NK	Belle Vue, Manchester
21/03/1945	George Gregory Vs Iron Duke	NK	Belle Vue, Manchester
28/03/1945	George Gregory Vs Farmers boy	Boy won, GGDQ	Dundee, Scotland
31/03/1945	George Gregory Vs Vic Hessell	NK	Belle Vue, Manchester
03/04/1945	George Gregory Vs Alf Robinson	NK	Belle Vue, Manchester
07/04/1945	George Gregory Vs Harry Brooks	NK	Newcastle, England
20/04/1945	George Gregory Vs Vic Hessell	NK	Belle Vue, Manchester
05/06/1945	George Gregory Vs Charlie Green	Gregory won	Edinburgh, Scotland
16/06/1945	George Gregory Vs Harry Brooks	Gregory won	Newcastle, England
02/07/1945	George Gregory Vs Farmers Boy	NK	Leeds, West yorkshire
09/07/1945	George Gregory Vs Dave Armstrong	Gregory won	Edinburgh, Scotland
14/07/1945	George Gregory Vs Bob Silcock	NK	Newcastle, England
21/07/1945	George Gregory Vs George Clark	NK	Aberdeen, Scotland
23/07/1945	George Gregory Vs Farmers boy	NK	Leeds, West yorkshire
28/07/1945	George Gregory Vs Dave Armstrong	NK	Newcastle, England
11/08/1945	George Gregory Vs Dave Armstrong	NK	Newcastle, England
13/08/1945	George Gregory Vs Bill Garnon	Garnon won	Edinburgh, Scotland
01/09/1945	George Gregory Vs Black Angel	Angel won	Newcastle, England
03/09/1945	George Gregory Vs Tony Baer	Baer won	Edinburgh, Scotland

Date	Match	Result	Venue
22/09/1945	George Gregory Vs Dave Armstrong	NK	Newcastle, England
24/09/1945	George Gregory Vs Anaconda	Anaconda won	Edinburgh, Scotland
29/09/1945	George Gregory Vs Farmers boy	NK	Belle Vue, Manchester
24/10/1945	George Gregory Vs Ernie Baldwin	NK	Belle Vue, Manchester
27/10/1945	George Gregory Vs Bill Garnon	NK	Belle Vue, Manchester
03/11/1945	George Gregory Vs Charlie Green	NK	Belle Vue, Manchester
10/11/1945	George Gregory Vs George Clark	NK	Newcastle, England
12/11/1945	George Gregory Vs George Clark	Clark won	Edinburgh, Scotland
14/11/1945	George Gregory Vs Bill Garnon	NK	Belle Vue, Manchester
17/11/1945	George Gregory Vs Vic Hessell	NK	Belle Vue, Manchester
24/11/1945	George Gregory Vs Anaconda	NK	Belle Vue, Manchester
03/12/1945	George Gregory Vs Anaconda	Anaconda won	Edinburgh, Scotland
15/12/1945	George Gregory Vs Chic Knight	NK	Belle Vue, Manchester
26/01/1946	George Gregory Vs Terry Ricardo	Gregory won	Belle Vue, Manchester
06/02/1946	Geroge Gregory Vs Louis Loew	NK	Belle Vue, Manchester
16/02/1946	George Gregory Vs Komeschenko	NK	Belle Vue, Manchester
27/02/1946	George Gregory Vs Anaconda	NK	Belle Vue, Manchester
02/03/1946	George Gregory Vs King Curtis	NK	Belle Vue, Manchester
08/03/1946	George Gregory Vs Chic Elliott	NK	Belfast, Ireland
16/03/1946	George Gregory Vs Tony Baer	NK	Belle Vue, Manchester
27/03/1946	George Gregory Vs Maxie Martinschultz	NK	Belle Vue, Manchester
06/04/1946	George Gregory Vs Ernie Baldwin	NK	Belle Vue, Manchester
13/04/1946	George Gregory Vs Roland Bonneville	NK	Belle Vue, Manchester
22/04/1946	George Gregory Vs Mitchell Gill	NK	Belle Vue, Manchester
11/05/1946	George Gregory Vs Steven Novotny	NK	Belle Vue, Manchester
22/05/1946	George Gregory Vs Mitchell Gill	NK	Belle Vue, Manchester
27/05/1946	George Gregory Vs Bert Assirati	Draw	Edinburgh, Scotland
29/05/1946	George Gregory Vs Alf Robinson	NK	Belle Vue, Manchester
19/06/1946	George Gregory Vs Mitchell Gill	NK	Belle Vue, Manchester
29/06/1946	George Gregory Vs Steven Novotny	NK	Belle Vue, Manchester
06/07/1946	George Gregory Vs Chich Knight	NK	Belle Vue, Manchester
17/07/1946	George Gregory Vs Chic Knight	NK	Belle Vue, Manchester
03/08/1946	George Gregory Vs Chic Knight	NK	Belle Vue, Manchester
10/08/1946	George Gregory Vs Bert Assirati	NK	Belle Vue, Manchester
13/09/1946	George Gregory Vs Charlie Green	NK	Hale
14/09/1946	George Gregory Vs Bill Garnon	NK	Belle Vue, Manchester
21/09/1946	George Gregory Vs Dave Armstrong	NK	Belle Vue, Manchester
23/09/1946	George Gregory Vs Dave Armstrong	Gregory won	Edinburgh, Scotland
09/10/1946	George Gregory Vs Bill Garnon	NK	Belle Vue, Manchester
19/10/1946	George Gregory Vs Chic Knight	NK	Belle Vue, Manchester
02/11/1946	George Gregory Vs Anaconda	NK	Belle Vue, Manchester
13/11/1946	George Gregory Vs Anaconda	NK	Belle Vue, Manchester
16/11/1946	George Gregory Vs Steve Casey	Steve won	Nottingham, England
16/11/1946	George Gregory Vd Black Angel	Gregory won	Newcastle, England
20/11/1946	George Gregory Vs Kiwi Kingston	NK	Belle Vue, Manchester
23/11/1946	George Gregory Vs Bill Garnon	NK	Belle Vue, Manchester

Date	Match	Result	Location
25/11/1946	George Gregory Vs Douglas Clark	Clark won	Edinburgh, Scotland
29/11/1946	George Gregory Vs Bill Garnon	NK	Hale
07/12/1946	George Gregory Vs Vic Hessell	NK	Belle Vue, Manchester
12/02/1947	George Gregory Vs Stanislaus Borienkow	NK	Belle Vue, Manchester
24/02/1947	George Gregory Vs Charlie Green	NK	Doncaster, South Yorkshire
22/03/1947	George Gregory Vs Chic Knight	NK	Belle Vue, Manchester
02/04/1947	George Gregory Vs Charlie Green	NK	Belle Vue, Manchester
12/04/1947	George Gregory Vs Kiwi Kingston	NK	Belle Vue, Manchester
23/04/1947	George Gregory Vs Dave Armstrong	NK	Belle Vue, Manchester
24/04/1947	George Gregory Vs Chic Knight	NK	Redruth, England
17/05/1947	George Gregory Vs Francis St Clair Gregory	NK	Belle Vue, Manchester
26/05/1947	George Gregory Vs Tony Baer	NK	Belle Vue, Manchester
05/06/1947	George Gregory Vs Sandy McLaren	NK	Redruth, England
11/06/1947	George Gregory Vs Sandy McLaren	NK	Belle Vue, Manchester
14/06/1947	George Gregory Vs Bill Benny	Gregory won	Newcastle, England
16/06/1947	George Gregory Vs Jim Foy	George Won	Edinburgh, Scotland
16/06/1947	George Gregory Vs Jim Foy	Gregory won	Edinburgh, Scotland
21/06/1947	George Gregory Vs Tony Mancelli	NK	Belle Vue, Manchester
09/07/1947	George Gregory Vs Pat O'Reilly	NK	Belle Vue, Manchester
26/07/1947	George Gregory Vs Francis St Clair Gregory	NK	Belle Vue, Manchester
30/07/1947	George Gregory Vs Chic Knight	NK	Belle Vue, Manchester
02/08/1947	George Gregory Vs Rex Gable	NK	Belle Vue, Manchester
13/08/1947	George Gregory Vs Clem Lawrence	NK	Belle Vue, Manchester
10/09/1947	George Gregory Vs Tony Mancelli	NK	Belle Vue, Manchester
19/09/1947	George Gregory Vs Chic Knight	NK	Hale, England
25/10/1947	George Gregory Vs Abdul the Turk	NK	Belle Vue, Manchester
27/10/1947	George Gregory Vs Rex Maxine	NK	Derby, England
07/11/1947	George Gregory Vs Ernie Baldwin	NK	Hale, England
15/11/1947	George Gregory Vs Ray St. Bernard	NK	Belle Vue, Manchester
26/11/1947	George Gregory Vs Phil Siki	NK	Belle Vue, Manchester
29/11/1947	George Gregory Vs Pat O'Reilly	NK	Belle Vue, Manchester
25/02/1948	George Gregory Vs Anaconda	NK	Belle Vue, Manchester
12/03/1948	George Gregory Vs Phil Siki	NK	Hale, England
10/04/1948	George Gregory Vs Mike Byrne	NK	Belle Vue, Manchester
20/04/1948	George Gregory Vs Dave Jones	NK	Aberdeen, Scotland
21/04/1948	George Gregory Vs Bill Garnon	NK	Belle Vue, Manchester
07/05/1948	George Gregory Vs Albert Van Der Auwera	NK	Hale, England
14/05/1948	George Gregory Vs Dave Armstrong	NK	Belle Vue, Manchester
09/06/1948	George Gregory Vs Anaconda	NK	Belle Vue, Manchester
23/06/1948	George Gregory Vs Francis St. Clair Gregory	NK	Belle Vue, Manchester
07/07/1948	George Gregory Vs Joe Fletcher	NK	Belle Vue, Manchester
13/07/1948	George Gregory Vs Farmers boy	Boy won, GGDQ	Aberdeen, Scotland
17/07/1948	George Gregory Vs Chic Elliott	NK	Belle Vue, Manchester
05/08/1948	George Gregory Vs Man Mountain	NK	Cheltensham, England
07/08/1948	George Gregory Vs Francis St Clair Gregory	NK	Belle Vue, Manchester

Date	Match	Result	Venue
25/08/1948	George Gregory Vs Anaconda	NK	Belle Vue, Manchester
15/09/1948	George Gregory Vs Alf Robinson	NK	Belle Vue, Manchester
17/09/1948	George Gregory Vs Kiwi Kingston	NK	Fleetwood, England
01/10/1948	George Gregory Vs Martin Bucht	NK	Fleetwood, England
02/10/1948	George Greogory Vs Fred Norman	NK	Belle Vue, Manchester
16/10/1948	George Gregory Vs Jim Burnett	NK	Belle Vue, Manchester
10/11/1948	George Gregory Vs Albert Van Der Auwera	NK	Belle Vue, Manchester
20/11/1948	George Gregory Vs Jim Burnett	NK	Belle Vue, Manchester
10/12/1948	George Gregory Vs Pat O'Reilly	NK	Hale, England
18/12/1948	George Gregory Vs Chic Elliott	NK	Belle Vue, Manchester
28/12/1948	George Gregory Vs Don Mendoza	George Won	Hamilton, Scotland
28/12/1948	George Gregory Vs Douglas Clark	Gregory won DGDQ	Aberdeen, Scotland
31/01/1949	George Greogory Vs Ted Fletcher	NK	Blackpool, England
21/02/1949	George Gregory Vs Kiwi Kingston	NK	Blackpool, England
23/02/1949	George Gregory Vs Dean Rockwell	NK	Newcastle, England
02/03/1949	George Gregory Vs Alf Robinson	NK	Belle Vue, Manchester
04/03/1949	George Gregory Vs Alf Robinson	NK	Hale, England
30/03/1949	George Gregory Vs Ernie Baldwin	NK	Belle Vue, Manchester
15/04/1949	George Gregory Vs Dave Armstrong	NK	Belle Vue, Manchester
11/06/1949	George Gregory Vs Farmers boy	NK	Belle Vue, Manchester
22/06/1949	George Gregory Vs Anaconda	NK	Belle Vue, Manchester
16/07/1949	George Gregory Vs Ron Jackson	Draw	Belle Vue, Manchester
30/07/1949	George Gregory Vs Farmers boy	NK	Belle Vue, Manchester
17/08/1949	George Gregory Vs Chic Knight	NK	Belle Vue, Manchester
31/08/1949	George Gregory Vs Chic Knight	NK	Belle Vue, Manchester
14/09/1949	George Gregory Vs Jim Burnett	NK	Belle Vue, Manchester
21/09/1949	George Gregory Vs Jim Andrews	NK	Blackpool, England
15/10/1949	George Gregory Vs Francis St Clair Gregory	NK	Belle Vue, Manchester
24/10/1949	George Gregory Vs Harry Pye	NK	Blackpool, England
05/11/1949	George Gregory Vs Vic Hessell	NK	Belle Vue, Manchester
21/11/1949	George Gregory Vs Bob McMasters	NK	Blackpool, England
07/12/1949	George Gregory Vs Leo Demetral	NK	Belle Vue, Manchester
25/02/1950	George Gregory Vs Alf Robinson	NK	Belle Vue, Manchester
08/04/1950	George Gregory Vs Jack Pye	Pye won	Belle Vue, Manchester
14/04/1950	George Gregory Vs Jim Burnett	NK	Rhyl, Wales
29/04/1950	George Gregory Vs Harry Pye	NK	Belle Vue, Manchester
20/05/1950	George Gregory Vs Rex Gable	NK	Belle Vue, Manchester
24/05/1950	George Gregory Vs Al Wilson	NK	Belle Vue, Manchester
29/05/1950	George Gregory Vs Anaconda	NK	Belle Vue, Manchester
01/07/1950	George Gregory Vs Harry Pye	NK	Belle Vue, Manchester
19/07/1950	George Gregory Vs Freddie Rex	NK	Belle Vue, Manchester
05/08/1950	George Gregory Vs Rex Gable	NK	Belle Vue, Manchester
12/08/1950	George Gregory Vs Alf Rawlings	NK	Belle Vue, Manchester
04/11/1950	George Gregory Vs Bill Benny	Gregory won	Belle Vue, Manchester
18/11/1950	George Gregory Vs Ken Davies	NK	Rhyl, Wales

Date	Match	Result	Venue
25/11/1950	George Gregory Vs Alf Robinson	George won	Manchester, England
29/11/1950	George Gregory Vs Ken Davies	NK	Belle Vue, Manchester
16/12/1950	George Gregory Vs Bob McMaster	George won	Manchester, England
30/12/1950	George Gregory Vs Dave Armstrong	George won	Manchester, England
20/01/1951	George Gregory Vs Alf Robinson	George won	Manchester, England
20/01/1951	George Gregory Vs Alf Robinson	George won	Manchester, England
17/02/1951	George Gregory Vs Ron Jackson	George won	Manchester, England
28/02/1951	George Gregory Vs Rene Bukovac	Gregory won	Belle Vue, Manchester
14/03/1951	George Gregory Vs Francis St Clair Gregory	NK	Belle Vue, Manchester
31/03/1951	George Gregory Vs Ken Davies	Gregory won	Belle Vue, Manchester
14/04/1951	George Gregory Vs Kiwi Kingston	George won	Manchester, England
05/05/1951	George Gregory Vs Emil Foy	Gregory won	Belle Vue, Manchester
11/08/1951	George Gregory Vs Bob McMasters	Gregory won	Belle Vue, Manchester
25/08/1951	George Gregory Vs Alf Robinson	George won	Manchester, England
08/10/1951	George Gregory Vs Sandy Orford	NK	Altrincham, England
14/11/1951	George Gregory Vs Dave Armstrong	Gregory won	Belle Vue, Manchester
01/12/1951	George Gregory Vs Bill Verna	Gregory won	Belle Vue, Manchester
23/02/1952	George Gregory Vs Alf Robinson	Gregory won	Belle Vue, Manchester
25/02/1952	Geroge Gregory Vs Emil Foy	NK	Altrincham, England
19/04/1952	George Gregory Vs Karel Istaz	Gregory won	Manchester
10/05/1952	George Gregory Vs Jack Pye	Gregory won	Belle Vue, Manchester
02/06/1952	George Gregory Vs Bill McDonald	NK	Belle Vue, Manchester
04/06/1952	George Gregory Vs Francis St Clair Gregory	NK	Belle Vue, Manchester
14/06/1952	George Gregory Vs Chic Knight	Gregory won	Belle Vue, Manchester
01/07/1952	George Gregory Vs Francis St Clair Gregory	Gregory won	Aberdeen, Scotland
02/07/1952	George Gregory Vs Tony Baer	Gregory won	Glasgow, Scotland
05/07/1952	George Gregory Vs Chic Knight	Gregory won	Belle Vue, Manchester
04/08/1952	George Gregory Vs Flash Ed Gordon	NK	Aberdeen, Scotland
23/09/1952	George Gregory Vs Kiwi Kingston	Gregory won	Aberdeen, Scotland
13/12/1952	George Gregory Vs Hassan Ali Bey	NK	Belle Vue, Manchester
20/06/1953	George Gregory Vs Karel Istaz	Gregory won	Manchester
13/07/1954	George Gregory Vs Ernie Baldwin	NK	Douglas, Isle of Man
20/07/1954	George Gregory Vs Ken Davies	NK	Douglas, Isle of Man
27/07/1954	George Gregory Vs The Ghoul	NK	Douglas, Isle of Man
31/07/1954	George Gregory Vs Charlie Scott	NK	Belle Vue, Manchester
14/08/1954	George Gregory Vs Karel Istaz	Istaz won	Belle Vue, Manchester
28/08/1954	George Gregory Vs Anaconda	NK	Belle Vue, Manchester
06/10/1954	George Gregory Vs Dominic Pye	NK	Belle Vue, Manchester
20/10/1954	George Gregory Vs Farmers Boy	NK	Belle Vue, Manchester
01/08/1955	George Gregory Vs Alf Robinson	NK	Belle Vue, Manchester

Karl Gotch

Date	Match	Outcome	Venue
10/03/1951	Karel Istaz Vs Bi Bill Benny	Karel won	Manchester, England
10/03/1951	Karel Istaz Vs Big Bell Benny	Istaz won	Manchester
17/03/1951	Karel Istaz Vs Alf Robinson	Karel won	Manchester, England
04/04/1951	Karel Istaz Vs Jack Pye	Istaz won	Manchester
07/04/1951	Karel Istaz Vs Dave Armstrong	Karel won	Manchester, England
07/04/1951	Karel Istaz Vs Dave Armstrong	Karel won	Manchester, England
07/04/1951	Karel Istaz Vs Dave Armstrong	Istaz won	Manchester
11/04/1951	Karel Istaz Vs Ernest Baldwin	NK	Manchester
20/04/1951	Karel Istaz Vs The Bat	The Bat won	Morecambe, Lancashire
04/05/1951	Karel Istaz Vs Dave Armstrong	Istaz won	Liverpool
05/05/1951	Karel Istaz Vs Vic Hesselle	Karel won	Manchester, England
05/05/1951	Karel Istaz Vs The Bat	NK	Levenshulme
12/05/1951	Karel Istaz Vs Sandy Orford	Karel won	Manchester, England
12/05/1951	Karel Istaz Vs Sandy Orford	Istaz won	Manchester
19/05/1951	Karel Istaz Vs Bob McMaster	Karel won	Manchester, England
19/05/1951	Karel Istaz Vs Bob McMasters	Istaz won	Manchester
23/05/1951	Karel Istaz Vs Ernie Kiwi Kingston	NK	Manchester
25/05/1951	Karel Istaz Vs Francis Gregory	Istaz won	Liverpool
28/05/1951	Karel Istaz Vs Dave Armstrong	Karel won	Edinburgh, Scotland
28/05/1951	Karel Istaz Vs Dave Armstrong	Istaz won	Edinburgh, Scotland
02/06/1951	Karel Istaz Vs Big Bill Benny	Karel won	Manchester, England
02/06/1951	Karel Istaz Vs Big Bill Benny	Istaz won	Manchester
31 Aug-1 Oct 1951	Karel Istaz Vs Jean Benoy	Karel won	Frankfurt, Germany
31 Aug-1 Oct 1951	Kare Istaz Vs Willi Bunge	Karel won	Frankfurt, Germany
31 Aug-1 Oct 1951	Karel Istaz Vs Erich Ecker	Karel won FL	Frankfurt, Germany
31 Aug-1 Oct 1951	Karel Istaz Vs Frank Hewitt	Karel won	Frankfurt, Germany
31 Aug-1 Oct 1951	Karel Istaz Vs Erich Koltschak	Karel won	Frankfurt, Germany
31 Aug-1 Oct 1951	Karel Istaz Vs Lado Kovarek	Karel won	Frankfurt, Germany
31 Aug-1 Oct 1951	Karel Istaz Vs Jean Prevost	Karel won	Frankfurt, Germany
31 Aug-1 Oct 1951	Karel Istaz Vs Hans Schwarz	Hans won	Frankfurt, Germany
31 Aug-1 Oct 1951	Karel Istaz Vs Josef Stofan	Karel won	Frankfurt, Germany
31 Aug-1 Oct 1951	Karel Istaz Vs Josef Vavra	Karel won F	Frankfurt, Germany
31 Aug-1 Oct 1951	Karel Istaz Vs Josef Stofan	Karel won	Frankfurt, Germany
31 Aug-1 Oct 1951	Karel Istaz Vs Josef Stofan	Karel won	Frankfurt, Germany
31 Aug-1 Oct 1951	Karel Istaz Vs Charles Ulsemar	Karel won	Frankfurt, Germany
21st May-8th Jul 1952	Karel Istaz Vs Bill Verna	Karel won	Berlin, Germany
07/04/1952	Karel Istaz Vs Dave Armstrong	Istaz won	Manchester

Date	Match	Result	Location
16/04/1952	Karel Istaz Vs Big Bill Benny	Karel won, BBB DQ	Manchester, England
16/04/1952	Karel Istaz Vs Big Bill Benny	Istaz won BBBDQ	Manchester
19/04/1952	Karel Istaz Vs George Gregory	George won	Manchester, England
19/04/1952	Karel Istaz Vs George Gregory	Gregory won	Manchester
05/05/1952	Karel Istaz Vs Vic Hesselle	Istaz won	Manchester
10/05/1952	Karel Istaz Vs Farmer's Boy	Karel won	Manchester, England
10/05/1952	Karel Istaz Vs The Farmer	Istaz won	Manchester
23/05/1952	Karel Istaz Vs Hubert Gensheimer	Istaz won	Berlin, Deutschland
26/05/1952	Karel Istaz Vs Erich Ecker	Istaz won EEDQ	Berlin, Deutschland
27/05/1952	Karel Istaz Vs Les Herberts	Istaz won	Berlin, Deutschland
28/05/1952	Karel Istaz Vs Josef Vavra	NC	Berlin, Deutschland
29/05/1952	Karel Istaz Vs Big Bill Verna	Istaz won	Berlin, Deutschland
01/06/1952	Karel Istaz Vs Paul BErger	NC	Berlin, Germany
01/06/1952	Karel Istaz Vs Paul Berger	NC Istaz inj left tournament	Berlin, Deutschland
19/01/1953	Karel Istaz Vs Dave Armstrong	Draw	Leeds, England
22/01/1953	Karel Istaz Vs Jack Pye	Jack won	Morecambe, Lancashire
21/02/1953	Karel Istaz Vs Tony Mancelli	Istaz won	Manchester
25/02/1953	Karel Istaz Vs Rex Gable	NK	Manchester
20/04/1953	Karel Istaz Vs Adolf Porizek	Istaz won	Hanover, Germany
21/04/1953	Karel Istaz Vs Ray Apollon	Istaz won	Hanover, Germany
22/04/1953	Karel Istaz Vs Erich Ecker	Istaz won	Hanover, Germany
23/04/1953	Karel Istaz Vs Emil Grosjean	Istaz won	Hanover, Germany
24/04/1953	Karel Istaz Vs Billy Joyce	Joyce won	Hanover, Germany
26/04/1953	Karel Istaz Vs Binder	Istaz won	Hanover, Germany
27/04/1953	Karel Istaz Vs Iska Khan Tiki	Tiki won	Hanover, Germany
29/04/1953	Karel Istaz Vs Sebastian Hering	Karel won	Munich, Germany
29/04/1953	Karel Istaz Vs Sebastian Hering	Istaz won	Munich, Germany
30/04/1953	Karel Istaz Vs Pedro Carnero	Karel won	Munich, Germany
30/04/1953	Karel Istaz Vs Pero Carnero	Istaz won	Munich, Germany
01/05/1953	Karel Istaz Vs JK 11	Karel won	Munich, Germany
01/05/1953	Karel Istaz Vs I.K.II	Istaz won	Munich, Germany
02/05/1953	Karel Istaz Vs Ivar Martinson	Karel won, IM DQ	Munich, Germany
02/05/1953	Karel Istaz Vs Yvar Martinson	Istaz won YMDQ	Munich, Germany
03/05/1953	Karel Istaz Vs Jimmy Dula	Jimmy won	Munich, Germany
03/05/1953	Karel Istaz Vs Jimmy Dula	Dula won	Munich, Germany
04/05/1953	Karel Istaz Vs Wolfgang Ehrl	Karel won	Munich, Germany
04/05/1953	Karel Istaz Vs Wolfgang Ehrl	Istaz won	Munich, Germany
05/05/1953	Karel Istaz Vs Erich Gottschalk	Karel won	Munich, Germany
05/05/1953	Karel Istaz Vs Erich Gottschalk	Istaz won	Munchen, Bayern, Deutschland
05/05/1953	Karel Istaz Vs Erich Gottschalk (F)	Istaz won	Munich, Germany
10/05/1953	Karel Istaz Vs King Kong Taverne	Karel won	Berlin, Germany
10/05/1953	Karel Istaz Vs King Kong Taverne	Istaz won	Berlin, Deutschland
10/05/1953	Karel Istaz Vs Francisco Tabola	Istaz won	Berlin, Deutschland

Date	Match	Result	Location
11/05/1953	Karel Istaz Vs Bilyl Virag	Istaz won	Berlin, Deutschland
11/05/1953	Karel Istaz Vs Billy Virag	Virag won	Berlin, Deutschland
13/05/1953	Karel Istaz Vs Salvatore Font	Karel won	Berlin, Germany
13/05/1953	Karel Istaz Vs Salvatore Font	Istaz won	Berlin, Deutschland
13/05/1953	Karel Istaz Vs Salvatore Font	Istaz won	Berlin, Deutschland
14/05/1953	Karel Istaz Vs Mico Selenkowitsch	Karel won	Berlin, Germany
14/05/1953	Karel Istaz Vs Nicola Selenkowitsch	Istaz won	Berlin, Deutschland
14/05/1953	Karel Istaz Vs Nicola Selenkowitsch	Istaz won	Berlin, Deutschland
15/05/1953	Karel Istaz Vs IK	IK won	Berlin, Deutschland
15/05/1953	Karel Istaz Vs I.K (Franz Krivinka)	I.K won	Berlin, Deutschland
21/05/1953	Kael Istaz Vs Wolfgang Ehrl	Karel won	Berlin, Germany
21/05/1953	Karel Istaz Vs Wolfgang Ehrl	Istaz won	Berlin, Deutschland
21/05/1953	Karel Istaz Vs Wolfgang Ehrl	Istaz won	Berlin, Deutschland
23/05/1953	Karel Istaz Vs Jimmy Dula	NK	Berlin, Germany
23/05/1953	Karel Istaz Vs Jimmy Dula	NK	Berlin, Deutschland
27/05/1953	Karel Istaz Vs Ray Hunter	Ray won	Berlin, Germany
27/05/1953	Karel Istaz Vs Ray Hunter	Hunter won	Berlin, Deutschland
27/05/1953	Karel Istaz Vs Ray Hunter	Hunter won	Berlin, Deutschland
28/05/1953	Karel Istaz Vs Josef Vavra	Josef won	Berlin, Germany
28/05/1953	Karel Istaz Vs Josef Vavra	Vavra won	Berlin, Deutschland
28/05/1953	Karel Istaz Vs Josef Vavra	Vavra won	Berlin, Deutschland
17/06/1953	Karel Istaz Vs Rex Gable	Istaz won	Manchester
20/06/1953	Karel Istaz Vs George Gregory	Gregory won	Manchester
31/07/1953	Karel Istaz Vs Pat O'Reilly	Istaz won	Liverpool
04/09/1953	Karel Istaz Vs Hassam Ali Bey	Karel won	Liverpool, England
05/09/1953	Karel Istaz Vs Jim Hussey	Jim won	Manchester, England
11/09/1953	Karel Istaz Vs Jack Pye	Jack won	Liverpool, England
19/09/1953	Karel Istaz Vs Vic Hesselle	Vic won	Manchester, England
14/11/1953	Karel Istaz Vs Ernie Kiwi Kingston	Istaz won	Manchester
1954	Carl Istaz Vs I.K	I.K won	Cologne
1954	Carl Istaz Vs Hans Dillinger	Istaz won	Cologne
1954	Carl Istaz Vs Adolf Porizek	Porizek won	Cologne
1954	Carl Istaz Vs Raphael Sampson	Istaz won	Cologne
04/03/1954	Karel Istaz Vs Fritz Muller	Draw	Berlin, Deutschland
05/03/1954	Karel Istaz Vs Rudi Schumacher	Istaz won	Berlin, Deutschland
08/03/1954	Karel Istaz Vs Lado Kovarek	Istaz won	Berlin, Deutschland
09/03/1954	Karel Istaz Vs Fritz Muller	Draw	Berlin, Deutschland
10/03/1954	Karel Istaz Vs Hermann Iffland	Draw	Berlin, Deutschland
12/03/1954	Karel Istaz Vs Sitting Ward	Draw	Berlin, Deutschland
15/03/1954	Karel Istaz Vs Herman Iffland	Iffland won	Berlin, Deutschland
21/03/1954	Karel Istaz Vs Paul Berger	Draw	Berlin, Deutschland
23/03/1954	Karel Istaz Vs Salvatore Font	Istaz won	Berlin, Deutschland
27/03/1954	Karel Istaz Vs Sitting Ward	Ward won	Berlin, Deutschland
29/03/1954	Karel Istaz Vs Harry Pinetzki	Draw	Berlin, Deutschland
30/03/1954	Karel Istaz Vs Erich Ecker	Istaz won	Berlin, Deutschland
31/03/1954	Karel Istaz Vs Nicolai Zigulinoff	Zigulinoff	Berlin, Deutschland

		won	
01/04/1954	Karel Istaz Vs Oskar Muller	Istaz won	Berlin, Deutschland
02/04/1954	Karel Istaz Vs Martyn Chenok	Istaz won	Berlin, Deutschland
03/04/1954	Karel Istaz Vs Harry Pinetzki	Draw	Berlin, Deutschland
04/04/1954	Karel Istaz Vs Isidor Jakobson	Istaz won	Berlin, Deutschland
05/04/1954	Karel Istaz Vs Herman Iffland	Draw	Berlin, Deutschland
06/04/1954	Karel Istaz Vs Nico Selenkowitsch	Istaz won	Berlin, Deutschland
07/04/1954	Karel Istaz Vs Richard Grupe	Istaz won	Berlin, Deutschland
08/04/1954	Karel Istaz Vs Harry Pinetzki	Istaz won	Berlin, Deutschland
09/04/1954	Karel Istaz Vs Juan Salessa	Istaz won	Berlin, Deutschland
10/04/1954	Karel Istaz Vs Samuel Popescu	Popescu won	Berlin, Deutschland
17/04/1954	Karel Istaz Vs Andre Bollet	Karel won	Karlsruhe, Germany
17/04/1954	Karel Istaz Vs Andre Bollet	Istaz won	Karlsruhe, Germany
18/04/1954	Karel Istaz Vs Antonio Litta	Karel won	Karlsruhe, Germany
18/04/1954	Karel Istaz Vs Antonio Litta	Istaz won	Karlsruhe, Germany
19/04/1954	Karel Istaz Vs Josef Miazio	Karel won	Karlsruhe, Germany
19/04/1954	Karel Istaz Vs Josef Miazio	Istaz won	Karlsruhe, Germany
20/04/1954	Karel Istaz Vs Rene Lasartesse	Karel won	Karlsruhe, Germany
20/04/1954	Karel Istaz Vs Rene Lasartesse	Istaz won	Karlsruhe, Germany
21/04/1954	Karel Istaz Vs Gedeon Gida	NC	Karlsruhe, Germany
21/04/1954	Karel Istaz Vs Gedeon Gida	NC	Karlsruhe, Germany
22/04/1954	Karel Istaz Vs Herbert Audersch	NC	Karlsruhe, Germany
22/04/1954	Karel Istaz Vs Herbert Audersch	NC	Karlsruhe, Germany
23/04/1954	Karel Istaz Vs Johnny Morand	Karel won	Karlsruhe, Germany
23/04/1954	Karel Istaz Vs Jean Morandi	Istaz won	Karlsruhe, Germany
24/04/1954	Karel Istaz Vs Black Panther	Karel won	Karlsruhe, Germany
24/04/1954	Karel Istaz Vs Black Panther	Istaz won	Karlsruhe, Germany
25/04/1954	Karel Istaz Vs Hermann Iffland	Karel won	Karlsruhe, Germany
25/04/1954	Karel Istaz Vs Herman Iffland	Istaz won	Karlsruhe, Germany
26/04/1954	Karel Istaz Vs Rene Lasartesse	NC	Karlsruhe, Germany
26/04/1954	Karel Istaz Vs Rene Lasartesse	NC	Karlsruhe, Germany
27/04/1954	Karel Istaz Vs Gaby Calderon	Karel won	Karlsruhe, Germany
27/04/1954	Karel Istaz Vs Gabriel Calderon	Istaz won	Karlsruhe, Germany
28/04/1954	Karel Istaz Vs Mr. M	Karel won	Karlsruhe, Germany
28/04/1954	Karel Istac Vs Francois Miquet	Istaz won	Karlsruhe, Germany
29/04/1954	Karel Istaz Vs Gedeon Gida	Gedeon won	Karlsruhe, Germany
29/04/1954	Karel Istaz Vs Gedeon Gida	Gida won	Karlsruhe, Germany
30/04/1954	Karel Istaz Vs Mathias Rosges	Karel won	Karlsruhe, Germany
30/04/1954	Karel Istaz Vs Mathias Rosges	Istaz won	Karlsruhe, Germany
1 May-31 Jul 1954	Karel Istaz Vs Black Panther	Karel won	Hamburg, Germany
1 May-31 Jul 1954	Karel Istaz Vs Kun Atscha	Karel won	Hamburg, Germany
1 May-31 Jul 1954	Karel Istaz Vs Herbert Westphal	Karel won	Hamburg, Germany
1 May-31 Jul 1954	Karel Istaz Vs Paul Berger	Karel won	Hamburg, Germany
1 May-31 Jul 1954	Karel Istaz Vs Maz DeGohm	Karel won	Hamburg, Germany

Date	Match	Result	Location
1 May-31 Jul 1954	Karel Istaz Vs Der Wurger	Der won	Hamburg, Germany
1 May-31 Jul 1954	Karel Istaz Vs Arabet Said	Karel won	Hamburg, Germany
1 May-31 Jul 1954	Karel Istaz Vs Ici	Ici won	Hamburg, Germany
1 May-31 Jul 1954	Karel Istaz Vs Gedeon Gida	Gedeon won	Hamburg, Germany
1 May-31 Jul 1954	Karel Istaz Vs Pierre Martine	Pierre won	Hamburg, Germany
1 May-31 Jul 1954	Karel Istaz Vs Leonhard Marciniak	Karel won	Hamburg, Germany
1 May-31 Jul 1954	Karel Istaz Vs Henri Bury	Draw	Hamburg, Germany
1 May-31 Jul 1954	Karel Istaz Vs Manuel Grosso	Karel won	Hamburg, Germany
1 May-31 Jul 1954	Karel Istaz Vs Jimmy Dula	Draw	Hamburg, Germany
1 May-31 Jul 1954	Karel Istaz Vs Conrad Fey	Karel won	Hamburg, Germany
1 May-31 Jul 1954	Karel Istaz Vs Dr. Primo Vitos	Dr. won	Hamburg, Germany
1 May-31 Jul 1954	Karel Istaz Vs Manuel Grosso	Karel won	Hamburg, Germany
16/05/1954	Karel Istaz Vs Leonhard Marciniak	Istaz won	Hamburg, Germany
17/05/1954	Karel Istaz Vs Paul Berger	Draw	Hamburg, Germany
18/05/1954	Karel Istaz Vs Gedeon Gida	Draw	Hamburg, Germany
19/05/1954	Karel Istaz Vs Arabet Said	Draw	Hamburg, Germany
21/05/1954	Karel Istaz Vs Hans Waldherr	Waldherr won	Hamburg, Germany
22/05/1954	Karel Istaz Vs Manuel Grosso	Istaz won	Hamburg, Germany
23/05/1954	Karel Istaz Vs Herbert Westphal	Istaz won	Hamburg, Germany
24/05/1954	Karel Istaz Vs Pierre Martinec	Draw	Hamburg, Germany
25/05/1954	Karel Istaz Vs Henri Bury	Draw	Hamburg, Germany
26/05/1954	Karel Istaz Vs Arabet Said	Istaz won	Hamburg, Germany
27/05/1954	Karel Istaz Vs Paul Berger	Istaz won	Hamburg, Germany
28/05/1954	Karel Istaz Vs Jimmy Dula	Draw	Hamburg, Germany
29/05/1954	Karel Istaz Vs Max Degohm	Draw	Hamburg, Germany
30/05/1954	Karel Istaz Vs Monsieur Ici	ICI won	Hamburg, Germany
31/05/1954	Karel Istaz Vs Pierre Martinec	Martinec won	Hamburg, Germany
12-19/07/1954	Karel Istaz Vs Hans Dillinger	Karel won	Cologne, Germany
12-19/07/1954	Karel Istaz Vs Jan Krivinska	JK won	Cologne, Germany
12-19/07/1954	Karel Istaz Vs Adolf Poricek	Adolf won	Cologne, Germany
12-19/07/1954	Karel Istaz Vs Raphael Sampson	Raphael won	Cologne, Germany
12-19/07/1954	Karel Istaz Vs Raphael Sampson	Karel won	Cologne, Germany
25/08/1954	Karel Istaz Vs Hans Lerche	Karel won	Lubeck, Germany
25/08/1954	Karel Istaz Vs Hans Lerche	Istaz won	Lubeck, Germany
26/08/1954	Karel Istaz Vs Black Panther	Karel won	Lubeck, Germany
26/08/1954	Karel Istaz Vs Black Panther	Istaz won	Lubeck, Germany
27/08/1954	Karel Istaz Vs Lloyd Barnett	Karel won	Lubeck, Germany
27/08/1954	Karel Istaz Vs Lloyd Barnett	Istaz won	Lubeck, Germany
28/08/1954	Karel Istaz Vs Golden Apollon	Karel won	Lubeck, Germany
28/08/1954	Karel Istaz Vs Ray Apollon	Istaz won	Lubeck, Germany

Date	Match	Result	Location
29/08/1954	Karel Istaz Vs Mathieu Rosges	Karel won	Lubeck, Germany
29/08/1954	Karel Istaz Vs Mathias Rosges	Istaz won	Lubeck, Germany
30/08/1954	Karel Istaz Vs Georg Blemenschutz	Georg won	Lubeck, Germany
30/08/1954	Karel Istaz Vs George Blemenschutz	Blemenschutz won	Lubeck, Germany
31/08/1954	Karel Istaz Vs Paul Kusch	Karel won	Lubeck, Germany
31/08/1954	Karel Istaz Vs Paul Kusch	Istaz won	Lubeck, Germany
01/09/1954	Karel Istaz Vs Gedeon Gida	Gedeon won	Lubeck, Germany
01/09/1954	Karel Istaz Vs Gedeon Gida (F)	Gida won	Lubeck, Germany
02/09/1954	Karel Istaz Vs Jules Delmee	Karel won	Hamburg, Germany
02/09/1954	Karel Istaz Vs Jules Delme	Istaz won	Hamburg, Germany
04/09/1954	Karel Istaz Vs Gedeon Gida	draw	Hamburg, Germany
04/09/1954	Karel Istaz Vs Gedeon Gida	Draw	Hamburg, Germany
05/09/1954	Karel Istaz Vs Black Panther	Karel won	Hamburg, Germany
05/09/1954	Karel Istaz Vs Black Panther	Istaz won	Hamburg, Germany
06/09/1954	Karel Istaz Vs Lloyd Barnett	Karel won	Hamburg, Germany
06/09/1954	Karel Istaz Vs Lloyd Barnett	Istaz won	Hamburg, Germany
07/09/1954	Karel Istaz Vs Georg Blemenschutz	Draw	Hamburg, Germany
07/09/1954	Karel Istaz Vs Georg Blemenschutz	Draw	Hamburg, Germany
08/09/1954	Karel Istaz Vs Paul Kusch	draw	Hamburg, Germany
08/09/1954	Karel Istaz Vs Paul kusch	Draw	Hamburg, Germany
10/09/1954	Karel Istaz Vs Franz Orlick	draw	Hamburg, Germany
10/09/1954	Karel Istaz Vs Franz Orlik	Draw	Hamburg, Germany
11/09/1954	Karel Istaz Vs Georg Blemenschutz	Georg won	Hamburg, Germany
11/09/1954	Karel Istaz Vs Georg Blemenschutz	Blemenschutz won	Hamburg, Germany
12/09/1954	Karel Istaz Vs Golden Apollon	Draw	Hamburg, Germany
12/09/1954	Karel Istaz Vs Ray Apollon	Draw	Hamburg, Germany
13/09/1954	Karel Istaz Vs Al Cabrol	NC, KI Inj	Hamburg, Germany
13/09/1954	Karel Istaz Vs Al Cabrol	NC Istaz inj	Hamburg, Germany
30/10/1954	Karel Istaz Vs Henri Bury	Istaz won	Liege, Belgium
01/12/1954	Karel Istaz Vs Bill Benny	Karel won	Manchester, England
01/12/1954	Karel Istaz Vs Billy Joyce	Billy won	Manchester, England
15/12/1954	Karel Istaz Vs Franz Koller	NK	Liege, Belgium
12/03/1955	Karel Istaz Vs Koolman	NK	Verviers, Belgium
03/05/1955	Karel Istaz Vs Hermann Iffland	NK	Antwerp, Belgium
08/05/1955	Karel Istaz Vs Lino DiSanto	Istaz won	Krefeld, Germany
09/05/1955	Karel Istaz Vs Leo Marciniak	Draw	Krefeld, Germany
10/05/1955	Karel Istaz Vs Wilson Kohlbrecher	Draw	Krefeld, Germany
11/05/1955	Karel Istaz Vs Antonio Litta	Istaz won	Krefeld, Germany
12/05/1955	Karel Istaz Vs Hermann Iffland	Draw	Krefeld, Germany
12/05/1955	Karel Istaz Vs Hermann Iffland	Draw	Krefeld, Germany
13/05/1955	Karel Istaz Vs Roger Guettier	Karel won	Krefeld, Germany
13/05/1955	Karel Istaz Vs Roger Guettier	Istaz won	Krefeld, Germany
14/05/1955	Karel Istaz Vs Pat Curry	Draw	Krefeld, Germany
14/05/1955	Karel Istaz Vs Pat Curry	Draw	Krefeld, Germany
15/05/1955	Karel Istaz Vs Ray Apollon	Draw	Krefeld, Germany

Date	Match	Result	Location
15/05/1955	Karel Istaz Vs Ray Apollon	Draw	Krefeld, Germany
16/05/1955	Karel Istaz Vs Gedeon Gida	Draw	Krefeld, Germany
16/05/1955	Karel Istaz Vs Gedeon Gida	Draw	Krefeld, Germany
17/05/1955	Karel Istaz Vs Ray Apollon	NC, Ray injured	Krefeld, Germany
17/05/1955	Karel Istaz Vs Ray Apollon	NC	Krefeld, Germany
18/05/1955	Karel Istaz Vs George Blemenschutz	Draw	Krefeld, Germany
18/05/1955	Karel Istaz Vs Georg Blemenschutz	Draw	Krefeld, Germany
19/05/1955	Karel Istaz Vs Leon Marciniak	Karel won	Krefeld, Germany
19/05/1955	Karel Istaz Vs Leo Marciniak	Istaz won	Krefeld, Germany
20/05/1955	Karel Istaz Vs Franz Orlick	Karel won	Krefeld, Germany
20/05/1955	Karel Istaz Vs Franz Orlik	Istaz won	Krefeld, Germany
21/05/1955	Karel Istaz Vs Ray Apollon	Karel won	Krefeld, Germany
21/05/1955	Karel Istaz Vs Ray Apollon	Istaz won	Krefeld, Germany
22/05/1955	Karel Istaz Vs Wilson Kohlbrecher	NC, wilson inj	Krefeld, Germany
22/05/1955	Karel Istaz Vs Wilson Kohlbrecher	NC	Krefeld, Germany
24/05/1955	Karel Istaz Vs Jacques Deen	Karel won	Krefeld, Germany
24/05/1955	Karel Istaz Vs Jacques Deen	Istaz won	Krefeld, Germany
25/05/1955	Karel Istaz Vs Hermann Iffland	Karel won	Krefeld, Germany
25/05/1955	Karel Istaz Vs Herman Iffland	Istaz won	Krefeld, Germany
26/05/1955	Karel Istaz Vs Pat Curry	Pat won	Krefeld, Germany
26/05/1955	Karel Istaz Vs Pat Curry	Curry won	Krefeld, Germany
27/05/1955	Karel Istaz Vs Wilson Kohlbrecher	Karel won	Krefeld, Germany
27/05/1955	Karel Istaz Vs Wilson Kohlbrecher	Istaz won	Krefeld, Germany
28/05/1955	Karel Istaz Vs Gedeon Gida	Karel won	Krefeld, Germany
28/05/1955	Karel Istaz Vs Gedeon Gida	Istaz won	Krefeld, Germany
30/05/1955	Karel Istaz Vs Jose Calderon	Draw	Krefeld, Germany
30/05/1955	Karel Istaz Vs Jose Calderon	Draw	Krefeld, Germany
01/06/1955	Karel Istaz Vs Black Green	Karel won	Krefeld, Germany
01/06/1955	Karel Istaz Vs Black Green	Istaz won	Krefeld, Germany
02/06/1955	Karel Istaz Vs Michael Ujevic	Karel won	Krefeld, Germany
02/06/1955	Karel Istaz Vs Michael Ujevic	Istaz won	Krefeld, Germany
03/06/1955	Karel Istaz Vs Roman Waniek	Karel won	Krefeld, Germany
03/06/1955	Karel istaz Vs Roman Waniek	Istaz won	Krefeld, Germany
04/06/1955	Karel Istaz Vs George Blemenschutz	Karel won, GB DQ	Krefeld, Germany
04/06/1955	Karel Istaz Vs Georg Blemenschutz	Istaz won	Krefeld, Germany
05/06/1955	Karel Istaz Vs Rene Lasartesse	Karel won	Krefeld, Germany
05/06/1955	Karel Istaz Vs Rene Lasartesse	Istaz won	Krefeld, Germany
06/06/1955	Karel Istaz Vs Gedeon Gida	Gedeon won	Krefeld, Germany
06/06/1955	Karel Istaz Vs Gedeon Gida (F)	Gida won	Krefeld, Germany
8-21/06/1955	Karel Istaz Vs Ray Apollon	Karel won	Monchen-Gladbach, Germany
8-21/06/1955	Karel Istaz Vs George Blemenschutz	Karel won	Monchen-Gladbach, Germany
8-21/06/1955	Karel Istaz Vs Jose Calderon	Karel won	Monchen-Gladbach, Germany
8-21/06/1955	Karel Istaz Vs Andre Coutoula	Karel won	Monchen-Gladbach, Germany
8-	Karel Istaz Vs Pat Curry	Karel won	Monchen-Gladbach, Germany

Date	Match	Result	Location
21/06/1955 8-21/06/1955	Karel Istaz Vs Gideon Gida	Gideon won	Monchen-Gladbach, Germany
8-21/06/1955	Karel Istaz Vs Hermann Iffland	Karel won	Monchen-Gladbach, Germany
8-21/06/1955	Karel Istaz Vs Leonhard Marciniak	Karel won	Monchen-Gladbach, Germany
21/06/1955	Karel Istaz Vs Hermann Iffland (F)	Istaz won	Monchengladbach, Germany
09/07/1955	Karel Istaz Vs Leonhard Marciniak	Istaz won	Vienna
11/07/1955	Karel Istaz Vs Adolf Porizek	Draw	Vienna
12/07/1955	Karel Istaz Vs Michael Ujevic	Draw	Vienna
13/07/1955	Karel Istaz Vs Herbert Westphal	Karel won	Vienna, Austria
13/07/1955	Karel Istaz Vs Herbert Westphal	Istaz won	Vienna
16/07/1955	Karel Istaz Vs Gedeon Gida	Draw	Vienna, Austria
16/07/1955	Karel Istaz Vs Gedeon Gida	Draw	Vienna
17/07/1955	Karel Istaz Vs Black Green	Draw	Vienna, Austria
17/07/1955	Karel Istaz Vs Black Green	Draw	Vienna
18/07/1955	Karel Istaz Vs Michael Ujevic	Karel won, MU DQ	Vienna, Austria
18/07/1955	Karel Istaz Vs Michael Ujevic	Istaz won	Vienna
21/07/1955	Karel Istaz Vs Hans Lerche	Karel won	Vienna, Austria
21/07/1955	Karel Istaz Vs Hans Lerche	Istaz won	Vienna
07/09/1955	Karel Istaz Vs Roger Guettier	Draw	Krefeld, Germany
09/02/1956	Karel Istaz Vs Jose Arroyo	NK	Antwerp, Belgium
20/03/1956	Karel Istaz Vs Robert Duranton	Istaz won	Antwerp, Belgium
02/05/1956	Karel Istaz Vs Wilson Kohlbrecher	Istaz won	Brussells, Belgium
15/11/1956	Karel Istaz Vs Gustav Meulenaere	Karel won	Ghent, Belgium
29/11/1956	Karel Istaz Vs Bob Martin	Karel won	Ghent, Belgium
29/11/1956	Karel Istaz Vs Bob Martin	Istaz won	Gent, Belgium
06/12/1956	Karel Istaz Vs Bob Martin	Karel won	Ghent, Belgium
06/12/1956	Karel Istaz Vs Bob Martin	Istaz won	Gent, Belgium
26/05/1959	Karel Istaz Vs Raoul Guettier	Istaz won	Antwerp, Belgium
07/07/1960	Karol Krauser Vs Arnold Skoaland	Karol won	Washington DC
21/07/1960	Karol Krauser Vs Marvin Mercer	Karol won	Washington DC
18/08/1960	Karol Krauser Vs Angelo Savoldi	Karol won	Washington DC
19/08/1960	Karl Krauser Vs Moose Cholak	Gotch won	Comiskey Park, Chicago. Illinois
25/08/1960	Karol Krauser Vs Eddie Graham	Karol won	Washington DC
01/09/1960	Karol Krauser Vs Buddy Rosen	Karol won	Washington DC
20/09/1960	Karol Krauser Vs Oyama Kato	Karol won	Dayton, Ohio
27/09/1960	Karol Krauser & Don Eagle & Golden Superman Vs Johnny Barend & Magnificent Maurice & The Phantom	Karol et al won	Dayton, Ohio
03/10/1960	Karol Krauser Vs Killer Ted Christy	Karol won	Dayton, Ohio
11/10/1960	Karol Krauser Vs Donn Lewin	Karol won, DL DQ	Dayton, Ohio
15/10/1960	Karol Krauser Vs Magnificent Maurice	Karol won	Cincinnatti, Ohio
18/10/1960	Karol Krauser&Billy Darnell&Frankie Talaber Vs Johnny Barend & Donn Levin& Magnificent Maurice	Karol et al won	Dayton, Ohio
01/11/1960	Karol Krauser Vs Tony Cosenza	Karol won	Long Island City
12/11/1960	Karol Krauser &Pancho Villa Vs Billy Cox & Big Bill Miller	Karol et al won	Columbus, Ohio
12/11/1960	Karol Krauser Vs Big Bill Miller	Karol won	Columbus, Ohio

Date	Match	Result	Location
15/11/1960	Karol Krauser Vs Al Smith	Karol won	Long Island City
03/12/1960	Karol Krauser Vs Bill Miller	Draw	Columbus, Ohio
04/12/1960	Karol Krauser Vs Donn Lewin	Karol won	Marion, Ohio
06/12/1960	Karel Krauser Vs Happy Humphrey	Karol won	Dayton, Ohio
10/12/1960	Karol Krauser Vs Fritz Von Goering	Karol won	Cincinnatti, Ohio
13/12/1960	Karol Krauser Vs Billy Darnell	Draw	Dayton, Ohio
17/12/1960	Karol Krauser Vs Bill Miller	Karol won	Columbus, Ohio
27/12/1960	Karol Krauser Vs The Shadow	Karol won	Dayton, Ohio
30/12/1960	Karol Krauser&Gene Stanlee& Frank Talaber Vs Johnny Barend & Magnificent Maurice & Fritz Von Goering	Karol et al won	Cincinnatti, Ohio
29/08/1961	Karl Krauser Vs Tiny Mills	Gotch won	Minneapolis, Minnesota
05/09/1961	Karl Krauser Vs Tiny Mills	Gotch won	Minneapolis, Minnesota
12/09/1961	Karl Krauser Vs Bill Wright	Gotch won	Minneapolis, Minnesota
13/09/1961	Karl Krauser & Wilbur Snyder Vs Bob Geigel & Hard Boiled Haggerty	Geigel et al won	Fargo, North Dakota
15/09/1961	Karl Krauser & Verne Gagne Vs Gene Kiniski & Hard Boiled Haggerty	Geigel et al won	Winnipeg, Manitoba, Canada
19/09/1961	Karl Krauser Vs Emil Dusek	Gotch won	Minneapolis, Minnesota
27/09/1961	Karl Krauser Vs Frank Marconi	Gotch won	Minneapolis, Minnesota
27/09/1961	Karl Krauser Vs Bob Geigel	Gotch won by DQ	Fargo, North Dakota
04/10/1961	Karl Krauser Vs Juan Hernandez	Gotch won	Mankato, Minnesota
10/10/1961	Karl Krauser Vs Maurice LaPointe	Gotch won	Minneapolis, Minnesota
11/10/1961	Karl Krauser Vs Bob Geigel	Draw	Fargo, North Dakota
13/10/1961	Karl Krauser & Dale Lewis Vs Bob Geigel & Otto Von Krupp	Gotch et al won	Winnipeg, Manitoba, Canada
16/10/1961	Karl Krauser Vs Hard Boiled Haggerty	Hard boiled won	Mankato, Minnesota
17/10/1961	Karl Krauser Vs Ernie Dusek	Gotch won	Minneapolis, Minnesota
21/10/1961	Karl Krauser Vs Hard Boiled Haggerty	Gotch won by DQ	St. Paul, Minnesota
27/10/1961	Karl Krauser Vs Mr. M	Mr. M won	Civic Auditorium, Winnipeg, Manitoba, Canada
30/10/1961	Karl Krauser Vs Hard Boiled Haggerty	NC	Mankato, Minnesota
31/10/1961	Karl Krauser Vs Mr. M	Mr. M won	Minneapolis, Minnesota
02/11/1961	Karl Krauser Vs Bob Geigel	Geigel won	Grand Forks, North Dakota
04/11/1961	Karl Krauser Vs Hard Boiled Haggerty	Draw	St. Paul, Minnesota
07/11/1961	Karl Krauser Vs Mr. M	Mr. M won	Minneapolis, Minnesota
11/11/1961	Karl Krauser Vs Bob Geigel	Gotch won	St. Paul, Minnesota
11/11/1961	Karl Krauser & Tex McKenzie Vs Bob Geigel & Hard Boiled Haggerty	Geigel et al won	St. Paul, Minnesota
13/11/1961	Karl Krauser Vs Hard Boiled Haggerty	Gotch won via DQ	Mankato, Minnesota
14/11/1961	Karl Krauser Vs Harry Sampson	Gotch won	Auditorium, Minneapolis, Minnesota
15/11/1961	Karl Krauser Vs Dale Lewis	Gotch won	Fargo, North Dakota
16/11/1961	Karl Krauser & Harry Sampson Vs Larry Hennig & Otto Von Krupp	NC	Grand Forks, North Dakota
16/11/1961	Karl Krauser Vs Otto Von Krupp	Gotch won	Grand Forks, North Dakota
17/11/1961	Karl Krauser Vs Mr. M	Mr. M won	Civic Auditorium, Winnipeg, Manitoba, Canada
22/11/1961	Karl Krauser Vs Otto Von Krupp	Krupp won	Fargo, North Dakota
27/11/1961	Karl Krauser Vs Dale Lewis	Gotch won	Mankato, Minnesota
30/11/1961	Karl Krauser Vs Larry Hennig	Gotch won	Grand Forks, North Dakota
01/12/1961	Karl Gotch Vs Bob Geigel	Gotch won	Civic Auditorium, Winnipeg,

Date	Match	Result	Location
02/12/1961	Karl Krauser Vs Mr. M	Draw	St Paul, Minnesota, USA
05/12/1961	Karl Krauser Vs Mr. M	Mr. M Won	Minneapolis, Minnesota
08/12/1961	Karl Krauser Vs Mr. M	Mr. M won	Civic Auditorium, Winnipeg, Manitoba, Canada
09/12/1961	Karl Krauser & Larry Hennig Vs Bob Geigel & Mr. M	Mr. M et al won	St Paul, Minnesota, USA
24/03/1962	Karl Gotch Vs Don Whittler	Gotch won	National Guard Armory, Lakeland, Florida
29/03/1962	Karl Gotch Vs Hans Schmidt	Gotch won	Jacksonville, Florida
02/09/1963	Karl Gotch Vs Lou Thesz	Draw	Columbus, Ohio
25/11/1963	Karl Gotch Vs Danny Plechas	Gotch won	St. Louis, Missouri
27/12/1963	Karl Gotch Vs Lou Thesz	Thesz won	St Louis, Missouri
18/01/1964	Karl Gotch Vs Lou Thesz	Draw	Columbus, Ohio
18/04/1964	Karl Gotch Vs Lou Thesz	Draw	Cincinnatti, Ohio
02/05/1964	Karl Gotch Vs Lou Thesz	Draw	Detroit, Michigan
12/05/1964	Karl Gotch Vs Bill Miller	Gotch won	Tydall Armory, Indianopolis, Indiana
18/08/1964	Karl Gotch Vs Lou Thesz	Thesz won	Tampa, Florida
18/08/1964	Karl Gotch Vs Lou Thesz	Thesz won	Tampa, Florida
07/09/1964	Karl Gotch Vs Lou Thesz	Thesz won	NK
23/11/1964	Karl Gotch Vs Lou Thesz	Draw	Vancouver, British Columbia
24/04/1965	Karl Gotch & Whipper Billy Watson Vs Professor Hiro & the Beast	Gotch et al won	Maple Leaf Gardens, Toronto, Ontario
22/12/1965	Karl Gotch Vs Joe Scarpa	Draw	Honolulu, Hawaii
16/05/1966	Karl Gotch & alex Medina Vs Henry Von Stroheim & kurt Von Stroheim	NK	Park Center, Charlotte, North Carolina
21/09/1966	Karl Gotch Vs Kongozan	Draw	Honlulu International Center, Honolulu, Hawaii
28/09/1966	Karl Gotch Vs Beauregarde	Gotch won	Civic Auditorium, Honolulu, Hawaii
05/10/1966	Karl Gotch & Billy White Wolf Vs Beauregarde & Ripper Collins	Gotch et al won	Civic Auditorium, Honolulu, Hawaii
12/10/1966	Karl Gotch & The Mongolian Stomper Vs Johnny Barend & Mighty Atlas	Atlas et al won	Civic Auditorium, Honolulu, Hawaii
19/10/1966	Karl Gotch & Billy White Wolf Vs Beauregarde & Tarzan Tyler	Draw	Honlulu International Center, Honolulu, Hawaii
26/10/1966	Karl Gotch Vs Lou Newman	Draw	Civic Auditorium, Honolulu, Hawaii
02/11/1966	Karl Gotch Vs Billy White Wolf	Draw	Civic Auditorium, Honolulu, Hawaii
09/11/1966	Karl Gotch Vs Mike Paidousis	Draw	Civic Auditorium, Honolulu, Hawaii
16/11/1966	Karl Gotch Vs The Mighty Atlas	Gotch won	Civic Auditorium, Honolulu, Hawaii
23/11/1966	Karl Gotch Vs Ripper Collins	Collins won	Civic Auditorium, Honolulu, Hawaii
23/11/1966	Karl Krauser Vs Maurice LaPointe	Gotch won	Minneapolis, Minnesota
25/11/1966	Karl Krauser Vs Maurice LaPointe	Gotch won	St Paul, Minnesota, USA
30/11/1966	Karl Gotch Vs Sonny Myers	Gotch won	Civic Auditorium, Honolulu, Hawaii
07/12/1966	Karl Gotch & Jim Hady & Billy White Wolf Vs Johnny Barend, Ripper Collins & Skull Murphy	Gotch et al won via DQ	Civic Auditorium, Honolulu, Hawaii
14/12/1966	Karl Gotch & Pampero Firpo Vs Beauregarde & Mighty Atlas	Gotch et al won	Civic Auditorium, Honolulu, Hawaii
21/12/1966	Karl Gotch Vs Johnny Barend	Barend won	Civic Auditorium, Honolulu, Hawaii
25/12/1966	Karl Gotch Vs Tarzan Tyler	Draw	Honlulu International Center, Honolulu, Hawaii
17/06/1967	Karl Gotch Vs Paul Diamond	NK	San Bernardino Arena

Date	Match	Result	Venue
24/06/1967	Karl Gotch & Ron Romano Vs Nick Buckwinkle & Ricki Romero	NK	NK
27/06/1967	Karl Gotch & Mike Dibiase Vs Riki Romero & Nick Buckwinkle	Gotch et al won	Municipal Auditorium
08/07/1967	Karl Gotch & Mike Dibiase Vs Vicxtor Rivera & Nicky Bockwinkle	NK	San Bernardino Arena
11/07/1967	Karl Gotch & Mike Dibiase Vs Kintaro Oki & Mr. Moto	NK	Municipal Auditorium
08/08/1967	Karl Gotch Vs Mark Lewin	Lewin wom	Municipal Auditorium
12/08/1967	Karl Gotch Vs Mark Lewin	Draw	NK
09/09/1967	Karl Gtoch Vs Hard Boiled Haggerty	Draw	San Bernardino Arena
17/09/1967	Karl Gotch Vs Ricki Romero	NK	San Bernardino Arena
19/12/1967	Karl Gotch Vs Gene Kiniski	NK	Grensboro Coliseum North Carolina,
25/08/1971	Karl Gotch & Mike Pappas Vs Beautiful Bobby & Jimmy Valiant	Valiant et al won	Freeport Stadium, Long Island, New York
30/08/1971	Karl Gotch Vs The Black Demon	Gotch won	Madison Square Garden, New York City
09/09/1971	Karl Gotch Vs Bull Molino	Gotch won	National Arena, Washington, Columbia
10/09/1971	Karl Gotch Vs Bull Molino	Gotch won	Zembo Mosque, Harrisburg, Pennsylvania
11/09/1971	Karl Gotch Vs Mike Monroe	Gotch won	Boston Garden, Boston, Massachusetts
14/09/1971	Karl Gotch Vs Chuck Richards	Gotch won	Fieldhouse, Hamburg, Pennsylvania
16/09/1971	Karl Gotch & Ramon Lopez Vs Bull Molino & The Black Demon	Gotch et al won	National Arena, Washington, Columbia
27/09/1971	Karl Gotch & Victor Rivera Vs Luke Graham & tarzan Tyler	Draw	Washington Coliseum, Washington, Columbia
28/09/1971	Karl Gotch Vs Killer Brooks	Gotch won	Philadelphia Arena, Philadelphia, Pennsylvania
28/09/1971	Karl Gotch Vs Mickey Doyle	Gotch won	Philadelphia Arena, Philadelphia, Pennsylvania
01/10/1971	Karl Gotch Vs Moose Monroe	Gotch won	Witachi's Sports Arena, North Attleboro
02/10/1971	Karl Gotch & Rene Goulet Vs The Rugged Russians (Igor & Ivan)	NC	Philadelphia Arena, Philadelphia, Pennsylvania
09/10/1971	Karl Gotch Vs The Black Demon	Gotch won	Boston Garden, Boston, Massachusetts
25/10/1971	Karl Gotch Vs Beautiful Bobby	Gotch won	Madison Square Garden, New York City
01/11/1971	Karl Gotch Vs Beautiful Bobby	Gotch won	Washington Coliseum, Washington, Columbia
10/11/1971	Karl Gotch Vs Jimmy Valiant	Valiant won	Belfast, maine
11/11/1971	Karl Gotch Vs Mike Monroe	Gotch won	Augusta Armory, Augusta, Maine
13/11/1971	Karl Gotch Vs Moose Monroe	Gotch won	Boston Garden, Boston, Massachusetts
15/11/1971	Karl Gotch Vs Mike Monroe	Gotch won	Madison Square Garden, New York City
19/11/1971	Karl Gotch Vs Rene Goulet	Gotch won	Zembo Mosque, Harrisburg, Pennsylvania
22/11/1971	Karl Gotch Vs Mike Monroe	Gotch won	Civic Center, Baltimore, Maryland
29/11/1971	Karl Gotch Vs Rene Goulet	Time limit draw	Washington Coliseum, Washington, Columbia
02/12/1971	Karl Gotch Vs Igor	Gotch won	Cherry Hill, New Jersey
06/12/1971	Karl Gotch & Rene Goulet Vs Luke Graham & Tarzan Tyler	Gotch et al won	Madison Square Garden, New York City
07/12/1971	Karl Gotch Vs Stan Stasiak	NC	Portland, Maine
10/12/1971	Karl Gotch Vs Jimmy Valiant	Valiant won	North Attleboro, Massachusetts
11/12/1971	Karl Gotch Vs Manuel Soto	Gotch won	Boston Garden, Boston, Massachusetts
15/12/1971	Karl Gotch & Gorilla Monsoon Vs The Rugged Russians (Igor & Ivan)	Russians won	Civic Center, Baltimore, Maryland

Date	Match	Result	Venue
18/12/1971	Karl Gotch & Rene Goulet Vs The Rugged Russians (Igor & Ivan)	Gotch et al won	Philadelphia Arena, Philadelphia, Pennsylvania
01/01/1972	Karl Gotch Vs Manuel Soto	Gotch won	Philadelphia, Pennsylvania
07/01/1972	Karl Gotch Vs Jimmy Valiant	Draw	North Attleboro, Massachusetts
07/01/1972	Karl Gotch Vs The Black Demon	Gotch won	International Arena, Philadelphia, Pennsylvania
17/01/1972	Karl Gotch Vs Jimmy Valiant	NC	North Attleboro, Massachusetts
22/01/1972	Karl Gotch & Rene Goulet Vs The Rugged Russians (Igor & Ivan)	Gotch et al won	Boston Garden, Boston, Massachusetts
31/01/1972	Karl Gotch & Rene Goulet Vs The Rugged Russians (Igor & Ivan)	Gotch et al won	Madison Square Garden, New York City
01/02/1972	Karl Gotch & Rene Goulet Vs Baron Mikel Scicluna & King Curtis	Scicluna & King won	Philadelphia, Pennsylvania
06/03/1972	Karl Gotch Vs Antonio Inoki	Gotch won	Ota Ward Gymnasium, Tokyo
10/03/1972	Karl Gotch Vs John Durango	Gotch won	City Gymnasium, Takasaki, Gunma
14/03/1972	Karl Gotch Vs Jim Durango	Gotch won	Kiryu, Gunma
04/10/1972	Karl Gotch Vs Antonio Inoki	Inoki won	Kuramae Kokugikan, Tokyo
05/10/1972	Karl Gotch Vs Pat Roach	Gotch won	Izumiya Shopping Center, Kyoto
09/10/1972	Karl Gotch Vs Prince Kumali	Gotch won	Hiroshima Prefectural Gymnasium, Hiroshima
10/10/1972	Karl Gotch Vs Antonio Inoki	Gotch won	Osaka Prefectural Gymnasium, Osaka
12/10/1972	Karl Gotch & Red Pimpernel & Sean Regan Vs Antonio Inoki & Katsuhisa Shibata & Kotetsu Yamamoto	Inoki et al won	Yamaguchi Prefectural Gymnasium, Yamaguchi
13/10/1972	Karl Gotch Vs Pat Roach	Gotch won	Mihagino Gymnasium, Kitakyushu, Fukuoka
15/10/1972	Karl Gotch Vs Sean Regan	Gotch won	Tanushimaru Station Gardener Market, Kitsuki, Fukuoka
16/10/1972	Karl Gotch Vs John Tolley	Gotch won	Usa, Oita
17/10/1972	Karl Gotch Vs Pat Roach	Gotch won	City Gymnasium, Shimabara, Nagasaki
18/10/1972	Karl Gotch & Red Pimpernel & Sean Regan Vs Antonio Inoki & Katsuhisa Shibata & Kotetsu Yamamoto	Inoki et al won	City Gymnasium, Oita
20/10/1972	Karl Gotch Vs Sean Regan	Gotch won	City Gymnasium, Nara
14/10/1973	Karl Gotch & Lou Thesz Vs Antonio Inoki & Seiji Sakaguchi	Inoki & Sakaguchi won	Kuramae Kokugikan, Tokyo
01/08/1974	Karl Gotch Vs Antonio Inoki	Inoki won	Osaka Prefectural Gymnasium, Osaka
04/08/1974	Karl Gotch Vs Osamu Kido	Gotch won	City Gymnasium, Ogori, Fukuoka
05/08/1974	Karl Gotch Vs Jacky Carpentier	Gotch won	Yamaga Junior High School Gymnasium, Yamaga, Kumamoto
06/08/1974	Karl Gotch Vs El Greco	Gotch won	Oguni, Kumamoto
07/08/1974	Karl Gotch Vs Reginald Love	Gotch won	City Gymnasium, Nogata, Fukuoka
08/08/1974	Karl Gotch Vs Antonio Inoki	Inoki won	Nihon University Hall, Tokyo
01/01/1982	Karl Gotch Vs Yoshiaki Fujiwara	Gotch won	Korakuen Hall, Tokyo
08/01/1982	Karl Gotch Vs Osamu Kido	Gotch won	Korakuen Hall, Tokyo

Billy Robinson

Date	Match	Outcome	Venue
01/12/1957	Bill Robinson Vs Chris Sheady	Robinson won	Albert Hall, London
23/01/1958	Bill Robinson Vs Billy Howes	NK	Nottingham
28/01/1958	Bill Robinson Vs Gordon Kilmartin	NK	Scarborough
29/01/1958	Bill Robinson Vs Billy Joyce	Joyce won	Lincoln, Lincolnshire
11/02/1958	Bill Robinson Vs Norman Walsh	NK	Lime Grove, England
22/02/1958	Bill Robinson Vs Vic Hessell	NK	Belle Vue, Manchester
26/02/1958	Bill Robinson Vs Buddy Cody	NK	Brighton, England
11/03/1958	Bill Robinson Vs Gene Murphy	NK	Lime Grove, England
13/03/1958	Bill Robinson Vs Johnny Allan	NK	Nottingham
18/03/1958	Bill Robinson Vs Frank O'Donnel	Robinson won	Leeds, England
19/03/1958	Bill Robinson Vs Dean Stockton	NK	Scunthorpe, England
20/03/1958	Bill Robinson Vs Cyril Knowles	Robinson won	Morecambe, Lancashire
21/03/1958	Bill Robinson Vs Francis Sullivan	Robinson won	Willenhall, England
22/03/1958	Bill Robinson Vs Tony Baer	Robinson won	Belfast, Ireland
24/03/1958	Bill Robinson Vs Tommy Kilmartin	Robinson won	Glasgow, Scotland
25/03/1958	Bill Robinson Vs Billy Joyce	NK	Wakefield
02/04/1958	Bill Robinson Vs Charlie Fisher	NK	Harringay
05/04/1958	Bill Robinson Vs Cyril Morris	Robinson won	Newcastle, England
08/04/1958	Bill Robinson Vs Francis Sullivan	Francis won	Lime Grove, England
12/04/1958	Bill Robinson Vs Billy Howes	Robinson won	Middlesborough, North Yorkshire
14/04/1958	Bill Robinson Vs Jack Beaumont	NK	Altrincham
15/04/1958	Bill Robinson Vs Masambula	NK	Wakefield
18/04/1958	Bill Robinson Vs Tommy Kilmartin	Robinson won	Glasgow, Scotland
22/04/1958	Bill Robinson Vs Gordon Kilmartin	NK	Bridlington
24/04/1958	Bill Robinson Vs Jim Rawlings	Robinson won	Morecambe, Lancashire
26/04/1958	Bill Robinson Vs Gwyn Davies	Davies won	Newcastle, England
29/04/1958	Bill Robinson Vs Arthur Beaumont	NK	Wakefield
03/05/1958	Bill Robinson Vs Don Mendoza	Draw	Manchester, England
10/05/1958	Bill Robinson Vs Johnny Allan	Johnny won	Middlesborough, North Yorkshire
19/05/1958	Bill Robinson Vs Tibor Szakacs	NK	Blackpool, England
22/05/1958	Bill Robinson Vs Joe Cornelius	Robinson won	Bristol, England
23/05/1958	Bill Robinson Vs Mike Marino	Mike won	Liverpool, England
24/05/1958	Bill Robinson Vs Tibor Szakacs	Robinson won	Newcastle, England
26/05/1958	Bill Robinson Vs Charlie Fisher	NK	Ramsgate
28/05/1958	Bill Robinson Vs Black Kwango	Robinson won	Bath, England
29/05/1958	Bill Robinson Vs Tibor Szakacs	NK	Luton, England
31/05/1958	Bill Robinson Vs Francis St Clair Gregory	NK	Belle Vue, Manchester
14/06/1958	Bill Robinson Vs Johnny Allan	NK	Grantham, England
21/06/1958	Bill Robinson Vs Charlie Fisher	NK	Belle Vue, Manchester
03/07/1958	Bill Robinson Vs Josef Zaranoff	Josef won	Bristol, England
04/07/1958	Bill Robinson Vs Charlie Fisher	NK	Ramsgate
05/07/1958	Bill Robinson Vs Charlie Fisher	Robinson won	Salisbury, England

Date	Match	Result	Location
07/07/1958	Bill Robinson Vs Gwyn Davies	Draw	Leeds, England
07/07/1958	Bill Robinson Vs Bob McDonald	Robinson won, BMDQ	Leeds, England
08/07/1958	Bill Robinson Vs Josef Zaranoff	NK	Reading, Berkshire
12/07/1958	Bill Robinson Vs Tibor Szakacs	Robinson won	Middlesborough, North Yorkshire
17/07/1958	Bill Robinson Vs Charlie Fisher	NK	Walthamstow, London
26/07/1958	Bill Robinson Vs Francis Sullivan	NK	Middlesborough, England
29/07/1958	Bill Robinson Vs Eric Taylor	NK	Scarborough
31/07/1958	Bill Robinson Vs Josef Zaranoff	Draw	Bristol, England
03/08/1958	Bill Robinson Vs Lew Roseby	Robinson won	Salisbury, England
09/08/1958	Bill Robinson Vs Ernest Baldwin	Robinson won	Newcastle, England
09/08/1958	Bill Robinson Vs Dennis Mitchell	Robinson won	Newcastle, England
09/08/1958	Bill Robinson Vs Eric Taylor	Eric won	Newcastle, England
19/08/1958	Bill Robinson Vs Johnny Allan	Robinson won	Birmingham, England
22/08/1958	Bill Robinson Vs Johnny Czeslaw	Robinson won	Liverpool, England
23/08/1958	Billy Robinson Vs Geoff portz	Geoff won	Middlesborough, North Yorkshire
26/08/1958	Bill Robinson Vs Bud Cody	Robinson won	Purley, England
29/08/1958	Bill Robinson Vs Werner Lehmann	Robinson won	Krefeld, Germany
30/08/1958	Bill Robinson Vs Hans Dillinger	Robinson won, HSDQ	Krefeld, Germany
31/08/1958	Bill Robinson Vs Joschi Kovacs	Joschi won	Krefeld, Germany
01/09/1958	Bill Robinson Vs James Brown	Draw	Krefeld, Germany
02/09/1958	Bill Robinson Vs Hermann Iffland	Hermann won	Krefeld, Germany
03/09/1958	Bill Robinson Vs Horst Hoffman	Draw	Krefeld, Germany
04/09/1958	Bill Robinson Vs Jim Hussey	Jim won	Krefeld, Germany
05/09/1958	Bill Robinson Vs Geoff Portz	Geoff won	Krefeld, Germany
06/09/1958	Bill Robinson Vs Rudi Schumacher	Draw	Krefeld, Germany
07/09/1958	Bill Robinson Vs Peter Kaiser	Draw	Krefeld, Germany
08/09/1958	Bill Robinson & James Brown Vs Joe Cornelius & Jim Hussey	Joe & jim won	Krefeld, Germany
09/09/1958	Bill Robinson Vs Horst Hoffman	Horst won	Krefeld, Germany
10/09/1958	Bill Robinson & Geoff Portz Vs Joe Cornelius & Jim Hussey	Draw	Krefeld, Germany
11/09/1958	Bill Robinson Vs Gedeon Gida	Gedeon won	Krefeld, Germany
23/09/1958	Bill Robinson Vs El Arabet Said	Robinson won	Purley, England
01/10/1958	Billy Robinson Vs John Lees	Robinson won	Leeds, England
06/10/1958	Bill Robinson Vs El Said Arabet	Robinson won	Tunbridge Wells, England
07/10/1958	Bill Robinson Vs John DaSilva	NK	Colchester, England
08/10/1958	Bill Robinson Vs Henri Bury	Robinson won	Cardiff, Wales
09/10/1958	Bill Robinson Vs Daula Singh	Robinson won	Bristol, England
10/10/1958	Bill Robinson Vs Charlie Fisher	Robinson won	Ipswich, England
11/10/1958	Bill Robinson Vs Buddy Cody	NK	Luton, England
16/10/1958	Bill Robinson Vs Charlie Fisher	Robinson won	Beckenham, England
18/10/1958	Bill Robinson Vs Dennis Mitchell	Robinson won	Newcastle, England
20/10/1958	Bill Robinson Vs Jose Calderon	NK	Altrincham
21/10/1958	Bill Robinson Vs Daula Singh	NK	Reading, Berkshire
25/10/1958	Bill Robinson Vs Ken Davies	NK	Belle Vue, Manchester
30/10/1958	Bill Robinson Vs Ernie Riley	NC	Nottingham, England

Date	Match	Result	Location
31/10/1958	Bill Robinson Vs Tibor Szakacs	Draw	Glasgow, Scotland
01/11/1958	Bill Robinson Vs Don Mendoza	Robinson won	Middlesborough, North Yorkshire
03/11/1958	Bill Robinson Vs Tibor Szakacs	Tibor won	Tunbridge Wells, England
07/11/1958	Bill Robinson Vs Jose Calderon	Robinson won	Beckenham, England
08/11/1958	Bill Robinson Vs Josef Kovacs	NK	Norwich
11/11/1958	Bill Robinson Vs Alan Garfield	NK	Purley
13/11/1958	Bill Robinson Vs Ray Apollon	Ray won	Beckenham, England
18/11/1958	Bill Robinson Vs Toni Olivera	NK	Colchester, England
20/11/1958	Bill Robinson Vs Conrad Fey	Conrad won	Bristol, England
21/11/1958	Bill Robinson Vs Tony Mancelli	Tony won	Ipswich, England
22/11/1958	Bill Robinson Vs Ray Apollon	NK	Norwich
24/11/1958	Bill Robinson Vs Johnny Czeslaw	NK	Bradford, West Yorkshire
25/11/1958	Bill Robinson Vs Don Mendoza	NK	Wakefield
27/11/1958	Bill Robinson Vs Alan Garfield	NK	Nottingham
01/12/1958	Bill Robinson Vs Bill Hargreaves	Robinson won	Brierley Hill, England
02/12/1958	Bill Robinson Vs ?	Draw	Lime Grove, England
03/12/1958	Bill Robinson Vs Billy Howes	Robinson won	Lincoln, Lincolnshire
04/12/1958	Bill Robinson Vs Norman Walsh	NK	Blackburn, Lancashire
05/12/1958	Bill Robinson Vs Johnny Allan	Johnny won	Glasgow, Scotland
06/12/1958	Bill Robinson Vs Billy Joyce	Joyce won	Middlesborough, North Yorkshire
15/12/1958	Bill Robinson Vs Ray Hunter	Ray won	High Wycombe, England
20/12/1958	Bill Robinson Vs Charlie Fisher	NK	Eastbourne, England
27/12/1958	Bill Robinson Vs Don Mendoza	Don won	Newcastle, England
31/12/1958	Bill Robinson Vs Don Mendoza	Robinson won	Lincoln, Lincolnshire
03/01/1959	Bill Robinson Vs Billy Joyce	Joyce won	Middlesborough, North Yorkshire
10/01/1959	Bill Robinson Vs Jamie Dula	Robinson won	Hanley
15/01/1959	Bill Robinson Vs Wolfgang Ehrl	Robinson won	Nottingham, England
16/01/1959	Bill Robinson Vs Norman Walsh	Robinson won	Glasgow, Scotland
17/01/1959	Bill Robinson Vs Wolfgang Ehrl	Draw	Grantham, England
23/01/1959	Bill Robinson Vs Billy Howes	NK	Liverpool, England
24/01/1959	Bill Robinson Vs Reg Williams	Williams won	Hanley
27/01/1959	Bill Robinson Vs Ernie Riley	Draw	Wolverhampton, West Midlands
28/01/1959	Bill Robinson Vs Jim Hady	Draw	Lincoln, Lincolnshire
28/01/1959	Bill Robinson Vs Albert Wall	Robinson won	Lincoln, Lincolnshire
29/01/1959	Bill Robinson Vs Norman Walsh	Robinson won	Nottingham, England
30/01/1959	Bill Robinson Vs Norman Walsh	NK	Chesterfield
31/01/1959	Bill Robinson Vs Don Mendoza	Robinson won	Lincoln, Lincolnshire
31/01/1959	Bill Robinson Vs Ernie Baldwin	Ernie won	Middlesborough, North Yorkshire
05/02/1959	Bill Robinson Vs Jack Bence	Jack won	Beckenham, England
06/02/1959	Bill Robinson Vs Ernie Riley	Draw	Willenhall, England
13/02/1959	Bill Robinson Vs Dennis Mitchell	NK	Bolton, Lancashire
14/02/1959	Bill Robinson Vs Gordon Nelson	NK	Doncaster, England
16/02/1959	Bill Robinson Vs Eric Taylor	NK	Bradford, England
19/02/1959	Bill Robinson Vs Reg Williams	Robinson won	Nottingham, England

Date	Match	Result	Location
24/02/1959	Bill Robinson Vs Billy Howes	Howes won	Birmingham, England
26/02/1959	Bill Robinson Vs Mike Marino	NK	Hastings, England
27/02/1959	Bill Robinson Vs Vic Stewart	Robinson won	Willenhall, England
27/02/1959	Bill Robinson Vs Eric Taylor	Robinson won	Willenhall, England
27/02/1959	Bill Robinson Vs Alf Cadman (final)	Robinson won	Willenhall, England
28/02/1959	Bill Robinson Vs Gordon Nelson	Draw	Hanley
05/03/1959	Bill Robinson Vs Tibor Szakacs	Draw	Morecambe, Lancashire
07/03/1959	Bill Robinson Vs John DaSilva	NK	Dudley, England
10/03/1959	Bill Robinson Vs Dennis Mitchell	NK	Wakefield
12/03/1959	Bill Robinson Vs Norman Walsh	Robinson won	Nottingham, England
13/03/1959	Bill Robinson Vs Dennis Mitchell	NK	Chesterfield
14/03/1959	Bill Robinson Vs Dennis Mitchell	Draw	Middlesborough, North Yorkshire
18/03/1959	Bill Robinson Vs Johnny Czeslaw	Robinson won	Lincoln, Lincolnshire
20/03/1959	Bill Robinson Vs Spencer Churchill	Robinson won	Liverpool, England
21/03/1959	Bill Robinson Vs Tibor Szakacs	NK	Doncaster, England
25/03/1959	Bill Robinson Vs Joe Cornelius	Robinson won	Royal Albert Hall, London
26/03/1959	Bill Robinson Vs Georges Gordienko	NK	Beckenham
27/03/1959	Bill Robinson Vs John DaSilva	Robinson won	Brighton, England
27/03/1959	Bill Robinson Vs Gideon Gidea	Robinson won	Brighton, England
27/03/1959	Bill Robinson Vs Herman Iffland	Iffland won	Brighton, England
28/03/1959	Bill Robinson Vs John DaSilva	NK	Luton, England
30/03/1959	Bill Robinson Vs Al Hayes	NK	Belle Vue, Manchester
03/04/1959	Bill Robinson Vs Jim Hussey	Robinson won	Glasgow, Scotland
11/04/1959	Bill Robinson Vs Dai Sullivan	Robinson won	Hanley
12/04/1959	Bill Robinson Vs John DaSilva	Robinson won	Birmingham, England
15/04/1959	Bill Robinson Vs Tibor Szakacs	NK	Sheffield, South Yorkshire
18/04/1959	Bill Robinson Vs Francis Sullivan	NK	Alfreton
22/04/1959	Bill Robinson Vs Felix Kerschitz	Robinson won	Cardiff, Wales
24/04/1959	Bill Robinson Vs Ernest Baldwin	NC	Glasgow, Scotland
02/05/1959	Bill Robinson Vs Erik Koltschak	Robinson won	Hanley
07/05/1959	Bill Robinson Vs Erik Koltschak	Robinson won	Bristol, England
10/05/1959	Bill Robinson Vs Erik Koltschak	NK	Brighton, England
11/05/1959	Bill Robinson Vs Dean Stockton	Robinson won	High Wycombe, England
11/05/1959	Bill Robinson Vs Peter Deakin	Robinson won	High Wycombe, England
11/05/1959	Bill Robinson Vs Tony Mancelli	Robinson won	High Wycombe, England
15/05/1959	Bill Robinson Vs Ernie Riley	NK	Dudley, England
16/05/1959	Bill Robinson Vs Billy Joyce	Joyce won	Middlesborough, North Yorkshire
17/05/1959	Bill Robinson Vs Don Mendoza	Robinson won	Birmingham, England
20/05/1959	Bill Robinson Vs Masambula	NK	Sheffield, South Yorkshire
23/05/1959	Bill Robinson Vs Alex Wenzl	NK	Belle Vue, Manchester
29/05/1959	Bill Robinson Vs Steve Logan	NK	Liverpool, England
07/06/1959	Bill Robinson Vs Al Hayes	NK	Brighton, England
08/06/1959	Bill Robinson Vs Al Hayes	NK	High Wycombe, England
12/06/1959	Bill Robinson Vs Alan Garfield	NK	Ramsgate
16/06/1959	Bill Robinson Vs Alf Cadman	Robinson won	Birmingham, England

Date	Match	Result	Location
18/06/1959	Bill Robinson Vs Francis Sullivan	Robinson won	Morecambe, Lancashire
30/07/1959	Bill Robinson Vs Francis Sullivan	Draw	Morecambe, Lancashire
04/08/1959	Bill Robinson Vs Masambula	Robinson won	Birmingham, England
06/08/1959	Bill Robinson Vs Mike Marino	NK	Morecambe, Lancashire
14/08/1959	Bill Robinson Vs Ray Apollon	NK	Rochester
15/08/1959	Bill Robinson Vs Billy Howes	NK	Newcastle, England
18/08/1959	Bill Robinson Vs Count Bartelli	Draw	Birmingham, England
21/08/1959	Bill Robinson Vs Al Hayes	NK	Bolton, Lancashire
22/08/1959	Bill Robinson Vs Reg Williams	Robinson won	Hanley
04/09/1959	Bill Robinson Vs Francis St Clair Gregory	NK	Dudley, England
08/09/1959	Bill Robinson Vs Masambula	NK	Wolverhampton, West Midlands
11/09/1959	Bill Robinson Vs Gwyn Davies	NK	Liverpool, England
14/09/1959	Bill Robinson Vs Francis St Clair Gregory	NK	Bedford, England
16/09/1959	Bill Robinson Vs Doug Joyce	Robinson won	Cardiff, Wales
19/09/1959	Bill Robinson Vs Doug Joyce	NK	Norwich
21/09/1959	Bill Robinson Vs Kiwi Kingston	NK	Shoreditch, London
24/09/1959	Bill Robinson Vs Iskha Khan	Draw	Bristol, England
26/09/1959	Bill Robinson Vs Dave Armstrong	NK	Norwich
01/10/1959	Bill Robinson Vs Geoff Portz	NK	Blackburn, Lancashire
03/10/1959	Bill Robinson Vs Mike Marino	Draw	Newcastle, England
06/10/1959	Bill Robinson Vs Kurt Wenzl	NK	Wolverhampton, West Midlands
09/10/1959	Bill Robinson Vs Masambula	NK	Liverpool, England
14/10/1959	Bill Robinson Vs Francis Sullivan	NK	Sheffield, South Yorkshire
15/10/1959	Bill Robinson Vs Francis Sullivan	NK	Morecambe, Lancashire
20/10/1959	Bill Robinson Vs Geoff Portz	NK	Welling
24/10/1959	Bill Robinson Vs Billy Two Rivers	NK	Norwich
26/10/1959	Bill Robinson Vs Billy Howes	NK	Blackpool, England
30/10/1959	Bill Robinson Vs Billy Howes	NK	Liverpool, England
31/10/1959	Bill Robinson Vs Dave Armstrong	NK	Shrewsbury
02/11/1959	Bill Robinson Vs John DaSilva	NK	Aylesbury, Buckinghamshire
04/11/1959	Bill Robinson Vs Francis St Clair Gregory	Robinson won	Royal Albert Hall, London
07/11/1959	Bill Robinson Vs Bill Verna	NK	Luton, England
14/11/1959	Bill Robinson Vs John DaSilva	Draw	Middlesborough, North Yorkshire
18/11/1959	Bill Robinson Vs Al Hayes	NK	Sheffield, South Yorkshire
20/11/1959	Bill Robinson Vs Johnny Allan	NK	Bolton, Lancashire
23/11/1959	Bill Robinson Vs Steve Logan	Robinson won	Loughborough, England
26/11/1959	Bill Robinson Vs Seamus Dunleavy	NK	Nottingham
30/11/1959	Bill Robinson Vs Willem Hall	NK	Blackpool, England
10/12/1959	Bill Robinson Vs Zebra Kid	NK	Bury, St. Edmunds
11/12/1959	Bill Robinson Vs Alan Garfield	NK	Barnehurst
12/12/1959	Bill Robinson Vs Jose Arroyo	NK	Gloucester
15/12/1959	Bill Robinson Vs Ernie Baldwin	NK	Scarborough
21/12/1959	Bill Robinson Vs Norman Walsh	NK	Eltham
04/01/1960	Bill Robinson Vs Francis Sullivan	NK	Leeds, West yorkshire

Date	Match	Result	Location
05/01/1960	Bill Robinson Vs Les Kellett	NK	Hull
06/01/1960	Bill Robinson Vs Norman Walsh	NK	Grimsby
08/01/1960	Bill Robinson Vs Mike Marino	NK	Rotherham, South Yorkshire
11/01/1960	Bill Robinson Vs Bill McDonald	NK	Blackpool, England
12/01/1960	Bill Robinson Vs Jack Bence	Robinson won, JBDQ	Bath, England
14/01/1960	Bill Robinson Vs Mike Marino	NK	Barrow
15/01/1960	Bill Robinson Vs Bill McDonald	Robinson won	Liverpool, England
16/01/1960	Bill Robinson Vs Johnny Yearsley	Robinson won	Hanley
18/01/1960	Bill Robinson Vs Jean Chausson-Bel	Robinson won	Bedford, England
20/01/1960	Bill Robinson Vs Jack Bence	Robinson won, JBDQ	Bath, England
22/01/1960	Bill Robinson Vs John DaSilva	NK	Barnehurst
23/01/1960	Billy Robinson vs Sammy Berg 'Mr/ Canada'	NK	Purley
26/01/1960	Bill Robinson Vs Axel Dieter	NK	Watford
29/01/1960	Bill Robinson Vs Mike Marino	Marino won	Ipswich, England
30/01/1960	Bill Robinson Vs Johnny Yearsley	NK	Norwich
01/02/1960	Bill Robinson Vs Joe Cornelius	NC	Loughborough, England
02/02/1960	Bill Robinson Vs Billy Two Rivers	NK	Huddersfield, England
03/02/1960	Bill Robinson Vs Reg Williams	NK	Grimsby
04/02/1960	Bill Robinson Vs Ernie Baldwin	NK	Kirkcaldy
05/02/1960	Bill Robinson Vs Joe Cornelius	NK	Glasgow, Scotland
06/02/1960	Bill Robinson Vs Alf Rawlings	NK	Middlesborough, North Yorkshire
08/02/1960	Bill Robinson Vs Dennis Mitchell	NK	Halifax, West Yorkshire
09/02/1960	Bill Robinson Vs Dennis Mitchell	NK	Wakefield
10/02/1960	Bill Robinson Vs Norman Walsh	Draw	Lincoln, England
11/02/1960	Bill Robinson Vs Achim Chall	NK	Nottingham
12/02/1960	Bill Robinson Vs Dai Sullivan	NK	Chesterfield
13/02/1960	Bill Robinson Vs Norman Walsh	NK	Grantham, England
15/02/1960	Bill Robinson Vs Kiwi Kingston	NK	Leeds, West yorkshire
17/02/1960	Bill Robinson Vs Pedro Bengochea	NK	Sheffield, South Yorkshire
20/02/1960	Bill Robinson Vs Rocky Wall	Robinson won	Newcastle, England
22/02/1960	Bill Robinson Vs Francis St Clair Gregory	NK	Colwyn Bay, Wales
23/02/1960	Bill Robinson Vs Zebra Kid	NK	Welling
24/02/1960	Bill Robinson Vs Gideon Gidea	NK	Hove
25/02/1960	Bill Robinson Vs Tibor Szakacs	NK	Walthamstow, London
26/02/1960	Bill Robinson Vs Norman Walsh	NK	Bolton, Lancashire
27/02/1960	Bill Robinson Vs Emile Poilve	Robinson won, EPDQ	Hanley
27/02/1960	Bill Robinson Vs Reg Williams	Robinson won	Hanley
27/02/1960	Bill Robinson Vs Billy Howes	Robinson won	Hanley
28/02/1960	Bill Robinson Vs Billy Howes	Robinson won	Birmingham, England
01/03/1960	Bill Robinson Vs Andre Drapp	NK	Wembley, London
02/03/1960	Bill Robinson Vs Frank Hurley	NK	Southend
03/03/1960	Bill Robinson Vs Ray Apollon	NK	Exeter
05/03/1960	Bill Robinson Vs Alan Garfield	NK	Norwich
07/03/1960	Bill Robinson Vs Gwyn Davies	NK	Carlisle

Date	Match	Result	Venue
08/03/1960	Bill Robinson Vs Ernie Baldwin	NK	Lime Grove, England
09/03/1960	Bill Robinson Vs Primo Carnera	NK	Newcastle, England
10/03/1960	Bill Robinson Vs Ian Campbell	NK	Scarborough
11/03/1960	Bill Robinson Vs Billy Two Rivers	NK	Chesterfield
12/03/1960	Bill Robinson Vs Bill McDonald	NK	Middlesborough, North Yorkshire
14/03/1960	Bill Robinson Vs Geoff Portz	NK	York
16/03/1960	Bill Robinson Vs Geoff Portz	NK	Grimsby
17/03/1960	Bill Robinson Vs Dai Sullivan	NK	Nottingham
18/03/1960	Bill Robinson Vs Billy Joyce	NK	Glasgow, Scotland
19/03/1960	Bill Robinson Vs Billy Howes	NK	Huddersfield, England
21/03/1960	Bill Robinson Vs Ray Hunter	NK	Leeds, West yorkshire
22/03/1960	Bill Robinson Vs Tony Mancelli	NK	Bridlington
24/03/1960	Bill Robinson Vs Eric Taylor	NK	Barrow
25/03/1960	Bill Robinson Vs Alf Rawlings	NK	Rotherham, South Yorkshire
26/03/1960	Bill Robinson Vs Eric Taylor	Draw	Newcastle, England
28/03/1960	Bill Robinson Vs Reg Williams	NK	Preston, Lancashire
01/04/1960	Bill Robinson Vs Masambula	NK	Liverpool, England
02/04/1960	Bill Robinson Vs Ernie Riley	NK	Doncaster, England
05/04/1960	Bill Robinson Vs Eric Koltschak	NK	Wolverhampton
06/04/1960	Bill Robinson Vs Bill Rawlings	NK	Sheffield, South Yorkshire
07/04/1960	Bill Robinson Vs John DaSilva	NK	Bradford
08/04/1960	Bill Robinson Vs Count Bartelli	NK	Bolton, Lancashire
09/04/1960	Billy Robinson Vs Dennis Mitchell	Robinson won	Hanley
13/04/1960	Bill Robinson Vs Kiwi Kingston	Robinson won	Bath, England
13/04/1960	Bill Robinson Vs Kiwi Kingston	Robinson won	Bath, England
14/04/1960	Bill Robinson Vs Masambula	NK	Bradford, England
15/04/1960	Bill Robinson Vs Geoff Portz	NK	Belle Vue, Manchester
16/04/1960	Bill Robinson Vs Zebra Kid	NC	Newcastle, England
18/04/1960	Bill Robinson Vs Eric Taylor	Robinson won	Hanley
19/04/1960	Bill Robinson Vs Norman Walsh	NK	Middlesborough, North Yorkshire
20/04/1960	Bill Robinson Vs Tibor Szakacs	NK	Dunstable, Bedfordshire
21/04/1960	Bill Robinson Vs Ian Campbell	NK	Hove
22/04/1960	Bill Robinson Vs Josef Zaranoff	NK	Liverpool, England
23/04/1960	Bill Robinson Vs John DaSilva	NK	Doncaster, England
25/04/1960	Bill Robinson Vs Jim Rawlings	NK	Preston, Lancashire
27/04/1960	Bill Robinson Vs Ian Campbell	Robinson won, ICDQ	Lincoln, England
29/04/1960	Bill Robinson Vs Billy Joyce	NK	Glasgow, Scotland
30/04/1960	Bill Robinson Vs Alf Rawlings	NK	Middlesborough, North Yorkshire
02/05/1960	Bill Robinson Vs Bob Sweeney	NK	Halifax, West Yorkshire
04/05/1960	Bill Robinson Vs Norman Walsh	NK	Grimsby
06/05/1960	Bill Robinson Vs John DaSilva	NK	Bradford, England
07/05/1960	Bill Robinson Vs Bill McDonald	NK	Grantham, England
13/05/1960	Bill Robinson Vs Jim Hussey	NK	Liverpool, England
14/05/1960	Bill Robinson Vs Tony Mancelli	NK	Doncaster, England

Date	Match	Result	Location
16/05/1960	Bill Robinson Vs Reg Williams	NK	Walsall, England
21/05/1960	Billy Robinson Vs Dennis Mitchell	NK	Ellesmere Port
23/05/1960	Bill Robinson Vs Ian Campbell	Campbell won	Bedford, England
24/05/1960	Bill Robinson Vs Ray Apollon	Robinson won	Purley
25/05/1960	Bill Robinson Vs Gwyn Davies	NK	Cardiff, Wales
27/05/1960	Bill Robinson Vs Kiwi Kingston	NK	Barnehurst
30/05/1960	Bill Robinson Vs Alf Rawlings	Robinson Won	Portobello
31/05/1960	Bill Robinson Vs Tony Mancelli	NK	Leicester, Leicestershire
02/06/1960	Bill Robinson Vs Geoff Portz	NK	Belle Vue, Manchester
02/06/1960	Bill Robinson Vs Billy Howes	NK	Nottingham, England
07/06/1960	Bill Robinson Vs Zebra Kid	NK	Bridlington
10/06/1960	Bill Robinson Vs Johnny Allan	NK	Liverpool, England
11/06/1960	Bill Robinson Vs Gwyn Davies	NK	Middlesborough, North Yorkshire
13/06/1960	Bill Robinson Vs Zebra Kid	NK	Preston, Lancashire
17/06/1960	Bill Robinson Vs Gwyn Davies	NK	Bradford
18/06/1960	Bill Robinson Vs Billy Howes	NK	Belle Vue, Manchester
20/06/1960	Bill Robinson Vs Doug Joyce	NK	Leeds, West yorkshire
23/06/1960	Bill Robinson Vs Nikki Selenkowich	Robinson won	Morecambe, Lancashire
24/06/1960	Bill Robinson Vs Joe Cornelius	NK	Fleetwood
25/06/1960	Bill Robinson Vs Rawlings	NK	Middlesborough, North Yorkshire
26/06/1960	Bill Robinson Vs Ian Campbell	NK	Brighton, England
28/06/1960	Bill Robinson Vs Vic Stewart	Robinson won	Birmingham, England
30/06/1960	Bill Robinson Vs Billy Howes	NK	Crewe, England
24/07/1960	Bill Robinson Vs Alan Garfield	NK	Folkestone
02/08/1960	Bill Robinson Vs Norman Walsh	NK	Aberdeen
03/08/1960	Bill Robinson Vs Ernie Baldwin	NK	Grimsby
04/08/1960	Bill Robinson Vs Gwyn Davies	NK	Scarborough
06/08/1960	Bill Robinson Vs Ernie Riley	NK	Middlesborough, North Yorkshire
21/08/1960	Bill Robinson Vs Pat Barrett	NK	Brighton, England
22/09/1960	Bill Robinson Vs Johnny Yearsley	NK	Walthamstow, London
29/09/1960	Bill Robinson Vs Zebra Kid	NK	Dunstable, Bedfordshire
04/10/1960	Bill Robinson Vs Alan Garfield	Garfield won	Purley
05/10/1960	Bill Robinson Vs The Zebra Kid	Zebra kid won	Cardiff, Wales
06/10/1960	Bill Robinson Vs Ramon Napolitano	Ramon won	Bristol, England
10/10/1960	Bill Robinson Vs Mihalyi Kuti	NK	Preston, Lancashire
13/10/1960	Bill Robinson Vs Zebra Kid	NK	Dunstable, Bedfordshire
14/10/1960	Bill Robinson Vs Mike Marino	NK	Bradford
15/10/1960	Bill Robinson Vs Zebra Kid	NK	Middlesborough, North Yorkshire
17/10/1960	Bill Robinson Vs Alf Cadman	NK	Blackpool, England
20/10/1960	Bill Robinson Vs Johnny Czeslaw	NK	Leigh, Lancashire
21/10/1960	Bill Robinson Vs Dennis Mitchell	NK	Liverpool, England
22/10/1960	Bill Robinson Vs Raphael Blascoe	NK	Doncaster, England
24/10/1960	Bill Robinson Vs Ramon Napolitano	NK	York, Yorkshire
25/10/1960	Bill Robinson Vs Dennis Mitchell	NK	Trowell

Date	Match	Result	Location
26/10/1960	Bill Robinson Vs Billy Howes	NK	Grimsby
27/10/1960	Bill Robinson Vs Colin Williamson	NK	Nottingham
28/10/1960	Bill Robinson Vs Dennis Mitchell	NK	Glasgow, Scotland
29/10/1960	Bill Robinson Vs Black Mask	Nk	Middlesborough, North Yorkshire
01/11/1960	Bill Robinson Vs Bill Rawlings	Robinson won	Wakefield
02/11/1960	Bill Robinson Vs Reg Williams	Robinson won	Lincoln, England
03/11/1960	Bill Robinson Vs Geoff Portz	NC	Bradford
04/11/1960	Bill Robinson Vs Geoff Portz	NK	Bolton, Lancashire
05/11/1960	Bill Robinson Vs Billy Joyce	NK	Belle Vue, Manchester
12/11/1960	Bill Robinson Vs Great Togo	NK	Norwich
14/11/1960	Bill Robinson Vs Vic Hessell	NK	Warrington
17/11/1960	Bill Robinson Vs Matthias Rosges	NK	Smethwick
18/11/1960	Bill Robinson Vs Francis St. Clair Gregory	NK	Bolton, Lancashire
19/11/1960	Bill Robinson Vs Felix Lamban	NK	Belle Vue, Manchester
21/11/1960	Bill Robinson Vs Norman Walsh	NK	Bradford
23/11/1960	Bill Robinson Vs Billy Howes	NK	Grimsby, England
23/11/1960	Bill Robinson Vs Billy Howes	NK	Grimsby
24/11/1960	Bill Robinson Vs Matthias Rosges	NK	Nottingham
25/11/1960	Bill Robinson Vs Norman Walsh	NK	Leicester, Leicestershire
26/11/1960	Bill Robinson Vs Geoff Portz	NK	Middlesborough, North Yorkshire
28/11/1960	Bill Robinson Vs Geoff Portz	NK	Bradford
30/11/1960	Bill Robinson Vs Geoff Portz	NK	Preston, Lancashire
02/12/1960	Bill Robinson Vs Dennis Mitchell	NK	Leicester, Leicestershire
03/12/1960	Bill Robinson Vs Geoff Portz	NK	Middlesborough, North Yorkshire
05/12/1960	Bill Robinson Vs Billy Howes	NK	Blackpool, England
06/12/1960	Bill Robinson Vs Gideon Gidea	NK	Wolverhampton
07/12/1960	Bill Robinson Vs Gideon Gidea	Robinson won	Royal Albert Hall, London
08/12/1960	Bill Robinson Vs John Lees	NK	Ellesmere Port
09/12/1960	Bill Robinson Vs Billy Howes	NK	Liverpool, England
10/12/1960	Bill Robinson Vs Billy Joyce	NK	Belle Vue, Manchester
12/12/1960	Bill Robinson Vs Gideon Gidea	NK	Leeds, West yorkshire
13/12/1960	Bill Robinson Vs Mike Marino	NK	Hull
14/12/1960	Bill Robinson Vs Norman Walsh	NK	Sheffield, South Yorkshire
17/12/1960	Bill Robinson Vs Johnny Allan	NK	Halifax, West Yorkshire
23/12/1960	Bill Robinson Vs Billy Howes	NK	Bolton, Lancashire
26/12/1960	Bill Robinson Vs Billy Howes	NK	Blackpool, England
30/12/1960	Bill Robinson Vs Billy Howes	NK	Liverpool, England
31/12/1960	Bill Robinson Vs Bud Cody	Robinson won	Coventry, England
02/01/1961	Bill Robinson Vs Felix Lamban	NK	York
03/01/1961	Bill Robinson Vs Geoff Portz	NK	Trowell
04/01/1961	Bill Robinson Vs Rocky Wall	NK	Grimsby
06/01/1961	Bill Robinson Vs Geoff Portz	Draw	Glasgow, Scotland
07/01/1961	Bill Robinson Vs Geoff Portz	NK	Halifax, West Yorkshire
09/01/1961	Bill Robinson Vs Dennis Mitchell	NK	Huddersfield, England
10/01/1961	Bill Robinson Vs Dennis Mitchell	NK	Wakefield

Date	Match	Result	Location
11/01/1961	Bill Robinson Vs Ernie Baldwin	Robinson won	Lincoln
12/01/1961	Bill Robinson Vs Mike Marino	NK	Nottingham
13/01/1961	Bill Robinson Vs Bill Rawlings	NK	Chesterfield
14/01/1961	Bill Robinson Vs Mike Marino	NK	Grantham, England
16/01/1961	Bill Robinson Vs Norman Walsh	NK	Leeds, West yorkshire
17/01/1961	Bill Robinson Vs Terry Ricardo	NK	Hull
18/01/1961	Bill Robinson Vs Francis Sullivan	NK	Sheffield, South Yorkshire
19/01/1961	Bill Robinson Vs Mike Marino	NK	Goole
21/01/1961	Bill Robinson Vs Gomez Maximilliano	NK	Purley
23/01/1961	Bill Robinson Vs Al Garmain	NK	Blackpool, England
25/01/1961	Bill Robinson Vs Bill McDonald	Robinson won BMDQ	Scunthorpe, England
26/01/1961	Bill Robinson Vs Arthur Ricardo	NK	Crewe, England
27/01/1961	Bill Robinson Vs Reg Williams	NK	Leicester, Leicestershire
28/01/1961	Bill Robinson Vs Digger Rowell	NK	Doncaster, England
03/02/1961	Bill Robinson Vs Felix Lamban	NK	Bermondsey
04/02/1961	Bill Robinson Vs Kiwi Kingston	NK	Seymour Hall, Marylebone, London
07/02/1961	Bill Robinson Vs Gideon Gidea	Draw	Lime Grove, England
08/02/1961	Bill Robinson Vs Gideon Gidea	NK	Preston, Lancashire
09/02/1961	Bill Robinson Vs Ian Campbell	NK	Nelson, England
10/02/1961	Bill Robinson Vs Rocky Wall	NK	Leicester, Leicestershire
11/02/1961	Bill Robinson Vs Gideon Gidea	NK	Middlesborough, North Yorkshire
13/02/1961	Bill Robinson Vs Gordon Nelson	Robinson won	Loughborough, England
14/02/1961	Bill Robinson Vs Mike Marino	NK	Trowell
15/02/1961	Bill Robinson Vs Gideon Gidea	Robinson won	Royal Albert Hall, London
16/02/1961	Bill Robinson Vs Gideon Gidea	NK	Nottingham
17/02/1961	Bill Robinson Vs Geoff Portz	NK	Glasgow, Scotland
18/02/1961	Bill Robinson Vs Mike Marino	NK	Halifax, West Yorkshire
20/02/1961	Bill Robinson Vs Billy Joyce	NK	Leeds, West yorkshire
21/02/1961	Bill Robinson Vs Jack Pye	Robinson won JPDQ	Hull
22/02/1961	Bill Robinson Vs Pat Barrett	NK	Newark
23/02/1961	Bill Robinson Vs Mike Marino	NK	Barrow
27/02/1961	Bill Robinson Vs Eric Taylor	Robinson won	Eltham
28/02/1961	Bill Robinson Vs Gideon Gidea	Gidea won	Lime Grove, England
01/03/1961	Bill Robinson Vs Gideon Gidea	NK	Preston, Lancashire
02/03/1961	Bill Robinson Vs Johnny allan	NK	Kirkcaldy
03/03/1961	Bill Robinson Vs Gwyn Davies	NK	Bradford
04/03/1961	Bill Robinson Vs Norman Walsh	NK	Middlesborough, North Yorkshire
06/03/1961	Bill Robinson Vs Hans Streiger	NK	Colwyn Bay, Wales
08/03/1961	Bill Robinson Vs Dino Bravo	NK	Sheffield, South Yorkshire
09/03/1961	Bill Robinson Vs Dennis Mitchell	NK	Ellesmere Port
10/03/1961	Bill Robinson Vs Billy Howes	NK	Bolton, Lancashire
11/03/1961	Bill Robinson Vs Francis St. Clair Gregory	Robinson won	Doncaster, England
13/03/1961	Bill Robinson Vs George Harris	NK	Worcester
15/03/1961	Bill Robinson Vs Gideon Gidea	NK	Preston, Lancashire

Date	Match	Result	Location
17/03/1961	Bill Robinson Vs Norman Walsh	NK	Leicester, Leicestershire
18/03/1961	Bill Robinson Vs Dennis Mitchell	NK	Bradford
20/03/1961	Bill Robinson Vs Masambula	NK	Hamilton, Scotland
23/03/1961	Bill Robinson Vs Ernie Riley	NK	Smethwick
24/03/1961	Bill Robinson Vs Bill McDonald	NK	Liverpool, England
27/03/1961	Bill Robinson Vs The Mask	NK	York
28/03/1961	Bill Robinson Vs Ian Campbell	NK	Trowell
30/03/1961	Bill Robinson Vs Billy Howes	NK	Nottingham
31/03/1961	Bill Robinson Vs Ernie Baldwin	Draw	Glasgow, Scotland
01/04/1961	Bill Robinson Vs Norman Walsh	NK	Scarborough
03/04/1961	Bill Robinson Vs Jamie Olivera	NK	Kilmarnock
04/04/1961	Bill Robinson Vs Geoff Portz	NK	Huddersfield, England
05/04/1961	Bill Robinson Vs Pat Barrett	Robinson won	Lincoln
07/04/1961	Bill Robinson Vs Dennis Mitchell	Draw	Glasgow, Scotland
08/04/1961	Bill Robinson Vs Count Daidone	NK	Halifax, West Yorkshire
11/04/1961	Bill Robinson Vs Dennis Mitchell	NK	Wolverhampton,
12/04/1961	Bill Robinson Vs Gwyn Davies	NK	Scunthorpe, England
13/04/1961	Bill Robinson Vs Hans Streiger	NK	Leigh
14/04/1961	Bill Robinson Vs Billy Howes	NK	Hanley
15/04/1961	Bill Robinson Vs Josef Zaranoff	NK	Hanley
21/04/1961	Bill Robinson Vs Geoff Portz	NK	Liverpool, England
22/04/1961	Bill Robinson Vs Francis St. Clair Gregory	NK	Doncaster, England
24/04/1961	Bill Robinson Vs Tony Mancelli	Robinson won	High Wycombe, England
25/04/1961	Bill Robinson Vs Alan Garfield	Robinson won AGDQ	Welling
26/04/1961	Bill Robinson Vs Sammy Cohen	Robinson won	Cardiff, Wales
26/04/1961	Bill Robinson Vs Mike Marino	Robinson won	Cardiff, Wales
27/04/1961	Bill Robinson Vs Gordon Nelson	NK	Dunstable, Bedfordshire
29/04/1961	Bill Robinson Vs Alan Garfield	NK	Norwich
01/05/1961	Bill Robinson Vs Billy Howes	NK	Huddersfield, England
01/05/1961	Bill Robinson Vs Billy Howes	NK	Huddersfield, England
03/05/1961	Bill Robinson Vs Billy Howes	NK	Grimsby
04/05/1961	Bill Robinson Vs Billy Howes	NK	Kirkcaldy
05/05/1961	Bill Robinson Vs Alf Rawlings	NK	Chesterfield
06/05/1961	Bill Robinson Vs Billy Howes	NK	Grantham, England
08/05/1961	Bill Robinson Vs Mike Marino	NK	Leeds, West yorkshire
09/05/1961	Bill Robinson Vs George Gordienko	NK	Wolverhampton
11/05/1961	Bill Robinson Vs Alan Garfield	NK	Paddington
12/05/1961	Bill Robinson Vs Mike Marino	NK	Liverpool, England
13/05/1961	Bill Robinson Vs Gwyn Davies	NK	Middlesborough, North Yorkshire
15/05/1961	Bill Robinson Vs Ian Campbell	NK	Worksop
16/05/1961	Bill Robinson Vs Mike Marino	NK	Scarborough
17/05/1961	Bill Robinson Vs Kiwi Kingston	NK	Cradley Heath, England
19/05/1961	Bill Robinson Vs Mike Marino	NK	Chesterfield
22/05/1961	Bill Robinson Vs Dai Sullivan	NK	Belle Vue, Manchester
23/05/1961	Bill Robinson Vs Michael Allary	Robinson won	Welling

Date	Match	Result	Location
24/05/1961	Bill Robinson Vs Alan Garfield	Robinson won	Royal Albert Hall, London
24/05/1961	Bill Robinson Vs Gordon Nelson	Robinson won	Royal Albert Hall, London
24/05/1961	Bill Robinson Vs Joe Cornelius	Robinson won	Royal Albert Hall, London
26/05/1961	Bill Robinson Vs Dennis Mitchell	NK	Northampton
27/05/1961	Billy Robinson Vs George Gordienko	Draw	Purley
28/05/1961	Bill Robinson Vs Tibor Szakacs	Draw	Brighton, England
31/05/1961	Bill Robinson Vs Eric Koltschak	Robinson won	Cardiff, Wales
31/05/1961	Bill Robinson Vs Billy Joyce	Joyce won	Cardiff, Wales
01/06/1961	Bill Robinson Vs Tibor Szakacs	NK	Walthamstow, London
03/06/1961	Bill Robinson Vs Mike Marino	Marino won	Coventry, England
05/06/1961	Bill Robinson Vs Matthias Rosges	NK	Wembley, London
06/06/1961	Bill Robinson Vs Billy Howes	Robinson won	Swindon, England
08/06/1961	Bill Robinson Vs Matthias Rosges	NK	Dunstable, Bedfordshire
09/06/1961	Bill Robinson Vs Bill Verna	Robinson won	Barking
15/06/1961	Bill Robinson Vs Johnny allan	NK	Barrow
17/06/1961	Bill Robinson Vs Billy Howes	Robinson won	Glasgow, Scotland
19/06/1961	Bill Robinson Vs Doug Joyce	NK	Leeds, West yorkshire
23/06/1961	Bill Robinson Vs Bill McDonald	NK	Liverpool, England
28/06/1961	Bill Robinson Vs Bernard Vignal	Robinson won	Cardiff, Wales
29/06/1961	Bill Robinson Vs Hans Streiger	NK	Scarborough
02/07/1961	Bill Robinson Vs Geoff Portz	NK	Liverpool, England
03/07/1961	Bill Robinson Vs Joe Cornelius	NK	Shoreditch, London
04/07/1961	Bill Robinson Vs Ray Apollon	NK	Weston Super Mare, England
06/07/1961	Bill Robinson Vs Hans Streiger	NK	Scarborough
02/09/1961	Bill Robinson Vs Rocky Wall	NK	Newcastle, England
11/09/1961	Bill Robinson Vs Dai Sullivan	NK	York
05/10/1961	Bill Robinson Vs Dino Bravo	NC	Walthamstow, London
06/10/1961	Bill Robinson Vs Terry Garvin	NK	Caledonian Road, London
07/10/1961	Bill Robinson Vs Dino Bravo	Robinson won	Norwich
09/10/1961	Bill Robinson Vs Willem Hall	NK	Catford
10/10/1961	Bill Robinson Vs George Gordienko	Gordienko won	Bournemouth, England
11/10/1961	Bill Robinson Vs Iskha Khan	Robinson won	Cardiff, Wales
12/10/1961	Bill Robinson Vs Tibor Szakacs	NK	Cambridge, England
14/10/1961	Bill Robinson Vs Iskha Khan	Robinson won IKDQ	Coventry, England
16/10/1961	Bill Robinson Vs Thomas Riandi	NK	Bedford, England
18/10/1961	Bill Robinson Vs Gomez Maximilliano	NK	Kingston
19/10/1961	Bill Robinson Vs Gomez Maximilliano	Robinson won	Peterborough, England
21/10/1961	Bill Robinson Vs George Gordienko	NK	Brighton, England
23/10/1961	Bill Robinson Vs Josef Zaranoff	NK	Preston, Lancashire
24/10/1961	Bill Robinson Vs Roy Bull Davis	NK	Wakefield
25/10/1961	Bill Robinson Vs Willem Hall	NK	Grimsby
26/10/1961	Bill Robinson Vs Terry Garvin	NK	Nottingham
27/10/1961	Bill Robinson Vs Ricky Waldo	NK	Leicester, Leicestershire
28/10/1961	Bill Robinson Vs Josef Zaranoff	Robinson won	Middlesborough, North Yorkshire
30/10/1961	Bill Robinson Vs Thomas Riandi	Robinson won	Cheltenham, England

Date	Match	Result	Location
31/10/1961	Bill Robinson Vs Norman Walsh	Draw	Purley
01/11/1961	Bill Robinson Vs Thomas Riandi	NK	Shoreditch, London
03/11/1961	Bill Robinson Vs Thomas Riandi	Robinson won	Ipswich, England
04/11/1961	Bill Robinson Vs Genghis Khan	NK	Camberwell
06/11/1961	Bill Robinson Vs Johnny Czeslaw	NK	Worthing
07/11/1961	Bill Robinson Vs Thomas Riandi	Robinson won	Watford
10/11/1961	Bill Robinson Vs Dave Armstrong	NK	Chesterfield
13/11/1961	Bill Robinson Vs Luther Lindsay	NK	Bradford
14/11/1961	Bill Robinson Vs Gwyn Davies	Robinson won	Plymouth, England
15/11/1961	Bill Robinson Vs Geoff Portz	NK	Preston, Lancashire
16/11/1961	Bill Robinson Vs Geoff Portz	NK	Hayes
18/11/1961	Bill Robinson Vs Tony Mancelli	NK	Portsmouth
20/11/1961	Bill Robinson Vs Sandy Mckay Scott	Draw	West Ham, England
22/11/1961	Bill Robinson Vs Gerry DeJaegar	Robinson won	Cardiff, Wales
23/11/1961	Bill Robinson Vs Bill Verna	NK	Deptford
24/11/1961	Bill Robinson Vs Thomas Riandi	Robinson won	Streatham
25/11/1961	Bill Robinson Vs Jim Hussey	NK	Norwich
27/11/1961	Bill Robinson Vs Sandy Mckay Scott	NK	Loughborough, England
28/11/1961	Bill Robinson Vs Sandy Mckay Scott	NK	Scarborough
29/11/1961	Bill Robinson Vs Dai Sullivan	Draw	Lincoln
30/11/1961	Bill Robinson Vs Willem Hall	NK	Nottingham
01/12/1961	Bill Robinson Vs Sandy Mckay Scott	Robinson won	Glasgow, Scotland
02/12/1961	Bill Robinson Vs Josef Zaranoff	NK	Falkirk
04/12/1961	Bill Robinson Vs Herman Iffland	NK	Seymour Hall, Marylebone, London
06/12/1961	Bill Robinson Vs Herman Iffland	Robinson won	Cardiff, Wales
07/12/1961	Bill Robinson Vs Willem Hall	NK	Cambridge, England
11/12/1961	Bill Robinson Vs Terry Garvin	NK	Bradford
12/12/1961	Bill Robinson Vs John Lees	NK	Leicester, Leicestershire
13/12/1961	Bill Robinson Vs Frankie Townsend	NK	Preston, Lancashire
14/12/1961	Bill Robinson Vs Frankie Townsend	NK	Hayes
17/12/1961	Bill Robinson Vs Gwyn Davies	NK	Middlesborough, North Yorkshire
17/12/1961	Bill Robinson Vs Tibor Szakacs	NK	Catford
18/12/1961	Bill Robinson Vs Willem Hall	NK	York
19/12/1961	Bill Robinson Vs John Lees	NK	Trowell
20/12/1961	Bill Robinson Vs Joe Cornelius	NK	Grimsby
21/12/1961	Bill Robinson Vs Billy Joyce	NK	Nottingham
22/12/1961	Bill Robinson Vs Willem Hall	Robinson won	Glasgow, Scotland
23/12/1961	Bill Robinson Vs Geoff Portz	NK	Hayes
01/01/1962	Bill Robinson Vs Joe Cornelius	Robinson won	Seymour Hall, Marylebone, London
02/01/1962	Bill Robinson Vs Terry Garvin	Robinson won	Purley
04/01/1962	Bill Robinson Vs George Gordienko	NK	Poplar
05/01/1962	Bill Robinson Vs Great Togo	NK	Rochester
06/01/1962	Bill Robinson Vs Johnny Czeslaw	NK	Eastbourne, England
08/01/1962	Bill Robinson Vs Billy Howes	Robinson won	Bradford
09/01/1962	Bill Robinson Vs Dennis Mitchell	Mitchell won	Lime Grove, England

Date	Match	Result	Location
12/01/1962	Bill Robinson Vs Syed Saif Shah	NK	Leicester, Leicestershire
13/01/1962	Bill Robinson Vs Terry Ricardo	Robinson won	Middlesborough, North Yorkshire
15/01/1962	Bill Robinson Vs Syed Saif Shah	NK	York
16/01/1962	Bill Robinson Vs Joe Cornelius	NK	Trowell
17/01/1962	Bill Robinson Vs Syed Saif Shah	Robinson won	Lincoln
19/01/1962	Bill Robinson Vs Syed Saif Shah	Shah won	Glasgow, Scotland
24/01/1962	Bill Robinson Vs Ski Hi Lee	Robinson won Lee DQ	Walthamstow, London
26/01/1962	Bill Robinson Vs Saaddee Mansourri	NK	Rochester
27/01/1962	Bill Robinson Vs Dino Bravo	Robinson won	Brighton, England
29/01/1962	Bill Robinson Vs Frankie Townsend	Robinson won	Bradford
30/01/1962	Bill Robinson Vs Frankie Townsend	NK	Lime Grove, England
02/02/1962	Bill Robinson Vs Gwyn Davies	NK	Leicester, Leicestershire
05/02/1962	Bill Robinson Vs Norman Walsh	NK	Derby
07/02/1962	Bill Robinson Vs Geoff Portz	NK	Preston, Lancashire
09/02/1962	Bill Robinson Vs Geoff Portz	NK	Chesterfield
14/02/1962	Bill Robinson Vs Great Togo	Robinson won	Cardiff, Wales
15/02/1962	Bill Robinson Vs Gideon Gidea	NK	Dunstable, Bedfordshire
16/02/1962	Bill Robinson Vs El Grande Apachee	NK	Streatham
19/02/1962	Bill Robinson Vs Tibor Szakacs	Draw	Bradford
20/02/1962	Bill Robinson Vs Gwyn Davies	NK	Dundee, Scotland
20/02/1962	Bill Robinson Vs Horst Hoffman	Draw	Munster, Germany
21/02/1962	Bill Robinson Vs Roy Bull Davis	NK	Preston, Lancashire
21/02/1962	Bill Robinson Vs Great Zorro	Draw	Munster, Germany
22/02/1962	Bill Robinson Vs Dino Bravo	NK	Hayes
22/02/1962	Bill Robinson Vs Peter Kayser	Robinson won	Munster, Germany
23/02/1962	Bill Robinson Vs Gwyn Davies	NK	Leicester, Leicestershire
23/02/1962	Bill Robinson Vs Ian Campbell	Robinson won	Munster, Germany
24/02/1962	Bill Robinson Vs Ray Apollon	Apollon won	Middlesborough, North Yorkshire
24/02/1962	Bill Robinson Vs Ossie Mueller	Robinson won	Munster, Germany
26/02/1962	Bill Robinson Vs Marius Daniels	NK	York
28/02/1962	Bill Robinson Vs Jan Brouwers	Robinson won	Lincoln
03/03/1962	Bill Robinson Vs Jan Brouwers	NK	Falkirk
09/03/1962	Bill Robinson Vs Alf Rawlings	NK	Chesterfield
17/08/1962	Bill Robinson Vs Hans Dillinger	Robinson won	Munster, Germany
18/08/1962	Bill Robinson Vs Josef Molnar	Robinson won	Munster, Germany
19/08/1962	Bill Robinson Vs Eric Taylor	Robinson won	Munster, Germany
02/09/1962	Bill Robinson Vs Ian Campbell	Draw	Karlsruhe, Germany
03/09/1962	Bill Robinson Vs Horst Hoffman	Draw	Karlsruhe, Germany
04/09/1962	Bill Robinson Vs Josef Molnar	Robinson won	Karlsruhe, Germany
05/09/1962	Bill Robinson Vs Ian Campbell	Robinson won	Karlsruhe, Germany
06/09/1962	Bill Robinson Vs Josef Kovacs	Draw	Karlsruhe, Germany
07/09/1962	Bill Robinson Vs Mihalyi Kuti	Draw	Karlsruhe, Germany
08/09/1962	Bill Robinson Vs Gideon Gidea	Gidea won	Karlsruhe, Germany
09/09/1962	Bill Robinson Vs Josef Kovacs	Robinson won	Karlsruhe, Germany
10/09/1962	Bill Robinson Vs Dennis Mitchell	Mitchell won	Karlsruhe, Germany

Date	Match	Result	Location
11/09/1962	Bill Robinson VS Hemran Ifflund	NC	Karlsruhe, Germany
12/09/1962	Bill Robinson Vs Mihalyi Kuti	Robinson won	Karlsruhe, Germany
13/09/1962	Bill Robinson & Dennis Mitchell Vs Josef Kovacs & Peter Kayser	Kovacs and Kayser won	Karlsruhe, Germany
14/09/1962	Bill Robinson VS Hemran Ifflund	Robinson won	Karlsruhe, Germany
16/09/1962	Bill Robinson & Horst Hoffman Vs Josef Kovacs & Ivor Martinson	Robinson & Hoffman won	Karlsruhe, Germany
18/09/1962	Bill Robinson Vs Ossie Mueller	Robinson won	Karlsruhe, Germany
19/09/1962	Bill Robinson Vs Horst Hoffman	Hoffman won	Karlsruhe, Germany
22/09/1962	Bill Robinson Vs Josef Kovacs	Draw	Krefeld, Germany
23/09/1962	Bill Robinson Vs Ivor Martinson	Robinson won	Krefeld, Germany
24/09/1962	Bill Robinson Vs Peter Kayser	Draw	Krefeld, Germany
26/09/1962	Bill Robinson & Dennis Mitchell Vs Jose Arroyo & Peter Kayser	Draw	Krefeld, Germany
27/09/1962	Bill Robinson Vs Gideon Gidea	Gida won	Krefeld, Germany
28/09/1962	Bill Robinson & Dennis Mitchell Vs Peter Kayser & Josef Kovacs	Kayser & Kovacs won	Krefeld, Germany
29/09/1962	Bill Robinson VS Hemran Ifflund	Robinson won	Krefeld, Germany
30/09/1962	Bill Robinson Vs Josef Kovacs	Robinson won	Krefeld, Germany
01/10/1962	Bill Robinson Vs Mihalyi Kuti	Robinson won	Krefeld, Germany
02/10/1962	Bill Robinson Vs Dennis Mitchell	Robinson won	Krefeld, Germany
03/10/1962	Bill Robinson Vs Horst Hoffman	Robinson won	Krefeld, Germany
12/10/1962	Bill Robinson Vs Josef Kovacs	Draw	Hamburg, Germany
13/10/1962	Bill Robinson Vs Gideon Gidea	Draw	Hamburg, Germany
14/10/1962	Bill Robinson VS Hemran Ifflund	Robinson won	Hamburg, Germany
15/10/1962	Bill Robinson Vs Peter Kayser	Draw	Hamburg, Germany
16/10/1962	Bill Robinson Vs Horst Hoffman	Draw	Hamburg, Germany
17/10/1962	Bill Robinson Vs Hans Dillinger	Robinson won	Hamburg, Germany
18/10/1962	Bill Robinson Vs Josef Kovacs	Robinson won JKDQ	Hamburg, Germany
19/10/1962	Bill Robinson Vs Bolo Hawaka	Robinson won	Hamburg, Germany
20/10/1962	Bill Robinson Vs Ski Hi Lee	Draw	Hamburg, Germany
21/10/1962	Bill Robinson Vs Dennis Mitchell	Draw	Hamburg, Germany
22/10/1962	Bill Robinson & Dennis Mitchell Vs Ski Hi Lee	Robinson & Mitchell won	Hamburg, Germany
23/10/1962	Bill Robinson Vs Horst Hoffman	Draw	Hamburg, Germany
24/10/1962	Bill Robinson Vs Ivor Martinson	Robinson won	Hamburg, Germany
25/10/1962	Bill Robinson & Herman Ifflund Vs Josef Kovacs & Ivor Martinson	Draw	Hamburg, Germany
26/10/1962	Bill Robinson & Dennis Mitchell Vs Ski Hi Lee	Ski Hi Lee won	Hamburg, Germany
27/10/1962	Bill Robinson Vs Horst Hoffman	Hoffman won	Hamburg, Germany
28/10/1962	Bill Robinson & Dennis Mitchell Vs Josef Kovacs & Ivor Martinson	Kovacs & Martinson won	Hamburg, Germany
29/10/1962	Bill Robinson Vs Miha Lyi Kuti	Robinson won	Hamburg, Germany
30/10/1962	Bill Robinson Vs Fritz Mueller	Draw	Hamburg, Germany
31/10/1962	Bill Robinson Vs Hans Dillinger	Robinson won	Hamburg, Germany
01/11/1962	Bill Robinson Vs Gordon Kilmartin	Robinson won	Hamburg, Germany
02/11/1962	Bill Robinson Vs Ski Hi Lee	Robinson won	Hamburg, Germany
03/11/1962	Bill Robinson Vs Gideon Gidea	Robinson won	Hamburg, Germany
04/11/1962	Bill Robinson Vs Peter Kayser	Robinson won	Hamburg, Germany
05/11/1962	Bill Robinson Vs Josef Kovacs	NK	Hamburg, Germany

Date	Match	Result	Location
06/11/1962	Bill Robinson Vs Gideon Gidea	Robinson won	Hamburg, Germany
07/11/1962	Bill Robinson Vs Josef Kovacs	Kovacs won	Hamburg, Germany
08/11/1962	Bill Robinson Vs Gordon Kilmartin	Robinson won	Hamburg, Germany
09/11/1962	Bill Robinson Vs Horst Hoffman	Hoffman won	Hamburg, Germany
10/11/1962	Bill Robinson & Horst Hoffman Vs Josef Kovacs & Ivor Martinson	Robinson & Hoffman won	Hamburg, Germany
11/11/1962	Bill Robinson Vs Fritz Mueller	Robinson won	Hamburg, Germany
12/11/1962	Bill Robinson & Horst Hoffman Vs Josef Kovacs & Gideon Gidea	Robinson & Hoffman won	Hamburg, Germany
13/11/1962	Bill Robinson Vs Erik Koltschak	Robinson won	Hamburg, Germany
14/11/1962	Bill Robinson Vs Herman Iffland	Iffland won	Hamburg, Germany
15/11/1962	Bill Robinson Vs Peter Kayser	Robinson won	Hamburg, Germany
16/11/1962	Bill Robinson Vs Ski Hi Lee	Robinson won	Hamburg, Germany
17/11/1962	Bill Robinson Vs Josef Kovacs	Robinson won	Hamburg, Germany
03/12/1962	Bill Robinson Vs John DaSilva	NK	York
04/12/1962	Bill Robinson Vs John DaSilva	NK	Lime Grove, England
07/12/1962	Bill Robinson Vs Norman Walsh	Draw	Glasgow, Scotland
08/12/1962	Bill Robinson Vs Dai Sullivan	NK	Grimsby
10/12/1962	Bill Robinson Vs Billy Joyce	Joyce won	Loughborough, England
11/12/1962	Bill Robinson Vs Pietro Capello	NK	Trowell
12/12/1962	Bill Robinson Vs Perdro Bengochea	Robinson won	Lincoln
13/12/1962	Bill Robinson Vs Bruno Elrington	NK	Kirkcaldy
15/12/1962	Bill Robinson Vs Billy Howes	Robinson won	Newcastle, England
20/12/1962	Bill Robinson Vs Tibor Szakacs	NK	Cambridge, England
21/12/1962	Bill Robinson Vs Josef Zaranoff	NK	Rochester
22/12/1962	Bill Robinson Vs Josef Zaranoff	NK	Brighton, England
28/12/1962	Bill Robinson Vs Jack Bence	NK	Bermondsey
02/01/1963	Bill Robinson Vs Gerry DeJaegar	Robinson won	Oxford
03/01/1963	Bill Robinson Vs Jack Bence	NK	Bristol
05/01/1963	Bill Robinson Vs Bruno Elrington	Robinson won	Norwich
07/01/1963	Bill Robinson Vs Bruno Elrington	Robinson won	Bradford
08/01/1963	Bill Robinson Vs Bruno Elrington	NK	Lime Grove, England
10/01/1963	Bill Robinson Vs John DaSilva	NK	Nottingham
11/01/1963	Bill Robinson Vs Bruno Elrington	NK	Leicester, Leicestershire
12/01/1963	Bill Robinson Vs Bruno Elrington	NK	Middlesborough, North Yorkshire
14/01/1963	Bill Robinson Vs Joe Cornelius	NK	West Ham, England
15/01/1963	Bill Robinson Vs Josef Kovacs	NK	Bournemouth, England
16/01/1963	Bill Robinson Vs Ian Campbell	NK	Hastings
17/01/1963	Bill Robinson Vs Johnny Czeslaw	NK	Wimbledon
18/01/1963	Bill Robinson Vs Ray Apollon	NK	Streatham
21/01/1963	Bill Robinson Vs John DaSilva	NK	Harrogate
23/01/1963	Bill Robinson Vs Bruno Elrington	Robinson won	London
24/01/1963	Bill Robinson Vs Norman Walsh	NK	Nottingham
25/01/1963	Bill Robinson Vs Dave Armstrong	Robinson won	Glasgow, Scotland
26/01/1963	Bill Robinson Vs Alf Rawlings	NK	Falkirk
28/01/1963	Bill Robinson Vs Willem Hall	NK	York
29/01/1963	Bill Robinson Vs Willem Hall	Robinson won	Huddersfield, England

Date	Match	Result	Location
31/01/1963	Bill Robinson Vs Norman Walsh	NK	Kirkcaldy
01/02/1963	Bill Robinson Vs Dai Sullivan	NK	Chesterfield
04/02/1963	Bill Robinson Vs Eric Taylor	Draw	Bradford
06/02/1963	Bill Robinson Vs Eric Taylor	NK	Preston, Lancashire
08/02/1963	Bill Robinson Vs Eric Taylor	NK	Leicester, Leicestershire
09/02/1963	Bill Robinson Vs Eric Taylor	NC	Middlesborough, North Yorkshire
11/02/1963	Bill Robinson Vs Johnny Allan	NK	Derby
13/02/1963	Bill Robinson Vs Rocky Wall	Draw	Lincoln
14/02/1963	Bill Robinson Vs Sandy Orford	NK	Nottingham
15/02/1963	Bill Robinson Vs Billy Howes	Robinson won BHDQ	Glasgow, Scotland
16/02/1963	Bill Robinson Vs Dennis Mitchell	Robinson won	Belle Vue, Manchester
18/02/1963	Bill Robinson Vs Ray Apollon	NK	Eltham
20/02/1963	Bill Robinson Vs Joe Cornelius	NK	Dorking
21/02/1963	Bill Robinson Vs Ray Apollon	NK	Beckenham
22/02/1963	Bill Robinson Vs Joe Cornelius	Robinson won	Ipswich, England
23/02/1963	Bill Robinson Vs Mihalyi Kuti	NK	Norwich
25/02/1963	Bill Robinson Vs Geoff Portz	Robinson won	Bradford
26/02/1963	Bill Robinson Vs Geoff Portz	Robinson won	Lime Grove, England
28/02/1963	Bill Robinson Vs Dennis Mitchell	NK	Blackburn, Lancashire
02/03/1963	Billy Robinson Vs Wilhelm Hall	NK	Limegrove Hall, Shepherd's Bush, London
04/03/1963	Bill Robinson Vs Rocky Wall	Draw	Loughborough, England
05/03/1963	Bill Robinson Vs Dennis Mitchell	Draw	Huddersfield, England
07/03/1963	Bill Robinson Vs Dennis Mitchell	NK	Nottingham
08/03/1963	Bill Robinson Vs Geoff Portz	Draw	Glasgow, Scotland
09/03/1963	Bill Robinson Vs Pietro Capello	NK	Grantham, England
11/03/1963	Bill Robinson Vs Geoff Portz	NK	Bradford
13/03/1963	Bill Robinson Vs Geoff Portz	NK	Preston, Lancashire
15/03/1963	Bill Robinson Vs Billy Howes	NK	Leicester, Leicestershire
16/03/1963	Bill Robinson Vs John Lees	Nk	Falkirk
19/03/1963	Bill Robinson Vs Kiwi Kingston	NC	Kidderminster
20/03/1963	Bill Robinson Vs Jim Hussey	NK	Sheffield, South Yorkshire
21/03/1963	Bill Robinson Vs Willem Hall	NK	Morecambe, Lancashire
22/03/1963	Bill Robinson Vs Willem Hall	Robinson won	Rotherham
23/03/1963	Bill Robinson Vs Dai Sullivan	Robinson won DSDQ	Newcastle, England
25/03/1963	Bill Robinson Vs Gideon Gidea	NK	West Ham, England
27/03/1963	Bill Robinson Vs John DaSilva	NK	Shoreditch, London
28/03/1963	Bill Robinson Vs Willem Hall	NK	Wimbledon
29/03/1963	Bill Robinson Vs Josef Zaranoff	Draw	Rochester
30/03/1963	Bill Robinson Vs Georges Gordienko	Gordienko won	Coventry, England
01/04/1963	Bill Robinson Vs Geoff Portz	Robinson won	Bradford
02/04/1963	Bill Robinson Vs Geoff Portz	NK	Lime Grove, England
03/04/1963	Bill Robinson Vs Geoff Portz	NK	Preston, Lancashire
04/04/1963	Bill Robinson Vs Geoff Portz	NK	Brierly Hill
06/04/1963	Bill Robinson Vs Geoff Portz	Robinson won	Middlesborough, North Yorkshire

Date	Match	Result	Location
09/04/1963	Bill Robinson Vs Bruno Elrington	NK	Croydon, England
10/04/1963	Bill Robinson Vs Johnny Kostas	NK	Cardiff, Wales
11/04/1963	Bill Robinson Vs John DaSilva	NK	Cambridge, England
15/04/1963	Bill Robinson Vs John DaSilva	NK	Kirkby, Ashfield
16/04/1963	Bill Robinson Vs Dennis Mitchell	Nk	Huddersfield, England
17/04/1963	Bill Robinson Vs Dennis Mitchell	Nk	Preston, Lancashire
18/04/1963	Bill Robinson Vs Willem Hall	NK	Morecambe, Lancashire
20/04/1963	Bill Robinson Vs Geoff Portz	Portz won	Middlesborough, North Yorkshire
22/04/1963	Bill Robinson Vs John Lees	NK	York
24/04/1963	Bill Robinson Vs Pietro Capello	NK	Lincoln
25/04/1963	Bill Robinson Vs Tibor Szakacs	NK	Barrow
26/04/1963	Bill Robinson Vs Dai Sullivan	NK	Chesterfield
27/04/1963	Bill Robinson Vs Billy Joyce	Joyce won	Belle Vue, Manchester
29/04/1963	Bill Robinson Vs Peter Maivia	Robinson won	Leeds, West yorkshire
30/04/1963	Bill Robinson Vs Dai Sullivan	NK	Aberdeen, Scotland
01/05/1963	Bill Robinson Vs Pietro Capello	NK	Sheffield, South Yorkshire
02/05/1963	Bill Robinson Vs Ian Campbell	NK	Brierly Hill
04/05/1963	Bill Robinson Vs John DaSilva	Draw	Newcastle, England
06/05/1963	Bill Robinson Vs Bill Rawlings	Robinson won	Hamilton, Scotland
07/05/1963	Bill Robinson Vs Dennis Mitchell	Draw	Huddersfield, England
09/05/1963	Bill Robinson Vs Ernie Riley	NK	Brierly Hill
10/05/1963	Bill Robinson Vs Billy Howes	Robinson won BHDQ	Glasgow, Scotland
11/05/1963	Bill Robinson Vs Billy Howes	NK	Grimsby
14/05/1963	Bill Robinson Vs Geoff Portz	NK	Harrogate
15/05/1963	Bill Robinson Vs Billy Howes	NK	Sheffield, South Yorkshire
16/05/1963	Bill Robinson Vs Bill McDonald	NK	Morecambe, Lancashire
17/05/1963	Bill Robinson Vs Billy Howes	NK	Bridlington
18/05/1963	Bill Robinson Vs Billy Joyce	Draw	Belle Vue, Manchester
20/05/1963	Bill Robinson Vs Johnny Yearsley	Robinson won	Shoreditch, London
21/05/1963	Bill Robinson Vs George Gordienko	NK	Croydon, England
22/05/1963	Bill Robinson Vs Ian Campbell	Draw	Royal Albert Hall, London
23/05/1963	Bill Robinson Vs Herman Iffland	NK	Bristol
24/05/1963	Bill Robinson Vs Prince Kumali	NK	Rochester
25/05/1963	Bill Robinson Vs Ray Apollon	NK	Norwich
26/05/1963	Bill Robinson Vs Steve Veidor	Robinson won	Brighton, England
27/05/1963	Bill Robinson Vs Billy Joyce	Robinson won	Bradford
28/05/1963	Bill Robinson Vs Geoff Portz	NK	Trowell
01/06/1963	Bill Robinson Vs Billy Joyce	Draw	Middlesbrough
01/06/1963	Bill Robinson Vs Billy Joyce	Draw	Middlesborough, North Yorkshire
03/06/1963	Bill Robinson Vs Yasim Ghulam Gama	Robinson won	Belle Vue, Manchester
03/06/1963	Bill Robinson Vs Pietro Capello	Robinson won	Belle Vue, Manchester
03/06/1963	Bill Robinson Vs Josef Kovacs	Robinson won	Belle Vue, Manchester
07/06/1963	Bill Robinson Vs Josef Kovacs	Robinson won	Glasgow, Scotland
08/06/1963	Bill Robinson Vs Rocky Wall	Draw	Newcastle, England
10/06/1963	Bill Robinson Vs Bruno Elrington	NK	Leeds, West yorkshire

Date	Match	Result	Location
11/06/1963	Bill Robinson Vs Roy Bull Davis	NK	Bridlington
13/06/1963	Bill Robinson Vs Billy Joyce	NK	Morecambe
13/06/1963	Bill Robinson Vs Billy Joyce	NK	Morecambe, Lancashire
14/06/1963	Bill Robinson Vs Gwyn Davies	Robinson won	Glasgow, Scotland
15/06/1963	Billy Robinson Vs Norman Walsh	Draw	Chesterfield
17/06/1963	Bill Robinson Vs Billy Howes	NK	York
24/06/1963	Bill Robinson Vs Henri Pierlot	Robinson won	Cheltenham, England
25/06/1963	Bill Robinson Vs Johnny Czeslaw	NK	Kings Lynn
26/06/1963	Bill Robinson Vs Ray Apollon	NK	Cardiff, Wales
27/06/1963	Bill Robinson Vs Tibor Szakacs	NK	Walthamstow, London
28/06/1963	Bill Robinson Vs Rocky Wall	Robinson won	Glasgow, Scotland
01/07/1963	Billy Robinson Vs Geoff Portz	NK	Bradford, West Yorkshire
02/07/1963	Bill Robinson Vs John DaSilva	NK	Bridlington
04/07/1963	Bill Robinson Vs John Lees	NK	Leeds, West yorkshire
06/07/1963	Bill Robinson Vs Geoff Portz	NK	Middlesborough, North Yorkshire
07/07/1963	Bill Robinson Vs Johnny Yearsley	Robinson won	Brighton, England
08/07/1963	Bill Robinson Vs Ray Apollon	NK	Wembley, London
09/07/1963	Bill Robinson Vs Ian Campbell	NK	Croydon, England
11/07/1963	Bill Robinson Vs Tibor Szakacs	NK	Bournemouth, England
12/07/1963	Bill Robinson Vs Geoff Portz	Robinson won	Glasgow, Scotland
13/07/1963	Bill Robinson Vs Gwyn Davies	Robinson won	Newcastle, England
15/07/1963	Bill Robinson Vs Dennis Mitchell	NK	York
16/07/1963	Bill Robinson Vs Peter Maivia	Robinson won	Hove
17/07/1963	Bill Robinson Vs Roy Bull Davis	NK	Margate
19/07/1963	Bill Robinson Vs Gwyn Davies	Davies won	Glasgow, Scotland
20/07/1963	Bill Robinson Vs Dennis Mitchell	Robinson won	Newcastle, England
23/07/1963	Bill Robinson Vs Rocky Wall	NK	Aberdeen, Scotland
25/07/1963	Bill Robinson Vs Jim Hussey	NK	Morecambe, Lancashire
26/07/1963	Bill Robinson Vs Billy Joyce	NK	Glasgow, Scotland
26/07/1963	Bill Robinson Vs Billy Joyce	NK	Glasgow, Scotland
27/07/1963	Bill Robinson Vs Norman Walsh	NK	Cleethorpes
12/08/1963	Bill Robinson Vs Hans Streiger	Robinson won	Douglas, Isle of Man
02/09/1963	Bill Robinson Vs Billy Joyce	Draw	Bradford
03/09/1963	Bill Robinson Vs Ian Campbell	NK	Bridlington
07/09/1963	Bill Robinson Vs Billy Howes	Robinson won	Belle Vue, Manchester
07/09/1963	Bill Robinson Vs Billy Howes	NK	Belle Vue, Manchester
09/09/1963	Bill Robinson Vs Arthur Ricardo	NK	York
12/09/1963	Bill Robinson Vs Gwyn Davies	NK	Morecambe, Lancashire
13/09/1963	Bill Robinson Vs Joe Cornelius	NK	Leicester, Leicestershire
14/09/1963	Bill Robinson Vs Joe Cornelius	Robinson won	Portsmouth
16/09/1963	Bill Robinson Vs Gwyn Davies	Draw	Leeds, West yorkshire
17/09/1963	Bill Robinson Vs Francis Sullivan	NK	Bridlington
18/09/1963	Bill Robinson Vs Billy Howes	NK	Sheffield, England
18/09/1963	Bill Robinson Vs Billy Howes	NK	Sheffield, South Yorkshire
19/09/1963	Bill Robinson Vs Billy Joyce	NK	Morecambe, Lancashire

Date	Match	Result	Location
21/09/1963	Bill Robinson Vs John Lees	Robinson won	Grantham, England
24/09/1963	Bill Robinson Vs Henri Pierlot	NK	Wolverhampton
28/09/1963	Bill Robinson Vs Billy Joyce	Robinson won	Middlesbrough
28/09/1963	Bill Robinson Vs Billy Joyce	Robinson won	Middlesborough, North Yorkshire
30/09/1963	Bill Robinson Vs Zebra Kid	NC	Loughborough, England
01/10/1963	Bill Robinson Vs Billy Joyce	Robinson won	Huddersfield
01/10/1963	Bill Robinson Vs Billy Joyce	Robinson won	Huddersfield, England
02/10/1963	Bill Robinson Vs Zebra Kid	Kid won	Lincoln
03/10/1963	Bill Robinson Vs Bob Sweeney	NK	Kirkcaldy
04/10/1963	Bill Robinson Vs John Lees	NC	Glasgow, Scotland
05/10/1963	Bill Robinson Vs Bob Sweeney	NK	Falkirk
07/10/1963	Bill Robinson Vs Billy Joyce	Draw	Bradford
08/10/1963	Bill Robinson Vs Norman Walsh	NK	Preston, Lancashire
10/10/1963	Bill Robinson Vs Hans Streiger	NK	Nottingham
11/10/1963	Bill Robinson Vs Gwyn Davies	NK	Chesterfield
12/10/1963	Bill Robinson Vs Gwyn Davies	NK	Grimsby
13/10/1963	Bill Robinson Vs Steve Veidor	NK	Kirkby, Ashfield
14/10/1963	Bill Robinson Vs Tibor Szakacs	Draw	Birmingham, England
16/10/1963	Bill Robinson Vs Dennis Mitchell	NC	Lincoln
17/10/1963	Bill Robinson Vs Ernie Riley	NK	Crewe
18/10/1963	Bill Robinson Vs Dennis Mitchell	Draw	Glasgow, Scotland
19/10/1963	Billy Robinson Vs Dave Armstrong	Robinson won	Hull
21/10/1963	Bill Robinson Vs Bill Rawlings	NK	Leeds, West yorkshire
22/10/1963	Bill Robinson Vs Bill Rawlings	Robinson won	Aberdeen, Scotland
25/10/1963	Bill Robinson Vs Johnny Allan	Robinson won	Bolton, Lancashire
26/10/1963	Bill Robinson Vs Billy Joyce	NK	Middlesbrough
26/10/1963	Bill Robinson Vs Billy Joyce	NK	Middlesborough, North Yorkshire
28/10/1963	Bill Robinson Vs Francis Sullivan	NK	Carlisle, England
29/10/1963	Bill Robinson Vs Zando Zabo	Draw	Hull
30/10/1963	Bill Robinson Vs Billy Howes	NK	Sheffield, South Yorkshire
31/10/1963	Bill Robinson Vs Billy Howes	NK	Barrow
31/10/1963	Bill Robinson Vs Billy Howes	NK	Barrow
01/11/1963	Bill Robinson & Billy Howes Vs Jim Rawlings & Bill Rawlings	NK	Morecambe, Lancashire
04/11/1963	Bill Robinson Vs Eric Froelich	Robinson won	Cheltenham, England
05/11/1963	Bill Robinson Vs Ken Ackles	NK	Croydon, England
07/11/1963	Bill Robinson Vs Zando Zabo	NK	Bristol
08/11/1963	Bill Robinson Vs Eric Froelich	Robinson won	Ipswich, England
09/11/1963	Bill Robinson Vs Felix Greegor	NK	Salisbury
11/11/1963	Bill Robinson Vs Zebra Kid	Draw	Loughborough, England
12/11/1963	Bill Robinson Vs John Lees	NK	Harrogate
13/11/1963	Bill Robinson Vs Rocky Wall	NK	Preston, Lancashire
14/11/1963	Bill Robinson Vs Frikki Alberta	NK	Nottingham
15/11/1963	Bill Robinson Vs Norman Walsh	NK	Glasgow, Scotland
16/11/1963	Bill Robinson Vs John Lees	NK	Falkirk
18/11/1963	Bill Robinson Vs Zando Zabo	NK	Leeds, West yorkshire

Date	Match	Result	Location
19/11/1963	Bill Robinson Vs Tony Cassio	Robinson won	Hull
20/11/1963	Bill Robinson Vs Dave Armstrong	Robinson won	Sheffield, South Yorkshire
21/11/1963	Bill Robinson Vs Billy Joyce	NK	Morecambe
21/11/1963	Bill Robinson Vs Billy Joyce	NK	Morecambe, Lancashire
22/11/1963	Bill Robinson Vs Ian Campbell	Campbell won	Rotherham
23/11/1963	Billy Robinson Vs Frikki Alberts	NK	Halifax, West Yorkshire
25/11/1963	Bill Robinson Vs Geoff Portz	NK	Bradford
26/11/1963	Bill Robinson Vs Billy Howes	NK	Trowell
26/11/1963	Bill Robinson Vs Billy Howes	NK	Trowell
28/11/1963	Bill Robinson Vs Dennis Mitchell	NK	Nottingham
29/11/1963	Bill Robinson Vs Dennis Mitchell	NC	Glasgow, Scotland
30/11/1963	Bill Robinson Vs Billy Howes	NK	Grantham,
30/11/1963	Bill Robinson Vs Billy Howes	NK	Grantham, England
02/12/1963	Bill Robinson Vs Digger Rowell	NK	Leeds, West yorkshire
03/12/1963	Bill Robinson Vs Pietro Capello	Robinson won	Hull
04/12/1963	Bill Robinson Vs Billy Howes	NK	Sheffield, England
04/12/1963	Bill Robinson Vs Billy Howes	NK	Sheffield, South Yorkshire
05/12/1963	Bill Robinson Vs Bruno Elrington	NK	Nelson
09/12/1963	Bill Robinson Vs Con Papalazarou	NK	Southampton, England
10/12/1963	Bill Robinson Vs Joe Cornelius	Robinson won	Croydon, England
11/12/1963	Bill Robinson Vs Con Papalazarou	Robinson won	Shoreditch, London
12/12/1963	Bill Robinson Vs Francis Sullivan	NK	Gloucester, England
13/12/1963	Bill Robinson Vs George Gordienko	Draw	Rochester
14/12/1963	Bill Robinson Vs Prince Kumali	NK	Brighton, England
16/12/1963	Bill Robinson Vs Josef Kovacs	Kovacs won	Bradford
17/12/1963	Bill Robinson Vs Josef Kovacs	NK	Lime Grove, England
19/12/1963	Bill Robinson Vs Bruno Elrington	NK	Dunfermline
20/12/1963	Bill Robinson Vs Rocky Wall	Robinson won	Glasgow, Scotland
21/12/1963	Bill Robinson Vs Earl Maynard	NK	Middlesborough, North Yorkshire
23/12/1963	Bill Robinson Vs Josef Kovacs	NK	Birmingham, England
28/12/1963	Bill Robinson Vs John Lees	Robinson won	Grantham, England
30/12/1963	Bill Robinson Vs Geoff Portz	NK	Nelson
02/01/1964	Bill Robinson Vs Bruno Elrington	NK	Nottingham
03/01/1964	Bill Robinson Vs Rocky Wall	Robinson won	Glasgow, Scotland
04/01/1964	Bill Robinson Vs Bruno Elrington	NK	Falkirk
08/01/1964	Bill Robinson Vs Ian Campbell	NK	Chesterfield
09/01/1964	Bill Robinson Vs Bruno Elrington	NK	Brierly Hill
10/01/1964	Bill Robinson Vs Johnny Kostas	NK	Rotherham
11/01/1964	Bill Robinson Vs John Lees	NK	Middlesborough, North Yorkshire
14/01/1964	Bill Robinson Vs Billy Joyce	NK	Wellington
15/01/1964	Bill Robinson Vs Tibor Szakacs	NK	Preston, Lancashire
16/01/1964	Bill Robinson Vs Roy Bull Davis	NK	Crewe
17/01/1964	Bill Robinson Vs John DaSilva	Robinson won	Bolton, Lancashire
18/01/1964	Bill Robinson Vs Gwyn Davies	Robinson won	Doncaster
20/01/1964	Bill Robinson Vs Ray Apollon	Robinson won	Leeds, West yorkshire

Date	Match	Result	Location
22/01/1964	Bill Robinson Vs Ian Campbell	NK	Sheffield, South Yorkshire
23/01/1964	Bill Robinson Vs Billy Howes	NK	Barrow
24/01/1964	Bill Robinson Vs Norman Walsh	NK	Leicester, Leicestershire
25/01/1964	Bill Robinson Vs Johnny Allan	NK	Grantham, England
27/01/1964	Bill Robinson Vs Luc Straub	Robinson won	West Ham, England
30/01/1964	Bill Robinson Vs Andre Bollett	Robinson won	Bristol
31/01/1964	Bill Robinson Vs Andre Bollett	Robinson won ABDQ	Streatham
03/02/1964	Bill Robinson Vs Norman Walsh	NK	Bradford
04/02/1964	Bill Robinson Vs Bill Rawlings	NK	Huddersfield, England
05/02/1964	Bill Robinson Vs Josef Kovacs	NK	Leicester, Leicestershire
06/02/1964	Bill Robinson Vs Josef Zaranoff	NK	Nottingham
07/02/1964	Bill Robinson Vs Norman Walsh	Robinson won	Rotherham
08/02/1964	Billy Robinson Vs Geoff Portz	Portz won, BR DQ	Limegrove Hall, Shepherd's Bush, London
10/02/1964	Bill Robinson Vs Billy Joyce	Robinson won	Cheltenham, England
13/02/1964	Bill Robinson Vs Billy Howes	NK	Crewe
14/02/1964	Bill Robinson Vs Tibor Szakacs	NK	Liverpool
15/02/1964	Bill Robinson Vs Tibor Szakacs	Draw	Hanley
18/02/1964	Bill Robinson Vs Josef Kovacs	NK	Wolverhampton
20/02/1964	Bill Robinson Vs Masambula	NK	Brierly Hill
21/02/1964	Bill Robinson Vs Franz Orlik	NK	Willenhall
25/02/1964	Bill Robinson Vs Zebra Kid	NK	Trowell
27/02/1964	Bill Robinson Vs The Mask	NK	Kirkcaldy
28/02/1964	Bill Robinson Vs The Mask	Draw	Glasgow, Scotland
29/02/1964	Bill Robinson Vs Henri Pierlot	NK	Falkirk
03/03/1964	Bill Robinson Vs Gideon Gidea	NK	Wolverhampton
04/03/1964	Bill Robinson Vs Norman Walsh	NK	Preston, Lancashire
05/03/1964	Bill Robinson Vs Frikki Alberta	NK	Nottingham
06/03/1964	Bill Robinson Vs Zebra Kid	NK	Liverpool
07/03/1964	Bill Robinson Vs Josef Kovacs	NK	Croydon, England
09/03/1964	Bill Robinson Vs Jack Bence	NK	Bedford
10/03/1964	Bill Robinson Vs Josef Kovacs	NK	Croydon, England
11/03/1964	Bill Robinson Vs Le Grande Vladimir	NK	Watford
12/03/1964	Bill Robinson Vs Gideon Gidea	Robinson won	Bristol
13/03/1964	Bill Robinson Vs Jack Bence	NK	Rochester
14/03/1964	Bill Robinson Vs Josef Kovacs	Robinson won JKDQ	Coventry, England
16/03/1964	Bill Robinson Vs Josef Kovacs	NK	Bradford
18/03/1964	Bill Robinson Vs Josef Kovacs	NK	Leicester, Leicestershire
19/03/1964	Bill Robinson Vs Ray Apollon	NK	Blackburn, Lancashire
21/03/1964	Billy Robinson Vs John Cox	Robinson won	Limegrove Hall, Shepherd's Bush, London
25/03/1964	Bill Robinson Vs Josef Kovacs	NK	Scarborough
26/03/1964	Bill Robinson Vs Billy Howes	NK	Liverpool
04/04/1964	Bill Robinson Vs Josef Kovacs	Nk	Falkirk
08/04/1964	Bill Robinson Vs Hans Streger	NK	Welshpool
09/04/1964	Bill Robinson Vs Roy Bull Davis	NK	Crewe

Date	Match	Result	Location
24/07/1964	Bill Robinson Vs Horst Hoffman	Draw	Nurenberg, Germany
25/07/1964	Bill Robinson Vs Tibor Szakacs	Robinson won	Nurenberg, Germany
26/07/1964	Bill Robinson Vs Fritz Mueller	Draw	Nurenberg, Germany
27/07/1964	Bill Robinson Vs Sean Regan	Robinson won	Nurenberg, Germany
28/07/1964	Bill Robinson Vs Horst Hoffman	Draw	Nurenberg, Germany
29/07/1964	Bill Robinson Vs Josef Molnar	Robinson won	Nurenberg, Germany
30/07/1964	Bill Robinson Vs Fritz Mueller	Robinson won	Nurenberg, Germany
05/11/1964	Bill Robinson Henri Pierlot	NK	Wimbledon
10/11/1964	Bill Robinson Vs Josef Zaranoff	NK	Croydon, England
01/01/1965	Bill Robinson Vs John Lees	Robinson won	Liverpool
02/01/1965	Bill Robinson Vs Alan Garfield	Robinson won	Hanley
04/01/1965	Bill Robinson Vs Norman Walsh	NK	Bradford
05/01/1965	Bill Robinson Vs Lucky Simonovich	Robinson won	Huddersfield, England
06/01/1965	Bill Robinson Vs Rocky Wall	NK	Ossett
07/01/1965	Bill Robinson Vs Zebra Kid	NK	Nottingham
08/01/1965	Bill Robinson Vs Zebra Kid	NK	Glasgow, Scotland
09/01/1965	Bill Robinson Vs Zebra Kid	NK	Grimsby
11/01/1965	Bill Robinson Vs Masambula	Robinson won	Birmingham, England
12/01/1965	Bill Robinson Vs Gideon Gidea	Draw	Wolverhampton
15/01/1965	Bill Robinson Vs Lucky Simonovich	Robinson won	Bolton, Lancashire
16/01/1965	Bill Robinson Vs Gideon Gidea	Robinson won	Hanley
18/01/1965	Bill Robinson Vs Geoff Portz	NK	Bradford
19/01/1965	Bill Robinson Vs Geoff Portz	NK	Leicester, Leicestershire
20/01/1965	Bill Robinson Vs Geoff Portz	NK	Middlesborough, North Yorkshire
21/01/1965	Bill Robinson Vs Earl Maynard	Robinson won	Rotherham
23/01/1965	Bill Robinson Vs Billy Howes	Robinson won	Wellington
23/01/1965	Bill Robinson Vs Dennis Mitchell	Robinson won	Newcastle, England
25/01/1965	Bill Robinson Vs Johnny Yearsley	NK	Wembley, London
27/01/1965	Bill Robinson Vs Johnny Kostas	Robinson won	Cardiff, Wales
28/01/1965	Bill Robinson Vs Josef Zaranoff	Robinson won	Bristol
30/01/1965	Bill Robinson Vs Syed Saif Shah	Robinson won	Brighton, England
01/02/1965	Bill Robinson Vs Eric Taylor	NK	Bradford
02/02/1965	Bill Robinson Vs Rocky Wall	NK	Leicester, Leicestershire
03/02/1965	Bill Robinson Vs Lucky Simonovich	Robinson won	Middlesborough, North Yorkshire
04/02/1965	Bill Robinson Vs John DaSilva	NK	Nottingham
05/02/1965	Bill Robinson Vs Rocky Wall	Wall won	Preston, Lancashire
06/02/1965	Bill Robinson Vs Rocky Wall	NK	Newcastle, England
08/02/1965	Bill Robinson Vs Ramon Napolitano	NK	Halifax
09/02/1965	Bill Robinson Vs Rocky Wall	NK	Trowell
11/02/1965	Bill Robinson Vs Lucky Simonovich	NK	Kirkcaldy
12/02/1965	Bill Robinson Vs Rocky Wall	NK	Glasgow, Scotland
13/02/1965	Bill Robinson Vs Rocky Wall	NK	Falkirk
15/02/1965	Bill Robinson Vs Bruno Elrington	NK	Blackpool
16/02/1965	Bill Robinson Vs Joe Cornelius	NK	Colchester
19/02/1965	Bill Robinson Vs Billy Joyce	Robinson won	Liverpool

Date	Match	Result	Location
19/02/1965	Bill Robinson Vs Billy Joyce	Robinson won	Liverpool
20/02/1965	Bill Robinson Vs Gideon Gidea	NK	Doncaster
22/02/1965	Bill Robinson Vs Enrique Marquess	NK	York
23/02/1965	Bill Robinson Vs Norman Walsh	NK	Wellington
24/02/1965	Bill Robinson Vs Tosh Togo	NK	Scarborough
25/02/1965	Bill Robinson Vs Josef Zaranoff	NK	Nottingham
27/02/1965	Bill Robinson Vs Josef Kovacs	Robinson won	Belle Vue, Manchester
01/03/1965	Bill Robinson Vs Billy Howes	Robinson won	Birmingham
01/03/1965	Bill Robinson Vs Billy Howes	Robinson won	Birmingham, England
05/03/1965	Bill Robinson Vs Hans Dillinger	Robinson won	Willenhall
06/03/1965	Bill Robinson Vs Dennis Mitchell	Robinson won	Doncaster
09/03/1965	Bill Robinson Vs Billy Howes	Robinson won	Wellington
10/03/1965	Bill Robinson Vs Josef Kovacs	NK	Uttoxeter
11/03/1965	Bill Robinson Vs Billy Howes	NK	Whitchurch
11/03/1965	Bill Robinson Vs Billy Howes	NK	Whitchurch
12/03/1965	Bill Robinson Vs Zebra Kid	Draw	Liverpool
13/03/1965	Bill Robinson Vs Bruno Elrington	Robinson won BEDQ	Hanley
15/03/1965	Bill Robinson Vs Jim Hussey	NK	Blackpool
16/03/1965	Bill Robinson Vs Arthur Ricardo	NK	Leicester, Leicestershire
17/03/1965	Bill Robinson Vs Rocky Wall	NK	Middlesborough, North Yorkshire
19/03/1965	Bill Robinson Vs Dennis Mitchell	NK	Chesterfield
20/03/1965	Bill Robinson Vs Norman Walsh	Draw	Newcastle, England
22/03/1965	Bill Robinson Vs Zebra Kid	NK	Blackpool
24/03/1965	Bill Robinson Vs Hans Streger	Robinson won HSDQ	Lincoln
26/03/1965	Bill Robinson Vs Zebra Kid	Draw	Liverpool
27/03/1965	Bill Robinson Vs Dennis Mitchell	Robinson won	Doncaster
29/03/1965	Bill Robinson Vs Geoff Portz	NK	Loughborough, England
30/03/1965	Bill Robinson Vs Geoff Portz	Draw	Huddersfield, England
03/04/1965	Bill Robinson Vs Geoff Portz	NK	Falkirk
06/04/1965	Bill Robinson Vs Joe Cornelius	Robinson won	Wolverhampton
08/04/1965	Bill Robinson Vs Dennis Mitchell	NK	Corwen
09/04/1965	Bill Robinson Vs John Lees	Robinson won	Liverpool
10/04/1965	Bill Robinson Vs Johnny Allan	Draw	Doncaster
12/04/1965	Bill Robinson Vs Zebra Kid	Draw	Birmingham, England
13/04/1965	Bill Robinson Vs Bill Verna	NK	Colchester
15/04/1965	Bill Robinson Vs Geoff Portz	Robinson won	Peterborough, England
16/04/1965	Bill Robinson Vs Gordon Nelson	Robinson won GNDQ	Belle Vue, Manchester
17/04/1965	Bill Robinson Vs Josef Kovacs	Robinson won JKDQ	Hanley
19/04/1965	Bill Robinson Vs Tibor Szakacs	NK	Wembley, London
20/04/1965	Bill Robinson Vs Josef Zaranoff	NK	Croydon, England
21/04/1965	Bill Robinson Vs Geoff Portz	Portz won	Middlesborough, North Yorkshire
22/04/1965	Bill Robinson Vs Paul Vachon	Robinson won PVDQ	Bristol
23/04/1965	Bill Robinson Vs Paul Vachon	Robinson won	Rochester
24/04/1965	Bill Robinson Vs Peter Maivia	Draw	Maidstone

Date	Match	Result	Location
26/04/1965	Bill Robinson Vs John Lees	Robinson won	Bradford
27/04/1965	Bill Robinson Vs Rocky Wall	Robinson won	Leicester, Leicestershire
29/04/1965	Bill Robinson Vs Gwyn Davies	NK	Crewe
30/04/1965	Bill Robinson Vs Rocky Wall	NK	Glasgow, Scotland
01/05/1965	Bill Robinson Vs Timmy Geoghegan	Robinson won	Newcastle, England
03/05/1965	Bill Robinson Vs Tibor Szakacs	NK	Blackpool
04/05/1965	Bill Robinson Vs Billy Howes	NK	Solihull
04/05/1965	Bill Robinson Vs Billy Howes	NK	Solihull
07/05/1965	Bill Robinson Vs Gwyn Davies	Robinson won	Liverpool
08/05/1965	Bill Robinson & Joe Cornelius Vs Jim Hussey & Roy Bull Davis	Robinson won	Hanley
10/05/1965	Bill Robinson Vs Hans Streiger	NK	Loughborough, England
11/05/1965	Bill Robinson Vs Billy Howes	Robinson won	Huddersfield
11/05/1965	Bill Robinson Vs Billy Howes	Robinson won	Huddersfield, England
13/05/1965	Bill Robinson Vs Billy Joyce	NK	Nottingham, England
13/05/1965	Bill Robinson Vs Billy Joyce	NK	Nottingham
14/05/1965	Bill Robinson Vs Billy Joyce	Robinson won	Glasgow, Scotland
14/05/1965	Bill Robinson Vs Billy Joyce	Robinson won	Glasgow, Scotland
15/05/1965	Bill Robinson Vs Billy Joyce	Robinson won	Belle Vue, Manchester
15/05/1965	Bill Robinson Vs Billy Joyce	Robinson won	Belle Vue, Manchester
17/05/1965	Bill Robinson Vs Roy Bull Davis	Robinson won	Birmingham, England
18/05/1965	Billy Howes Vs Bill Robinson	Robinson won	Rochdale
18/05/1965	Bill Robinson Vs Billy Howes	Robinson won	Rochdale
21/05/1965	Bill Robinson Vs Roy Bull Davis	Robinson won	Bolton, Lancashire
22/05/1965	Bill Robinson Vs Billy Howes	Robinson won	Hanley
22/05/1965	Bill Robinson Vs Billy Howes	Robinson won	Hanley
24/05/1965	Bill Robinson Vs Peter Maivia	Robinson won	Worthing
26/05/1965	Bill Robinson Vs John DaSilva	Draw	Shoreditch, London
28/05/1965	Bill Robinson Vs Gomez Maximilliano	Robinson won	Northampton
29/05/1965	Bill Robinson Vs Bill Verna	NK	Eastbourne, England
31/05/1965	Bill Robinson Vs Geoff Portz	NK	Bradford
02/06/1965	Bill Robinson Vs Geoff Portz	Draw	Middlesborough, North Yorkshire
05/06/1965	Bill Robinson Vs Johnny Allan	NC	Newcastle, England
07/06/1965	Bill Robinson Vs Johnny Allan	Robinson won	Birmingham, England
08/06/1965	Bill Robinson Vs Josef Kovacs	NK	Wolverhampton
09/06/1965	Bill Robinson Vs Roy Bull Davis	NK	Uttoxeter
11/06/1965	Bill Robinson Vs Josef Kovacs	Robinson won JKDQ	Liverpool
12/06/1965	Bill Robinson Vs Billy Joyce	Robinson won	Belle Vue, Manchester
14/06/1965	Bill Robinson Vs Johnny Allan	NK	York
15/06/1965	Bill Robinson Vs Billy Joyce	Draw	Trowell
15/06/1965	Bill Robinson Vs Billy Joyce	Draw	Trowell
18/06/1965	Bill Robinson Vs Dennis Mitchell	Robinson won	Glasgow, Scotland
23/06/1965	Bill Robinson Vs Dennis Mitchell	NK	Falkirk
28/06/1965	Bill Robinson Vs Tibor Szakacs	Robinson won	Bradford
29/06/1965	Bill Robinson Vs Billy Joyce	NK	Scarborough, England
29/06/1965	Bill Robinson Vs Billy Joyce	NK	Scarborough

Date	Match	Result	Location
02/07/1965	Bill Robinson Vs Billy Joyce	Joyce won	Glasgow, Scotland
03/07/1965	Bill Robinson Vs Rocky Wall	Robinson won	Newcastle, England
04/07/1965	Bill Robinson Vs Josef Kovacs	NK	Bromsgrove
05/07/1965	Bill Robinson Vs Billy Howes	Robinson won	Bolton
06/07/1965	Bill Robinson Vs Josef Kovacs	Robinson won JKDQ	Wolverhampton
07/07/1965	Billy Robinson Vs Billy Howes	NK	Bolton, Lancashire
08/07/1965	Bill Robinson Vs Roy Bull Davis	NK	Torquay
11/07/1965	Bill Robinson Vs John DaSilva	Robinson won	Brighton, England
12/07/1965	Bill Robinson Vs Bruno Elrington	Robinson won	Wembley, London
13/07/1965	Bill Robinson Vs Roy Bull Davis	Robinson won	Croydon, England
14/07/1965	Bill Robinson Vs Josef Zaranoff	Robinson won	Great Yarmouth, England
15/07/1965	Bill Robinson Vs Roy Bull Davis	Robinson won RBDDQ	Bristol
16/07/1965	Bill Robinson Vs Gordon Nelson	Robinson won	Rochester
17/07/1965	Bill Robinson Vs Bruno Elrington	Robinson won BEDQ	Hanley
19/07/1965	Bill Robinson Vs Gwyn Davies	Draw	Birmingham, England
20/07/1965	Bill Robinson Vs Billy Howes	NK	Skegness
20/07/1965	Bill Robinson Vs Billy Howes	NK	Skegness
22/07/1965	Bill Robinson Vs Gwyn Davies	NK	Aberystwyth, Wales
23/07/1965	Bill Robinson Vs Roy Bull Davis	Robinson won	Liverpool
26/07/1965	Bill Robinson Vs Steve Veidor	Robinson won	Hastings
27/07/1965	Bill Robinson Vs Tom Dowie	NK	Weymouth
28/07/1965	Billy Robinson Vs Johnny Da Silva	NK	Shoreditch, London
28/07/1965	Bill Robinson Vs Paul Vachon	Robinson won	Watford
30/07/1965	Bill Robinson Vs Earl Maynard	NK	Ramsgate
31/07/1965	Bill Robinson Vs Tibor Szakacs	Robinson won	Rhyl, Wales
03/08/1965	Bill Robinson Vs Rocky Wall	NK	Scarborough
06/08/1965	Bill Robinson Vs Jim Hussey	Robinson won	Bolton, Lancashire
07/08/1965	Bill Robinson Vs Billy Joyce	Robinson won	Belle Vue, Manchester
07/08/1965	Bill Robinson Vs Billy Joyce	Robinson won	Belle Vue, Manchester
12/08/1965	Bill Robinson Vs Henri Pierlot	NK	Morecambe, Lancashire
13/08/1965	Bill Robinson Vs Ezzard Hart	Robinson won	Glasgow, Scotland
17/08/1965	Bill Robinson Vs John Lees	Robinson won	Wolverhampton
20/08/1965	Bill Robinson Vs Billy Howes	Robinson won	Bolton
20/08/1965	Bill Robinson Vs Billy Howes	Robinson won	Bolton, Lancashire
22/08/1965	Bill Robinson Vs Tibor Szakacs	Robinson won	Blackpool
23/08/1965	Bill Robinson Vs Roy Bull Davis	Robinson won	Wembley, London
24/08/1965	Bill Robinson Vs Roy Bull Davis	Robinson won	Reading, England
25/08/1965	Bill Robinson Vs Roy Bull Davis	NK	Great Yarmouth, England
26/08/1965	Bill Robinson Vs Josef Zaranoff	NK	Bournemouth, England
27/08/1965	Bill Robinson Vs Tibor Szakacs	NK	Hornsey
28/08/1965	Bill Robinson Vs Remy Bale	Robinson won	Maidstone
29/08/1965	Bill Robinson Vs Prince Kumali	Robinson won	Brighton, England
30/08/1965	Bill Robinson Vs Earl Maynard	NK	Watford
31/08/1965	Bill Robinson Vs Rocky Wall	NK	Scarborough
15/09/1965	Bill Robinson Vs Hansi Rocks	Robinson won	Krefeld, Germany

Date	Match	Result	Location
16/09/1965	Bill Robinson Vs Mihalyi Kuti	Draw	Krefeld, Germany
18/09/1965	Bill Robinson Vs Peter Kayser	Robinson won	Krefeld, Germany
19/09/1965	Bill Robinson Vs Hans Dillinger	Robinson won	Krefeld, Germany
20/09/1965	Bill Robinson Vs Ray Apollon	Robinson won	Krefeld, Germany
22/09/1965	Bill Robinson Vs Horst Hoffman	Hoffman won	Krefeld, Germany
20/10/1965	Bill Robinson Vs Horst Hoffman	Draw	Munich, Germany
21/10/1965	Bill Robinson Vs Peter Kayser	Robinson won	Munich, Germany
22/10/1965	Bill Robinson Vs Mihalyi Kuti	Draw	Munich, Germany
23/10/1965	Bill Robinson Vs Gideon Gidea	Draw	Munich, Germany
24/10/1965	Bill Robinson Vs Josef Molnar	Robinson won	Munich, Germany
25/10/1965	Bill Robinson Vs Horst Hoffman	Draw	Munich, Germany
26/10/1965	Bill Robinson Vs Geoff Portz	Draw	Munich, Germany
27/10/1965	Bill Robinson Vs Hans Dillinger	Robinson won	Munich, Germany
28/10/1965	Bill Robinson Vs Mihalyi Kuti	Robinson won	Munich, Germany
29/10/1965	Bill Robinson Vs Hansi Rocks	Robinson won	Munich, Germany
30/10/1965	Bill Robinson Vs Ray Apollon	Draw	Munich, Germany
31/10/1965	Bill Robinson Vs Gideon Gidea	Robinson won	Munich, Germany
02/11/1965	Bill Robinson Vs Franz Orlik	Robinson won	Munich, Germany
03/11/1965	Bill Robinson Vs Ian Campbell	Robinson won	Munich, Germany
04/11/1965	Bill Robinson Vs Ray Apollon	Robinson won	Munich, Germany
05/11/1965	Bill Robinson Vs Geoff Portz	Robinson won	Munich, Germany
06/11/1965	Bill Robinson Vs Horst Hoffman	Robinson won	Munich, Germany
07/11/1965	Bill Robinson Vs Hansi Rocks	Robinson won	Hamburg, Germany
08/11/1965	Bill Robinson Vs Horst Hoffman	Draw	Hamburg, Germany
09/11/1965	Bill Robinson Vs Mihalyi Kuti	Robinson won	Hamburg, Germany
10/11/1965	Bill Robinson Vs Geoff Portz	Robinson won	Hamburg, Germany
11/11/1965	Bill Robinson Vs Josef Kovacs	Robinson won JKDQ	Hamburg, Germany
12/11/1965	Bill Robinson Vs Horst Hoffman	Hoffman won	Hamburg, Germany
13/11/1965	Bill Robinson Vs Gideon Gidea	Robinson won	Hamburg, Germany
14/11/1965	Bill Robinson Vs Hans Dillinger	Robinson won	Hamburg, Germany
15/11/1965	Bill Robinson Vs Josef Kovacs	Kovacs won	Hamburg, Germany
16/11/1965	Bill Robinson Vs Ray Apollon	Robinson won	Hamburg, Germany
01/12/1965	Bill Robinson Vs Paul Vachon	NK	Sheffield, South Yorkshire
03/12/1965	Bill Robinson Vs Ian Campbell	Robinson won	Liverpool
04/12/1965	Billy Robinson Vs Josef Zaranoff	NK	Wallasey, merseyside
06/12/1965	Bill Robinson Vs Gwyn Davies	Robinson won	Birmingham, England
07/12/1965	Bill Robinson Vs Gwyn Davies	Robinson won	Huddersfield, England
09/12/1965	Bill Robinson Vs Tibor Szakacs	NK	Nottingham
10/12/1965	Bill Robinson Vs Earl Maynard	NK	Glasgow, Scotland
11/12/1965	Bill Robinson Vs Bruno Elrington	Robinson won	Hanley
13/12/1965	Bill Robinson Vs Billy Joyce	NK	Leeds, West yorkshire
17/12/1965	Bill Robinson Vs Ian Campbell	Draw	Rotherham
18/12/1965	Bill Robinson Vs Earl Maynard	Robinson won	Belle Vue, Manchester
20/12/1965	Bill Robinson Vs Earl Maynard	NK	Blackpool
21/12/1965	Bill Robinson Vs Ian Campbell	NK	Wolverhampton

Date	Match	Result	Location
01/01/1966	Billy Robinson Vs Albert Wall	NK	The Coronation Hall, Kingston Upon Thames
03/01/1966	Bill Robinson Vs Gwyn Davies	Robinson won	Blackpool
06/01/1966	Bill Robinson Vs Prince Kumali	NK	Nottingham
07/01/1966	Bill Robinson Vs Paul Vachon	Robinson won	Liverpool
10/01/1966	Bill Robinson Vs Roy Bull Davis	NK	York
14/01/1966	Bill Robinson Vs Gwyn Davies	Robinson won	Glasgow, Scotland
15/01/1966	Bill Robinson Vs Syed Saif Shah	NC	Falkirk
21/01/1966	Bill Robinson Vs Billy Howes	NK	Willenhall
21/01/1966	Bill Robinson Vs Billy Howes	NK	Willenhall
26/01/1966	Bill Robinson Vs John Lees	NK	Welshpool
15/02/1966	Bill Robinson Vs Billy Joyce	NK	Harrogate, north Yorkshire
15/02/1966	Bill Robinson Vs Billy Joyce	NK	Harrogate
18/02/1966	Bill Robinson Vs Tibor Szakacs	Robinson won	Glasgow, Scotland
21/02/1966	Bill Robinson Vs Ian Campbell	Robinson won	Blackpool
22/02/1966	Bill Robinson Vs Dennis Mitchell	NK	Solihull
23/02/1966	Bill Robinson Vs Billy Howes	Howes won BRDQ	Sheffield, South Yorkshire
23/02/1966	Bill Robinson Vs Billy Howes	Howes won	Sheffield, South Yorkshire
25/02/1966	Billy Robinson Vs Geoff Portz	Robinson won	Liverpool, England
09/03/1966	Billy Robinson Vs Roy Bull Davies	NK	Leominster
18/03/1966	Billy Robinson Vs Hans Streiger	Robinson won	Bolton, Lancashire
19/03/1966	Billy Robinson Vs Tibor Szakacs	Robinson won	Hanley, England
21/03/1966	Billy Robinson Vs Hans Streiger	NK	Blackpool, England
22/03/1966	Billy Robinson Vs Count Bartelli	NK	Solihull, England
25/03/1966	Billy Robinson Vs Hans Streiger	Robinson won, HSDQ	Liverpool, England
28/03/1966	Billy Robinson Vs Barry Douglas	Robinson won	Carlisle, England
29/03/1966	Billy Robinson Vs Hans Streiger	Robinson won	Aberdeen, Scotland
30/03/1966	Billy Robinson Vs Geoff Portz	Robinson won	Scunthorpe, England
31/03/1966	Billy Robinson Vs Tibor Szakacs	NK	Nottingham, England
01/04/1966	Billy Robinson Vs Geoff Portz	Robinson won	Rotherham, England
02/04/1966	Billy Robinson Vs Gwynn Davies	Robinson won	Belle Vue, Manchester
05/04/1966	Billy Robinson Vs Count Bartelli	Draw	Worsley
06/04/1966	Billy Robinson Vs Hans Streiger	Robinson won	Liverpool, England
07/04/1966	Bilyl Robinson Vs Gwynn Davies	NK	Willenhall
09/04/1966	Billy Robinson Vs Jim Hussey	Robinson won	Belle Vue, Manchester
12/04/1966	Billy Robinson Vs Dennis Mitchell	Robinson won	Huddersfield
13/04/1966	Bill Robinson Vs Billy Joyce	NK	Lincoln, Lincolnshire
13/04/1966	Billy Robinson Vs Billy Joyce	NK	Lincoln, England
18/04/1966	Billy Robinson Vs Johnny Allan	Robinson won	Leeds, England
20/04/1966	Billy Robinson Vs Dennis Mitchell	Robinson won	Sheffield, England
21/04/1966	Billy Robinson Vs Hans Streiger	NK	Morecambe, Lancashire
23/04/1966	Billy Robinson Vs Billy Joyce	Robinson won	Belle Vue, Manchester
29/04/1966	Billy Robinson Vs Jim Hussey	Robinson won	Bolton, Lancashire
30/04/1966	Billy Robinson Vs Geoff Portz	NK	Grimsby, England
02/05/1966	Billy Robinson Vs Dennis Mitchell	NK	Blackpool, England
05/05/1966	Billy Robinson Vs John Lees	Robinson won	Crewe, England

Date	Match	Result	Location
06/05/1966	Billy Robinson Vs Dennis Mitchell	Robinson won	Liverpool, England
07/05/1966	Billy Robinson Vs John Lees	Robinson won	Hanley
13/05/1966	Bill Robinson Vs Billy Joyce	Robinson won	Glasgow
13/05/1966	Billy Robinson Vs Billy Joyce	Robinson won	Glasgow, Scotland
14/05/1966	Billy Robinson Vs Billy Joyce	Joyce won	Belle Vue, Manchester
17/05/1966	Billy Robinson Vs Syed Saif Shah	Robinson won	Solihull, England
19/05/1966	Billy Robinson Vs Syed Saif Shah	NK	Brierley Hill, England
20/05/1966	Billy Robinson Vs Hans Streiger	Robinson won	Liverpool, England
23/05/1966	Billy Robinson Vs Geoff Portz	Robinson won	Leeds, England
24/05/1966	Billy Robinson Vs Geoff Portz	NK	Harrogate
25/05/1966	Billy Robinson Vs Tibor Szakacs	NK	Prestatyn Holiday Camp Ballroom, Denbighshire
25/05/1966	Billy Robinson Vs Gwynn Davies	NK	Newtown
26/05/1966	Bill Robinson Vs Billy Joyce	NK	Nelson
26/05/1966	Billy Robinson Vs Billy Joyce	NK	Nelson
28/05/1966	Billy Robinson Vs Togo Tami	NK	The Pavillion, Hemel Hempstead, Hertfordshire
30/05/1966	Billy Robinson Vs Josef Zaranoff	Nk	York, England
03/06/1966	Billy Robinson Vs Ernie Riley	NK	Dumfries
06/06/1966	Bill Robinson Vs Wildman of Borneo	Robinson won	Birmingham, England
07/06/1966	Bill Robinson Vs John Cox	NK	Wolverhampton, England
08/06/1966	Bill Robinson Vs Wildman of Borneo	Robinson won	Southport
10/06/1966	Bill Robinson Vs Steve Veidor	Robinson won	Liverpool, England
11/06/1966	Bill Robinson Vs Bruno Elrington	Robinson won	Hanley
14/06/1966	Billy Robinson Vs Syed Saif Shah	Robinson won	Solihull, England
18/06/1966	Billy Robinson Vs Dennis Mitchell	NK	Watford Town Hall, Hertfordshire
22/06/1966	Billy Robinson Vs Billy Joyce	Robinson won	Glasgow, Scotland
23/06/1966	Bill Robinson Vs Billy Joyce	NK	Glasgow
23/06/1966	Billy Robinson Vs The Outlaw	NK	Nelson
24/06/1966	Bill Robinson Vs Tibor Szakacs	NC	Liverpool, England
25/06/1966	Bill Robinson Vs Zebra Kid	Robinson won, ZKDQ	Belle Vue, Manchester
28/06/1966	Billy Robinson Vs Geoff Portz	NK	Aberdeen, Scotland
29/06/1966	Bill Robinson Vs Billy Joyce	Robinson won	Sheffield, South Yorkshire
29/06/1966	Billy Robinson Vs Billy Joyce	Robinson won	Sheffield, England
30/06/1966	Billy Robinson Vs Ian Campbell	NK	Morecambe, Lancashire
09/07/1966	Bill Robinson Vs Pat Roach	Robinson won	Newcastle, England
14/07/1966	Bill Robinson Vs Steve Veidor	Robinson won	Bristol, England
16/07/1966	Billy Robinson Vs Geoff Portz	NK	Liverpool Stadium, Merseyside
16/07/1966	Bill Robinson Vs Billy Howes	Robinson won	Hanley
19/07/1966	Bill Robinson Vs Sean Regan	NK	Wolverhampton, England
21/07/1966	Bill Robinson Vs Mike Marino	Robinson won	Middlesborough, North Yorkshire
22/07/1966	Bill Robinson Vs John Lees	Robinson won	Bolton, Lancashire
23/07/1966	Bill Robinson Vs Hans Streiger	NK	Rhyl, Wales
26/07/1966	Bill Robinson Vs Roy Bull Davis	NK	Solihull, England
27/07/1966	Bill Robinson Vs Roy Bull Davis	Robinson won	Southport
29/07/1966	Bill Robinson Vs Steve Veidor	Robinson won	Liverpool, England

Date	Match	Result	Location
30/07/1966	Bill Robinson Vs Ian Campbell	NK	Portsmouth, England
31/07/1966	Bill Robinson Vs Henri Pierlot	Robinson won	Blackpool, England
02/08/1966	Bill Robinson Vs Dennis Mitchell	NK	Bridlington, England
04/08/1966	Bill Robinson Vs John Lees	Robinson won	Morecambe, Lancashire
05/08/1966	Bill Robinson Vs Billy Joyce	Joyce won	Hindley
05/08/1966	Bill Robinson Vs Billy Joyce	Robinson won	Hindley
06/08/1966	Bill Robinson Vs Hans Streiger	Robinson won	Belle Vue, Manchester
08/08/1966	Bill Robinson Vs Dave Larsen	NK	Birmingham, England
09/08/1966	Bill Robinson Vs Jim Hussey	Draw	Solihull, England
12/08/1966	Bill Robinson Vs Wayne Bridges	Robinson won	Liverpool, England
13/08/1966	Billy Robinson Vs John Cox	NK	Spa Royal Hall, Bridlington
14/08/1966	Bill Robinson Vs Jim Hussey	Robinson won	Blackpool, England
20/08/1966	Bill Robinson Vs Ian Campbell	Robinson won	Newcastle, England
22/08/1966	Bill Robinson Vs Count Bartelli	NK	Uttoxeter, England
23/08/1966	Bill Robinson Vs Josef Zaranoff	NK	Solihull, England
24/08/1966	Bill Robinson Vs Josef Zaranoff	Robinson won	Southport
27/08/1966	Bill Robinson Vs Ian Campbell	Robinson won	Belle Vue, Manchester
30/08/1966	Bill Robinson Vs John Lees	NK	Bridlington, England
31/08/1966	Bill Robinson Vs Zebra Kid	Zebra kid won	Great Yarmouth, England
01/09/1966	Bill Robinson Vs Bruno Elrington	Robinson won	Walthamstow
02/09/1966	Bill Robinson Vs Ian Campbell	NK	Rochester
03/09/1966	Bill Robinson Vs Billy Joyce	Joyce won	Newcastle, England
03/09/1966	Bill Robinson Vs Billy Joyce	Joyce won	Newcastle, England
21/09/1966	Bill Robinson Vs John Lees	Robinson won	Sheffield, England
23/09/1966	Bill Robinson Vs Jim Hussey	NK	Dumfries
24/09/1966	Bill Robinson Vs Billy Joyce	Robinson won	Newcastle, England
24/09/1966	Bill Robinson Vs Billy Joyce	Robinson won	Newcastle, England
30/09/1966	Bill Robinson Vs Count Bartelli	Draw	Bolton, Lancashire
01/10/1966	Bill Robinson Vs Reg Williams	Robinson won	Hanley
02/10/1966	Bill Robinson Vs Syed Saif Shah	NK	Blackpool, England
05/10/1966	Bill Robinson Vs Billy Joyce	Robinson won	Glasgow
05/10/1966	Bill Robinson Vs Billy Joye	NK	Glasgow, Scotland
07/10/1966	Bill Robinson Vs John Lees	NK	Dumfries
08/10/1966	Bill Robinson Vs Zebra Kid	Robinson won, ZKDQ	Belle Vue, Manchester
17/10/1966	Bill Robinson Vs Crusher Verdu	NK	Tunbridge Wells
18/10/1966	Bill Robinson Vs Crusher Verdu	Robinson won	Watford, England
19/10/1966	Bill Robinson Vs Crusher Verdu	Robinson won	Bath, England
22/10/1966	Bill Robinson Vs Steve Veidor	Robinson won	Belle Vue, Manchester
23/10/1966	Bill Robinson Vs Hans Streiger	Robinson won, HSDQ	Blackpool, England
17/11/1966	Bill Robinson Vs Gwyn Davies	NK	Nottingham, England
18/11/1966	Bill Robinson Vs Zebra Kid	NK	Scarborough
19/11/1966	Bill Robinson Vs Billy Joye	Joyce won	Newcastle, England
22/11/1966	Bill Robinson Vs Pat Roach	Nk	Wolverhampton, England
24/11/1966	Bill Robinson Vs Ian Campbell	NK	Nelson
25/11/1966	Bill Robinson Vs Tibor Szakacs	Tibor won	Liverpool, England

Date	Match	Result	Location
26/11/1966	Bill Robinson Vs Dennis Mitchell	Robinson won	Hanley
28/11/1966	Bill Robinson Vs Hans Streiger	Robinson won	Wembley, England
29/11/1966	Bill Robinson Vs Bruno Elrington	NK	Reading, England
30/11/1966	Bill Robinson Vs Zebra Kid	NK	Banbury, England
07/12/1966	Bill Robinson Vs Jim Hussey	NK	Leominster
10/12/1966	Bill Robinson Vs Billy Howes	Robinson won	Hanley
10/12/1966	Billy Robinson Vs Gwyn Davies	NK	The Floral Hall, Southport, Merseyside
12/12/1966	Bill Robinson Vs Billy Joyce	Joyce won	Bradford
12/12/1966	Bill Robinson Vs Billy Joye	Joyce won	Bradford
14/12/1966	Bill Robinson Vs Zebra Kid	NK	Lincoln, England
15/12/1966	Bill Robinson Vs Gwyn Davies	NK	Nottingham, England
17/12/1966	Bill Robinson Vs John Lees	Robinson won	Newcastle, England
19/12/1966	Bill Robinson Vs Mike Marino	NK	Leeds, England
20/12/1966	Bill Robinson Vs Jack Rowlands	Robinson won	Hull, England
21/12/1966	Bill Robinson Vs Kendo Nagasaki	NK	Grimsby, England
24/12/1966	Billy Robinson Vs Roy 'Bull' Davies	NK	Wryton Stadium, Bolton
26/12/1966	Bill Robinson Vs The Outlaw	NK	Sheffield, England
01/01/1967	Billy Robinson Vs Albert Wall	NK	The Coronation Hall, Kingston Upon Thames
02/01/1967	Bill Robinson Vs The Outlaw	NK	Derby, England
05/01/1967	Bill Robinson Vs Dennis Mitchell	Draw	Nottingham, England
07/01/1967	Bill Robinson Vs Leon Arras	Robinson won	Newcastle, England
11/01/1967	Bill Robinson Vs Billy Joye	NC	Leicester
12/01/1967	Bill Robinson Vs Zebra Kid	Zebra Kid Won, BRDQ	Nelson
14/01/1967	Bill Robinson Vs Bobby Graham	NK	Portsmouth, England
16/01/1967	Bill Robinson Vs Pat Roach	NK	Blackpool, England
17/01/1967	Bill Robinson Vs Jim Hussey	NK	Wolverhampton, England
18/01/1967	Bill Robinson Vs Billy Joye	Robinson won	Manchester
19/01/1967	Bill Robinson Vs Tibor Szakacs	NK	Caernarvon, Wales
20/01/1967	Bill Robinson Vs Pat Roach	Robinson won	Liverpool, England
21/01/1967	Bill Robinson Vs Hans Streiger	Robinson won	Hanley
23/01/1967	Bill Robinson Vs Billy Joye	Robinson won	Bradford
26/01/1967	Bill Robinson Vs Zebra Kid	Robinson won	Nelson
30/01/1967	Bill Robinson Vs Tibor Szakacs	Robinson won	Leeds, England
31/01/1967	Bill Robinson Vs John Lees	Robinson won	Hull, England
02/02/1967	Bill Robinson Vs John Lees	Robinson won	Preston, England
06/02/1967	Bill Robinson Vs Steve Haggetty	NK	Carlisle, England
07/02/1967	Bill Robinson Vs Count Bartelli	Draw	Solihull, England
08/02/1967	Bill Robinson Vs Count Bartelli	NC	Ellesmere Port
09/02/1967	Bill Robinson Vs Dennis Mitchell	Draw	Nottingham, England
10/02/1967	Bill Robinson Vs Jack Rowlands	Robinson won	Bolton, Lancashire
11/02/1967	Bill Robinson Vs John Lees	Robinson won	Hanley
13/02/1967	Bill Robinson Vs Josef Zaranoff	Robinson won	Cheltenham, England
14/02/1967	Bill Robinson Vs Peter Maivia	Robinson won	Colchester
15/02/1967	Bill Robinson Vs Nikita Mulkovich	Robinson won	Royal Albert Hall, London
16/02/1967	Bill Robinson Vs Gomez Maximilliano	Robinson won	Walthamstow

Date	Match	Result	Location
17/02/1967	Bill Robinson Vs Johnny Yearsley	NK	Ipswich
18/02/1967	Bill Robinson Vs Bruno Elrington	Robinson won	Hove
20/02/1967	Bill Robinson Vs John Lees	Robinson won	Bradford
25/02/1967	Bill Robinson Vs John Lees	Robinson won	Preston, England
27/02/1967	Bill Robinson Vs Hans Streiger	Robinson won	Blackpool, England
28/02/1967	Bill Robinson Vs Rocky Wall	Robinson won	Wolverhampton, England
03/03/1967	Bill Robinson Vs Wayne Bridges	Robinson won	Liverpool, England
04/03/1967	Bill Robinson Vs Count Bartelli	Count won	Hanley
06/03/1967	Bill Robinson Vs Gwyn Davies	Robinson won	Leeds, England
08/03/1967	Bill Robinson Vs John Lees	NK	Glasgow, Scotland
13/03/1967	Bill Robinson Vs Billy Joyce	NK	Derby, England
14/03/1967	Bill Robinson Vs Don Vines	Robinson won	Hull, England
16/03/1967	Bill Robinson Vs Rocky Wall	NK	Nottingham, England
17/03/1967	Bill Robinson Vs Josef Kovacs	Robinson won, JKDQ	Willenhall
18/03/1967	Bill Robinson Vs Pat Roach	NK	Solihull, England
20/03/1967	Bill Robinson Vs Josef Kovacs	Robinson won, JKDQ	Birmingham, England
21/03/1967	Bill Robinson Vs Syed Saif Shah	Robinson won	Spalding
21/03/1967	Bill Robinson Vs Les Herberts	Robinson won	Spalding
21/03/1967	Bill Robinson Vs Josef Zaranoff	Robinson won	Spalding
22/03/1967	Billy Robinson Vs Pat Roach	NK	The Civic Hall, Solihull
23/03/1967	Bill Robinson Vs Josef Kovacs	NK	Caernarvon, Wales
25/03/1967	Bill Robinson Vs Count Bartelli	NK	Shrewsbury
27/03/1967	Bill Robinson Vs Roy Bull Davis	Robinson won	Belle Vue, Manchester
28/03/1967	Bill Robinson Vs Mike Marino	Robinson won	Wolverhampton, England
29/03/1967	Bill Robinson Vs Prince Kumali	NK	Ross On Wye, England
31/03/1967	Bill Robinson Vs Josef Kovacs	Robinson won, JKDQ	Bolton, Lancashire
01/04/1967	Bill Robinson Vs Count Bartelli	Robinson won	Hanley
03/04/1967	Bill Robinson Vs Pat Roach	Robinson won	Bradford
04/04/1967	Bill Robinson Vs Steve Veidor	NK	Solihull, England
05/04/1967	Bill Robinson Vs Steve Veidor	NK	Leominster
07/04/1967	Bill Robinson Vs Johnny Allan	NK	Coalville
08/04/1967	Bill Robinson Vs Pat Roach	Robinson won	Newcastle, England
10/04/1967	Bill Robinson Vs Hans Streiger	NK	Leeds, England
12/04/1967	Bill Robinson Vs Gwyn Davies	Robinson won	Leicester
13/04/1967	Bill Robinson Vs Bruno Elrington	Robinson won	Nelson
14/04/1967	Bill Robinson Vs Bobo Matu	Robinson won	Liverpool, England
15/04/1967	Billy Robinson Vs Gil Voiney	NK	The Royal Hall, Harrogate, North Yorkshire
15/04/1967	Bill Robinson Vs Gil Voiney	Robinson won	Harrogate
21/04/1967	Bill Robinson Vs Steve Veidor	Robinson won	Glasgow, Scotland
22/04/1967	Bill Robinson Vs Josef Zaranoff	Robinson won	Belle Vue, Manchester
24/04/1967	Bill Robinson Vs Rocky Wall	Robinson won	Hamilton, Scotland
25/04/1967	Bill Robinson Vs Tibor Szakacs	Robinson won	Aberdeen, Scotland
09/05/1967	Bill Robinson Vs Tibor Szakacs	Robinson won	Wolverhampton, England
12/05/1967	Bill Robinson Vs Johnny Allan	Robinson won	Bolton, Lancashire

Date	Match	Result	Location
13/05/1967	Bill Robinson Vs Rocky Wall	NC	Newcastle, England
18/05/1967	Bill Robinson Vs Bruno Elrington	Robinson won	Bristol, England
19/05/1967	Bill Robinson Vs Syed Saif Shah	Robinson won	Liverpool, England
20/05/1967	Billy Robinson Vs Robert Gastel	NK	The Clifton Hall, Rotherham, South Yorkshlre
20/05/1967	Bill Robinson Vs Robert Gastel	Robinson won	Rotherham, England
21/05/1967	Bill Robinson Vs Geoff Portz	Robinson won	Cleethorpes
22/05/1967	Bill Robinson Vs The Outlaw	Robinson won, ODQ	Bradford
24/05/1967	Bill Robinson Vs Roy Bull Davis	NK	Leominster
25/05/1967	Bill Robinson Vs Gwyn Davies	Robinson won	Nelson
26/05/1967	Bill Robinson Vs Count Bartelli	Robinson won	Bolton, Lancashire
27/05/1967	Bill Robinson Vs Geoff Portz	Draw	Newcastle, England
29/05/1967	Bill Robinson Vs Rocky Wall	Robinson won	Belle Vue, Manchester
30/05/1967	Bill Robinson Vs Syed Saif Shah	NK	Solihull, England
31/05/1967	Bill Robinson Vs Steve Haggetty	Robinson won	Wordsley
02/06/1967	Bill Robinson Vs Rocky Wall	Robinson won	Liverpool, England
03/06/1967	Billy Robinson Vs Gwyn Davies	NK	Prestatyn Holiday Camp Ballroom, Denbighshire
03/06/1967	Bill Robinson Vs Syed Saif Shah	Robinson won	Hanley
05/06/1967	Bill Robinson Vs Rocky Wall	NK	York, England
10/06/1967	Bill Robinson Vs John Lees	Robinson won	Belle Vue, Manchester
12/06/1967	Bill Robinson Vs Syed Saif Shah	Draw	Birmingham, England
13/06/1967	Bill Robinson Vs Billy Howes	NK	Skegness
16/06/1967	Bill Robinson Vs Gwyn Davies	Robinson won	Bolton, Lancashire
17/06/1967	Bill Robinson Vs Steve Veidor	Robinson won	Hanley
20/06/1967	Bill Robinson Vs Mike Marino	Robinson won	Wolverhampton
21/06/1967	Billy Robinson Vs Steve Bell	NK	Victorial Hall, Hanley, Staffordshire
21/06/1967	Bill Robinson Vs Tibor Szakacs	NK	Royal Albert Hall, London
23/06/1967	Bill Robinson Vs Geoff Portz	Robinson won	Liverpool, England
24/06/1967	Bill Robinson Vs Geoff Portz	Draw	The Winter Gardens, Malvern, Worcestershire
25/06/1967	Bill Robinson Vs Josef Zaranoff	Robinson won	Blackpool, England
26/06/1967	Bill Robinson Vs Pat Barrett	NK	Bournemouth, England
27/06/1967	Bill Robinson Vs Crusher Verdu	Robinson won	Croydon
28/06/1967	Bill Robinson Vs Roy Bull Davis	Robinson won	Great Yarmouth, England
29/06/1967	Bill Robinson Vs Yure Borienko	Robinson won	Bristol, England
30/06/1967	Bill Robinson Vs Crusher Verdu	Robinson won	Rochester
01/07/1967	Bill Robinson Vs Bruno Elrington	Robinson won	Maidstone
04/07/1967	Bill Robinson Vs John Lees	NK	Aberdeen, Scotland
06/07/1967	Bill Robinson Vs John Lees	Robinson won	Morecambe, Lancashire
08/07/1967	Bill Robinson Vs The Outlaw	Robinson won, ODQ	Newcastle, England
10/07/1967	Bill Robinson Vs Roy Bull Davis	Robinson won	Birmingham, England
11/07/1967	Bill Robinson Vs Steve Veidor	NK	Solihull, England
12/07/1967	Bill Robinson Vs Rocky Wall	Robinson won	Southport
14/07/1967	Bill Robinson Vs Steve Veidor	Robinson won	Liverpool
15/07/1967	Bill Robinson Vs Steve Veidor	Robinson won	Hanley

Date	Match	Result	Location
16/07/1967	Bill Robinson Vs Steve Veidor	Robinson won	Blackpool, England
18/07/1967	Bill Robinson Vs John Lees	Draw	Wolverhampton, England
21/07/1967	Bill Robinson Vs Ron Marino	Robinson won	Bolton, Lancashire
22/07/1967	Bill Robinson Vs John Lees	NK	Rhyl, Wales
25/07/1967	Bill Robinson Vs Jim Hussey	NK	Bridlington, England
27/07/1967	Bill Robinson Vs Don Vines	NK	Morecambe, Lancashire
29/07/1967	Bill Robinson Vs Rocky Wall	Robinson won	Rhyl, Wales
31/07/1967	Bill Robinson Vs Count Bartelli	Robinson won	Birmingham, England
02/08/1967	Bill Robinson Vs John Cox	Robinson won	Southport
05/08/1967	Billy Robinson Vs Josef Zaranoff	NK	The Floral Hall, Southport, Merseyside
05/08/1967	Bill Robinson Vs Josef Zaranoff	NK	Southport
07/08/1967	Bill Robinson Vs Paul Vachon	Robinson won	Great Yarmouth, England
08/08/1967	Bill Robinson Vs Pat Roach	NK	Weymouth
09/08/1967	Bill Robinson Vs Crusher Verdu	Robinson won	Watford, England
10/08/1967	Bill Robinson Vs Johnny Yearsley	Robinson won	Southampton, England
11/08/1967	Bill Robinson Vs Les Kellett	NK	Dumfries
12/08/1967	Bill Robinson Vs Kendo Nagasaki	Draw	Newcastle, England
15/08/1967	Bill Robinson Vs Tibor Szakacs	Robinson won	Wolverhampton, England
16/08/1967	Bill Robinson Vs Tibor Szakacs	NK	Southport
18/08/1967	Bill Robinson Vs Tibor Szakacs	NK	Liverpool, England
19/08/1967	Bill Robinson Vs Count Bartelli	NK	Rhyl, Wales
22/08/1967	Bill Robinson Vs Bruno Elrington	NK	Herne Bay
25/08/1967	Bill Robinson Vs John Cox	Robinson won	Ayr
26/08/1967	Bill Robinson Vs Geoff Portz	NC	Belle Vue, Manchester
27/08/1967	Bill Robinson Vs Tibor Szakacs	Draw	Cleethorpes
28/08/1967	Bill Robinson Vs John Lees	Robinson won	Birmingham, England
29/08/1967	Bill Robinson Vs John Lees	NK	Bridlington, England
01/09/1967	Bill Robinson Vs Billy Howes	Robinson won	Bolton, Lancashire
02/09/1967	Bill Robinson Vs Tibor Szakacs	Robinson won	Southport
04/09/1967	Bill Robinson Vs The Outlaw	NK	Folkestone
06/09/1967	Bill Robinson Vs Bruno Elrington	NK	Felixstowe
07/09/1967	Bill Robinson Vs Roy Bull Davis	Roy won, BR Retired injury	Wimbledon, England
09/09/1967	Bill Robinson Vs Jim Hussey	Robinson won	Hanley
11/09/1967	Bill Robinson Vs Dennis Mitchell	Robinson won	Bradford
12/09/1967	Bill Robinson Vs Steve Veidor	Robinson won	Hemel Hempstead
13/09/1967	Bill Robinson Vs Bruno Elrington	NK	Banbury, England
14/09/1967	Bill Robinson Vs Tibor Szakacs	Robinson won	Bristol, England
16/09/1967	Bill Robinson Vs Dennis Mitchell	Robinson won	Newcastle, England
18/09/1967	Bill Robinson Vs Johnny Yearsley	NK	Folkestone
19/09/1967	Bill Robinson Vs Tibor Szakacs	NK	Plymouth
21/09/1967	Bill Robinson Vs Taras Bulba	Robinson won	Southampton, England
22/09/1967	Bill Robinson Vs Tibor Szakacs	Robinson won	Rochester
23/09/1967	Bill Robinson Vs Taras Bulba	Robinson won	Maidstone, Kent
25/09/1967	Bill Robinson Vs Kendo Nagasaki	NC	Bradford
26/09/1967	Bill Robinson Vs Hans Streiger	Robinson won	Croydon

Date	Match	Result	Location
27/09/1967	Bill Robinson Vs Roy Bull Davis	NK	Oxford
28/09/1967	Bill Robinson Vs Roy Bull Davis	Robinson won	Wimbledon, England
30/09/1967	Bill Robinson Vs Kendo Nagasaki	Draw; double DQ	Newcastle, England
02/10/1967	Bill Robinson Vs Kendo Nagasaki	Robinson won	Bradford
03/10/1967	Bill Robinson Vs Mike Marino	NK	Solihull, England
04/10/1967	Bill Robinson Vs Geoff Portz	Robinson won	Sheffield, England
06/10/1967	Bill Robinson Vs Geoff Portz	Robinson won	Liverpool, England
07/10/1967	Bill Robinson Vs Geoff Portz	Draw; double DQ	Hanley
08/10/1967	Bill Robinson Vs Geoff Portz	Robinson won	Blackpool, England
09/10/1967	Bill Robinson Vs Dennis Mitchell	NK	York, England
10/10/1967	Bill Robinson Vs Tibor Szakacs	Robinson won	Huddersfield
12/10/1967	Bill Robinson Vs Steve Veidor	Robinson won	Nottingham, England
13/10/1967	Bill Robinson Vs Paul Luty	Robinson won	Glasgow, Scotland
14/10/1967	Bill Robinson Vs Dennis Mitchell	NK	Falkirk
16/10/1967	Bill Robinson Vs Wild Angus	Robinson won	Bedford
17/10/1967	Bill Robinson Vs Tibor Szakacs	NK	Bournemouth, England
19/10/1967	Bill Robinson Vs Wild Angus	Robinson won	Peterborough, England
20/10/1967	Bill Robinson Vs Wolfgang Starck	Robinson won	Ipswich
21/10/1967	Bill Robinson Vs Crusher Verdu	Robinson won	Bracknell
23/10/1967	Bill Robinson Vs Wild Angus	Robinson won	Birmingham, England
27/10/1967	Bill Robinson Vs Mike Marino	Robinson won	Bolton, Lancashire
28/10/1967	Bill Robinson Vs Prince Kumali	Robinson won	Hanley
30/10/1967	Bill Robinson Vs Johnny Yearsley	Robinson won	Wembley, England
31/10/1967	Bill Robinson Vs Josef Zaranoff	Robinson won	Croydon
01/11/1967	Bill Robinson Vs Crusher Verdu	Robinson won, CVDQ	Bath, England
02/11/1967	Bill Robinson Vs Bruno Elrington	NK	Bury St. Edmunds
03/11/1967	Bill Robinson Vs Bruno Elrington	Robinson won	Bridgewater
04/11/1967	Bill Robinson Vs Rocky Wall	Robinson won	Liverpool Stadium, Merseyside
06/11/1967	Bill Robinson Vs Kendo Nagasaki	Draw	Bradford
07/11/1967	Bill Robinson Vs Kendo Nagasaki	Draw; double DQ	Lime Grove, England
08/11/1967	Bill Robinson Vs John Cox	NK	Perth
10/11/1967	Bill Robinson Vs Roy Bull Davis	Robinson won	Willenhall
11/11/1967	Bill Robinson Vs Kendo Nagasaki	Nagasaki won; BR DQ	Newcastle, England
13/11/1967	Bill Robinson Vs John Cox	NK	Blackpool, England
14/11/1967	Bill Robinson Vs Mike Marino	NK	Solihull, England
15/11/1967	Bill Robinson Vs Jack Rowlands	Rowlands won; BR retired injured	Bolton, Lancashire
20/11/1967	Bill Robinson Vs Wild Angus	NK	Derby, England
23/11/1967	Bill Robinson Vs Kendo Nagasaki	NK	Nottingham, England
30/11/1967	Bill Robinson Vs Kendo Nagasaki	NK	Brierley Hill, England
01/12/1967	Bill Robinson Vs Kendo Nagasaki	NK	Carlisle, England
02/12/1967	Bill Robinson Vs Luc Barreto	NK	Bridlington, England
13/12/1967	Bill Robinson Vs Mario Yugerous	NK	Sheffield, England
15/12/1967	Bill Robinson & Les Kellett Vs Halcons D'Orco	NK	Carlisle, England
16/12/1967	Bill Robinson Vs Sean Regan	NK	Limegrove Hall, Shepherd's Bush, London

Date	Match	Result	Location
18/12/1967	Bill Robinson Vs Johnny Allan	NK	Darlington
21/12/1967	Bill Robinson Vs Kendo Nagasaki	NK	Nottingham, England
23/12/1967	Bill Robinson Vs Roy Bull Davis	Robinson won	Bolton, Lancashire
29/12/1967	Bill Robinson Vs Ian Campbell	NK	Liverpool, England
01/01/1968	Billy Robinson Vs Dennis Mitchell	NK	York, England
02/01/1968	Billy Robinson Vs Rocky Wall	NC	Huddersfield
06/01/1968	Billy Robinson Vs Rocky Wall	Robinson won	Newcastle, England
08/01/1968	Billy Robinson Vs Lee Sharron	Robinson won	Hamilton, Scotland
10/01/1968	Billy Robinson Vs kendo Nagaski	Nagasaki won; BR DQ	Sheffield, England
11/01/1968	Billy Robinson Vs Syed Saif Shah	NK	Nelson
12/01/1968	Billy Robinson Vs kendo Nagaski	NK	Carlisle
16/01/1968	Billy Robinson Vs kendo Nagaski	Nagasaki won; BR DQ	Lime Grove
20/01/1968	Billy Robinson Vs Josef Kovacs	NK	Shrewsbury
22/01/1968	Billy Robinson Vs Hans Streiger	Robinson won	Wembley, England
23/01/1968	Billy Robinson Vs Jim Osborn	Robinson won	Hastings
24/01/1968	Billy Robinson Vs Bruno Elrington	Robinson won	Great yarmouth
25/01/1968	Billy Robinson Vs Lee Sharron	Robinson won	Peterborough, England
26/01/1968	Billy Robinson Vs Johnny Yearsley	NK	Herne Bay
27/01/1968	Billy Robinson Vs Al Hayes	Robinson won	Eastbourne, England
29/01/1968	Billy Robinson Vs kendo Nagaski	Robinson won	Bradford
30/01/1968	Billy Robinson Vs kendo Nagaski	Robinson won	Lime Grove
01/02/1968	Billy Robinson Vs kendo Nagaski	Draw	Lime Grove
02/02/1968	Billy Robinson Vs Geoff Portz	NK	Dumfries
05/02/1968	Billy Robinson Vs Steve Veidor	Robinson won	Blackpool, England
06/02/1968	Billy Robinson Vs Josef Zaranoff	Robinson won	Solihull, England
09/02/1968	Billy Robinson Vs kendo Nagaski	Nagasaki won	Liverpool, England
10/02/1968	Billy Robinson Vs Dennis Mitchell	Robinson won	Belle Vue, Manchester
12/02/1968	Billy Robinson Vs Gargantua	Robinson won	Bradford
13/02/1968	Billy Robinson Vs kendo Nagaski	Nagasaki won	Huddersfield
15/02/1968	Billy Robinson Vs Roy Bull Davies	NK	Nottingham
16/02/1968	Billy Robinson Vs kendo Nagaski	NK	Glasgow, Scotland
19/02/1968	Billy Robinson Vs Steve Veidor	NK	Harrogate
20/02/1968	Billy Robinson Vs Josef Zaranoff	Robinson won	Edinburgh, Scotland
23/02/1968	Billy Robinson Vs Steve Veidor	Robinson won	Stafford, England
24/02/1968	Billy Robinson Vs Josef Zaranoff	Robinson won	Newcastle, England
26/02/1968	Bill Robinson Vs Billy Joyce	Robinson won	Leeds
26/02/1968	Billy Robinson Vs Billy Joyce	Robinson won	Leeds
27/02/1968	Billy Robinson Vs John Lees	Robinson won	Wolverhampton, England
03/04/1968	Bill Robinson Vs Masao Kimura	Robinson won	Yokohoma
07/04/1968	Bill Robinson & John Lees & Colin Joynson Vs Masao Kimura & Thunder Sugiyama & Toyonobori	Kimura et al won	Himeji
07/04/1968	Billy Robinson & John Lees & Colin Joynson Vs Masao Kimura & Thunder Sugiyama & Toyonobori	Kimura et al won	Himeji, Japan
08/04/1968	Bill Robinson Vs Thunder Sugiyama	Draw DKO	Iwakuni
08/04/1968	Billy Robinson Vs Thunder Sugiyama	draw	Iwakuni, Japan
11/04/1968	Bill Robinson Vs Shozo Kobyashi	Robinson won	Kure

Date	Match	Result	Location
11/04/1968	Billy Robinson Vs Shozo Kobayashi	Robinson won	Kure, Japan
14/04/1968	Bill Robinson & Tony Charles Vs Great Kusatsu & Tadaharu Tanaka	Kusatsu et al won BRDQ	Kashima
14/04/1968	Billy Robinson & Tony Charles Vs Great Kusatsu & Tadaharu Tanaka	Kusatsu & Tanaka won	Kashima, Japan
17/04/1968	Bill Robinson Vs Great kusatsu	Robinson won	Karatsu
17/04/1968	Billy Robinson Vs Great Kusatsu	NK	Karatsu, Japan
20/04/1968	Bill Robinson Vs Shozo Kobyashi	Robinson won	Higashiosaka
24/04/1968	Bill Robinson & Tony Charles Vs Thunder Sugiyama & Toyonobor	Thunder et al won	Kumagaya
24/04/1968	Billy Robinson & Tony Charles Vs Toyonobori & Thunder Sugiyama	Toyonobori & Sugiyama won	Kumagaya, Japan
29/04/1968	Bill Robinson & John Lees Vs Great Kusatsu & thunder Sugiyama	Kusatsu et al won	Gamagori
29/04/1968	Billy Robinson & John Lees Vs Great Kusatsu & Thunder Sugiyama	Kusatsu & Sugiyama]	Gamagori, Japan
30/04/1968	Bill Robinson Vs Toyonobori	Draw DKO	Tokyo
30/04/1968	Billy Robinson Vs Toyonobori	Draw	Tokyo, Japan
05/05/1968	Bill Robinson Vs Masao Kimura	Robinson won	Joetsu
05/05/1968	Billy Robinson Vs Masao Kimura	Robinson won	Naoetsu, Japan
08/05/1968	Bill Robinson & John lees Vs Thunder Sugiyama & Toyonobori	Thunder et al won	Funabashi
08/05/1968	Billy Robinson & John Lees Vs Thunder Sugiyama & Toyonobori	Sugiyama &toyonobori won	Funabashi, Japan
11/05/1968	Billy Robinson Vs John Lees	Robinson won	Yokohoma, Japan
12/05/1968	Bill Robinson Vs Shozo Kobayashi	Robinson won	Hachioji
12/05/1968	Billy Robinson Vs Shozo Kobayashi	Robinson won	Hachioji, Japan
03/10/1968	Billy Robinson Vs Syed Saif Shah	NK	Morecambe, Lancashire
04/10/1968	Billy Robinson Vs Rocky Wall	Robinson won	Liverpool, England
06/10/1968	Billy Robinson Vs John Lees	Robinson won	Blackpool, England
07/10/1968	Billy Robinson Vs Mal Kirk	Robinson won	Bradford
08/10/1968	Billy Robinson Vs Geoff Portz	Robinson won	Lime Grove
09/10/1968	Billy Robinson Vs Mal Kirk	Robinson won	Leicester
10/10/1968	Billy Robinson Vs Gargantua	Robinson won	Nelson
11/10/1968	Billy Robinson Vs Gwyn Davies	Robinson won	Bolton, Lancashire
12/10/1968	Billy Robinson Vs Gargantua	Robinson won	Newcastle, England
14/10/1968	Billy Robinson Vs Gargantua	NK	Derby, England
16/10/1968	Billy Robinson Vs Mike Marino	NK	Leeds, West Yorkshire
17/10/1968	Billy Robinson Vs Tony Charles	Robinson won	Malvern, England
18/10/1968	Billy Robinson Vs Ian Campbell	Robinson won	Liverpool, England
19/10/1968	Billy Robinson Vs Roy Bull Davies	Robinson won RDDQ	Hanley
21/10/1968	Billy Robinson Vs Gargantua	NK	Derby, England
22/10/1968	Billy Robinson Vs Ian Campbell	Draw	Aberdeen, Scotland
24/10/1968	Billy Robinson Vs Hans Streiger	NK	Nottingham
25/10/1968	Billy Robinson Vs Prince Kumali	NK	Carlisle
26/10/1968	Billy Robinson Vs Sean Regan	NK	Belfast, Ireland
29/10/1968	Billy Robinson Vs Kendo Nagaski	NK	Edinburgh, Scotland
30/10/1968	Billy Robinson Vs Steve Veidor	Robinson won	Sheffield, England
31/10/1968	Billy Robinson Vs Geoff Portz	NK	Barrow
04/11/1968	Billy Robinson Vs George Gordienko	Draw	Sapporo, Japan
05/11/1968	Billy Robinson & John DaSilva Vs Tadaharu Tanaka & Mammoth Suzuki	Robinson & Dasilva won	Asahikawa, Japan

Date	Match	Result	Location
06/11/1968	Billy Robinson & Ray Apollon Vs Great Kusatsu & Takeshi Oiso	Robinson & Apollon won	Wakkanai, Japan
07/11/1968	Billy Robinson & Ray Hunter Vs Masao Kimura & Thunder Sugiyama	Robinson & Hunter won	Iwamizawa, Japan
08/11/1968	Billy Robinson & Mihalyi Kuti Vs Masao Kimura & Thunder Sugiyama	Robinson & Kuti won	Kushiro, Japan
09/11/1968	Billy Robinson Vs Peter Maivia	Robinson won	Furano, Japan
11/11/1968	Billy Robinson & Peter Maivia & Ray Hunter Vs Great Kusatsu & Tadaharu Tanaka & Toyonobori	Kusatsu et al won	Aomori, Japan
12/11/1968	Billy Robinson Vs Peter Maivia	Robinson won	Tsuruoka, Japan
13/11/1968	Billy Robinson & Peter Maivia Vs Masao Kimura & Great Kusatsu	Robinson & Maivia won	Morioka, Japan
14/11/1968	Billy Robinson & John DaSilva Vs Masao Kimura & Tadaharu Tanaka	Robinson & Dasilva won	Mizusawa, Japan
18/11/1968	Billy Robinson & John DaSilva & Ray Apollon Vs Great kusatsu & Tadaharu Tanaka & Toyonobori	Kusatsu et al won	Sendai, Japan
19/11/1968	Billy Robinson & Mihalyi Kuti & John DaSilva Vs Masao kimura & Great Kusatsu & Thunder Sugiyama	Draw	Takasaki, Japan
21/11/1968	Billy Robinson & Ray Apollon Vs Masao Kimura & Tadaharu Tanaka	Robinson & Apollon won	Toyohashi, Japan
22/11/1968	Billy Robinson Vs Mihalyi Kuti	Robinson won	Nagoya, Japan
23/11/1968	Billy Robinson & Ray Hunter Vs Great Kusatsu & Tadaharu Tanaka	Robinson & Hunter won	Yokkaichi, Japan
25/11/1968	Billy Robinson & Peter Maivia Vs Thunder Sugiyama & Masao Kimura	sugiyama & Kimura won	Shibata, Japan
26/11/1968	Billy Robinson Vs Ray Apollon	Robinson won	Niigata, Japan
28/11/1968	Billy Robinson & John DaSilva Vs Great Kusatsu & takeshi Oiso	Robinson & DaSilva won	Noshiro, Japan
30/11/1968	Billy Robinson Vs Peter Maivia	Maivia won BR DQ	Tokyo, Japan
02/12/1968	Billy Robinson Vs John DaSilva	Robinson won	Kumamoto, Japan
07/12/1968	Billy Robinson Vs Great Kusatsu	Robinson won	Karatsu, Japan
09/12/1968	Billy Robinson & John DaSilva Vs Great Kusatsu & Thunder Sugiyama	Draw	Onomichi, Japan
10/12/1968	Billy Robinson Vs Toyonobori	Draw	Kure, Japan
14/12/1968	Billy Robinson Vs Peter Maivia	Robinson won	Tokyo, Japan
15/12/1968	Billy Robinson Vs Thunder Sugiyama	Robinson won	Kofu, Japan
16/12/1968	Billy Robinson Vs George Gordienko	Robinson won	Nagano, Japan
19/12/1968	Billy Robinson Vs Toyonobori	Draw	Okayama, Japan
01/01/1969	Billy Robinson Vs Great Kusatsu	Robinson won	Miyazaki, Japan
02/01/1969	Billy |Robinson & robert gastel & Andre Bollett Vs great Kusatsu & takeshi Oiso & Toyonobori	Robinson et al won	Fukuoka, Japan
03/01/1969	Billy Robinson & Great Kusatsu & toyonobori Vs Joe Cornelius & robert Gastel & Billy White Wolf		
05/01/1969	Billy Robinson & Rusher Kimura Vs Andre Bollet & Robert Gastel	Robinson & Kimura won	Himeji, Japan
07/01/1969	Billy Robinson & Great Kusatsu Vs Robert gastel & Mike Marino	Robinson & Kusatsu won	wakayama, Japan
09/01/1969	Billy Robinson Vs Takeshi Oiso & Enzo Inoue	Robinson won	Shirahama, Japan
11/01/1969	Billy Robinson & great kusatsu Vs Robert Gastel & Billy White Wolf	Robinson & Kusatsu won	Machida, Japan
25/01/1969	Billy Robinson Vs joe Cornelius	Robinson won	Atami, Japan
28/01/1969	Billy Robinson Vs Billy White Wolf	Robinson won	Tokyo, Japan
01/02/1969	Billy Robinson Vs Andre Bollett	Robinson won	Shimoneski, Japan
02/02/1969	Billy Robinson Vs Mike Marino	Robinson won	Ogawa, Japan
04/02/1969	Billy Robinson & Great Kusatsu Vs Joe Cornelius & Mike Marino	Robinson & Kusatsu won	Ohmuta, japan
06/02/1969	Billy Robinson & Tadaharu Tanaka & Toyonobori Vs Andre bollet & Billy white Wolf & robert gastel	Robinson et al won	kitakyushi, Japan
08/02/1969	Billy Robinson Vs joe Cornelius	Robinson won	Mitaka, Japan

Date	Match	Result	Location
12/02/1969	Billy Robinson & Thunder Sugiyama & Toyonobori Vs Andre Bollet & Joe Cornelius & Billy White Wolf	Robinson et al won	Ichihara, Japan
25/02/1969	Billy Robinson & Thunder Sugiyama & Toyonobori Vs Pat Roach & Al Hobman & Dave Ruhl	Robinson et al won	Tokyo, Japan
04/03/1969	Billy Robinson Vs Rusher kimura	Robinson won	Tokorozawa
08/03/1969	Billy Robinson Vs pat roach	robinson won	Tokyo, Japan
10/03/1969	Billy Robinson Vs Danny lynch	Robinson won	Sendai, Japan
16/03/1969	Billy Robinson Vs Dave Ruhl	Robinson won	Saijo, Japan
17/03/1969	Billy Robinson vs Tadaharu Tanaka	Robinson won	Takamatsu, japan
18/03/1969	Billy Robinson & Toyonobori Vs Al Hobman & Dave Ruhl	Robinson & Toyonobori won	Kochi, Japan
20/03/1969	Billy Robinson Vs Al Hobman	Robinson won	Okayama, Japan
22/03/1969	Billy Robinson & Toyonobori Vs Danny lynch & Al Hobman	Robinson & Toyonobori won	kitsugi, japan
23/03/1969	Billy Robinson & Toyonobori Vs Danny Lynch & Dave Ruhl	Robinson & Toyonobori won	Hamada, Japan
29/03/1969	Billy Robinson Vs Great Kusatsu	Robinson won	Owase, Japam
01/04/1969	Billy Robinson & Rusher Kimura Vs Jose Arroyo & Rocky Wall	Robinson won	Koganei, Japan
05/04/1969	Billy Robinson & thunder Sugiyama Vs Tank Morgan & Stan Stasiak	Robinson & Sugiyama won	Tsu, Japan
08/04/1969	Billy Robinson Vs Great Kusatsu	Robinson won	Toyama, Japan
10/04/1969	Billy Robinson Vs Takeshi Oiso	Robinson won	Eukui, Japan
12/04/1969	Billy Robinson & Rusher Kimura Vs Rocky Wall & Dory Dixon	Robinson won	Kumagaya, Japan
13/04/1969	Billy Robinson Vs Rocky Wall	Robinson won	Wakuya, Japan
14/04/1969	Billy Robinson Vs Dory Dixon	Robinson won	Iwasaki, Japan
15/04/1969	Billy Robinson & Great Kusatsu Vs Stan Stasiak & Rocky Wall	Robinson won	Fukuoka, Japan
18/04/1969	Billy Robinson Vs Takeshi Oiso	Robinson won	Kakuda, Japan
19/04/1969	Billy Robinson Vs Jose Arroyo	Robinson won	Tokyo, Japan
20/04/1969	Billy Robinson & Toyonobori Vs Jose Arroyo & Dory Dixon	Robinson won	Nagoya, Japan
21/04/1969	Billy Robinson Vs Rusher kimura	Robinson won	Kisarazu, Japan
22/04/1969	Billy Robinson Vs stan Stasiak	Robinson won	Tokyo, Japan
23/04/1969	Billy Robinson Vs Rocky Wall	Robinson won	Tokyo, Japan
24/04/1969	Billy Robinson Vs Tank Morgan	Robinson won	Semmaya, Japan
26/04/1969	Billy Robinson Vs Takeshi Oiso	Robinson won	kamaishi, Japan
27/04/1969	Billy Robinson Vs Rusher kimura	Robinson won	Miyako, Japan
28/04/1969	Billy Robinson Vs Takeshi Oiso	Robinson won	Kuji, Japan
29/04/1969	Billy Robinson Vs Rusher kimura	Robinson won	Nishine, japan
01/05/1969	Billy Robinson Vs Takeshi Oiso	Robinson won	Shiogamsa, Japan
03/05/1969	Billy Robinson Vs Dory Dixon	Robinson won	Gosen, Japan
04/05/1969	Billy Robinson Vs Great Kusatsu	Robinson won	Tokamachi, Japan
05/05/1969	Billy Robinson Vs Rusher kimura	Robinson won	Niigata, Japan
15/01/1970	Billy Robinson Vs Alex the Butcher (Gil poisson)	Robinson won	Regina, Canada
18/01/1970	Billy Robinson Vs Alex the Butcher (Gil poisson)	NK	Edmonton, Canada
22/01/1970	Billy Robinson Vs Dan Kroffat	Robinson won	Regina, Canada
23/01/1970	Billy Robinson Vs Gil hayes	Robinson won	Calgary, Canada
25/01/1970	Billy Robinson Vs Gil hayes	NK	Edmonton, Canada
05/02/1970	Billy Robinson Vs jose Quintero	Robinson won	Regina, Canada
06/02/1970	Billy Robinson Vs Abdullah the Butcher	Butcher won	Corral, Canada
13/02/1970	Billy Robinson Vs Abdullah the Butcher	Butcher won	Calgary, Canada

Date	Match	Result	Location
20/02/1970	Billy Robinson Vs Abdullah the Butcher	Robinson won	Calgary, Canada
22/02/1970	Billy Robinson Vs Abdullah the Butcher	NK	Edmonton, Canada
26/02/1970	Billy Robinson Vs Bill Dromo	Robinson won	Regina, Canada
27/02/1970	Billy Robinson Vs Abdullah the Butcher	Butcher won	Calgary, Canada
05/03/1970	Billy Robinson Vs Abdullah the Butcher	Butcher won	Regina, Canada
17/07/1971	Billy Robinson Vs Kendo Nagasaki	NK	Wembley, London
23/07/1971	Billy Robinson Vs Big K	Robinson won	Winnipeg, Canada
01/09/1971	Billy Robinson Vs Bobby heenan	Robinson won	Winnipeg, Canada
07/10/1971	Billy Robinson & Don Muraco Vs Larry Hennig & Lars Anderson	Hennig & anderson won	Winnipeg, Canada
04/11/1971	Billy Robinson Vs Ray Stevens	Robinson won RSDQ	Winnipeg, Canada
18/11/1971	Billy Robinson Vs Lars Anderson	Robinson won RSDQ	Winnipeg, Canada
02/12/1971	Billy Robinson & Dr X Vs Larry hennig & Lars Anderson	Robinson won RSDQ	Winnipeg, Canada
15/05/1972	Billy Robinson Vs Jack Bence	Robinson won	Vancouver, Canada
15/06/1972	Billy Robinson Vs Ivan Koloff	Robinson won IJDQ	Winnipeg, Canada
17/08/1972	Billy Robinson Vs Ivan Koloff	Robinson won	Winnipeg, Canada
09/11/1972	Billy Robinson Vs Butcher Vachon	Robinson won	Winnipeg, Canada
31/01/1973	Billy Robinson & Don Muraco Vs Dusty Rhodes & Dick Murdoch	Robinson won DR DM DQ	Winnipeg, Canada
05/04/1973	Billy Robinson & Wahoo McDaniel & Gene Kiniski Vs Billy Graham &Ivan Koloff & Dick Murdoch	Robinson won	Winnipeg, Canada
24/05/1973	Billy Robinson Vs Horst Hoffman	NK	Winnipeg, Canada
14/06/1973	Billy Robinson Vs Nick Bockwinkel	Bockwinkel won BR DQ	Winnipeg, Canada
05/07/1973	Billy Robinson Vs Billy Graham	Graham won BRDQ	Winnipeg, Canada
13/09/1973	Billy Robinson Vs Buddy Wolff	Robinson won	Winnipeg, Canada
15/11/1973	Billy Robinson & Geoff Portz Vs Buddy Wolff & Larry Heinemi	Robinson won	Winnipeg, Canada
06/12/1973	Billy Robinson & Geoff Portz Vs Ray Stevens & Nick Bockwinkel	Stevens & Bockwinkel won	Winnipeg, Canada
04/04/1974	Billy Robinson Vs Baron Von Raschke	Robinson won BVRDQ	Winnipeg, Canada
15/08/1974	Billy Robinson Vs Ray Stevens	Stevens won	Winnipeg, Canada
03/10/1974	Billy Robinson Vs Hugo Babich	NK	Winnipeg, Canada
06/03/1975	Billy Robinson Vs Buddy Wolff	Robinson won	Winnipeg, Canada
27/03/1975	Billy Robinson Vs Boris Breznikoff	Robinson won	Winnipeg, Canada
17/04/1975	Billy Robinson Vs Nick Bockwinkel	Robinson won	Winnipeg, Canada
01/05/1975	Billy Robinson Vs Guy Mitchell	Robinson won	Winnipeg, Canada
03/05/1975	Billy Robinson won 15 man Battle Royale	N/A	Winnipeg, Canada
02/10/1975	Billy Robinson Vs Baron Von Raschke	Draw	Winnipeg, Canada
13/11/1975	Billy Robinson Vs Nick Bockwinkel	Robinson won	Winnipeg, Canada
07/04/1977	Billy Robinson Vs Jack Lanza	Robinson won	Winnipeg, Canada
19/05/1977	Billy Robinson Vs Roger Kirby	Robinson won	Winnipeg, Canada
28/05/1977	Billy Robinson Vs Bob Backlund	Robinson won	Winnipeg, Canada
09/06/1977	Billy Robinson Vs Wilbur Snyder	Robinson won	Winnipeg, Canada
07/07/1977	Billy Robinson Vs Mad Dog Vachon	Robinson won	Winnipeg, Canada
18/08/1977	Billy Robinson Vs Moose Morowski	Robinson won	Winnipeg, Canada
06/10/1977	Billy Robinson Vs Nick Bockwinkel	Draw	Winnipeg, Canada
02/02/1978	Billy Robinson Vs Angelo Mosca	Mosca won	Winnipeg, Canada

Date	Match	Result	Location
23/02/1978	Billy Robinson Vs Jack Lanza	Robinson won	Winnipeg, Canada
05/04/1978	Billy Robinson & Verne gane Vs Angelo Mosca & Destroyer II	Robinson & gagne won	Winnipeg, Canada
17/08/1978	Billy Robinson Vs Bob Orton	Draw	Winnipeg, Canada
14/09/1978	Billy Robinson Vs Ray Stevens	Robinson won	Winnipeg, Canada
16/09/1978	Billy Robinson Vs Lee Bronson	NK	St. Albans, Hertfordshire
22/02/1979	Billy Robinson Vs Bobby Duncum	Robinson won	Winnipeg, Canada
15/03/1979	Billy Robinson Vs Cecil Dubois	Robinson won	Winnipeg, Canada
28/06/1979	Billy Robinson Vs Al Hayes	Robinson won	Winnipeg, Canada
15/08/1979	Billy Robinson Vs Destroyer II	Destroyer won	Winnipeg, Canada
25/10/1979	Billy Robinson Vs Destroyer II	Destroyer won	Winnipeg, Canada

Billy Howes

Date	Match	Outcome	Venue
16/04/1949	Billy Howes Vs Ted Buckley	NK	Bury, England
09/12/1949	Billy Howes Vs Bert Royal	Bert won	Glasgow, Scotland
09/12/1949	Billy Howes Vs Bert Royal	Royal won	Glasgow, Scotland
06/05/1950	Billy Howes Vs Billy Joyce	NK	Belle Vue, Manchester
03/03/1951	Billy Howes Vs Cliff Beaumont	NK	Bury, England
16/04/1951	Billy Howes Vs Jim Boyle	Bill won	Edinburgh, Scotland
30/04/1951	Billy Howes Vs Bert Royal	NC	Edinburgh, Scotland
04/05/1951	Billy Howes Vs Cliff Belshaw	Cliff won	Glasgow, Scotland
04/05/1951	Billy Howes Vs Cliff Belshaw	Cliff won	Glasgow, Scotland
05/05/1951	Billy Howes Vs Tony Vallon	NK	Hanley, England
21/05/1951	Billy Howes Vs Danny Flynn	Danny won	Edinburgh, Scotland
21/09/1951	Billy Howes Vs Danny Flynn	Billy won	Glasgow, Scotland
21/09/1951	Billy Howes Vs Danny Flynn	Billy won	Glasgow, Scotland
18/10/1951	Billy Howes Vs The Phantom	Phantom won	Morecambe, Lancashire
22/10/1951	Billy Howes Vs Johnny Stead	Billy won	Edinburgh, Scotland
26/10/1951	Billy Howes Vs Tiger Woods	NK	Willenhall, England
16/11/1951	Billy Howes Vs Jack Beaumont	NK	Willenhall, England
17/11/1951	Billy Howes Vs Jack Beaumont	NK	Willenhall, England
23/11/1951	Billy Howes Vs Fred Woolley	Fred won	Glasgow, Scotland
07/12/1951	Billy Howes Vs Jimmy Munlack	NK	Willenhall, England
22/12/1951	Billy Howes Vs Johnny Stead	Howes won	Newcastle, England
11/01/1952	Billy Howes Vs Laurie Bailey	Draw	Glasgow, Scotland
12/01/1952	Billy Howes Vs Laurie Bailey	Draw	Glasgow, Scotland
26/01/1952	Billy Howes Vs Tony Lawrence	Tony won	Middlesborough, North Yorkshire
01/02/1952	Billy Howes Vs Bobby Steele	NK	Levenshulme
11/02/1952	Billy Howes Vs Chic Purvey	Chic won	Edinburgh, Scotland
23/02/1952	Billy Howes Vs Tiger Woods	NK	Bury, England
27/02/1952	Billy Howes Vs Les Stent	NK	Lincoln, England
29/02/1952	Billy Howes Vs Dennis Mitchell	Dennis won	Glasgow, Scotland
12/03/1954	Billy Howes Vs Rex harrison	Rex won	Glasgow, Scotland
13/03/1954	Billy Howes Vs Johnny Stead	Johnny won	Middlesborough, North Yorkshire
19/03/1954	Billy Howes Vs Rex Harrison	Harrison won	Glasgow, Scotland
27/03/1954	Billy Howes Vs Alex Bray	Billy won	Middlesborough, North Yorkshire
03/04/1954	Billy Howes Vs Black Beau Jack	black won	Newcastle, England
08/04/1954	Billy Howes Vs Spencer Churchill	Spencer won	Morecambe, Lancashire
16/04/1954	Billy Howes Vs Martin Conroy	NK	Levenshulme
23/04/1954	Bilyl Howes Vs jack Atherton	Jack won	Glasgow, Scotland
08/05/1954	Billy Howes Vs Ron Johnson	Ron won	Newcastle, England
14/05/1954	Billy Howes Vs Johnny Peters	NK	Ramsgate
25/05/1954	Billy Howes Vs Frankie Hughes	NK	Birmingham, England
17/06/1954	Billy Howes Vs Johnny Peters	NK	Southampton
27/08/1954	Billy Howes Vs Masambula	Masambula won	Middlesborough, North Yorkshire

07/09/1954	Billy Howes Vs Masambula	Bilyl won	Morecambe, Lancashire
10/09/1954	Billy Howes Vs Francis Sullivan	NK	Manchester
16/09/1954	Bilyl Howes Vs Cyril Knowles Peters	Bilyl won	Bristol, England
16/09/1954	Billy Howes Vs Steve Logan	Howes won	Bristol, England
17/09/1954	Billy Howes Vs Harry Kendall	NK	Ramsgate
27/09/1954	Billy Howes Vs Masambula	Masambula won	Edinburgh, Scotland
08/10/1954	Billy Howes Vs Frank Hughes	Frank won	Glasgow, Scotland
22/10/1954	Billy Howes Vs Vic Stewart	Billy won	Leicester, England
25/10/1954	Billy Howes Vs Bobby Wayne	Billy won	Edinburgh, Scotland
01/11/1954	Billy Howes Vs Vic Coleman	Vic won	High Wycombe, England
01/11/1954	Billy Howes Vs Vic Coleman	Coleman won	High Wycombe
05/11/1954	Billy Howes Vs Frank Hughes	Billy won	Glasgow, Scotland
15/11/1954	Billy Howes Vs Ernie Robertson	Ernie won	Edinburgh, Scotland
19/11/1954	Billy Howes Vs Jim Rawlings	Billy won	Glasgow, Scotland
10/12/1954	Billy Howes Vs Harry Fields	Fields won	Ipswich
05/01/1955	Billy Howes Vs Gori Ed Mangotich	Billy won, Gori DQ	Cardiff, Wales
19/01/1955	Billy Howes Vs Masambula	Billy won	Cardiff, Wales
24/01/1955	Billy Howes Vs Tommy Pye	NK	Altrincham
04/02/1955	Billy Howes Vs Ted Beech	Billy won	Belfast, Ireland
16/02/1955	Bilyl Howes Vs Harry Fields	Draw	Albert Hall, London
17/02/1955	Billy Howes Vs Johnny Kwango	NK	Hove
28/02/1955	Billy Howes Vs Steve Logan	Steve won	Edinburgh, Scotland
01/03/1955	Billy Howes Vs Earl McGrath	Billy won	Dundee, Scotland
25/03/1955	Billy Howes Vs Spencer Churchill	Billy won	Leicester, England
28/03/1955	Billy Howes Vs Harry Fields	Billy won	Edinburgh, Scotland
30/03/1955	Billy Howes Vs Steve Logan	Billy won	Cardiff, Wales
01/04/1955	Billy Howes Vs Danny Flynn	NK	Willenhall
05/04/1955	Billy Howes Vs Masambula	Masambula won	Hamilton, Scotland
07/04/1955	Billy Howes Vs Steve Logan	Billy won	Wimbledon, England
15/04/1955	Billy Howes Vs Bert Royal	Bilyl won	Albert Hall, London
19/04/1955	Billy Howes Vs Gori Ed Mangotich	Billy won	Swindon, England
02/05/1955	Bilyl Howes Vs Eric Taylor	Eric won	Leeds, England
11/05/1955	Billy Howes Vs Terence Ricardo	Billy won	Cardiff, Wales
12/05/1955	Billy Howes Vs Charlie Fisher	NK	Bristol, England
21/05/1955	Billy Howes Vs Harry Fields	Harry won	Wimbledon, England
28/05/1955	Billy Howes Vs Tommy Mann	Draw	Newcastle, England
06/06/1955	Billy Howes Vs Tommy Mann	Bilyl won	Edinburgh, Scotland
07/06/1955	Billy Howes Vs Arjit Singh	Arjit won	Aberdeen, Scotland
11/06/1955	Billy Howes Vs Bob McDonald	Bilyl won	New Brighton, England
02/07/1955	Billy Howes Vs Tommy Pye	Tommy won	Middlesborough, North Yorkshire
14/07/1955	Billy Howes Vs Eric Taylor	Erice won	Morecambe, Lancashire
21/07/1955	Billy Howes Vs Charlie Fisher	NC	Wimbledon, England
26/07/1955	Billy Howes Vs Johnny Allan	Allan won	Birmingham, England
04/08/1955	Billy Howes Vs Reg Williams	Reg won	Morecambe, Lancashire
25/08/1955	Billy Howes Vs Joe Hill	Billy won	Morecambe, Lancashire
07/09/1955	Billy Howes Vs Tommy Pye	Tommy won	Douglas, Isle of Man

Date	Match	Result	Location
10/09/1955	Billy Howes Vs Rex Harrison	Rex won	Newcastle, England
16/09/1955	Billy Howes Vs Francis Sullivan	NK	Manchester, England
17/09/1955	Billy Howes Vs Jack Proctor	Jack won	Middlesborough, North Yorkshire
19/09/1955	Billy Howes Vs Gerry DeJaegar	Draw	Leeds, England
07/10/1955	Billy Howes Vs Jack Proctor	Billy won	Glasgow, Scotland
10/10/1955	Billy Howes Vs Ernie Riley	Ernie won	Edinburgh, Scotland
13/10/1955	Billy Howes Vs Cubano Badu	Cubano won	Bristol, England
17/10/1955	Billy Howes Vs Jan Jacobs	Draw	Bedford, England
18/10/1955	Billy Howes Vs Mike Demitre	Billy won	Swindon, England
04/11/1955	Billy Howes Vs Dean Stockton	NK	Willenhall
21/11/1955	Billy Howes Vs Johnny Peters	Draw	Tunbridge Wells, England
23/11/1955	Billy Howes Vs Charro Montes	Billy won	Cardiff, Wales
01/12/1955	Billy Howes Vs jean Morandi	Billy won	Morecambe, Lancashire
05/12/1955	Billy Howes Vs Wolfgang Ehrl	Wolfgang won	Edinburgh, Scotland
10/12/1955	Billy Howes Vs Steve Logan	NK	Norwich, England
19/12/1955	Billy Howes Vs Frank O'Donnell	Frank won	Edinburgh, Scotland
20/12/1955	Billy Howes Vs Ernie Riley	Ernie won	Aberdeen, Scotland
27/12/1955	Billy Howes Vs Charlie Fisher	NK	Lime Grove, London
31/12/1955	Billy Howes Vs Doug Joyces	Billy won	Tunbridge Wells, England
04/01/1956	Billy Howes Vs Buddy Cody	Draw	Cardiff, Wales
05/01/1956	Billy Howes Vs Les Kellett	NK	Bristol, England
06/01/1956	Billy Howes Vs Ernie Riley	NK	Ramsgate
12/01/1956	Billy Howes Vs Jack Dempsey	NK	Wimbledon, England
23/01/1956	Billy Howes competed in KO tournament	NK	Altrincham
26/01/1956	Billy Howes Vs Tony Vallon	NK	Manchester, England
01/02/1956	Billy Howes Vs Marty Jacobs	Billy won	Cardiff, Wales
02/02/1956	Billy Howes Vs Flash Edwards	NK	Bury St. Edmunds
24/02/1956	Billy Howes Vs Arjit Singh	Draw	Ipswich, England
29/02/1956	Billy Howes Vs Jean Morandi	Billy won	Cardiff, Wales
01/03/1956	Billy Howes Vs Jean Morandi	Billy won	Bristol, England
09/04/1956	Billy Howes Vs Tommy Mann	Billy won	Tunbridge Wells, England
10/04/1956	In KO tournament	NK	Colchester
12/04/1956	Billy Howes Vs Charlie Fisher	NK	Bristol, England
21/06/1956	Billy Howes Vs Terence Ricardo	Terence won	Morecambe, Lancashire
23/06/1956	Billy Howes Vs Rex Harrison	NC	Newcastle, England
28/06/1956	Billy Howes Vs Steve Logan	NK	Wimbledon, England
29/06/1956	Billy Howes Vs Eric Taylor	NK	Liverpool, England
02/07/1956	Billy Howes Vs Alf Cadman	Billy won	Middleton Towers, England
07/07/1956	Billy Howes Vs Johnny Allan	Billy won	Aberdeen, Scotland
16/07/1956	Billy Howes Vs Johnny Peters	Johnny won	Edinburgh, Scotland
21/07/1956	Billy Howes Vs Harry Fields	Harry won	Newcastle, England
06/08/1956	Billy Howes Vs Bobby Watts	Billy won	Edinburgh, Scotland
16/08/1956	Billy Howes Vs Johnny Peters	NK	Wimbledon, England
25/08/1956	Billy Howes Vs Eric Taylor	Eric won	Newcastle, England
04/09/1956	Billy Howes Vs Gwyn Davies	Gwyn won	Swindon, England
06/09/1956	Billy Howes Vs Arjit Singh	NK	Southampton

Date	Match	Result	Location
08/09/1956	Billy Howes Vs Cyril Knowles	Cyril won	Middlesborough, North Yorkshire
15/09/1956	Billy Howes Vs Johnny Allan	Allan won	Hanley
17/09/1956	Billy Howes Vs Tommy Kilmartin	Billy won	Edinburgh, Scotland
18/09/1956	Billy Howes Vs Robert McDonald	Bilyl won, Rob DQ	Aberdeen, Scotland
20/09/1956	Billy Howes Vs Bert Royal	NK	Southampton
29/09/1956	Billy Howes Vs Jack Dillon	Billy won	Newcastle, England
01/10/1956	Billy Howes Vs Don Mendoza	Billy won	Edinburgh, Scotland
03/10/1956	Billy Howes Vs Tony Vallon	Draw	Lincoln, Lincolnshire
07/10/1956	Billy Howes Vs Jack Procter	Billy won	Glasgow, Scotland
10/10/1956	Billy Howes Vs Steve Logan	Draw	Cardiff, Wales
11/10/1956	Billy Howes Vs Lee Edwards	Billy won	Aylesbury, Buckinghamshire
12/10/1956	Billy Howes Vs Les Kellett	Les won	Glasgow, Scotland
15/10/1956	Billy Howes Vs Aaron Vargyas	Billy won	Leeds, West yorkshire
17/10/1956	Billy Howes Vs Tony Vallon	Draw	Lincoln, Lincolnshire
19/10/1956	Billy Howes Vs Alf Cadman	Billy won	Glasgow, Scotland
20/10/1956	Billy Howes Vs Paul Kowalik	Billy won	Middlesborough, North Yorkshire
24/10/1956	Billy Howes Vs Les Kellett	Les won	Belfast, Ireland
28/10/1956	Billy Howes Vs Francis Sullivan	NK	Blackpool, England
01/11/1956	Billy Howes Vs Johnny Peters	NK	Wimbledon, England
06/11/1956	Billy Howes Vs Alf Cadman	Billy won	Hamilton, Scotland
07/11/1956	Billy Howes Vs Judo Al Hayes	Judo Al Hayes won	Albert Hall, London
08/11/1956	Billy Howes Vs Kid Zamboa	Draw	Bristol, England
12/11/1956	Billy Howes Vs Doug Joyce	Billy won Doug DQ	Edinburgh, Scotland
13/11/1956	Billy Howes Vs Emile Poilve	Billy won	Aberdeen, Scotland
17/11/1956	Billy Howes Vs Wolfgang Earl	NC	Middlesborough, North Yorkshire
24/11/1956	Billy Howes Vs Alf Cadman	Howes won	Hanley
01/12/1956	Billy Howes Vs Wolfgang Earl	Billy won	Middlesborough, North Yorkshire
03/12/1956	Billy Howes Vs Ernie Riley	NK	Altrincham
04/12/1956	Billy Howes Vs Gwyn Davies	Gwyn won	Swindon, England
07/12/1956	Billy Howes Vs Grant Fotheringham	Billy won	Liverpool , England
11/12/1956	Billy Howes Vs Don Mendoza	Don Mendoza won	Hamilton, Scotland
15/12/1956	Billy Howes Vs Al Hayes	Hayes won	Hanley
18/12/1956	Billy Howes Vs Judo Al Hayes	Judo Al Hayes won	Hanley, England
20/12/1956	Billy Howes Vs Alf Cadman	Billy won	Bristol, England
27/12/1956	Billy Howes Vs Tiger Lombardo	NK	Beckenham, England
02/01/1957	Billy Howes Vs Ernie Riley	Ernie won	Lincoln, Lincolnshire
18/01/1957	Billy Howes Vs Francis Sullivan	Draw	Glasgow, Scotland
19/01/1957	Billy Howes Vs Jack Dillon	Billy won	Middlesborough, North Yorkshire
21/01/1957	Billy Howes Vs Masambula	NK	Blackpool, England
22/01/1957	Billy Howes Vs Vic Hesselle	Billy won	Dundee, Scotland
25/01/1957	Billy Howes Vs Rudi Schumacher	Draw	Liverpool, England
26/01/1957	Billy Howes Vs Emile Poilve	Howes won	Doncaster, England
26/01/1957	Billy Howes Vs Tony Vallon	Vallon won BHDQ	Doncaster, England
30/01/1957	Billy Howes Vs Buddy Cody	NK	Hove
31/01/1957	Billy Howes Vs Ernie Riley	Draw	Bristol, England
02/02/1957	Billy Howes Vs Leong Lee Foo	Leong won	Newcastle, England

Date	Match	Result	Location
04/02/1957	Billy Howes Vs Masambula	NK	Blackpool, England
05/02/1957	Billy Howes Vs Tiger Lombardo	Howes won	Hull, England
08/02/1957	Billy Howes Vs Oskar Muller	Draw	Liverpool, England
09/02/1957	Billy Howes Vs Alf Cadman	NK	Doncaster, England
12/02/1957	Billy Howes Vs Tumac Amaru	Billy won	Lime Grove, England
16/02/1957	Billy Howes Vs Rudi Schumacher	Billy won	Newcastle, England
18/02/1957	Billy Howes Vs Tumac Amaru	Billy won	Leeds, England
22/02/1957	Billy Howes Vs Masambula	NC	Belfast, Ireland
28/02/1957	Billy Howes Vs jean Morandi	Billy won	Harringay, England
02/03/1957	Billy Howes Vs Bill McDonald	McDonald won BHDQ	Hanley
04/03/1957	Billy Howes Vs Count Bartelli	NK	Blackpool, England
05/03/1957	Billy Howes Vs Steve Logan	NK	Swindon
08/03/1957	Billy Howes Vs Bob McDonald	Bob won	Liverpool, England
09/03/1957	Billy Howes Vs Johnny Allan	Johnny won	Newcastle, England
13/03/1957	Billy Howes Vs Tony Quarmby	Billy won	Lincoln, Lincolnshire
22/03/1957	Billy Howes Vs Reg Williams	Billy won	Liverpool, England
23/03/1957	Billy Howes Vs Tony Mancelli	Mancelli	Hanley
26/03/1957	Billy Howes Vs Mike Marino	NK	Colchester
27/03/1957	Billy Howes Vs Ernie Riley	Billy won	Belfast, Ireland
30/03/1957	Billy Howes Vs Tony Vallon	Howes won	Doncaster, England
05/04/1957	Billy Howes Vs Johnny Peters	Billy won	Liverpool, England
06/04/1957	Billy Howes Vs Johnny Allan	Howes won	Hanley
12/04/1957	Billy Howes Vs Black Kwango	Billy won	Belfast, Ireland
13/04/1957	Billy Howes Vs Francis Gregory	NC	Middlesborough, North Yorkshire
18/04/1957	Billy Howes Vs Paul DeBusne	Billy won	Edinburgh, Scotland
20/04/1957	Billy Howes Vs Jack Beaumont	NK	Doncaster, England
25/04/1957	Billy Howes Vs Tamaru Radak	NK	Blackburn, England
03/05/1957	Billy Howes Vs Masambula	Masambula won	Liverpool, England
04/05/1957	Billy Howes Vs Johnny Allan	Allan won	Newcastle, England
11/05/1957	Billy Howes Vs Tony Mancelli	Mancelli won BH Inj	Hanley
21/05/1957	Billy Howes in KO Tournament	NK	Colchester
22/05/1957	Billy Howes Vs Kid Zamboa	NK	Cardiff, Wales
24/05/1957	Billy Howes Vs Black Butcher Johnson	Draw	Coventry, England
01/06/1957	Billy Howes Vs Eddie Saxon	NK	Blackpool, England
06/06/1957	Bilyl Howes Vs Bernard Vignal	Bernard won	Morecambe, Lancashire
08/06/1957	Billy Howes Vs Tibor Szakacs	NK	Newcastle, England
11/06/1957	Billy Howes Vs Johnny Peters	Billy won	Swindon, England
14/06/1957	Billy Howes Vs Johnny Kwango	Nk	Dudley, England
29/06/1957	Billy Howes Vs Johnny Allan	Billy won	Newcastle, England
01/07/1957	Billy Howes Vs Johnny Allan	Billy won	Edinburgh, Scotland
02/07/1957	Billy Howes Vs Arjit Singh	Arjit won	Aberdeen, Scotland
06/07/1957	Billy Howes Vs Ernie Riley	Riley won	Blackpool, England
13/07/1957	Billy Howes Vs Robert McDonald	Rob won	Middlesborough, North Yorkshire
19/07/1957	Billy Howes Vs Johnny Yearsley	NK	Dudley, England
20/07/1957	Billy Howes Vs Masambula	NK	Ramsgate

Date	Match	Result	Location
26/07/1957	Billy Howes Vs Masambula	NK	Ramsgate
29/07/1957	Billy Howes Vs Tibor Szakacs	Szakacs won	Shoreditch, England
05/08/1957	Billy Howes Vs Johnny Allan	NK	Belle Vue, Manchester
09/08/1957	Billy Howes Vs Johnny Allan	Draw	Liverpool, England
10/08/1957	Billy Howes Vs Bob McDonald	Billy won, bob DQ	Middlesborough, North Yorkshire
12/08/1957	Billy Howes Vs Ron Johnson	Billy won	Edinburgh, Scotland
13/08/1957	Billy Howes Vs Johnny Peters	Draw	Aberdeen, Scotland
15/08/1957	Billy Howes Vs Mike Demitre	Billy won	Morecambe, Lancashire
17/08/1957	Billy Howes Vs Jack Beaumont	Jack won	Newcastle, England
23/08/1957	Billy Howes Vs Jack Beaumont	NK	Dudley, England
29/08/1957	Billy Howes Vs Harry Fields	NK	Wimbledon, England
30/08/1957	Billy Howes Vs Mike Marino	Mike won	Dudley, England
31/08/1957	Billy Howes Vs Don Mendoza	Don won	Middlesborough, North Yorkshire
02/09/1957	Billy Howes Vs Lew Roseby	Billy won	Edinburgh, Scotland
05/09/1957	Billy Howes Vs Don Mendoza	NC	Morecambe, Lancashire
07/09/1957	Billy Howes Vs Paul Lincoln	Billy won	Portsmouth, England
11/09/1957	Billy Howes Vs Dai Morgan	Billy won	Cardiff, Wales
16/09/1957	Billy Howes Vs Raschid Anwar	Raschid won	Edinburgh, Scotland
18/09/1957	Billy Howes Vs Count Bartelli	NK	Wolverhampton, England
19/09/1957	Billy Howes Vs Roger Trigeaud	NK	Liverpool, England
19/09/1957	Billy Howes Vs Ernie Riley	NK	Crewe, England
21/09/1957	Billy Howes Vs Alf Cadman	NK	Kings Lynn, England
23/09/1957	Billy Howes Vs Gori Ed Mangotich	Draw	Tunbridge Wells, England
24/09/1957	Billy Howes Vs Masambula	Masambula won	Harringay, England
28/09/1957	Billy Howes Vs Frankie Townsend	NK	Belle Vue, Manchester
03/10/1957	Billy Howes Vs Ernie Riley	NK	Southampton
05/10/1957	Billy Howes Vs Ernie Riley	NK	Luton, London
07/10/1957	Billy Howes Vs Tony Vallon	Tony won	Hamilton, Scotland
12/10/1957	Bilyl Howes Vs Gordon Nelson	Gordon won	Newcastle, England
14/10/1957	Billy Howes Vs Tony olivera	Tony won	Leeds, England
16/10/1957	Billy Howes Vs Bert Craddock	Billy won	Lincoln, Lincolnshire
17/10/1957	Billy Howes Vs Spencer Churchill	NK	Wimbledon, England
24/10/1957	Billy Howes Vs Johnny Peters	NK	Wimbledon, England
08/11/1957	Billy Howes Vs Alf Cadman	NK	Liverpool, England
29/11/1957	Billy Howes Vs Buddy Cody	NK	Ipswich, England
02/12/1957	Billy Howes Vs Alec Bray	NK	Altrincham
07/12/1957	Billy Howes Vs Hans Schnabl	NK	Hanley
13/12/1957	Billy Howes Vs Bud Kent	Bud won	Willenhall, England
06/01/1958	Billy Howes Vs Bill McDonald	NK	Blackpool, England
14/01/1958	Billy Howes Vs Dai Sullivan	NK	Scarborough
15/01/1958	Billy Howes Vs Alex Wenzl	Alex won, BH DQ	Lincoln, Lincolnshire
16/01/1958	Billy Howes Vs Gordon Kilmartin	NK	Blackburn, England
17/01/1958	Bilyl Howes Vs Johan Dillinger	NK	Chesterfield, England
20/01/1958	Billy Howes Vs Johnny Allan	NK	Blackpool, England
23/01/1958	Billy Howes Vs Billy Robinson	NK	Nottingham
29/01/1958	Billy Howes Vs Dai Sullivan	Sullivan won	Cardiff, Wales

Date	Match	Result	Location
30/01/1958	Billy Howes Vs Charlie Fisher	NK	Bristol, England
03/02/1958	Blly Howes Vs Don Mendoza	Don won	Leeds, England
04/02/1958	Billy Howes Vs Gerry DeJaegar	Draw	Hull, England
11/02/1958	Billy Howes Vs Gordon Nelson	NK	Wolverhampton, England
15/02/1958	Billy Howes Vs Tony Vallon	2-1 to Billy	Hanley
18/02/1958	Billy Howes Vs Charlie Fisher	Draw	Swindon, England
19/02/1958	Billy Howes Vs Steve Logan	Steve won	Harringay, England
21/02/1958	Billy Howes Vs Joe Cornelius	Draw	Ipswich, England
27/02/1958	Billy Howes Vs Alex Wenzl	NK	Liverpool, England
03/03/1958	Billy Howes Vs Francis Sullivan	NK	Seymour Hall, London
06/03/1958	Billy Howes Vs Tony Vallon	NK	Nottingham, England
21/03/1958	Billy Howes Vs Alex Wenzl	Billy won	Liverpool, England
12/04/1958	Billy Howes Vs Bill Robinson	Bill Won	Middlesborough, North Yorkshire
14/04/1958	Billy Howes Vsw Ivan Zarinov	Billy won	Edinburgh, Scotland
18/04/1958	Billy Howes Vs Gordon Nelson	Gordon won	Belfast, Ireland
22/04/1958	Billy Howes Vs Johnny Czeslaw	Billy won	Aylesbury, Buckinghamshire
22/04/1958	Billy Howes Vs Judo Al Hayes	Judo won	Aylesbury, Buckinghamshire
28/04/1958	Billy Howes & Norman Walsh Vs Jim Hussey & Bob McDonald	Jim & Bob won	Edinburgh, Scotland
29/04/1958	Billy Howes Vs Josef Zaranoff	NK	Wakefield, England
05/05/1958	Billy Howes Vs Les Kellett	Les won	Edinburgh, Scotland
08/05/1958	Billy Howes Vs Les Kellett	Les won	Morecambe, Lancashire
09/05/1958	Billy Howes Vs Johnny Allan	NK	Chesterfield, England
10/05/1958	Billy Howes Vs Alf Cadman	NK	Hanley, England
12/05/1958	Billy Howes Vs Bert Royal	NK	Altrincham
16/05/1958	Billy Howes Vs Bobby Graham	Billy won	Crewe, England
17/05/1958	Billy Howes Vs Bill Malloy	Bill M. Won	Middlesborough, North Yorkshire
18/05/1958	Billy Howes Vs Steve Logan	Billy won	Birmingham, England
19/05/1958	Billy Howes Vs Josef Zaranoff	Billy won	Leeds, England
30/05/1958	Billy Howes Vs Ernie Riley	Billy won	Liverpool, England
01/06/1958	Billy Howes Vs Black Kwango	Billy won	Birmingham, England
07/06/1958	Billy Howes Vs Bill McDonald	Howes won	Newcastle, England
09/06/1958	Billy Howes Vs Tommy Kilmartin	Billy won	Edinburgh, Scotland
15/06/1958	Billy Howes Vs Emile Poilve	Billy won	Birmingham, England
30/06/1958	Billy Howes Vs Charlie Fisher	Draw	Shoreditch, London
03/07/1958	Billy Howes Vs Gori Ed Mangotich	Billy won	Bristol, England
05/07/1958	Billy Howes Vs Johnny Yearsley	Billy won	Salisbury, England
12/07/1958	Billy Howes Vs Gene Murphy	Billy won	Newcastle, England
14/07/1958	Billy Howes Vs Dave Finch	Billy won	Edinburgh, Scotland
18/07/1958	Billy Howes Vs Steve Logan	Draw	Liverpool, England
20/07/1958	Bilyl Howes Vs Ernie Riley	Billy won	Birmingham, England
22/07/1958	Billy Howes & Tony Mancelli Vs Les Kellett & Lew Roseby	Les won	Leeds, England
24/07/1958	Billy Howes Vs Black Kwango	Billy won	Morecambe, Lancashire
25/07/1958	Billy Howes Vs Alf Cadman	NK	Bolton, England
28/07/1958	Bilyl Howes Vs Lew Roseby	Lew won, BH DQ	Edinburgh, Scotland
31/07/1958	Billy Howes Vs Vic Hesselle	Billy won	Bristol, England

Date	Match	Result	Location
02/08/1958	Bilyl Howes Vs Frank O'Donnel	Billy won	Middlesborough, North Yorkshire
09/08/1958	Billy Howes Vs Gene Murphy	Gene won	Maidstone, England
10/08/1958	Billy Howes Vs Bert Royal	Bilyl won	Birmingham, England
14/08/1958	Billy Howes Vs Eric Taylor	Billy won	Bristol, England
16/08/1958	Billy Howes Vs Jack Beaumont	NK	Llandudno, Wales
23/08/1958	Billy Howes Vs Harry Fields	Billy won	Newcastle, England
23/08/1958	Billy Howes Vs Don Mendoza	Don won	Newcastle, England
29/08/1958	Billy Howes Vs Steve Logan	Billy won	Liverpool, England
01/09/1958	Billy Howes Vs Ernie Riley	NK	Bridlington
08/09/1958	Billy Howes Vs Ray Hunter	NK	Shoreditch, England
09/09/1958	Billy Howes Vs Tony Vallon	Draw	Purley, England
10/09/1958	Billy Howes Vs Tony Vallon	Billy won	Cardiff, Wales
12/09/1958	Billy Howes Vs Pat Barrett	NK	Wisbech
13/09/1958	Billy Howes Vs Gwyn Davies	NC	Middlesborough, North Yorkshire
14/09/1958	Billy Howes Vs Dean Stockton	Billy won	Birmingham, England
14/09/1958	Billy Howes Vs Francis Sullivan	Billy won	Birmingham, England
14/09/1958	Billy Howes Vs Alf Cadman (F)	Alf won	Birmingham, England
17/09/1958	Billy Howes Vs Gordon Nelson	Gordon won	Bath, England
19/09/1958	In KO tournament	NK	Hove
20/09/1958	Billy Howes Vs Black Panther	Billy won	Salisbury, England
20/09/1958	Billy Howes Vs Arthur Beaumont	Arthur won	Salisbury, England
25/09/1958	Billy Howes Vs Steve Logan	NK	Peterborough, England
27/09/1958	Billy Howes Vs Johnny Yearsley	NK	Norwich, England
01/10/1958	Billy Howes Vs Gene Murphy	Gene won	Lincoln, Lincolnshire
02/10/1958	Billy Howes Vs Mike Marino	NK	Blackburn, England
03/10/1958	Billy Howes Vs Gene Murphy	Billy won	Glasgow, Scotland
04/10/1958	Billy Joyce Vs Geoff Portz	NC	Middlesborough, North Yorkshire
07/10/1958	Billy Howes Vs Eric Taylor	NK	Wakefield, England
10/10/1958	Billy Howes Vs Mighty Zaranoff	NK	Bolton, Lancashire
12/10/1958	Billy Howes Vs Ernie Riley	Ernie won	Birmingham, England
13/10/1958	Billy Howes Vs jean Morandi	Billy won	Edinburgh, Scotland
16/10/1958	Billy Howes Vs Black Kwango	Billy won	Morecambe, Lancashire
20/10/1958	Billy Howes Vs Roger Gueret	Billy won	Leeds, England
01/11/1958	Billy Howes Vs Johnny Yearsley	Billy won	Maidstone, England
01/11/1958	Billy Howes Vs Georges Gueret	Bilyl won	Leeds, England
04/11/1958	Billy Howes Vs Tony Olivera	Billy won	Purley, England
05/11/1958	Billy Howes Vs Gori Ed Mangotich	Billy won, Gori DQ	Cardiff, Wales
07/11/1958	Billy Howes Vs Johnny Yearsley	Billy won	Ipswich, England
15/11/1958	Billy Howes Vs Ernie Riley	Ernie won	Middlesborough, North Yorkshire
15/11/1958	Billy Howes Vs Don Branch	Billy won	Middlesborough, North Yorkshire
19/11/1958	Billy Howes Vs Karl Von Cramm	Billy won	Cardiff, Wales
20/11/1958	Billy Howes Vs Tony Olivera	Billy won	Bristol, England
21/11/1958	Billy Howes Vs Rudi Schumacher	Billy won	Liverpool, England
22/11/1958	Billy Howes Vs Emile Poilve	Billy won	Shrewsbury, England
27/11/1958	Billy Howes Vs Bob McDonald	Billy won	Morecambe, Lancashire
29/11/1958	Billy Howes Vs Bill McDonald	NK	Belle Vue, Manchester

Date	Match	Result	Location
03/12/1958	Billy Howes Vs Bill Robinson	Bill won	Lincoln, Lincolnshire
04/12/1958	Billy Howes Vs Josef Zaranoff	Josef won, BH DQ	Nottingham, England
09/12/1958	Billy Howes Vs Reg Williams	Reg won	Wolverhampton, West Midlands
12/12/1958	Billy Howes Vs Alec Bray	NK	Liverpool, England
19/12/1958	Billy Howes Vs Reg Williams	NK	Rotherham
26/12/1958	Billy Howes Vs Alf Cadman	NK	Bolton, Lancashire
02/01/1959	Billy Howes Vs Alec Bray	Howes won	Liverpool, England
07/01/1959	Billy Howes Vs John King	NK	Sheffield, England
09/01/1959	Billy Howes Vs Reg Williams	Reg won	Liverpool, England
10/01/1959	Billy Howes Vs Vic Stewart	Draw	Shrewsbury, England
13/01/1959	Billy Howes Vs Johnny Allan	NK	Wakefield, England
14/01/1959	Billy Howes Vs Tony Mancelli	Tony won, BH DQ	Lincoln, Lincolnshire
15/01/1959	Billy Howes Vs Peter Deakin	Peter won, BH DQ	Nottingham, England
17/01/1959	Billy Howes Vs Peter Deakin	NK	Grantham, England
23/01/1959	Billy Howes Vs Bill Robinson	NK	Liverpool, England
24/01/1959	Billy Howes Vs Alf Cadman	Billy won, AC DQ	Shrewsbury, England
30/01/1959	Billy Howes Vs Ernie Riley	NK	Bolton, Lancashire
06/02/1959	Billy Howes Vs Mike Marino	Mike won	Nottingham, England
07/02/1959	Billy Howes Vs Gwyn Davies	Billy won	Newcastle, England
11/02/1959	Billy Howes Vs Tony Mancelli	Billy won	Lincoln, Lincolnshire
13/02/1959	Billy Howes Vs Axel Dieter	NK	Brighton, England
14/02/1959	Billy Howes Vs Alf Cadman	Draw	Shrewsbury, England
16/02/1959	Billy Howes Vs Josef Zaranoff	Zaranoff won	High Wycombe, England
17/02/1959	Billy Howes Vs Johnny Allan	NK	Wakefield, England
18/02/1959	Billy Howes Vs Tony Vallon	Billy won	Albert Hall, London
19/02/1959	Billy Howes Vs Johan Dillinger	NK	Luton, London
21/02/1959	Billy Howes Vs Axel Dieter	Billy won	Purley, England
24/02/1959	Billy Howes Vs Bill Robinson	Billy won	Birmingham, England
27/02/1959	Billy Howes Vs Tony Mancelli	NK	Bolton, Lancashire
06/03/1959	Billy Howes Vs Reg Williams	Billy won	Liverpool, England
07/03/1959	Billy Howes Vs Alf Cadman	Alf won	Shrewsbury, England
10/03/1959	Billy Howes Vs Masambula	Masambula won	Hull, England
11/03/1959	Billy Howes Vs Horst Hoffman	NK	Scunthorpe, England
13/03/1959	Billy Howes Vs Ernie Riley	NK	Bolton, Lancashire
16/03/1959	Billy Howes Vs John Lees	NK	Bradford, England
17/03/1959	Billy Howes Vs Ernie Riley	NK	Wakefield, England
18/03/1959	Billy Howes Vs Peter Deakin	NK	Grimsby, England
19/03/1959	Billy Howes Vs Dai Sullivan	Billy won, DS DQ	Nottingham, England
31/03/1959	Billy Howes Vs Joe Cornelius	NK	Swindon, England
01/04/1959	Billy Howes Vs Bill McDonald	Billy won	Bath, England
04/04/1959	Billy Howes Vs Joe Cornelius	Draw	Coventry, England
07/04/1959	Billy Howes Vs Eric Taylor	Eric won	Birmingham, England
11/04/1959	Billy Howes Vs Bert Royal	Draw	Hanley
15/04/1959	Billy Howes Vs Reg Williams	NK	Llandudno, Wales
21/04/1959	Billy Howes Vs Rocky Wall	NK	Scarborough
25/04/1959	Billy Howes Vs Frank O'Donnell	NK	Belle Vue, Manchester

Date	Match	Result	Location
26/04/1959	Billy Howes Vs Reg Williams	Bill won, RW DQ	Birmingham, England
28/04/1959	Billy Howes Vs Erich Koltschak	Erich won	Swindon, England
29/04/1959	Billy Howes Vs Eric Taylor	NK	Albert Hall, London
30/04/1959	Billy Howes Vs Masambula	NK	Luton, London
02/05/1959	Billy Howes Vs Johnny Czeslaw	Howes won	Newcastle, England
04/05/1959	Billy Howes Vs Ernie Riley	Riley won	Blackpool, England
08/05/1959	Billy howes & Tommy Mann Vs Bert Royal & Ernie Riley	NK	Liverpool, England
09/05/1959	Billy Howes Vs Eric Koltschak	NK	Dudley, England
12/05/1959	Billy Howes Vs Johnny Czeslaw	Howes won	Wolverhampton, England
20/05/1959	Billy Howes Vs Norman Walsh	NK	Cardiff, Wales
21/05/1959	Billy Howes Vs Mike Marino	Marino won	Peterborough, England
23/05/1959	Billy howes Vs The Mask	Mask won	Newcastle, England
27/05/1959	Billy Howes Vs Vic Stewart	NK	Sheffield, England
02/06/1959	Billy Howes Vs Bert Royal	Howes won	Birmingham, England
04/06/1959	Billy Howes Vs Doug Joyce	NK	Bristol, England
05/06/1959	Billy Howes Vs Les Kellett	NK	Bolton, Lancashire
08/06/1959	Billy Howes Vs Steve Logan	NK	Shoreditch, England
20/06/1959	Billy Howes Vs Pat Barrett	NK	Norwich, England
23/06/1959	Billy Howes Vs Geoff Portz	NK	Wakefield, England
14/07/1959	Billy Howes Vs Bert Royal	Howes won, BRDQ	Birmingham, England
24/07/1959	Billy Howes Vs Bill McDonald	Howes won	Dudley, England
25/07/1959	Billy Howes Vs Vic Stewart	Nk	Grantham, England
26/07/1959	Billy howes Vs Steve Logan	Howes won	Brighton, England
27/07/1959	Billy Howes Vs Tibor Szakacs	NK	Shoreditch, England
29/07/1959	Billy Howes Vs Bill Rawlings	NK	Southend
11/08/1959	Billy Howes Vs Dennis Dean	Howes won	Withernsea
11/08/1959	Billy Howes Vs Ernie Baldwin (F)	Baldwin won	Withernsea
15/08/1959	Billy Howes Vs Bill Robinson	NK	Newcastle, England
20/08/1959	Billy Howes Vs Masambula	Masambula won	Withernsea
25/08/1959	Billy Howes Vs Reg Williams	NK	Wolverhampton, England
31/08/1959	Billy Howes Vs Doug joyce	NK	Folkestone
04/09/1959	Billy Howes & Frank O'Donnell Vs Bert Royal & Tony Vallon	Nk	Dudley, England
09/09/1959	Billy howes Vs Ray Apollon	Nk	Ashford
10/09/1959	Billy howes Vs Tony Vallon	Howes won	Bristol, England
11/09/1959	Billy Howes johnny Allan	Nk	Liverpool, England
12/09/1959	Billy Howes Vs Gwyn Davies	Davies won	Hanley
14/09/1959	Billy Howes Vs Masambula	Masambula won	Hamilton, Scotland
15/09/1959	Billy Howes Vs Don Branch	NK	Wakefield, England
23/09/1959	Billy Howes Vs Antonio Montorro	Nk	Sheffield, England
25/09/1959	Billy Howes Vs Ernie Riley	Nk	Dudley, England
28/09/1959	Billy Howes Vs Johnny Yearsley	Nk	Bedford, England
29/09/1959	Billy Howes Vs Charlie Fisher	Nk	Welling
07/10/1959	Billy Howes Vs Antonio Montorro	NK	Sheffield, England
14/10/1959	Billy Howes Vs Johnny Czeslawa	Howes won	Royal Albert Hall, London
17/10/1959	Billy Howes Vs Kurt Wenzl	Howes won	hanley

Date	Match	Result	Location
19/10/1959	Billy Howes Vs Jamie Dula	NK	Shoreditch, England
20/10/1959	Billy Howes Vs Johnny Yearsley	NK	Welling
21/10/1959	Billy Howes Vs Les Kellett	Kellett won	Bridlington
22/10/1959	Billy Howes Vs Eric Taylor	NK	Bristol, England
26/10/1959	Billy Howes Vs Bill Robinson	NK	Blackpool, England
28/10/1959	Billy Howes Vs Bill Rawlings	Rawlings won	Lincoln, England
30/10/1959	Billy Howes Vs Bill Robinson	NK	Liverpool, England
31/10/1959	Billy Howes Vs Arthur Ricardo	NK	Shrewsbury
03/11/1959	Billy Howes Vs Bill Rawlings	Draw	Welling
06/11/1959	Billy Howes Vs Johnny Allan	NK	Bolton, Lancashire
06/11/1959	Billy howes Vs johnny Allan	NK	Bolton, England
09/11/1959	Billy Howes Vs Tibor Szakacs	Szakacs won	High Wycombe, England
14/11/1959	Billy howes Vs Roman Wanniek	NK	Kings Lynn, England
18/11/1959	Billy Howes Vs Gordon Nelson	NK	Sheffield, England
23/11/1959	Billy Howes Vs jim Rawlings	NK	Kirkby, Ashfield
10/12/1959	Billy Howes Vs Bert Royal	NK	Nottingham, England
11/12/1959	Billy Howes Vs Francis Sullivan	NK	Rotherham
16/12/1959	Billy Howes Vs Alec Bray	Howes won	Lincoln, England
19/12/1959	Billy Howes Vs Billy Two Rivers	NK	Barrow
26/12/1959	Billy Howes Vs Ernie Riley	NK	Bolton, Lancashire
05/01/1960	Billy Howes Vs Dennis Mitchell	NK	Birmingham, England
06/01/1960	Billy Howes Vs Alf Cadman	NK	Smethwick, England
09/01/1960	Billy Howes Vs Reg Williams	NK	Doncaster, England
12/01/1960	Billy Howes Vs Ernie Riley	NK	Lime Grove, London
16/01/1960	Billy Howes Vs Ron Fury	NK	Middlesborough, England
19/01/1960	Billy Howes Vs Franz Orlik	NK	Welling
20/01/1960	Billy Howes Vs Jean Chausson-Bel	Howes won	Royal Albert Hall, London
22/01/1960	Billy Howes Vs Tibor Szakas	NK	Wembley, London
23/01/1960	Billy Howes Vs Doug Joyce	Howes won	Coventry, England
26/01/1960	Billy Howes Vs Ernie Riley	Howes won	Lime Grove, London
28/01/1960	Billy Howes Vs Peter Deakin	NK	Nottingham, England
01/02/1960	Billy Howes Vs Pedro Bengochea	NK	Leeds, England
02/02/1960	Billy Howes Vs Perdro Bengochea	NK	Hull, England
10/02/1960	Billy Howes Vs Francis St Clair Gregory	NK	Llandudno, Wales
13/02/1960	Billy Howes Vs Pedro Bengochea	NK	Doncaster, England
15/02/1960	Billy Howes Vs Mike Marino	NK	Leeds, England
16/02/1960	Billy Howes Vs Ernie Baldwin	NK	Bridlington, England
17/02/1960	Billy Howes Vs Bob Sweeney	NK	Grimsby, England
20/02/1960	Billy Howes Vs Bert Royal	NK	Halifax, West Yorkshire
22/02/1960	Billy Howes Vs Bert Nuttall	NK	Colwyn Bay, Wales
24/02/1960	Billy Howes Vs Francis Sullivan	NK	Shoreditch
25/02/1960	Billy Howes Vs Doug Joyce	NK	Walthamstow
26/02/1960	Billy Howes Vs Johnny Allan	NK	Bolton, England
27/02/1960	Billy Howes Vs Bill Robinson	Robinson won	Hanley
27/02/1960	Billy Howes Vs Tony Vallon	Howes won	Hanley
27/02/1960	Billy Howes Vs Norman Walsh	Howes won	Hanley

Date	Match	Result	Location
28/02/1960	Billy Howes Vs Bill Robinson	Robinson won	Birmingham, England
04/03/1960	Billy Howes Vs Eric Taylor	NK	Bradford, England
05/03/1960	Billy Howes Vs Eric Taylor	NK	Middlesborough, England
07/03/1960	Billy Howes Vs Enriqu Marquess	NK	Blackpool, England
08/03/1960	Billy Howes Vs Ernie Riley	NK	Wolverhampton, England
09/03/1960	Billy Howes Vs Bert Royal	NK	Smethwick, England
11/03/1960	Billy Howes Vs Enriqu Marquess	NK	Liverpool, England
12/03/1960	Billy Howes Vs Ernie Riley	Riley won	Hanley
14/03/1960	Billy Howes Vs Black Angel	NK	York, England
15/03/1960	Billy Howes Vs Billy Joyce	NK	Scarborough, England
17/03/1960	Billy Howes Vs Enrique Marquess	Howes won	Nottingham, England
18/03/1960	Billy Howes Vs Bob Sweeney	NK	Glasgow, Scotland
19/03/1960	Billy Howes Vs Bill Robinson	NK	Huddersfield, England
21/03/1960	Billy Howes Vs Reg Williams	NK	Walsall
22/03/1960	Billy Howes Vs Alf Cadman	Draw	Birmingham, England
23/03/1960	Billy Howes Vs Tibor Szakacs	NK	Banbury, England
24/03/1960	Billy Howes Vs Vittorio Ochoa	Howes won	Bristol, England
25/03/1960	Billy Howes Vs Vic Stewart	NK	Willenhall
26/03/1960	Billy Howes Vs Reg Williams	draw	Wellington, England
01/04/1960	Billy Howes Vs Joseph Zaranoff	Zaranoff won	Northampton, England
02/04/1960	Billy Howes Vs Alex Wenzl	Draw	Coventry, England
04/04/1960	Billy Howes Vs Billy Two Rivers	NK	Halifax, England
06/04/1960	Billy Howes Vs Eric Taylor	NK	Preston, England
07/04/1960	Billy Howes Vs Eric Taylor	NK	Bradford, England
09/04/1960	Billy Howes Vs Ernie Riley	NK	Middlesborough, England
12/04/1960	Billy Howes Vs Ernie Riley	NK	Lime Grove, London
13/04/1960	Billy Howes Vs Norman Walsh	Draw	Bath, England
13/04/1960	Billy Howes Vs Norman Walsh	Draw	Bath, England
15/04/1960	Billy Howes Vs Vic Stewart	NK	Willenhall
19/04/1960	Billy Howes Vs Ed Mangotich	NK	Leeds, England
20/04/1960	Billy Howes Vs Francis Sullivan	Draw	Albert Hall, London
23/04/1960	Billy Howes Vs Bert Royal	NK	Halifax, England
26/04/1960	Billy Howes Vs Clayton Thomson	NK	Hull, England
27/04/1960	Billy Howes Vs Barry Douglas	NK	Sheffield, England
28/04/1960	Billy Howes Vs Bert Royal	Draw	Barrow, England
30/04/1960	Billy Howes Vs Bob Sweeney	NK	Festival inn, Trwell, Nottinghamshire
02/05/1960	Billy Howes Vs Adolf Kaiser	Howes won	Leeds, England
03/05/1960	Billy Howes Vs Seamus Dunleavy	NK	Bridlington, England
05/05/1960	Billy Howes Vs Remy Bayle	Bayle won	Morecambe, Lancashire
06/05/1960	Billy Howes Vs Arthur Ricardo	NK	Bradford, England
07/05/1960	Billy Howes Vs Alf Cadman	NK	Leeds, England
09/05/1960	Billy Howes Vs Masambula	Howes won	Bedford, England
10/05/1960	Billy Howes Vs Doug Joyce	Howes won	Purley
16/05/1960	Billy Howes Vs Eric Taylor	NK	Portobello
17/05/1960	Billy Howes Vs Johnny Allan	NK	Trowell

Date	Match	Result	Location
24/05/1960	Billy Howes Vs Alf Cadman	Howes won	Birmingham, England
25/05/1960	Billy Howes Vs Joe Cornelius	Howes won	Cardiff, Wales
27/05/1960	Billy Howes Vs Jim Hart	NK	Liverpool, England
28/05/1960	Billy Howes Vs Francis St Clair Gregory	Gregory won	Hanley
31/05/1960	Billy Howes Vs Norman Walsh	NK	Scarborough, England
02/06/1960	Billy Howes Vs Bill Robinson	NK	Nottingham, England
09/06/1960	Billy Howes Vs Clayton Thomson	NK	Hornsea
10/06/1960	Billy Howes Vs Seamus Dunleavy	NK	Fleetwood
11/06/1960	Billy Howes Vs Clayton Thomson	NK	Middlesborough, England
15/06/1960	Billy Howes Vs Johnny Allan	Howes won	Cardiff, Wales
16/06/1960	Billy Howes Vs Arthur Beaumont	Howes won	Bristol, England
17/06/1960	Billy Howes Vs Norman Walsh	Draw	Bradford, England
18/06/1960	Billy Howes Vs Bill Robinson	NK	Belle Vue, Manchester
22/06/1960	Billy Howes Vs Ernie Riley	NK	Southend
23/06/1960	Billy Howes Vs Ernie Riley	Draw	Bath, England
26/06/1960	Billy Howes Vs Joseph Zaranoff	NK	Folkestone
30/06/1960	Billy Howes Vs Bill Robinson	NK	Crewe, England
01/07/1960	Billy Howes Vs Arthur Ricardo	Howes won	Bradford, England
02/07/1960	Billy Howes Vs Norman Walsh	NK	Middlesborough, England
04/07/1960	Billy Howes Vs Vic Stewart	NK	Skegness, England
07/07/1960	Billy Howes Vs Bert Royal	NK	Southport
08/07/1960	Billy Howes Vs Remy Bayle	NK	Liverpool, England
09/07/1960	Billy Howes Vs John Lees	NK	Doncaster, England
15/07/1960	Billy Howes Vs Eric Taylor	Taylore won	Bradford, England
18/07/1960	Billy Howes Vs Seamus Dunleavy	NK	Skegness, England
19/07/1960	Billy Howes Vs Remy Bayle	NK	Wolverhampton, England
22/07/1960	Billy Howes Vs Reg Williams	NK	Liverpool, England
23/07/1960	Billy Howes Vs Johnny Yearsley	NK	Hanley
27/07/1960	Billy Howes Vs Ernie Riley	NK	Withernsea
29/07/1960	Billy Howes Vs Bill Rawlings	NK	Fleetwood
30/07/1960	Billy Howes Vs Norman Walsh	NK	Halifax, England
01/08/1960	Billy Howes Vs Les Kellett	NK	Colwyn Bay, Wales
04/08/1960	Billy Howes Vs Francis Sullivan	NK	Scarborough, England
05/08/1960	Billy Howes Vs Arthur Ricardo	Howes won	Bolton, England
05/08/1960	Billy Howes Vs Les Kellett	Kellett won	Bolton, England
09/08/1960	Billy Howes Vs Joe Cornelius	NK	Welling
10/08/1960	Billy Howes Vs Johnny Yearsley	NK	Dunstable
13/08/1960	Billy Howes Vs Norman Walsh	NK	Middlesborough, England
15/08/1960	Billy Howes & Bobby Steele Vs Alf Cadman & Frank O'Donnell	NK	York, England
18/08/1960	Billy Howes Vs Dai Sullivan	NK	Scarborough, England
20/08/1960	Billy Howes Vs Jack Beaumont	NK	Newcastle, England
24/08/1960	Billy Howes Vs Johnny Czeslaw	NK	Felixstowe
14/09/1960	Billy Howes Vs Alf Cadman	NK	Aberystwyth, Wales
15/09/1960	Billy Howes Vs Spencer Churchill	NK	Ellesmere
17/09/1960	Billy Howes Vs Francis St Clair Gregory	NK	Hanley

Date	Match	Result	Location
20/09/1960	Billy Howes Vs Frank O'Donnell	NK	Wakefield, England
23/09/1960	Billy Howes Vs Tibor Szakacs	NK	Bradford, England
24/09/1960	Billy Howes Vs Tony Mancelli	NK	Middlesborough, England
28/09/1960	Billy Howes Vs Bert Royal	NK	Grimsby, England
01/10/1960	Billy Howes Vs Cyril Morris	Morris won	Newcastle, England
04/10/1960	Billy Howes Vs Clayton Thomson	NK	Wakefield, England
07/10/1960	Billy Howes Vs Arthur Ricardo	NK	Bolton, England
08/10/1960	Billy Howes Vs Bert Royal	NK	Doncaster, England
11/10/1960	Billy Howes Vs Eric Taylor	NK	Hull
12/10/1960	Billy Howes Vs Antonio Montorro	NK	Sheffield, England
14/10/1960	Billy Howes Vs Bobby Graham	NK	Rotherham, England
15/10/1960	Billy Howes Vs Eric Taylor	NK	Belle Vue, Manchester
19/10/1960	Billy Howes Vs Pat Roach	NK	Banbury
21/10/1960	Billy Howes Vs Great Togo	Howes won	Norwich, England
24/10/1960	Billy Howes Vs Bob Sweeney	NK	Loughborough, England
25/10/1960	Billy Howes Vs Colin Williamson	NK	Trowell
26/10/1960	Billy Howes Vs Bill Robinson	NK	Grimsby
27/10/1960	Billy Howes Vs Eric Liederman	NK	Nottingham, England
28/10/1960	Billy Howes Vs Frank O'Donnell	NK	Glasgow, Scotland
05/11/1960	Billy Howes Vs Johnny Yearsley	NK	Luton, England
07/11/1960	Billy Howes Vs Jean Morandi	NK	Bradford, England
09/11/1960	Billy Howes Vs Eric Taylor	NK	Grimsby, England
10/11/1960	Billy Howes Zebra Kid	NK	Kirkcaldy
11/11/1960	Billy Howes Vs Jean Morandi	NK	Leicester, England
12/11/1960	Billy Howes Vs Gunther Nordhoff	NK	Middlesborough, England
15/11/1960	Billy Howes Vs Harry Fields	NK	Wakefield, England
16/11/1960	Billy Howes Vs Billy Two Rivers	Bill Rivers won	Lincoln, England
16/11/1960	Billy Howes Vs Billy Two Rivers	Rivers won	Lincoln, England
17/11/1960	Billy Howes Vs Geoff Portz	NK	Nottingham, England
18/11/1960	Billy Howes Vs Eric Taylor	NK	Leicester, England
21/11/1960	Billy Howes Vs Dai Sullivan	NK	Loughborough, England
23/11/1960	Billy Howes Vs Bill Robinson	NK	Grimsby
23/11/1960	Billy Howes Vs Bill Robinson	NK	Grimsby, England
24/11/1960	Billy Howes Vs John Lees	NK	Ellesmere Port
25/11/1960	Billy Howes Vs Arthur Beaumont	NK	Bolton, England
26/11/1960	Billy Howes Vs Jamie Oliver	NK	Chesterfield
30/11/1960	Billy Howes Vs Ernie Baldwin	NK	Preston, England
01/12/1960	Billy Howes Vs Eric Liederman	Howes won	Hastings,
01/12/1960	Billy Howes Vs Tony Mancelli	Howes won	Hastings,
03/12/1960	Billy Howes Vs Jamie Olivera	NK	Kings Lynn, London
05/12/1960	Billy Howes Vs Bill Robinson	NK	Blackpool, England
08/12/1960	Billy Howes Vs Bolo Hawaka	NK	Smethwick
09/12/1960	Billy Howes Vs Bill Robinson	NK	Liverpool, England
15/12/1960	In KO Tournament	NK	Walthamstow
16/12/1960	Billy Howes Vs Josef Zaranoff	Draw	Ipswich, England
17/12/1960	Billy Howes Vs Jamie Olivera	NK	Middlesborough, England

Date	Match	Result	Location
19/12/1960	Billy Howes Vs Seamus Dunleavy	NK	Colwyn Bay, Wales
21/12/1960	Billy Howes Vs Alf Cadman	NK	Preston, England
23/12/1960	Billy Howes Vs Bill Robinson	NK	Bolton, Lancashire
24/12/1960	Billy Howes Vs Alf Cadman	NK	New Brighton
26/12/1960	Billy Howes Vs Bill Robinson	NK	Blackpool, England
30/12/1960	Billy Howes Vs Bill Robinson	NK	Liverpool, England
31/12/1960	Billy Howes Vs Arthur Ricardo	Howes won	Middlesborough, England
04/01/1961	Billy Howes Vs Al Hayes	NK	Grimsby, England
06/01/1961	Billy Howes Vs Bob Sweeney	Howes won	Glasgow, Scotland
09/01/1961	Billy Howes Vs Bill McDonald	NK	Hamilton, Scotland
10/01/1961	Billy Howes Vs Norman Walsh	Draw	Aberdeen, Scotland
12/01/1961	Billy Howes Vs Bobby Graham	NK	Barrow, England
13/01/1961	Billy Howes Vs Doug Joyce	NK	Belfast
14/01/1961	Billy Howes Vs Ian Campbell	NK	Halifax, England
16/01/1961	Billy Howes Vs Clayton Thomson	NK	Eltham
17/01/1961	Billy Howes Vs Rudi Martinez	NK	Lime Grove, London
19/01/1961	Billy Howes Vs Dai Sullivan	NK	Nottingham, England
20/01/1961	Billy Howes Vs Masambula	NK	Leicester, England
21/01/1961	Billy Howes Vs Clayton Thomson	NK	Middlesborough, England
23/01/1961	Billy Howes Vs Joe Cornelius	Cornelius won	Aylesbury
28/01/1961	In KO Tournament	NK	Luton, England
31/01/1961	Billy Howes Vs Buddy Cody	Howes won	Purley
02/02/1961	Billy Howes Vs Count Bartelli	NK	Ellesmere Port
03/02/1961	Billy Howes Vs Reg Williams	NK	Liverpool, England
04/02/1961	Billy Howes Vs Vic Stewart	NK	Hanley
07/02/1961	Billy Howes Vs Norman Walsh	NK	Wakefield, England
08/02/1961	Billy Howes Vs Francis SUllivan	NK	Preston, England
09/02/1961	Billy Howes Vs Felix Lamban	NK	Nottingham, England
13/02/1961	Billy Howes Vs Bill Rawlings	NK	Hamilton, Scotland
15/02/1961	Billy Howes Vs Count Daidone	NK	Sheffield, England
16/02/1961	Billy Howes Vs Count Daidone	Draw	Morecambe, Lancashire
18/02/1961	Billy Howes Vs Bill Rawlings	NK	Halifax, England
20/02/1961	Billy Howes Vs Norman Walsh	NK	Huddersfield, England
21/02/1961	Billy Howes Vs Joe Cornelius	Cornelius won	Purley
22/02/1961	Billy Howes Vs Norman Walsh	Draw	Lincoln, England
24/02/1961	Billy Howes Vs Bill McDonald	NK	Glasgow, Scotland
28/02/1961	Billy Howes Vs Buddy Cody	NK	Welling
03/03/1961	Billy Howes Vs Hans Streiger	NK	Streatham
06/03/1961	Billy Howes Vs Arthur Ricardo	NK	Walsall
09/03/1961	Billy Howes Vs Bob Sweeney	NK	Blackpool, England
10/03/1961	Billy Howes Vs Bill Robinson	NK	Bolton, Lancashire
11/03/1961	Billy Howes Vs Emile Poilve	Howes won	Hanley
15/03/1961	Billy Howes Vs Eric Taylor	NK	Scunthorpe
23/03/1961	Billy Howes Vs Vic Hessle	NK	Crewe
24/03/1961	Billy Howes Vs Tony Olivera	NK	Liverpool, England
27/03/1961	Billy Howes Vs Dai Sullivan	NK	York, England

Date	Match	Result	Location
28/03/1961	Billy Howes Vs Billy Two Rivers	NK	Wolverhampton, England
30/03/1961	Billy Howes Vs Bill Robinson	NK	Nottingham
06/04/1961	Billy Howes Vs Count Daidone	NK	Barrow, England
14/04/1961	Billy Howes Vs Bill Robinson	NK	Hanley
22/04/1961	In KO Tournament	NK	Luton, England
26/04/1961	Billy Howes Vs Pat Barrett	NK	Sheffield, England
27/04/1961	Billy Howes Vs Gerry De Jaegar	NK	Goole
29/04/1961	Billy Howes Vs Gerry De Jaegar	Howes won	Hanley
29/04/1961	Billy Howes Vs Jack Beaumont	Howes won	Hanley
29/04/1961	Billy Howes Vs Francis St Clair Gregory (F)	Howes won	Hanley
01/05/1961	Billy Howes Vs Bill Robinson	NK	Huddersfield, England
01/05/1961	Billy Howes Vs Bill Robinson	NK	Huddersfield, England
03/05/1961	Billy Howes Vs Bill Robinson	NK	Grimsby
04/05/1961	Billy Howes Vs Bill Robinson	NK	Kirkcaldy
05/05/1961	Billy Howes Vs Gordon Kilmartin	NK	Bulwell
06/05/1961	Billy Howes Vs Bill Robinson	NK	Grantham, England
09/05/1961	Billy Howes Vs Barry Douglas	NK	Aberdeen, Scotland
10/05/1961	Billy Howes Vs Billy Two Rivers	NK	Scunthorpe
11/05/1961	Billy Howes Vs Mike Marino	Marino won	Morecambe, Lancashire
16/05/1961	Billy Howes Vs Doug Joyce	Draw	Colchester, England
17/05/1961	Billy Howes Vs Norman Walsh	NK	Hove
18/05/1961	Billy Howes Vs Doug Joyce	NK	Dunstable
19/05/1961	Billy Howes Vs Masambula	NK	Liverpool, England
22/05/1961	Billy Howes Vs Eric Taylor	NK	York, England
23/05/1961	Billy Howes Vs Billy Two Rivers	NK	Wolverhampton, England
25/05/1961	Billy Howes Vs Ernie Riley	NK	Birkenhead
26/05/1961	Billy Howes Vs Count Bartelli	NK	Bolton, England
28/05/1961	Billy Howes Vs Eric Taylor	NK	Dudley, England
31/05/1961	Billy Howes Vs Alan Garfield	Howes won	Cardiff, Wales
31/05/1961	Billy Howes Vs Mike Marino	Marino won	Cardiff, Wales
05/06/1961	Billy Howes Vs Johnny Yearsley	Howes won	Bedford
06/06/1961	Billy Howes Vs Bill Robinson	Robinson won	Swindon, England
08/06/1961	Billy Howes Vs Johnny Czeslaw	NK	Southampton, England
12/06/1961	Billy Howes Vs Masambula	NK	Preston, England
13/06/1961	Billy Howes Vs Vic Stewart	NK	Southport
17/06/1961	Billy Howes Vs Bill Robinson	Robinson won	Glasgow, Scotland
20/06/1961	Billy Howes Vs Norman Walsh	NK	Wolverhampton, England
21/06/1961	Billy Howes Vs Jim Armstrong	NK	Scunthorpe
23/06/1961	Billy Howes Vs Steve Logan	Draw	Barking
26/06/1961	Billy Howes Vs Phil Fogg	NK	Walsall
28/06/1961	Billy Howes Vs Hans Streiger	NK	Llanwrst, Wales
30/06/1961	Billy Howes Vs Hassan Ali Bey	NK	Chester, England
02/07/1961	Billy Howes Vs Jim Armstrong	NK	Dudley, England
05/07/1961	Billy Howes Vs Mike Marino	NK	Scunthorpe
07/07/1961	Billy Howes Vs Johnny Czeslaw	NK	Liverpool, England
08/07/1961	Billy Howes Vs Josef Zaranoff	Draw	Hanley

Date	Match	Result	Location
12/07/1961	Billy Howes Vs Seamus Dunleavy	NK	Sheffield, England
13/07/1961	Billy Howes Vs Masambula	NK	Scarborough, England
14/07/1961	Billy Howes Vs jim Hussey	Howes won JH DQ	Bolton, England
15/07/1961	Billy Howes Vs Norman Walsh	Draw	Newcastle, England
17/07/1961	Billy Howes Vs Doug Joyce	Howes won	Shoreditch
18/07/1961	Billy Howes Vs Mike Marino	NK	Welling
20/07/1961	Billy Howes Vs Masambula	NK	Scarborough, England
24/07/1961	Billy Howes Vs Alf Cadman	NK	Llandudno, Wales
26/07/1961	Billy Howes Vs Hans Streiger	NK	Withernsea
27/07/1961	Billy Howes Vs jim Hussey	NK	Southport
28/07/1961	Billy Howes Vs Ed Mangotich	NK	Liverpool, England
01/08/1961	Billy Howes Vs Johnny Allan	Nk	Aberdeen, Scotland
03/08/1961	Billy Howes Vs Reg Williams	NK	Hornsea
04/08/1961	Billy Howes Vs John Lees	Howes won	Fleetwood
05/08/1961	Billy Howes Vs Geoff Portz	NK	Middlesborough, England
17/08/1961	Billy Howes Vs Hassan Ali Bey	NK	Birkenhead
26/08/1961	Billy Howes Vs Johnny Allan	Howes won	Middlesborough, England
26/08/1961	Billy Howes Vs Eric taylor	Taylor won	Middlesborough, England
29/08/1961	Billy Howes Vs Johnny Czeslaw	NK	Welling
30/08/1961	Billy Howes Vs Eric taylor	Draw	Watford, England
31/08/1961	Billy Howes Vs Al Garmain	NK	Dunstable
05/09/1961	Billy Howes Vs Les Kellett	NK	Bridlington, England
06/09/1961	Billy Howes Vs Reg Williams	NK	Sheffield, England
09/09/1961	Billy Howes Vs Josef Zaranoff	NK	Stirling
13/09/1961	Billy Howes & Alf Cadman Vs Bert Royal & Eric Taylor	NK	Preston, England
18/09/1961	Billy Howes Vs Geoff Portz	NK	Halifax, England
19/09/1961	Billy Howes Vs Harry Fields	NK	Wakefield, England
21/09/1961	Billy Howes Vs Masambula	NK	Kirkcaldy
22/09/1961	Billy Howes Vs Masambula	Masambula won	Glasgow, Scotland
05/10/1961	Billy Howes Vs Francis St Clair Gregory	NK	Crewe
06/10/1961	Billy Howes Vs Enrie Riley	NK	Wellington
07/10/1961	Billy Howes Vs Count Bartelli	NK	Shrewsbury, England
10/10/1961	Billy Howes Vs Gerry De Jaegar	DeJaegar won	Chelmsford, England
11/10/1961	Billy Howes Vs Gerry De Jaegar	DeJaegar won	Dorking
12/10/1961	Billy Howes Vs Gerry De Jaegar	Howes won	Bristol, England
14/10/1961	Billy Howes Vs Majid Ackra	2-1 to Billy	Tottenham
17/10/1961	Billy Howes Vs Bill Rawlings	NK	Scarborough, England
18/10/1961	Billy Howes Vs Francis SUllivan	Sullivan BHDQ	Lincoln, England
19/10/1961	Billy Howes Vs Steve Logan	NK	Hayes
20/10/1961	Billy Howes Vs Billy Joyce	NK	Leicester, England
23/10/1961	Billy Howes Vs Joe Cornelius	NK	Walsall
24/10/1961	Billy Howes Vs Bobby Graham	NK	Wakefield, England
25/10/1961	Billy Howes Vs Billy Joyce	NK	Scunthorpe
26/10/1961	Billy Howes Vs Chief Maretana	NK	Barrow, England
30/10/1961	Billy Howes Vs billy Two Rivers	NK	Bradford, England

Date	Match	Result	Location
01/11/1961	Billy Howes Vs billy Two Rivers	Draw	Lincoln, England
02/11/1961	Billy Howes Vs Ricky Waldo	NK	Nottingham, England
03/11/1961	Billy Howes Vs Ernie Riley	Howes won	Glasgow, Scotland
06/11/1961	Billy Howes Vs Norman Walsh	NK	Blackpool, England
07/11/1961	Billy Howes Vs Ricky Waldo	NK	Wolverhampton, England
10/11/1961	Billy Howes Vs Norman Walsh	NK	Liverpool, England
11/11/1961	Billy Howes Vs Count Bartelli	NK	Doncaster, England
13/11/1961	Billy Howes Vs Jim Hussey	NK	Colwyn Bay, Wales
14/11/1961	Billy Howes Vs Billy Joyce	NK	Harrogate
15/11/1961	Billy Howes Vs Josef Zaranoff	NK	Aberystwyth, Wales
16/11/1961	Billy Howes Vs Francis St Clair Gregory	NK	Crewe
20/11/1961	Billy Howes Vs Seamus Dunleavy	Howes won	West Ham, England
22/11/1961	In KO Tournament	NK	Banbury
23/11/1961	Billy Howes Vs Gomez Maximilliano	Howes won	Bristol, England
24/11/1961	Billy Howes Vs Johnny Morgan	Morgan won	Streatham
27/11/1961	Billy Howes Vs Ray Apollon	NK	Warrington
29/11/1961	Billy Howes Vs Chief Maretana	Nk	Preston, England
30/11/1961	Billy Howes Vs Great Togo	NK	Smethwick
02/12/1961	Billy Howes Vs Great Togo	NK	Hanley
06/12/1961	Billy Howes Vs Charles Verhulst	NK	Sheffield, England
07/12/1961	Billy Howes Vs Charles Verhulst	NK	Hereford, England
08/12/1961	Billy Howes Vs Josef Zaranoff	NK	Eltham
13/12/1961	Billy Howes Vs Masambula	Draw	Lincoln, England
15/12/1961	Billy Howes Vs Count Bartelli	Count won	Bolton, England
23/12/1961	Billy Howes Vs Ernie Riley	2-1 to Billy	Trowell, Nottinghamshire
02/01/1962	Billy Howes Vs Gomez Maximilliano	Max won	Welling
04/01/1962	Billy Howes Vs Lucky Simonovich	Howes won	Bristol, England
05/01/1962	Billy Howes Vs Doug Joyce	NK	Barking
06/01/1962	Billy Howes Vs Gomez Maximilliano	NK	Norwich, England
08/01/1962	Billy Howes Vs Bill Robinson	Robinson won	Bradford
13/01/1962	Billy Howes Vs Bob Taylor	KO	Leicester, Leicestershire
15/01/1962	Billy Howes Vs Bill McDonald	Howes won	Blackpool, England
17/01/1962	Billy Howes Vs El Saaddee Mansourri	Howes won	Royal Albert Hall, London
18/01/1962	Billy Howes Vs Great Togo	Togo won BH Inj	Smethwick
20/01/1962	Billy Howes Vs Great Togo	Togo won BHDQ	Doncaster, England
22/01/1962	Billy Howes Vs Bill Rawlings	NK	Halifax, England
23/01/1962	Billy Howes Vs Willem Hall	Draw	Huddersfield, England
24/01/1962	Billy Howes Vs Enrique Marquess	NK	Sheffield, England
26/01/1962	Billy Howes Vs Dennis Mitchell	Mitchell won	Glasgow, Scotland
27/01/1962	Billy Howes Vs Terry Garvin	NK	Falkirk
29/01/1962	Billy Howes Vs Jim Armstrong	NK	Birmingham
02/02/1962	Billy Howes Vs Count Bartelli	NK	Liverpool, England
03/02/1962	Billy Howes Vs Jose Arroyo	Howes won	Doncaster, England
05/02/1962	Billy Howes Vs Enrique Marquess	Draw	Blackpool, England
08/02/1962	Billy Howes Vs Bert Royal	NK	Crewe
10/02/1962	Billy Howes Vs Count Bartelli	NK	Hanley

Date	Match	Result	Location
13/02/1962	Billy Howes Vs Josef Zaranoff	NK	Lime Grove, London
14/02/1962	Billy Howes Vs Norman Walsh	NK	Preston, England
15/02/1962	Billy Howes Vs Sandy Orford	NK	Nottingham, England
16/02/1962	Billy Howes Vs Josef Zaranoff	NK	Leicester, England
17/02/1962	Billy Howes Vs Billy Joyce	Howes won	Middlesborough, England
17/02/1962	Billy Howes Vs Bobo Matu	Matu won BHDQ	Middlesborough, England
19/02/1962	Billy Howes Vs Willem Hall	NK	Manor Baths, London
22/02/1962	Billy Howes Vs Great Togo	NK	Smethwick
23/02/1962	Billy Howes Vs Hans Streiger	Howes won	Bolton, England
24/02/1962	Billy Howes Vs billy Two Rivers	NK	Shrewsbury, England
26/02/1962	Billy Howes Vs Bill McDonald	NK	Blackpool, England
27/02/1962	Billy Howes Vs Count Bartelli	Draw	Wolverhampton, England
01/03/1962	Billy Howes Vs Iskha Khan	NK	Nottingham, England
03/03/1962	Billy Howes Vs Count Bartelli	Howes Inj	Doncaster, England
06/03/1962	Billy Howes Vs Bill Rawlings	Howes won	Huddersfield, England
07/03/1962	Billy Howes Vs Bob Sweeney	NK	Grimsby, England
09/03/1962	Billy Howes Vs The Monster	Monster won	Glasgow, Scotland
10/03/1962	Billy Howes Vs Bob Sweeney	NK	Grantham,
12/03/1962	Billy Howes Vs Bobo Matu	Howes won	Blackpool, England
13/03/1962	Billy Howes Vs John lees	NK	Hull
14/03/1962	Billy Howes Vs Masambula	NK	Caernarvon, Wales
15/03/1962	Billy Howes Vs Billy Joyce	NK	Blackburn, England
16/03/1962	Billy Howes Vs Hans Streiger	NC	Bolton, England
19/03/1962	Billy Howes Vs Dennis Mitchell	Mitchell won	Colwyn Bay, Wales
22/03/1962	Billy Howes Vs Hassan Ali Bey	NK	Crewe
24/03/1962	Billy Howes Vs Dennis Mitchell	Mitchell won	Hanley
26/03/1962	Billy Howes Vs Roger Gueret	Howes won	High Wycombe, England
27/03/1962	In 4 man KO Tournament	NK	Welling
28/03/1962	Billy Howes Vs Johnny Czeslaw	NK	Shoreditch
28/03/1962	Billy Howes Vs Tony Cassio	NK	Shoreditch
03/04/1962	Billy Howes Vs Alf Cadman	NK	Dundee, Scotland
04/04/1962	Billy Howes Vs Johnny Allan	NK	Sheffield, England
06/04/1962	Billy Howes Vs Jim Hussey	NK	Liverpool, England
09/04/1962	Billy Howes Vs Dennis Mitchell	NK	York
10/04/1962	Billy Howes Vs Count Bartelli	Bartelli won	Wolverhampton, England
12/04/1962	Billy Howes Vs Masambula	Howes won	Peterborough
14/04/1962	Billy Howes Vs Billy Joyce	Joyce won	Middlesborough, England
16/04/1962	Billy Howes Vs Gerry DeJaegar	NK	Leeds, England
19/04/1962	Billy Howes Vs Dai Sullivan	NK	Rotherham
23/04/1962	Billy Howes Vs Roy Bull Davis	NK	Buxton, England
26/04/1962	Billy Howes Vs Rocco Colombo	Howes won	Bristol, England
28/04/1962	Billy Howes Vs Count Bartelli	Bartelli won	Doncaster, England
30/04/1962	Billy Howes Vs Bobo Matu	NK	Birmingham
02/05/1962	Billy Howes Vs Johnny Allan	NK	Sheffield, England
03/05/1962	Billy Howes Vs Count Bartelli	Bartelli won	Crewe
04/05/1962	Billy Howes Vs Hans Streiger	Howes won	Bolton, England

Date	Match	Result	Venue
05/05/1962	Billy Howes (EMHWC) Vs Jacques Lageott (French Champ)	NK	Wembley, London
05/05/1962	Billy Howes Vs Jacques Lagaet	Howes won	Barking
07/05/1962	Billy Howes & Roy St Clair Vs Frank Hurley & Ed Mangotich	NK	Walthamstow
08/05/1962	Billy Howes Vs Rocco Colombo	Howes won	Hove
11/05/1962	Billy Howes Vs Johnny Czeslaw	Howes won	Welling
14/05/1962	Billy Howes Vs Jim Hussey	NK	Colwyn Bay, Wales
16/05/1962	Billy Howes Vs Gwyn Davies	NK	Leicester, England
18/05/1962	Billy Howes Vs Jim Hussey	NK	Liverpool, England
19/05/1962	Billy Howes Vs Billy Joyce	Howes won	Middlesborough, England
22/05/1962	Billy Howes Vs Masambula	NK	Trowell
23/05/1962	Billy Howes Vs Dai Sullivan	Draw	Lincoln, England
25/05/1962	Billy Howes Vs The Monster	Monster won	Glasgow, Scotland
26/05/1962	Billy Howes Vs Norman Walsh	Draw	Middlesborough, England
28/05/1962	Billy Howes Vs Johnny Allan	NK	Leeds, England
29/05/1962	Billy Howes Vs Masambula	NK	Bridlington, England
30/05/1962	Billy Howes Vs Dai Sullivan	NK	Grimsby, England
31/05/1962	Billy Howes Vs Terry Ricardo	NK	Morecambe, Lancashire
01/06/1962	Billy Howes Vs Bobby Graham	Howes won	Bolton, England
02/06/1962	Billy Howes Vs Hans Streiger	Streiger won BHDQ	Newcastle, England
04/06/1962	Billy Howes Vs Ernie Riley	NK	Buxton, England
05/06/1962	Billy Howes Vs Steve Logan	NK	Wolverhampton, England
07/06/1962	Billy Howes Vs Bobby Graham	NK	Barrow, England
08/06/1962	Billy Howes Vs Norman Walsh	NK	Liverpool, England
13/06/1962	Billy Howes Vs Francis SUllivan	NK	Sheffield, England
14/06/1962	Billy Howes Vs Johnny Allan	NK	Morecambe, Lancashire
15/06/1962	Billy Howes Vs Jim Hussey	NK	Bolton, England
16/06/1962	Billy Howes Vs Count Bartelli	NK	Doncaster, England
18/06/1962	Billy Howes Vs Gerry DeJaegar	Howes won	Bedford, England
19/06/1962	Billy Howes Vs Navarro Moyans	NK	Swindon, England
20/06/1962	Billy Howes Vs Johnny Yearsley	NK	Banbury
21/06/1962	Billy Howes Vs Frank Hurley	NK	Southampton, England
22/06/1962	Billy Howes Vs Seamus Dunleavy	NK	Northampton, England
23/06/1962	Billy Howes Vs Johnny Czeslaw	Draw	Maidstone
25/06/1962	Billy Howes Vs Alf Cadman	NK	Bradford, England
27/06/1962	Billy Howes Vs Jim Hussey	NK	Douglas, Isle of Man
28/06/1962	Billy Howes Vs Dai Sullivan	NK	Scarborough, England
29/06/1962	Billy Howes Vs Bill McDonald	NK	Glasgow, Scotland
30/06/1962	Billy Howes Vs Norman Walsh	Walsh won	Middlesborough, England
06/07/1962	Billy Howes Vs Francis St Clair Gregory	Howes won	Liverpool, England
08/07/1962	Billy Howes Vs Bill McDonald	NK	Blackpool, England
17/07/1962	Billy Howes Vs Francis Sullivan	NK	Bridlington, England
20/07/1962	Billy Howes Vs Steve Veidor	NK	Withernsea
21/07/1962	Billy Howes Vs Bruno Elrington	NK	Portsmouth, England
23/07/1962	Billy Howes Vs Reg Williams	NK	Skegness
27/07/1962	Billy Howes Vs Jim Hussey	NK	Bolton, England

Date	Match	Result	Location
29/07/1962	Billy Howes Vs Masambula	NK	Blackpool, England
11/08/1962	Billy Howes Vs Tibor Szakacs	NK	Newcastle, England
13/08/1962	Billy Howes Vs John DaSilva	Nk	York
14/08/1962	Billy Howes Vs Steve Logan	NK	Wolverhampton, England
17/08/1962	Billy Howes Vs Masambula	NK	Liverpool, England
18/08/1962	Billy Howes Vs Dai Sullivan	NK	Middlesborough, England
21/08/1962	Billy Howes Vs Norman Walsh	NK	Bridlington, England
24/08/1962	Billy Howes Vs Norman Walsh	NK	Glasgow, Scotland
25/08/1962	Billy Howes Vs Tibor Szakacs	Howes won	Newcastle, England
01/09/1962	Billy Howes Vs Johnny Czeslaw	NK	Maidstone
02/09/1962	Billy Howes Vs Francis Sullivan	Draw	Brighton
03/09/1962	Billy Howes Vs Vic Stewart	NK	Birmingham
04/09/1962	Billy Howes Vs Syed Saif Shah	NK	Wellington
08/09/1962	Billy Howes Vs Norman Walsh	NK	Bolton, Lancashire
09/09/1962	Billy Howes Vs Mario Matassa	NK	Blackpool, England
10/09/1962	Billy Howes Vs Johnny Czeslaw	NK	Cheltenham
13/09/1962	Billy Howes Vs Masambula	Howes won	Bristol, England
14/09/1962	Billy Howes Vs Joe Cornelius	Cornelius won	Barking
17/09/1962	Billy Howes Vs Norman Walsh	NK	Bradford, England
21/09/1962	Billy Howes Vs Norman Walsh	Howes won NMDQ	Glasgow, Scotland
22/09/1962	Billy Howes Vs Dai Sullivan	NK	Middlesborough, England
25/09/1962	Billy Howes Vs Syed Saif Shah	NK	Leicester, England
26/09/1962	Billy Howes Vs Seamus Dunleavy	NK	Cardiff, Wales
27/09/1962	Billy Howes Vs Johnny Czeslaw	NK	Dunstable
28/09/1962	Billy Howes & Dai Sullivan Vs Ian Campbell & Bill McDonald	NK	Liverpool, England
02/10/1962	Billy Howes Vs Dai Sullivan	NK	Harrogate
04/10/1962	Billy Howes Vs Ezzard Hart	Nk	Kirkcaldy
05/10/1962	Billy Howes Vs Roy Bull Davis	Howes won	Glasgow, Scotland
12/10/1962	Billy Howes Vs Norman Walsh	NK	Rotherham
13/10/1962	Billy Howes Vs Hassan Ali Bey	NK	Coventry, England
15/10/1962	Billy Howes Vs Reg Williams	NK	Birmingham
19/10/1962	Billy Howes Vs Johnny Czeslaw	NK	Liverpool, England
20/10/1962	Billy Howes Vs Josef Zaranoff	NK	Hanley
21/10/1962	Billy Howes Vs Josef Zaranoff	Howes won	Dudley, England
26/10/1962	Billy Howes Vs Angelo Romeiro	Howes won	Streatham
01/11/1962	Billy Howes Vs Eric Taylor	NK	Blackburn, England
02/11/1962	Billy Howes Vs El Greco	NK	Leicester, England
05/11/1962	Billy Howes Vs Emile Poilve	Howes won	Blackpool, England
08/11/1962	Billy Howes Vs Masambula	Masambula won BHDQ	Smethwick
09/11/1962	Billy Howes Vs Pierre Bernhardt	NK	Liverpool, England
10/11/1962	Billy Howes Vs Michael Allary	Howes won	Doncaster, England
11/11/1962	Billy Howes Vs Arthur Ricardo	Howes won	Dudley, England
13/11/1962	Billy Howes Vs Norman Walsh	Draw	Hull, England
23/11/1962	Billy Howes Vs Norman Walsh	Walsh won	Glasgow, Scotland
27/11/1962	Billy Howes Vs Syed Saif Shah	NK	Wellington

Date	Match	Result	Location
28/11/1962	Billy Howes Vs Dai Sullivan	Howes won	Lincoln, England
29/11/1962	Billy Howes Vs Joe Cornelius	NK	Blackburn, England
01/12/1962	Billy Howes Vs The Headhunter	NK	Hanley
03/12/1962	Billy Howes Vs Antonio Morlans	Howes won	Blackpool, England
04/12/1962	Billy Howes Vs Norman Walsh	NK	Leicester, England
06/12/1962	Billy Howes Vs Jacquerez	Jacquerez won	Smethwick
06/12/1962	Billy Howes Vs Antonio Morlans	Howes won	Smethwick
08/12/1962	Billy Howes Vs Masambula	Howes won	Doncaster, England
10/12/1962	Billy Howes Vs The Professor	NK	Bradford, England
12/12/1962	Billy Howes Vs Jack bence	Draw	Royal Albert Hall, London
13/12/1962	Billy Howes Vs Dennis Mitchell	NK	Nottingham, England
14/12/1962	Billy Howes Vs Norman Walsh	Draw	Leicester, England
15/12/1962	Billy Howes Vs Bill Robinson	Robinson won	Newcastle, England
18/12/1962	Billy Howes Vs Tony Cassio	NK	Wolverhampton, England
21/12/1962	Billy Howes Vs Steve Veidor	NK	Willenhall
22/12/1962	Billy Howes Vs Antonio Morlans	Howes won	Doncaster, England
31/12/1962	Billy Howes Vs Dennis Mitchell	NK	York
02/01/1963	Billy Howes Vs Dai Sullivan	Sullivan won	Lincoln, England
04/01/1963	Billy Howes Vs Dennis Mitchell	NK	Chesterfield, England
09/01/1963	Billy Howes Vs Doug Joyce	NK	Sheffield, England
10/01/1963	Billy Howes Vs Arjit Singh	NK	Smethwick
12/01/1963	Billy Howes Vs Pierre La Chappelle	NK	Trowell, Nottinghamshire
12/01/1963	Billy Howes Vs Steve Bell	Howes won	Trowell
12/01/1963	Billy Howes Vs Eric Taylor	NK	Middlesborough, England
15/01/1963	Billy Howes Vs Enrique Marquess	NK	Wolverhampton, England
16/01/1963	Billy Howes Vs Alf Cadman	NK	Wallasey
17/01/1963	Billy Howes Vs Dai Sullivan	NK	Nottingham, England
18/01/1963	Billy Howes Vs Quasimodo	Quasimodo won	Liverpool, England
19/01/1963	Billy Howes Vs Quasimodo	NK	Hanley
21/01/1963	Billy Howes Vs Gomez Maximilliano	NK	Eltham
22/01/1963	Billy Howes Vs Josef Molnar	NK	Colchester, England
25/01/1963	Billy Howes Vs Syed Saif Shah	NK	Northampton, England
29/01/1963	Billy Howes Vs Johnny Czeslaw	NK	Lime Grove, London
30/01/1963	Billy Howes Vs Dai Sullivan	NC	Lincoln, England
31/01/1963	Billy Howes Vs Rocky Wall	NK	Blackburn, England
01/02/1963	Billy Howes Vs Iskha Khan	NK	Leicester, England
05/02/1963	Billy Howes Vs Quasimodo	NK	Caernarvon, Wales
06/02/1963	Billy Howes Vs Quasimodo	NK	Hanley
08/02/1963	Billy Howes Vs Quasimodo	Quasimodo won	Liverpool, England
09/02/1963	Billy Howes Vs Tibor Szakacs	draw 1 each	Solihull, West Midlands
11/02/1963	Billy Howes Vs Billy Joyce	NK	York
12/02/1963	Billy Howes Vs Masambula	Masambula won	Huddersfield, England
15/02/1963	Billy Howes Vs Bill Robinson	Robinson won BH DQ	Glasgow, Scotland
18/02/1963	Billy Howes Vs Les Kellett	Howes won	Leeds, England
19/02/1963	Billy Howes Vs Bill McDonald	McDonal won	Aberdeen, Scotland

Date	Match	Result	Location
20/02/1963	Billy Howes Vs Norman Walsh	NK	Sheffield, England
21/02/1963	Billy Howes & Bert Royal Vs Les kellett & Bill McDonald	NK	Morecambe, Lancashire
22/02/1963	Billy Howes Vs Bill McDonald	NK	Rotherham
27/02/1963	Billy Howes Vs Earl Maynard	NK	Southend
02/03/1963	Billy Howes Vs Vic Stewart	NK	Hanley
07/03/1963	Billy Howes Vs Josef Zaranoff	Zaranoff won	East Grinstead
08/03/1963	Billy Howes Vs Gerry DeJaegar	NK	Rochester
11/03/1963	Billy Howes Vs Alf Cadman	NK	Bradford, England
12/03/1963	Billy Howes Vs John Lees	NK	Scarborough, England
13/03/1963	Billy Howes Vs Dai Sullivan	Sullivan won	Lincoln, England
14/03/1963	Billy Howes Vs Youssef Gama	NK	Blackburn, England
15/03/1963	Billy Howes Vs Bill Robinson	NK	Leicester, Leicestershire
16/03/1963	Billy Howes Vs Peter Maivia	Maivia won	Newcastle, England
18/03/1963	Billy Howes Vs Count Bartelli	NK	Blackpool, England
20/03/1963	Billy Howes Vs Roy Bull Davis	Howes won RDDQ	Banbury
21/03/1963	Billy Howes Vs Count Bartelli	NK	Crewe
23/03/1963	Billy Howes Vs Roy Davis	Howes won	Bolton, Lancashire
26/03/1963	Billy Howes Vs Rocky Wall	Wall won BHDQ	Huddersfield, England
28/03/1963	Billy Howes Vs Count Bartelli	NK	Rawtenstall
29/03/1963	Billy Howes Vs Geoff Portz	Portz won BHDQ	Glasgow, Scotland
01/04/1963	Billy Howes Vs Eric Taylor	Howes won	Birmingham
02/04/1963	Billy Howes Vs Roy Bull Davis	NK	Dudley
03/04/1963	Billy Howes Vs Peter Maivia	Howes won	Lincoln
04/04/1963	Billy Howes Vs Dennis Mitchell	NK	Rotherham
05/04/1963	Billy Howes Vs Tibor Szakacs	NC	Bolton
06/04/1963	Billy Howes & Norman Walsh Vs Roy Bull Davis & Jim Hussey	NK	Hanley
08/04/1963	Billy Howes Vs Reg Williams	Howes won	Birmingham
11/04/1963	Billy Howes Vs Count Bartelli	NK	Willenhall
12/04/1963	Billy Howes Vs Count Bartelli	NK	Willenhall
13/04/1963	Billy Howes Vs Josef Zaranoff	Howes won	Doncaster
16/04/1963	Billy Howes Vs Steve Veidor	NK	Huddersfield
17/04/1963	Billy Howes Vs Arthur Ricardo	NK	Preston
20/04/1963	Billy Howes Vs Arthur Ricardo	Howes won	Middlesborough
22/04/1963	Billy Howes Vs Jim Hussey	Hussey won	Carlisle
23/04/1963	Billy Howes Vs Masambula	NK	Wellington
24/04/1963	Billy Howes Vs Yousseff Gama	Howes won	Scunthorpe
25/04/1963	Billy Howes Vs Roy Bull Davis	NK	Brierly Hill
26/04/1963	Billy Howes Vs Tibor Szakacs	Howes won	Bolton
27/04/1963	Billy Howes Vs Josef Zaranoff	Draw	Doncaster
29/04/1963	Billy Howes Vs Eric Taylor	Howes won	Bradford
30/04/1963	Billy Howes Vs Bob Sweeney	NK	Solihull
02/05/1963	Billy Howes Vs Hans Streiger	NK	Crewe
03/05/1963	Billy Howes Vs Count Bartelli	Bartelli won	Liverpool
08/05/1963	Billy Howes Vs Peter Maivia	Howes won	Lincoln
10/05/1963	Billy Howes Vs Bill Robinson	Robinson won BHDQ	Glasgow, Scotland

Date	Match	Result	Venue
11/05/1963	Billy Howes Vs Bill Robinson	NK	Grimsby
14/05/1963	Billy Howes Vs Dai Sullivan	NK	Trowell
15/05/1963	Billy Howes Vs Bill Robinson	NK	Sheffield, South Yorkshire
16/05/1963	Billy Howes Vs Terry O'Neill	NK	Morecambe
17/05/1963	Billy Howes Vs Bill Robinson	NK	Bridlington
18/05/1963	Billy Howes Vs Jack Pye	Howes won JPDQ	Belle Vue, Manchester
20/05/1963	Billy Howes Vs Leon Arras	Arras won	Leeds
21/05/1963	Billy Howes Vs Henri Pierlot	NK	Wolverhampton
22/05/1963	Billy Howes Vs Warnia Zarzecki	Howes won	Royal Albert Hall, London
23/05/1963	Billy Howes Vs Doug Joyce	NK	Barrow
24/05/1963	Billy Howes Vs Count Bartelli	Bartelli won BHDQ	Liverpool
27/05/1963	Billy Howes Vs Dai Sullivan	Howes won	Bradford
30/05/1963	Billy Howes Vs Leon Arras	NK	Brierly Hill
01/06/1963	Billy Howes Vs The Professor	Draw	Middlesbrough
04/06/1963	Billy Howes Vs Leon Arras	Howes won	Wolverhampton
05/06/1963	Billy Howes Vs Gerry DeJaegar	Howes won	Cardiff, Wales
12/06/1963	Billy Howes Vs Seamus Dunleavy	NK	Malvern
13/06/1963	Bilyl Howes Vs Ernie Riely	NK	Crewe
14/06/1963	Billy Howes Vs Dennis Mitchell	Mitchell won	Liverpool
17/06/1963	Billy Howes Vs Bill Robinson	NK	York
18/06/1963	Billy Howes Vs Ezzard Hart	NK	Croydon
19/06/1963	Billy Howes Vs Masambula	NK	Felixstowe
20/06/1963	Billy Howes Vs Francis Sullivan	NK	Bournemouth, England
21/06/1963	Billy Howes Vs John Lees	Lees won	Glasgow, Scotland
24/06/1963	Billy Howes Vs Dennis Mitchell	NK	Bradford
25/06/1963	Billy Howes Vs Les Kellett	NK	Bridlington, England
27/06/1963	Billy Howes Vs Norman Walsh	NK	Morecambe
28/06/1963	Billy Howes Vs Masambula	Howes won	Bolton
29/06/1963	Billy Howes Vs Doug Joyce	NK	Belle Vue, Manchester
01/07/1963	Billy Howes Vs Hans Streiger	NK	Skegness
05/07/1963	Billy Howes Vs Dennis Mitchell	Howes won	Liverpool
06/07/1963	Billy Howes Vs Count Bartelli	Bartelli won	Doncaster
07/07/1963	Billy Howes Vs Jim Hussey	NK	Blackpool, England
23/07/1963	Billy Howes Vs Masambula	Masambula won	Solihull
02/08/1963	Billy Howes Vs Norman Walsh	Howes won	Glasgow, Scotland
05/08/1963	Billy Howes Vs Johnny Allan	NK	Skegness
06/08/1963	Billy Howes Vs Tibor Szakacs	NK	Bridlington, England
07/08/1963	Billy Howes Vs Ernie Riley	Draw (DKO)	Douglas, Isle of Man
09/08/1963	Billy Howes Vs Johnny allan	Howes won	Liverpool
10/08/1963	Billy Howes Vs Dai Sullivan	Sullivan won	Cleethorpes
11/08/1963	Bilyl Howes Vs Hans Streiger	Howes won	Blackpool, England
15/08/1963	Billy Howes Vs Gerry DeJaegar	NK	Clacton
16/08/1963	Billy Howes Vs Majid Ackra	NK	Rochester
17/08/1963	Billy Howes Vs Eric Taylor	NK	Middlesbrough
19/08/1963	Bilyl Howes Vs Hans Streiger	Howes won HSDQ	Hamilton, Scotland
20/08/1963	Billy Howes Vs Les Kellett	Howes won	Aberdeen, Scotland

Date	Match	Result	Location
23/08/1963	Billy Howes Vs Norman Walsh	Walsh won BHDQ	Glasgow, Scotland
24/08/1963	Billy Howes Vs Norman Walsh	NK	Middlesbrough
27/08/1963	Billy Howes Vs Dai Sullivan	Sullivan won	Wolverhampton
30/08/1963	Billy Howes Vs Alf Cadman	Howes won	Liverpool
31/08/1963	Billy Howes Vs Dai Sullivan	NK	Middlesbrough
01/09/1963	Billy Howes Vs Alf Cadman	Howes won	Blackpool, England
02/09/1963	Billy Howes Vs Eric Taylor	Draw	Bradford
03/09/1963	Billy Howes Vs Josef Zaranoff	NK	Finsbury Park
04/09/1963	Billy Howes Vs Tony Cassio	NK	Felixstowe
06/09/1963	Billy Howes Vs Norman Walsh	Walsh won	Glasgow, Scotland
07/09/1963	Billy Howes Vs Bill Robinson	NK	Belle Vue, Manchester
07/09/1963	Billy Howes Vs Bill Robinson	Robinson won	Belle Vue, Manchester
09/09/1963	Billy Howes Vs Eric Leiderman	Howes won	Leeds
11/09/1963	Billy Howes Vs Bill Rawlings	NK	Bridlington, England
14/09/1963	Billy Howes Vs Norman Walsh	Howes inj	Middlesbrough
18/09/1963	Billy Howes Vs Bill Robinson	NK	Sheffield, South Yorkshire
18/09/1963	Billy Howes Vs Bill Robinson	NK	Sheffield, England
19/09/1963	Billy Howes Vs Francis Sullivan	NK	Barrow
23/09/1963	Billy Howes Vs Billy Two Rivers	NK	Birmingham
24/09/1963	Billy Howes Vs Billy Two Rivers	NK	Wellington
27/09/1963	Billy Howes Vs Gerry DeJaegar	Howes won	Bolton
28/09/1963	Billy Howes Vs Masambula	Howes won	Doncaster
30/09/1963	Billy Howes Vs Achmed The Turk	NK	High Wycombe, England
01/10/1963	Billy Howes Vs Hans Streiger	NK	Colchester, England
02/10/1963	Billy Howes Vs Eric Froelich	Howes won	Cardiff, Wales
03/10/1963	Billy Howes Vs Warnia Zarzecki	Howes won	Peterborough, England
04/10/1963	Billy Howes Vs Eric Froelich	Howes won	Rochester
05/10/1963	Billy Howes Vs Johnny Apollo	Billy KO Johnny	Wimbledon
07/10/1963	Billy Howes Vs John Lees	Lees won	Bradford
10/10/1963	Billy Howes Vs The Professor	NK	Blackburn, England
11/10/1963	Billy Howes Vs Norman Walsh	Walsh won	Glasgow, Scotland
12/10/1963	Billy Howes Vs Billy Joyce	Joyce won	Newcastle, England
14/10/1963	Billy Howes Vs Billy Two Rivers	Rivers won	Birmingham
16/10/1963	Billy Howes Vs Barry Douglas	Howes won	Lincoln
17/10/1963	Billy Howes Vs Franz Orlik	Howes won	Bolton, England
18/10/1963	Billy Howes Vs Norman Walsh	Walsh won	Liverpool, England
19/10/1963	Billy Howes Vs Tibor Szakacs	NK	Hanley
21/10/1963	Billy Howes Vs Tony Cassio	NK	York, England
22/10/1963	Billy Howes Vs Tony Cassio	Howes won	Huddersfield
23/10/1963	Billy Howes Vs Bruno Elrington	NK	Preston
26/10/1963	Billy Howes Vs Henri Pierlot	Howes won	Belle Vue, Manchester
30/10/1963	Billy Howes Vs Bill Robinson	NK	Sheffield, South Yorkshire
31/10/1963	Billy Howes Vs Bill Robinson	NK	Barrow
31/10/1963	Billy Howes Vs Bill Robinson	NK	Barrow
01/11/1963	Billy Howes & Bill Robinson Vs Bill & Jim Rawlings	NK	Morecambe, Lancashire

Date	Match	Result	Location
04/11/1963	Billy Howes Vs Masambula	Howes	Blackpool, England
05/11/1963	Billy Howes Vs Billy Two Rivers	NK	Wolverhampton
08/11/1963	Billy Howes Vs Masambula	NK	Liverpool
09/11/1963	Billy Howes Vs Count Bartelli	NK	Shrewsbury
12/11/1963	Billy Howes Vs Johnny Czeslaw	NK	Colchester, England
13/11/1963	Billy Howes Vs Manuel Polman	Howes won	Royal Albert Hall, London
15/11/1963	Billy Howes Vs Johnny Yearsley	NK	Northampton, England
19/11/1963	Billy Howes Vs Jim Hussey	NK	Kidderminster
21/11/1963	Billy Howes Vs Manuel Polman	NK	Nottingham, England
22/11/1963	Billy Howes Vs John Lees	NK	Leicester, England
25/11/1963	Billy Howes Vs Johnny Allan	Draw (DKO)	Loughborough
26/11/1963	Billy Howes Vs Bill Robinson	NK	Trowell
26/11/1963	Billy Howes Vs Bill Robinson	NK	Trowell
28/11/1963	Billy Howes Vs Rocky Wall	NK	Huddersfield
29/11/1963	Billy Howes Vs Inca Wiracogha	Howes won	Glasgow, Scotland
30/11/1963	Billy Howes Vs Bill Robinson	NK	Grantham, England
30/11/1963	Billy Howes Vs Bill Robinson	NK	Grantham,
02/12/1963	Billy Howes Vs Steve Veidor	NK	Leeds
04/12/1963	Billy Howes Vs Bill Robinson	NK	Sheffield, South Yorkshire
04/12/1963	Billy Howes Vs Bill Robinson	NK	Sheffield, England
06/12/1963	Billy Howes Vs Steve Veidor	Howes won	
07/12/1963	Billy Howes Vs Inca Wirracocha	NK	Barrow
10/12/1963	Billy Howes Vs Jim Hussey	NK	Kidderminster
11/12/1963	Billy Howes Vs Norman Walsh	NK	Preston
14/12/1963	Billy Howes Vs Hans Streiger	NK	Hanley
16/12/1963	Billy Howes Vs Count Bartelli	Bartelli won	
17/12/1963	Billy Howes Vs Billy Two Rivers	NK	Wellington
18/12/1963	Billy Howes Vs Billy Two Rivers	NK	Welshpool
20/12/1963	Billy Howes Vs Great Togo	NK	Liverpool
26/12/1963	Billy Howes Vs Zebra Kid	NK	Nottingham, England
28/12/1963	Billy Howes Vs Andy Robbins	Howes won	Middlesbrough
30/12/1963	Billy Howes V Josef Zaranoff	Zaranoff won	Blackpool, England
04/01/1964	Billy Howes Vs Josef Zaranoff	draw 1 each	Wolverhampton, West Midlands
23/01/1964	Billy Howes Vs Bill Robinson	NK	Barrow
13/02/1964	Billy Howes Vs Bill Robinson	NK	Crewe
26/03/1964	Billy Howes Vs Bill Robinson	NK	Liverpool
28/03/1964	Billy Howes Vs Josef Zaranoff	draw 1 each	Wallasey, merseyside
11/04/1964	Billy Howes (DQ) Vs Norman Walsh	NK	York
09/05/1964	Billy Howes Vs Norman Walsh	NK	Trowell, Nottinghamshire
23/06/1964	Billy Howes Vs Johnny Allan (NC)	NK	Scarborough
25/07/1964	Billy Howes Vs Joe Cornelius	NK	Barking Assembly Hall
12/09/1964	Billy Howes Vs Charlie Fisher	NK	Walthamstow, London
09/01/1965	Billy Howes Vs Roy Davis	NK	Bolton, Lancashire
09/01/1965	Billy Howes Vs Roy Bull Davis	Howes won RBDDQ	Bolton
12/01/1965	Billy Howes Vs Count Bartelli	NL	Solihull
14/01/1965	Billy Howes Vs John Lees	Lees won	Blackburn, England

Date	Match	Result	Location
15/01/1965	Billy Howes Vs Eric Taylor	Howes won	Bolton
21/01/1965	Billy Howes Vs Roy St Clair	NK	Airdrie
22/01/1965	Billy Howes Vs Masambula	NK	Glasgow, Scotland
23/01/1965	Billy Howes Vs Bill Robinson	Robinson won	Wellington
26/01/1965	Billy Howes Vs Ramon Napolitano	Howes won	Warrington
28/01/1965	Billy Howes Vs Bill Rawlings	NK	Normanton
29/01/1965	Billy Howes Vs Johnny Allan	Allan won BHDQ	Preston
30/01/1965	Billy Howes Vs Gerry DeJaegar	DeJaegar won	Hanley
01/02/1965	Billy Howes Vs Jim Hussey	NK	Blackpool, England
02/02/1965	Billy Howes Vs Bob Taylor	Howes won	Wellington
03/02/1965	Billy Howes Vs Bob Taylor	Howes won	Pontypool, Wales
05/02/1965	Billy Howes Vs Jim Hussey	Howes won JHDQ	Liverpool
15/02/1965	Billy Howes Vs Zebra Kid	NK	Loughborough
16/02/1965	Billy Howes Vs Masambula	Masambula won	Huddersfield
18/02/1965	Billy Howes Vs John Lees	NK	Nottingham, England
19/02/1965	Billy Howes Vs Masambula	NK	Chesterfield, England
22/02/1965	Billy Howes Vs Gerry Hogan	NK	Leeds
24/02/1965	Billy Howes Vs Harry Fields	NK	Scunthorpe
26/02/1965	Billy Howes Vs Harry Fields	Draw	Rotherham
01/03/1965	Billy Howes Vs Bill Robinson	Robinson won	Birmingham, England
01/03/1965	Billy Howes Vs Bill Robinson	Robinson won	Birmingham
03/03/1965	Billy Howes & Jim Hussey Vs Eric Taylor & Harry Fields	NK	Middlesbrough
04/03/1965	Billy Howes Vs Timmy Geogeghan	Geogeghan won	Crewe
05/03/1965	Billy Howes Vs Enrique Marquess	Howes won	Willenhall
06/03/1965	Billy Howes Vs Enrique Marquess	Howes won	Hanley
08/03/1965	Billy Howes Vs Doug Joyce	NK	Blackpool, England
09/03/1965	Billy Howes Vs Bill Robinson	Robinson won	Wellington
11/03/1965	Billy Howes Vs Bill Robinson	NK	Whitchurch
11/03/1965	Billy Howes Vs Bill Robinson	NK	Whitchurch
15/03/1965	Billy Howes Vs Dennis Mitchell	NK	Derby
20/03/1965	Billy Howes Vs Jim Hussey	NK	Wolverhampton, West Midlands
20/03/1965	Billy Howes Vs Jim Hussey	Hussey won	Wolverhampton, West Midlands
22/03/1965	Billy Howes Vs Dennis Mitchell	NK	Blackpool, England
23/03/1965	Billy Howes Vs Timmy Geogeghan	Timmy won	Wolverhampton, West Midlands
24/03/1965	Billy Howes Vs Jim Hussey	NK	Scarborough, England
05/04/1965	Billy Howes Vs Tibor Szakacs	Szakacs won BH DQ	Bradford
06/04/1965	Billy Howes Vs Tibor Szakacs	Howes won	Lime Grove, London
07/04/1965	Billy Howes Vs Norman Walsh	Howes won	Middlesbrough
07/04/1965	Billy Howes Vs Ricky Starr (F)	Starr won	Middlesbrough
12/04/1965	Billy Howes Vs Chris Spyros	Howes won	Birmingham
20/04/1965	Billy Howes Vs jim Hussey	NK	Solihull
21/04/1965	Billy Howes Vs hassan Ali Bey	NK	Coedpoeth
26/04/1965	Billy Howes Vs Norman Walsh	NK	Blackpool, England
27/04/1965	Billy Howes Vs Billy Two Rivers	Howes won	Wolverhampton, West Midlands
29/04/1965	Billy Howes Vs Billy Two Rivers	NK	Chester

Date	Match	Result	Location
30/04/1965	Billy Howes Vs Jim Hussey	Howes won	Liverpool
01/05/1965	Billy Howes Vs Hans Streiger	Howes won HSDQ	Belle Vue, Manchester
03/05/1965	Billy Howes Vs Steve Veidor	Howes won	Worksop
03/05/1965	Billy Howes Vs Rocky Wall (F)	Wall won	Worksop
04/05/1965	Billy Howes Vs Bill Robinson	NK	Solihull
04/05/1965	Billy Howes Vs Billy Robinson	NK	Solihull
05/05/1965	Billy Howes Vs Tibor Szakacs	NK	Uttoxeter
07/05/1965	Billy Howes Vs Ernie Riley	Howes won	Bolton
08/05/1965	Billy Howes Vs Masambula	NK	Doncaster
11/05/1965	Billy Howes Vs Bill Robinson	Robinson won	Huddersfield, England
11/05/1965	Billy Howes Vs Bill Robinson	Robinson won	Huddersfield
13/05/1965	Billy Howes Vs Eric Liederman	NK	Nottingham, England
17/05/1965	Billy Howes Vs Seamus Dunleavy	Howes won	Birmingham
18/05/1965	Billy Howes Vs Bill Robinson	Robinson won	Rochdale
18/05/1965	Bill Robinson Vs Billy Howes	Robinson won	Rochdale
21/05/1965	Billy Howes Vs Count Bartelli	Bartelli won	Bolton
22/05/1965	Billy Howes Vs Bill Robinson	Robinson won	Hanley
22/05/1965	Billy Howes Vs Bill Robinson	Robinson won	Hanley
25/05/1965	Billy Howes Vs Doug Joyce	Howes won	Wolverhampton, West Midlands
25/05/1965	Billy Howes Vs Les Kellett	Howes won	Wolverhampton, West Midlands
25/05/1965	Billy Howes Vs Ernie Riley (F)	Howes won	Wolverhampton, West Midlands
28/05/1965	Billy Howes Vs Jean Morandi	Howes won	Bolton
28/05/1965	Billy Howes Vs Masambula	Howes won	Bolton
28/05/1965	Billy Howes Vs Ernie Riley (F)	Riley won	Bolton
29/05/1965	Billy Howes Vs Johnny Czeslaw	Howes won	Hanley
29/05/1965	Billy Howes Vs Les Kellett	Howes won	Hanley
29/05/1965	Billy Howes Vs Ernie Riley (F)	Howes won	Hanley
31/05/1965	Billy Howes Vs Hans Streiger	NK	York
01/06/1965	Billy Howes Vs Peter Maivia	NK	Cleethorpes
09/06/1965	Billy Howes Vs Johnny Czeslaw	NK	Uttoxeter
11/06/1965	Billy Howes Vs Roy Bull Davis	Davis won	Liverpool
12/06/1965	Billy Howes Vs Jim Hussey	Howes won	Doncaster
15/06/1965	Billy Howes Vs Johnny Allan	NK	Scarborough, England
18/06/1965	Billy Howes Vs Steve Veidor	NK	Solihull, West Midlands
05/07/1965	Billy Howes Vs Bill Robinson	Robinson won	Bolton
07/07/1965	Billy Howes Vs Billy Robinson	NK	Bolton, Lancashire
12/07/1965	Billy Howes Vs Les Kellett	NK	York
13/07/1965	Billy Howes Vs Les Kellett	NK	Cleethorpes
17/07/1965	Billy Howes Vs Ernie Riley	Howes won	Newcastle, England
19/07/1965	Billy Howes Vs Syed Saif Shah	Syed won	Birmingham
20/07/1965	Billy Howes Vs Bill Robinson	NK	Skegness
20/07/1965	Billy Howes Vs Bill Robinson	NK	Skegness
23/07/1965	Billy Howes Vs Ezzard Hart	Howes won	Liverpool
24/07/1965	Billy Howes & Jim Hussey Vs Kendo Nagasaki & Count Bartelli	Nagasaki et al won	Doncaster
31/07/1965	Billy Howes & Francis Sullivan Vs Doug Joyce & Pietro Capello	Howes et al won	Belle Vue, Manchester

Date	Match	Result	Location
11/08/1965	Billy Howes Vs Vic Stewart	NK	Wolverhampton, West Midlands
12/08/1965	Billy Howes Vs Eric Taylor	NK	Denbigh
20/08/1965	Billy Howes Vs Bill Robinson	Robinson won	Bolton, Lancashire
20/08/1965	Billy Howes Vs Bill Robinson	Robinson won	Bolton
23/08/1965	Billy Howes Vs Les Kellett	NK	York
24/08/1965	Billy Howes Vs Les Kellett	NK	Cleethorpes
28/08/1965	Billy Howes Vs Alf Cadman	NK	Prestatyn
30/08/1965	Billy Howes & Frank O'Donnell Vs Masambule & Ezzard Hart	Howes & O'Donnell won	Belle Vue, Manchester
01/09/1965	Billy Howes Vs Alf Cadman	NK	Bolton, Lancashire
02/09/1965	Billy Howes Vs Seamus Dunleavy	NK	Ross on Wye
03/09/1965	Billy Howes Vs Syed Saif Shah	Howes won	Bolton
07/09/1965	Billy Howes Vs Peter Maivia	NK	Wellington
10/09/1965	Billy Howes Vs Masambula	Howes won	Liverpool
11/09/1965	Billy Howes Vs Masambula	Howes won	Doncaster
12/09/1965	Billy Howes Vs Timmy Geogeghan	Howes won	Blackpool, England
13/09/1965	Billy Howes Vs Norman Walsh	NK	Bradford
17/09/1965	Billy Howes Vs Norman Walsh	NK	Leicester
18/09/1965	Billy Howes Vs Norman Walsh	Howes won	Newcastle, England
21/09/1965	Billy Howes Vs Roy Bull Davis	Davis won	Solihull
23/09/1965	Billy Howes Vs Count Bartelli	Both disq	Crewe
25/09/1965	Billy Howes Vs Pietro Capello	Howes won	Belle Vue, Manchester
29/09/1965	Billy Howes Vs Yure Borienko	NK	Uttoxeter
01/10/1965	Billy Howes Vs Steve Veidor	Howes won	Liverpool
02/10/1965	Billy Howes Vs Johnny Allan	Howes won	Hanley
02/10/1965	Billy Howes Vs Honeyboy Zimba	Howes won	Hanley
02/10/1965	Billy Howes Vs Alf Cadman (F)	Howes won	Hanley
03/10/1965	Billy Howes Vs Geoff Portz	Portz won	Blackpool, England
07/10/1965	Billy Howes Vs Billy Joyce	NK	Nelson
09/10/1965	Billy Howes Vs Vic Stewart	Howes won	Doncaster
11/10/1965	Billy Howes Vs Norman Walsh	NK	Spenymoor
13/10/1965	Billy Howes Vs Norman Walsh	NK	Boston
14/10/1965	Billy Howes Vs Eric Taylor	NK	Malvern
15/10/1965	Billy Howes Vs Johnny Allan	NK	Liverpool
19/10/1965	Billy Howes Vs Henri Pierlot	NK	Solihull
25/10/1965	Billy Howes Vs Norman Walsh	NK	Bradford
26/10/1965	Billy Howes Vs Joe Cornelius	NK	Kidderminster
27/10/1965	Billy Howes Vs Gwyn Davies	Billy Howes	Middlesbrough
01/11/1965	Billy Howes Vs Norman Walsh	NK	Blackpool, England
03/11/1965	Billy Howes Vs Kendo Nagasaki	NK	Ross on Wye
04/11/1965	Billy Howes Vs Count Bartelli	Howes won	Crewe
05/11/1965	Billy Howes Vs Norman Walsh	Walsh won	Liverpool
08/11/1965	Billy Howes Vs Rocky Wall	NK	Selby
10/11/1965	Billy Howes Vs John Lees	NK	Scarborough, England
11/11/1965	Billy Howes Vs Masambula	NK	Nottingham, England
13/11/1965	Billy Howes Vs Les Kellett	NK	Hull

Date	Match	Result	Location
17/11/1965	Billy Howes Vs Les Kellett	NK	Kingston Upon Hull, East Riding of Yorkshire
17/11/1965	Billy Howes Vs Chris Spyros	NK	Lincoln
23/11/1965	Billy Howes Vs Reg Williams	Howes won	Wolverhampton, West Midlands
24/11/1965	Billy Howes Vs Gerry DeJaegar	NK	Buckley
26/11/1965	Billy Howes Vs Jim Hussey	Draw	Liverpool
02/12/1965	Billy Howes Vs johnny Allan	NK	Morecambe, Lancashire
07/12/1965	Billy Howes Vs Syed Saif Shah	Syed won	Wolverhampton, West Midlands
08/12/1965	Billy Howes Vs Billy Joyce	NC	Hindley
11/12/1965	Billy Howes Vs Syed Saif Shah	Syed won	Doncaster
13/12/1965	Billy Howes Vs Paul Luty	NK	Blackpool, England
03/01/1966	Billy Howes & Barry Cannon Vs Earl Maynard & Majid Ackra	NK	Derby, Derbyshire
04/01/1966	Billy Howes Vs Syed Saif Shah	Howes DQ	Huddersfield
06/01/1966	Billy Howes Leon Arras	NK	Nottingham
11/01/1966	Billy Howes Vs Peter Maivia	NK	Solihull, West Midlands
12/01/1966	Billy Howes Vs Quasimodo	NK	Spalding
14/01/1966	Billy Howes Vs Quasimodo	Howes won Quas DQ	Liverpool, Merseyside
21/01/1966	Billy Howes Vs Bill Robinson	NK	Willenhall
21/01/1966	Billy Howes Vs Bill Robinson	NK	Willenhall
22/01/1966	Billy Howes Vs Quasimodo	NK	Shrewsbury
24/01/1966	Billy Howes Vs Geoff Portz	NK	Bradford
25/01/1966	Billy Howes Vs Bert Nuttall	NK	Kidderminster
28/01/1966	Billy Howes Vs Ricky Starr	NK	Worksop
31/01/1966	Billy Howes Vs Quasimodo	NK	Blackpool, England
01/02/1966	Billy Howes Vs Kendo Nagasaki	NK	Wellington
04/02/1966	Billy Howes Vs Quasimodo	Howes won	Liverpool
07/02/1966	Billy Howes Vs Kendo Nagasaki	Kendo won	Birmingham
11/02/1966	Billy Howes Vs Quasimodo	NK	Willenhall
12/02/1966	Billy Howes Vs Peter Maivia	NK	Horncastle
14/02/1966	Billy Howes Vs Geoff Portz	Draw	Bradford
15/02/1966	Billy Howes Vs Masambula	Masambula won	Huddersfield
22/02/1966	Billy Howes Vs Jim Hussey	NK	Wellington
23/02/1966	Billy Howes Vs Bill Robinson	Howes won	Sheffield, South Yorkshire
23/02/1966	Billy Howes Vs Bill Robinson	Howes won BRDQ	Sheffield, South Yorkshire
24/02/1966	Billy Howes Vs billy Joyce	NK	Nelson
26/02/1966	Billy Howes Vs Josef Zaranoff	Zaranoff won	Belle Vue, Manchester
28/02/1966	Billy Howes Vs Kendo Nagasaki	Nagasaki won BHDQ	Birmingham
01/03/1966	Billy Howes Vs El Greco	Wolverhampton	Wolverhampton, West Midlands
02/03/1966	Billy Howes Vs Les Kellett	Howes won	Hindley
05/03/1966	Billy Howes Vs Masambula	NK	Shrewsbury
07/03/1966	Billy Howes Vs Rocky Wall	NC	Bradford
12/03/1966	Billy Howes Vs Rocky Wall	Wall won	Newcastle, England
16/03/1966	Billy Howes Vs Tibor Szakacs	NK	Welshpool
25/03/1966	Billy Howes Vs Ricky Starr	Starr won	Liverpool
26/03/1966	Billy Howes Vs Count Bartelli	Bartelli won	Worsley
30/03/1966	Billy Howes Vs Syed Saif Shah	Shah won BHDQ	Lincoln, Lincolnshire

Date	Match	Result	Venue
01/04/1966	Billy Howes Vs Dennis Mitchell	NK	Chesterfield
04/04/1966	Billy Howes Vs Bobby Graham	NK	Leeds
09/04/1966	Billy Howes Vs Don Mendoza	Howes won	Belle Vue, Manchester
14/04/1966	Billy Howes Vs Count Bartelli	Bartelli won	Southport, Merseyside
18/04/1966	Billy Howes Vs Josef Zaranoff	NK	York
23/04/1966	Billy Howes Vs Geoff Portz	Howes won	Newcastle, England
25/04/1966	Billy Howes Vs Hans Streiger	NK	Blackpool, England
29/04/1966	Billy Howes Vs Hans Streiger	Streiger won	Liverpool
02/05/1966	Billy Howes Vs Les kellett	NK	Leeds
04/05/1966	Billy Howes Vs Paul Kozak	Howes won	Sheffield, South Yorkshire
07/05/1966	Billy Howes Vs Les Kellett	Kellett won BHDQ	Belle Vue, Manchester
10/05/1966	Billy Howes Vs The Outlaw	NK	Wellington
16/05/1966	Billy Howes Vs Dennis Mitchell	NK	Bradford
19/05/1966	Billy Howes Vs Honeyboy Zimba	NK	Brierly Hill
21/05/1966	Billy Howes Vs Count Bartelli	NK	Prestatyn Holiday Camp Ballroom, Denbighshire
21/05/1966	Billy Howes Vs Count Bartelli	Bartelli won BHDQ	Prestatyn
22/05/1966	Billy Howes Vs Les kellett	Kellett won BHDQ	Leeds
26/05/1966	Billy Howes Vs Bobby Graham	NK	Morecambe, Lancashire
31/05/1966	Billy Howes Vs Count Bartelli	Bartelli won	Worsley
03/06/1966	Billy Howes Vs Roy Bull Davis	Howes won RBDDQ	Bolton, Lancashire
04/06/1966	Billy Howes & Rocky Wall Vs Hans Streiger & Jim Hussey	Howes et al won	Hanley
06/06/1966	Billy Howes Vs Count Bartelli	NK	Warrington Fete
10/06/1966	Billy Howes Vs Wildman of Borneo	Howes won WOBDQ	Liverpool
11/06/1966	Billy Howes Vs The Outlaw	NK	The Winter Gardens, Morecambe, Lancashire
11/06/1966	Billy Howes Vs The Outlaw	NC	Morecambe, Lancashire
18/06/1966	Billy Howes Vs Jim Moser	Howes won	Newcastle, England
26/06/1966	Billy Howes Vs Roy Bull Davis	Davis won BH Inj	Blackpool, England
02/07/1966	Billy Howes & Johnny Allan Vs Ezzard Hart & Honeyboy Zimba	Ezzard et al won	Newcastle, England
09/07/1966	Billy Howes Vs Geoff Portz	NK	The Winter Gardens, Morecambe, Lancashire
09/07/1966	Billy Howes Vs The Outlaw	Outlaw won	Belle Vue, Manchester
16/07/1966	Billy Howes Vs Jim Hussey	NK	Liverpool Stadium, Merseyside
16/07/1966	Billy Howes Vs Bill Robinson	Robinson won	Hanley
16/07/1966	Billy Howes Vs Jim Hussey	Howes won JHDQ	Liverpool
17/07/1966	Billy Howes Vs Kendo Nagasaki	Kendo won	Blackpool, England
19/07/1966	Billy Howes Vs Kendo Nagasaki	NK	Bridlington
21/07/1966	Billy Howes Vs Geoff Portz	Draw	Middlesborough, North Yorkshire
22/07/1966	Billy Howes Vs The Outlaw	Outlaw won BH Inj	Bolton, Lancashire
09/08/1966	Billy Howes Vs The Outlaw	NK	Skegness
14/08/1966	Billy Howes Vs The Outlaw	Outlaw won	Blackpool, England
19/08/1966	Billy Howes Vs Roy Bull Davis	Howes won RBD DQ	Bolton, Lancashire
27/08/1966	Billy Howes Vs Steve Veidor	NK	Halifax
31/08/1966	Billy Howes Vs Steve Bell	NK	New Victoria Hall, Halifax
31/08/1966	Billy Howes Vs Wildman of Borneo	Howes won WOBDQ	Southport, Merseyside
02/09/1966	Billy Howes Vs Tibor Szakacs	Szakacs won	Bolton, Lancashire

Date	Match	Result	Location
02/09/1966	Billy Howes Vs Rocky Wall	Wall won BHDQ	Bolton, Lancashire
04/09/1966	Billy Howes Vs Hans Streiger	Howes won HSDQ	Blackpool, England
14/09/1966	Billy Howes Vs Dennis Mitchell	NK	Coalville
19/09/1966	Billy Howes Vs Roy St Clair	Howes won	Leeds
23/09/1966	Billy Howes Vs hans Streiger	Streiger won	Liverpool
25/09/1966	Billy Howes Vs Kendo Nagasaki	NK	Blackpool, England
26/09/1966	Billy Howes Vs Jim Hussey	NK	Bradford
11/10/1966	Billy Howes Vs Wayne Bridges	NK	Wolverhampton, West Midlands
15/10/1966	Billy Howes Vs Bill Rawlings	Howes won	Hanley
09/12/1966	Billy Howes Vs Hans Streiger	Howes won	Bolton, Lancashire
10/12/1966	Billy Howes Vs Bill Robinson	Robinson won	Hanley
12/12/1966	Billy Howes Vs Pat Roach	NK	Blackpool, England
21/01/1967	Billy Howes Vs Wayne Bridges	NK	Lime Grove Baths, Shepherd's Bush, London
13/05/1967	Billy Howes Vs Les Kellett	NK	Liverpool Stadium, Merseyside
03/06/1967	Billy Howes Vs Tony Charles	NK	Prestatyn Holiday Camp Ballroom, Denbighshire
13/06/1967	Billy Howes Vs Bill Robinson	NK	Skegness
01/09/1967	Billy Howes Vs Bill Robinson	Robinson won	Bolton, Lancashire
01/01/1968	Billy Howes Vs Youri Borienko	Howes won	Birmingham
08/01/1968	Billy Howes Vs Geoff Portz	Portz won	Blackpool, England
26/01/1968	Billy Howes Vs Gwyn Davies	Davies won	Liverpool
27/01/1968	Billy Howes Vs Jim Hussey	Howes won	Hanley
09/02/1968	Billy Howes Vs Jack Rowlands	Howes won	Liverpool
26/02/1968	Billy Howes Vs Jim Hussey	Howes won	Blackpool, England
22/04/1968	Billy Howes Vs Rocky Wall	Wall won	Blackpool, England
17/05/1968	Billy Howes Vs Josef Zaranoff	Howes won	Liverpool
22/05/1968	Billy Howes Vs Les kellett	Draw	Hindley
21/06/1968	Billy Howes Vs John Lees	Lees won	Liverpool
02/08/1968	Billy Howes Vs John lees	Draw DKO	Liverpool
11/08/1968	Billy Howes Vs Jack Rowlands	Howes won	Blackpool, England
16/08/1968	Billy Howes & Steve Haggetty Vs Jim Hussey & Hans Streiger	Hussey et al won	Liverpool
27/08/1968	Billy Howes Vs Red Scorpion	Scorpion won	Aberdeen, Scotland
27/08/1968	Billy Howes Vs John Cox	Howes won	Liverpool
28/08/1968	Billy Howes Vs Mike Marino	Marino won BHDQ	Hanley
29/08/1968	Billy Howes Vs John Cox	Cox won BHDQ	Blackpool, England
30/10/1968	Billy Howes Vs John Cox	NK	Bolton, Lancashire
30/10/1968	Billy Howes Vs John Cox	NC	Bolton, Lancashire
07/11/1968	Billy Howes Vs Steve Logan	Howes won	Warrington
08/11/1968	Billy Howes Vs Wildman of Borneo	Howes won	Liverpool
15/11/1968	Billy Howes Vs Jim Hussey	Howes won JHDQ	Bolton, Lancashire
16/11/1968	Billy Howes Vs Roy Bull Davis	Howes won RDDQ	Hanley
19/11/1968	Billy Howes Vs Leon Arras	Howes won	Wolverhampton, West Midlands
25/11/1968	Billy Howes & Judd Harris Vs Seamus Donlevy & Mike Donlevy	NK	Derby, Derbyshire
06/12/1968	Billy Howes Vs Roy Bull Davis	Howes won	Bolton, Lancashire
07/12/1968	Billy Howes Vs John Cox	Howes won	Hanley

Date	Match	Result	Location
09/12/1968	Billy Howes Vs Shozo Kobayashi	Howes won	Altrincham
10/12/1968	Billy Howes Vs Bobo Matu	Howes won	Solihull, West Midlands
16/12/1968	Billy Howes Vs Rocky Wall	NC	Bradford
17/12/1968	Billy Howes Vs Les Kellett	Howes won	Wolverhampton, West Midlands
18/12/1968	Billy Howes Vs Rocky Wall	NK	Bradford, West Yorkshire
01/01/1969	Billy Howes Vs jim Hussey	Hussey won	Bolton, Lancashire
06/01/1969	Billy Howes Vs henri Pierlot	Howes won	Blackpool, England
08/01/1969	Billy Howes Vs Jim Hussey	NK	Southport, Merseyside
11/01/1969	Billy Howes Vs Jim Hussey	Hussey won	Southport, Merseyside
13/01/1969	Billy Howes Vs Kendo Nagasaki	NK	Derby, Derbyshire
21/01/1969	Billy Howes Vs Jim Hussey	Hussey won	Solihull, West Midlands
22/01/1969	Billy Howes Vs Rocky Wall	Howes won	Blackburn
25/01/1969	Billy Howes Vs Albert Wall	NK	Blackburn, Lancashire
25/01/1969	Billy Howes Vs Jim Hussey	Howes won	Hanley
04/02/1969	Billy Howes Vs Jim Hussey	NK	Oakengates
06/02/1969	Billy Howes Vs Honeyboy Zimba	Howes won	Nelson
17/03/1969	Billy Howes Vs Quasimodo	Howes won	Blackpool, England
21/03/1969	Billy Howes Vs Quasimodo	Howes won	Liverpool
08/04/1969	Billy Howes Vs Hans Streiger	Howes won HSDQ	Wolverhampton, West Midlands
09/04/1969	Billy Howes Vs Steve Logan	Howes won SLDQ	Winsford
12/04/1969	Billy Howes Vs Steve Logan	NK	Winsford, Cheshire
14/04/1969	Billy Howes & Johnny Eagles Vs The Black Diamonds	Howes et al won	Altrincham
23/04/1969	Billy Howes Vs henri Pierlot	NK	Southport, Merseyside
26/04/1969	Billy Howes Vs Al Martin	Howes won	Hanley
01/05/1969	Billy Howes Vs Mike Marino	Howes won	Blackburn
16/05/1969	Billy Howes Vs Reg Williams	Williams won	Middlesborough, England
24/05/1969	Billy Howes Vs Jim Hussey	Howes won	Hanley
06/06/1969	Billy Howes Vs Pete Roberts	Howes won	Liverpool
10/06/1969	Billy Howes Vs Abe Ginsberg	NK	Solihull, West Midlands
17/06/1969	Billy Howes Vs Mike Marino	Howes won	Wolverhampton, West Midlands
20/06/1969	Billy Howes Vs Paul Duval	NC	Bolton, Lancashire
27/06/1969	Billy Howes Vs Jim Hussey	Howes won	Liverpool
02/07/1969	Billy Howes Vs Hans Streiger	Howes won	Southport, Merseyside
13/07/1969	Billy Howes Vs John Lees	Draw	Blackpool, England
03/08/1969	Billy Howes Vs Al Martin	Howes won	Blackpool, England
16/08/1969	Billy Howes Vs Pete Curry	Howes won	Hanley
05/09/1969	Billy Howes Vs Colin Joynson	Howes won	Liverpool
19/09/1969	Billy Howes Vs Pete Roberts	Howes won	Liverpool
07/10/1969	Billy Howes Vs Pete Roberts	NC	Wolverhampton, West Midlands
26/10/1969	Billy Howes Vs Pete Roberts	Howes won	Blackpool, England
01/11/1969	Billy Howes Vs Steve Veidor	Howes won	Hanley
05/11/1969	Bily Howes Vs Luis Salazaar	NK	Bolton, Lancashire
10/11/1969	Billy Howes Vs Pete Roberts	Draw	Derby, Derbyshire
20/11/1969	Billy Howes & Keith Williams Vs White Eagles	NK	Caernarvon, Wales
19/09/1970	Billy Howes Vs Ray Steele	NK	Leicester, Leicestershire

Date	Match	Result	Location
28/11/1970	Billy Howes Vs Jim Moser	NK	Derby, Derbyshire
13/02/1971	Billy Howes Vs Pete Stewart	NK	Liverpool, Merseyside
24/03/1971	Billy Howes Vs Mike Marino	NK	Preston, Lancashire
02/06/1971	Billy Howes Vs Kendo Nagasaki	NK	Leeds, West Yorkshire
31/07/1971	Billy Howes Vs Kendo Nagasaki	NK	Catterick, North Yorkshire
13/11/1971	Billy Howes Vs Kendo Nagasaki	NK	Bradford, West Yorkshire
04/12/1971	Billy Howes Vs Geoff Portz	NK	Leicester, Leicestershire
01/01/1972	Billy Howes Vs Tony Charles	NK	Bradford, West Yorkshire
19/01/1972	Billy Howes Vs Steve Veidor	NK	Doncaster, South Yorkshire
01/04/1972	Billy Howes Vs Tony Charles	NK	Halifax, West Yorkshire
16/01/1973	Billy Howes Vs Lee Sharron	Howes won LSDQ	Huddersfield
17/02/1973	Billy Howes Vs Gwyn Davies	Davies won	Belle Vue, Manchester
06/03/1973	Billy Howes Vs John Lees	Howes won	Wolverhampton, West Midlands
04/04/1973	Billy Howes Vs Steve Veidor	Veidor won BHDQ	Sheffield, South Yorkshire
06/04/1973	Billy Howes Vs Kendo Nagasaki	Nagasaki won	Liverpool
12/04/1973	Billy Howes Vs Syd Askins	Askins won BHDQ	Nelson
13/04/1973	Billy Howes Vs Al Martin	Howes won	Bolton, Lancashire
14/04/1973	Billy Howes Vs Kendo Nagasaki	Nagasaki won	Chesterfield
16/04/1973	Billy Howes Vs Tony St Clair	NK	Bradford
24/04/1973	Billy Howes Vs John Lees	NK	Leicester, Leicestershire
11/05/1973	Billy Howes & tibor Szakacs Vs Thundercloud & Whitecloud	Howes et al won clouds DQ	Liverpool
01/06/1973	Billy Howes Vs Honeyboy Zimba	Howes won	Liverpool
04/06/1973	Billy Howes Vs Masambula	Howes won	Leeds
05/06/1973	Billy Howes Vs Count Bartelli	Howes inj	Solihull, West Midlands
09/06/1973	Billy Howes Vs Gwyn Davies	NK	Hanley
18/06/1973	Billy Howes Vs Count Bartelli	Howes won	Newcastle, England
27/06/1973	Billy Howes Vs Count Bartelli	Bartelli won	Brierly Hill
30/06/1973	Billy Howes Vs Count Bartelli	NK	Brierley Hill, West Midlands
26/07/1973	Billy Howes Vs Tibor Szakacs	Szakacs won	Morecambe, Lancashire
08/09/1973	Billy Howes Vs Gwyn Davies	Davies won	Belle Vue, Manchester
09/09/1973	Billy Howes Vs John lees	Lees won BHDQ	Blackpool, England
30/09/1973	Billy Howes & Karl Schultz Vs Johnny Czeslaw & Ivan Penzekoff	Czeslaw et al won BHKSDQ	Blackpool, England
08/10/1973	Billy Howes & Karl Schultz Vs Johnny South & Paul Mitchell	South et al won BHKSDQ	Nantwich
26/10/1973	Billy Howes & Hans Streiger Vs Honeyboy Zimba & Bobo Matu	Howes et al won	Liverpool
27/10/1973	Billy Howes & Hans Streiger Vs Masambula & Bobo Matu	Masambula et al won BHHSDQ	Belle Vue, Manchester
01/12/1973	Billy Howes Vs Honeyboy Zimba	Howes won	Hanley
05/12/1973	Billy Howes Vs Billy Two Rivers	NK	Winsford
10/12/1973	Billy Howes Vs Goro Tanaka	NK	Bradford
21/09/1974	Billy Howes Vs Terry Swann	Howes won	Birkinhead
21/09/1974	Billy Howes Vs Kendo Nagasaki	Nagasaki won	Birkinhead
27/11/1975	Billy Howes Vs Alan Wood	Draw	Preston
14/01/1976	Billy Howes Vs Alan Wood	NK	Guildhall Preston, Lancashire
28/01/1976	Billy Howes Vs Lee Thomas	Draw DKO	Bradford
31/01/1976	Billy Howes Vs Lee Thomas	NK	Bradford, West Yorkshire

Date	Match	Result	Location
31/01/1976	Billy Howes Vs Count Bartelli	Bartelli won	Hanley
03/02/1976	Billy Howes Vs Bob Matu	NK	Oakengates
06/02/1976	Billy Howes Vs Honeyboy Zimba	Howes won	Bolton, Lancashire
09/02/1976	Billy Howes Vs Count Bartelli	NK	Shrewsbury
11/02/1976	Billy Howes Vs Ali Shan	NK	Lincoln
13/02/1976	Billy Howes Vs Count Bartelli	Bartelli won	Liverpool
14/02/1976	Billy Howes Vs Count Bartelli	Howes won	Hanley
26/02/1976	Billy Howes Vs Ray Steele	NK	Nelson
02/03/1976	Billy Howes Vs Lee Thomas	Thomas won	Dundee, Scotland
03/03/1976	Billy Howes Vs Harry Palin	Palin won BHDQ	Hindley
13/03/1976	Billy Howes Vs Roy St/ Clair	NK	Walkden, Greater Manchester
15/03/1976	Billy Howes Vs Roy St Clair	NK	Newcastle, England
16/03/1976	Billy Howes & Kevin Conneally Vs Skinheads	Howes et al won	Wolverhampton, West Midlands
22/03/1976	Alan Wood & Kevin Conneally Vs John Naylor & Mo Hunter	Naylor et al won	Derby, Derbyshire
29/03/1976	Billy Howes Vs Count Bartelli	Bartelli won	Buxton
02/04/1976	Billy Howes Vs Jonny Czeslaw	Czeslaw won BHDQ	Liverpool

Jimmy Hart

Date	Match	Outcome	Venue
29/08/1955	Jim Hart Vs Saxon Smith	Jim won	Plymouth, England
13/04/1958	Jimmy Hart Vs Ron Johnson	Jim won	Birmingham, England
27/04/1958	Jim Hart Vs Dean Stockton	Jim won	Birmingham, England
06/05/1958	Jim Hart Vs Jim Holden	Jim Hart won	Birmingham, England
08/06/1958	Jim Hart Vs Jim Holden	Draw	Birmingham, England
17/08/1958	Jim Hart Vs Cyril Morris	Draw	Birmingham, England
02/09/1958	Jim Hart Vs Jim Holden	Hart won	Birmingham, England
16/09/1958	Jim Hart Vs Bill Hargreaves	Jim won	Birmingham, England
28/09/1958	Jim Hart Vs Dean Stockton	Dean won	Birmingham, England
02/10/1958	Jim Hart Vs Jack Dempsey	NK	Blackburn, England
04/10/1958	Jim Hart Vs Dean Stockton	Dean won	Shrewsbury, England
10/10/1958	Jim Hart Vs Archer O'Brien	Archer won	Glasgow, Scotland
14/10/1958	Jim Hart Vs Gerry Hogan	Gerry won	Birmingham, England
24/10/1958	Jim Hart Vs Ernie Saxon Smith	Jim won	Dudley, England
08/11/1958	Jim Hart & Reg Ray Vs Brian Burke & Danny Flynn	Hart & Ray won	Shrewsbury, England
02/12/1958	Jim Hart Vs Chick Booth	Chick won	Birmingham, England
05/12/1958	Jim Hart Vs Billy Joyce	Billy won	Glasgow, Scotland
06/12/1958	Jim Hart Vs John Foley	John won	Middlesborough, North Yorkshire
03/01/1959	Jim Hart Vs Tommy Mann	Tommy won	Newcastle, England
17/01/1959	Jim Hart Vs Cliff Belshaw	Cliff won	Newcastle, England
19/02/1959	Jim Hart Vs Francis Sullivan	NK	Stretford, England
12/03/1959	Jim Hart Vs Jean Morandi	Jim won	Bristol, England
28/03/1959	Jim Hart Vs Francis Sullivan	NK	Dudley, England
02/04/1959	Jim Hart Vs Francis Sullivan	NK	Hulme
26/04/1959	Jim Hart Vs Cyril Knowles	Jim won	Birmingham, England
13/06/1959	Jim Hart Vs Francis Sullivan	NK	NK
19/09/1959	Jim Hart Vs Bobby Graham	NK	Wulfrun Hall, Wolverhampton
24/09/1959	Jim Hart Vs Francis Sullivan	Nk	Hulme
17/10/1959	Jim Hart Vs Jack Dempsey	Dempsey won	hanley
07/02/1960	Jim Hart Vs Bobby Graham	NC	Hamilton, Scotland
27/05/1960	Jim Hart Vs Billy Howes	NK	Liverpool, England
02/06/1960	Jim Hart Vs Gene Riscoe	NK	Manchester, England
04/08/1960	Jim Hart Vs Brian Burke	NK	Southport
07/12/1960	Jim Hart Vs Harry Fields	Harry won	Cardiff, Wales
10/12/1960	Jim Hart Vs Black Kwango	NK	Purley
18/03/1961	Jim Hart Vs Gerry Hogan	NK	Wallasey, merseyside
02/12/1961	Jim Hart Vs Spencer Churchill (KO)	NK	Lewisham, London
25/12/1961	Jim Hart Vs Joe Critchley	NK	Ellesmere Port
12/05/1962	Jim Hart Vs Roy St Clair	NK	Wembley, London
08/06/1963	Jim Hart Vs Spencer Churchill	NK	Watford
07/12/1963	Jim Hart Vs Andy Robbins	NK	Barrow
28/12/1963	Jim Hart Vs Johnny Kwango	NK	Seymour Hall, Marylebone, London

Date	Match	Result	Location
11/01/1965	Jim Hart & Ken Cadman Vs Vic & Peter Stewart	NK	Altrincham
16/01/1965	Jim Hart Vs Dave Phillips	NK	Kingston Upon Hull, East Riding of Yorkshire
16/04/1965	Jim Hart & Francis Sullivan Vs Stewarts	Stewarts won	Bolton
19/06/1965	Jim Hart Vs Gerry Hogan	NK	Solihull, West Midlands

Melvyn Riss

Date	Match	Outcome	Venue
19/07/1952	Mel Riss Vs John Foley	NK	Costa Green, Birmingham
06/01/1953	Melwyn Riss Vs Andre DuBarry	Andre won	Warrington, England
20/01/1953	Melwyn Riss Vs Joe Egan	Joe won	Warrington, England
18/02/1953	Melwyn Riss Vs Ray Young Foley	NC	Hawick, Scotland
05/03/1953	Melwyn Riss Vs Ray Foley	Draw	Albert Hall, London
16/04/1953	Melwyn Riss Vs Babe Foley	Babe won	Albert Hall, London
12/12/1953	Melwyn Riss Vs Jack Beaumont	Jack won	Manchester, England
08/02/1954	Melwyn Riss Vs Bob Archer O'Brien	Archer won, MR Injured	Bedford
09/02/1954	Mewlyn Riss Vs Peter Rann	Peter won,	Swindon, England
12/02/1954	Melwyn Riss Vs Jack Cunningham	Cunnigham won	Ipswich
05/03/1954	Melwyn Riss Vs Tony Lawrence	Tony won	Leicester, England
22/03/1954	Melwyn Riss Vs Andy Anderson	Andy won	Edinburgh, Scotland
30/11/1954	Melwyn Riss Vs Babe Foley	Draw	Harringay, England
15/12/1954	Melwyn Riss Vs Alan Kimber	NK	Belle Vue, Manchester
18/12/1954	Melwyn Riss Vs John Foley	Foley won	Belle Vue, Manchester
31/03/1956	Mel Riss Vs Chic Linton	NK	Belle Vue, Manchester
09/06/1956	Mel Riss Vs Al Nicol	Riss won	Hanley
16/06/1956	Mel Riss Vs Stefan Milla	Riss won	New Brighton
23/06/1956	Mel Riss Vs Stefan Milla	NK	Cheetham
30/06/1956	Mel Riss Vs Bernard Murray	Bernard won	Newcastle, England
18/08/1956	Melwyn Riss Vs George Kidd	George won	Newcastle, England
15/09/1956	Mel Riss Vs Danny Flynn	Riss won	Hanley
24/09/1956	Melwyn Riss Vs Harry Hall	NK	Altrincham
01/12/1956	Melwyn Riss Vs Danny Flynn	Danny won	Shrewsbury, England
14/12/1956	Mel Riss Vs Fred Woolley	NK	Willenhall
06/01/1957	Melvyn Riss Vs Jim Mellor	Mel won	Shrewsbury, England
19/01/1957	Melvyn Riss Vs John Foley	Draw	Shrewsbury, England
01/02/1957	Mel Riss Vs Brian Trevors	NK	Willenhall
02/02/1957	Mel Riss Vs Jim Mellor	Mellor won	Hanley
09/02/1957	Melvyn Riss Vs John Foley	John won	Shrewsbury, England
01/03/1957	Melvyn Riss Vs Jim Mellor	NK	Liverpool, England
02/03/1957	Mel Riss Vs John Foley	NK	Doncaster, England
13/03/1957	Melvyn Riss Vs Mick McManus	Mick won	Albert Hall, London
29/03/1957	Mel Riss & Martin Conroy Vs Joe Critchley & Jim Lewis	NK	Willenhall
12/04/1957	Melvyn Riss Vs Jim Mellor	Jim won	Willenhall, England
13/04/1957	Melvyn Riss Vs Jim Mellor	Riss won	Doncaster, England
25/04/1957	Mel Riss Vs George Kidd	NK	Blackburn, England
25/05/1957	Melvyn Riss Vs Chick Booth	NC	New Brighton, England
13/06/1957	Mel Riss Vs Jim Mellor	NK	Wolverhampton, England
02/08/1957	Melvyn Riss Vs Jim Mellor	Mel won	Liverpool, England
03/08/1957	Melvyn Riss Vs Al Nicol	Al won	Newcastle, England
24/08/1957	Melvyn Riss Vs Jim Berry	Jim won	Middlesborough, North

Date	Match	Result	Location
			Yorkshire
30/09/1957	Melwyn Riss Vs Jim Lewis	Mel won	Edinburgh, Scotland
07/10/1957	Melwyn Riss Vs Andy Anderson	Mel won	Edinburgh, Scotland
17/12/1957	Melwyn Riss Vs Chic Purvey	NK	Lime Grove, London
08/01/1958	Melwyn Riss Vs Brian Trevors	NK	Nelson
10/01/1958	Melwyn Riss Vs Jim Mellor	NK	Willenhall
11/01/1958	Melwyn Riss Vs Ted Hannon	NK	Shrewsbury, England
22/01/1958	Melwyn Riss Vs John Foley	NK	Scunthorpe, England
31/01/1958	Melwyn Riss Vs Brian Burke	NK	Willenhall
29/03/1958	Melwyn Riss Vs Peter Rann	NK	Belle Vue, Manchester
10/04/1958	Melwyn Riss Vs Fred Woolley	NK	Hulme
12/04/1958	Melwyn Riss Vs Alan Colbeck	Alan won	Newcastle, England
13/04/1958	Mel Riss Vs john Foley	John won	Birmingham, England
21/04/1958	Melwyn Riss Vs John Foley	NK	Kirkby, Ashfield
24/04/1958	Melwyn Riss Vs Jim Mellor	NK	Hulme
10/05/1958	Melwyn Riss Vs Brian Burke	NK	Grantham, England
31/05/1958	Melwyn Riss Vs Johnny Rudd	NK	Rhyl, North Wales
02/06/1958	Melwyn Riss Vs Jim Mellor	Jim won	Edinburgh, Scotland
02/06/1958	Melwyn Riss Vs Les Kellett	Kellett won	Edinburgh, Scotland
05/06/1958	Melwyn Riss Vs Brian Burke	NK	Hulme
07/06/1958	Mewlyn Riss Vs Al Nicol	NK	Belle Vue, Manchester
24/06/1958	Mel Riss Vs Jimmy Rudd	Draw	Birmingham, England
08/07/1958	Mel Riss Vs Al Nicols	Mel won	Birmingham, England
19/07/1958	Melwyn Riss Vs Fred Woolley	Fred won	Newcastle, England
11/08/1958	Mewlyn Riss Vs Al Nicol	Riss won	Bridlington
14/08/1958	Melwyn Riss Vs Fred Woolley	NK	Hulme
21/08/1958	Melvyn Riss Vs Ted Hannon	Mel won	Morecambe, Lancashire
24/08/1958	Melwyn Riss Vs Brian Burke	Mel won	Birmingham, England
17/09/1958	Melwyn Riss Vs Brian Burke	Brian won	Lincoln, Lincolnshire
09/10/1958	Melwyn Riss Vs John Foley	Draw	Nottingham, England
10/10/1958	Mewlyn Riss Vs Ted Hannon	NK	Chesterfield, England
14/10/1958	Melwyn Riss Vs Alan Dennison	NK	Wakefield, England
20/10/1958	Melwyn Riss Vs Bob Archer O'Brien	NK	Welling
28/10/1958	Melwyn Riss Vs Lazlo Bajko	NK	Scarborough
31/10/1958	Melwyn Riss Vs Bakjo Lazlo	Mel won	Glasgow, Scotland
02/11/1958	Melwyn Riss Vs Jackie Pallo	NK	West Ham, England
26/11/1958	Melwyn Riss Vs Stefan Milla	Stefan won	Albert Hall, London
27/11/1958	Melwyn Riss Vs Chic Purvey	Chic won	Morecambe, Lancashire
09/12/1958	Melwyn Riss Vs Fred Woolley	NK	Hull, England
02/01/1959	Melwyn Riss Vs Don Branch	Don won	Glasgow, Scotland
06/01/1959	Mewlyn Riss Vs Alan Dennison	NK	Scarborough
09/01/1959	Melwyn Riss Vs Alan Dennison	NK	Scarborough
12/01/1959	Melwyn Riss Vs Peter Szakacs	Mel won	Aylesbury, Buckinghamshire
15/01/1959	Melwyn Riss Vs Len Wilding	Mel won	Bristol, England
16/01/1959	Melwyn Riss Vs Tony Charles	Draw	Ipswich, England
17/01/1959	Melwyn Riss Vs Brian Sparks	NK	Luton, London

Date	Match	Result	Location
11/02/1959	Melwyn Riss Vs Eric Sands	Draw	Cardiff, Wales
12/02/1959	Melwyn Riss Vs Stefan Milla	Mel won	Bristol, England
13/02/1959	Melwyn Riss Vs Stefan Milla	Mel won	Ipswich, England
14/02/1959	Melwyn Riss Vs Mick McManus	NK	Luton, London
17/02/1959	Melwyn Riss Vs Alf Cadman	Draw	Cardiff, Wales
28/02/1959	Melwyn Riss Vs Dick Swales	Mel won	Middlesborough, North Yorkshire
04/03/1959	Mewlyn Riss Vs Jackie Pallo	Draw	Bath, England
05/03/1959	Melwyn Riss Vs Jackie Pallo	Mel won	Beckenham, England
05/03/1959	Melwyn Riss Vs Jackie Pallo	Riss won	Beckenham, England
06/03/1959	Melwyn Riss Vs Al Miquet	Mel won	Ipswich, England
07/03/1959	Melwyn Riss Vs Peter Szakacs	NK	Eastbourne
09/03/1959	Melwyn Riss Vs Dick Swales	Mel won	Hamilton, Scotland
10/03/1959	Melwyn Riss Vs Dickie Swailes	Riss won	Hull, England
12/03/1959	Melwyn Riss Vs Brian Burke	Draw	Bristol, England
16/03/1959	Melwyn Riss Vs Mick McManus	McManus won	Bedford, England
17/03/1959	Melwyn Riss Vs Eric Sands	NK	Swindon, England
18/03/1959	Melwyn Riss Vs Eric Sands	NK	Ashford
20/03/1959	Melwyn Riss Vs Len Wilding	Mel won	Ipswich, England
04/04/1959	Melwyn Riss Vs Jack Cunningham	Nk	Eastbourne
08/04/1959	Melwyn Riss Vs Peter Szakacs	Riss won	Cardiff, Wales
09/04/1959	Melwyn Riss Vs Peter Szakacs	Mel won	Cardiff, Wales
09/04/1959	Melwyn Riss Vs Jackie Pallo	Draw	Bristol, England
09/04/1959	Melwyn Riss Vs Jackie Pallo	Draw	Bristol, England
13/04/1959	Melwyn Riss Vs Jack Dempsey	NK	Folkestone
23/04/1959	Melwyn Riss Vs Mick McManus	Draw	Peterborough, England
24/04/1959	Melwyn Riss Vs Eddie Saxon	Riss won	Ramsgate
24/04/1959	Melwyn Riss Vs Arthur Fisher	Fisher won	Ramsgate
25/04/1959	In KO tournament	NK	Luton, London
26/04/1959	Melwyn Riss Vs Tony Lawrence	NK	Brighton, England
04/05/1959	Melwyn Riss Vs Stefan Milla	NK	Aylesbury, England
06/05/1959	In KO tournament	NK	Hereford, England
07/05/1959	Melwyn Riss Vs Tony Lawrence	Riss won	Bristol, England
09/05/1959	Melwyn Riss Vs Len Wilding	NK	Luton, London
18/05/1959	Melwyn Riss Vs Tony Skarlo	NK	Ramsgate
23/05/1959	In KO tournament	NK	Coventry, England
25/05/1959	Melwyn Ris Vs Etienne Gobi	Riss won	Blackpool, England
01/06/1959	Melwyn Riss Vs Bob Archer O'Brien	NK	Shoreditch, England
18/06/1959	Melwyn Riss Vs Bob Anthony	Riss won	Peterborough, England
18/06/1959	Melwyn Riss Vs Jackie Pallo	Riss won	Peterborough, England
18/06/1959	Melwyn Riss Vs Mick McManus (F)	Riss won	Peterborough, England
23/06/1959	Melwyn Riss Vs Fred Woolley	NK	Wakefield, England
25/06/1959	Melwyn Riss Vs Chic Purvey	NK	Luton, London
22/07/1959	Mlwyn Riss Vs Julien Morice	Nk	Watford, England
11/08/1959	Melwyn Riss Vs tony Lawrence	Nk	Purley, England
14/08/1959	Melwyn Riss Vs jackie Pallo	NK	Rochester

Date	Match	Result	Venue
15/08/1959	Melwyn Riss Vs Brian Burke	NK	Belle Vue, Manchester
18/08/1959	Melwyn Riss Vs Bernard Murray	Draw	Bridlington
31/08/1959	Melwyn Riss Vs jackie Pallo	NK	Folkestone
08/09/1959	Melwyn Riss Vs Peter Szakacs	Nk	Hinckley, England
09/09/1959	Melwyn Riss Vs Len Wilding	Nk	Ashford
14/09/1959	Melwyn Riss Vs jackie Pallo	Nk	Bedford, England
15/09/1959	Melwyn Riss Vs joe Critchley	Nk	Wakefield, England
21/09/1959	Melwyn Riss Vs Peter Szakacs	Nk	Shoreditch, England
26/09/1959	Melwyn Riss Vs Bob Archer O'Brien	NK	Luton, London
03/10/1959	Melwyn Riss Vs Roy Briggs	NK	Belle Vue, Manchester
08/10/1959	Melwyn Riss Vs Jack Dempsey	Dempsey won	Bristol, England
09/10/1959	Melwyn Riss Vs Tony Charles	Draw	Ipswich, England
10/10/1959	Melwyn Riss Vs Bob Archer O'Brien	NK	Norwich, England
12/10/1959	Melwyn Riss Vs Peter Szakacs	NK	Folkestone
14/10/1959	Melwyn Riss Vs Carlo Valdez	Riss won	Royal Albert Hall, London
15/10/1959	Melwyn Riss Vs Stefan Milla	NK	Beckenham, England
19/10/1959	Mlwyn Riss Vs Len Wilding	NK	Shoreditch, England
20/10/1959	Melwyn Riss Vs Bob Archer O'Brien	NK	Welling
21/10/1959	Melwyn Riss Vs peter Szakacs	NK	Kingston
22/10/1959	Melwyn Riss Vs Peter Szakacs	Riss won	Peterborough, England
23/10/1959	Melwyn Riss Vs Bob Anthony	Draw	Ipswich, England
03/11/1959	Melwyn Riss Vs Bobby Steele	NK	Purley, England
07/11/1959	In KO tournament	NK	Norwich, England
11/11/1959	Melwyn Riss Vs Brian Burke	NK	Grimsby, England
23/11/1959	Melwyn Riss Vs Alan Dennison	NK	Loughborough, England
04/01/1960	Melwyn Riss Vs Bob Archer O'Brien	Draw	Bedford, England
06/01/1960	Melwyn Riss Vs Bobby Steele	NK	Kingston, England
09/01/1960	Mewlyn Riss Vs Bob Anthony	NK	Kings Lynn, London
16/01/1960	Melwyn Riss Vs Alan Dennison	Riss won	Newcastle, England
19/01/1960	Melwyn Riss Vs Jim Breaks	NK	Huddersfield, England
27/01/1960	Melwyn Riss Vs Jim Breaks	NK	Preston
30/01/1960	Mewlyn Riss Vs Mick McMichael	Riss won	Newcastle, England
01/02/1960	Melwyn Riss Vs Alan Miquet	Riss won	High Wycombe, England
02/02/1960	Melwyn Riss Vs Len Wilding	NK	Welling
11/02/1960	Melwyn Riss Vs Bob Anthony	NK	Peterborough, England
12/02/1960	Melwyn Riss Vs Bernard Murray	NK	Bradford, England
17/02/1960	Melwyn Riss Vs El Kader	NK	Preston, England
22/02/1960	Melwyn Riss Vs Peter Szakacs	Mel won	Cheltenham, England
23/02/1960	Melwyn Riss Vs Julien Morice	Morice won	Purley
01/03/1960	Melwyn Riss Vs Gil Cesca	NK	Welling
02/03/1960	Melwyn Riss Vs Tony Charles	Charles won	Bath, England
15/03/1960	Melwyn Riss Vs Brian Burke	Draw	Welling
19/03/1960	Melwyn Riss Vs Julien Morice	Draw	Coventry, England
28/03/1960	Melwyn Riss Vs Jackie Pallo	Draw	Bedford, England
02/04/1960	Melwyn Riss Vs Bob Anthony	NK	Eastbourne, England
12/04/1960	Melwyn Riss Vs Stefan Milla	NK	Welling

Date	Match	Result	Location
13/04/1960	Melwyn Riss Vs Jackie Pallo	Mel won	Bath, England
13/04/1960	Melwyn Riss Vs Jackie Pallo	Riss won	Bath, England
14/04/1960	Melwyn Riss Vs Chic Osmond	NK	Luton, England
20/04/1960	Melwyn Riss Vs Modesto Aledo	Riss won	Royal Albert Hall, London
21/04/1960	Melwyn Riss Vs Jean Rabutt	NK	Hove
23/04/1960	Melwyn Riss Vs Brian Burke	Riss won	Halifax, England
25/04/1960	Melwyn Riss Vs Jean Rabutt	Rabutt won	High Wycombe, England
26/04/1960	Melwyn Riss Vs Bob Anthony	NK	Chelmsford, England
29/04/1960	Melwyn Riss Vs Julien Morice	NK	Barnehurst
11/05/1960	Melwyn Riss Vs Bob Archer O'Brien	NK	Southend
14/05/1960	Melwyn Riss Vs jackie Pallo	NK	Norwich, England
18/05/1960	Melwyn Riss Vs Pasquale Salvo	NK	Ashford
23/05/1960	Melwyn Riss Vs Bob Anthony	NK	Aylesbury
24/05/1960	Melwyn Riss Vs Bob Archer O'Brien	NK	Welling
26/05/1960	Melwyn Riss Vs Len Wilding	NK	Cambridge, England
28/05/1960	Melwyn Riss Vs Len Wilding	Riss won	Coventry, England
30/05/1960	Melwyn Riss Vs Cliff Beaumont	NK	Leeds, England
01/06/1960	Melwyn Riss Vs Joe Critchley	NK	Sheffield, England
07/06/1960	Melwyn Riss Vs Jim Breaks	NK	Trowell
13/06/1960	Melwyn Riss Vs Cliff Beaumont	NK	Leeds, England
20/06/1960	Melwyn Riss Vs Bob Anthony	NK	Bedford, England
21/06/1960	Melwyn Riss Vs Bob Archer O'Brien	Draw	Purley
22/06/1960	Melwyn Riss Vs Bob Anthony	NK	Southend
24/06/1960	Melwyn Riss Vs Len Wilding	NK	Barnehurst
30/06/1960	Melwyn Riss Vs Joe Critchley	Riss won	Morecambe, Lancashire
01/07/1960	Melwyn Riss Vs Jack Dempsey	NK	Fleetwood
02/07/1960	Melwyn Riss Vs Boy Briggs	NK	Belle Vue, Manchester
18/07/1960	Melwyn Riss Vs Bernard Murray	NK	Shoreditch
20/07/1960	Melwyn Riss Vs Peter Szakacs	NK	Southend
24/07/1960	Melwyn Riss Vs Bernard Murray	NK	Brighton, England
04/08/1960	Melwyn Riss Vs Al Nicol	Riss won	Morecambe, Lancashire
09/08/1960	Melwyn Riss Vs Julien Morice	NK	Welling
10/08/1960	Melwyn Riss Vs Len Wilding	NK	Dunstable
13/08/1960	Melwyn Riss Vs Bernard Murray	NK	Belle Vue, Manchester
16/08/1960	Melwyn Riss Vs Jack Dempsey	Riss won	Bridlington, England
24/08/1960	Melwyn Riss Vs Mick McManus	NK	Southend
25/08/1960	Melwyn Riss Vs Bob Archer O'Brien	NK	Walthamstow
01/09/1960	Melwyn Riss Vs Ted Hannon	Riss won	Morecambe, Lancashire
05/09/1960	Melwyn Riss Vs Bobby Steele	NK	High Wycombe, England
06/09/1960	Melwyn Riss Vs Mick McManus	NK	Colchester, England
08/09/1960	Melwyn Riss Vs Jack Dempsey	NK	Walthamstow
14/09/1960	Melwyn Riss Vs jackie Pallo	NK	Southend
17/09/1960	Melwyn Riss Vs Alan Miquet	NK	Blackburn, England
22/09/1960	Melwyn Riss Vs Jack Dempsey	Dempsey won	Morecambe, Lancashire
24/09/1960	Melwyn Riss Vs Al Nicol	NK	Grantham,
01/10/1960	Mel Riss Vs Al Micquet	NK	Purley

Date	Match	Result	Location
04/10/1960	Melwyn Riss Vs Len Wilding	NK	Welling
05/10/1960	Melwyn Riss Vs Al Nicols	Mel won	Cardiff, Wales
05/10/1960	Melwyn Riss Vs Al Nicol	Riss won	Cardiff, Wales
06/10/1960	Melwyn Riss Vs Archer O'Brien	Mel won	Bristol, England
06/10/1960	Melwyn Riss Vs Bob Archer O'Brien	Riss won	Bristol, England
07/10/1960	Melwyn Riss Vs Bob Anthony	NK	Chesterfield, England
11/10/1960	Melwyn Riss Vs Jim Breaks	NK	Trowell
18/10/1960	Melwyn Riss Vs Pasquale Salvo	Riss won	Purley
20/10/1960	Melwyn Riss Vs Len Wilding	Riss won	Peterborough, England
21/10/1960	Melwyn Riss Vs Bob Anthony	NK	Taunton, England
22/10/1960	Melwyn Riss Vs Peter Szakacs	NK	Wembley, England
26/10/1960	Melwyn Riss Vs Pasquale Salvo	NK	Hastings,
01/11/1960	Melwyn Riss Vs Al Nicol	Draw	Hinckley
05/11/1960	Melwyn Riss Vs jackie Pallo	NK	Luton, England
16/11/1960	Melwyn Riss Vs Len Wilding	NK	Cardiff, Wales
17/11/1960	Melwyn Riss Vs Bernard Murray	Draw	Beckenham, England
23/11/1960	Melwyn Riss Vs Julien Morice	NK	Preston, England
26/11/1960	Melwyn Riss Vs Cliff Beaumont	NK	Middlesborough, England
28/11/1960	Melwyn Riss Vs Alan Colbeck	NK	Hamilton, Scotland
01/12/1960	Melwyn Riss Vs Jack Cunningham	NK	Barrow, England
02/12/1960	Melwyn Riss Vs Jim Breaks	Riss won	Glasgow, Scotland
08/12/1960	Melwyn Riss Vs Jim Breaks	NK	Kirkcaldy
12/12/1960	Melwyn Riss Vs Bernard Murray	NK	Blackpool, England
14/12/1960	Melwyn Riss Vs George Adams	NK	Preston, England
24/12/1960	Melwyn Riss Vs Jim Breaks	Mel won	Middlesborough, North Yorkshire
24/12/1960	Melwyn Riss Vs Jim Breaks	Riss won	Middlesborough, England
27/12/1960	Melwyn Riss Vs Ted Hannon	NK	Leeds, England
28/12/1960	Melwyn Riss Vs Jim Breaks	Mel won	Lincoln, England
30/12/1960	Melwyn Riss Vs Jim Breaks	NK	Liverpool, England
31/12/1960	Melwyn Riss Vs Alan Colbeck	NK	Grantham,
02/01/1961	Melwyn Riss Vs Julien Morices	Draw	Seymour Hall, London
03/01/1961	Melwyn Riss Vs Ted Hannon	NK	Welling
05/01/1961	Melwyn Riss Vs Ted Hannon	NK	Cambridge, England
07/01/1961	Melwyn Riss Vs Alan Colbeck	Colbeck won	Newcastle, England
11/01/1961	Melwyn Riss Vs Julien Morice	Draw	Banbury
16/01/1961	Melwyn Riss Vs Bob Archer O'Brien	NK	Seymour Hall, London
17/01/1961	Melwyn Riss Vs Ted Hannon	NK	Chelmsford, England
21/01/1961	Melwyn Riss Vs Ted Hannon	Riss won	Camberwell
23/01/1961	Melwyn Riss Vs Julien Morice	NK	Leeds, England
24/01/1961	Melwyn Riss Vs Jack Dempsey	NK	Hull, England
30/01/1961	Melwyn Riss Vs Jim Breaks	NK	Hamilton, Scotland
04/02/1961	Melwyn Riss Vs Ted Hannon	NK	Coventry, England
06/02/1961	Melwyn Riss Vs Stefan Milla	Riss won	Seymour Hall, London
07/02/1961	Melwyn Riss Vs keith Williams	NK	Welling
08/02/1961	Melwyn Riss Vs Julien Morice	NK	Cardiff, Wales

Date	Match	Result	Location
10/02/1961	Melwyn Riss Vs Len Wilding	Riss won	Ipswich, England
11/02/1961	Melwyn Riss Vs Julien Morice	NK	Portsmouth, England
13/02/1961	Melwyn Riss Vs Joe Critchley	NK	Blackpool, England
20/02/1961	Melwyn Riss Vs Bob Anthony	Draw	Aylesbury
22/02/1961	Melwyn Riss Vs Julien Morice	NK	Cardiff, Wales
25/02/1961	Melwyn Riss Vs Ted Hannon	NK	Coventry, England
27/02/1961	Melwyn Riss Vs Bob Archer O'Brien	NK	High Wycombe, England
04/03/1961	Melwyn Riss Vs Sid Cooper	NK	Middlesborough, England
06/03/1961	Melwyn Riss Vs Julien Morice	NK	Worksop
07/03/1961	Melwyn Riss Vs Peter Szakacs	Szakacs won, Mel Inj	Cheltenham, England
08/03/1961	Melwyn Riss Vs Mick McManus	McManus won	Lincoln, England
09/03/1961	Melwyn Riss Vs Mick McMichael	NK	Nottingham, England
10/03/1961	Melwyn Riss Vs Julien Morice	NK	Glasgow, Scotland
11/03/1961	Melwyn Riss Vs Julien Morice	NK	Grantham,
18/03/1961	Melwyn Riss Vs Julien Morice	NK	Portsmouth, England
20/03/1961	Melwyn Riss Vs Bob Anthony	Draw	Aylesbury
21/03/1961	Melwyn Riss Vs Johnny Major	Riss won	Purley
23/03/1961	Melwyn Riss Vs Pasquale Salvo	NK	Luton, England
25/03/1961	Mel Riss Vs Len Wilding	NK	Beckenham
25/03/1961	Melwyn Riss Vs Johnny Major	Riss won	Brighton, England
25/03/1961	Melwyn Riss Vs Len Wilding	Riss won	Beckenham, England
28/03/1961	Melwyn Riss Vs Bernard Murray	NK	Chelmsford, England
29/03/1961	Melwyn Riss Vs Chic Purvey	NK	Liverpool, England
31/03/1961	Melwyn Riss Vs Bob Archer O'Brien	NK	Northampton, England
04/04/1961	Melwyn Riss Vs Julien Morice	NK	Welling
05/04/1961	Melwyn Riss Vs Billy Stock	Riss won	Cardiff, Wales
07/04/1961	Melwyn Riss Vs Gil Cesca	NK	Bermondsey
08/04/1961	Melwyn Riss Vs Julien Morice	NK	Grantham,
10/04/1961	Melwyn Riss Vs Bobby Steele	NK	Worthing
12/04/1961	Melwyn Riss Vs jackie Pallo	NK	Ashford
22/04/1961	Melwyn Riss Vs Julien Morice	NK	Belle Vue, Manchester
01/05/1961	Melwyn Riss Vs jackie Pallo	Draw	Tunbridge Wells
02/05/1961	Melwyn Riss Vs Modesto Aledo	Riss won	Colchester, England
03/05/1961	Melwyn Riss Vs Bernard Murray	NK	Ashford
04/05/1961	Melwyn Riss Vs Julien Morice	Riss won	Walthamstow
16/05/1961	Melwyn Riss Vs Bob Anthony	Draw	Bournemouth
17/05/1961	Melwyn Riss Vs Bob Anthony	NK	Winchester
18/05/1961	Melwyn Riss Vs Jackie Pallo	NK	Dunstable
19/05/1961	Melwyn Riss Vs Julien Morice	NK	Caledonian Road, London
22/05/1961	Melwyn Riss Vs John Foley	Foley won	Purley
05/06/1961	Melwyn Riss Vs Len Wilding	NK	Edmonton
08/06/1961	Melwyn Riss Vs jackie Pallo	NK	Dunstable
09/06/1961	Melwyn Riss Vs Joe Critchley	NK	Liverpool, England
23/06/1961	Melwyn Riss Vs julien Morice	NK	Bridgewater
24/06/1961	Melwyn Riss Vs Joe Murphy	NK	Norwich, England

Date	Match	Result	Location
29/06/1961	Melwyn Riss Vs Stefan Milla	Riss won	Dagenham
01/07/1961	In KO Tournament	NK	Luton, England
03/07/1961	Melwyn Riss Vs Cyril Knowles	NK	Buxton
08/07/1961	Melwyn Riss Vs Jim Breaks	Riss won	Belle Vue, Manchester
10/07/1961	Melwyn Riss Vs Bernard Murray	Draw	Shoreditch
11/07/1961	Melwyn Riss Vs Ted Hannon	NK	Weston Super Mare
12/07/1961	Melwyn Riss Vs Ted Hannon	Draw	Felixstowe
13/07/1961	Melwyn Riss Vs Peter Szakacs	NK	Torquay
31/07/1961	Melwyn Riss Vs Jim Mellor	NK	Warwick
02/08/1961	Melwyn Riss Vs Jack Dempsey	Dempsey won	Watford, England
02/09/1961	Melwyn Riss Vs Eric Wasburg	Riss won	Kings Lynn, London
06/09/1961	Melwyn Riss Vs Al Nicol	NK	Winchester
07/09/1961	Melwyn Riss Vs Jack Dempsey	NK	Torquay
10/09/1961	Melwyn Riss Vs Gil Cesca	NK	Brighton, England
11/09/1961	Melwyn Riss Vs Len Wilding	NK	High Wycombe, England
12/09/1961	Melwyn Riss Vs Stefan Milla	Riss won	Weston Super Mare
12/09/1961	Melwyn Riss Vs Jack Pallo (F)	Pallo won	Weston Super Mare
23/09/1961	Melwyn Riss Vs Bernard Murray	Riss won	Newcastle, England
04/10/1961	Melwyn Riss Vs Stefan Milla	NK	Felixstowe
07/10/1961	Melwyn Riss Vs Pasquale Salvo	Draw	Coventry, England
16/10/1961	Melwyn Riss Vs Julien Morice	NK	Cheltenham, England
18/10/1961	Melwyn Riss Vs keith Williams	Draw	Bath
19/10/1961	Melwyn Riss Vs Billy Stock	Riss won	Walthamstow
15/11/1961	Melwyn Riss Vs Billy Stock	Riss won	Royal Albert Hall, London
18/11/1961	Melwyn Riss Vs Billy Stock	Riss won	Coventry, England
20/11/1961	Melwyn Riss Vs Dick Conlon	Riss won	Seymour Hall, London
21/11/1961	Melwyn Riss Vs Johnny Major	NK	Purley
22/11/1961	Melwyn Riss Vs Billy Stock	Stock won	Dorking
24/11/1961	Melwyn Riss Vs Peter Szakacs	Riss won	Taunton, England
25/11/1961	Melwyn Riss Vs Bobby Steele	NK	Norwich, England
04/12/1961	Melwyn Riss Vs Len Wilding	Riss won	High Wycombe, England
04/12/1961	Melwyn Riss Vs Bob Archer O'Brien (F)	Riss won	High Wycombe, England
06/12/1961	Melwyn Riss Vs Len Wilding	NK	Southend
07/12/1961	Melwyn Riss Vs Pasquale Salvo	NK	Southampton, England
09/12/1961	Melwyn Riss Vs Bob Archer O'Brien	NK	Eastbourne
15/12/1961	Melwyn Riss Vs Alan Miquet	NK	Bermondsey
16/12/1961	Melwyn Riss Vs Peter Szakacs	NK	Kings Lynn, London
20/12/1961	Melwyn Riss Vs Adrian Street	NK	Cambridge, England
27/12/1961	Melwyn Riss Vs Kalmen Gaston	Riss won	Shoreditch
27/12/1961	Melwyn Riss Vs Pasquale Salvo (F)	Riss won	Shoreditch
03/01/1962	Melwyn Riss Vs Dick Conlon	NK	Banbury
04/01/1962	Melwyn Riss Vs Jack Cunningham	NK	Dunstable
05/01/1962	Melwyn Riss Vs Peter Szakacs	NK	Barking
06/01/1962	Melwyn Riss Vs jackie Pallo	NK	Maidstone
17/01/1962	Melwyn Riss Vs Bob Anthony	NK	Southen
18/01/1962	Melwyn Riss Vs Vassilios Mantopolous	Riss won	Brighton

Date	Match	Result	Location
19/01/1962	Melwyn Riss Vs Bernard Murray	Murray won	Ipswich
20/01/1962	Melwyn Riss Vs Joe Murphy	NK	Norwich
29/01/1962	Melwyn Riss Vs Bob Archer O'Brien	NK	Tunbridge Wells
31/01/1962	Melwyn Riss Vs Julien Morice	Draw	Cardiff, Wales
02/02/1962	Melwyn Riss Vs Alan Colbeck	NK	Rochester
03/02/1962	Melwyn Riss Riss Vs Jack Dempsey	NK	Coventry, England
05/02/1962	Melwyn Riss Vs Eric Coates	NK	Derby
06/02/1962	Melwyn Riss Vs Reg Ray	NK	Kidderminster
12/02/1962	Melwyn Riss Vs Vassilios Mantopolous	NK	Cheltenham
13/02/1962	Melwyn Riss Vs Tony Skarlo	Riss won	Plymouth, England
15/02/1962	Melwyn Riss Vs Billy Stock	NK	Dunstable
16/02/1962	Melwyn Riss Vs Eric Sands	NK	Streatham
17/02/1962	Melwyn Riss Vs Mick McMichael	NK	Southall
22/02/1962	Melwyn Riss Vs Peter Szakacs	Riss won	Peterborough
23/02/1962	Melwyn Riss Vs Mick McManus	NK	Rochester
27/02/1962	Melwyn Riss Vs Len Wilding	NK	Chelmsford
17/03/1962	Melwyn Riss Vs Al Nicol	NK	Brighton, England
19/03/1962	Melwyn Riss Vs Vic Faulkner	NK	Worcester, England
27/03/1962	Melwyn Riss Vs Len Wilding	NK	Hastings
29/03/1962	Melwyn Riss Vs Pasquale Salvo	Draw	Bristol, England
02/04/1962	Melwyn Riss Vs Bernard Murray	Murray won	Blackpool, England
09/04/1962	Melwyn Riss Vs Chic Purvey	NK	Nelson
13/04/1962	Melwyn Riss Vs Julien Morice	Riss won	Ipswich
24/04/1962	Melwyn Riss Vs Alan Miquet	NK	Ilford
25/04/1962	Melwyn Riss Vs Stefan Milla	Riss won	Oxford, England
26/04/1962	Melwyn Riss Vs Pasquale Salvo	NK	Cambridge, England
15/05/1962	Melwyn Riss Vs Billy Stock	NK	Colchester, England
17/05/1962	Melwyn Riss Vs Len Wilding	Riss won	Wimbledon
17/05/1962	Melwyn Riss Vs Eric Sands	Sands won	Wimbledon
18/05/1962	Melwyn Riss Vs Tony Skarlo	NK	Ramsgate
21/05/1962	Melwyn Riss Vs Stefan Milla	NK	Tunbridge Wells
24/05/1962	Melwyn Riss Vs Julien Morice	NK	Wimbledon
06/06/1962	Melwyn Riss Vs Eric Wasburg	Riss won	Bath, England
06/06/1962	Melwyn Riss Vs Joe Murphy	Murphy won	Bath, England
08/06/1962	Melwyn Riss Vs Eric Wasburg	NK	Northampton, England
21/06/1962	Melwyn Riss Vs Pasquale Salvo	Riss won	Worthing
25/06/1962	Melwyn Riss Vs Bob Archer O'Brien	NK	Folkestone
27/06/1962	Melwyn Riss Vs Pasquale Salvo	Riss won	Great Yarmouth, England
28/06/1962	Melwyn Riss Vs Jackie Pallo	Pallo won	Walthamstow
02/07/1962	In KO Tournament	NK	Weston Super Mare
03/07/1962	Melwyn Riss Vs Len Wilding	Riss won	Hove
05/07/1962	In KO Tournament	NK	Southampton, England
06/07/1962	Melwyn Riss Vs Len Wilding	NK	Herne Bay
09/07/1962	Melwyn Riss Vs Bernard Murray	Draw	Shoreditch
17/07/1962	Melwyn Riss Vs Adrian Street	NK	Hastings
20/07/1962	Melwyn Riss Vs Julien Morice	NK	Barking

Date	Match	Result	Location
31/07/1962	Melwyn Riss Vs Eddie Capelli	NK	Ilford
02/08/1962	Melwyn Riss Vs Leon Fortuna	NK	Torquay, England
10/08/1962	Melwyn Riss Vs Eric Sands	Draw	Barking
12/08/1962	Melwyn Riss Vs Johnny Mack	Draw	Blackpool, England
20/08/1962	Melwyn Riss Vs Leon Fortuna	NK	Wembley
27/08/1962	Melwyn Riss Vs Eddie Capelli	NK	High Wycombe, England
30/08/1962	Melwyn Riss Vs Joe Murphy	Murphy won	Wimbledon
31/08/1962	Melwyn Riss Vs Joe Murphy	NK	Redruth, England
17/09/1962	Melwyn Riss Vs Jackie Pallo	NK	Weston Super Mare
18/09/1962	Melwyn Riss Vs Peter Szakacs	NK	Swindon, England
22/09/1962	Melwyn Riss Vs Alan Miquet	NK	Kings Lynn, London
03/10/1962	Melwyn Riss Vs Bobby Steele	Riss won	Cardiff, Wales
15/10/1962	Melwyn Riss Vs Alan Miquet	NK	Cheltenham
19/10/1962	Melwyn Riss Vs Manuel Lopez	NK	Herne Bay
29/10/1962	Melwyn Riss Vs Jim Breaks	NK	Nelson
06/11/1962	Melwyn Riss Vs Julien Morice	Morice won	Hove
08/11/1962	Melwyn Riss Vs Julien Pizzaro	Riss won	Wimbledon
10/11/1962	Melwyn Riss Vs Nino Pizzaro	NK	Maidstone
30/11/1962	Melwyn Riss Vs Ted Hannon	Draw	Northampton, England
01/12/1962	Melwyn Riss Vs Len Wilding	NK	Eastbourne
05/12/1962	Melwyn Riss Vs Alan Miquet	NK	Dorking
20/12/1962	Melwyn Riss Vs Adrian Street	NK	Cambridge, England
04/01/1963	Melwyn Riss Vs Stefan Milla	Riss won	Farnham
07/01/1963	Melwyn Riss Vs Vic Faulkner	NK	High Wycombe, England
09/01/1963	Melwyn Riss Vs Adrian Street	NK	Kingston
11/01/1963	Melwyn Riss Vs Vic Faulkner	NK	Streatham
14/01/1963	Melwyn Riss Vs Terry Nylands	NK	Derby, England
15/01/1963	Melwyn Riss Vs Terry Nylands	Riss won	Kidderminster
18/01/1963	Melwyn Riss Vs Terry Nylands	NK	Dumfries
21/01/1963	Melwyn Riss Vs Pasquale Salvo	NK	Weston Super Mare
22/01/1963	Melwyn Riss Vs Peter Szakacs	NK	Croydon
25/01/1963	Melwyn Riss Vs Adrian Street	NK	Northampton, England
02/02/1963	Mel Riss Vs Young Vulcan	Mel won	Preston, Lancashire
04/02/1963	Melwyn Riss Vs Joe Critchley	NK	Worcester, England
11/02/1963	Melwyn Riss Vs Bob Archer O'Brien	Draw	Worthing
19/02/1963	Melwyn Riss Vs Leon Fortuna	Riss won	Plymouth, England
25/02/1963	Melwyn Riss Vs Ian Gilmour	NK	Cheltenham
26/02/1963	Melwyn Riss Vs Tony Skarlo	Riss won	Swindon, England
01/03/1963	Melwyn Riss Vs Adrian Street	NK	Rochester
02/03/1963	Melwyn Riss Vs Tony Skarlo	Riss won	Coventry, England
04/03/1963	Melwyn Riss Vs Joe Critchley	NK	Worcester, England
11/03/1963	Melwyn Riss Vs Len Wilding	NK	West Ham, England
12/03/1963	Melwyn Riss Vs Jim Breaks	Draw	Tottenham
14/03/1963	Melwyn Riss Vs Alan Miquet	NK	Wimbledon
25/03/1963	Melwyn Riss Vs Adrian Street	Riss won	Wisbech
27/03/1963	Melwyn Riss Vs Julien Morice	Morice won	Croydon

Date	Match	Result	Location
30/03/1963	Melwyn Riss Vs Al Patterson	Riss won	Coventry, England
08/04/1963	Melwyn Riss Vs Stefan Milla	Riss won	Tunbridge Wells
09/04/1963	Melwyn Riss Vs Tony Skarlo	NK	Chelmsford
10/04/1963	Melwyn Riss Vs Ted Hannon	Draw	Lincoln
11/04/1963	Melwyn Riss Vs Alan Miquet	Draw	Bristol, England
13/04/1963	Mel Riss (RSF) Vs Adrian Street	Riss won	Croydon, London
15/04/1963	Melwyn Riss Vs Terry Downs	NK	Kirkby, Ashfield
22/04/1963	Melwyn Riss Vs Leon Fortuna	NK	Reading, England
23/04/1963	Melwyn Riss Vs Bernard Murray	Draw	Croydon
24/04/1963	Melwyn Riss Vs Adrian Street	NK	Hastings
25/04/1963	Melwyn Riss Vs Julien Morice	Draw	Southampton, England
26/04/1963	Melwyn Riss Vs Len Wilding	NK	Ramsgate
01/05/1963	Melwyn Riss Vs Leon Fortuna	NK	Winchester
04/05/1963	Melwyn Riss Vs Julien Morice	NK	Southall
06/05/1963	Melwyn Riss Vs Cliff Beaumont	Draw	Bradford
20/05/1963	Melwyn Riss Vs Linde Caulder	NK	Tunbridge Wells
21/05/1963	Melwyn Riss Vs Jim Breaks	Riss won	Croydon
23/05/1963	Melwyn Riss Vs Julien Morice	NK	Wimbledon
24/05/1963	Melwyn Riss Vs Stefan Milla	NK	Barking
25/05/1963	Melwyn Riss Vs Eddie Capelli	NK	Kings Lynn, London
17/06/1963	Melwyn Riss Vs Alan Miquet	NK	Folkestone
18/06/1963	Melwyn Riss Vs Leon Fortuna	NK	Croydon
18/06/1963	Melwyn Riss Vs Billy Stock	NK	Westbury
19/06/1963	Melwyn Riss Vs Stefan Milla	NK	Bognor Regis
20/06/1963	Melwyn Riss Vs Billy Stock	Riss won	Bristol, England
22/06/1963	Melwyn Riss Vs Leon Fortuna	NK	Salisbury
26/06/1963	Melwyn Riss Vs Leon Fortuna	NK	Bournemouth, England
28/06/1963	Melwyn Riss Vs Miquel Santos	NK	Herne bay
01/07/1963	Mel Riss Vs Eric Sands	Sands won	Bradford, West Yorkshire
02/07/1963	Melwyn Riss Vs Peter Szakacs	NK	Barnstaple
15/07/1963	Melwyn Riss Vs Leon Fortuna	NK	Weston Super Mare
16/07/1963	Melwyn Riss Vs Julien Morice	NK	Finsbury Park
29/07/1963	Melwyn Riss Vs Pasquale Salvo	Draw	Southampton, England
01/08/1963	Melwyn Riss Vs Adrian Street	NK	Bournemouth, England
02/08/1963	Melwyn Riss Vs Alan Miquet	NK	Bognor Regis
03/08/1963	Melwyn Riss Vs Tony Skarlo	NK	Maidstone
13/08/1963	Melwyn Riss Vs Mick McManus	NK	Hastings
14/08/1963	Melwyn Riss Vs Dick Conlon	NK	Margate
16/08/1963	In KO Tournament	NK	Barking
27/08/1963	Melwyn Riss Vs Jim Breaks	Riss won	Hove
29/08/1963	Melwyn Riss Vs Peter Szakacs	NK	Torquay
30/08/1963	Melwyn Riss Vs Leon Fortuna	NK	Rochester
31/08/1963	Melwyn Riss Vs Jim Breaks	NK	Kings Lynn, London
10/09/1963	Melwyn Riss Vs Tony Skarlo	NK	Hove
11/09/1963	Melwyn Riss Vs Cliff Beaumont	NK	Felixstowe
12/09/1963	Melwyn Riss Vs Jackie Pallo	NK	Dunstable

Date	Match	Result	Location
13/09/1963	In KO Tournament	NK	Ramsgate
14/09/1963	Melwyn Riss Vs Jackie Pallo	Pallo won	Maidstone
23/09/1963	Melwyn Riss Vs Bob Archer O'Brien	Draw	Tunbridge Wells
24/09/1963	Melwyn Riss Vs Alan Miquet	NK	Swindon, England
25/09/1963	Melwyn Riss Vs Jim Breaks	NK	Salisbury
26/09/1963	Melwyn Riss Vs Jackie Pallo	Pallo won	Longleat
05/10/1963	Mel Riss Vs Adrian Street	NK	Wimbledon
12/10/1963	Melwyn Riss Vs Leon Fortuna	NK	Eastbourne
14/10/1963	Melwyn Riss Vs Eric Sands	NK	Bradford
17/10/1963	Melwyn Riss Vs Leon Fortuna	NK	Exeter
25/10/1963	Melwyn Riss Vs Jim Breaks	Breaks won	Ipswich
28/10/1963	Melwyn Riss Vs Jack Cunningham	Cunningham won	Catford
29/10/1963	Melwyn Riss Vs Miquel Santos	NK	Hertford
31/10/1963	Melwyn Riss Vs Ted Hannon	NK	Wimbledon
01/11/1963	Melwyn Riss Vs Steve Sipos	Riss won	Rochester
02/11/1963	Melwyn Riss Vs Bernard Murray	NK	Luton, England
06/11/1963	Melwyn Riss Vs Bernard Murray	Draw	Cardiff, Wales
07/11/1963	Melwyn Riss Vs Pasquale Salvo	NK	Bury St Edmunds
09/11/1963	Melwyn Riss Vs Peter Szakacs	NK	Camberwell
21/11/1963	Melwyn Riss Vs Dick Conlon	Riss won	Bristol
23/11/1963	Melwyn Riss Vs Peter Szakacs	NK	Maidstone
30/11/1963	Melwyn Riss Vs Danny Shay	NK	Sutton, Ashfield
07/12/1963	Melwyn Riss Vs Billy Catanzaro	NK	Kings Lynn, London
09/12/1963	Melwyn Riss Vs jack Dempsey	NK	Derby
17/12/1963	Melwyn Riss Vs Billy Catanzaro	NK	Swindon, England
19/12/1963	Melwyn Riss Vs Eddie Capelli	NK	Bury St Edmunds
20/12/1963	Melwyn Riss Vs Michael Saulnier	Draw	Ipswich
21/12/1963	Melwyn Riss Vs Leon Fortuna	Draw	Camberwell
11/01/1964	Mel Riss Vs Vassilios Mantopolous (Greek Champ)	NK	Bermondsey
01/01/1965	Melwyn Riss Vs Al Nicol	Riss won	Bolton
02/01/1965	Melwyn Riss Vs Terry Downs	Riss won	Doncaster
06/01/1965	Melwyn Riss Vs jim Mellor	NK	Leominster
09/01/1965	Melwyn Riss Vs Bobby Steele	NK	Llandudno
13/01/1965	Melwyn Riss Vs jim Mellor	NK	Southport
18/01/1965	Melwyn Riss Vs Jim Mellor	NK	Birmingham
28/01/1965	Melwyn Riss Vs Terry Downs	NK	Northwich
01/02/1965	Melwyn Riss Vs Al Brown	Riss won	Birmingham
04/02/1965	Melwyn Riss Vs Cliff Beaumont	Riss won	Malvern
08/02/1965	Melwyn Riss Vs Bernard Murray	Murray won	Blackpool, England
12/02/1965	Melwyn Riss Vs Bernard Murray	NK	Liverpool
13/02/1965	Melwyn Riss Vs Joe Critchley	Draw	Doncaster
15/02/1965	Melwyn Riss Vs Sid Cooper	NK	Derby
23/02/1965	Melwyn Riss Vs jack Dempsey	NK	Kidderminster
24/02/1965	Melwyn Riss Vs Joe Critchley	Riss won	Alfreton
25/02/1965	Melwyn Riss Vs Keith Williams	NK	Nelson
09/03/1965	Melwyn Riss Vs Alan Wood	NK	Solihull

Date	Match	Result	Location
10/03/1965	Melwyn Riss Vs Colin Joynson	NK	Leominster
11/03/1965	Melwyn Riss Vs jim Mellor	NK	Whitchurch
13/03/1965	Melwyn Riss Vs Alan Wood	Riss won	Doncaster
16/03/1965	Melwyn Riss Vs Terry Downs	NK	Welshpool
17/03/1965	Melwyn Riss Vs Terry Nylands	NK	Southport
26/03/1965	Melwyn Riss Vs Jim McKenzie	NK	Dumfries
29/03/1965	Melwyn Riss Vs Bernard Murray	NK	Blackpool, England
02/04/1965	Melwyn Riss Vs Bernard Murray	Riss won	Liverpool
10/04/1965	Melwyn Riss Vs Al Nicol	Draw	Doncaster
12/04/1965	Melwyn Riss Vs Bernard Murray	NK	Worcester, England
13/04/1965	Melwyn Riss Vs Keith Williams	Draw	Warrington
16/04/1965	Melwyn Riss Vs Alan Wood	Draw	Bolton
01/05/1965	Melwyn Riss Vs jack Dempsey	Dempsey won	Doncaster
11/07/1965	Melwyn Riss & Joe Critchley Vs Keith Williams & Mick McMichael	Williams & McMichael won	Blackpool, England
17/07/1965	Melwyn Riss Vs Jim Mellor	NK	Rhyl, Wales
24/07/1965	Melwyn Riss Vs Shem Singh	Riss won	Belle Vue, Manchester
30/07/1965	Melwyn Riss & Jim Breaks Vs Joe Critchley & Bernard Murray	Riss et al won	Liverpool
01/08/1965	Melwyn Riss & Jim Breaks Vs Joe Critchley & Bernard Murray	Critchley et al won	Blackpool, England
12/08/1965	Melwyn Riss Vs Keith Williams	NK	Aberystwyth, Wales
20/08/1965	Melwyn Riss Vs Joe Critchley	Riss won	Glasgow, Scotland
27/08/1965	Melwyn Riss Vs Joe Critchley	Riss won	Liverpool
30/08/1965	Melwyn Riss Vs Jim Mellor	Riss won	Birmingham
31/08/1965	Melwyn Riss Vs Jim Mellor	Riss won	Wolverhampton, West Midlands
01/09/1965	Melwyn Riss Vs Jim Mellor	NK	Hinckley
02/09/1965	Melwyn Riss Vs Jim Mellor	NK	Ross on Wye
03/09/1965	Melwyn Riss Vs Jim Mellor	Riss won	Bolton
24/09/1965	Melwyn Riss Vs Barry Cannon	Riss won	Liverpool
26/09/1965	Melwyn Riss & Joe Critchley Vs Mick McMichael & Barry Cannon	McMichael et al won	Blackpool, England
01/10/1965	Melwyn Riss Vs Leon Fortuna	NK	Chesterfield, England
01/11/1965	Melwyn Riss & Terry Downs Vs Jeff Kaye & Keith Williams	NK	Derby
04/11/1965	Melwyn Riss Vs Alan Wood	NK	Nelson
06/11/1965	Melwyn Riss Vs Al Brown	NK	Shrewsbury
16/11/1965	Melwyn Riss Vs Al Brown	NK	Solihull
22/11/1965	Melwyn Riss Vs Keith Williams	NK	Blackpool, England
08/12/1965	Melwyn Riss & Al Brown Vs Jackie Cheers & Alan Wood	Riss et al won	Hindley
27/12/1965	Melwyn Riss Vs Jim Breaks	Breaks won	Blackpool, England
03/01/1966	Melwyn Riss Vs jack Dempsey	NK	Derby, Derbyshire
07/01/1966	Melwyn Riss & Alan Wood Vs Reg Ray & Barry Cannon	NK	Dumfries
15/01/1966	Melwyn Riss Vs Alan Wood	NK	Sutton, Ashfield
24/01/1966	Melwyn Riss Vs Mir Zaffar Ealam	NK	Derby, Derbyshire
07/02/1966	Melwyn Riss Vs jack Dempsey	NK	Derby, Derbyshire
09/02/1966	Melwyn Riss Vs Nick Dallas	NK	Alfreton
21/02/1966	Melwyn Riss Vs jack Dempsey	Dempsey won	Derby, Derbyshire

Date	Match	Result	Location
07/03/1966	Melwyn Riss Vs jack Dempsey	NK	Derby, Derbyshire
10/03/1966	Melwyn Riss Vs jack Dempsey	NK	Nelson
28/03/1966	Melwyn Riss Vs jack Dempsey	Dempsey won	Derby, Derbyshire
01/04/1966	Melwyn Riss Vs jack Dempsey	NK	Dumfries
09/04/1966	Melwyn Riss & Joe Critchley Vs Ted Hannon & Terry Downs	Hannon et al won	Blackpool, England
20/04/1966	Melwyn Riss Vs jack Dempsey	NK	Nelson
26/05/1966	Melwyn Riss Vs jack Dempsey	Draw	Malvern
05/06/1966	Melwyn Riss Vs Mike Bennett	NK	Douglas, Isle of Man
26/06/1966	Melwyn Riss & Joe Critchley Vs Leon Arras & Barry Cannon	Arras et al won	Blackpool, England
24/07/1966	Melwyn Riss & Joe Critchley Vs The White Eagles	Eagles won	Blackpool, England
12/08/1966	Melwyn Riss Vs Peter Cortez	Cortez won	Redruth
18/10/1966	Melwyn Riss Vs Alan Wood	NK	Kidderminster
05/12/1966	Melwyn Riss Vs joe Critchley	NK	Blackpool, England
02/09/1967	Melvyn Riss Vs Al Nicol	NK	The Floral Hall, Southport, Merseyside
06/01/1968	Melwyn Riss Vs Bill Connor	NK	Shrewsbury
15/01/1968	Melwyn Riss Vs Alan Wood	NK	Derby, Derbyshire
29/01/1968	Melwyn Riss Vs Alan Wood	NK	Derby, Derbyshire
12/02/1968	Melwyn Riss Vs Bill Connor	NK	Altrincham
15/02/1968	Melwyn Riss Vs joe Critchley	Riss won	Malvern
24/02/1968	Melwyn Riss Vs Bill Connor	NK	Shrewsbury
26/02/1968	Melwyn Riss Vs Roy Wood	Wood won MRDQ	Blackpool, England
18/03/1968	Melwyn Riss Vs Peter Preston	NK	Blackpool, England
29/03/1968	Melwyn Riss Vs Alan Wood	Draw	Bolton, Lancashire
16/05/1968	Melwyn Riss Vs Bill Connor	NK	Malvern
24/05/1968	Melwyn Riss Vs Dave Barrie	NK	Dumfries
04/06/1968	Melwyn Riss & Alan Kilby Vs Peter Preston & Chic Purvey	Riss et al won	Skegness
11/06/1968	Melwyn Riss Vs Ian Gilmour	NK	Bromsgrove
01/07/1968	Melwyn Riss Vs Bill Connor	Draw	Birmingham
02/07/1968	Melwynr Riss Vs Chic Purvey	Draw	Oakengates
06/07/1968	Melwyn Riss Vs Jim Mellor	NK	Rhyl, Wales
07/07/1968	Melwyn Riss Vs Steve Best	NK	Blackpool, England
27/07/1968	Melwyn Riss Vs Chic Purvey	Draw	Hanley
30/07/1968	Melwyn Riss Vs Chic Purvey	Riss won	Wolverhampton, West Midlands
05/08/1968	Melwyn Riss Vs Alan Wood	Draw	Coedpoeth
06/08/1968	Melwyn Riss & terry Jowett Vs The Black Diamonds	Diamonds won	Skegness
06/08/1968	Melwyn Riss Vs Alan Kilby	Riss inj	Skegness
07/08/1968	Melwyn Riss Vs Jim Mellor	Riss won	Southport, Merseyside
13/08/1968	Melwyn Riss Vs Steve Best	Riss won	Skegness
24/08/1968	Melwyn Riss Vs Alan Kilby	NK	Rhyl, Wales
28/08/1968	Melwyn Riss Vs Alan Wood	Draw	Southport, Merseyside
29/08/1968	Melwyn Riss Vs Asheik Hussein	NC	Buxton
30/08/1968	Melwyn Riss Vs Asheik Hussein	NK	Holyhead
31/08/1968	Melwyn Riss Vs Dave Barrie	Riss won	Rhyl, Wales
16/09/1968	Melwyn Riss & Steve Best Vs Mick McMichael & Alan Colbeck	McMichae et al won	Brierly Hill

Date	Match	Result	Venue
01/10/1968	Melwyn Riss Vs Alan Wood	Wood won	Solihull, West Midlands
04/10/1968	Melwyn Riss Vs Alan Wood	NK	Dumfries
14/11/1968	Melwyn Riss Vs Al Nicol	Riss won	Nelson
18/11/1968	Melwyn Riss Vs Peter Preston	Riss won	Blackpool, England
20/11/1968	Melwyn Riss Vs Jack Fallon	NK	Coedpoeth
05/12/1968	Melwyn Riss Vs Dave Barrie	NK	Brierly Hill
10/12/1968	Melwyn Riss Vs Steve Best	Riss won	Spalding
07/01/1969	Melwyn Riss Vs Steve Best	Riss won	Oakengates
10/01/1969	Melwyn Riss & Terry Downs Vs The Terriers	Terriers won	Dumfries
06/02/1969	Melwyn Riss Vs Asheik Hussein	NK	Nelson
14/02/1969	Melwyn Riss Vs Alan Wood	Wood won	Malvern
10/03/1969	Melwyn Riss Vs Joe Keegan	Riss won	Altrincham
11/04/1969	Melwyn Riss Vs Bobby Ryan	Riss won	Bolton, Lancashire
15/04/1969	Melwyn Riss Vs Dave Barrie	Barrie won	Solihull, West Midlands
27/06/1969	Melwyn Riss Vs Jim McKenzie	NK	Dumfries
02/09/1969	Melwyn Riss Vs Alan Wood	Wood won	Solihull, West Midlands
11/09/1969	Melwyn Riss Vs Alan Wood	Wood won	Malvern
29/10/1969	Melwyn Riss Vs Sabu	Riss won	Buxton, England
14/11/1969	Melwyn Riss Vs Jackie Robinson	NK	Dumfries

Francis Sullivan (Alan Latham)

Date	Match	Outcome	Venue
13/01/1950	Francis Sullivan Vs Taffy Jones	NK	Hereford
03/02/1950	Francis Sullivan Vs Rik St. Just	NK	Hereford, England
01/03/1950	Francis Sullivan Vs Ron Jackson	NK	Belle Vue, Manchester
08/03/1950	Francis Sullivan Vs Pat Ryan	NK	Belle Vue, Manchester
22/03/1950	Francis Sullivan Vs Young Apollo	NK	Belle Vue, Manchester
04/04/1950	Francis Sullivan Vs Jack Atherton	NK	Rhyl, Wales
07/04/1950	Francis Sullivan Vs Lew Roseby	NK	Belle Vue, Manchester
26/04/1950	Francis Sullivan Vs Freddie Rex	NK	Belle Vue, Manchester
06/05/1950	Francis Sullivan Vs Louis Loew	NK	Belle Vue, Manchester
01/06/1950	Francis Sullivan Vs Johnny Douglas	NK	Rhyl, Wales
03/06/1950	Francis Sullivan Vs Neil McBride	NK	Belle Vue, Manchester
13/06/1950	Francis Sullivan Vs Ted Beckley	Sullivan Won TBDQ	Rhyl, Wales
21/06/1950	Francis Sullivan Vs Rene Bukovac	NK	Belle Vue, Manchester
12/08/1950	Francis Sullivan Vs Cab Cashford	NK	Belle Vue, Manchester
06/12/1950	Francis Sullivan Vs Charlie Fisher	Draw	Bognor Regis, England
07/12/1950	Francis Sullivan Vs Charlie Fisher	Charlie won	Beckenham, England
19/12/1950	Francis Sullivan Vs Mike Marino	NK	Kingston, England
03/01/1951	Francis Sullivan Vs Dave Armstrong	Armstrong won	Paddington, London
04/01/1951	Francis Sullivan Vs Jim Anderson	Jim won	Beckenham, England
04/01/1951	Francis Sullivan Vs Jim Anderson	Jim won	Beckenham, England
05/01/1951	Francis Sullivan Vs Jim Anderson	Anderson won	Beckenham, England
25/01/1951	Francis Sullivan Vs Arthur Beaumont	Arthur won	Beckenham, England
01/03/1951	Francis Sullivan Vs Jim Anderson	Francis won	Bury, England
15/03/1951	Francis Sullivan Vs Len Britton	Draw	Beckenham, England
27/03/1951	Francis Sullivan Vs Mike Marino	Francis won	Kingston, England
04/04/1951	Francis Sullivan Vs Bob Robinson	Bob won	Worthing, England
04/04/1951	Francis Sullivan Vs Bob Robinson	Bob won	Worthing, England
06/04/1951	Francis Sullivan Vs Tommy Pye	NK	Liverpool, England
10/04/1951	Francis Sullivan Vs Don Steadman	NK	Colchester, England
26/04/1951	Francis Sullivan Vs Charles Fisher	NK	Southampton, England
03/05/1951	Francis Sullivan Vs Val Cerino	NK	Southampton, England
01/06/1951	Francis Sullivan Vs Emile Poilve	NK	Liverpool, England
07/06/1951	Francis Sullivan Vs The Ghoul	Ghoul won	Morecambe, Lancashire
29/06/1951	Francis Sullivan Vs Emile Poilve	NK	Liverpool, England
03/08/1951	Francis Sullivan Vs Alf Cadman	NK	Plymouth, England
04/08/1951	Francis Sullivan Vs Lew Roseby	Roseby won	Belle Vue, Manchester
07/08/1951	Francis Sullivan Vs Johnny Douglas	NK	Rhyl, Wales
21/08/1951	Francis Sullivan Vs Johnny Douglas	NK	Rhyl, Wales
24/08/1951	Francis Sullivan Vs Emile Poilve	NK	Liverpool, England
02/10/1951	Francis Sullivan Vs Len Britton	Len won	Swindon, England
03/10/1951	Francis Sullivna Vs Bob Robinson	NK	Cambridge, England
13/10/1951	Francis Sullivan Vs Tommy Mann	Tommy won	Manchester, England

Date	Match	Result	Venue
13/11/1951	Francis Sullivan Vs Lew Roseby	Lew won, FS DQ	Lime Grove, London
26/11/1951	Francis Sullivan Vs Johnny Doulas	Francis won	Edinburgh, Scotland
03/12/1951	Francis Sullivan Vs Alf Cadman	NK	Blackpool, England
14/12/1951	Francis Sullivan Vs Tommy Mann	NK	Liverpool, England
22/02/1952	Francis Sullivan Vs Tommy Mann	NK	Liverpool, England
28/02/1952	Francis Sullivan Vs Dennis Mithcell	Francis won	Morecambe, Lancashire
03/03/1952	Francis Sullivan Vs Norman Walsh	NC	Leeds, England
18/03/1952	Francis Sullivan Vs Francis St Clair Gregory	Gregory won	Aberdeen, Scotland
27/03/1952	Francis Sullivan Vs Mike Marino	Francis won	Kingston, England
28/04/1952	Francis Sullivan & Lew Roseby Vs Alf Cadman & Norman Walsh	Alf & Norman won	Leeds, England
30/04/1952	Francis Sullivan Vs Don Mendoza	NK	Belle Vue, Manchester
22/05/1952	Francis Sullivan Vs Reg Williams	NK	Norwich, England
31/05/1952	Francis Sullivan Vs Ron Harrison	Ron won	Manchester, England
27/06/1952	Francis Sullivan Vs Dai Sullivan	NK	Liverpool, England
18/07/1952	Francis Sullivan Vs Neil McBride	NK	Manchester, England
19/07/1952	Francis Sullivan Vs Billy Joyce	NK	Costa Green, Birmingham
28/08/1952	Francis Sullivan Vs Earl McGrath	Earl won	Morecambe, Lancashire
06/09/1952	Francis Sullivan Vs Rex Reagan	NK	Bury, England
13/09/1952	Francis Sullivan Vs Brendan Moriarty	NK	Hanley, England
02/10/1952	Francis Sullivan Vs Francis St Clair Gregory	NK	Bristol, England
03/10/1952	Francis Sullivan Vs Count Bartelli	NK	Willenhall, England
04/10/1952	Francis Sullivan Vs Rex Reagan	NK	Peterborough, England
16/10/1952	Francis Sullivan Vs Jack Fay	Francis won	Morecambe, Lancashire
20/10/1952	Francis Sullivan Vs Joe Hill	Joe won	Leeds, England
25/10/1952	Francis Sullivan Vs Jim Anderson	NK	Hanley, England
01/11/1952	Francis Sullivan Vs Vic Stewart	NK	Kings Lynn, England
06/11/1952	Francis Sullivan Vs Charles Fisher	NK	Southampton, England
07/11/1952	Francis Sullvian Vs Masambula	NK	Willenhall, England
14/11/1952	Francis Sullivan Vs Emile Poilve	NK	Liverpool, England
29/11/1952	Francis Sullivan Vs Chic Knight	NK	Hanley, England
01/12/1952	Francis Sullivan Vs Jackie Faye	Jackie won	Aberdeen, Scotland
01/12/1952	Francis Sullivan Vs Mike Demitre	Mike won	Aberdeen, Scotland
12/12/1952	Francis Sullivan Vs Emile Poilve	NK	Liverpool, England
05/01/1953	Francis Sullivan Vs Ernie Riley	Ernie won	Blackpool, England
16/05/1953	Francis Sullivan Vs Masmbula	NK	Liverpool, England
22/05/1953	Francis Sullivan Vs Arthur Belshaw	NK	Liverpool, England
03/07/1953	Francis Sullivan Vs Arthur Belshaw	NK	Liverpool, England
10/09/1953	Francis Sullivan Vs Jim Anderson	Jim won	Morecambe, Lancashire
08/01/1954	Francis Sullivan Vs Alan Wilson	NK	Levenshulme
16/01/1954	Francis Sullivan Vs Tomas Riandi	NK	Willenhall
25/01/1954	Francis Sullivan Vs Ron Johnson	Ron won	Edinburgh, Scotland
05/02/1954	Francis Sullivan Vs Emile Poilve	NK	Liverpool, England
06/02/1954	Francis Sullivan Vs Geoff Portz	NK	Hanley
11/03/1954	Francis Sullivan Vs Jack Keegan	Jack won	Morecambe, Lancashire
15/03/1954	Francis Sullivan Vs Count Bartelli	Count won	Leeds, England

Date	Match	Result	Location
22/03/1954	Francis Sullivan Vs Spencer Churchill	Spencer won	Edinburgh, Scotland
03/04/1954	Francis Sullivan Vs Ted Beech	NK	New Brighton
09/04/1954	Francis Sullivan Vs Martin Conroy	NK	Willenhall
04/06/1954	Francis Sullivan Vs Tony Mancelli	NK	Levenshulme
18/06/1954	Francis Sullivan Vs Martin Conroy	NK	Levenshulme
19/06/1954	Francis Sullivan Vs Tiger Shark	NK	New Brighton
06/07/1954	Francis Sullivan Vs Jim Breen	NK	Douglas, Isle of Man
09/07/1954	Francis Sullivan Vs Count Bartelli	NK	Levenshulme
10/09/1954	Francis Sullivan Vs Billy Howes	NK	Manchester
08/10/1954	Francis Sullivan Vs Les Kellett	NK	Liverpool, England
01/11/1954	Francis Sullivan Vs Tony Vallon	NK	Worcester
06/01/1955	Francis Sullivan Vs Masambula	NK	Liverpool, England
10/01/1955	Francis Sullivan Vs Rex Harrison	NK	Blackpool, England
11/01/1955	Francis Sullivan Vs Geoff Portz	Francis won	Lime Grove, England
15/01/1955	Francis Sullivan Vs Don Mendoza	Francis won	Middlesborough, North Yorkshire
22/01/1955	Francis Sullivan Vs Johnny Allan	NK	Hanley
04/02/1955	Francis Sullivan Vs Francis Gregory	Gregory won	Leicester, England
05/02/1955	Francis Sullivan Vs Tommy Robinson	Francis won	Newcastle, England
11/02/1955	Francis Sullivan Vs Ted Beech	NK	Willenhall
25/02/1955	Francis Sullivan Vs Eric Taylor	NK	Altrincham
25/02/1955	Francis Sullivan Vs Emil Foy	NK	Willenhall
04/03/1955	Francis Sullivan Vs Alf Cadman	NK	Liverpool, England
05/03/1955	Francis Sullivan Vs Ernie Smith	Sullivan won	Newcastle, England
17/03/1955	Francis Sullivan Vs Ray Apollon	Apollon won	Wimbledon, England
01/04/1955	Francis Sullivan Vs Les Kellett	NK	Liverpool, England
02/04/1955	Francis Sullivan Vs Tommy Pye	Francis won	Middlesborough, North Yorkshire
07/04/1955	Francis Sullivan Vs Martin Conroy	NK	Willenhall
14/05/1955	Francis Sullivan Vs Sandy Orford	Sandy won	Middlesborough, North Yorkshire
14/05/1955	Francis Sullivan Vs Sandy Orford	Orford won	Middlesborough, England
21/05/1955	Francis Sullivan Vs Rex Harrison	Francis won	Newcastle, England
28/05/1955	Francis Sullivan Vs Spencer Churchill	NK	Hanley
04/06/1955	Francis Sullivan Vs Sandy Orford	Sandy won	Middlesborough, North Yorkshire
11/06/1955	Francis Sullivan Vs Masambula	NK	Hanley
02/07/1955	Francis Sullivan Vs Tomas Riandi	NK	New Brighton
08/07/1955	Francis Sullivan Vs Shirley Crabtree	NK	Liverpool, England
09/07/1955	Francis Sullivan Vs Rex Harrison	Francis won	Middlesborough, North Yorkshire
16/07/1955	Francis Sullivan Vs Terence Ricardo	Francis won	Newcastle, England
06/08/1955	Francis Sullivan Vs Sandy Orford	Sandy won	Newcastle, England
20/08/1955	Francis Sullivan Vs Martin Conroy	NK	New Brighton
23/08/1955	Francis Sullivan Vs Ghoul	Ghoul won	Douglas, Isle of Man
27/08/1955	Francis Sullivan Vs Les Kellett	NK	New Brighton
03/09/1955	Francis Sullivan Vs Alan Garfield	Francis won	Newcastle, England
03/09/1955	Francis Sullivan Vs Ray Hunter	Ray won	Newcastle, England
16/09/1955	Francis Sullivan Vs Billy Howes	NK	Manchester, England

Date	Match	Result	Location
17/09/1955	Francis Sullivan Vs Masambula	NK	Hanley
14/10/1955	Francis Sullivan Vs Tommy Pye	NK	Liverpool, England
15/10/1955	Francis Sullivan Vs Johnny Kwango	Sullivan won	Hanley
29/10/1955	Francis Sullivan Vs Ray Apollon	Francis won	Middlesborough, North Yorkshire
07/11/1955	Francis Sullivan Vs Alf Cadman	Francis won	Edinburgh, Scotland
11/11/1955	Francis Sullivan Vs Ray Apollon	Ray won	Glasgow, Scotland
10/12/1955	Francis Sullivan Vs Rex Harrison	Francis won	Middlesborough, North Yorkshire
16/12/1955	Francis Sullivan Vs Francis Gregory	Francis S won	Glasgow, Scotland
23/12/1955	Francis Sullivan Vs Johnny Allan	NK	Willenhall
30/12/1955	Francis Sullivan Vs Don Mendoza	Don won	Liverpool, England
31/12/1955	Francis Sullivan Vs Johnny Alln	Francis won	Middlesborough, North Yorkshire
17/01/1956	Francis Sullivan Vs Ernest Baldwin	Ernest held the Lord Mountevans Challenge Belt	Lime Grove Baths, Shepherd's Bush, London
20/01/1956	Francis Sullivan Vs Norman Walsh	Sullivan won	Glasgow, Scotland
21/01/1956	Francis Sullivan Vs Tony Vallon	Vallon won	Hanley
23/01/1956	Francis Sullivan in KO Tournament	NK	Altrincham
27/01/1956	Francis Sullivan Vs Emile Poilve	NK	Willenhall
03/02/1956	Francsis Sullivan Vs Tony Mancelli	Tony won	Liverpool, England
09/02/1956	Francis Sullivan Vs Anton Vargas	NK	Nottingham, England
10/02/1956	Francis Sullivan Vs Marty Jacobs	Francis won	Glasgow, Scotland
14/02/1956	Francis Sullivan Vs Gwyn Davies	Gwyn won	Lime Grove, England
18/02/1956	Francis Sullivan Vs Ali Riza Bey	Francis won	Middlesborough, North Yorkshire
20/02/1956	Francis Sullivan Vs Tommy Tucker	NK	Blackpool, England
25/02/1956	Francis Sullivan Vs Masambula	Masambula won	Newcastle, England
27/02/1956	Francis Sullivan Vs Gwyn Davies	Gwyn won	Leeds, West yorkshire
06/03/1956	Francis Sullivan Vs Gwyn Davies	Francis won	Lime Grove, London
10/03/1956	Francis Sullivan Vs Masambula	Masambula won	Middlesborough, North Yorkshire
20/03/1956	Francis Sullivan	Billy Won	Hamilton, Scotland
29/03/1956	Francis Sullvian Vs Don Stedman	NK	Wimbledon, England
31/03/1956	Frances Sullivan Vs Masambula	Francis won	Newcastle, England
31/03/1956	Francis Sullivan Vs Horst Hoffman	NK	Hanley
07/04/1956	Francis Sullivan Vs Tony Vallon	Vallon won	Hanley
13/04/1956	Francis Sullivan Vs Alf Cadman	NK	Liverpool, England
17/04/1956	Francis Sullivan Vs Norman Walsh	Francis won	Dundee, Scotland
23/04/1956	Francis Sullivan Vs Judo Al Hayes	Draw	Leeds, West yorkshire
05/05/1956	Ernie Riley & Francis Sullivan Vs John Grant & Masambula	Ernie & Francis won	Middlesborough, North Yorkshire
11/05/1956	Francis Sullivan Vs John Grant	Francis won	Glasgow, Scotland
18/05/1956	Francis Sullivan Vs Bill McDonald	NK	Liverpool, England
26/05/1956	Francis Sullivan Vs Johnny Allan	Sullivan won	Newcastle, England
02/06/1956	Francis Sullivan Vs Mike Marino	NC	Middlesborough, North Yorkshire
04/06/1956	Francis Sullivan Vs Les Kellett	Les won	Edinburgh, Scotland
16/06/1956	Francis Sullivan Vs Masambula	Francis won	Middlesborough, North Yorkshire
21/06/1956	Francsi Sullivan Vs Ernest Baldwin	Ernest won	Morecambe, Lancashire
23/06/1956	Francis Sullivan Vs Mike Marino	mike won	Newcastle, England

Date	Match	Result	Location
09/07/1956	Francis Sullivan Vs Masambula	Masambula won	Leeds, West yorkshire
13/07/1956	Francis Sullivan Vs Alf Cadman	NK	Liverpool, England
14/07/1956	Francis Sullivan Vs Don Mendoza	Mendoza won	New Brighton
21/07/1956	Francis Sullivan Vs The Ghoul	The ghoul won	Newcastle, England
23/07/1956	Francis Sullivan Vs Paul Kowalik	Paul won	Edinburgh, Scotland
24/07/1956	Francis Sullivan Vs The Ghoul	Ghoul won	Douglas, Isle of Man
04/08/1956	Francis Sullivan Vs Mike Marino	Francis won, Mike DQ	Newcastle, England
18/08/1956	Francis Sullivan Vs Norman Walsh	Walsh won, FS Inj	New Brighton
25/08/1956	Francis Sullivan Vs Mike Marino	Mike won	Middlesborough, North Yorkshire
30/08/1956	Francis Sullivan Vs Jim Hussey	NK	Wimbledon, England
08/09/1956	Francis Sullivan Vs Dave Armstrong	Dave won	Newcastle, England
10/09/1956	Francis Sullivan Vs Tommy Kilmartin	Francis won	Edinburgh, Scotland
21/09/1956	Francis Sullivan Vs Johnny Yearsley	Sullivan won	Liverpool, England
29/09/1956	Francis Sullivan Vs Cyril Morris	Francis won	Middlesborough, North Yorkshire
12/10/1956	Francis Sullivan Vs Billy Joyce	Sullivan won	Glasgow, Scotland
15/10/1956	Francis Sullivan Vs Robert Mcdonald	Robert won	Leeds, West yorkshire
17/10/1956	Francis Sullivan Vs Reg Williams	Draw	Lincoln, Lincolnshire
28/10/1956	Francis Sullivan Vs Billy Howes	NK	Blackpool, England
12/11/1956	Francis Sullivan Vs Buddy Cody	Francis won	Leeds, West yorkshire
30/11/1956	Francis Sullivan Vs Billy Joyce	Francis won	Glasgow, Scotland
04/12/1956	Francis Sullivan Vs Sandy Orford	NK	Lime Grove, London
07/12/1956	Francis Sullivan Vs Black Kwango	Francis won	Belfast, Ireland
07/01/1957	Francis Sullivan Vs Black Butcher Johnson	NK	Derby, England
08/01/1957	Francis Sullivan Vs Ossie Mueller	Sullivan won	Hull, England
18/01/1957	Frances Sullivan Vs Billy Howes	Draw	Glasgow, Scotland
24/01/1957	Francis Sullivan Vs Leong Lee Fu	NK	Blackburn, England
25/01/1957	Francis Sullivan Vs Dean Stockton	Francis won	Liverpool, England
31/01/1957	Francis Sullivan Vs Billy Joyce	NK	Nottingham, England
06/02/1957	Francis Sullivan Vs Dave McLean	Francis won	Dundee, Scotland
13/02/1957	Francis Sullivan Vs Tumac Amaru	Tumac won	Lincoln, Lincolnshire
20/02/1957	Francis Sullivan Vs Rudi Schumacher	Sullivan won	Grimsby, England
13/03/1957	Francis Sullivan Vs Don Mendoza	Don won	Glasgow, Scotland
24/04/1957	Francis Sullivan Vs Mario Matassa	Mario won	Lincoln, Lincolnshire
27/04/1957	Francis Sullivan in KO tournament	NK	Luton, London
25/05/1957	Francis Sullvian Vs Kid Zamboa	NK	Blackpool, England
01/06/1957	Francis Sullivan Vs Gordon Nelson	NK	Belle Vue, Manchester
29/06/1957	Francis Sullivan Vs Masambula	Masambula won	Blackpool, England
20/07/1957	Francis Sullivan Vs Billy Joyce	Billy Won	Middlesborough, North Yorkshire
02/08/1957	Francis Sullivan Vs Masambula	Masambula won	Liverpool, England
03/08/1957	Francis Sullivan Vs Jim Hussey	Draw	Newcastle, England
10/08/1957	Francis Sullivan Vs Ernest Baldwin	NC	Middlesborough, North Yorkshire
24/08/1957	Francis Sullivan Vs Ken Davies	Francis won	Middlesborough, North Yorkshire
30/08/1957	Francis Sullivan Vs Alf Cadman	Alf won	Dudley, England
07/09/1957	Francis Sullivan Vs Billy Joyce	Francis won	Newcastle, England

Date	Match	Result	Venue
21/09/1957	Raschid Anwar, Adjit Singh & Dara Singh Vs Francis Sullivan, Eric Taylor & Bill Verna	NC	Leeds, England
12/10/1957	Francis Sullivan Vs Rex Gable	NK	Belle Vue, Manchester
19/10/1957	Francis Sullivan Vs Alan Garfield	Garfield won FS Inj	Hanley
25/10/1957	Francis Sullivan Vs Reg Williams	NK	Willenhall
08/11/1957	Francis Sullivna Vs Gordon Nelson	NK	Chesterfield, England
20/11/1957	Francis Sullivan Vs Ernie Baldwin	NK	Harringay
30/11/1957	Francis Sullivan Vs Milo Popocopolis	Milo won	Hanley
01/12/1957	Francis Sullivan Vs Mike Marino	Francis won	Kingston, England
06/12/1957	Francis Sullivan Vs Norman Walsh	NK	Leicester, England
11/12/1957	Francis Sullivan Vs Milo Popocopolis	NK	Grimsby, England
08/01/1958	Francis Sullivan Vs Les Kellett	NK	Sheffield, England
13/01/1958	Francis Sullivan Vs Jamie Dula	NK	Blackpool, England
17/01/1958	Rocky' Francis Sullivan Vs Bud Cody	Bud won	Willenhall, England
25/01/1958	Francis Sullivan Vs Don Mendoza	NK	Shrewsbury, England
01/02/1958	Francis Sullivan Vs Bill Coverdale	Sullivan won	Newcastle, England
03/02/1958	Francis Sullivan Vs Terence Ricardo	Terence won	Leeds, England
05/02/1958	Francis Sullivan Vs Jack Beaumont	NK	Scunthorpe, England
25/02/1958	Francis Sullivan Vs Francis Gregory	NK	Lime Grove, England
26/02/1958	Francis Sullivan Vs Tony Mancelli	NK	Brighton, England
03/03/1958	Francis Sullivan Vs Billy Howes	NK	Seymour Hall, London
14/03/1958	Francis Sullivan Vs Jean Morandi	Francis won	Liverpool, England
21/03/1958	Francis Sullivan Vs Bill kenton	Bill won	Willenhall, England
21/03/1958	Francis Sullivna Vs Bill Robinson	Robinson won	Willenhall, England
23/03/1958	Francis Sullivan Vs Ernie Baldwin	NK	NK
23/03/1958	Francis Sullivan Vs Ski Hi Lee	Francis won	Bristol, England
27/03/1958	Francis Sullivan Vs Tony Mancelli	NK	Wimbledon, England
04/04/1958	Francis Sullivan Vs Reg Williams	NK	Chesterfield, England
05/04/1958	Francis Sullivan Vs Bert Craddock	Francis won	Middlesborough, North Yorkshire
08/04/1958	Francis Sullivan Vs Bill Robinson	Francis won	Lime Grove, England
15/04/1958	Francis Sullivan Vs Gordon Nelson	Francis won	Lime Grove, England
25/04/1958	Francis Sullivan Vs Billy Joyce	NK	Brierley
05/05/1958	Francis Sullivan Vs Masambula	NK	Kirkby, Ashfield
06/05/1958	Francis Sullivan Vs Arthur Ricardo	NK	Wakefield, England
24/05/1958	Francis Sullivan Vs Masambula	NK	Blackpool, England
31/05/1958	Francis Sullivan Vs Charles Fisher	Francis won	Newcastle, England
06/06/1958	Francis Sullivan Vs Archie Popplewell	Sullivan won	Redruth, England
07/06/1958	Francis Sullivan Vs Jack Beaumont	NK	Rhyl, North Wales
19/06/1958	Francis Sullivan Vs Alec Bray	NK	Hulme
28/06/1958	Francis Sullivan Vs Daula Singh	Francis won	Newcastle, England
04/07/1958	Francis Sullivan Vs Masambula	NK	Bolton, England
12/07/1958	Francis Sullivan Vs Johnny Allan	Johnny won	Middlesborough, North Yorkshire
17/07/1958	Francis Sullivan Vs Terry Ricardo	NK	Hulme
19/07/1958	Francis Sullivan Vs Alec Bray	NK	Rhyl, North Wales
26/07/1958	Francis Sullivan Vs Bill Robinson	NK	Middlesborough, England
08/08/1958	Francis Sullivan Vs Bill Kenton	NK	Bolton, England

Date	Match	Result	Location
14/08/1958	Francis Sullivan Vs Emile Poilve	NK	Hulme
16/08/1958	Francis Sullivan Vs Alf Rawlings	Alf won	Newcastle, England
30/08/1958	Francis Sullivan Vs Josef Zaranoff	Josef won	Wellington, England
05/09/1958	Francis Sullivan Vs Emile Poilve	NK	Bolton, Lancashire
11/09/1958	Francis Sullivan Vs Gwyn Davies	NK	Blackburn, England
13/09/1958	Francis Sullivan Vs Masambula	Masambula won	Newcastle, England
14/09/1958	Francis Sullivan vs Emile Poilve	Francis won	Birmingham, England
14/09/1958	Francis Sullivan Vs Billy Howes	Billy won	Birmingham, England
21/09/1958	Francis Sullivan Vs Alan Garfield	NK	Brighton, England
02/10/1958	Francis Sullivan Vs Emile Poilve	NK	Hulme
10/10/1958	Francis Sullivan Vs Terry Ricardo	NK	Dumfries, Scotland
16/10/1958	Francis Sullivan Vs Alf Cadman	NK	Hulme
18/10/1958	Francis Sullivan Vs Ernie Riley	Ernie won	Shrewsbury, England
21/10/1958	Francis Sullivan Vs Alf Rawlings	NK	Wakefield, England
23/10/1958	Francis Sullivan Vs Dai Sullivan	NK	Blackburn, England
29/10/1958	Francis Sullivan Vs Ernie Riley	NK	Dudley, England
01/11/1958	Francis Sullivan Vs Francis Gregory	Gregory won	Shrewsbury, England
01/11/1958	Francis Sullivan Vs Alf Rawlings	Alf won	Wakefield, England
06/11/1958	Francis Sullivan Vs Alf Cadman	NK	Hulme
07/11/1958	Francis Sullivan Vs Albert Wall	Francis won	Willenhall, England
11/11/1958	Francis Sullivan Vs Emile Poilve	NK	Birmingham, England
17/11/1958	Francis Sullivan Vs Tony Vallon	NK	Altrincham
25/11/1958	Francis Sullivan Vs Johnny Czeslaw	NK	Wakefield, England
09/12/1958	Francis Sullivan Vs Francis Gregory	Gregory won	Wolverhampton, West Midlands
13/12/1958	Francis Sullivan Vs Rudi Schumacher	Francis won	Newcastle, England
16/12/1958	Francis Sullivan Vs Nikki Selenkowich	NK	Wakefield, England
19/12/1958	Francis Sullivan Vs Alf Cadman	Francis won	Liverpool, England
21/12/1958	Francis Sullivan Vs Bill Coverdale	Bill won	Birmingham, England
30/12/1958	Francis Sullivan Vs Bob McDonald	Bob won	Birmingham, England
02/01/1959	Francis Sullivan Vs Doug Joyce	Joyce won	Willenhall
03/01/1959	Francis Sullivan Vs Masambula	Masambula won	Shrewsbury, England
10/01/1959	Francis Sullivan Vs Don Mendoza	Don won	Middlesborough, North Yorkshire
11/01/1959	Francis Sullivan Vs Eric Taylor	Francis won	Birmingham, England
29/01/1959	Francis Sullivan Vs Vic Stewart	NK	Stretford, England
31/01/1959	Francis Sullivan Vs Peter Deakin	Sullivan won	Hanley
13/02/1959	Francis Sullivan Vs Cyril Morris	Francis won	Willenhall, England
14/02/1959	Francis Sullivan Vs Cyril Morris	NK	Doncaster, England
19/02/1959	Francis Sullivan Vs Jim Hart	NK	Stretford, England
20/02/1959	Francis Sullivan Vs Norman Walsh	Norman won, FS DQ	Willenhall, England
21/02/1959	Francis Sullivan Vs Emile Poilve	Draw	Shrewsbury, England
21/02/1959	Francis Sullivan Vs Gordon Nelson	Gordon won	Shrewsbury, England
23/02/1959	Francis Sullivan Vs Saxon Smith	NK	Sutton, Ashfield
27/02/1959	Francis Sullivan Vs Alf Cadman	Alf won	Willenhall, England
27/02/1959	Francis Sullivan Vs Dean Stockton	Sullivan won	Willenhall
04/03/1959	Francis Sullivan Vs Dave Armstrong	NK	Newcastle, England

Date	Match	Result	Location
05/03/1959	Francis Sullivan Vs Saxon Smith	NK	Hulme
07/03/1959	Francis Sullivan Vs Don Mendoza	NK	Belle Vue, Manchester
10/03/1959	Francis Sullivan Vs Arthur Ricardo	Arthur won	Birmingham, England
13/03/1959	Francis Sullivan Vs Alec Bray	Alec won	Willenhall, England
14/03/1959	Francis Sullivan Vs Alec Bray	NK	Shrewsbury, England
18/03/1959	Francis Sullivan Vs Tony Vallon	Tony won	Smethwick, England
21/03/1959	Francis Sullivan Vs Vic Stewart	Stewart won	Hanley
28/03/1959	Francis Sullivan Vs Jim Hart	NK	Dudley, England
02/04/1959	Francis Sullivan Vs Dave Armstrong	Dave won	Camberwell, England
02/04/1959	Francis Sullivan Vs Jim Hart	NK	Hulme
07/04/1959	Francis Sullivan Vs Bill Rawlings	Nk	Wakefield, England
10/04/1959	Francis Sullivan Vs Vic Stewart	NK	Bolton, Lancashire
13/04/1959	Francis Sullivan Vs Eugene Steczycki	NK	Seymour Hall, London
18/04/1959	Francis Sullivan Vs Bill Robinson	NK	Alfreton
20/04/1959	Francis Sullivan Vs George Harris	Sullivan won	Loughborough, England
21/04/1959	Francis Sullivan Vs Emile Poilve	Francis won	Birmingham, England
23/04/1959	Francis Sullivan Vs Cyril Morris	NK	Hulme
25/04/1959	Francis Sullivan & Dai Sullivan & Arthur Ricardo Vs Alf, Bill & Jim Rawlings	Rawlings won	Middlesborough, North Yorkshire
19/05/1959	Francis Sullivan Vs Jim Rawlings	NK	Wakefield, England
23/05/1959	Francis Sullivan Vs Reg Williams	Sullivan won	Hanley
23/05/1959	Francis Sullivan Vs Vic Stewart	Stewart won	Hanley
29/05/1959	Francis Sullivan Vs Dean Stockton	NK	Dudley, England
05/06/1959	Francis Sullivan Vs Frank O'Donnell	NK	Bolton, Lancashire
11/06/1959	Francis Sullivan Vs Alf Cadman	NK	Hulme
13/06/1959	Francis Sullivan Vs Jim hart	NK	NK
18/06/1959	Francis Sullivan Vs Bill Robinson	Robinson won	Morecambe, Lancashire
30/06/1959	Francis Sullivan Vs Saxon Smith	NK	Bridlington
16/07/1959	Francis Sullivan Vs Ernie Riley	NK	Hulme
18/07/1959	Francis Sullivan Vs Piet Slabbett	Sullivan won	Hanley
23/07/1959	Francis Sullivan Vs Johnny Allan	Allan won	Morecambe, Lancashire
30/07/1959	Francis Sullivan Vs Bill Robinson	Draw	Morecambe, Lancashire
26/08/1959	Francis Sullivan Vs Tony Mancelli	NK	Withernsea
28/08/1959	Francis Sullivan Vs Seamus Dunlevy	NK	Bolton, Lancashire
18/09/1959	Francis Sullivan Vs Seamus Dunlevy	NK	Bolton, Lancashire
19/09/1959	Francis Sullivana Vs Emile poilve	Poilve won	Hanley
24/09/1959	Francis Sullivan Vs Jim hart	Nk	Hulme
30/09/1959	Francis Sullivan Vs Kurt Wenzl	Nk	Sheffield, England
03/10/1959	Francis Saullivan Vs Eric Leiderman	NK	Belle Vue, Manchester
06/10/1959	Francis Sullivan Vs Saxon Smith	Sullivan won	Birmingham, England
14/10/1959	Francis Sullivan Vs Bill Robinson	NK	Sheffield, South Yorkshire
15/10/1959	Francis Sullivan Vs Bill Robinson	NK	Morecambe, Lancashire
23/10/1959	Francis Sullivan Vs Emile Poilve	Nk	Liverpool, England
04/11/1959	Francis Sullivan Vs Saxon Smith	Nk	Scunthorpe, England
12/11/1959	Francis Sullivan Vs Alf Cadman	NK	Hulme
13/11/1959	Francis Sullvian Vs Saxon Smith	NK	Bolton, Lancashire

28/11/1959	Francis Sullivan Vs Steve Logan	Nk	Belle Vue, Manchester
01/12/1959	Francis Sullivan Vs Wilson Sheppard	Sullivan won	Wakefield, England
04/12/1959	Francis Sullivan Vs Ray Webster	NK	Bolton, Lancashire
09/12/1959	Francis Sullivan Vs Masambula	NK	Scunthorpe
10/12/1959	Francis Sullivan Vs Ernie Derbyshire	NK	Hulme
11/12/1959	Francis Sullivan Vs Billy Howes	NK	Rotherham
26/12/1959	Francis Sullivan Vs Bert Royal	NK	Bolton, Lancashire
28/12/1959	Francis Sullivan Vs Ron johnson	NK	Sutton, Ashfield
04/01/1960	Francis Sullivan Vs Bill Robinson	NK	Leeds, West yorkshire
05/01/1960	Francis Sullivan Vs Geoff Portz	NK	Huddersfield, England
07/01/1960	Francis Sullivan Vs Emile Poilve	NK	Hulme
08/01/1960	Francis Sullivan Vs Sandy Orford	NK	Rotherham, England
12/01/1960	Francis Sullivan Vs Jim Rawlings	NK	Scarborough, England
13/01/1960	Francis Sullivan Vs Billy Two Rivers	Billy won	Lincoln, England
15/01/1960	Francis Sullivan Vs Johnny Allan	NK	Leicester, England
15/01/1960	Francis Sullivan Vs Billy Two Rivers	NK	Chesterfield, England
18/01/1960	Francis Sullivan Vs Count Bartelli	NK	Derby, England
20/01/1960	Francis Sullivan Vs Achim Chall	Francis won	Bath, England
22/01/1960	Francis Sullivan Vs Hassan Ali Bey	NK	Bradford, England
23/01/1960	Francis Sullivan Vs Joe Cornelius	Sullivan won	Newcastle, England
29/01/1960	Francis Sullivan Vs Sandy Orford	NK	Leicester, England
30/01/1960	Francis Sullivan Vs Johnny Czeslaw	NK	Hanley
05/02/1960	Francis Sullivan Vs Vittorio Ochoa	NK	Bradford, England
06/02/1960	Francis Sullivan Vs Bill Rawlings	NK	Middlesborough, England
09/02/1960	Francis Sullivan Vs Masambula	NK	Trowell
11/02/1960	Francis Sullivan Vs Pedro Bengochea	NK	Barrow, England
13/02/1960	Francis Sullivan Vs Laurent Baranyi	NK	Middlesborough, England
15/02/1960	Francis Sullivan Vs Billy Two Rivers	NK	Leeds, England
16/02/1960	Francis Sullivan Vs Spencer Churchill	NK	Bridlington, England
18/02/1960	Francis Sullivan Vs Vic Stewart	NK	Hulme
23/02/1960	Francis Sullivan Vs Johnny Allan	NK	Wakefield, England
24/02/1960	Francis Sullivan Vs Billy Howes	NK	Shoreditch
27/02/1960	Francis Sullivan Vs Reg Williams	Williams won	Hanley
02/03/1960	Francis Sullivan Vs Remy Bayle	NK	Banbury
05/03/1960	Francis Sullivan Vs Billy Two Rivers	NK	Nottingham
05/03/1960	Francis Sullivan Vs Billy Two Rivers	Billy won	Nottingham, England
09/03/1960	Francis Sullivan Vs Eric Leiderman	NK	Preston, England
11/03/1960	Francis Sullivan Vs Cyril Morris	Sullivan won	Bradford, England
14/03/1960	Francis Sullivan Vs Vic Stewart	NK	Carlisle
15/03/1960	Francis Sullivan Vs Les Kellett	NK	Hull, England
17/03/1960	Francis Sullivan Vs Ray Webster	NK	Hulme
22/03/1960	Francis Sullivan Vs Ray Hunter	NK	Reading, England
24/03/1960	Francis Sullivan Vs Andraes Lambrakis	Sullivan won	Bristol, England
26/03/1960	Francis Sullivan Vs Gordon Nelson	NK	Luton, England
28/03/1960	Francis Sullivan Vs Norman Walsh	Sullivan inj	Hamilton, Scotland
29/03/1960	Francis Sullivan Vs Gordon Nelson	NK	Aberdeen, Scotland

Date	Match	Result	Location
31/03/1960	Francis Sullivan Vs Frank O'Donnell	NK	Leigh, Lancashire
08/04/1960	Francis Sullivan Vs The Mask	NK	Glasgow, Scotland
09/04/1960	Francis Sullivan Vs Peter Deakin	NK	Falkirk
11/04/1960	In KO Tournament	NK	Preston, England
12/04/1960	Francis Sullivan Vs Bill McDonald	NK	Wakefield, England
14/04/1960	Francis Sullivan Vs Ernie Riley	NK	Bradford, England
16/04/1960	Francis Sullivan Vs Ernie Riley	Riley won	Newcastle, England
18/04/1960	Francis Sullivan Vs Joe Cornelius	Cornelius won	Tunbridge Wells
20/04/1960	Francis Sullivan Vs Billy Howes	Draw	Albert Hall, London
21/04/1960	Francis Sullivan Vs Ray Apollon	Ray won	Bristol, England
22/04/1960	Francis Sullivan Vs Mike Marino	Marino won	Ipswich, England
25/04/1960	Francis Sullivan Vs Bill Rawlings	NK	Preston, England
28/04/1960	Francis Sullivan Vs Alf Rawlings	NK	Nelson
30/04/1960	Francis Sullivan Vs Bill Rawlings	NK	Middlesborough, England
03/05/1960	Francis Sullivan Vs Peter Deakin	Deakin won	Purley
04/05/1960	Francis Sullivan Vs Dave Armstrong	Draw	Cardiff, Wales
05/05/1960	Francis Sullivan Vs Gordon Nelson	Sullivan won	Peterborough, England
07/05/1960	Francis Sullivan Vs Charlie Fisher	Sullivan won	Coventry, England
09/05/1960	Francis Sullivan Vs Geoff Portz	Portz won	Loughborough, England
12/05/1960	Francis Sullivan Vs Nikki Selenkowich	Sullivan won	Barrow, England
14/05/1960	Francis Sullivan Vs Don Mendoza	Draw	Newcastle, England
15/05/1960	Francis Sullivan Vs Peter Kaiser	NK	Folkestone
17/05/1960	Francis Sullivan Vs Nikki Selenkowich	Sullivan won	Purley
18/05/1960	Francis Sullivan Vs Kiwi Kingston	NK	Dunstable
19/05/1960	Francis Sullivan Vs Doug Joyce	NK	Walthamstow
21/05/1960	Francis Sullivan Vs George Gordienko	NK	Luton, England
23/05/1960	Francis Sullivan Vs Bill McDonald	NK	York, England
24/05/1960	Francis Sullivan Vs Franz Orlik	NK	Scarborough, England
25/05/1960	Francis Sullivan Vs Masambula	Draw	Lincoln, England
26/05/1960	Francis Sullivan Vs Cyril Morris	NK	Hulme
28/05/1960	Francis Sullivan Vs Colin Williamson	NK	Middlesborough, England
31/05/1960	Francis Sullivan Vs Iskha Kham	Draw	Purley
31/05/1960	Francis Sullivan & Frank O'Donnell Vs Alf & Bill Rawlings	NK	Leicester, England
04/06/1960	Francis Sullivan Vs Bill McDonald	NK	Belle Vue, Manchester
07/06/1960	Francis Sullivan Vs John DaSilva	NK	Welling
08/06/1960	Francis Sullivan Vs Peter Deakin	NK	Hove
11/06/1960	Francis Sullivan Vs Digger Rowell	Draw	Coventry, England
12/06/1960	Francis Sullivan Vs Alec Bray	NK	Dudley, England
14/06/1960	Francis Sullivan Vs Johnny Czeslaw	Czeslaw won	Birmingham, England
16/06/1960	Francis Sullivan Vs Vic Stewart	NK	Hulme
17/06/1960	Francis Sullivan Vs Johnny Czeslaw	NK	Bolton, England
18/06/1960	Francis Sullivan Vs Rocky Wall	NK	Doncaster, England
04/07/1960	Francis Sullivan Vs Bill McDonald	NK	York, England
07/07/1960	Francis Sullivan Vs Gwyn Davies	NK	Scarborough, England
12/07/1960	Francis Sullivan Vs Norman Walsh	Draw	Purley

Date	Match	Result	Location
15/07/1960	Francis Sullivan Vs Rocky Wall	Sullivan won	Bradford, England
16/07/1960	Francis Sullivan Vs Gwyn Davies	NK	Middlesborough, England
21/07/1960	Francis Sullivan Vs Seamus Dunleavy	NK	Hulme
23/07/1960	Francis Sullivan Vs Gwyn Davies	NK	Belle Vue, Manchester
03/08/1960	Francis Sullivan & Eric Taylor Vs Alf Cadman & Frank O'Donnell	NK	Grimsby, England
04/08/1960	Francis Sullivan Vs Billy Howes	NK	Scarborough, England
06/08/1960	Francis Sullivan Vs Frank O'Donnell	NK	Middlesborough, England
08/08/1960	Francis Sullivan Vs Alf Cadman	NK	Skegness, England
09/08/1960	Francis Sullivan Vs Bert Royal	Draw	Birmingham, England
12/08/1960	Francis Sullivan Vs Bobby Graham	NK	Bolton, England
18/08/1960	Francis Sullivan Vs Alf Cadman	NK	Scarborough, England
20/08/1960	Francis Sullivan Vs Reg Williams	NK	Newcastle, England
22/08/1960	Francis Sullivan Vs John Lees	NK	Colwyn Bay, Wales
23/08/1960	Francis Sullivan Vs Eric Liederman	NK	Aberdeen, Scotland
25/08/1960	Francis Sullivan Vs Les Kellett	Sullivan won	Morecambe, Lancashire
26/08/1960	Francis Sullivan Vs Eric Liederman	NK	Fleetwood
30/08/1960	Francis Sullivan Vs Doug Joyce	NK	Welling
01/09/1960	Francis Sullivan Vs Michael Allary	NK	Southampton, England
02/09/1960	Francis Sullivan Vs Michael Allary	Sullivan won	Northampton, England
04/09/1960	Francis Sullivan Vs Frank Hurley	Sullivan won	Brighton, England
07/09/1960	Francis Sullivan Vs Josef Zaranoff	Draw	Cardiff, Wales
12/09/1960	Francis Sullivan Vs Bendy	NK	Leeds, England
13/09/1960	Francis Sullivan Vs Ernie Riley	NK	Wakefield, England
15/09/1960	Francis Sullivan Vs Ernie Baldwin	Baldwin won	Morecambe, Lancashire
17/09/1960	Francis Sullivan & Frank o'Donnell Vs Bert Royal & Eric Taylor	NK	Blackburn, England
19/09/1960	Francis Sullivan Vs Bill McDonald	NK	Carlisle
21/09/1960	Francis Sullivan Vs Iskha Khan	Khan won	Royal Albert Hall, London
23/09/1960	Francis Sullivan Vs Johnny Allan	NK	Glasgow, Scotland
24/09/1960	Francis Sullivan Vs Bob Sweeney	NK	Falkirk
27/09/1960	Francis Sullivan Vs Rocky Wall	Wall won	Wakefield, England
30/09/1960	Francis Sullivan Vs Harry Fields	NK	Bolton, England
01/10/1960	Francis Sullivan Vs Rocky Wall	NK	Middlesborough, England
06/10/1960	Francis Sullivan Vs Bilyl Two Rivers	NK	Barrow, England
10/10/1960	Francis Sullivan Vs Johnny Allan	NK	Worcester, England
12/10/1960	Francis Sullivan Vs George Gordienko	George won	Bath, England
12/10/1960	Francis Sullivan Vs George Gordienko	Gordienko won	Bath, England
13/10/1960	Francis Sullivan Vs Gordon Nelson	Draw	Beckenham, England
17/10/1960	Francis Sullivan Vs Josef Zaranoff	NK	Leeds, England
18/10/1960	Francis Sullivan Vs Roman Wanniek	NK	Hull
24/10/1960	Francis Sullivan Vs Gwyn Davies	Davies won	Hamilton, Scotland
26/10/1960	Francis Sullivan Vs Les Kellett	NK	Sheffield, England
28/10/1960	Francis Sullivan Vs Rocky Wall	NK	Glasgow, Scotland
02/11/1960	Francis Sullivan Vs Mathias Rosges	NK	Sheffield, England
03/11/1960	Francis Sullivan Vs Pierre Angellini	NK	Nottingham, England
04/11/1960	Francis Sullivan Vs Johnny Allan	NK	Glasgow, Scotland

Date	Match	Result	Venue
05/11/1960	Francis Sullivan Vs Felix Lamban	NK	Belle Vue, Manchester
09/11/1960	In KO Tournament	NK	Hove
12/11/1960	Francis Sullivan Vs Mike Marino	Sullivan won	Camberwell
14/11/1960	Francis Sullivan Vs Harry Fields	NK	Bradford, England
19/11/1960	Francis Sullivan Vs Ian Campbell	NK	Falkirk
21/11/1960	Francis Sullivan Vs Toni Olivera	NK	York, England
22/11/1960	Francis Sullivan Vs Bill Rawlings	NK	Wakefield, England
24/11/1960	Francis Sullivan Vs Reg Williams	NK	Nottingham, England
25/11/1960	Francis Sullivan Vs Jamie Olivera	NK	Glasgow, Scotland
26/11/1960	Francis Sullivan Vs Jim Rawlings	NK	Chesterfield
29/11/1960	Francis Sullivan Vs Felix Lamban	Sullivan won	Hull, England
01/12/1960	Francis Sullivan Vs Frank O'Donnell	NK	Barrow, England
03/12/1960	Francis Sullivan Vs Johnny Czeslaw	NK	Shrewsbury, England
05/12/1960	Francis Sullivan Vs Vic Hessle	NK	Bradford, England
08/12/1960	Francis Sullivan Vs Johnny Apollo	NK	Hulme
09/12/1960	Francis Sullivan Vs Johnny Allan	NK	Leicester, England
10/12/1960	Francis Sullivan Vs Gwyn Davies	Sullivan won	Middlesborough, England
12/12/1960	Francis Sullivan Vs Gordon Nelson	NK	Aylesbury
19/12/1960	Francis Sullivan Vs Reg Williams	NK	Bradford, England
23/12/1960	Francis Sullivan Vs Eric Taylor	NK	Leicester, England
24/12/1960	Francis Sullivan Vs Gwyn Davies	Gwyn won	Middlesborough, North Yorkshire
26/12/1960	Francis Sullivan & Dean Stockton Vs Cadmans	NK	Hanley
29/12/1960	Francis Sullivan Vs Reg Williams	NK	Rotherham, England
31/12/1960	Francis Sullivan Vs Gwyn Davies	Sullivan won	Newcastle, England
02/01/1961	Francis Sullivan Vs Bob Sweeney	NK	York, England
04/01/1961	Francis Sullivan Vs Rudi Martinez	NK	Preston, England
06/01/1961	Francis Sullivan & Steve Logan Vs Al Hayes & Ray Hunter	NK	Leicester, England
07/01/1961	Francis Sullivan Vs Bill Rawlings	Sullivan won	Middlesborough, England
12/01/1961	Francis Sullivan Vs Kurt Stein	Stein won	Bristol, England
14/01/1961	Francis Sullivan Vs Kurt Stein	NK	Coventry, England
16/01/1961	Francis Sullivan Vs Gordon Nelson	NK	Leeds, England
17/01/1961	Francis Sullivan Vs Al Hayes	Sullivan won	Purley
18/01/1961	Francis Sullivan Vs Bill Robinson	NK	Sheffield, South Yorkshire
21/01/1961	Francis Sullivan Vs Kenny Hogan	NK	Shrewsbury, England
24/01/1961	Francis Sullivan Vs Billy Joyce	NK	Lime Grove, London
27/01/1961	Francis Sullivan Vs Bob Sweeney	NK	Bradford, England
30/01/1961	Francis Sullivan Vs Francis St Clair Gregory	NK	Hamilton, Scotland
31/01/1961	Francis Sullivan Vs Felix Lamban	NK	Bridlington, England
03/02/1961	Francis Sullivan Vs Arthur Ricardo	NK	Willenhall
07/02/1961	Francis Sullivan Vs Harry Fields	NK	Wakefield, England
08/02/1961	Francis Sullivan Vs Billy Howes	NK	Preston, England
10/02/1961	Francis Sullivan Vs Tony Mancelli	NK	Leicester, England
13/02/1961	Francis Sullivan Vs Herman Iffland	NK	Seymour Hall, London
14/02/1961	Francis Sullivan Vs Felix Lamban	NK	Purley
18/02/1961	Francis Sullivan Vs Herman Iffland	NK	Norwich, England

Date	Match	Result	Location
21/02/1961	Francis Sullivan Vs Sandy Orford	NK	Wakefield, England
22/02/1961	Francis Sullivan Vs Masambula	NK	Preston, England
24/02/1961	Francis Sullivan Vs Harry Fields	NK	Leicester, England
02/03/1961	Francis Sullivan Vs Franz Orlik	NK	Exeter
06/03/1961	Francis Sullivan Vs Masambula	Draw	Eltham
07/03/1961	Francis Sullivan Vs Billy Joyce	NK	Wakefield, England
08/03/1961	Francis Sullivan Vs Ernie Riley	NK	Preston, England
09/03/1961	Francis Sullivan Vs Norman Walsh	Sullivan won	Bristol, England
11/03/1961	Francis Sullivan Vs Masambula	NK	Middlesborough, England
13/03/1961	Francis Sullivan Vs Tony Mancelli	NK	Kilmarnock
14/03/1961	Francis Sullivan Vs Enrique Marquess	Sullivan won	Hull, England
15/03/1961	Francis Sullivan Vs Rocky Wall	NK	Sheffield, England
16/03/1961	Francis Sullivan Vs Barry Douglas	NK	Goole
18/03/1961	Francis Sullivan Vs Gordon Nelson	NK	Brighton, England
20/03/1961	Francis Sullivan Vs Jose Arroyo	NK	Catford
21/03/1961	Francis Sullivan Vs Gideon Gida	Draw	Welling
22/03/1961	Francis Sullivan Vs Al Hayes	NK	Cardiff, Wales
23/03/1961	Francis Sullivan Vs Ski Hi Lee	Sullivan won	Bristol, England
25/03/1961	Francis Sullivan Vs Gideon Gida	Gidea won	Coventry, England
27/03/1961	Francis Sullivan Vs Billy Joyce	Joyce won	Eltham
28/03/1961	Francis Sullivan Vs Bert Royal	NK	Lime Grove, London
31/03/1961	Francis Sullivan Vs Masambula	Sullivan won	Belle Vue, Manchester
14/04/1961	Francis Sullivan Vs Billy Joyce	NK	Bradford, England
15/04/1961	Francis Sullivan Vs Bobby Graham	Sullivan won	Newcastle, England
19/04/1961	Francis Sullivan Vs Johnny Allan	NK	Grimsby, England
22/04/1961	Francis Sullivan Vs John Lees	Sullivan won	Newcastle, England
24/04/1961	Francis Sullivan Vs Eric Liederman	NK	Preston, England
27/04/1961	Francis Sullivan Vs Dean Stockton	NK	Hulme
28/04/1961	Francis Sullivan Vs Seamus Dunleavy	NK	Bolton, England
29/04/1961	Francis Sullivan Vs Arthur Ricardo	Sullivan won	Newcastle, England
06/05/1961	Francis Sullivan Vs Billy Two Rivers	NK	Wembley, London
08/05/1961	Francis Sullivan Vs Hans Streiger	NK	York, England
09/05/1961	Francis Sullivan Vs Bob Sweeney	NK	Aston
10/05/1961	Francis Sullivan Vs John Lees	NK	Lanwrst
12/05/1961	Francis Sullivan Vs Ernie Riley	NK	Bradford, England
13/05/1961	Francis Sullivan Vs Bobby Graham	Sullivan won	Newcastle, England
15/05/1961	Francis Sullivan Vs Rocky Wall	NK	Leeds, England
17/05/1961	Francis Sullivan Vs Reg Williams	NK	Sheffield, England
20/05/1961	Francis Sullivan Vs Black Mask	Mask won	Newcastle, England
21/05/1961	Francis Sullivan Vs Alf Cadman	NK	Dudley, England
22/05/1961	Francis Sullivan Vs Dennis Mitchell	Sullivan won	Purley
24/05/1961	Francis Sullivan Vs Gordon Nelson	Nelson won	Royal Albert Hall, London
28/05/1961	Francis Sullivan Vs Josef Zaranoff	NK	Folkestone
03/06/1961	Francis Sullivan Vs Alf Cadman	Sullivan won	Glasgow, Scotland
08/06/1961	Francis Sullivan Vs Martin Contoy	NK	Hulme
09/06/1961	Francis Sullivan Vs Bob Sweeney	NK	Bolton, England

Date	Match	Result	Location
11/06/1961	Francis Sullivan Vs Dave Armstrong	NK	Dudley, England
13/06/1961	Francis Sullivan Vs Tony Mancelli	NK	Welling
14/06/1961	Francis Sullivan Vs John Lees	Sullivan won	Cardiff, Wales
15/06/1961	Francis Sullivan Vs Ray Apollon	Apollon won	Bristol, England
16/06/1961	Francis Sullivan Vs Matthias Rogers	Sullivan won	Felixstowe
17/06/1961	Francis Sullivan Vs Bernard Vignall	NK	Luton, England
21/06/1961	Francis Sullivan Vs Bill McDonald	Sullivan won BM DQ	Sheffield, England
22/06/1961	Francis Sullivan Vs Ian Campbell	Sullivan won ICDQ	Morecambe, Lancashire
26/06/1961	Francis Sullivan Vs Ian Campbell	Campbell won	Hamilton, Scotland
27/06/1961	Francis Sullivan Vs Reg Williams	NK	Aberdeen, Scotland
28/06/1961	Francis Sullivna Vs Johnny Allan	NK	Sheffield, England
01/07/1961	Francis Sullivan Vs Gordon Kilmartin	NK	Newcastle, England
03/07/1961	Francis Sullivan Vs Ray Apollon	NK	Edmonton
04/07/1961	Francis Sullivan Vs Johnny Czeslaw	NK	Purley
05/07/1961	Francis Sullivan Vs Baron Von Heczy	NK	Exeter
06/07/1961	Francis Sullivan Vs Josef Zaranoff	NK	Worthing
10/07/1961	Francis Sullivan Vs Doug Joyce	NK	Leeds, England
14/07/1961	Francis Sullivan Vs Dean Stockton	Sullivan won	Bolton, England
15/07/1961	Francis Sullivan Vs Bert Royal	NK	Middlesborough, England
18/07/1961	Francis Sullivan Vs Ramon Napolitano	NK	Weymouth
19/07/1961	Francis Sullivan Vs Eric Liederman	Sullivan won	Great Yarmouth, England
20/07/1961	Francis Sullivan Vs Martin Contoy	Conroy won	Hulme
22/07/1961	Francis Sullivan Vs Eric Liederman	Sullivan won	Newcastle, England
28/07/1961	Francis Sullivan Vs Don Branch	NK	Chester, England
30/07/1961	Francis Sullivan Vs Josef Zaranoff	NK	Brighton, England
31/07/1961	Francis Sullivan Vs Josef Zaranoff	NK	Skegness
02/08/1961	Francis Sullivan Vs Tony Mancelli	Sullivan won	Felixstowe
03/08/1961	Francis Sullivan Vs Alan Garfield	NK	Dunstable
04/08/1961	Francis Sullivan Vs Doug Joyce	Draw	Barking
05/08/1961	Francis Sullivan Vs Buddy Cody	NK	Soham
09/08/1961	Francis Sullivan Vs Norman Walsh	Walsh won	Great Yarmouth, England
11/08/1961	Francis Sullivan Vs Dean Stockton	Sullivan won	Bolton, England
12/08/1961	Francis Sullivan Vs Reg Williams	NK	Belle Vue, Manchester
14/08/1961	Francis Sullivan Vs Alf Rawlings	NK	Scarborough, England
17/08/1961	Francis Sullivan Vs Jim Rawlings	NK	Rhyl, Wales
19/08/1961	Francis Sullivan Vs Digger Rowell	Sullivan won	Newcastle, England
19/08/1961	Francis Sullivan Vs Bob Sweeney	Sullivan won	Newcastle, England
21/08/1961	Francis Sullivan Vs Ernie Riley	Draw	Hamilton, Scotland
22/08/1961	Francis Sullivan Vs Johnny Allan	NK	Aberdeen, Scotland
25/08/1961	Francis Sullivan Vs Ernie Riley	Riley won	Belfast, Ireland
26/08/1961	Francis Sullivan Vs Eric Taylor	Taylor won	Middlesborough, England
28/08/1961	Francis Sullivan Vs Johnny Allan	NK	York, England
29/08/1961	Francis Sullivan Vs Bob Sweeney	NK	Bridlington, England
31/08/1961	Francis Sullivan Vs Baron Von Heczy	NK	Scarborough, England
01/09/1961	Francis Sullivan Vs Johnny Allan	Draw	Glasgow, Scotland
02/09/1961	Francis Sullivan Vs Clayton Thomson	NK	Acton

Date	Match	Result	Location
07/09/1961	Francis Sullivan Vs George Gordienko	NK	Worthing
09/09/1961	Francis Sullivan Vs Jamie Dula	NK	Coventry, England
11/09/1961	Francis Sullivan Vs Jim Grosert	Sullivan won	Shoreditch
13/09/1961	Francis Sullivan Vs Earl Maynard	NK	Aberystwyth, Wales
19/09/1961	Francis Sullivan Vs Gordon Kilmartin	NK	Bridlington, England
20/09/1961	Francis Sullivan Vs Sheik Wadih Ayoub	NK	Sheffield, England
21/09/1961	Francis Sullivan Vs Arthur Jackson	NK	Morecambe, Lancashire
23/09/1961	Francis Sullivan Vs Norman Walsh	NK	Stirling
26/09/1961	Francis Sullivan Vs Gerry DeJaegar	NK	Swindon, England
29/09/1961	Francis Sullivan Vs Johnny Yearsley	Sullivan won	Taunton, England
30/09/1961	Francis Sullivan Vs Bill Verna	NK	Norwich, England
05/10/1961	Francis Sullivan Vs Colin Williamson	NK	Scarborough, England
09/10/1961	Francis Sullivan Vs Vic Stewart	NK	York, England
14/10/1961	Francis Sullivan Vs Dennis Mitchell	NK	Middlesborough, England
16/10/1961	Francis Sullivan Vs Alf Rawlings	NK	Halifax, England
17/10/1961	Francis Sullivan Vs Bob Sweeney	Sullivan won	Huddersfield, England
18/10/1961	Francis Sullivan Vs Billy Howes	Sullivan BHDQ	Lincoln, England
19/10/1961	Francis Sullivan Vs Jamie Dula	Sullivan won	Coventry, England
20/10/1961	Francis Sullivan Vs Sandy Scott	Sullivan won	Glasgow, Scotland
21/10/1961	Francis Sullivan Vs Sheik Wadih Yousseff	NK	Falkirk
23/10/1961	Francis Sullivan Vs Chief Maretana	NK	Bradford, England
25/10/1961	Francis Sullivan Vs Ian Campbell	Campbell won	Watford, England
26/10/1961	Francis Sullivan Vs Gomez Maximilliano	NK	Southampton, England
28/10/1961	Francis Sullivan Vs Great Togo	NK	Norwich, England
30/10/1961	Francis Sullivan Vs Mike Marino	NK	Carlisle, England
31/10/1961	Francis Sullivan Vs Frank O'Donnell	Sullivan won	Hull
01/11/1961	Francis Sullivan Vs Earl Maynard	Sullivan won	Scunthorpe
03/11/1961	Francis Sullivan Vs George Gordienko	Gordienko won	London
13/11/1961	Francis Sullivan Vs Ernie Riley	Sullivan won	Hamilton, Scotland
14/11/1961	Francis Sullivan Vs Emile Poilve	NK	Bridlington, England
21/11/1961	Francis Sullivan Vs Johnny Morgan	Sullivan won	Lime Grove, London
22/11/1961	Francis Sullivan Vs Josef Zaranoff	NK	Preston, England
24/11/1961	Francis Sullivan Vs Dave Armstrong	Armstrong won	Glasgow, Scotland
25/11/1961	Francis Sullivan Vs Seamus Dunleavy	Sullivan won	Belle Vue, Manchester
27/11/1961	Francis Sullivan Vs Great Togo	NK	Bradford, England
28/11/1961	Francis Sullivan Vs Johnny Czeslaw	Draw	Plymouth
01/12/1961	Francis Sullivan Vs Dino Bravo	NK	Eltham
08/12/1961	Francis Sullivan Vs Axel Dieter	NK	Streatham
09/12/1961	Francis Sullivan Vs Axel Dieter	Sullivan won	Brighton, England
12/12/1961	Francis Sullivan Vs Jim Rawlings	NK	Huddersfield, England
13/12/1961	Francis Sullivan Vs Willem Hall	NK	Lemington
14/12/1961	Francis Sullivan Vs Hans Streiger	NK	Kirkcaldy
15/12/1961	Francis Sullivan Vs Billy Two Rivers	Rivers won	Glasgow, Scotland
16/12/1961	Francis Sullivan Vs Sandy Orford	Orford won	Bolton, England
16/12/1961	Francis Sullivan Vs Billy Two Rivers	Rivers won	Belle Vue, Manchester
19/12/1961	Francis Sullivan Vs Digger Rowell	Nk	Aberdeen, Scotland

Date	Match	Result	Venue
22/12/1961	Francis Sullivan Vs Roy Bull Davis	Sullivan won	Streatham
29/12/1961	Francis Sullivan Vs Gerry DeJaegar	Sullivan won	Ipswich, England
01/01/1962	Francis Sullivan Vs Earl Maynard	NK	Leeds, England
03/01/1962	Francis Sullivan Vs Barry Douglas	NK	Sheffield, England
06/01/1962	Francis Sullivan Vs Eric Liederman	Sullivan won	Newcastle, England
08/01/1962	Francis Sullivna Vs Dino Bravo	Sullivan won	Weston Super Mare
11/01/1962	Francis Sullivan Vs Doug Joyce	Sullivan won	Walthamstow
12/01/1962	Francis Sullivan Vs Bobo Matu	Sullivan won	Belfast, Ireland
13/01/1962	Francis Sullivan Vs Frankie Townsend	NK	Norwich, England
18/01/1962	Francis Sullivan Vs Jim Rawlings	NK	Blackburn, England
22/01/1962	Francis Sullivan Vs Gomez Maximilliano	NK	Wembley, England
24/01/1962	Francis Sullivan Vs Roy Bull Davis	NK	Shoreditch
27/01/1962	Francis Sullivan Vs Josef Kovacs	NK	Luton, England
29/01/1962	Francis Sullivan & Alan Dennison Vs Enriqe Marquess & Bernard Murray	Marquess et al won	Leeds, England
31/01/1962	Francis Sullivan Vs Reg Williams	NK	Sheffield, England
05/02/1962	Francis Sullivan Vs El Saaddee Mansourri	NK	Margate
08/02/1962	Francis Sullivan Vs Dino Bravo	Sullivan won	Weston Super Mare
09/02/1962	Francis Sullivan Vs Josef Kovacs	NK	Rochester
10/02/1962	Francis Sullivan Vs Gomez Maximilliano	NK	Brighton
12/02/1962	Francis Sullivan Vs Vic Stewart	NK	Leicester, England
13/02/1962	Francis Sullivan Vs Joe Cornelius	NK	Lime Grove, London
16/02/1962	Francis Sullivan Vs Clay Thomson	NC	Glasgow, Scotland
17/02/1962	Francis Sullivan Vs Masambula	Masambula won	Belfast, Ireland
19/02/1962	Francis Sullivan Vs Bert Nuttall	Sullivan won	Hamilton, Scotland
21/02/1962	Francis Sullivan Vs Masambula	Masambula won	Belfast, Ireland
24/02/1962	Francis Sullivan Vs Iskha Khan	NK	Coventry, England
02/03/1962	Francis Sullican Vs Johnny Allan	NK	Bermondsey
03/03/1962	Francis Sullivan Vs Great Togo	NK	Belle Vue, Manchester
05/03/1962	Francis Sullivan Vs Willem Hall	Sullivan won	Leeds, England
07/03/1962	Francis Sullivan Vs Apachee Arnaize	NK	Preston, England
08/03/1962	Francis Sullivan Vs The monster	NK	Kirkcaldy
12/03/1962	Francis Sullivan Vs Vic Hessle	NK	Buxton, England
13/03/1962	Francis Sullivan Vs Ernie Riley	Riley won	Kidderminster
15/03/1962	Francis Sullivan Vs Les Kellett	NK	Rotherham
17/03/1962	Francis Sullivan Vs Eric Taylor	NK	Lime Grove, London
20/03/1962	Francis Sullivan Vs Bob Sweeney	NK	Lime Grove, London
21/03/1962	Francis Sullivan Vs Roy Bull Davis	NK	Acton
22/03/1962	Francis Sullivan Vs Tug Holton	NK	Hayes
23/03/1962	Francis Sullivan Vs Roy Bull Davis	NK	Leicester, England
24/03/1962	Francis Sullivan Vs Reg Williams	Draw	Newcastle, England
30/03/1962	Francis Sullivan Vs Dino Bravo	Sullivan won	Streatham
31/03/1962	Francis Sullivan Vs Al Jarmain	NK	Tottenham
02/04/1962	Francis Sullivan Vs Max Crabtree	NK	Leeds, England
07/04/1962	Francis Sullivan & Peters Vs Lucky Simonivich & Dutch Zorro	Sullivan et al won, others DQ	Brighton
11/04/1962	Francis Sullivan Vs Rocco Colombo	Colombo won	Royal Albert Hall, London

Date	Match	Result	Venue
12/04/1962	Francis Sullivan Vs Horst Hoffman	NK	Poplar
14/04/1962	Francis Sullivan Vs Lucky Simonovich	NK	Southall
18/04/1962	Francis Sullivan Vs Steve Logan	NK	Winchester
19/04/1962	Francis Sullivan Vs Joe Cornelius	NK	Westbury
20/04/1962	Francis Sullivan Vs Bob Sweeney	Sullivan won	Belle Vue, Manchester
21/04/1962	Francis Sullivan Vs George Gordienko	NK	Brighton
01/05/1962	Francis Sullivan Vs Roy Bull Davis	NK	Colchester, England
04/05/1962	Francis Sullivan Vs Bill Rawlings	Draw	Glasgow, Scotland
07/05/1962	Francis Sullivan Vs The Mask	Mask won	Falkirk
08/05/1962	Francis Sullivan Vs Johnny Allan	NK	Hamilton, Scotland
09/05/1962	Francis Sullivan Vs Bobby Graham	NK	Aberdeen, Scotland
11/05/1962	Francis Sullivan Vs Rocky Wall	NK	Chesterfield, England
12/05/1962	Francis Sullivan Vs Ernie Riley	Sullivan won	Belle Vue, Manchester
14/05/1962	Francis Sullivan Vs Bill Verna	NK	Cheltenham
15/05/1962	Francis Sullivan Vs Charlie Fisher	NK	Purley
16/05/1962	Francis Sullivan Vs Bruno Elrington	Sullivan won BE DQ	Cardiff, Wales
17/05/1962	Francis Sullivan Vs Iskha Khan	Sullivan won	Peterborough, England
18/05/1962	Francis Sullivan Vs Bruno Elrington	NK	Rochester
23/05/1962	Francis Sullivan Vs Bobby Graham	NK	Sheffield, England
25/05/1962	Francis Sullivan Vs Vic Stewart	Draw	Glasgow, Scotland
26/05/1962	Francis Sullivan Vs Jim Armstrong	Draw	Middlesborough, England
29/05/1962	Francis Sullivan Vs Ian Campbell	Campbell won	Peckham, England
30/05/1962	Francis Sullivan Vs Bruno Elrington	Sullivan won	Banbury
31/05/1962	Francis Sullivan Vs Max Crabtree	NK	Walthamstow
02/06/1962	Francis Sullivan Vs Navarro Moyans	NK	Barking Assembly Hall
08/06/1962	Francis Sullivan Vs Jean Morandi		Liverpool, England
09/06/1962	Francis Sullivan Vs The Monster	NK	Portsmouth, England
11/06/1962	Francis Sullivan Vs Gwyn Davies	Davies won	Belle Vue, Manchester
13/06/1962	Francis Sullivan Vs Billy Howes	NK	Sheffield, England
15/06/1962	Francis Sullivan Vs Johnny Czeslaw	NK	Rochester
18/06/1962	Francis Sullivan Vs Mihalyi Kuti	Sullivan won	Bedford, England
19/06/1962	Francis Sullivan Vs Mario Matassa	NK	Worthing
23/06/1962	Francis Sullivan Vs Charlie Fisher	NK	Gravesend
24/06/1962	Francis Sullivan Vs Johnny Yearsley	Sullivan won JYDQ	Brighton
25/06/1962	Francis Sullivan Vs Josef Zaranoff	NK	Cheltenham
27/06/1962	Francis Sullivan Vs Josef Zaranoff	Zaranoff won	Cardiff, Wales
28/06/1962	Francis Sullivan Vs Tibor Szakacs	Szakacs won	Peterborough
30/06/1962	Francis Sullivan Vs Johnny Yearsley	NK	Southall
02/07/1962	Francis Sullivan Vs Ian Campbell	Campbell won	Shoreditch
03/07/1962	Francis Sullivan Vs Josef Zaranoff	NK	Weymouth
04/07/1962	Francis Sullivan Vs Max Crabtree	Crabtree won	Oxford, England
05/07/1962	Francis Sullivan Vs Max Crabtree	NK	Torquay, England
07/07/1962	Francis Sullivan Vs Bernard Vignall	Sullivan won	Barking
17/07/1962	Francis Sullivan Vs Billy Howes	NK	Bridlington, England
19/07/1962	Francis Sullivan Vs Barry Douglas	NK	Morecambe, Lancashire
20/07/1962	Francis Sullivan Vs Bill McDonald	McDonald won	Glasgow, Scotland

Date	Match	Result	Venue
21/07/1962	Francis Sullivan Vs Gerry DeJaegar	Sullivan won	Belle Vue, Manchester
28/07/1962	Francis Sullivan Vs Gordon Kilmartin	Sullivan won	Newcastle, England
01/08/1962	Francis Sullivan Vs Doug Joyce	Joyce won	Purley
04/08/1962	Francis Sullivan Vs Reg Williams	Sullivan won	Belle Vue, Manchester
06/08/1962	Francis Sullivan Vs Masambula	NK	Hamilton, Scotland
07/08/1962	Francis Sullivan Vs Bill McDonald	McDonald won FSinjured	Aberdeen, Scotland
09/08/1962	Francis Sullivan Vs Bill McDonald	NK	Morecambe, Lancashire
10/08/1962	Francis Sullivan Vs Masambula	NK	Withernsea
11/08/1962	Francis Sullivan Vs Bill McDonald	NK	Middlesborough, England
12/08/1962	Francis Sullivan & Don Mendoza Vs Frank Hurley & Johnny Yearsley	NK	Brighton, England
13/08/1962	Francis Sullivan Vs Ray Apollon	Apollon won	Catford
15/08/1962	Francis Sullivan Vs Seamus Dunleavy	Sullivan won	Carlyon Bay
16/08/1962	Francis Sullivan Vs Josef Zaranoff	NK	Torquay, England
18/08/1962	Francis Sullivan Vs Ray Apollon	NK	Great Yarmouth, England
20/08/1962	Francis Sullivan Vs Tibor Szakacs	NK	Wembley
22/08/1962	Francis Sullivan Vs Max Crabtree	NK	Deal
24/08/1962	Francis Sullivan Vs Ezzard Hart	NK	Glasgow, Scotland
28/08/1962	Francis Sullivan & Dai Sullivan Vs Bob Sweeney & Reg Williams	NK	Bridlington, England
02/09/1962	Francis Sullivan Vs Billy Howes	Draw	Brighton
03/09/1962	Francis Sullivan Vs John DaSilva	DaSilva won	Tunbridge Wells
04/09/1962	Francis Sullivan Vs Frank Hurley	NK	Peckham, England
06/09/1962	Francis Sullivan Vs Bill Rawlings	NK	Morecambe, Lancashire
10/09/1962	Francis Sullivan Vs Syed Saif Shah	NK	Weston Super Mare
12/09/1962	Francis Sullivan Vs Johnny Czeslaw	NK	Dorking
15/09/1962	Francis Sullivan Vs Bruno Elrington	Elrington won	Newcastle, England
22/09/1962	Francis Sullivan Vs Ray Apollon	NK	Norwich
01/10/1962	Francis Sullivan Vs arjit Singh	Sullivan won	Leeds, England
03/10/1962	Francis Sullivan Vs Leon Arras	Nk	Sheffield, England
04/10/1962	Francis Sullivan Vs Steve Bell	Nk	Morecambe, Lancashire
06/10/1962	Francis Sullivan Vs Steve Veidor	Sullivan won	Newcastle, England
09/10/1962	Francis Sullivan Vs Tibor Szakacs	Szakacs won	Plymouth, England
10/10/1962	Francis Sullivan Vs Steve Veidor	Sullivan won	Watford,
11/10/1962	Francis Sullivan Vs Ray Apollon	NK	Hounslow
12/10/1962	Francis Sullivan Vs Angelo Romeiro	NK	Rochester
13/10/1962	Francis Sullivan & Gerry DeJaegar Vs Johnny Yearsley &Frank Hurley	Yearsey & Hurley won	Brighton
15/10/1962	Francis Sullivan Vs Josef Zaranoff	NK	Seymour Hall, London
19/10/1962	Francis Sullivan Vs Ron Johnson	Sullivan won	Leicester, England
20/10/1962	Francis Sullivan Vs El Greco	Sullivan won	Newcastle, England
22/10/1962	Francis Sullivan Vs Antonio Morlans	NK	Kilmarnock
24/10/1962	Francis Sullivan Vs Johnny Allan	Draw	Scunthorpe
26/10/1962	Francis Sullivan Vs Frikki Alberta	NK	Rotherham
27/10/1962	Francis Sullivan Vs Ernie Riley	NK	Middlesborough, England
29/10/1962	Francis Sullivan Vs Gerry DeJaegar	NK	Cheltenham
30/10/1962	Francis Sullivan Vs Pedro Bengochea	Sullivan won	Bournemouth, England
01/11/1962	Francis Sullivan Vs Bruno Elrington	NK	Walthamstow

Date	Match	Result	Venue
02/11/1962	Francis Sullivan Vs Angelo Romeiro	NK	Bermondsey
03/11/1962	Francis Sullivan Vs Charles Fisher	NK	Wembley, London
10/11/1962	Francis Sullivan Vs Joe Cornelius	Cornelius won	Brighton, England
12/11/1962	Francis Sullivan & Leon Arras Vs Eric Liederman & Jesse Hodgson	NK	Bradford, England
17/11/1962	Francis Sullivan Vs The Legionaire	Legionaire won	Newcastle, England
19/11/1962	Francis Sullivan Vs Pedro Bengochea	Sullivan won	Catford
20/11/1962	Francis Sullivan Vs Prince Kumali	NK	Folkestone
21/11/1962	Francis Sullivan Vs Norman Walsh	NK	Sheffield, England
23/11/1962	Francis Sullivan Vs Jack Bence	NK	Bermondsey
26/11/1962	Francis Sullivan Vs The Professor	NK	Bradford, England
27/11/1962	Francis Sullivan Vs Jack Bence	NK	Colchester, England
01/12/1962	Francis Sullivan Vs The Legionaire	NC	Newcastle, England
03/12/1962	Francis Sullivan Vs Tony Mancelli	NK	Kettering
04/12/1962	Francis Sullivan Vs Jim Rawlings	Sullivan won	Hove
04/12/1962	Francis Sullivan Vs Eric Koltschak	Sullivan won	Hove
06/12/1962	Francis Sullivan Vs Dai Sullivan	Francis won	Wimbledon
07/12/1962	Francis Sullivan Vs Pietro Capello	Sullivan won	Rochester
10/12/1962	Francis Sullivan Vs Juan Tarres	Sullivan won	Leeds, England
11/12/1962	Francis Sullivan Vs Sandy Orford	Orford won	Plymouth, England
13/12/1962	Francis Sullivan Vs Tibor Szakacs	Szakacs won	Walthamstow
15/12/1962	Francis Sullivan Vs Horst Hoffman	NK	Camberwell
18/12/1962	Francis Sullivan Vs Tibor Szakacs	NK	Croydon
21/12/1962	Francis Sullivan Vs Roy Bull Davis	Sullivan won	Streatham
22/12/1962	Francis Sullivan Vs Charlie Fisher	Sullivan won	Brighton
04/01/1963	Francis Sullivan Vs Bill Verna	Sullivan won	Rochester
05/01/1963	Francis Sullivan Vs Eric Taylor	Taylor won	Newcastle, England
08/01/1963	Francis Sullivan Vs Charlie Fisher	NK	Finsbury Park
09/01/1963	Francis Sullivan Vs Quasimodo	Sullivan won QDQ	Cardiff, Wales
11/01/1963	Francis Sullivan Vs Roy Bull Davis	NK	Bermondsey
12/01/1963	Francis Sullivan Vs Seamus Dunleavy	NK	Luton, England
14/01/1963	Francis Sullivan Vs Josef Molnar	Sullivan won	Leeds, England
19/01/1963	Francis Sullivan Vs Don Mendoza	NK	Kings Lynn, London
21/01/1963	Francis Sullivan Vs George Gordienko	NK	Weston Super Mare
23/01/1963	Francis Sullivan Vs Jack Bence	Bence won	Great Yarmouth, England
24/01/1963	Francis Sullivan Vs Jack Bence	Sullivan won	Peterborough, England
25/01/1963	Francis Sullivan Vs Jack Bence	NK	Rochester
26/01/1963	Francis Sullivan Vs George Gordienko	NK	Camberwell
30/01/1963	Francis Sullivan Vs Les Kellett	Sullivan won	Cardiff, Wales
31/01/1963	Francis Sullivan Vs Henri Pierlot	Sullivan won	Bristol, England
04/02/1963	Francis Sullivan Vs Bruno Elrington	Elrington won	Tunbridge Wells
08/02/1963	Francis Sullivan Vs Jack Bence	NK	Bermondsey
15/02/1963	Francis Sullivan Vs Friki Alberta	Sullivan won	Streatham
16/02/1963	Francis Sullivan Vs Masambula	NK	Middlesborough, England
18/02/1963	Francis Sullivan Vs Mihalyi Kuti	NK	Wembley
19/02/1963	Francis Sullivan Vs Quasimodo	Sullivan won	Finsbury Park

Date	Match	Result	Location
20/02/1963	Francis Sullivan Vs Charlie Fisher	Sullivan won	Cardiff, Wales
20/02/1963	Francis Sullivan Vs John DaSilva	DaSilva won	Cardiff, Wales
21/02/1963	Francis Sullivan Vs Frikki Alberta	NK	Northampton, England
23/02/1963	Francis Sullivan Vs Lucky Simonovich	NK	Luton, England
27/02/1963	Francis Sullivan Vs Les Kellett	NK	Banbury
28/02/1963	Francis Sullivan Vs Jim Garner	Sullivan won	Bristol, England
01/03/1963	Francis Sullivan Vs Pietro Capello	Sullivan won	Barking
06/03/1963	Francis Sullivan Vs Mihalyi Kuti	NK	Hastings
07/03/1963	Francis Sullivan Vs Mihalyi Kuti	Sullivan won	Exeter, England
09/03/1963	Francis Sullivan Vs Syed Saif Shah	Draw	Barnet
11/03/1963	Francis Sullivan Vs Tony Cassio	NK	Leeds, England
13/03/1963	Francis Sullivan Vs Gideon Gida	NK	Kingston
15/03/1963	Francis Sullivan Vs Josef Zaranoff	NK	Rotherham
16/03/1963	Francis Sullivan Vs Karl Von Chenok	Sullivan won	Belle Vue, Manchester
18/03/1963	Francis Sullivan Vs Karl Von Chenok	Sullivan won	Tunbridge Wells
19/03/1963	Francis Sullivan Vs El Saaddee Mansourri	Sullivan won	Plymouth, England
20/03/1963	Francis Sullivan Vs Gideon Gida	Gidea won	Croydon
22/03/1963	Francis Sullivan Vs Tibor Szakacs	NK	Ventnor, Isle of Wight
23/03/1963	Francis Sullivan Vs Ray Apollon	NK	Eastbourne
25/03/1963	Francis Sullivan Vs Norman Walsh	NK	Kilmarnock
30/03/1963	Francis Sullivan Vs Willem Hall	Hall won	Belle Vue, Manchester
04/05/1963	Francis Sullivan Vs Frikki Alberta (KO)	NK	Wembley, London
17/09/1963	Francis Sullivan Vs Bill Robinson	NK	Bridlington
19/09/1963	Francis Sullivan Vs Billy Howes	NK	Barrow
28/10/1963	Francis Sullivan Vs Bill Robinson	NK	Carlisle, England
12/12/1963	Francis Sullivan Vs Bill Robinson	NK	Gloucester, England
14/12/1963	Francis Sullivan Vs Ernest Baldwin	Baldwin won Francis replaced Joyce	Lime Grove, Shepherd's Bush, London
08/01/1964	Francis Sullivan Vs Earl Maynard	NK	Croydon, London
11/01/1964	Francis Sullivan Vs George Drake	George Won	Bermondsey
04/01/1965	Francis Sullivan Vs Lee Sharron	NK	Derby
15/01/1965	Francis Sullivan Vs Syed Saif Shah	Syed won	Willenhall
16/01/1965	Francis Sullivan Vs Rocky Wall	Wall won	Newcastle, England
19/01/1965	Francis Sullivan Vs Zebra Kid	NK	Margate
20/01/1965	Francis Sullivan Vs Alan Garfield	Garfield won	Shoreditch
25/01/1965	Francis Sullivan Vs Billy Joyce	NK	Worcester, England
28/01/1965	Francis Sullivan Vs Jim Hussey	NK	Nelson
01/02/1965	Francis Sullivan Vs John Lees	NK	Derby
04/02/1965	Francis Sullivan Vs Ian Campbell	Campbell won	Malvern
08/02/1965	Francis Sullivan Vs Billy Joyce	NK	Worcester, England
13/02/1965	Francis Sullivan Vs Harry Kendall	NK	Preston, Lancashire
13/02/1965	Francis Sullivan Vs Dennis Mitchell	Mitchell won	Newcastle, England
01/03/1965	Francis Sullivan Vs Harry Fields	NK	Bradford
02/03/1965	Francis Sullivan Vs Josef Kovacs	NK	Dundee, Scotland
03/03/1965	Francis Sullivan Vs Ian Campbell	NK	Hindley
06/03/1965	Francis Sullivan Vs Terry Ricardo	NC	Newcastle, England

Date	Match	Result	Location
22/03/1965	Francis Sullivan Vs Billy Joyce	NK	Bradford
23/03/1965	Francis Sullivan Vs Josef Zaranoff	Draw	Lime Grove, London
27/03/1965	Francis Sullivan Vs Billy Joyce	Joyce won	Newcastle, England
08/04/1965	Francis Sullivan Vs Jim Hussey	NK	Nelson
12/04/1965	Francis Sullivan Vs Josef Zaranoff	Draw (DKO)	Carlisle
16/04/1965	Francis Sullivan & Jim Hart Vs Stewarts	Stewarts won	Bolton
29/04/1965	Francis Sullivan Vs Masambula	NK	Chester
08/05/1965	Francis Sullivan Vs Ernie Riley	NK	Doncaster
10/05/1965	Francis Sullivan Vs Reg Williams	NK	Leeds
12/05/1965	Francis Sullivan Vs Geoff Portz	Portz won	Sheffield, South Yorkshire
15/05/1965	Francis Sullivan Vs Syed Saif Shah	Syed won	Hanley
19/05/1965	Francis Sullivan & Les Kellett Vs Black Diamonds	NK	Hindley
14/06/1965	Francis Sullivan Vs Geoff Portz	NK	Leeds
19/06/1965	Francis Sullivan Vs Jim Hussey	Sullivan won JHDQ	Newcastle, England
25/06/1965	Francis Sullivan Vs Roy Bull Davis	NC	Ayr
26/06/1965	Francis Sullivan Vs Timmy Geogeghan	Sullivan won	Belle Vue, Manchester
28/06/1965	Francis Sullivan Vs Masambula	Sullivan inj	Hamilton, Scotland
29/06/1965	Francis Sullivan Vs Geoff Portz	Portz won	Aberdeen, Scotland
01/07/1965	Francis Sullivan Vs Masambula	NK	Morecambe, Lancashire
10/07/1965	Francis Sullivan Vs Jim Hussey	Sullivan inj	Newcastle, England
18/07/1965	Francis Sullivan Vs Ernie Riley	NK	Douglas, Isle of Man
22/07/1965	Francis Sullivan Vs Les Kellett	NK	Morecambe, Lancashire
26/07/1965	Francis Sullivan Vs Frank O'Donnell	NK	Arbroath
30/07/1965	Francis Sullivan Vs Reg Williams	Williams won	Bolton
31/07/1965	Francis Sullivan & Billy Howes Vs Doug Joyce & Pietro Capello	Howes et al won	Belle Vue, Manchester
12/08/1965	Francis Sullivan Vs Masambula	NK	Morecambe, Lancashire
20/09/1965	Francis Sullivan Vs Paul Luty	NK	Worcester, England
25/09/1965	Francis Sullivan Vs Roy Bull Davis	Davis won	Doncaster
09/10/1965	Francis Sullivan Vs Ezzard Hart	NK	Kirkby, Ashfield
23/10/1965	Francis Sullivan Vs Norman Walsh	Walsh won	Belle Vue, Manchester
27/10/1965	Francis Sullivan Vs Johnny Allan	Francis Sullivan	Hindley
14/11/1965	Francis Sullivan Vs Mihalvi Kuti	NK	Camberwell
27/11/1965	Francis Sullivan Vs Count Bartelli	NK	Sutton, Ashfield
14/02/1966	Francis Sullivan Vs Gwyn Davies	NK	Derby, Derbyshire
20/04/1966	Francis Sullivan Vs Syed Saif Shah	NK	Nelson
08/06/1966	Francis Sullivan Vs Ian Campbell	NK	Hindley
16/05/1969	Francis Sullivan Vs Bill Rawlings	NK	Newcastle, England
29/02/1954	Francis Sullivan Vs Arthur Beaumont	NK	Blackpool, England

Bob Sherry (Jimmy Nibblett)

Date	Match	Outcome	Venue
01/12/1948	Bob Sherry won amateur welter and middleweight championships of Lancashire	N/A	N/A
15/09/1950	Bob Sherry Vs Johnny Stead	Johnny won	Glasgow, Scotland
27/10/1950	Bob Sherry Vs Fred Woolley	Fred won	Glasgow, Scotland
01/12/1950	Bob Sherry won amateur welterweight and middleweight championship of Lancashire	N/A	N/A
01/12/1950	Bob Sherry Vs Jack Dempsey	Jack Won	Glasgow, Scotland
05/02/1951	Bob Sherry Vs Steve Kilroy	Sherry won	Peterborough, England
07/02/1951	Bob Sherry Vs Russ Bishop	NK	Cardiff, Wales
16/02/1951	Bob Sherry Vs Chick Linton	Chick won	Caledonian Road, London
06/03/1951	Bob Sherry Vs Bob Russell	Draw	Hastings, England
21/03/1951	Bob Sherry Vs College Boy	College won	Cardiff, Wales
12/04/1951	Bob Sherry Vs Ken Wilson	Wilson won	Wimbledon, England
02/05/1951	Bob Sherry Vs Ken Wilson	Draw	Cardiff, Wales
02/05/1951	Bob Sherry Vs Ken Wilson	Draw	Cardiff, Wales
25/06/1951	Bob Sherry Vs Ken Joyce	Joyce won	Peterborough, England
07/11/1951	Bob Sherry Vs Arthur Fisher	Arthur won	Cardiff, Wales
12/11/1951	Bob Sherry Vs Arthur Fisher	Fisher won	Cardiff, Wales
27/11/1951	Bob Sherry Vs John Lipman	Johnny won	Chelmsford, England
28/11/1951	Bob Sherry Vs College Boy	College won	Cardiff, Wales
10/12/1951	Bob Sherry Vs Johnny Williams	Williams won	Peterborough, England
13/12/1951	Bob Sherry Vs Len Britton	Britton won	Wimbledon, England
07/02/1952	Bob Sherry Vs Cab Cashford	Cashford won	Beckenham, England
11/02/1952	Bob Sherry Vs Gerry DeJaegar	DeJaegar won	Hull, England
25/02/1952	Bob Sherry Vs Len Britton	Britton won	Croydon, England
06/03/1952	Bob Sherry Vs Steve Logan	NK	Southampton, England
10/03/1952	Bob Sherry Vs Pat Brennan	Sherry won	High Wycombe, England
27/03/1952	Bob Sherry Vs Johnny Peters	NK	Bristol, England
09/04/1952	Bob Sherry Vs Johnny Peters	NK	Cardiff, Wales
17/04/1952	Bob Sherry Vs Steve Logan	Sherry won	Wimbledon, England
22/05/1952	Bob Sherry Vs Stan Stone	Stone won	Bristol, England
17/07/1952	Bob Sherry Vs Johnny Peters	Sherry won	Bristol, England
23/07/1952	Bob Sherry Vs Jack Dale	Dale won	Bournemouth, England
28/08/1952	Bob Sherry Vs Kid Pitman	Pitman won	Bristol, England
10/12/1952	Bob Sherry Vs Vic Coleman	Vic won	Paddington, England
02/02/1953	Bob Sherry Vs Don Branch	Bob won	Leeds, England
23/04/1953	Bob Sherry Vs Johnny Peters	NK	Wimbledon, England
02/07/1953	Bob Sherry Vs Steve Logan	NK	Wimbledon, England
11/09/1953	Bob Sherry Vs Cliff Belshaw	Cliff won	Liverpool, England
26/05/1954	Bob Sherry Vs John Foley	NK	Belle Vue, Manchester
07/06/1954	Bob Sherry Vs Tiger Woods	NK	Belle Vue, Manchester
07/08/1954	Bob Sherry Vs Jack Beaumont	Beaumont won	Belle Vue, Manchester

Date	Match	Result	Location
13/10/1954	Bob Sherry Vs Alan Kimber	Kimber won	Belle Vue, Manchester
27/10/1954	Bob Sherry Vs Jack Beaumont	NK	Belle Vue, Manchester
06/11/1954	Bob Sherry Vs John Foley	NK	Belle Vue, Manchester
01/03/1955	Bob Sherry Vs Pat Kloke	Pat won	Dundee, Scotland
11/03/1955	Bob Sherry Vs Jim Mellor	Mellor won	Leicester, England
12/03/1955	Bob Sherry Vs Chic Purvey	Chic won	Middlesborough, North Yorkshire
17/03/1955	Bob Sherry Vs Joe Queseck	NK	Wimbledon, England
19/03/1955	Bob Sherry Vs Steve Logan	Steve won	Newcastle, England
17/02/1956	Bob Sherry Vs Frank O'Donnel	Frank won	Glasgow, Scotland
17/02/1956	Bob Sherry Vs Cyril Knowles	Cyril won	Glasgow, Scotland
21/02/1956	Bob Sherry Vs Frank O'Donnel	Frank won	Hamilton, Scotland
07/03/1956	Bob Sherry Vs Tony Lawrence	NK	Scunthorpe, England
17/03/1956	Bob Sherry Vs Jim Lewis	Lewis won	Middlesborough, England
21/03/1956	Bob Sherry Vs Eric Sands	NK	Scunthorpe, England
31/03/1956	Bob Sherry Vs Mick McManus	Mick won	Newcastle, England
14/04/1956	Bob Sherry Vs Reg Ray	Sherry won	Middlesborough, England
18/01/1957	Bob Sherry Vs Peter Muirhead	Bob won	Glasgow, Scotland
22/06/1957	Bob Sherry Vs Keith Walbach	Bob won	New Brighton, England
22/07/1957	Bob Sherry Vs Ron Knight	Bob won	Merry Fiddlers, England
31/07/1957	Bob Sherry Vs Norman Thomas	NK	Watford, England
07/08/1957	Bob Sherry Vs Norman Thomas	Draw	Watford, England
19/08/1957	Bob Sherry Vs Red Callaghan	Draw	Merry Fiddlers, England
02/09/1957	Bob Sherry Vs Keith Walbach	Bob won	Merry Fiddlers, England
10/10/1957	Bob Sherry Vs Red Callaghan	Draw	Alexandra Palace, London
28/11/1957	Bob Sherry Vs Terry Nylands	NK	Cleethorpes, England
10/05/1958	Bob Sherry Vs Rufus Riley	Rufus won, BS DQ	New Brighton, England
30/05/1958	Bob Sherry Vs Red Callaghan	Bob won	New Brighton, England
19/07/1958	Bob Sherry Vs Red Callaghan	Red won	New Brighton, England
23/08/1958	Bob Sherry Vs Rufus Riley	Bob won	New Brighton, England
19/09/1958	Bob Sherry Vs Red Callaghan	Red won	Blyth, Scotland
24/09/1958	Bob Sherry Vs Arturio Martinelli	Bob won	Harrogate, north Yorkshire
06/10/1958	Bob Sherry Vs Ken Shaw	Draw	Loughborough, England
16/10/1958	Bob Sherry Vs Frankie Hughes	NK	Wimbledon, England
17/11/1958	Bob Sherry Vs Maurice DuBois	Maurice won	Reading, Berkshire
01/01/1959	Bob Sherry Vs Eddie Capelli	NK	Wimbledon, England
06/02/1959	Bob Sherry Vs Bobo Matu	Draw	Ilkeston, England
03/03/1959	Bob Sherry Vs Spike O'Reilly	NK	Nottingham, England
17/06/1959	Bob Sherry Vs Gerard Dubois	NK	Blackpool, England
27/08/1959	Bob Sherry Vs Bobo Matu	NK	Southport
02/10/1959	Bob Sherry Vs Bobo Matu	NK	Burnley
23/10/1959	Bob Sherry Vs Bobo Matu	Nk	Scunthorpe, England
28/01/1960	Bob Sherry Vs Emile Poilve	NK	Hulme
05/02/1960	Bob Sherry Vs Bobo Matu	NK	Birmingham, England
05/05/1960	Bob Sherry Vs George Bullock	NK	Hulme

Date	Match	Result	Location
01/06/1960	Bob Sherry Vs Bobo Matu	NK	Hulme
28/11/1960	Bob Sherry Vs Jim Lewis	NK	Long Eaton
11/01/1962	Bob Sherry Vs Dusty Rhodes	NK	Barnsley
23/04/1962	Bob Sherry Vs Keith Williams	NK	Kirkby, Ashfield
03/05/1962	Bob Sherry Vs Tiger Ryan	NK	Cradley Heath
21/05/1962	Bob Sherry Vs Keith Martinelli	NK	Nelson
06/08/1962	Bob Sherry Vs Bobo Matu	NK	Colwyn Bay, Wales
14/09/1962	Bob Sherry Vs jack Dempsey	NK	Burton on trent, England
01/10/1962	Bob Sherry Vs Keith Martinelli	NK	Worcester, England
11/10/1962	Bob Sherry Vs Al Brown	NK	Chester, England
17/10/1962	Bob Sherry Vs Brian Burke	Sherry won	Rawtenstall
29/10/1962	Bob Sherry Vs Keith Martinelli	NK	Nelson
08/04/1963	Bob Sherry Vs Mike Donlevy	NK	Worcester, England
08/01/1965	Bob Sherry Vs Bobo Matu	NK	Cheam
22/01/1965	Bob Sherry Vs Bobo Matu	NK	Tipton
25/01/1965	Bob Sherry Vs Pedro The Gypsy	NK	Harrogate
08/01/1966	Bob Sherry Vs Lee Sharron	NK	Derby, Derbyshire
20/12/1966	Bob Sherry & Jack Cassidy Vs Ken Davies & Bertie Topham	Sherry et al won	Digbeth

John Foley

Date	Match	Outcome	Venue
19/07/1952	John Foley Vs Mel Riss	NK	Costa Green, Birmingham
08/12/1952	John Foley Vs Jim Mellor	John won	Warrington, England
01/01/1953	Competed in Germany	NK	Miscellaneous
5 Aug- 17 Sep/1953	John Foley Vs Eduardo Castillo	Eduardo won	Hamburg, Germany
5 Aug- 17 Sep/1953	John Foley Vs Martin Chenok	John won	Hamburg, Germany
5 Aug- 17 Sep/1953	John Foley Vs Bob McDonald	Bob won	Hamburg, Germany
5 Aug- 17 Sep/1953	John Foley Vs Erhard Grimm	John won	Hamburg, Germany
5 Aug- 17 Sep/1953	John Foley Vs Guy Laroche	Guy won	Hamburg, Germany
5 Aug- 17 Sep/1953	John Foley Vs Leonhard Marciniak	Leon won	Hamburg, Germany
5 Aug- 17 Sep/1953	John Foley Vs Pierre Martine	Pierre won	Hamburg, Germany
5 Aug- 17 Sep/1953	John Foley Vs Juan Salessa	Juan won	Hamburg, Germany
5 Aug- 17 Sep/1953	John Foley Vs Josef Ski	Josef won	Hamburg, Germany
5 Aug- 17 Sep/1953	John Foley Vs Benedict Trinkgeld	Benedict won	Hamburg, Germany
5 Aug- 17 Sep/1953	John Foley Vs Sepp Wenzl	Sepp won	Hamburg, Germany
5 Aug- 17 Sep/1953	John Foley Vs Carl Van Wurden	Carl won	Hamburg, Germany
5 Aug- 17 Sep/1953	John Foley Vs MP	MP won	Hamburg, Germany
17/10/1953	John Foley Vs Tony McDonald	John won	Manchester, England
03/04/1954	John Foley Vs Jim Mellor	NK	Willenhall, England
17/04/1954	John Foley Vs Fred Woolley	John won	Manchester, England
26/05/1954	John Foley Vs Bob Sherry	NK	Belle Vue, Manchester
06/11/1954	John Foley Vs Bob Sherry	NK	Belle Vue, Manchester
01/12/1954	John Foley Vs Ernest Smith	Draw	Manchester, England
18/12/1954	John Foley Vs Melwyn Riss	Foley won	Belle Vue, Manchester
29/08/1955	John Foley Vs Jack Beaumont	John won	Plymouth, England
30/07/1956	John Foley Vs Jack Beaumont	Jack won	Becontree Heath, England
15/12/1956	John Foley Vs Jim Holden	John won	Manchester, England
19/01/1957	John Foley Vs Mel Riss	Draw	Shrewsbury, England
09/02/1957	John Foley Vs Mel Riss	John won	Shrewsbury, England
02/03/1957	John Foley Vs Mel Riss	NK	Doncaster, England
09/03/1957	John Foley Vs Jim Mellor	john won	Shrewsbury, England
12/04/1957	John Foley Vs Eric Sands	NK	Liverpool, England
15/04/1957	John Foley Vs Jack Dempsey	NK	Altrincham
19/11/1957	John Foley Vs Joe Critchley	john won	Leeds, England
16/12/1957	John Foley Vs Mick McManus	Mick won	Leeds, England
14/03/1958	John Foley Vs Alan Colbeck	Alan won	Belfast, Ireland
21/03/1958	John Foley Vs Joe Critchley	Draw	Willenhall, England
24/03/1958	John Foley Vs Joe Critchley	John won	Leeds, England
27/03/1958	John Foley Vs Reg Ray	Reg won	Gainsborough, England

Date	Match	Result	Location
04/04/1958	John Foley Vs Jim Mellor	Jim won	Willenhall, England
05/04/1958	John Foley Vs Alan Colbeck	Alan won	Manchester, England
11/04/1958	John Foley Vs Jim Lewis	Jim won	Glasgow, Scotland
13/04/1958	John Foley Vs Mel Riss	John won	Birmingham, England
21/04/1958	John Foley Vs Mel Riss	NK	Kirkby, Ashfield
15/05/1958	John Foley Vs Chic Purvey	John won	Morecambe, Lancashire
15/05/1958	John Foley Vs Tony Zale	Tony won	Belfast, Ireland
03/06/1958	John Foley Vs Brian Burke	Draw	Birmingham, England
24/06/1958	John Foley Vs Al Miquet	John won	Birmingham, England
05/07/1958	John Foley Vs Bakjo Lazlo	John won	Newcastle, England
19/08/1958	John Foley Vs Al nicols	John won	Birmingham, England
30/08/1958	John Foley Vs Tony Quarmby	John won	Wellington, England
08/09/1958	John Foley Vs Bakjo Lazlo	John won	Edinburgh, Scotland
21/09/1958	John Foley Vs Reg Ray	John won	Birmingham, England
09/10/1958	John Foley Vs Melwyn Riss	Draw	Nottingham, England
10/10/1958	John Foley Vs Dave Finch	John won	Glasgow, Scotland
10/10/1958	John Foley Vs Alan Colbeck	John won, alan DQ	Glasgow, Scotland
10/10/1958	John Foley Vs Bert Toyal	Bert won	Glasgow, Scotland
23/10/1958	John Foley Vs Josef Sky	Josef won	Morecambe, Lancashire
24/10/1958	John Foley Vs Jack Dempsey	NK	Bolton, Lancashire
15/11/1958	John Foley Vs Al Nicol	John won	Shrewsbury, England
20/11/1958	John Foley Vs Arthur Fisher	John won	Bristol, England
21/11/1958	John Foley Vs Tony Charles	John won	Ipswich, England
05/12/1958	John Foley Vs Tommy Dowie	John won	Glasgow, Scotland
06/12/1958	John Foley Vs Jim Hart	John won	Middlesborough, North Yorkshire
13/12/1958	John Foley Vs George Robb	John won	Newcastle, England
18/12/1958	John Foley Vs Inca Peruano	Draw	Bristol, England
30/12/1958	John Foley Vs Jack Dempsey	Jack won	Birmingham, England
13/01/1959	John Foley Vs jack Dempsey	Foley won JD DQ	Hull, England
23/01/1959	John Foley Vs Brian Burke	John won	Willenhall, England
25/01/1959	John Foley Vs Tony Charles	John won	Birmingham, England
26/01/1959	John Foley Vs Serge Reggiori	John won	Leeds, England
06/02/1959	John Foley Vs Arturo Martinelli	John won	Willenhall, England
13/02/1959	John Foley Vs Brian Burke	John won	Glasgow, Scotland
20/02/1959	John Foley Vs Bob Anthony	Bob won	Willenhall, England
07/03/1959	John Foley Vs Fred Woolley	Fred won	Shrewsbury, England
19/03/1959	John Foley Vs Reg Ray	Reg won	Morecambe, Lancashire
31/03/1959	John Foley Vs Jack Cunningham	Jack won	Swindon, England
22/05/1959	John Foley Vs Brian Burke	NK	Dudley, England
17/10/1959	John Foley Vs brian burke	NK	Dudley, England
29/10/1959	John Foley Vs Brian burke	NK	Hulme
15/01/1960	John Foley Vs Jack Dempsey	NK	Ipswich, England
27/02/1960	John Foley Vs Brian Burke	NK	Bolton, England
12/05/1960	John Foley Vs Jack Dempsey	Draw	Barrow, England
17/06/1960	John Foley Vs Brian Burke	NK	Liverpool, England

Date	Match	Result	Location
23/06/1960	John Foley Vs Brian Burke	NK	Leigh, Lancashire
20/09/1960	John Foley Vs Jean Morandi	John won	Reading, England
24/09/1960	John Foley Vs Brian Burke	NK	Grantham,
14/10/1960	John Foley Vs Brian Burke	NK	Glasgow, Scotland
17/10/1960	John Foley Vs Rene Ben Chemoul	Rene won	Paris, France
05/11/1960	John Foley Vs Jack Dempsey	NK	Grantham,
10/11/1960	John Foley Vs Jackie Cheers	NK	Hulme
15/12/1960	John Foley Vs Jack Dempsey	Foley won	Beckenham, England
17/12/1960	John Foley Vs Jack Dempsey	Foley won	Brighton, England
25/02/1961	John Foley Vs Jack Dempsey	NK	Middlesborough, England
03/04/1961	John Foley Vs Brian Burke	NK	Kilmarnock
08/04/1961	Johnny Foley Vs Jackie Pallo	NK	Shoreditch, London
29/04/1961	John Foley Vs Jack Dempsey	Draw	Coventry, England
06/05/1961	John Foley Vs Jack Dempsey	Draw	Coventry, England
22/05/1961	John Foley Vs Melwyn Riss	Foley won	Purley
02/09/1961	John Foley Vs Al Nicol	NK	Acton
11/09/1961	John Foley Vs Jack Dempsey	NK	Leeds, England
23/09/1961	John Foley Vs Brian Burke	NK	Grantham,
16/12/1961	John Foley Vs Brian Burke	NK	Norwich, England
10/02/1962	John Foley Vs Tony Charles	NK	Preston, Lancashire
14/03/1962	John Foley Vs Brian Burke	NK	Hastings
07/04/1962	John Foley Vs Ray Leslie	Foley 2 Leslie 1	Lime Grove, Shepherd's Bush, London
28/04/1962	John Foley Vs Roy St Clair	NK	Colne
05/06/1962	John Foley Vs Jack Dempsey	Foley won	Hove
21/06/1962	John Foley Vs Jack Dempsey	NK	Barrow, England
04/08/1962	John Foley Vs Jack Dempsey	Foley won	Maidstone
14/08/1962	John Foley Vs Jack Dempsey	Draw	Plymouth, England
10/11/1962	John Foley Vs Johnny Eagles	NK	Preston, Lancashire
17/11/1962	John Foley Vs Alan Dennison	NK	Lime Grove, Shepherd's Bush, London
11/12/1962	John Foley Vs Jack Dempsey	NK	Kidderminster
28/12/1962	John Foley Vs Jack Dempsey	Dempsey won	Ipswich
28/03/1963	John Foley Vs Jack Dempsey	NK	Brierly Hill
09/05/1963	John Foley Vs Jack Dempsey	NK	Brierly Hill
06/06/1963	John Foley Vs Jack Dempsey	Dempsey won	Wimbledon
11/10/1963	John Foley Vs Jack Dempsey	NK	Rotherham
09/11/1963	John Foley Vs Al Brown	Al won 1-0	Wallasey, merseyside
12/12/1963	John Foley Vs Jack Dempsey	NK	Nelson
21/12/1963	Bert Royal/Vic Faulkner (Royals) (W) v Abe Ginsberg/John Foley (Black Diamonds)	NK	Wallasey, merseyside
13/02/1965	Johnny Eagles/Terry Jowett (White Eagles) vs/ Abe Ginsberg/John Foley (Black Diamonds	NK	Preston, Lancashire
19/05/1965	Black Diamonds Vs Francis Sullivan & Les Kellett	NK	Hindley
23/07/1966	The Black Diamonds (John Foley and Abe Ginsergh) vs/ (The Silent Ones) Harry Kendall and Mike Eagers	NK	The Winter Gardens, Morecambe, Lancashire
17/02/1968	Black Diamonds (Abe Ginsberg/John Foley) vs/ The Untouchables	NK	Morecambe, Lancashire
22/08/1968	John Foley Vs Roy Wood	Wood won	Blackpool, England

02/07/1969	John Foley Vs Alan Wood	Foley won	Southport, Merseyside
08/10/1969	John Foley & Eric Cutler Vs Alan Wood & Terry Jowett	Wood et al won	Welshpool

Seamus Dunleavy

Date	Match	Outcome	Venue
01/12/1954	Won Northern Counties amateur title	Seamus won	Northern Counties
30/03/1959	Seamus Donlevy Vs Jackie Cheers	NK	Kirkby, Ashfield
28/08/1959	Seamus Dunlevy Vs Francis Sullivan	NK	Bolton, Lancashire
18/09/1959	Seamus Dunlevy Vs Francis Sullivan	NK	Bolton, Lancashire
26/11/1959	Seamus Dunleavy Vs Bill Robinson	NK	Nottingham
13/01/1960	Seamus Dunleavy Vs Reg Williams	draw	Lincoln, England
20/01/1960	Seamus Dunleavy Vs Billy Joyce	NK	Grimsby, England
21/01/1960	Seamus Dunleavy Vs Billy Joyce	NK	Kirkcaldy
10/02/1960	Seamus Dunleavy Vs Ernest Baldwin	Ernest won	Lincoln, England
26/03/1960	Seamus Dunleavy Vs Dean Stockton	Dean won	Wellington, England
06/04/1960	Seamus Donlevy Vs John Lees	John won	Lincoln, England
03/05/1960	Seamus Dunleavy Vs Billy Howes	NK	Bridlington, England
10/06/1960	Seamus Dunleavy Vs Billy Howes	NK	Fleetwood
18/07/1960	Seamus Dunleavy Vs Billy Howes	NK	Skegness, England
21/07/1960	Seamus Dunleavy Vs Francis Sullivan	NK	Hulme
02/11/1960	Seamus Dunleavy Vs Eric Taylor	Eric won	Cardiff, Wales
19/12/1960	Seamus Dunleavy Vs Billy Howes	NK	Colwyn Bay, Wales
28/04/1961	Seamus Dunleavy Vs Francis Sullivan	NK	Bolton, England
12/07/1961	Seamus Dunleavy Vs Billy Howes	NK	Sheffield, England
16/10/1961	Seamus Dunleavy Vs Gene Riscoe	NK	Derby, England
20/11/1961	Seamus Dunleavy Vs Billy Howes	Howes won	West Ham, England
25/11/1961	Seamus Dunleavy Vs Francis Sullivan	Sullivan won	Belle Vue, Manchester
20/06/1962	Seamus Dunleavy Vs Billy Joyce	Joyce won	Cardiff, Wales
22/06/1962	Seamus Dunleavy Vs Billy Howes	NK	Northampton, England
15/08/1962	Seamus Dunleavy Vs Francis Sullivan	Sullivan won	Carlyon Bay
26/09/1962	Seamus Dunleavy Vs Billy Howes	NK	Cardiff, Wales
12/01/1963	Seamus Dunleavy Vs Francis Sullivan	NK	Luton, England
12/06/1963	Seamus Dunleavy Vs Billy Howes	NK	Malvern
25/07/1963	Seamus Dunleavy Vs Billy Joyce	NK	Wimbledon
17/05/1965	Seamus Dunleavy Vs Billy Howes	Howes won	Birmingham
02/09/1965	Seamus Dunleavy Vs Billy Howes	NK	Ross on Wye
25/11/1968	Seamus Donlevy & Mike Donlevy Vs Billy Howes & Judd Harris	NK	Derby, Derbyshire
16/01/1969	Seamus Dunleavy & Alan Wood Vs Bobo Matu & Jim Moser	Wood & Dunleavy won	Malvern

Tony Zale

Date	Match	Outcome	Venue
12/10/1957	Tony Zale Vs Jim Holden	Jim won	Shrewsbury, England
13/12/1957	Tony Zale & Danny Flynn Vs Jim Mellor & Reg Ray	Tony won	Willenhall, England
11/05/1958	Tony Zale Vs Reg Ray	Draw	Birmingham, England
15/05/1958	Tony Zale Vs John Foley	Tony Won	Belfast, Ireland
24/05/1958	Tony Zale Vs Dave Finch	Tony won	Middlesborough, North Yorkshire
25/05/1958	Tony Zale Vs Archer O'Brien	Draw	Birmingham, England
19/06/1958	Tony Zale Vs Joe Critchley	Joe won	Morecambe, Lancashire
04/09/1958	Tony Zale Vs Bobby Steele	Bobby won	Oswestry, England
26/09/1958	Tony Zale Vs Joe Critchley	Tony won	Dudley, England
12/10/1958	Tony Zale Vs Jim Mellor	Jim won	Birmingham, England
18/10/1958	Tony Zale Vs Danny Flynn	Tony won	Shrewsbury, England
24/10/1958	Tony Zale Vs Cyril Knowles Peters	Cyril won	Glasgow, Scotland
06/11/1958	Tony Zale Vs Reg Williams	Reg won	Morecambe, Lancashire
15/11/1958	Tony Zale Vs Bobby Steele	Bobby won	Shrewsbury, England
26/11/1958	Tony Zale Vs Bert Royal	NK	Hastings, England
03/01/1959	Tony Zale Vs Jack Dempsey	NK	Doncaster, England
10/01/1959	Tony Zale Vs Joe Critchley	Tony won	Shrewsbury, England
12/01/1959	Tony Zale Vs Fred Wooley	Tony won	Leeds, England
30/01/1959	Tony Zale Vs Lew Roseby	NC	Shrewsbury, England
20/03/1959	Tony Zale & Cyril Morris Vs Joe Critchley & Chopper Conroy	Tony & Cyril won	Willenhall, England
21/03/1959	Tony Zale Vs Bobby Steele	Bobby won	Shrewsbury, England
09/04/1959	Tony Zale Vs Chic Purvey	Draw	Cardiff, Wales
19/09/1959	Tony Zale Vs Joe Critchley	NK	Wulfrun Hall, Wolverhampton
21/11/1959	Tony Zale Vs Frank O'Donnell	Frankie won	Hanley
08/12/1959	Tony Zale Vs Brian Burke	NK	Bridlington
29/01/1960	Tony Zale Vs Brian Burke	NK	**Dumfries, Scotland**
15/03/1960	Tony Zale Vs Johnny Czeslaw	Johnny won	Swindon, England
12/04/1960	Tony Zale Vs Brian Burke	NK	Trowell
23/04/1960	Tony Zale Vs Jean Morandi	NK	Halifax, West Yorkshire
01/09/1960	Tony Zale Vs Brian Burke	NK	Hulme
26/02/1963	Tony Zale Vs Newman	NK	Cudworth
11/05/1963	Tony Zale Vs Newman	Draw	Leicester, England
08/03/1965	Tony Zale Vs Dave Newman	NK	Southend

Joe Critchley

Date	Match	Outcome	Venue
01/11/1954	Joe Critchley Vs Alan Wood	NK	Worcester
09/02/1957	Joe Critchley Vs Henry Hall	Joe won	Shrewsbury, England
13/03/1959	Joe Critchley Vs Reg Ray	Reg won	Bolton, England
13/03/1959	Joe Critchley & Jim Mellor Vs Danny Flynn & Reg Ray	Joe & jim won	Willenhall, England
18/03/1959	Joe Critchley & Jim Mellor Vs Danny Flynn & Reg Ray	Joe & jim won	Willenhall, England
20/03/1959	Joe Critchley & Chopper Conroy Vs Tony Zale & Cyril Morris	Tony & Cyril won	Willenhall, England
02/04/1959	Joe Critchley Vs Reg Ray	Reg won	Doncaster, England
19/05/1959	Joe Critchley Vs Tony Zale	NK	Wulfrun Hall, Wolverhampton
02/07/1959	Joe Critchley Vs Brian Burke	NK	Hulme
15/09/1959	Joe Critchley Vs Melwyn Riss	Nk	Wakefield, England
12/12/1959	joe Critchley Vsa brian Burke	NK	Belle Vue, Manchester
18/01/1960	Joe Critchley Vs Brian Burke	NK	Altrincham, England
10/02/1960	Joe Critchley & Reg Ray Vs Brian Burke & Jim Mellor	NK	Llandudno, Wales
16/04/1960	Joe Critchley Vs Mick McMichael	NK	Grantham, England
05/05/1960	Joe Critchley Vs Brian Burke	NK	Hulme
01/06/1960	Joe Critchley Vs Melwyn Riss	NK	Sheffield, England
30/06/1960	Joe Critchley Vs Melwyn Riss	Riss won	Morecambe, Lancashire
21/07/1960	Joe Critchley Vs Brian Burke	NK	Hulme
10/09/1960	Joe Critchley Vs Keith Williamson	NK	Crewe, England
24/10/1960	Joe Critchley Vs Brian Burke	NK	Walsall
26/12/1960	Joe Critchley & Reg Ray Vs Brian Burke & Roy St Clair	Burke et al won	Bolton, England
03/02/1961	Joe Critchley Vs Jack Dempsey	Dempsey won	Glasgow, Scotland
13/02/1961	Joe Critchley Vs Melwyn Riss	NK	Blackpool, England
25/02/1961	Joe Critchley Vs Jim Hart	NK	Ellesmere Port
18/03/1961	Joe Critchley Vs Jim Mellor	NK	Wallasey, merseyside
25/03/1961	Joe Critchley Vs Brian Burke	Critchley won	Newcastle, England
09/06/1961	Joe Critchley Vs Melwyn Riss	NK	Liverpool, England
21/06/1961	Joe Critchley Vs Brian Burke	NK	Cradley Heath
12/02/1962	Joe Critchley & Brian Burke Vs Bobby Steele & Jack Taylor	Steele et al won	Bradford, England
01/03/1962	Joe Critchley Vs Jack Dempsey	Dempsey won	Bristol, England
06/10/1962	Joe Critchley Vs Tommy Mann	NK	Wolverhampton, West Midlands
05/11/1962	Joe Critchley Vs Jack Dempsey	NK	Derby, England
04/02/1963	Joe Critchley Vs Melwyn Riss	NK	Worcester, England
04/03/1963	Joe Critchley Vs Melwyn Riss	NK	Worcester, England
27/04/1963	Joe Critchley Vs Joe Keegan	Keegan won	Wolverhampton, West Midlands
08/06/1963	Joe Critchley Vs Downs	Downs won	Belle Vue, Manchester
09/11/1963	Joe Critchley Vs Abe Ginsbery	NK	Wallasey, merseyside
13/02/1965	Joe Critchley Vs Melwyn Riss	Draw	Doncaster
24/02/1965	Joe Critchley Vs Melwyn Riss	Riss won	Alfreton
16/03/1965	Joe Critchley Vs Roy Wood	Critchley won	Edinburgh

Date	Match	Result	Location
27/03/1965	Joe Critchley & Frank O'Donnell Vs Eric Sands & Alan Colbeck	NK	Blackburn, Lancashire
17/04/1965	Joe Critchley & Jackies Cheers Vs Roy Wood & Gene Riscoe	NK	Brierly Hill
22/05/1965	Joe Critchley Vs Jack Dempsey	Dempsey won	Doncaster
12/06/1965	Joe Critchley Vs Jack Dempsey	Dempsey won	Doncaster
11/07/1965	Joe Critchley & Melwyn Riss Vs Keith Williams & Mick McMichael	Williams & McMichael won	Blackpool, England
30/07/1965	Joe Critchley & Bernard Murray Vs Melwyn Riss & Jim Breaks	Riss et al won	Liverpool
01/08/1965	Joe Critchley & Bernard Murray Vs Melwyn Riss & Jim Breaks	Critchley et al won	Blackpool, England
20/08/1965	Joe Critchley Vs Melwyn Riss	Riss won	Glasgow, Scotland
27/08/1965	Joe Critchley Vs Melwyn Riss	Riss won	Liverpool
26/09/1965	Joe Critchley & Melwyn Riss Vs Mick McMichael & Barry Cannon	McMichael et al won	Blackpool, England
16/03/1966	Joe Critchley Vs Alan Wood	NK	Welshpool
09/04/1966	Joe Critchley & Melwyn Riss Vs Ted Hannon & Terry Downs	Hannon et al won	Blackpool, England
26/06/1966	Joe Critchley & Melwyn Riss Vs Leon Arras & Barry Cannon	Arras et al won	Blackpool, England
24/07/1966	Joe Critchley & Melwyn Riss Vs The White Eagles	Eagles won	Blackpool, England
25/09/1966	Joe Critchley Vs Alan Wood	NK	Blackpool, England
05/12/1966	Joe Critchley Vs Melwyn Riss	NK	Blackpool, England
15/02/1968	Joe Critchley Vs Melwyn Riss	Riss won	Malvern
15/04/1968	Joe Critchley Vs Alan Wood	Wood won	Blackpool, England
23/06/1968	Joe Critchley Vs Roy Wood	Critchley won	Blackpool, England
11/08/1968	Joe Critchley Vs Roy Wood	Wood won	Blackpool, England
20/10/1968	Joe Critchley Vs Roy Wood	Critchley won	Blackpool, England
08/12/1969	Joe Critchley & Kevin Conneally Vs Alan Wood & Monty Swann	Critchley et al won	Nantwich
24/01/1970	Joe Critchley & Les Kellett Vs Steve Logan & Colin Joynson	NK	NK

Brian Burke

Date	Match	Outcome	Venue
Jan-58	Brian Burke Debut	N/A	N/A
31/01/1958	Brian Burke Vs Melwyn Riss	NK	Willenhall
15/02/1958	Brian Burke Vs Chic Purvey	NK	Shrewsbury, England
28/03/1958	Brian Burke Vs Danny Flynn	Draw	Willenhall, England
12/04/1958	Brian Burke Vs Virag Lazlo	Virag won	Portsmouth, England
28/04/1958	Brian Burke Vs Tony Mancelli	NK	Blackpool, England
04/05/1958	Brian Burke Vs Jim Mellor	Brian won	Birmingham, England
10/05/1958	Brian Burke Vs Melwyn Riss	NK	Grantham, England
18/05/1958	Brian Burke Vs Danny Flynn	Danny won	Birmingham, England
03/06/1958	Brian Burke Vs John Foley	Draw	Birmingham, England
05/06/1958	Brian Burke Vs Melwyn Riss	NK	Hulme
29/06/1958	Brian Burke Vs Fred Woolley	Draw	Birmingham, England
12/07/1958	Brian Burke Vs Lazlo Bajko	NK	Belle Vue, Manchester
14/07/1958	Brian Burke Vs Fred Woolley	Fred won	Leeds, England
18/07/1958	Brian Burke Vs Bert Royal	NK	Bolton, England
29/07/1958	Brian Burke Vs Al Nicol	NK	Scarborough
07/08/1958	Brian Burke Vs Johnny Rudd	NK	Hulme
08/08/1958	Brian Burke Vs Danny Flynn	NK	Bolton, England
10/08/1958	Brian Burke Vs Danny Flynn	Draw	Birmingham, England
19/08/1958	Brian Burke Vs Jack Dempsey	NK	Scarborough
24/08/1958	Brian Burke Vs Melwyn Riss	Mel won	Birmingham, England
01/09/1958	In KO tournament	NK	High Wycombe, England
04/09/1958	Brian Burke Vs Fred Woolley	NK	Hulme
06/09/1958	Brian Burke Vs Arthur Fisher	NK	Kings Lynn, England
13/09/1958	Brian Burke Vs Bernard Murray	Bernard won	Newcastle, England
17/09/1958	Brian Burke Vs Melwyn Riss	Brian won	Lincoln, Lincolnshire
19/09/1958	Brian Burke Vs jack Dempsey	Jack won	Belfast, Ireland
25/09/1958	Brian Burke Vs Jim Mellor	NK	Hulme
04/10/1958	Brian Burke Vs Jack Dempsey	Jack won	Newcastle, England
06/10/1958	Brian Burke Vs Cliff Belshaw	Cliff won	Edinburgh, Scotland
08/10/1958	Brian Burke Vs Bob Anthony	NK	Sheffield, England
11/10/1958	Brian Burke Vs Jimmy Rudd	Brian won	Shrewsbury, England
13/10/1958	Brian Burke Vs Jackie Pallo	NK	Folkestone
17/10/1958	Brian Burke Vs Len Wilding	Brian won	Ipswich, England
18/10/1958	Brian Burke Vs Eddie Saxon	Eddie won	Coventry, England
24/10/1958	Brian Burke Vs Bobby Steele	NK	Chesterfield, England
25/10/1958	Brian Burke Vs Cliff Beaumont	NK	Grantham, England
02/11/1958	Brian Burke Vs Jimmy Rudd	Brian won	Birmingham, England
06/11/1958	Brian Burke Vs Jim Mellor	NK	Hulme
07/11/1958	Brian Burke Vs Al Nicol	Al won	Glasgow, Scotland
08/11/1958	Brian Burke & Danny Flynn Vs Jim Hart & Reg Ray	Hart & Ray won	Shrewsbury, England
10/11/1958	Brian Burke Vs Eric Sands	NK	Bradford, England

Date	Match	Result	Location
15/11/1958	Brian Burke Vs jack Dempsey	Jack won	Middlesborough, North Yorkshire
22/11/1958	Brian Burke Vs Ted Hannon	NK	Hanley
24/11/1958	Brian Burke Vs Jimmy Rudd	NK	Kirkby, Ashfield
26/11/1958	Brian Burke Vs Jack Dempsey	Jack won	Albert Hall, London
27/11/1958	Brian Burke Vs Tony Charles	Brian won	Beckenham, England
04/12/1958	Brian Burke Vs Fred Woolley	Fred won	Nottingham, England
05/12/1958	Brian Burke Vs Joe Critchley	Brian won, JC DQ	Glasgow, Scotland
06/12/1958	Brian Burke Vs Cliff Beaumont	NK	Grantham, England
09/12/1958	Brian Burke Vs jack Dempsey	Draw	Wolverhampton, West Midlands
21/12/1958	Brian Burke Vs Alan Dennison	Brian won	Birmingham, England
10/01/1959	Brian Burke Vs Peter Szakacs	NK	Eastbourne
11/01/1959	Brian Burke Vs Al Miquet	Brian won	Birmingham, England
23/01/1959	Brians Burke Vs John Foley	John won	Willenhall, England
24/01/1959	Brian Burke Vs Frank Robb	Frank won	Newcastle, England
27/01/1959	Brian Burke Vs Eddie Saxon	Eddie won	Purley, England
12/02/1959	Brian Burke Vs Ted Hannon	NK	Stretford, England
13/02/1959	Brian Burke Vs John Foley	John won	Glasgow, Scotland
16/02/1959	Brian Burke Vs Harry Hill	NK	Derby, England
19/02/1959	Brian Burke Vs Len Wilding	NK	Luton, London
20/02/1959	Brian Burke Vs Archer O'Brien	Draw	Ipswich, England
20/02/1959	Brian Burke Vs Vic Coleman	Vic won	Ipswich, England
21/02/1959	Brian Burke Vs Jackie Pallo	Jackie won	Purley, England
02/03/1959	Brian Burke Vs Jackie Cheers	NK	Kirkby, Ashfield
09/03/1959	Brian Burke Vs Arthur Fisher	Arthur won	Aylesbury, Buckinghamshire
10/03/1959	Brian Burke Vs Cliff Beaumont	Beaumont won	Purley, England
11/03/1959	Brian Burke Vs Jack Cunningham	Jack won	Cardiff, Wales
12/03/1959	Brian Burke Vs Melwyn Riss	Draw	Bristol, England
14/03/1959	Brian Burke Vs Jim Mellor	NK	Shrewsbury, England
21/03/1959	Brian Burke Vs Alan Miquet	NK	Dudley, England
02/04/1959	Brian Burke Vs Keith Williams	NK	Hulme
18/04/1959	Brian Burke Vs Keith Williams	NK	Doncaster, England
23/04/1959	Brian Burke Vs Fred Woolley	Fred won	Morecambe, Lancashire
25/04/1959	Brian Burke Vs Ted Hannon	NK	Belle Vue, Manchester
04/05/1959	Brian Burke Vs Len Wilding	NK	Aylesbury, England
07/05/1959	Brian Burke Vs Bob Archer O'Brien	Burke won	Peterborough, England
08/05/1959	Brian Burke Vs Eric Sands	Draw	Ramsgate
12/05/1959	Brian Burke Vs Rab Hannon	Burke won	Birmingham, England
22/05/1959	Brian Burke Vs John Foley	NK	Dudley, England
02/06/1959	Brian Burke Vs Fred Woolley	Burke won	Birmingham, England
11/06/1959	Brian Burke Vs Ken Wilson	NK	Hulme
02/07/1959	Brian Burke Vs Joe Critchley	NK	Hulme
07/07/1959	Brian Burke Vs jim Mellor	Burke won	Birmingham, England
15/08/1959	Brian Burke Vs Melwyn Riss	NK	Belle Vue, Manchester
20/08/1959	Brian Burke Vs Danny Flynn	NK	Hulme
25/09/1959	Brian Burke Vs Fred Woolley	Nk	Dudley, England

Date	Match	Result	Location
08/10/1959	Brian Burke Vs Jim mellor	NK	Hulme
17/10/1959	Brian Burke Vs john Foley	NK	Dudley, England
29/10/1959	Brian Burke Vs John Foley	NK	Hulme
11/11/1959	Brian Burke Vs Melwyn Riss	NK	Grimsby, England
12/11/1959	Brian Burke Vs John Hall	NK	Hulme
17/11/1959	Brian Burke Vs Ted Hannon	NK	Wakefield, England
26/11/1959	Brian Burkes Vs Pasquale Salvo	Nk	Luton, London
30/11/1959	Brian Burke Vs Alan Dennison	Nk	Kirkby, Ashfield
08/12/1959	Brian burke Vs Tony Zale	NK	Bridlington
12/12/1959	Brian Burke Vs joe Critchley	NK	Belle Vue, Manchester
26/12/1959	Brian Burke Vs Keith Williams	NK	Bolton, Lancashire
08/01/1960	brian Burke Vs Jack Dempsey	NK	Glasgow, Scotland
09/01/1960	brian Burke Vs Doug Reid	NK	Falkirk
11/01/1960	Brian Burke Vs Abe Ginsberg	NK	Warrington, England
14/01/1960	brian Burke Vs Alan Dennison	NK	Colne
15/01/1960	Brian Burke Vs Alan Dennison	NK	Burton On Trent, England
18/01/1960	Brian Burke Vs Joe Critchley	NK	Altrincham, England
20/01/1960	Brian Burke Vs Abe Ginsberg	NK	Smethwick, England
22/01/1960	Brian Burke Vs Abe Ginsberg	NK	Bolton, England
23/01/1960	Brian Burke Vs Jim Mellor	NK	Shrewsbury, England
27/01/1960	Brian Burke Vs Pasquale Slavo	NK	Ashford
29/01/1960	Brian Burke Vs Tony Zale	NK	Dumfries, Scotland
31/01/1960	Brian Burke Vs Dick Conlon	NK	Folkestone
04/02/1960	Brian Burke Vs Joe Critchley	NK	Crewe, England
06/02/1960	Brian Burke Vs Abe Ginsberg	NK	Shrewsbury, England
08/02/1960	Brian Burke Vs Jim Breaks	NK	Sutton, Ashfield
10/02/1960	Brian Burke & Jim Mellor Vs Reg Ray & Joe Critchley	NK	Llandudno, Wales
11/02/1960	Brian Burke Vs Jim Mellor	NK	Hulme
12/02/1960	Brian Burke Vs Reg Ray	NK	Bolton, England
15/02/1960	Brian Burke Vs Cliff Beaumont	NK	Derby, England
16/02/1960	Brian Burke Vs Bernard Murray	Murray won	Birmingham, England
27/02/1960	Brian Burke Vs John Foley	NK	Bolton, England
29/02/1960	Brian Burke Vs Peter Szakacs	Szakacs won	High Wycombe, England
02/03/1960	Brian Burke Vs Bob Anthony	NK	Banbury
05/03/1960	Brian Burke Vs Bob Anthony	NK	Norwich, England
10/03/1960	Brian Burke Vs Stefan Milla	NK	Hulme
12/03/1960	Brian Burke Vs Alan Miquet	NK	Grantham,
14/03/1960	Brian Burke Vs Tony Lawrence	Burke won	Bedford, England
15/03/1960	Brian Burke Vs Melwyn Riss	Draw	Welling
16/03/1960	Brian Burke Vs Jack Cunningham	NK	Ashford
19/03/1960	Brian Burke Vs Bob Archer O'Brien	NK	Norwich, England
26/03/1960	Brian Burke Vs Keith Williamson	NK	Canteen of Joseph Sankey & Sons Ltd, Hadley Castle, Wellington
27/03/1960	Brian Burke Vs Stefan Milla	Milla won	Birmingham, England
07/04/1960	Brian Burke vs Keith Williams	NK	Hulme
08/04/1960	Brian Burke Vs Abe Ginsberg	NK	Bolton, England

Date	Match	Result	Location
12/04/1960	Brian Burke Vs Tony Zale	NK	Trowell
16/04/1960	Brian Burke Vs Jim Mellor	NK	Doncaster, England
23/04/1960	Brian Burke Vs Melwyn Riss	Riss won	Halifax, England
25/04/1960	Brian Burke Vs Jim Mellor	NK	Walsall
26/04/1960	Brian Burke Vs Peter Szakacs	NK	Swindon, England
27/04/1960	Brian Burke Vs Julien Morice	NK	Southend
28/04/1960	Brian Burke Vs Eddie Saxon	NK	Luton, England
02/05/1960	Brian Burke Vs Ted Hannon	NK	Huddersfield, England
05/05/1960	Brian Burke Vs Joe Critchley	NK	Hulme
07/05/1960	Brian Burke Vs Al Nicol	NK	Belle Vue, Manchester
17/05/1960	Brian Burke vs Keith Williams	Burke won	Birmingham, England
17/05/1960	Brian Burke Vs Jim Mellor	Mellor won	Birmingham, England
24/05/1960	Brian Burke Vs Jack Dempsey	NK	Nelson
09/06/1960	Brian Burke Vs Frank O'Donell	O'Donnell won	Morecambe, Lancashire
10/06/1960	Brian Burke Vs Jack Dempsey	NK	Bolton, England
16/06/1960	Brian Burke vs Keith Williams	NK	Hulme
17/06/1960	Brian Burke Vs John Foley	NK	Liverpool, England
23/06/1960	Brian Burker Vs John Foley	NK	Leigh, Lancashire
19/07/1960	Brian Burke Vs Stefan Milla	Draw	Birmingham, England
21/07/1960	Brian Burke Vs Joe Critchley	NK	Hulme
29/07/1960	Brian Burke Vs Jim Mellor	NK	Bolton, England
30/07/1960	Brian Burke Vs Danny Flynn	NK	Rhyl, North Wales
04/08/1960	Brian Burke Vs Jim Hart	NK	Southport
27/08/1960	Brian Burke Vs Jack Dempsey	NK	Doncaster, England
01/09/1960	Brian Burke Vs Tony Zale	NK	Hulme
08/09/1960	Brian Burke Vs Chic Purvey	NK	Barrow, England
10/09/1960	Brian Burke Vs Cliff Beaumont	NK	Huddersfield, England
12/09/1960	Brian Burke Vs Clay Thomson	Thomson won	Hamilton, Scotland
13/09/1960	Brian Burke Vs Chic Purvey	NK	Aberdeen, Scotland
15/09/1960	Brian Burke Vs Cliff Beaumont	NK	Nelson
17/09/1960	Brian Burke Vs Al Nicol	NK	Belle Vue, Manchester
24/09/1960	Brian Burke Vs John Foley	NK	Grantham,
01/10/1960	Brian Burke Vs Tommy Mann	NK	Belle Vue, Manchester
12/10/1960	Brian Burke Vs Ted Hannon	NK	Scunthorpe
13/10/1960	Brian Burke Vs Dennis Dean	NK	Kirkcaldy
14/10/1960	Brian Burke Vs John Foley	NK	Glasgow, Scotland
19/10/1960	Brian Burke Vs Alan Miquet	NK	Coedpoeth
20/10/1960	Brian Burke Vs Alan Dennison	Burke won	Ellesmere Port
22/10/1960	Brian Burke Vs Kenny Hogan	NK	Grantham,
24/10/1960	Brian Burke Vs Joe Critchley	NK	Walsall
27/10/1960	Brian Burke Vs Stefan Milla	NK	Smethwick
27/10/1960	Brian Burke Vs Jim Mellor	NK	Hulme
29/10/1960	In KO Tournament	NK	Brighton, England
02/11/1960	Brian Burke Vs Tommy Mann	NK	Sleaford
07/11/1960	Brian Burke Vs Bob Bibby	NK	Derby, England

Date	Match	Result	Location
08/11/1960	Brian Burke Vs Abe Ginsberg	NK	Sutton, Ashfield
14/11/1960	Brian Burke Vs Abe Ginsberg	NK	Warrington
25/11/1960	Brian Burke Vs Alan Dennison	Dennison won	Redruth, England
28/11/1960	Brian Burke Vs Mick McMichael	NK	Blackpool, England
01/12/1960	Brian Burke Vs Monty Swann	NK	Hulme
05/12/1960	Brian Burke Vs Eric Cutler	NK	Worksop
12/12/1960	Brian Burke Vs Colin Joynson	NK	Warrington
15/12/1960	Brian Burke Vs Bill Hargreaves	NK	Hulme
23/12/1960	Brian Burke Vs Ray Leslie	NK	Glasgow, Scotland
26/12/1960	Brian Burke & Roy St Clair Vs Reg Ray & Joe Critchley	Burke et al won	Bolton, England
04/01/1961	Brian Burke Vs Tommy Mann	NK	Sheffield, England
07/01/1961	Brian Burke Vs Jack Dempsey	NK	Falkirk
13/01/1961	Brian Burke Vs Don Branch	NK	Chesterfield, England
14/01/1961	Brian Burke Vs Vic Coleman	NK	Kings Lynn, London
15/01/1961	Brian Burke Vs Mike Donlevy	NK	Brighton, England
19/01/1961	Brian Burke Vs Mick McMichael	NK	Leigh, Lancashire
20/01/1961	Brian Burke Vs Inca Peruano	NK	Willenhall
23/01/1961	Brian Burke Vs Cliff Beaumont	NK	Derby, England
27/01/1961	Brian Burke Vs Mick McMichael	NK	Chesterfield, England
06/02/1961	Brian Burke Vs Jim Breaks	NK	Walsall
08/02/1961	Brian Burke Vs Tommy Mann	NK	Sheffield, England
09/02/1961	Brian Burke Vs Roy St Clair	NK	Smethwick
10/02/1961	Brian Burke & Keith Williams Vs Mick McMichael & Jim Mellor	NK	Willenhall
11/02/1961	Brian Burke Vs Bobby Steele	NK	Stirling
13/02/1961	Brian Burke Vs Mick McMichael	NK	Warrington
18/02/1961	Brian Burke Vs Jim Mellor	NK	Shrewsbury, England
20/02/1961	Brian Burke Vs Vic Faulkner	NK	Sutton, Ashfield
22/02/1961	Brian Burke Vs Jack Dempsey	NK	Scunthorpe
24/02/1961	Brian Burke & Keith Williams Vs Mick McMichael & Jim Mellor	NK	Willenhall
25/02/1961	Brian Burke Vs Brian Trevors	NK	Doncaster, England
27/02/1961	Brian Burke Vs Tiger Ryan	NK	West Bromwich, England
07/03/1961	Brian Burke Vs Bob Anthony	NK	Welling
08/03/1961	Brian Burke Vs Tommy Mann	NK	Sheffield, England
11/03/1961	Brian Burke Vs Jack Dempsey	NK	Buxton
13/03/1961	Brian Burke Vs Roy St Clair	NK	Neath, Wales
14/03/1961	Brian Burke Vs Mick McMichael	NK	Scarborough, England
15/03/1961	Brian Burke Vs Brian Trevors	NK	Cradley Heath
16/03/1961	Brian Burke Vs Colin Joynson	NK	Leigh, Lancashire
17/03/1961	Brian Burke Vs Ken Else	NK	Bolton, England
18/03/1961	Brian Burke Vs Bernard Murray	NK	Shrewsbury, England
20/03/1961	Brian Burke Vs Basil Coloulias	NK	Seymour Hall, London
23/03/1961	Brian Burke Vs Majid Ackra	NK	Hulme
25/03/1961	Brian Burke Vs Joe Critchley	Critchley won	Newcastle, England
03/04/1961	Brian Burke Vs John Foley	NK	Kilmarnock

Date	Match	Result	Location
08/04/1961	Brian Burke Vs Jim Breaks	NK	Halifax, England
15/04/1961	Brian Burke Vs Alan Dennison	NK	Belle Vue, Manchester
15/04/1961	Brian Burke Vs Alan Dennison	NK	Wembley, England
19/04/1961	Brian Burke Vs Tiger Ryan	NK	Cradley Heath
27/04/1961	Brian Burke Vs Tommy Mann	NK	Hereford, England
29/05/1961	Brian Burke Vs Bob Archer O'Brien	Archer won	High Wycombe, England
30/05/1961	Brian Burke Vs Pasquale Salvo	NK	Welling
01/06/1961	Brian Burke Vs Jack Cunningham	Cunningham won	Bristol, England
21/06/1961	Brian Burke Vs Joe Critchley	NK	Cradley Heath
25/06/1961	Brian Burke Vs Brian Trevors	NK	Folkestone
28/06/1961	Brian Burke Vs Tony Charles	Charles won	Cardiff, Wales
29/06/1961	Brian Burke Vs Tony CHarles	Charles won	Bristol, England
02/07/1961	Brian Burke Vs Chic Purvey	NK	Liverpool, England
06/07/1961	Brian Burke Vs Mick Duffy	Burke won	Morecambe, Lancashire
07/07/1961	Brian Burke Vs Jim Breaks	NK	Fleetwood
10/07/1961	Brian Burke Vs Tommy Mann	NK	Leeds, England
12/07/1961	Brian Burke Vs Dick Conlon	NK	Winchester
13/07/1961	Brian Burke Vs Arthur Fisher	Fisher won	Dagenham
15/07/1961	In KO Tournament	NK	Grantham,
30/07/1961	Brian Burke Vs Bernard Murray	NK	Liverpool, England
31/07/1961	Brian Burke Vs Monty Swann	NK	York, England
09/08/1961	Brian Burke Vs Eric Wasburg	Burke won	Great Yarmouth, England
10/08/1961	Brian Burke Vs Jean Morandi	NK	Torquay
17/08/1961	Brian Burke Vs Jack Dempsey	Dempsey won	Morecambe, Lancashire
28/08/1961	Brian Burke Vs Don Branch	NK	Warwick
02/09/1961	Brian Burke Vs Ray Leslie	Burke won	Belle Vue, Manchester
15/09/1961	Brian Burke Vs Al Nicol	NK	Chesterfield, England
18/09/1961	Brian Burke Vs Roy St Clair	NK	Carlisle, England
23/09/1961	Brian Burke Vs John Foley	NK	Grantham,
09/10/1961	Brian Burke Vs Bernard Murray	NK	Bradford, England
13/10/1961	Brian Burke Vs Jackie Pallo	Draw	Bridgewater
18/10/1961	Brian Burke Vs Vic Faulkner	NK	Winchester
19/10/1961	Brian Burke Vs Keith Williams	Draw	Beckenham, England
21/10/1961	Brian Burke Vs Billy Stock	NK	Norwich, England
23/10/1961	Brian Burke Vs Julien Morice	NK	Leeds, England
28/10/1961	Brian Burke Vs Roy St Clair	Burke won	Belle Vue, Manchester
02/11/1961	Brian Burke Vs Don Branch	NK	Hereford, England
13/11/1961	Brian Burke Vs Arthur Fisher	Burke won	Cheltenham, England
13/11/1961	Brian Burke Vs Pasquale Salvo (F)	Salvo won	Cheltenham, England
14/11/1961	Brian Burke Vs Peter Szakacs	Burke won	Purley
18/11/1961	Brian Burke Vs Don Branch	Branch won	Newcastle, England
04/12/1961	Brian Burke Vs Jim McKenzie	NK	Kilmarnock
09/12/1961	Brian Burke Vs tom Dowie	NK	Stirling
16/12/1961	Brian Burke Vs John Foley	NK	Norwich, England
15/01/1962	Brian Burke Vs Jim Breaks	NK	Kilmarnock

Date	Match	Result	Location
19/01/1962	Brian Burke Vs Jackie Pallo	NK	Rochester
20/01/1962	Brian Burke Vs Bernard Murray	NK	Coventry, England
25/01/1962	Brian Burke Vs Peter Szakacs	Burke won	Beckenham, England
02/02/1962	Brian Burke Vs tony Cassio	NK	Gravesend
05/02/1962	Brian Burke Vs Julien Morice	NK	Aylesbury
12/02/1962	Brian Burke & Joe Critchley Vs Bobby Steele & Jack Taylor	Steele et al won	Bradford, England
20/02/1962	Brian Burke Vs Julien Morice	Draw	Purley
12/03/1962	Brian Burke Vs Alan Miquet	NK	Seymour Hall, London
14/03/1962	Brian Burke Vs John Foley	NK	Hastings
15/03/1962	Brian Burke Vs Peter Szakacs	NK	Gloucester
19/03/1962	Brian Burke Vs Mal Sample	NK	Carlisle, England
29/03/1962	Brian Burke Vs Bob Archer O'Brien	NK	Southampton, England
30/03/1962	Brian Burke Vs tony Cassio	Cassio won	Ipswich
19/04/1962	In KO Tournament	NK	Dagenham
28/04/1962	In KO Tournament	NK	Norwich
30/04/1962	Brian Burke Vs Jack Dempsey	NK	Kilmarnock
29/05/1962	Brian Burke Vs Stefan Milla	Burke won	Hove
30/05/1962	Brian Burke Vs Cliff Beaumont	Beaumont won	Felixstowe
31/05/1962	Brian Burke Vs Peter Szakacs	NK	Yeovil
13/06/1962	Brian Burke Vs Eric Sands	NK	Dorking
14/06/1962	Brian Burke Vs Eric Sands	Draw	Walthamstow
15/06/1962	Brian Burke Vs Joe Murphy	NK	Farnham
16/06/1962	Brian Burke Vs Frankie Price	NK	Salisbury
17/10/1962	Brian Burke Vs Bob Sherry	Sherry won	Rawtenstall
02/11/1962	Brian Burke Vs Newman	NK	Chorley, England
13/03/1963	Brian Burke Vs Gordon Kilmartin	NK	Southend
19/04/1963	Newman Vs The Gorilla	NK	Kings Lynn, London
11/05/1963	Newman Vs Tony Zale	Draw	Leicester, England
12/01/1965	Newman Vs Buddy Ward	NK	West Bromwich
18/02/1965	Dave Newman Vs Ted Beech	NK	Bloxwich
08/03/1965	Dave Newman Vs Tony Zale	NK	Southend
06/07/1965	Dave Newman Vs Andy McCormack	NK	Colwyn Bay
20/07/1965	Dave Newman Vs Brendan Moriarty	NK	Colwyn Bay
03/08/1965	Dave Newman Vs Jim Moser	NK	Abergele
10/08/1965	Dave Newman Vs Kevin Conneally	NK	Colwyn Bay
24/08/1965	Dave Newman Vs Dennis Tracey	NK	Colwyn Bay
08/09/1965	Dave Newman & Pat Roach Vs Jim Moser & Jack Rowlands	NK	Douglas, Isle of Man
05/10/1965	Dave Newman Vs Billy Yukon	NK	West Bromwich
19/10/1965	Dave Newman Vs Earl McCready	NK	West Bromwich
23/02/1966	Dave Newman Vs Fred Woolley	NK	Cardiff
16/07/1974	Dave Newman Vs Alan Miquet	NK	Llandudno, Wales
18/07/1974	Dave Newman Vs Alan Miquet	NK	Rhyl, Wales

Harry Litherland

Date	Match	Outcome	Venue
13/08/1955	Harry Hall Vs Red Callagham	Red won	New Brighton, England
24/09/1956	Harry Hall Vs Melwyn Riss	NK	Altrincham
21/12/1956	Harry Hall Vs Jack Dempsey	NK	Willenhall
12/01/1957	Harry Hall Vs Red Callagham	Harry won	Shrewsbury, England
09/02/1957	Henry Hall Vs Joe Critchley	Joe Won	Shrewsbury, England
24/01/1958	Harry Hall Vs Fred Woolley	Draw	Willenhall, England
07/03/1959	Harry Hall Vs Ted Hannan	Ted won	Shrewsbury, England

Alan Wood

Date	Match	Outcome	Venue
17/09/1979	Alan Wood Vs Bobby Ryan	Wood won	Derby, Derbyshire
23/08/1979	Alan Wood Vs Bert Royal	Royal won	Morecambe, Lancashire
18/08/1979	Alan Wood Vs Kid Chocolate	Chocolate won AWDQ	Belle Vue, Manchester
09/08/1979	Alan Wood Vs Bert Royal	Royal won	Morecambe, Lancashire
09/08/1979	Alan Wood & John Naylor & Jack Mulligan Vs Bert Royal & Johnny Saint & Jackie Robinson	Royal et al won	Morecambe, Lancashire
23/04/1979	Alan Wood Vs Young David	David won AWDQ	Shrewsbury
21/04/1979	Alan Wood Vs Terry McMahon	Wood won	Hanley
14/04/1979	Alan Wood Vs Honeyboy Zimba	Zimba won	Hanley
05/03/1979	Alan Wood Vs Jackie Robinson	Wood won	Bradford
19/02/1979	Alan Wood Vs Eddie Riley	Wood won	Crewe
18/02/1979	Alan Wood Vs Jack Mulligan	NK	Sutton, Ashfield
06/02/1979	Alan Wood Vs Bobby Ryan	Ryan won	Solihull, West Midlands
05/02/1979	Alan Wood Vs Chris Bailey	Bailey won	Derby, Derbyshire
27/11/1978	Alan Wood Vs Chris Bailey	Wood won	Derby, Derbyshire
27/11/1978	Alan Wood & Jackie Robinson Vs Chris Bailey & Bobby Ryan	Bailey & Ryan won	Derby, Derbyshire
25/11/1978	Alan Wood Vs John Naylor	Naylor won AWDQ	Belle Vue, Manchester
08/11/1978	Alan Wood Vs John Naylor	NK	Banbury
30/10/1978	Alan Wood Vs Kid Chocolate	Chocolate won AWDQ	Crewe
17/10/1978	Alan Wood Vs John Naylor	Naylor won	Leicester
05/10/1978	Alan Wood Vs John Naylor	Naylor won	Preston, Lancashire
02/10/1978	Alan Wood Vs Alan Dennison	Dennison won	Derby, Derbyshire
29/09/1978	Alan Wood Vs Honeyboy Zimba	Zimba won	Chester
21/09/1978	Alan Wood Vs Vic Faulkner	Faulkner won	Morecambe, Lancashire
10/09/1978	Alan Wood Vs Honeyboy Zimba	Zimba won	Blackpool, England
07/09/1978	Alan Wood & Tally Ho Kaye Vs The Royals	Royals won	Preston, Lancashire
05/09/1978	Alan Wood Vs Young David	NK	Oakengates
26/08/1978	Tiger Wood Vs Bert Royal	NK	Southport, Merseyside
20/08/1978	Alan Wood Vs Vic Faulkner	Faulkner won	Blackpool, England
19/08/1978	Alan Wood Vs UFO	Wood won	Rhyl, Wales
09/08/1978	Alan Wood Vs Bert Royal	Royal won	Southport, Merseyside
16/07/1978	Alan Wood Vs Honeyboy Zimba	NK	Cleethorpes
30/06/1978	Alan Wood Vs John Naylor	Naylor won	Bedworth
21/06/1978	Alan Wood Vs John Naylor	Naylor won	Southport, Merseyside
15/06/1978	Alan Wood Vs Brian Maxine	Maxine won	Malvern
08/06/1978	Alan Wood Vs Marty Jones	NK	Rhyl, Wales
06/06/1978	Alan Wood Vs Flash Jordan	Wood won	Wolverhampton, West Midlands
24/05/1978	Alan Wood Vs Kung Fu	NK	Preston
03/05/1978	Alan Wood Vs Alan Dennison	Dennison won	Winsford
26/04/1978	Alan Wood Vs Bernie Wright	Wright won	Lincoln
17/04/1978	Alan Wood & Tally Ho Kaye Vs The Royals	Royals won	Derby, Derbyshire

Date	Match	Result	Location
13/04/1978	Alan Wood Vs Jackie Turpin	Turpin won	Birmingham
07/04/1978	Alan Wood Vs Vic Faulkner	NK	Hindley
07/04/1978	Alan Wood & The Viking Vs The Royals	NK	Hindley
03/04/1978	Alan Wood Vs Flash Jordan	Jordan won	Crewe
20/03/1978	Alan Wood Vs Bernie Wright	Wood won	Shrewsbury
14/03/1978	Alan Wood Vs John Naylor	Naylor won	Wolverhampton, West Midlands
08/03/1978	Alan Wood Vs John Naylor	Naylor won	Buxton
06/03/1978	Alan Wood Vs Bernie Wright	Wood won	Bradford
28/02/1978	Alan Wood Vs Dynamite Kid	Kid won	Preston
16/02/1978	Alan Wood Vs King Ben	Wood won	Nottingham
16/02/1978	Alan Wood Vs John Naylor (F)	Naylor won	Nottingham
13/02/1978	Alan Wood Vs John Naylor	Naylor won	Shrewsbury
06/02/1978	Alan Wood Vs King Ben	Ben wn	Derby, Derbyshire
07/01/1978	Tiger Wood Vs Johnny Saint	NK	Harrogate, north Yorkshire
19/12/1977	Alan Wood Vs Honeyboy Zimba	Zimba won	Halifax
05/12/1977	Alan Wood Vs Dynamite Kid	Kid won	Crewe
26/11/1977	Alan Wood Vs Johnny Saint	Saint won	Hanley
30/10/1977	Alan Wood Vs Johnny Saint	Saint won	Kirkby, Ashfield
25/10/1977	Alan Wood Vs John Naylor	Naylor won	Keighley
10/08/1977	Alan Wood Vs Kid Chocolate	Chocolate won	Southport, Merseyside
11/07/1977	Alan Wood Vs Dynamite Kid	NK	Scarborough
23/06/1977	Alan Wood & tornado Torontos Vs Alan Dennison & Gypsy Smith	NK	Malvern
22/06/1977	Alan Wood Vs Dynamite Kid	Kid won	Leicester
26/05/1977	Alan Wood Vs John Naylor	Naylor won	Glasgow, Scotland
25/04/1977	Alan Wood Vs Bearcat Wright	Wood won	Bradford
23/04/1977	Alan Wood Vs John Naylor	Naylor won	Belle Vue, Manchester
20/04/1977	Alan Wood Vs John Naylor	Naylor won	Middleton
18/04/1977	Alan Wood Vs Bearcat Wright	Wood won	Shrewsbury
14/04/1977	Alan Wood Vs John Naylor	Naylor won	Birmingham
09/04/1977	Alan Wood Vs Ian Gilmour	Gilmour won	Hanley
06/04/1977	Alan Wood Vs John Naylor	Naylor won	Chesterfield
05/04/1977	Alan Wood Vs Roy Paul	Paul won	Solihull, West Midlands
03/04/1977	Alan Wood Vs Clive Myers	Wood won CMDQ	Kirkby, Ashfield
01/04/1977	Alan Wood Vs Flash Jordan	Draw DKO	Liverpool
31/03/1977	Alan Wood Vs Kenny Hogan	Hogan won	Colne
31/03/1977	Alan Wood & Dynamite Kid Vs Flash Jordan & Kenny Hogan	Wood et al won	Colne
30/03/1977	Alan Wood Vs Kung Fu	NK	Hindley
28/03/1977	Alan Wood Vs Ian Gilmour	Gilmour won	Harrogate
19/03/1977	Tiger Wood Vs Dynamite Kid	NK	Buxton, Derbyshire
11/03/1977	Alan Wood Vs John Naylor	Naylor won	Bolton, Lancashire
10/03/1977	Alan Wood Vs Mo Hunter	NK	Brierly Hill
07/03/1977	Tiger Wood Vs Kung Fu	NK	Sheffield, South Yorkshire
05/03/1977	Alan Wood Vs Dynamite Kid	Kid won	Hanley
28/02/1977	Alan Wood Vs John Naylor	Naylor won	Preston, Lancashire

Date	Match	Result	Location
17/02/1977	Alan Wood Vs Jackie Robinson	NK	Malvern
15/02/1977	Alan Wood Vs John Naylor	Naylor won	Wolverhampton, West Midlands
10/02/1977	Alan Wood Vs Clive Myers	Myers won	Brierly Hill
31/01/1977	Alan Wood Vs Jackie Robinson	Wood won	Derby, Derbyshire
27/01/1977	Alan Wood Vs Leon Arras	NK	Colne
20/01/1977	Alan Wood Vs Little Prince	Draw	Leeds
01/12/1976	Alan Wood Vs Jackie Robinson	Wood inj	Sheffield, South Yorkshire
22/11/1976	Alan Wood Vs Marty Jones	Jones won	Bradford
10/11/1976	Alan Wood Vs John Naylor	Naylor won	Dumfries
09/11/1976	Alan Wood Vs John Naylor	Naylor won	Trentham Gardens
08/11/1976	Alan Wood Vs Gil Singh	Singh won	Bradford
09/10/1976	Alan Wood Vs Marty Jones	Jones won	Hanley
24/09/1976	Alan Wood Vs Dynamite Kid	Kid wonn	Liverpool
09/09/1976	Alan Wood Vs Kenny Hogan	Wood won	Morecambe, Lancashire
08/09/1976	Alan Wood Vs Kung Fu	Kung fu won	Southport, Merseyside
08/09/1976	Alan Wood Vs Marty Jones	Wood won	Southport, Merseyside
03/09/1976	Alan Wood Vs John Naylor	Naylor won	MEM Birmingham
26/08/1976	Alan Wood Vs John Naylor	Naylor won AWDQ	Birmingham
08/08/1976	Alan Wood Vs Jackie Robinson	NK	Blackpool, England
07/08/1976	Alan Wood Vs Marty Jones	NK	Bedworth, Warwickshire
06/08/1976	Alan Wood Vs Bobby Ryan	Ryan won	Liverpool
04/08/1976	Alan Wood Vs John Naylor	Naylor won	Southport, Merseyside
03/08/1976	Alan Wood Vs Marty Jones	Jones won	Bedworth
22/07/1976	Alan Wood Vs Keith Williams	Wood won	Malvern
06/07/1976	Alan Wood Vs John Naylor	NK	Stoneleigh
04/07/1976	Alan Wood Vs John Naylor	Naylor won	Blackpool, England
01/07/1976	Alan Wood Vs John Peters	NK	Morecambe, Lancashire
23/06/1976	Alan Wood Vs John Naylor	Naylor won	Southport, Merseyside
31/05/1976	Alan Wood Vs John Naylor	Naylor won	Bradford
29/05/1976	Alan Wood Vs Vic Faulkner	NK	Rhyl, Wales
24/05/1976	Alan Wood Vs John Naylor	Naylor won	Liverpool
28/04/1976	Alan Wood Vs John Jenkins	Jenkins won AWDQ	Leicester
21/04/1976	In KO Tournament	NK	Leamington Spa
15/04/1976	Alan Wood Vs Vic Faulkner	Faulkner won	Nottingham
14/04/1976	Alan Wood Vs John Naylor	Naylor won	Lincoln
12/04/1976	Alan Wood Vs John Naylor	NK	Newcastle, England
09/04/1976	Alan Wood Vs Marty Jones	NK	Liverpool
08/04/1976	Alan Wood Vs Alan Dennison	Wood won	Bolton, Lancashire
07/04/1976	Alan Wood Vs Phil Halverson	Draw DKO	Sheffield, South Yorkshire
03/04/1976	Alan Wood Vs John Naylor	Naylor won	Newark
13/03/1976	Alan Wood Vs Marty Jones	Jones won	Belle Vue, Manchester
04/03/1976	Alan Wood & Hillbilly Jake Vs The Royals	Royal won	Brierly Hill
21/02/1976	Alan Wood Vs Roy St Clair	St Clair won	Hanley
20/02/1976	Alan Wood Vs Colin Bennett	Wood won	Liverpool
19/02/1976	Alan Wood Vs Ali Shan	Wood inj	Nottingham

Date	Match	Result	Location
09/02/1976	Alan Wood Vs Marty Jones	NK	Harrogate
07/02/1976	Alan Wood & Tally Ho Kaye Vs The Royals	Royals won	Halifax
03/02/1976	Alan Wood Vs John Naylor	NK	Oakengates
27/01/1976	Alan Wood Vs John Naylor	NC	Willenhall
15/01/1976	Alan Wood & Bobby Ryan Vs Bob Abbotts & King Ben	Wood et al won	Malvern
14/01/1976	Alan Wood Vs Billy Howes	NK	Guildhall Preston, Lancashire
11/01/1976	Alan Wood Vs John Naylor	Naylor won	Kirkby, Ashfield
09/01/1976	Alan Wood Vs Vic Faulkner	NK	Dumfries
12/12/1975	Alan Wood Vs King Ben	Wood won	Liverpool
11/12/1975	Alan Wood Vs keith Williams	Draw	Rotherham
27/11/1975	Alan Wood Vs Billy Howes	Draw	Preston
20/11/1975	Alan Wood Vs john Naylor	Naylor won	Nottingham
28/10/1975	Alan Wood Vs Steve Taylor	Wood won	Wolverhampton, West Midlands
06/10/1975	Alan Wood Vs john Naylor	Naylor won	Leicester
13/09/1975	Tiger Wood Vs Vic Faulkner	NK	Blackburn, Lancashire
30/08/1975	Alan Wood Vs john Naylor	NC	Hanley
24/08/1975	Alan Wood Vs john Naylor	Naylor won	Blackpool, England
21/08/1975	Alan Wood Vs keith Martinelli	NC	Malvern
21/08/1975	Alan Wood Vs Robby Baron	Draw	Malvern
20/08/1975	Alan Wood Vs Steve Taylor	Wood inj	Southport, Merseyside
17/08/1975	Alan Wood Vs john Naylor	Naylor won	Cleethorpes
27/07/1975	Alan Wood Vs john Naylor	Naylor won	Blackpool, England
26/07/1975	Alan Wood Vs john Naylor	Naylor won	Hanley
04/07/1975	Alan Wood Vs john Naylor	NC	Liverpool
25/06/1975	Alan Wood Vs john Naylor	Naylor won	Southport, Merseyside
21/06/1975	Alan Wood Vs john Naylor	Draw	Rhyl, Wales
30/05/1975	Alan Wood Vs Steve Taylor	Wood won	Nantwich
19/05/1975	Alan Wood Vs Tornado Torontos	NK	Leeds
17/05/1975	Alan Wood Vs Steve Taylor	NK	Nantwich, Cheshire
17/05/1975	Alan Wood Vs Bert Royal	Draw DKO	Hanley
15/05/1975	Alan Wood Vs Keith Williams	Wood won	Birmingham
08/05/1975	Alan Wood Vs john Naylor	Naylor won	Preston
15/04/1975	Alan Wood Vs Colin Bennett	Wood won	Wolverhampton, West Midlands
07/04/1975	Alan Wood Vs Alf Marqutte	Wood won	Shrewsbury
21/03/1975	Alan Wood Vs Colin Bennett	Wood won	Birmingham
15/03/1975	Alan Wood Vs john Naylor	Naylor won	Hanley
14/03/1975	Alan Wood Vs Harry Palin	Wood won	Liverpool
11/03/1975	Alan Wood Vs Leon Arras	Wood won	Solihull, West Midlands
11/03/1975	Alan Wood Vs Roger Green	Wood won	Solihull, West Midlands
10/03/1975	Alan Wood & john Naylor Vs Lapaques	Lapaques won	Bradford
09/03/1975	Alan Wood Vs Rollerball Rocco	Rocco won	Kirkby, Ashfield
28/02/1975	Alan Wood Vs Zolton Boscik	Wood won	Liverpool
23/02/1975	Alan Wood Vs Steve Taylor	Taylor won	Halifax
12/02/1975	Alan Wood Vs Jeff Kaye	Wood won	Sheffield, South Yorkshire
10/02/1975	Alan Wood Vs Bobby Barnes	NK	Leeds

Date	Match	Result	Location
27/01/1975	Alan Wood Vs Colin Bennett	NK	Bradford
23/01/1975	Alan Wood Vs Bull Carter	Wood won	Birmingham
21/01/1975	Alan Wood Vs Tug Wilson	NK	Solihull, West Midlands
20/01/1975	Alan Wood Vs John Naylor	NK	Nottingham
19/01/1975	Alan Wood Vs Colin Rice	Rice won AWDQ	Kirkby, Ashfield
15/01/1975	Alan Wood Vs Harry palin	NK	Malvern
07/01/1975	Alan Wood Vs Mick McMichael	McMichael won	Wolverhampton, West Midlands
02/01/1975	Alan Wood Vs Steve Taylor	Wood won	Birmingham
09/12/1974	Alan Wood Vs Mick McMichael	Draw	Sale
06/12/1974	Alan Wood Vs Harry palin	NK	Carlisle
02/12/1974	Alan Wood Vs Amet Chong	NK	Leeds
12/11/1974	Alan Wood Vs Harry Palin	NK	Nantwich, Cheshire
10/11/1974	Alan Wood Vs Bob Abbotts	NC	Kirkby, Ashfield
07/11/1974	Alan Wood Vs Terry Jowett	Wood won	Birmingham
06/11/1974	Alan Wood Vs Harry palin	Wood won	Nantwich
23/10/1974	Alan Wood Vs Mo Hunter	NK	Buxton
22/10/1974	Alan Wood Vs Pete McGowan	NK	Hull
21/10/1974	Alan Wood Vs Johnny Saint	NK	Leesd
19/10/1974	Alan Wood Vs Colin Bennett	Draw	Belle Vue, Manchester
18/10/1974	Alan Wood Vs Mick McMichael	Draw	Liverpool
16/10/1974	Alan Wood Vs Sid Cooper	Wood won	Sheffield, South Yorkshire
08/10/1974	Alan Wood Vs Mike Bennett	Wood won	Solihull, West Midlands
04/10/1974	Alan Wood Vs Clive Myers	NK	Worksop
03/10/1974	Alan Wood Vs Honeyboy Zimba	Honeyboy won	Birmingham
02/10/1974	Alan Wood Vs John Naylor	NK	Leamington Spa
10/09/1974	Alan Wood Vs Harry palin	Wood won	Skegness
26/08/1974	Alan Wood Vs Bobby Ryan	Wood won	Knowsley
22/08/1974	Alan Wood Vs Ace Allcard	Wood won	Birmingham
17/08/1974	Alan Wood Vs Marty Jones	Wood won	Rhyl, Wales
14/08/1974	Alan Wood Vs Jackie Robinson	NK	Southport, Merseyside
11/08/1974	Alan Wood Vs Mike McGowan	Draw	Blackpool, England
10/08/1974	Alan Wood Vs John Naylor	Naylor won	Belle Vue, Manchester
27/07/1974	Alan Wood Vs Llew Roberts	NC	Hanley
24/07/1974	Alan Wood Vs Colin Bennett	NC	Southport, Merseyside
09/07/1974	Alan Wood Vs Mo Hunter	Wood won	Skegness
30/06/1974	Alan Wood Vs John Naylor	Draw	Cleethorpes
13/06/1974	Alan Wood Vs Tug Wilson	Wilson won	Birmingham
12/06/1974	Alan Wood Vs Pete Roberts	Roberts won	Sheffield, South Yorkshire
04/06/1974	Alan Wood Vs Terry Jowett	NK	Oakengates
03/06/1974	Alan Wood Vs Clay Thomson	Thomson won	Leeds
28/05/1974	Alan Wood Vs Mo Hunter	Wood won	Wolverhampton, West Midlands
25/05/1974	Alan Wood Vs Marty Jones	Jones won	Barnsley
20/05/1974	Alan Wood Vs Ian Gilmour	Wood won	Leeds
19/05/1974	Alan Wood Vs Marty Jones	NK	Kirkby, Ashfield
03/05/1974	Alan Wood Vs Jackie Robinson	Draw	Liverpool

Date	Match	Result	Location
23/04/1974	Alan Wood Vs Mick McMichael	McMichael won	Solihull, West Midlands
21/04/1974	Alan Wood Vs John Naylor	Naylor won	Cleethorpes
20/04/1974	Alan Wood Vs Ian Beeston	Wood won	Hanley
19/04/1974	Alan Wood Vs Vic Faulkner	Draw	Liverpool
18/04/1974	Alan Wood Vs Ian Beeston	Wood won	Birmingham
08/04/1974	Alan Wood Vs Roger Green	Wood won	Altrincham
14/03/1974	Alan Wood Vs Harry Palin	Wood won	Malvern
26/02/1974	Alan Wood Vs Tug Wilson	Wilson won	Milton
20/02/1974	Alan Wood Vs Iggy Borg	Draw DKO	Sheffield, South Yorkshire
11/02/1974	Alan Wood Vs Terry Jowett	NK	Leeds
21/01/1974	Alan Wood Vs Jackie Robinson	NC	Shrewsbury
14/01/1974	Alan Wood Vs Tug Wilson	Wood won	Altrincham
20/12/1973	Alan Wood Vs Ian Gilmour	Draw	Birmingham
18/12/1973	Alan Wood Vs Tug Wilson	Wilson won	Solihull, West Midlands
08/12/1973	Alan Wood Vs Marty Jones	NC	Hanley
26/11/1973	Alan Wood Vs Mike McGowan	Wood inj	Derby, Derbyshire
24/11/1973	Alan Wood Vs John Naylor	Draw	Belle Vue, Manchester
21/11/1973	Alan Wood Vs Harry palin	NK	Blackpool, England
15/11/1973	Alan Wood Vs Mike McGowan	NK	Warrington
09/11/1973	Alan Wood Vs Adrian Street	Street won	Bolton, Lancashire
30/10/1973	Alan Wood Vs Brian Maxine	Maxine won	Wolverhampton, West Midlands
17/08/1973	Alan Wood Vs Vic Faulkner	Draw DKO	Birmingham
16/08/1973	Alan Wood Vs Marty Jones	Draw	Birmingham
04/04/1973	Alan Wood Vs Keith Williams	Draw	Connahs Quay
15/03/1973	Alan Wood Vs Tally Ho Kaye	both DQ	Nelson
08/03/1973	Alan Wood Vs Dave Barrie	Draw	Warrington
03/02/1971	Alan Wood Vs Peter Preston	NK	Derby, Derbyshire
09/01/1971	Alan Wood Vs Steve Wright	NK	Morecambe, Lancashire
31/10/1970	Alan Wood Vs Alan Dennison	NK	Bolton, Lancashire
13/05/1970	Alan Wood Vs Steve Wright	NK	Bolton, Lancashire
08/12/1969	Alan Wood & Monty Swann Vs Joe Critchley & Kevin Conneally	Critchley et al won	Nantwich
05/12/1969	Alan Wood Vs Steve Wright	Draw	Bolton, Lancashire
24/11/1969	Alan Wood Vs Steve Wright	Draw	Derby, Derbyshire
21/11/1969	Alan Wood Vs Alan Miquet	NK	Dumfries
19/11/1969	Alan Wood Vs Bob Anderson	Wood won	Ross on Wye
10/11/1969	Alan Wood Vs Keith Williams	Wood won KWDQ	Derby, Derbyshire
29/10/1969	Alan Wood & Jack Fallon Vs Steve Wright & Mike Dallas	Writght et al won JFAW DQ	Buxton, England
08/10/1969	Alan Wood & Terry Jowett Vs John Foley & Eric Cutler	Wood et al won	Welshpool
27/09/1969	Alan Wood Vs Bob Anderson	Wood won	Hanley
13/09/1969	Alan Wood Vs Jackie Robinson	NK	Rhyl, Wales
11/09/1969	Alan Wood Vs Melwyn RIss	Wood won	Malvern
02/09/1969	Alan Wood Vs Melwyn RIss	Wood won	Solihull, West Midlands
15/08/1969	Alan Wood Vs Dave Barrie	Wood won	Bolton, Lancashire
02/08/1969	In KO tournament	NK	Rhyl, Wales

Date	Match	Result	Location
26/07/1969	Alan Wood & Mohammed Meru Ullah Vs Artful Dodgers	Dodgers won	Hanley
20/07/1969	Alan Wood Vs Judd Harris	Wood won	Blackpool, England
18/07/1969	Alan Wood Vs Peter Preston	Wood won	Liverpool
02/07/1969	Alan Wood Vs John Foley	Foley won	Southport, Merseyside
29/06/1969	Alan Wood Vs Roy Paul	Wood won	Blackpool, England
24/06/1969	Alan Wood Vs Terry Downs	NK	Skegness
07/06/1969	Alan Wood Vs Terry Downs	NK	Wolverhampton, West Midlands
05/06/1969	Alan Wood Vs jack Fallon	Fallon won	Malvern
04/06/1969	Alan Wood Vs Bill Ross	Wood won	Buxton
03/06/1969	Alan Wood Vs Terry Downs	Wood won	Wolverhampton, West Midlands
31/05/1969	Alan Wood Vs Pete Danby	NK	Rhyl, Wales
27/05/1969	Alan Wood Vs Johnny Saint	NK	Solihull, West Midlands
23/05/1969	Alan Wood Vs Mick McMichael	Draw	Bolton, Lancashire
25/04/1969	Alan Wood Vs Vic Faulkner	Draw	Bolton, Lancashire
23/04/1969	Alan Wood Vs Joe Keegan	NK	Southport, Merseyside
22/04/1969	Alan Wood Vs Jackie Robinson	Wood won	Wolverhampton, West Midlands
21/04/1969	Alan Wood Vs Terry Downs	Wood won	Blackpool, England
19/04/1969	Alan Wood Vs Jackie Robinson	NK	Hanley
18/04/1969	Alan Wood Vs Al Simpson	Draw	Dumfries
14/04/1969	Alan Wood Vs Alan Dennison	Wood won	Altrincham
12/04/1969	Alan Wood Vs Johnny Eagles	NK	Winsford, Cheshire
10/04/1969	Alan Wood Vs Johnny Eagles	Wood won	Winsford
01/04/1969	Alan Wood Vs Jeff Kaye	NK	Solihull, West Midlands
28/03/1969	Alan Wood Vs Terry Downs	NK	Solihull, West Midlands
21/03/1969	Alan Wood Vs Roy Paul	Wood won	Liverpool
19/03/1969	Alan Wood Vs Alan Colbeck	Wood won	Buxton, England
17/03/1969	Alan Wood Vs Roy Paul	Wood won	Blackpool, England
13/03/1969	Alan Wood Vs Alan Sergeant	Wood won	Malvern
10/03/1969	Alan Wood Vs Alan Sergeant	NK	Derby, Derbyshire
21/02/1969	Alan Wood Vs Mike Dallas	NK	Bolton, Lancashire
15/02/1969	Alan Wood Vs Vic Faulkner	NK	Wolverhampton, West Midlands
14/02/1969	Alan Wood Vs Melwyn RIss	Wood won	Malvern
10/02/1969	Alan Wood Vs Vic Faulkner	Faulkner won	Altrincham
10/02/1969	Alan Wood Vs Bobby Ryan	Wood won	Altrincham
04/02/1969	Alan Wood Vs Ian Gilmour	NK	Solihull, West Midlands
31/01/1969	Alan Wood Vs Jeff Kaye	Wood won	Bolton, Lancashire
16/01/1969	Alan Wood & Seamus Dunleavy Vs Bobo Matu & Jim Moser	Wood & Dunleavy won	Malvern
11/01/1969	Alan Wood Vs Tally Ho Kaye	Wood won	Hanley
17/12/1968	Alan Wood Vs Mike Dallas	Draw	Wolverhampton, West Midlands
12/12/1968	Alan Wood Vs Alan Sergeant	Wood won	Malvern
10/12/1968	Alan Wood Vs Billy Yukon	Wood won	Solihull, West Midlands
09/12/1968	Alan Wood Vs Alan Sergeant	NK	Derby, Derbyshire
07/12/1968	Alan Wood Vs johnny Eagles	Draw	Hanley
30/11/1968	Alan Wood Vs Johnny Eagles	NK	Bolton, Lancashire

Date	Match	Result	Location
20/11/1968	Alan Wood Vs Dave Barrie	NK	Ross on Wye
16/11/1968	Alan Wood Vs Terry Downs	Downs won	Hanley
12/11/1968	Alan Wood Vs Al Nicol	Wood won	Solihull, West Midlands
11/11/1968	Alan Wood Vs Al Nicol	Wood won	Derby, Derbyshire
07/11/1968	Alan Wood Vs Steve Clements	Wood won	Warrington
04/11/1968	Alan Wood Vs Tery Downs	Wood won	Blackpool, England
02/11/1968	Alan Wood Vs Terry Downs	NK	Bolton, Lancashire
21/10/1968	Alan Wood Vs Frank Karalius	NK	Warrington
09/10/1968	Alan Wood Vs Ian Gilmour	Wood won	Coedpoeth
08/10/1968	Alan Wood Vs Ian Gilmour	Wood won	Worcester
04/10/1968	Alan Wood Vs Melwyn RIss	NK	Dumfries
02/10/1968	Alan Wood & Terry Jowett Vs The Terriers	Wood et al won	Welshpool
01/10/1968	Alan Wood Vs Melwyn RIss	Wood won	Solihull, West Midlands
17/09/1968	Alan Wood & Joe Keegan Vs Terry Jowett & Jim Mellor	NK	Aldridge
15/09/1968	Alan Wood Vs Chic Purvey	Wood won	Blackpool, England
13/09/1968	Alan Wood Vs Chic Purvey	Wood won	Liverpool
07/09/1968	Alan Wood Vs Steve Best	Wood won	Belle Vue, Manchester
28/08/1968	Alan Wood Vs Melwyn RIss	Draw	Southport, Merseyside
18/08/1968	Alan Wood Vs Tony St Clair	Draw	Buxton
09/08/1968	Alan Wood Vs Dave Barrie	Wood won	Liverpool
05/08/1968	Alan Wood Vs Melwyn RIss	Draw	Coedpoeth
28/07/1968	Alan Wood Vs Mike Bennett	Wood won	Blackpool, England
30/06/1968	Alan Wood Vs Dave Barrie	Wood won	Blackpool, England
29/06/1968	Alan Wood Vs Tally Ho Kaye	NK	Rhyl, Wales
26/06/1968	Alan Wood Vs Eric Cutler	NK	Ross on Wye
21/06/1968	Alan Wood Vs Mike Bennett	Draw	Bolton, Lancashire
11/06/1968	Alan Wood Vs joe Keegan	NK	Skegness
05/06/1968	Alan Wood Vs Alan Dennison	Draw	Oakengates
03/06/1968	Alan Wood Vs Sid Cooper	Wood won	Birmingham
23/05/1968	Alan Wood Vs Ted Heath	NK	Nelson
22/05/1968	Alan Wood Vs Frank Karalius	Wood won	Hindley
20/05/1968	Alan Wood Vs Steve Clements	Clements won	Birmingham
15/05/1968	Alan Wood Vs Jim Mellor	Wood won	Welshpool
07/05/1968	Alan Wood Vs Bill Connor	Wood won	Worcester
30/04/1968	Alan Wood Vs Leon Fortuna	NC	Solihull, West Midlands
23/04/1968	Alan Wood Vs Bill Connor	NK	Leominster
22/04/1968	Alan Wood Vs Bill Connor	Wood won	Altrincham
20/04/1968	Alan Wood Vs Bill Connor	NK	Wolverhampton, West Midlands
20/04/1968	Alan Wood Vs Bill Connor	Draw	Wolverhampton, West Midlands
18/04/1968	Alan Wood Vs Bill Connor	Wood won	Northwich
15/04/1968	Alan Wood Vs Joe Critchley	Wood won	Blackpool, England
05/04/1968	Alan Wood Vs Mike Dallas	NK	Horncastle
04/04/1968	Alan Wood Vs Ted Heath	NK	Nelson
29/03/1968	Alan Wood Vs Melwyn RIss	Draw	Bolton, Lancashire
19/03/1968	Alan Wood Vs Kid Chocolate	NK	Solihull, West Midlands

Date	Match	Result	Location
18/03/1968	Alan Wood Vs Mike Dallas	Wood won	Birmingham
11/03/1968	Alan Wood Vs Mike Dallas	Wood won	Blackpool, England
09/03/1968	Alan Wood Vs Keith Williams	NK	Shrewsbury
08/03/1968	Alan Wood Vs Joe Keegan	NK	Holyhead
05/03/1968	Alan Wood Vs Al Nicol	NK	Solihull, West Midlands
02/03/1968	Alan Wood Vs Johnny Williams	Williams won	Hanley
10/02/1968	Alan Wood Vs Judd Harris	NK	Shrewsbury
09/02/1968	Alan Wood Vs Bill Connor	Wood won	Newcastle, England
05/02/1968	Alan Wood Vs Billy Blackfort	Wood won	Blackpool, England
03/02/1968	Alan Wood Vs Jim Mellor	NK	Hanley
02/02/1968	Alan Wood Vs Dave Barrie	Wood won	Bolton, Lancashire
30/01/1968	Alan Wood Vs Peter Szakacs	Wood won	Worcester
29/01/1968	Alan Wood Vs Melwyn RIss	NK	Derby, Derbyshire
15/01/1968	Alan Wood Vs Melwyn RIss	NK	Derby, Derbyshire
13/01/1968	Alan Wood Vs Joe Keegan	Wood won	Hanley
11/01/1968	Alan Wood Vs Bill Connor	NK	Rhyl, Wales
09/01/1968	Alan Wood Vs Alan Dennison	NK	Solihull, West Midlands
30/12/1967	Alan Wood Vs Jim Mellor	NK	The Baths Hall, Shrewsbury
27/12/1966	Alan Wood Vs Bobby Steele	Steele won	Solihull, West Midlands
27/12/1966	Alan Wood Vs jack Fallon	Draw	Solihull, West Midlands
16/12/1966	Alan Wood Vs Terry Downs	NK	Willenhall
10/12/1966	Alan Wood Vs Terry Downs	NK	Shrewsbury
10/12/1966	Alan Wood Vs Cliff Beaumont	NK	Kidderminster
03/12/1966	Alan Wood Vs Terry Downs	NK	Wolverhampton, Civi Hall
26/11/1966	Alan Wood Vs Alan Sergeant	NK	The Pavillion, Hemel Hempstead, Hertfordshire
26/11/1966	Alan Wood Vs Jim Mellor	NK	Shrewsbury
25/11/1966	Alan Wood Vs Keith Williams	Wood inj	Bolton, Lancashire
23/11/1966	Alan Wood Vs Bobby Steele	NK	Welshpool
16/11/1966	Alan Wood Vs Peter Stewart	NK	Ross on Wye
12/11/1966	Alan Wood Vs Brian Maxine	NK	Brent Town Hall, Wembley
11/11/1966	Alan Wood Vs Joe Keegan	NK	Dumfries
10/11/1966	Alan Wood & Roy Wood Vs Cortez Brothers	NK	Nelson
09/11/1966	Alan Wood Vs Terry Downs	NK	Leominster
07/11/1966	Alan Wood Vs jack Fallon	NK	Derby, Derbyshire
05/11/1966	Alan Wood Vs Mike Bennett	NK	NK
05/11/1966	Alan Wood Vs Mike Bennett	Wood won	Watford
01/11/1966	Alan Wood Vs Mike Eagers	NK	Solihull, West Midlands
31/10/1966	Alan Wood & Terry Downs Vs Cortez brothers	NK	Blackpool, England
29/10/1966	Alan Wood Vs Terry Nylands	NK	Shrewsbury
27/10/1966	Alan Wood Vs Stefan Milla	NK	Warrington
26/10/1966	Alan Wood Vs Johnny Eagles	NK	Hindley
18/10/1966	Alan Wood Vs Melwyn RIss	NK	Kidderminster
08/10/1966	Alan Wood Vs Mike Dallas	NK	Shrewsbury
07/10/1966	Alan Wood Vs Terry Downs	Wood won	Bolton, Lancashire
06/10/1966	Alan Wood Vs Johnny Eagles	NK	Newtown

Date	Match	Result	Location
04/10/1966	Alan Wood Vs Peter Stewart	NK	Solihull, West Midlands
01/10/1966	Alan Wood Vs Mike Dallas	Wood won	Hanley
25/09/1966	Alan Wood Vs Joe Critchley	NK	Blackpool, England
16/09/1966	Alan Wood Vs Mike Eagers	Eagers won	Bolton, Lancashire
07/09/1966	Alan Wood Vs Cliff Beaumont	NK	Southport, Merseyside
05/09/1966	Alan Wood Vs Cliff Beaumont	NK	Birmingham
03/09/1966	Alan Wood Vs Jeff kaye	NK	Prestatyn Holiday Camp Ballroom, Denbighshire
03/09/1966	Alan Wood Vs Jeff Kaye	Draw	Prestatyn
22/08/1966	Alan Wood Vs Bobby Steele	NK	Uttoxeter
13/08/1966	Alan Wood Vs Jim Mellor	NK	Rhyl, Wales
23/07/1966	Alan Wood Vs Bobby Steele	NK	Rhyl, Wales
16/07/1966	Alan Wood Vs Jim Mellor	NK	Rhyl, Wales
06/07/1966	Alan Wood Vs Peter Preston	NK	Southport, Merseyside
05/07/1966	Alan Wood Vs Peter Preston	NK	Skegness
03/07/1966	Alan Wood Vs Barry Cannon	NK	Douglas, Isle of Man
11/06/1966	Alan Wood Vs Mick McMichael	McMichael won	Hanley
10/06/1966	Alan Wood Vs Dallas	NK	Altrincham
04/06/1966	Alan Wood Vs Mike Dallas	NK	Doncaster, South Yorkshire
03/06/1966	Alan Wood Vs Jim Breaks	NK	Dumfries
12/05/1966	Alan Wood Vs Mike Eagers	Eagers won	Southport, Merseyside
06/05/1966	Alan Wood Vs Keith Williams	Williams won	Bolton, Lancashire
02/05/1966	Alan Wood Vs Al Brown	NK	Birmingham
23/04/1966	Alan Wood Vs Peter Stewart	Wood won	Doncaster, South Yorkshire
20/04/1966	Alan Wood Vs Mike Dallas	Dalla won AWDQ	Warrington
11/04/1966	Alan Wood Vs Jack Fallon	NK	Kirkby, Ashfield
09/04/1966	Alan Wood Vs Micky Gold	NK	Skegness
02/04/1966	Alan Wood Vs Al Brown	NK	Doncaster, South Yorkshire
19/03/1966	Alan Wood Vs Jack Dempsey	Draw	Doncaster, South Yorkshire
16/03/1966	Alan Wood Vs Joe Critchley	NK	Welshpool
14/03/1966	Alan Wood Vs Jim Breaks	Breaks won	Birmingham
12/03/1966	Alan Wood Vs Jim Mellor	NK	Shrewsbury
22/02/1966	Alan Wood Vs Colin Bennett	NK	Wellington
19/02/1966	Alan Wood Vs Al Nicol	Wood won	Doncaster, South Yorkshire
12/02/1966	Alan Wood Vs Terry Downs	Downs won	Doncaster, South Yorkshire
03/02/1966	Alan Wood Vs Ken Cadman	NK	Warrington
02/02/1966	Alan Wood Vs Joe Keegan	NK	Leominster
29/01/1966	Alan Wood Vs Chic Purvey	NK	Doncaster, South Yorkshire
28/01/1966	Alan Wood Vs Terry Downs	Wood won	Bolton, Lancashire
25/01/1966	Alan Wood Vs Tally Ho Kaye	Wood won	Worsley
25/01/1966	Alan Wood & John Lees Vs Lee Sharron & Tally Ho Kaye	Wood et al won	Worsley
15/01/1966	Alan Wood Vs Melwyn RIss	NK	Sutton, Ashfield
11/01/1966	Alan Wood Vs Al Brown	NK	Solihull, West Midlands
07/01/1966	Alan Wood & Melwyn Riss Vs Reg Ray & Barry Cannon	NK	Dumfries
03/01/1966	Alan Wood Vs Jim Mellor	NK	Uttoxeter
08/12/1965	Alan Wood Vs Terry Downs	NK	Wallasey, merseyside

Date	Match	Result	Location
13/10/1965	Alan Wood Vs Ken Cadman	NK	Bolton, Lancashire
31/07/1965	Alan Wood Vs Peter Rann	NK	Hornsey Town Hall, London
13/09/1958	Tiger Wood Vs Jim Lewis	Tiger won	New Brighton, England
12/07/1958	Tiger Wood Vs Rufus Riley	Tiger won	New Brighton, England
30/05/1958	Tiger Wood Vs Tommy Bailey	Tiger won	New Brighton, England
10/05/1958	Tiger Wood Vs Les Thornton	Tiger won	New Brighton, England
02/04/1958	Tiger Wood Vs George Goldie	Tiger won	Manchester, England
08/07/1957	Tiger Wood Vs George Andrews	George Won	Merry Fiddlers, England
29/06/1957	Tiger Wood Vs George Goldie	George Won	New Brighton, England
08/12/1956	Tiger Wood Vs Jack Beaumont	Jack won	Manchester, England
27/10/1956	Tiger Wood Vs Bill Ogden	Bill won	Manchester, England
28/05/1955	Jim Lewis & Tiger Wood Vs Danny Flynn & Bill Hargreaves	Jim & Tiger won	New Brighton, England
20/12/1954	Tiger Wood Vs Eric Sands	Eric won	Edinburgh, Scotland
20/12/1954	Alan Wood Vs Eric Sands	Sands won	Edinburgh, Scotland
10/12/1954	Alan Wood Vs Bobby Steele	NK	Willenhall
01/12/1954	Alan Wood Vs Chic Purvey	NK	Scunthorpe
19/11/1954	Alan Wood Vs Jim Lewis	NK	Willenhall
12/11/1954	Alan Wood Vs Jim Lewis	NK	Manchester
01/11/1954	Alan Wood Vs Joe Critchley	NK	Worcester
23/10/1954	Alan Wood Vs Stefan Milla	NK	Hanley
19/10/1954	Tiger Wood Vs Jack Cunningham	Jack won	Hamilton, Scotland
18/10/1954	Tiger Wood Vs Jack Dempsey	Jack won	Edinburgh, Scotland
18/10/1954	Alan Wood Vs Jack Dempsey	Dempsey won	Edinburgh, Scotland
15/10/1954	Alan Wood Vs Martin Conroy	NK	Willenhall
26/04/1952	Tiger Wood Vs Tommy Mann	Tommy won	Middlesborough, North Yorkshire
12/04/1952	Tiger Wood Vs Johnny Allan	Johnny won	Newcastle, England
11/04/1952	Tiger Wood Vs Jim Boyle	Jim won, TW DQ	Glasgow, Scotland
28/01/1952	Tiger Wood Vs Ron Johnson	Ron won	Edinburgh, Scotland
06/06/1951	Tiger Wood Vs John Strang	Tiger won	Cardiff, Wales
21/05/1951	Tiger Wood Vs Bill Hargreaves	NC	Doncaster, Englanf
18/12/1950	Tiger Wood Vs Vic Coleman	Vic won	West Ham, England
21/11/1950	Tiger Wood Vs Archer O'Brien	Tiger won	West Ham, England
14/12/1965	Alan Wood Vs Jack Fallon	NK	Spalding
13/12/1965	Alan Wood Vs Keith Williams	NK	Blackpool, England
11/12/1965	Alan Wood Vs Micky Gold	NK	Shrewsbury
08/12/1965	Alan Wood & Jackie Cheers Vs Melwyn Riss & Al Brown	Riss et al won	Hindley
07/12/1965	Alan Wood Vs Wilf Darkus	NK	Kidderminster
06/12/1965	Alan Wood Vs Bobby Steele	Draw	Birmingham
26/11/1965	Alan Wood Vs Terry Downs	NK	Willenhall
20/11/1965	Alan Wood Vs Bobby Steele	NK	Shrewsbury
19/11/1965	Alan Wood Vs Bobby Steele	Steele won	Bolton
08/11/1965	Alan Wood Vs Terry Downs	NK	Blackpool, England
05/11/1965	Alan Wood Vs Terry Downs	NK	Dumfries
04/11/1965	Alan Wood Vs Melwyn Riss	NK	Nelson
27/10/1965	Alan Wood Vs Bobby Steele	Steele won	Scunthorpe

Date	Match	Result	Venue
25/10/1965	Alan Wood Vs Micky Gold	NK	Birmingham
23/10/1965	Alan Wood Vs Cliff Beaumont	Beaumont won	Hanley
21/10/1965	Alan Wood Vs Joe Keegan	NK	Northwich
19/10/1965	Alan Wood Vs Ian Gilmour	NK	Kidderminster
09/10/1965	Alan Wood Vs Ken Cadman	Cadman won	Bolton
08/10/1965	Alan Wood Vs Joe Keegan	NK	Bolton
07/10/1965	Alan Wood Vs Eric Cutler	Wood won	Crewe
03/10/1965	Alan Wood Vs Chic Purvey	Purvey won	Blackpool, England
23/09/1965	Alan Wood Vs Cliff Beaumont	NK	Malvern
12/09/1965	Alan Wood Vs Keith Williams	Williams won	Blackpool, England
17/08/1965	Alan Wood Vs Mick Duffy	Wood won	Skegness
15/08/1965	Alan Wood Vs Majid Ackra	Ackra won	Blackpool, England
13/08/1965	Alan Wood Vs Majid Ackra	Ackra won	Liverpool
07/08/1965	Alan Wood Vs Colin Joynson	NK	Rhyl, Wales
31/07/1965	Alan Wood Vs Peter Rann	NK	Hornsey
26/06/1965	Alan Wood Vs Sid Cooper	Draw	Doncaster
19/06/1965	Alan Wood Vs Jack Fallon	NK	Rhyl, Wales
16/06/1965	Alan Wood Vs Jack Fallon	NK	Malvern
28/05/1965	Alan Wood Vs Jim Lewis	Draw	Lowestoft
27/05/1965	Alan Wood Vs Peter Szakacs	Draw	Peterborough, England
26/05/1965	Alan Wood Vs Mick McMichael	NK	Kilmarnock
25/05/1965	Alan Wood Vs Kalmen Gaston	Draw	Finsbury Park
24/05/1965	Alan Wood Vs Peter Szakacs	Draw	Cheltenham
20/05/1965	Alan Wood Vs George Cohen	NK	Morecambe, Lancashire
15/05/1965	Alan Wood Vs Joe Murphy	NK	Shoreditch
12/05/1965	Alan Wood Vs Gerry Diprose	NK	Dorking
11/05/1965	Alan Wood Vs Ray Leslie	Wood won	Bournemouth
24/04/1965	Alan Wood Vs Kalmen Gaston	Gaston won	Coventry, England
23/04/1965	Alan Wood Vs Eddie Capelli	NK	Barking
22/04/1965	Alan Wood Vs Alan Miquet	NK	Southampton, England
19/04/1965	Alan Wood Vs Terry Jowett	NK	High Wycombe, England
16/04/1965	Alan Wood Vs Melwyn Riss	Draw	Bolton
08/04/1965	Alan Wood Vs Eric Sands	NK	Bury St Edmunds
06/04/1965	Alan Wood Vs Ivan Penzekoff	Ivan won	Croydon, London
05/04/1965	Alan Wood Vs Pasquale Salvo	Draw	Bedford
03/04/1965	Alan Wood Vs Jim Mellor	Mellor won	Hanley
24/03/1965	Alan Wood & Roy Wood Vs Eric Sands & Terry Nylands	Wood won ES TN DQ	Scunthorpe
16/03/1965	Alan Wood Vs Terry Camm	NK	Warrington
15/03/1965	Alan Wood Vs Sid Cooper	Alan inj	Carlisle
13/03/1965	Alan Wood Vs Melwyn Riss	Riss won	Doncaster
10/03/1965	Alan Wood Vs Jim Mellor	NK	Uttoxeter
09/03/1965	Alan Wood Vs Melwyn Riss	NK	Solihull
06/03/1965	Alan Wood Vs Peter Stewart	Stewart won	Shrewsbury
27/02/1965	Alan Wood Vs Jack Dempsey	Dempsey won	Shrewsbury
26/02/1965	Alan Wood Vs Terry Downs	NK	Caernarvon, Wales

25/02/1965	Alan Wood Vs Leon Fortuna	NK	Wimbledon
24/02/1965	In KO Tournament	NK	Hastings
23/02/1965	In KO Tournament	NK	Chelmsford
22/02/1965	Alan Wood Vs Pasquale Salvo	Salvo won	High Wycombe, England
15/02/1965	Alan Wood Vs Terry Downs	Draw	Birmingham
13/02/1965	Alan Wood Vs Peter Stewart	Stewart won	Shrewsbury
10/02/1965	Alan Wood Vs Jim Breaks	NK	Scunthorpe
09/02/1965	Alan Wood Vs Jim Mellor	NK	Warrington
30/01/1965	Alan Wood Vs Alan Miquet	NK	Sutton, Ashfield
18/01/1965	Alan Wood Vs Jack Dempsey	Dempsey won	Cheltenham
14/01/1965	Alan Wood & Terry Camm Vs Bobby Steele & Alan Miquet	NK	Nelson
03/10/1963	Alan Wood Vs Brian Trevors	NK	Brierly Hill

Jack Fallon

Date	Match	Outcome	Venue
01/11/1962	Jack Fallon Vs Ray	NK	Leyton Baths
10/10/1963	Jack Fallon Vs Jack Dempsey	NK	Nelson
22/10/1963	Jack Fallon Vs Danny Clough	NK	Kidderminster
02/01/1965	Jack Fallon Vs Terry Camm	NK	Sutton, Ashfield
19/01/1965	Jack Fallon Vs Ivan Penzekoff	NK	Kidderminster
30/01/1965	Jack Fallon Vs Ray Francis	NK	Brierly Hill
08/02/1965	Jack Fallon Vs Reg Ray	NK	Worcester, England
26/02/1965	Jack Fallon Vs Terry Nylands	Fallon won	Rotherham
02/03/1965	Jack Fallon Vs Al Brown	NK	Warrington
13/03/1965	Jack Fallon Vs Reg Ray	NK	Shrewsbury
15/03/1965	Jack Fallon Vs Barry Cannon	NK	Birmingham
18/03/1965	Jack Fallon Vs Al Brown	NK	Northwich
20/03/1965	Jack Fallon Vs Jack Dempsey	Dempsey won	Doncaster
27/03/1965	Jack Fallon & Johnny Mack Vs Roy Wood & Keith Williams	NK	Kirkby, Ashfield
12/04/1965	Jack Fallon Vs Derek Collins	NK	Kilmarnock
16/04/1965	Jack Fallon Vs Tim McAdam	Fallon won	Glasgow, Scotland
22/04/1965	Jack Fallon Vs Reg Ray	Ray won	Barrow
10/05/1965	Jack Fallon Vs Cliff Beaumont	NK	Altrincham
16/06/1965	Jack Fallon Vs Alan Wood	NK	Malvern
19/06/1965	Jack Fallon Vs Alan Wood	NK	Rhyl, Wales
13/08/1965	Jack Fallon Vs Tom Dowie	Dowie won	Glasgow, Scotland
08/11/1965	Jack Fallon Vs Gene Riscoe	NK	Derby
09/11/1965	Jack Fallon & Gene Riscoe Vs Mike Donlevy & O'Dooma	NK	Kidderminster
12/11/1965	Jack Fallon Vs Al Brown	NK	Bolton
13/11/1965	Jack Fallon Vs Micky Gold	NK	Shrewsbury
15/11/1965	Jack Fallon Vs Jim Mellor	NK	Birmingham
18/11/1965	Jack Fallon Vs Terry Downs	Downs won	Crewe
19/11/1965	Jack Fallon Vs Cliff Beaumont	NK	Willenhall
11/12/1965	Jack Fallon Vs Terry Downs	Fallon won	Doncaster
14/12/1965	Jack Fallon Vs Alan Wood	NK	Spalding
18/12/1965	Jack Fallon Vs Keith Williams	v	Shrewsbury
08/01/1966	Jack Fallon Vs Micky Gold	NK	Doncaster, South Yorkshire
10/01/1966	Jack Fallon Vs Lee Sharron	NK	Derby, Derbyshire
31/01/1966	Jack Fallon Vs Mike Dallas	NK	Derby, Derbyshire
15/02/1966	Jack Fallon Vs Roy St Clair	St Clair won	Edinburgh, Scotland
28/02/1966	Jack Fallon Vs Bobby Steele	NK	Derby, Derbyshire
18/03/1966	Jack Fallon Vs Leon Arras	Arras won	Liverpool
03/04/1966	Jack Fallon Vs Tally Ho Kaye	NK	Bromsgrove
06/04/1966	Jack Fallon Vs Alan Dennison	NK	Hindley
09/04/1966	Jack Fallon Vs Ezzard Hart	Draw	Falkirk
11/04/1966	Jack Fallon Vs Alan Wood	NK	Kirkby, Ashfield
16/05/1966	Jack Fallon Vs Barry Cannon	NK	Birmingham

Date	Match	Result	Location
17/05/1966	Jack Fallon Vs Ken Cadman	Cadman won	Worsley
26/05/1966	Jack Fallon Vs Honeyboy Zimba	NK	Nelson
12/06/1966	Jack Fallon Vs Johnny Eagles	NK	Douglas, Isle of Man
06/08/1966	Jack Fallon Vs Mike Dallas	NK	Rhyl, Wales
23/09/1966	Jack Fallon Vs Alan Dennison	NK	Harrogate, north Yorkshire
15/10/1966	Jack Fallon Vs Cliff Beaumont	NK	Shrewsbury
07/11/1966	Jack Fallon Vs Alan Wood	NK	Derby, Derbyshire
08/11/1966	Jack Fallon Vs Wildman of Borneo	NK	Kidderminster
13/11/1966	Jack Fallon Vs Brian Trevors	NK	Bromsgrove
14/11/1966	Jack Fallon Vs Alan Sergeant	Sergeant won	Birmingham
08/12/1966	Jack Fallon Vs Ricardo Negerete	NK	Nelson
27/12/1966	Jack Fallon Vs Alan Wood	Draw	Solihull, West Midlands
08/03/1968	Jack Fallon Vs Tony St Clair	NK	Liverpool
25/03/1968	Jack Fallon Vs Ivan Penzekoff	NK	Derby, Derbyshire
20/11/1968	Jack Fallon Vs Melwyn Riss	NK	Coedpoeth
28/11/1968	Jack Fallon Vs Judd Harris	NK	Nelson
07/01/1969	Jack Fallon Vs Adrian Street	Fallon won ASDQ	Worcester
10/01/1969	Jack Fallon Vs Steve young	Draw	Dumfries
20/01/1969	Jack Fallon Vs Jim Moser	NK	Derby, Derbyshire
10/02/1969	Jack Fallon Vs Johnny Czeslaw	NK	Derby, Derbyshire
10/03/1969	Jack Fallon Vs Peter Rann	NK	Derby, Derbyshire
04/06/1969	Jack Fallon & Vic Faulkner Vs The Black Diamonds	Fallon et al won	Buxton
05/06/1969	Jack Fallon Vs Alan Wood	Fallon won	Malvern
29/10/1969	Jack Fallon & Alan Wood Vs Steve Wright & Mike Dallas	Wrigtht et al won JFAW DQ	Buxton, England
03/11/1969	Jack Fallon Vs Billy Joyce	NK	Derby, Derbyshire
14/11/1969	Jack Fallon Vs Peter Preston	NK	Dumfries
09/12/1969	Jack Fallon Vs Reg Yates	Fallon won	Brierly Hill
28/11/1970	Jack Fallon Vs Pat Roach	NK	Derby, Derbyshire
20/01/1971	Jack Fallon Vs Pete Roberts	NK	NK
03/07/1971	Jack Fallon Vs Bobo Matu	NK	Southport, Merseyside
28/08/1971	Jack Fallon Vs Ray Glendenning	NK	Southport, Merseyside
19/04/1972	Jack Fallon Vs Tibor Szakacs	NK	Wolverhampton, West Midlands
11/01/1974	Jack Fallon Vs Ray Glendenning	Fallon won	Liverpool
18/07/1974	Jack Fallon Vs Jim Moser	NK	Rhyl, Wales

Paul Duval

Date	Match	Outcome	Venue
03/01/1966	Paul Duval Vs Dennis Mitchell	NK	Bradford
05/01/1966	Paul Duval Vs Billy Joyce	NK	Leicester, Leicestershire
06/01/1966	Paul Duval Vs Dennis Mitchell	NK	Preston, Lancashire
08/01/1966	Paul Duval Vs Bill Rawlings	Draw	Newcastle, England
27/01/1966	Paul Duval Vs Billy Joyce	NK	Kirkcaldy
28/01/1966	Paul Duval Vs Dennis Mitchell	Mitchell won	Glasgow
25/01/1968	Paul Duval Vs Wild Angus	NK	Nelson
30/01/1968	Paul Duval Vs Barry Douglas	Duval won	Worcester
09/12/1968	Paul Duval Vs Lee Sharron	Sharron won	Blackpool, England
26/04/1969	Paul Duval Vs Wild Angus	Angus won	Hanley
31/05/1969	Paul Duval Vs John Lees	NK	Rhyl, Wales
07/06/1969	Pete Duval Vs Pete Curry	Duval won	Hanley
08/06/1969	Paul Duval Vs Wild Angus	NK	Douglas, Isle of Man
10/06/1969	Paul Duval Vs Steve Veidor	NK	Solihull, West Midlands
17/06/1969	Pete Duval Vs Pete Curry	Duval won	Wolverhampton, West Midlands
20/06/1969	Paul Duval Vs Billy Howes	NC	Bolton, Lancashire
24/06/1969	Paul Duval Vs Roy Bull Davies	NK	Skegness
28/06/1969	Paul Duval Vs Wild Angus	NK	Rhyl, Wales
15/07/1969	Paul Duval Vs Bob Francini	Duval won	Skegness
26/07/1969	Paul Duval Vs henri Pierlot	Duval won	Hanley
15/08/1969	Paul Duval Vs Rocky Wall	Duval won	Bolton, Lancashire
23/08/1969	Paul Duval Vs Pat Roach	Duval won	Hanley
06/09/1969	Paul Duval Vs Al Martin	Duval won	Darlaston
10/09/1969	Paul Duval Vs Don Vines	Duval won DVDQ	Wigan, Lancashire
17/09/1969	Paul Duval Vs Kendo Nagasaki	Nagasaki won	Buxton, England
18/09/1969	Paul Duval Vs Kendo Nagasaki	Nagasaki won	Winsford
04/10/1969	Paul Duval Vs Pete Roberts	NK	Hanley
11/11/1969	Paul Duval Vs Henri Pierlot	Duval won HPDQ	Dundee, Scotland
18/11/1969	Paul Duval Vs Johnny South	NC	Huddersfield
01/12/1969	Paul Duval Vs Bob Francini	Duval won	York
07/01/1973	Paul Duval Vs Barry Douglas	Duval won	Kirkby, Ashfield

John Naylor

Date	Match	Outcome	Venue
23/09/1972	John Naylor Vs Marty Jones	NK	Bolton, Lancashire
28/10/1972	John Naylor Vs Brian Maxine	NK	Solihull, West Midlands
11/11/1972	John Naylor Vs Zolton Boscik	NK	Sheffield, South Yorkshire
09/12/1972	John Naylor Vs Tug Wilson	NK	Bolton, Lancashire
06/01/1973	John Naylor Vs Frank (Jacky) Rickard	NK	Solihull, West Midlands
28/07/1973	John Naylor Vs Keith Williams	NK	Wolverhampton, West Midlands
18/09/1973	John Naylor Vs Tally Ho Kay	NK	Southport, Merseyside
20/10/1973	John Naylor Vs Mike Bennett	NK	Middlesborough, North Yorkshire
10/11/1973	John Naylor Vs Raj Singh	NK	Bletchley, Buckinghamshire
24/11/1973	John Naylor Vs Alan Wood	Draw	Belle Vue, Manchester
22/12/1973	John Naylor Vs Alan Dennison	NK	Solihull, West Midlands
09/02/1974	John Naylor Vs Harry Palin	NK	Winsford, Cheshire
21/04/1974	John Naylor Vs Alan Wood	Naylor won	Cleethorpes
30/06/1974	John Naylor Vs Alan Wood	Draw	Cleethorpes
10/08/1974	John Naylor Vs Alan Wood	Naylor won	Belle Vue, Manchester
24/08/1974	John Naylor Vs Zolton Boscik	NK	Dunstable, Bedfordshire
02/10/1974	John Naylor Vs Alan Wood	NK	Leamington Spa
05/10/1974	John Naylor Vs Robby Barron	NK	Gravesend, Kent
09/11/1974	John Naylor Vs Jim Breaks	NK	Royal Lemington Spa, Warwickshire
17/12/1974	John Naylor Vs Steve Best	NK	Wolverhampton, West Midlands
20/01/1975	John Naylor Vs Alan Wood	NK	Nottingham
25/01/1975	John Naylor Vs Vic Faulkner	NK	Solihull, West Midlands
01/03/1975	John Naylor Vs Mick McManus	NK	Preston, Lancashire
10/03/1975	John Naylor & Alan Wood Vs Lapaques	Lapaques won	Bradford
15/03/1975	John Naylor Vs Alan Wood	Naylor won	Hanley
29/03/1975	John Naylor Vs Colin Bennett	NK	Solihull, West Midlands
19/04/1975	John Naylor Vs Steve Grey	NK	Gravesend, Kent
03/05/1975	John Naylor Vs Leon Fortuna	NK	Walthamstow, London
08/05/1975	John Naylor Vs Alan Wood	Naylor won	Preston
17/06/1975	John Naylor Vs Brian (Gold Belt) Maxine	NK	Royal Lemington Spa, Warwickshire
21/06/1975	John Naylor Vs Alan Wood	Draw	Rhyl, Wales
25/06/1975	John Naylor Vs Alan Wood	Naylor won	Southport, Merseyside
04/07/1975	John Naylor Vs Alan Wood	NC	Liverpool
26/07/1975	John Naylor Vs Alan Wood	Naylor won	Hanley
27/07/1975	John Naylor Vs Alan Wood	Naylor won	Blackpool, England
02/08/1975	John Naylor Vs Robby baron	NK	Crawley, West Sussex
17/08/1975	John Naylor Vs Alan Wood	Naylor won	Cleethorpes
24/08/1975	John Naylor Vs Alan Wood	Naylor won	Blackpool, England
30/08/1975	John Naylor Vs Alan Wood	NC	Hanley
20/09/1975	John Naylor Vs Alan Dennison	NK	Blackburn, Lancashire

Date	Match	Result	Location
06/10/1975	John Naylor Vs Alan Wood	Naylor won	Leicester
01/11/1975	John Naylor Vs Vic Faulkner	NK	Sheffield, South Yorkshire
20/11/1975	John Naylor Vs Alan Wood	Naylor won	Nottingham
10/01/1976	John Naylor Vs Steve Grey	NK	Gravesend, Kent
11/01/1976	John Naylor Vs Alan Wood	Naylor won	Kirkby, Ashfield
27/01/1976	John Naylor Vs Alan Wood	NC	Willenhall
03/02/1976	John Naylor Vs Alan Wood	NK	Oakengates
03/03/1976	John Naylor Vs Colin Bennett	NK	Solihull, West Midlands
06/03/1976	John Naylor Vs Bill Ross	NK	Sheffield, South Yorkshire
22/03/1976	John Naylor & Mo Hunter Vs Alan Wood & kevin Conneally	Naylor et al won	Derby, Derbyshire
03/04/1976	John Naylor Vs Alan Wood	Naylor won	Newark
12/04/1976	John Naylor Vs Alan Wood	NK	Newcastle, England
14/04/1976	John Naylor Vs Alan Wood	Naylor won	Lincoln
21/04/1976	John Naylor Vs Jackie Robinson	NK	Leeds, West yorkshire
24/05/1976	John Naylor Vs Alan Wood	Naylor won	Liverpool
31/05/1976	John Naylor Vs Alan Wood	Naylor won	Bradford
23/06/1976	John Naylor Vs Alan Wood	Naylor won	Southport, Merseyside
04/07/1976	John Naylor Vs Alan Wood	Naylor won	Blackpool, England
06/07/1976	John Naylor Vs Alan Wood	NK	Stoneleigh
10/07/1976	John Naylor Vs Bobby Ryan	NK	Lincoln, Lincolnshire
04/08/1976	John Naylor Vs Alan Wood	Naylor won	Southport, Merseyside
14/08/1976	John Naylor Vs Colin Bennett	NK	Bedworth, Warwickshire
26/08/1976	John Naylor Vs Alan Wood	Naylor won AWDQ	Birmingham
03/09/1976	John Naylor Vs Alan Wood	Naylor won	MEM Birmingham
09/11/1976	John Naylor Vs Alan Wood	Naylor won	Trentham Gardens
10/11/1976	John Naylor Vs Alan Wood	Naylor won	Dumfries
11/12/1976	John Naylor Vs Alan Dennison	NK	Solihull, West Midlands
15/02/1977	John Naylor Vs Alan Wood	Naylor won	Wolverhampton, West Midlands
28/02/1977	John Naylor Vs Alan Wood	Naylor won	Preston, Lancashire
11/03/1977	John Naylor Vs Alan Wood	Naylor won	Bolton, Lancashire
12/03/1977	John Naylor Vs Mick McManus	NK	Buxton, Derbyshire
06/04/1977	John Naylor Vs Alan Wood	Naylor won	Chesterfield
14/04/1977	John Naylor Vs Alan Wood	Naylor won	Birmingham
20/04/1977	John Naylor Vs Alan Wood	Naylor won	Middleton
23/04/1977	John Naylor Vs Alan Wood	Naylor won	Belle Vue, Manchester
26/05/1977	John Naylor Vs Alan Wood	Naylor won	Glasgow, Scotland
30/07/1977	John Naylor Vs Marty Jones	NK	Southport, Merseyside
20/08/1977	John Naylor Vs Johnny Saint	NK	Morecambe, Lancashire
25/10/1977	John Naylor Vs Alan Wood	Naylor won	Keighley
29/10/1977	John Naylor Vs Catweazle	NK	Chester, Cheshire
07/01/1978	John Naylor Vs Catweazle	NK	Harrogate, north Yorkshire
13/02/1978	John Naylor Vs Alan Wood	Naylor won	Shrewsbury
16/02/1978	John Naylor Vs Alan Wood (F)	Naylor won	Nottingham
08/03/1978	John Naylor Vs Alan Wood	Naylor won	Buxton

Date	Match	Result	Venue
14/03/1978	John Naylor Vs Alan Wood	Naylor won	Wolverhampton, West Midlands
01/04/1978	John Naylor Vs Bobby Ryan	NK	Leicester, Leicestershire
21/06/1978	John Naylor Vs Alan Wood	Naylor won	Southport, Merseyside
30/06/1978	John Naylor Vs Alan Wood	Naylor won	Bedworth
15/07/1978	John Naylor Vs Jim Breaks	NK	Bedworth, Warwickshire
28/08/1978	John Naylor Vs Alan Dennison	NK	Preston, Lancashire
05/10/1978	John Naylor Vs Alan Wood	Naylor won	Preston, Lancashire
17/10/1978	John Naylor Vs Alan Wood	Naylor won	Leicester
04/11/1978	John Naylor Vs Peter kaye	NK	Walton-On-Thames, Surrey
08/11/1978	John Naylor Vs Alan Wood	NK	Banbury
25/11/1978	John Naylor Vs Alan Wood	Naylor won AWDQ	Belle Vue, Manchester
24/02/1979	John Naylor Vs John England	NK	Reading, Berkshire
17/03/1979	John Naylor Vs Jim Breaks	NK	Rotherham, South Yorkshire
07/04/1979	John Naylor Vs Mike Jordan	NK	Hemel Hempstead, Hertfordshire
09/08/1979	John Naylor & Jack Mulligan & Alan Wood Vs Bert Royal & Johnny Saint & Jackie Robinson	Royal et al won	Morecambe, Lancashire
15/12/1979	John Naylor Vs Alan Dennison	NK	Aylesbury, Buckinghamshire
01/03/1980	John Naylor Vs Marty Jones	NK	Lincoln, Lincolnshire
26/05/1980	John Naylor Vs Jackie Robinson	NK	Croydon, London
09/08/1980	John Naylor Vs Peter Kaye	NK	Bedworth, Warwickshire
22/11/1980	John Naylor Vs Mick McManus	NK	Chester, Cheshire
28/02/1981	John Naylor Vs Kenny Hogan	NK	Bury, Greater Manchester
04/04/1981	John Naylor Vs Jackie Turpin	NK	Hemel Hempstead, Hertfordshire
15/07/1981	John Naylor Vs Bernie Wright	NK	Morecambe, Lancashire
14/11/1981	John Naylor Vs Mal Sanders	NK	Croydon, London
16/06/1982	John Naylor Vs Bernie Wright	NK	Southport, Merseyside
16/10/1982	John Naylor Vs Bob Walsh	NK	Derby, Derbyshire
11/12/1982	John Naylor Vs King Ben	NK	Halifax, West Yorkshire
26/03/1983	John Naylor Vs Johnny Apollon	NK	Aylesbury, Buckinghamshire
23/04/1983	John Naylor Vs Kid Chocolate Marty Jones/Clive Myers vs/ John Naylor/King Ben	NK	Harrogate, north Yorkshire
23/07/1983		NK	Derby, Derbyshire
07/01/1984	Ringo Rigby/John Naylor vs/ Bobby Barnes & Sid Cooper	NK	Macclesfield, Cheshire
18/08/1984	John Naylor Vs Rick Wiseman	NK	Southport, Merseyside
12/01/1985	John Naylor Vs Peter kaye	NK	Keighley, West Yorkshire
03/08/1985	John Naylor Vs Little Prince	NK	Bradford, West Yorkshire

Gene Riscoe (Tommy Heyes)

Date	Match	Outcome	Venue
04/01/1960	Gene Riscoe Vs Fred Walshe	NK	Derby, England
19/02/1960	Gene Riscoe Vs Alan Colbeck	NK	Dumfries, Scotland
22/02/1960	Gene Riscoe Vs ?	NK	Matlock
08/03/1960	Gene Riscoe Vs Jackie Cheers	NK	Alfreton
18/03/1960	Gene Riscoe Vs Jackie Cheers	NK	Alfreton
09/05/1960	Gene Riscoe Vs Bill Hargreaves	NK	Worcester, England
02/06/1960	Gene Riscoe Vs Jim Hart	NK	Manchester, England
10/06/1960	Gene Riscoe Vs Alec Bray	NK	Bolton, England
30/06/1960	Gene Riscoe Vs Dean Stockton	NK	Crewe, England
11/07/1960	Gene Riscoe Vs Emile Poilve	NK	Skegness, England
01/08/1960	Gene Riscoe Vs Jackie Cheers	Riscoe won	Douglas, Isle of Man
06/08/1960	Gene Riscoe Vs Bill Hargreaves	NK	Colne
18/08/1960	Gene Riscoe Vs Bill Hargreaves	NK	Hulme
22/08/1960	Gene Riscoe Vs Dean Stockton	NK	Skegness, England
05/09/1960	Gene Riscoe Vs Kenny Hogan	NK	Worcester, England
16/09/1960	Gene Riscoe Vs Jackie Cheers	NK	Redruth, England
19/09/1960	Gene Riscoe Vs Carl Dane	NK	Matlock
10/10/1960	Gene Riscoe Vs Bill Hargreaves	NK	Worcester, England
20/10/1960	Gene Riscoe Vs Dean Stockton	NK	Leigh, Lancashire
16/10/1961	Gene Riscoe Vs Seamus Dunleavy	NK	Derby, England
17/10/1961	Gene Riscoe Vs Micke Donlevy	Donlevy won	Kidderminster
30/10/1961	Gene Riscoe Vs Keith Martinelli	NK	Derby, England
12/02/1962	Gene Riscoe Vs Pete Lyons	NK	Sutton, Ashfield
15/02/1962	Gene Riscoe Vs Johnny Eagles	Eagles won	Malvern
16/02/1962	Gene Riscoe Vs Carl Dane	NK	Dumfries
09/03/1963	Gene Riscoe Vs Les Kellett	NK	Sutton, Ashfield
01/03/1965	Gene Riscoe Vs Jackie Cheers	NK	Worcester, England
02/03/1965	Gene Riscoe Vs Jackie Cheers	NK	Kidderminster
04/03/1965	Gene Riscos Vs Terry Nylands	NK	Malvern
01/04/1965	Gene Riscoe Vs Terry Nylands	NK	Malvern
17/04/1965	Gene Riscoe & Roy Wood Vs Jackie Cheers & Joe Critchley	NK	Brierly Hill
22/04/1965	Gene Riscoe Vs Roy Wood	NK	Nelson
08/11/1965	Gene Riscoe Vs Jack Fallon	NK	Derby
09/11/1965	Gene Riscoe & Jack Fallon Vs Mike Donlevy & O'Dooma	NK	Kidderminster
10/11/1965	Gene Riscoe Vs Keith Williams	NK	Hindley

Roy Wood

Date	Match	Outcome	Venue
30/01/1965	Roy Wood Vs Keith Williams	Wood won	Shrewsbury
16/03/1965	Roy Wood Vs Joe Critchley	Critchley won	Edinburgh
24/03/1965	Roy Wood & Alan Wood Vs Eric Sands & Terry Nylands	Wood won ES TN DQ	Scunthorpe
27/03/1965	Roy Wood & Keith Williams Vs Jack Fallon & Johnny Mack	NK	Kirkby, Ashfield
17/04/1965	Roy Wood & Gene Riscoe Vs Jackie Cheers & Joe Critchley	NK	Brierly Hill
22/04/1965	Roy Wood Vs Gene Riscoe	NK	Nelson
04/11/1965	Roy Wood Vs Peter Stewart	NK	Nelson
20/11/1965	Roy Wood Vs Jim Mellor	NK	Shrewsbury
11/12/1965	Roy Wood Vs Jim Mellor	NK	Shrewsbury
09/03/1966	Roy Wood Vs Chic Purvey	Wood won CPDQ	Sheffield, South Yorkshire
08/06/1966	Roy Wood Vs Mike Dallas	NK	Hindley
10/11/1966	Roy Wood & Alan Wood Vs Cortez Brothers	NK	Nelson
09/01/1968	Roy Wood & Johnny Eagles Vs The Dennisons	Wood et al won	Worcester
20/01/1968	Roy Wood Vs Jack Dempsey	NK	Shrewsbury
26/02/1968	Roy Wood Vs Melwyn Riss	Wood won MRDQ	Blackpool, England
08/03/1968	Roy Wood Vs Peter Stewart	NK	Horncastle
22/03/1968	Roy Wood Vs Bill Connor	Wood won	Willenhall
22/04/1968	Roy Wood Vs Dave Barrie	Wood won	Blackpool, England
02/05/1968	Roy Wood & terry Jowett Vs The Terriers	NK	Nelson
23/06/1968	Roy Wood Vs Joe Critchley	Critchley won	Blackpool, England
11/08/1968	Roy Wood Vs Joe Critchley	Wood won	Blackpool, England
22/08/1968	Roy Wood Vs John Foley	Wood won	Blackpool, England
20/10/1968	Roy Wood Vs Joe Critchley	Critchley won	Blackpool, England

Printed in Great Britain
by Amazon.co.uk, Ltd.,
Marston Gate.